THE
LONG ROAD
TO
ANTIETAM

HOW THE CIVIL WAR
BECAME A REVOLUTION

RICHARD SLOTKIN

"Delivers . . . vivid narrative, fresh thinking, and characters that spring from the page." —Geoffrey C. Ward, author of *A First-Class Temperament*

Praise for THE LONG ROAD TO ANTIETAM

"Historian Slotkin . . . moves from his path-breaking studies of America's cultural mythology of violence to a set piece of real-life carnage in this gripping, multifaceted history of the Civil War's bloodiest day. . . . Grounding military operations in political calculation and personal character, Slotkin gives us perhaps the richest interpretation yet of this epic of regenerative violence." —*Publishers Weekly*, starred review

"An absorbing account. . . . Slotkin paints a detailed portrait of the talented but flawed general who helped Lincoln bring about his revolution, if ever so unwillingly. . . . Slotkin's description of the battle is essential to completing his meticulous, maddening portrait of McClellan."

—John Swansburg, *Slate*

"Throughout the book, the author exhibits his vast knowledge of the numerous generals involved in both sides of the conflict. Slotkin's comprehensive descriptions of the battles of 1862 show his deep understanding of the terrain, the difficulties of communication, the impossible logistics and the characters that influenced the outcome. . . . The author deftly exposes [McClellan's] egocentric, messianic tendencies as he purposely prolonged the beginning of the conflict." —*Kirkus Reviews*

"Slotkin does an excellent job of tracing the strategies used by both sides."
—*Military Heritage* magazine

"Slotkin tells a great story and for those interested in battle narratives, I have little doubt that you will enjoy his narration of Antietam. . . . Slotkin does a great job laying out this conflict and how Lincoln managed to rid himself of the McClellan problem, issue the Emancipation Proclamation, and turn the Civil War into a holy war that ended slavery. . . . *The Long Road to Antietam* will change how I teach the first two years of the war. In my world, that's a pretty high compliment." —Erik Loomis, Lawyers, Guns & Money blog

"A remarkable piece of work, an eye-opening double history of a battle and a war." —Randy Dotinga, *Christian Science Monitor*

"Richard Slotkin has made us understand how very delicately the entire fate of the American nation trembled in the wind at the battle of Antietam—not only for the high military stakes between the Union and Confederate armies in this, the single bloodiest day in our history, but for his clear-eyed dissection of the ambitions that led George McClellan to the brink of a treason greater than that contemplated by Benedict Arnold." —Dr. Allen C. Guelzo, Henry R. Luce Professor of the Civil War Era, Gettysburg College

"A riveting, perceptive analysis of the Civil War campaigns of 1862, of the reasoning behind the Emancipation Proclamation and of the complex power struggle between President Abraham Lincoln and the 35-year-old Union Commander of the Army of the Potomac, Gen. George B. McClellan. . . . This is one of the most moving and incisive books on the Civil War that I have ever read." —Chris Patsilelis, *Tampa Bay Times*

"This is much more than another treatise on the battle itself. Yes, the movements and countermovements on the battlefield are there, but this sprawling book has multi-faceted tentacles which Slotkin, an award-winning author and former university professor, skillfully weaves into a cohesive narrative. . . . This is a thought-provoking book which goes well beyond the standard battle narratives and places Antietam in its full context as a significant point of change in U.S. domestic policy, a shift with far-reaching ramifications for the next century."—Scott Mingus, Cannonball blog

"In this engrossing book Richard Slotkin looks beyond that blood-drenched battlefield to explore how President Abraham Lincoln linked victory at Antietam to his decision to free slaves and declare that they could join the Union Army." —Thomas B. Allen, HistoryNet

ALSO BY **RICHARD SLOTKIN**

NONFICTION

Regeneration through Violence:
The Mythology of the American Frontier, 1600–1860

(1973) (Albert J. Beveridge Award—American Historical Association,
National Book Award Finalist, *New York Times* Notable Book of the Year)

So Dreadfull a Judgment: Puritan Responses to
King Philip's War, 1675–1677, with James K. Folsom (1978)

The Fatal Environment: The Myth of the Frontier in
the Age of Industrialization, 1800–1890

(1985) (Little Big Horn Associates Literary Award,
New York Times Notable Book of the Year)

Gunfighter Nation: The Myth of the Frontier
in Twentieth-Century America

(1992) (National Book Award Finalist,
New York Times Notable Book of the Year)

Lost Battalions: The Great War and the
Crisis of American Nationality (2005)

No Quarter: The Battle of the Crater, 1864 (2009)

FICTION

The Crater (1980) (*New York Times* Notable Book of the Year)

The Return of Henry Starr (1988)

Abe: A Novel of the Young Lincoln

(2000) (Michael Shaara Award for Civil War Fiction, *Salon* Best Book,
New York Times Notable Book of the Year)

THE
LONG ROAD to
ANTIETAM

HOW THE CIVIL WAR BECAME
A REVOLUTION

RICHARD SLOTKIN

LIVERIGHT PUBLISHING CORPORATION
a division of
W. W. NORTON & COMPANY | NEW YORK LONDON

Frontispiece: Lincoln and McClellan (photograph by
Alexander Gardner; courtesy of the Library of Congress).

Copyright © 2012 by Richard Slotkin

FIRST PUBLISHED AS A LIVERIGHT PAPERBACK 2013

All photographs courtesy of the Library of Congress,
unless otherwise indicated.

For information about permission to reproduce selections from this book,
write to Permissions, Liveright Publishing Corporation, a division of
W. W. Norton & Company, Inc., 500 Fifth Avenue, New York, NY 10110

For information about special discounts for bulk purchases, please contact
W. W. Norton Special Sales at specialsales@wwnorton.com or 800-233-4830

Maps by Sam DeFabbia-Kane

Manufacturing by Courier Westford
Book design by Barbara M. Bachman
Production manager: Anna Oler

LIBRARY OF CONGRESS CATALOGING-IN-PUBLICATION DATA
Slotkin, Richard, 1942–
The long road to Antietam : how the Civil War became
a revolution / Richard Slotkin. — 1st ed.
pages cm
Includes bibliographical references and index.
ISBN 978-0-87140-411-4 (hardcover)
1. Antietam, Battle of, Md., 1862. 2. Lincoln, Abraham, 1809–1865—
Military leadership. 3. United States. President (1861–1865 : Lincoln).
Emancipation Proclamation. I. Title.
E474.65.S57 2012
973.7'336—dc23   2012007795

978-0-87140-665-1 pbk.

Liveright Publishing Corporation
500 Fifth Avenue, New York, N.Y. 10110

www.wwnorton.com

W. W. Norton & Company Ltd.
Castle House, 75/76 Wells Street, London W1T 3QT

1 2 3 4 5 6 7 8 9 0

For Iris

CONTENTS

❧❧

LIST OF MAPS   XI
INTRODUCTION   XIII
A NOTE ON MILITARY TERMINOLOGY   XXIX

PART ONE

TURNING POINT: MILITARY STALEMATE AND STRATEGIC INITIATIVES

JULY 1862

CHAPTER 1   Lincoln's Strategy: Emancipation and the McClellan Problem   3

CHAPTER 2   McClellan's Strategy: Irresistible Force   40

CHAPTER 3   President Davis's Strategic Offensive   62

PART TWO

THE CONFEDERATE OFFENSIVE

AUGUST 1862

CHAPTER 4   Self-Inflicted Wounds: The Union High Command   85

CHAPTER 5   Both Ends Against the Middle: The Campaign of Second Bull Run   108

CHAPTER 6   McClellan's Victory   128

PART THREE

THE INVASION OF MARYLAND

SEPTEMBER 2–15, 1862

CHAPTER 7   Lee Decides on Invasion   141

CHAPTER 8   McClellan Takes the Offensive   170

CHAPTER 9   The Battles of South Mountain   193

CHAPTER 10   The Forces Gather   209

PART FOUR

THE BATTLE OF ANTIETAM

SEPTEMBER 16–18, 1862

CHAPTER 11   Preparation for Battle   231

CHAPTER 12   The Battle of Antietam: Hooker's Fight,
6:00–9:00 AM   253

CHAPTER 13   The Battle of Antietam: Sumner's Fight,
9:00 AM–Noon   283

CHAPTER 14   The Battle of Antietam: The Edge of Disaster,
Noon to Evening   311

CHAPTER 15   The Day When Nothing Happened   339

PART FIVE

THE REVOLUTIONARY CRISIS

SEPTEMBER 22–NOVEMBER 7, 1862

CHAPTER 16   Lincoln's Revolution   357

CHAPTER 17   The General and the President   379

CHAPTER 18   Dubious Battle: Everything Changed,
Nothing Settled   393

CHRONOLOGY   415

ANTIETAM ORDER OF BATTLE   429

NOTES   435

SELECTED BIBLIOGRAPHY   455

INDEX   463

LIST OF MAPS

❧ ❧

MAP 1: THE VIRGINIA THEATER, JULY 1–SEPT. 9, 1862   84

MAP 2: LEE DIVIDES HIS ARMY, SEPT. 9–13   140

MAP 3: SOUTH MOUNTAIN, SEPT. 14–15   192

MAP 4: ANTIETAM, 6:30–7:30 AM   252

MAP 5: ANTIETAM, 7:30–9:00 AM   268

MAP 6: ANTIETAM, 9:30–10:00 AM   282

MAP 7: ANTIETAM, 10:30 AM–NOON   298

MAP 8: ANTIETAM, NOON–1:00 PM   310

MAP 9: ANTIETAM, 3:00–5:00 PM   328

INTRODUCTION

❧ ❧

THE BATTLE OF ANTIETAM HAS LONG BEEN CONSIDERED THE TURN-
ing point of the Civil War. The defeat of Lee's army frustrated the Confederacy's best chance to win the war on the battlefield. The Union
army's narrow victory on September 17, 1862, enabled Abraham Lincoln to issue the Emancipation Proclamation, a political act that transformed the war and the future of United States by binding the defense
of the Union to the destruction of slavery. Paradoxically, the victory
also allowed Lincoln to fire the man who won the battle, Major General
George McClellan, and thereby begin the military reorganization that
would in the end produce victory for the Union.

In fact, neither the military nor the political results of the battle were
decisive. The military strength of the Confederacy was not substantially
weakened by the defeat. The political and military benefits of emancipation would prove substantial, perhaps decisive, in the long run. But
in the shorter term the costs offset the benefits. Emancipation gave the
disorganized Democratic opposition an issue around which to rally: the
defense of White supremacy. And although the president's proclamation made it more difficult for the British to recognize the Confederacy,
the policy of Lord Palmerston's government was ultimately determined
by a hardheaded calculation of the Confederacy's military prospects.
In short, after Antietam the outcome of the war was still uncertain and
would hinge on policies not yet enacted and battles still to be fought.

The significance of Antietam lies not in the battle itself but in the campaign that produced it. That campaign was the result of a radical turn in
the strategies of both Union and Confederacy—a series of political and
military decisions made over a four-month period in the summer and fall

of 1862 that transformed the policies, principles, and purposes that had hitherto governed the conduct of the war. Before Antietam it was still possible for Americans to imagine a compromise settlement of sectional differences. After Antietam, and the Emancipation Proclamation, the only way the war could end was by the outright victory of one side over the other. Either way, the result would be a revolutionary transformation of American politics and society.

The road to Antietam, however, began long before September 3, 1862, when General Lee gave orders for the invasion of Maryland. It had, in fact, begun nearly two months earlier, during the first two weeks of July, when—after six months of intense military engagement by land and naval forces all around the Confederate periphery—Presidents Lincoln and Davis were compelled to acknowledge that their existing strategies were incapable of producing decisive results, and that new and more radical policies were necessary.

STRATEGY IS MORE than the mechanics of military operations. All war is a form of politics, in which force and violence substitute for the civil exercise of power. That is especially true of the American Civil War, which was not fought over territory but over fundamental questions of social order, political organization, and human rights. Through strategic planning, the leaders of the warring parties define the aims and purposes of the conflict and develop a combination of political actions and military operations designed to control the action and achieve their objectives—which are always ultimately political.

Of course, strategy is not everything in war or politics. It is a truism of military science that no strategic or tactical plan outlives the first actual combat. The Antietam campaign is a pluperfect illustration of that maxim, in that almost nothing about it went as its planners intended. Presidents and generals cannot control the course of events that their orders may initiate. Their purposes and intentions will be crossed by those of their opponents and complicated by the motives and commitments of the people who do the actual fighting and the civilian societies that support or fail to support the war effort. Nevertheless, in modern warfare the role of a nation's political and military leadership is central. The ideas and intentions of these individuals shape the decision whether, when, and how to go to war or organize a campaign; their commands set the action in motion, determine its initial lines of operation, and set the conditions under which the conflict will begin. In studying the thoughts and actions of presidents and generals we gain insight into the motives and values that make wars and help to determine their course.

While it is easy to see how politics shapes strategy through the whole course of a war, it is harder to trace the connection between politics and the tactical decisions that shape war at the operational level. Thus most histories of the Antietam campaign treat the political decisions of the rival presidents and the operational decisions of their generals as if these occurred in separate spheres of thought and action—overlapping at the edges, but essentially different. Historians generally acknowledge that the outcome of the Battle of Antietam was given a vital political significance when Lincoln used the Union's narrow victory as the occasion to issue the Emancipation Proclamation. But in fact political concerns and priorities shaped the operational decision making of both presidents, and of their army commanders, at every stage of the campaign; and the interaction of politics with military operations drove leaders on each side to adopt increasingly radical and even revolutionary policies. *The Long Road to Antietam* differs from previous studies of the campaign in that it offers a narrative that integrates military and political developments and shows how each played with and against the other as events unfolded.

This book also differs from its predecessors in seeing the Civil War as a genuinely revolutionary crisis in American history. I think we cannot appreciate the character and significance of the strategic decisions taken by Lincoln and Davis unless we understand that they were not acting as the heads of stable national governments, defending well-established constitutional systems, but as leaders of embattled political movements whose regimes were vulnerable to the play of uncontrollable social and political forces. Both presidents would have to deal with the threat of new secessions by disaffected state governments and the threat of popular uprisings against their governments. Events would pressure both Lincoln and Davis to stretch their constitutional authority to or beyond the breaking point, to intensify the scope of combat operations beyond all precedent, and to inflict loss and suffering on civilian populations as an instrument of policy.

Lincoln's decision to issue the Emancipation Proclamation was the culmination of this movement: to defeat the Confederacy's political revolution he would inaugurate a social revolution, with class and race consequences far more like those of, say, the French or Russian revolutions than the Napoleonic Wars. The Proclamation was an unprecedented assertion of presidential and Federal power, which altered forever the constitutional balance of powers. Although it freed only those slaves held in Rebel territory, its application would legally annihilate several billion dollars in property. It would revolutionize the economy, social order, and politics of one-half of the country; and that transformation would be nationalized in the longer term, as freed slaves left the South and racial issues became a critical factor in the social, cultural, and political life of the entire nation. The Civil War may have ended as (in Eric Foner's phrase) an "unfinished revolution"—but revolution it certainly was.

But before he could put his new strategy into effect, Lincoln would have to overcome the most severe challenge of military to civilian authority in American history. Almost from the start of hostilities there had been movements in Washington to transfer the president's effective power as commander in chief to a professional soldier, who would be legally appointed to a temporary and limited dictatorship. That movement had found a focus and an active agent in General George B. McClellan, commander of the armies entrusted with the defense of the capital; and it would rise to the level of a explicit threat during the summer and fall of 1862.

The fact that, in the end, McClellan never acted to seize control has led most historians to discount the seriousness of the threat he represented. But historical actors, ignorant of the outcome, have to act with the full range of potential outcomes in mind. If we want to understand the quality and the content of decision making by Davis, Lincoln, and their military advisers, we need to know more than how things actually turned out. Any historical crisis has more potential outcomes than will actually be realized. Many of these possibilities have been codified in those lists of "might-have-beens" that historians and history buffs love to compile. The Antietam campaign is rife with such moments, most of them having to do with purely military events. What would have happened if McClellan had not accidentally learned Lee's plans through the finding of the lost order, or had moved with greater speed to attack?

What if Lee had chosen retreat instead of battle? Some of these are questions of real importance and will be addressed in this book.

Beyond the tactical might-have-beens are deeper questions, arising from the political crisis with which the presidents and their generals had to deal. Davis would be disappointed in his belief that a Confederate invasion would produce a political revolution in the Border States and an electoral revulsion against the administration. Was that failure inevitable, or were the decisions of Davis and Lee based on a realistic assessment of their chances to win the war on the battlefield in September 1862? In the end, the conflict between Lincoln and McClellan would not end in a military takeover. But Lincoln lacked the advantage of hindsight, and this book assesses the potential menace of the McClellan problem as Lincoln would have seen it.

History would have taught Lincoln that the political disruption of a revolutionary crisis, and the social violence of civil war, almost inevitably create the potential for the overthrow or abdication of civil authority in favor of a military dictatorship that promises to restore order. The Senate of Rome had surrendered republican powers to Caesar and his imperial successors. The English Revolution of 1640–52, which overthrew the monarchy and established a Parliamentary government, had ended in the dictatorship of Oliver Cromwell. The French Republic established by the Revolution of 1789 had given way in 1799 to the dictatorship of General Napoleon Bonaparte; and history repeated itself sixty years later when the Second Republic, formed in 1849, was overthrown by Napoleon III in 1852. Ten years after that debacle it was hardly inconceivable that the same fate might overtake the American republic.

What Lincoln also knew was that from the moment McClellan first assumed high command, in July 1861, the general had incessantly schemed and conspired and politicked to gain control of the administration. In August and September the president would come to believe that McClellan was deliberately sabotaging the war effort, and that the ideas espoused at army headquarters were increasingly disloyal and by some accounts treasonous. The threat of what Lincoln's aide John Hay called "the McClellan conspiracy" was serious, and a central theme of this study will be to show how Lincoln's decision making at every stage of the Antietam campaign was distorted by his need to deal with that threat.

Lincoln's conflict with McClellan was far more dangerous to constitutional government than the later clash between President Truman and General MacArthur during the Korean War. Truman enjoyed the presumption that the president has unquestioned constitutional authority as commander in chief to direct military policy—a presumption Lincoln did not enjoy in 1862. Moreover, the Lincoln-McClellan conflict occurred in the midst of civil war and revolution, when the authority of constitutional government itself was under challenge; and McClellan's army was not half a world away but was entrusted with defense of the president, his government, and the capital of the nation. Even a failed or abortive coup attempt by a few disgruntled officers would have done severe, perhaps irreparable, harm to the Union cause, and set a dangerous precedent for the future of constitutional government.

In the end Lincoln would succeed in transforming Federal strategy and putting the Union on the path to both victory and emancipation; and he would settle the question of civilian supremacy over the military in terms that would serve Harry Truman nearly a century later. Ironically, his initial attempt to both deal with McClellan and prepare the ground for the Emancipation Proclamation would give Jefferson Davis and Robert E. Lee their best opportunity to win the war in a single campaign.

THE STRATEGIC SETTING:
MILITARY OPERATIONS IN THE WAR'S FIRST YEAR

The secession of the Southern state was a political revolution—a fundamental disruption of national government, which challenged all existing constitutional relations. So too, in its way, was the decision of President Lincoln's government to suppress the secession movement by force of arms. The governments of states in the upper South denied his right to use force against the rebellious states and joined the secession. The constitutional authority for his action was held questionable by many Northern leaders as well as partisans of the new Confederacy; while even staunch Unionists like Democratic senator Stephen A. Douglas and Republican editor Horace Greeley questioned whether it was feasible, wise, or safe for a republican government to undertake so vast a political suppression.

The revolutionary character of the moment was obscured by the fact that both sides justified their actions by an appeal to conservative values. Each claimed to be acting on perfectly legal constitutional grounds, with the aim of preserving republican institutions and social order in their traditional form. They backed these rhetorical claims with policies that reflected the preponderance of genuinely conservative inclinations. The Confederate constitution retained the essential elements and wording of the Federal constitution, and its departures for the most part simply made explicit long-standing Southern interpretations of the original text. Unionists and Confederates also chose "conservative" presidents to lead them. Jefferson Davis had been among the more reluctant secessionists and was one of the few who defended secession as a constitutionally protected remedy rather than an assertion of the natural right of revolution. Among Republicans Lincoln was considered moderate to conservative on the slavery question, willing to give guarantees of protection to the institution in the states where it already existed. He was adamant on only two points: the specific insistence that slavery be banned from any new territory acquired by the United States; and the general principle that slavery be recognized as both a moral and a political wrong, and set on a path to "ultimate extinction" by peaceful means, at some indeterminate future date.

The strategies initially adopted by Lincoln and Davis reflected their wish that the conflict be resolved by some kind of compromise that would preserve the values and social order each man valued. They hoped that hostilities could be brought to an early end by the combination of successful but limited military actions with efforts to conciliate and compromise political differences. A few substantial and impressive victories might teach the North the futility of invasion and conquest or convince the South that the costs of resistance would be unbearable. If such successes were coupled with political measures designed to show that a peace settlement would not endanger vital interests, they might yield some kind of compromise peace.

So in defining the Confederacy's war aims, Davis denied any intention to invade the territory or threaten the political integrity of those states that remained in the Union. Davis was willing to give assurances that an independent Confederacy would not endanger vital Northern interests, for example by offering to sign a treaty guaranteeing the free passage of the Mississippi for the produce of farmers in the Ohio and upper Mississippi River valleys. Faced with the costs of a long and bloody war, reasonable men at the North might make peace if, as Davis said, "All we ask is to be left alone."[1]

Since the North's primary war aim was to restore the Union by force of arms, Lincoln had no choice but to assume the offensive. His strategy envisioned powerful military offensives on several fronts, designed to inflict demoralizing defeats on Southern armies, coupled with a blockade that would inflict significant but not ruinous damage on Southern economic interests. However, these offensive measures would be combined with a civil policy designed to reassure Southerners that their states could negotiate a return to "the Union as it was," with their rights and civil standing unimpaired. Central to this conservative policy was Lincoln's declared intent to leave slavery untouched in those states where it now existed. His stance was principled: the Constitution he hoped to preserve recognized and protected slave property. It was also politic: by declaring his intention to respect the rights of slaveholders, Lincoln was able to hold or win the allegiance of the slaveholding Border States of Maryland, Delaware, and Kentucky (which had remained in the Union). It also allowed him to make a plausible appeal to whatever peace or prounion sentiment existed in the Confederacy. In his first message to Congress, on December 3, 1861, he therefore declared that his policy would be to leave slavery alone, so that the war would not degenerate into "a remorseless revolutionary contest."[2]

Lincoln and Davis understood that a compromise settlement would be extraordinarily difficult to achieve, given the depth and intensity of their disagreement on the fundamental issues: the right of any state to secede from the Union, and the question whether slavery should be perpetuated and extended or put on a path to "ultimate extinction." Davis would accept no peace that did not concede Southern independence; Lincoln would reach no settlement that did not achieve the restoration of the Union and repudiation of the supposed "right of secession." Both therefore hoped that early and decisive victories on the battlefield would degrade, if not break, the enemy's political will to resist and bring them to make peace on acceptable terms.

The civil and military leadership of Union and Confederacy tried from the first to develop viable strategies for putting these nascent forces in play. It was clear that the Confederacy would have to stand on the defensive; clear as well that the Federals would have to take the offensive if they hoped to compel the South's return to the Union. But it was not at all obvious just how a strategic offensive might be conducted, or whether an armed reconquest of the South was even possible. Lieutenant General Winfield Scott, general in chief of the Federal army and an officer of vast military knowledge and experience, doubted whether the North could muster and equip enough land forces to successfully invade and occupy the South. At the outset, the only element on which Lincoln and Scott agreed was the necessity of establishing a naval blockade of Southern ports, which Lincoln declared on April 19, five days after the surrender of Fort Sumter. The press derided Scott's hope that the economic strangulation inflicted by a blockade—"Scott's Anaconda"—would bring the South to terms.

Military operations during the first phase of the conflict, which lasted from April 14 to the late summer of 1861, were sporadic, opportunistic, and badly organized. The firing on Fort Sumter on April 14, 1861, and Lincoln's call for troops, had brought out the militias of states North and South, and waves of recruits for newly formed volunteer regiments. But it was slow and frustrating work to form these gangs of enthusiasts into effective military units. The Regular Army of the United States was too small to provide a core combat force or an adequate supply of officers for either side. The state militias were generally neglected, poorly armed, and officered by local magnates and politicos. It would take each side months to recruit, equip, and concentrate enough regiments to form effective field armies; and their training was so poor that it was difficult if not impossible for commanders to maneuver troop combinations larger than a brigade of four or five regiments.

A premature attempt to take the offensive ended in disaster at the First Battle of Bull Run, on July 21, 1861. Ill-trained Federal troops were unable to mount organized attacks or conduct an orderly retreat when repulsed. The Federal army, commanded by General Irvin McDowell, simply fell apart, but managed to escape because the badly trained Rebel army was too disorganized by victory to pursue.

While each side was forming its field armies, the rival governments contended for control of Missouri, Kentucky, Maryland, and the western counties of Virginia, where slavery existed but Union sentiment remained strong. The struggle was made with a mixture of political chicanery, semilegal subversion, and small-scale actions by hastily gathered military forces, the proportions differing in each state. In Missouri Unionists in effect staged a military coup against the secessionist governor and legislature and won control of the northern half of the state. In Maryland, Lincoln mixed appeals to Unionist politicians with the military occupation of Annapolis, Baltimore, and the rail lines to Washington, and the threat to arrest secessionist legislators. In the end, the Maryland legislature rejected secession. In Kentucky the struggle was mostly political, though both sides smuggled arms to their supporters and both concentrated military forces on the state's borders anticipating invasion. The standoff lasted until September 1861, when, under threat of invasion, the Unionist legislature declared for the North. Only in western Virginia did success hinge entirely on action by regular military forces. In June 1861 a small Union army under General George McClellan crossed the Ohio River into the mountains and, in a campaign of maneuver punctuated by two small but decisive battles, drove Confederate forces out of the region. McClellan's success stood out sharply, juxtaposed with the Bull Run disaster and the disorder everywhere else, and led Lincoln to summon him to Washington.

McClellan took command of the Federal forces there on July 26 and became the president's most influential military adviser. In consultation with Lincoln and General Scott, he developed a general plan of operations, dated August 2, which laid down the general course of action Union armies would follow in their strategic offensive. Many of the plan's specific proposals would prove impractical, and McClellan's ideas would undergo numerous changes before they were finally put into effect. Nevertheless, certain general lines of operation laid down in McClellan's plan would become the basis of Federal strategy. The naval blockade, which had already been instituted, would be pressed by staging a series of amphibious operations to capture and hold key positions along the Atlantic and Gulf coasts. These beachheads would serve as supply bases for the blockading fleet and allow Union forces to seize or control access to Southern seaports. The invasion of the South would follow three primary lines of advance. On the Virginia front, the Army of the Potomac under McClellan's direct command would advance against the Rebel capital of Richmond. An army commanded by General Don Carlos

Buell, then forming around Louisville, Kentucky, would advance against Rebel forces based on Nashville in middle Tennessee—then turn east to capture Chattanooga, cutting the shortest rail link between Virginia and the Confederate West and liberating the pro-Union population there. A third army, or rather a group of armies and a fleet of navy gunboats, commanded by General Henry W. Halleck, would begin an offensive to recover the Mississippi River Valley—an army under General John Pope operating on the west bank of the river while another under U.S. Grant advanced on the eastern side.[3]

Lincoln pressed his generals to begin operations in the late summer and fall of 1861. However, none of the army commanders were willing to do so. All three believed it was unwise to risk a major battle before their forces were fully trained, organized and equipped. Halleck and Buell also needed time to arrange for transport and the supplies that would allow them to operate in the vast spaces of the western theater. Their objections were well founded: offensive operations were far more demanding and difficult than the defensive for raw troops and untried army staffs to organize and conduct. However, as we will see, McClellan's resistance was also driven by less reasonable factors.

The result was that, until January 1862, it was impossible for Lincoln to put any strategic concept into effect. However, the preparations made in the latter half of 1861 allowed Union forces to open a multipronged strategic offensive all around the Confederate periphery, starting in the winter of 1861–62 and culminating on July 1, 1862.

The opening gambits were a series of joint operations by the army and navy to seize key positions along the Atlantic coast. On November 7, 1861, they captured Port Royal, South Carolina, and soon gained control of the Sea Islands off the coasts of Georgia and South Carolina. Three months later, on February 1, a force under Brigadier General Ambrose Burnside entered the North Carolina sounds. It captured the Confederate force defending Roanoke Island on February 7, destroying the small defensive fleet. With complete naval superiority, Burnside would spend the next four months capturing the major towns along the coast, from Elizabeth City southward to Beaufort. The threat of invasions emanating from these Atlantic enclaves tied substantial numbers of Southern troops to local defense and limited the numbers that could be concentrated in the field armies.

While these operations went forward, another amphibious expedition, the largest of all, was organized to capture New Orleans. A fleet of mortar boats was sent in March 1862 to reinforce the navy's West Gulf Squadron and provide the big guns that would reduce the Confederate forts defending the city. A division of Union infantry was specially recruited and sent south to provide an initial garrison once the place was taken.

While the coastal operations were under way, Halleck's and Buell's armies were on the move in Missouri and Kentucky. The Confederates had a field army under General Albert Sidney Johnston facing Buell and defending Nashville, and two fortified posts, Forts Henry and Donelson, blocking a southward advance by U. S. Grant's army of Halleck's command via the Tennessee and Cumberland rivers. Grant's infantry, supported by navy gunboats, captured Fort Henry on February 6. Grant then made a rapid cross-country march to surround Fort Donelson, which surrendered on February 16 after a hard fight. Grant's victories compromised the Confederate defensive line and forced Johnston's army to retreat. Buell took Nashville on February 25 and marched with painful slowness to join forces with Grant, whose army was isolated in an advanced position on the Tennessee River, at Pittsburg Landing, Tennessee. Before Buell could get there, the Confederates under Johnston pulled their forces together and staged a surprise attack on Grant's army. Grant managed to salvage a victory in the ensuing Battle of Shiloh (April 7–8), at horrendous cost to both armies. The armies of Grant and Buell were then combined under Halleck's command and, after another painfully slow advance, captured the vital railroad junction of Corinth, Mississippi, on May 30.

While Halleck was moving against Corinth, Union naval forces under Admirals David Farragut and David Porter undertook a futile bombardment of Confederate forts below New Orleans from April 18 to April 24. On April 25 the fleet ran past the forts and it captured New Orleans on April 30, isolating the forts and forcing their surrender. The Union now had possession of the largest city and greatest seaport in the South, and it seemed possible for the navy to drive north and join forces with Halleck, clearing the Mississippi River in the process.

Operations under McClellan on the Virginia front took much longer to develop, for reasons that bear further discussion. But on March 17 the navy began transporting McClellan's Army of the Potomac, 120,000 strong, to Fort Monroe on the Virginia Peninsula—the tongue of land between the York and James rivers. The first skirmishes occurred on April 5, as McClellan moved against a Confederate trench line that spanned the Peninsula southeast from Yorktown. (Grant's fight at Shiloh came two days later.) Fort Monroe was only fifty miles from Richmond, but McClellan advanced with excruciating slowness. It took from April 5 to June 2 for his army to reach the Richmond suburbs—while fifteen hundred miles southwest Halleck's army crawled at a similar turtle's pace toward Corinth. Now McClellan was in position for a decisive battle, with an army of over 100,000.

The War Department considered that McClellan's prospects, when combined with the achievement of Halleck's western armies and the navy's successes at New Orleans and the Carolinas, gave such assurance of victory that it suspended recruitment to save money.

Then a series of bold Confederate countermoves, beginning in May and ending July 1, reversed the course of events.

On the Richmond front, General Robert E. Lee assumed command of Confederate forces on June 2. Rather than stand a siege by McClellan's superior infantry force and heavy artillery, Lee decided to seize the initiative and attack. He was aided by the operations of General Thomas J. "Stonewall" Jackson in the Shenandoah Valley. With a small command of about 15,000 men, Jackson had rampaged up and down the Shenandoah Valley from May 8 to June 9, defeating the Union forces holding the Valley, shaking the Union army's hold on northern Virginia, and appearing to threaten Washington itself. Reinforcements that ought to have gone to McClellan were distracted into a futile pursuit of Jackson. During the first week of June, Jackson broke contact with his pursuers, and Lee ordered him to bring his Valley army to Richmond. When Jackson arrived, Lee's force would be increased to about 95,000 men, nearly equal to McClellan's 105,000. Moreover, Federal units were in a bad position, divided by the Chickahominy River, with four corps to the south and only one to the north defending the army's line of supply.

Lee executed a daring tactical maneuver, using a fraction of his army to hold the line south of the Chickahominy and throwing two-thirds of his infantry, including Jackson's troops, against the lone Federal V Corps north of the river. In the Seven Days Battles that followed (June 25–

July 1), Lee smashed V Corps, compromised McClellan's supply line, and forced him to retreat to Harrison's Landing on the James River, leaving behind his wounded, thousands of prisoners, and vast stores of equipment with which Lee would reequip his army.

At the same time in the western theater, offensive operations by the Union army group under General Henry W. Halleck were stultified by poor leadership and tenuous logistics. Halleck ordered Buell's army to take up its original mission, which had been the invasion of east Tennessee and the capture of Chattanooga. But thanks to the concentration against Corinth, Buell would have to begin his advance from a point much farther from his goal than Louisville, along lateral lines exposed to Rebel cavalry raids. Meanwhile, Grant was ordered to prepare an advance against Vicksburg, the next major bastion on the Mississippi River. However, he was unable to begin his offensive, because he had to send several divisions to protect Buell's supply line.

As a result, the Confederate field armies in the theater were able to break contact with the Federals and maneuver freely. In mid-July—with Lee's force watching an immobilized McClellan—General Braxton Bragg, senior Confederate commander in the west, proposed a theater-wide offensive. He would shift most of his Army of Tennessee, 35,000 men strong, eastward by rail from Tupelo, Mississippi, to Chattanooga, easily outstripping Buell. Then, in conjunction with the small army in eastern Tennessee, led by General Kirby Smith, he would invade Kentucky. A victory there might compel Buell to abandon central Tennessee, and might even cause Kentuckians to reject their Unionist government and change sides.

THUS IN JULY OF 1862 the Civil War had reached a turning point. The strategies that had governed the actions of both sides for the first year of the war had exhausted their potential for producing decisive results. There was a brief moment of equipoise, a military standoff during which Presidents Lincoln and Davis and their military advisers could assess the lessons learned in a year of warfare and consider new military and political measures that might lead on to victory. Each president would reorganize his military commands and commit them to a new and more intensive program of offensive operations. Each would also adopt a more radical political course, taking actions and adopting policies that would test the limitations of the constitutional governments he served.

Although Confederate forces had managed to check the wave of Union offensives that had begun in January, the power of those offensives had taught President Davis that the South could not preserve slavery and independence by a purely defensive strategy. In the first two weeks of July 1862, Davis and General Lee began discussing the possibility of adopting a new and more radical strategy: a shift in military operations from the defensive to the offensive posture. By July 13 Davis would have authorized simultaneous counteroffensives by his three main field armies, whose ultimate goal was to disrupt and derange the political order that sustained the Union war effort. They would invade the slaveholding Border States of Maryland and Kentucky and invite their citizens to rise and throw off the yoke of Yankee oppression; and by raiding into Northern territory, they would bring home to the Northern people the pain and cost of war and so persuade them to reject Lincoln and the Republican Party in the upcoming midterm elections.

At the same moment, the failure of the Union offensives had made it clear to Lincoln that the forces deployed had failed to weaken the Confederacy's political will or power to resist; nor had the spirit of compromise been awakened by his assurances that slave property would be safe in a restored Union. Between June 28, when he first learned the dimensions of McClellan's defeat, and July 12, when he returned from a deeply disturbing conference with McClellan, Lincoln made a series of decisions that would transform Federal strategy in the most fundamental way. The centerpiece of his new strategy was the political decision to declare a general emancipation of all slaves held in Confederate territory. The effect of such a proclamation would be to make a compromise peace impossible and commit the Union to a war of subjugation. It would therefore entail a thoroughgoing reorganization of the military command, a drastic increase in force size, and an ambitious expansion of the army's strategic mission.

But Lincoln could not put this new strategy into effect until he had resolved "the McClellan problem."

A NOTE ON
MILITARY TERMINOLOGY

﹌﹌

FOR READERS UNFAMILIAR WITH MILITARY TERMINOLOGY, OR WITH the organization of Civil War armies, some brief definitions and descriptions may be useful.

CIVIL WAR MILITARY UNITS

The basic unit of Civil War military organization was the *regiment*, usually raised by state governments and recruited from a particular city or district. The initial strength of a regiment was 1,000–1,200 officers and men, but disease shrank that number before a unit reached the field, after which casualties and desertions took their toll. Veteran regiments in the Antietam campaign might number 150 or fewer, while "rookie" regiments mustered nearly a thousand. A regiment was supposed to be commanded by a colonel, but because of illness, wounds, or other causes, command often fell to lower-ranking officers.

A *brigade* is a group of four or five regiments, with an attached artillery battery. Brigades were supposed to be commanded by brigadier generals, and in the Confederate armies they generally were. But the Union was slow to grant general's stars, so many Federal brigades were led by colonels. The Confederate army was more assiduous than the Federals about organizing brigades by state but was not always able to do so. Rebel brigades were known by the name of their commander (for example, Hood's Brigade) or by an officially designated nickname (Stonewall Brigade). Union brigades were designated by number, though some earned unofficial nicknames: for example, the Iron Brigade and the Irish Brigade.

A *division* is a group of brigades. In the Antietam campaign, Confederate divisions ranged between four and six brigades, and were typically commanded by major generals; while Union divisions had three or four brigades and were commanded by colonels and brigadiers as well as major generals. Confederate divisions were named for their commanders; Union divisions were numbered.

A *corps* or *army corps* is a group of divisions. Two or more corps were sometimes combined to form a *wing*. During the Antietam campaign, the corps structure of Lee's army was not yet firmly established. Although Generals Longstreet and Jackson had commanded groups of divisions for months before Antietam, Lee had often altered the composition of their commands in response to events. How and why he did so is part of the story that follows. However, Lee consistently followed the principle of corps command, which was to delegate control of large-scale tactical operations to a single trusted commander with the rank of lieutenant general. Union corps were smaller than Confederate corps and usually commanded by major generals. When Confederate corps were finally established, they would be named for their commanders, while Union corps were numbered.

An *army* is a group of corps. Until 1864, the Federal government refused to authorize any grade higher than major general. Hence Union armies were commanded by major generals, while Confederate armies were led by generals or "full generals." Union armies were named after rivers, Southern armies after the territories they were initially assigned to defend. Thus McClellan's force was called the Army of the Potomac, while Lee's was the Army of Northern Virginia.

The basic artillery unit was the *battery*, consisting of four to six horse-drawn guns and their supporting equipment and ammunition, which was carried in wheeled limber-chests and supply wagons. Each battery was divided into two or more sections that might maneuver separately in action. Batteries were administratively organized into regiments and battalions, but in practice most were distributed to brigades and divisions as autonomous units. Lightweight, short-range batteries of smoothbore cannons (some called "Napoleons") were attached to brigades for action with the infantry. Divisions, corps, and the army also disposed of artillery reserves, which included both smoothbores and longer-range pieces with rifled barrels, which fired heavier-weight shells. At long ranges (800–1,800 yards), guns fired solid shot or explosive shells of various sizes, which were effective against infantry and enemy batteries. Exploding case-shot—a hollow shell packed with six large lead or iron balls— was used against infantry at ranges of 500 to 800 yards. The deadliest antipersonnel ammunition was canister, a cylinder of thin metal packed with 100–120 lead or iron balls bedded in sawdust. A cannon firing canister was like a giant shotgun, which was devastating at ranges up to 400 yards but could be effective up to 600 yards.

MILITARY TERMINOLOGY

Strategy is commonly used to describe large-scale military planning, from "grand strategy," which may be international in scope, to the planning of an entire war, to the design of a military campaign for the conquest of a region or theater of operations. In this book, *strategy* refers to the planning of a war as a whole, in which the use of military force is systematically tied to ideas about the nation's war aims—that is, the *political* objectives for which the war is being fought.

Operations are the actual movements planned or actually made by armies. A *campaign* is a series of operations designed to achieve a significant objective, such as the capture of a major city or the destruction of an opposing army. The region in which a campaign plays out is called a *theater* of operations. *Tactics* are the movements and actions of military units when in contact with the enemy.

Some of the operational and tactical maneuvers described in this book may require definition. Civil War armies fought in *lines*. The basic infantry weapon was the single-shot muzzle-loaded rifle-musket, and the only way to deliver massed fire on the battlefield was to form the infantry in two lines, one behind the other. The range and power of rifles and artillery were such that frontal assaults against strong battle lines were generally doomed to failure. If two hundred riflemen advance directly against another line of two hundred, the attackers have no advantage in firepower, and if they stop firing and attempt a charge they are at a disadvantage. The best way to break a battle line is to attack it from the *flank*, by finding a gap or open area, pushing troops through it, and wheeling one's battle line to face the end of the enemy's line—as if crossing the top of a capital "T." Now, instead of fronting an equal number of rifle-men, the attacker faces only two defenders; and his own fire *enfilades* the defender's line—rips down it from end to end. Since the attacker's line is wider than the defender's flank, the attacker also threatens to hit the enemy unit from the rear or cut it off from the rest of its army. The defenders have little choice but to retreat, or break and run.

That same principle of the flanking maneuver applies to the move-ment of armies. An army's defensive position inevitably took the form of an extended line, to defend its lines of supply and to bring its firepower into play. To drive an army from its position without attacking frontally, an attacker had to turn the defender's flank. By making a *turning maneu-ver* around the end of the defender's line, the attacker could reach a posi-tion from which he could either attack the endmost unit of the defending army, and "roll up" the line by striking each unit in turn from end to end; or strike at the defender's line of supply, cutting him off from food and ammunition and compelling him to retreat.

PART ONE

TURNING POINT: MILITARY STALEMATE AND STRATEGIC INITIATIVES

July 1862

CHAPTER 1

LINCOLN'S STRATEGY: EMANCIPATION AND THE McCLELLAN PROBLEM

APRIL 1861–FEBRUARY 1862

❧

UNION STRATEGY AT AN IMPASSE

JUNE 1–JULY 4, 1862

THE MONTH OF JUNE BRINGS SWELTERING HEAT AND HUMIDITY TO Washington, and in 1862 it also brought malaria and typhoid. For their health and comfort, President Lincoln moved his family out to a Gothic Revival cottage in the suburbs on the grounds of the Soldiers' Home, a government hospital and sanitarium for ill and disabled veterans. The president would dutifully ride into town on horseback or in an open carriage in order to work in his office at the White House or to sit anxiously by the telegraph in the War Department to get the latest intelligence from the fighting fronts.

For Lincoln the month was a time of frustration and forebodings of disaster. The depressive mood to which he was prone took hold. He left his meals half-eaten and remained up late into the night brooding. His dark, lean face went from gaunt to haggard.

On the surface the Union cause appeared to be riding a wave of success. The North Carolina sounds and Sea Islands of Georgia and South Carolina were now in Federal hands, and New Orleans had been captured. The western armies under General Halleck had driven the Rebel army out of Kentucky and the western half of Tennessee and seized Corinth as a base for further advances. In Virginia, "Stonewall" Jackson's apparent threat to Washington had been repelled, and General McClellan with the Army of the Potomac was at the gates of Richmond. There was a general consensus among both political leaders and military professionals that the victory there, which seemed imminent, would convince the Rebels to give up their attempt to gain independence. Secretary of War Edwin M. Stanton was so sanguine that he ordered the recruiting offices closed as a measure of economy.

Lincoln did not share that optimism. As he read the course of events, it seemed to him increasingly clear that the strategy of conciliation had failed. It had been based on the belief that the Southern people's commitment to secession was shallow, and could be broken by the combination of swift and decisive military action, with reassurances that slavery would be protected in the states where it already existed. But the military and the political assumptions behind that strategy had demonstrably been mistaken.

It had proved to be impossible for the Union to mount effective military offensives during the first nine months of war, and that interval had given the Confederacy time to build up substantial military forces and consolidate its hold on the loyalty of the populace. Although the first six months of 1862 had seen successful Federal offensives all around the Confederate periphery, none of these had been decisive. Southern armies had escaped destruction and continued to build their powers; and Southerners had accepted the losses suffered in these campaigns as sacrifices, which actually strengthened the public's commitment to the Rebel cause.

The slow, seemingly interminable pace of offensive operations was partly to blame. The western campaign had begun with swift victories by Grant at Forts Henry and Donelson in February 1862. But the near defeat of Grant's army at Shiloh on April 7 had given General Halleck a fright. Halleck was not an experienced field general; rather, he was a veteran of staff appointments in the prewar army, a military bureaucrat and scholar of strategic theory whose nickname was "Old Brains." It took Halleck and his army of over 100,000 men more than a month to cover the thirty miles between Shiloh and Corinth, because he insisted on marching only half the day, and spent the rest digging entrenchments to ward off a Confederate attack—which the Rebel army, outnumbered and weakened by battle losses, was incapable of mounting.

As a result, the Rebel army—known as the Army of Tennessee and commanded by General Braxton Bragg—was able to slip away from Corinth into northern Alabama, where it spent the month of June recovering its strength and mobility. From that position the Rebels could harass and disrupt the march of General Buell's army, which was supposed to march east from Corinth and capture Chattanooga, more than three hundred miles away. If Buell moved at Halleck's pace it would take him ten months to reach his goal. Lincoln was also worried about the possibility that Bragg might send reinforcements over the mountains to prevent McClellan from taking Richmond.

McClellan's advance up the Virginia Peninsula, which was nearly simultaneous with Halleck's march on Corinth, had stultified for similar reasons. McClellan mistakenly believed he was outnumbered, and therefore paused to lay siege to every Rebel defense line. He had landed on the Peninsula in the first week of April but did not close with the main Rebel army until May 31, in the Battle of Seven Pines, a little over six miles from Richmond. It would take McClellan nearly four weeks more, until June 25, to get his troops into positions from which it would be possible to assault the city. Even then, his position was an awkward one. Four of his five army corps were south of the Chickahominy River, directly fronting the Richmond defense lines. The V Corps, commanded by General Fitz-John Porter, was north of the river, separated from the rest of the army by a rain-swollen stream crossed by a few rickety bridges. Porter's position was both vulnerable and vital. He was exposed to attack by Stonewall Jackson's troops moving south from the Shenandoah Valley; and his was the only substantial body of troops positioned to defend the army's line of supply, which ran back over the Chickahominy to the small York River port of White House.

Whatever his ideas about the likelihood of McClellan taking Richmond, Lincoln was becoming convinced that it was no longer possible for the Union to defeat the Confederacy in a short war. He did not share the troubled drift of his ideas with anyone. For all his affability he was an extremely secretive man who kept his deepest thoughts to himself until he was ready to act upon them. But the effects were visible in his dark mood and loss of appetite, his frequent outbursts of dissatisfaction with his generals, and his new willingness to contemplate a major restructuring of the army command.

On June 23 he made a trip to West Point to consult retired lieutenant general Winfield Scott, who had been general in chief until forced into retirement by General McClellan. Scott was seventy-six, broken in health, his six-five frame swollen and crippled with arthritis, but Lincoln trusted his patriotism and his professionalism. Scott had served his country for fifty years and had already been a general in the War of 1812, and his conduct of the campaign against Mexico City in the Mexican American War of 1846–48 had earned him an international reputation as a strategist and field commander. Although Lincoln would not follow all of Scott's recommendations, the meeting did seem to clarify his ideas about the necessity of reorganizing the military commands. After his return to Washington he summoned General John Pope, one of Halleck's successful subordinates, to assume command of the armies that had been chasing Stonewall Jackson in northern Virginia. He also seems to have begun considering the idea of bringing Halleck himself to Washington, to take up the vacant position of general in chief and bring some coordination to the movements of the Federal armies. Neither move would have been needed if Lincoln had believed McClellan's success at Richmond would end the war.[1]

The event would prove worse than Lincoln had imagined. The messages that began rattling off the War Department telegraph on June 26 indicated that the Confederates had preempted McClellan's planned assault and staged their own surprise attack on the single army corps that defended the line of supply to the base at White House. Telegrams from McClellan's headquarters on the evening of the twenty-sixth and morning of the twenty-seventh reported the army holding firm against heavy attacks and ready to respond in kind. But by the afternoon and evening of the twenty-seventh McClellan was reporting attacks "by greatly superior numbers in all directions" that might force him to abandon his position and the White House base of supply and retreat toward the James River. That would be a costly, desperate, and dangerous move. Most of the ammunition and other supplies stored at White House would have to be destroyed, and the whole huge army would have to retreat down two narrow roads twisting through swamps and forests. They would be moving across the face of the Rebel positions in front of Richmond, and a strong offensive out of those lines could strike the retreating columns, turn retreat into rout, or even cut their escape route.

Then, just after midnight on the morning of the twenty-eighth, after Lincoln and Secretary of War Stanton had both gone home to bed, the telegraph delivered a long, rambling message from McClellan. Its extreme language and highly wrought emotional tone suggested a mind made distraught by sudden and utter catastrophe. The army had been "overwhelmed by vastly superior numbers," the last reserves had been committed and had failed to stem the attack, and the army would have to retreat with nothing intact but its honor. The message ended on a note of desperation and strident accusation: "The Government must not & cannot hold me responsible for the result. . . . I have seen too many dead & wounded comrades to feel otherwise than that the Govt has not sustained this Army. If you do not do so now the game is lost." The original telegram had contained an additional paragraph whose language was so intemperate in its arraignment of the government that Thomas Eckert, the head of the telegraph office at the War Department, deleted it from the text he forwarded to Stanton and Lincoln.[2]

Lincoln got the news early on the morning of June 28. Instead of the imperfect victory he had gloomily anticipated, McClellan's campaign seemed about to end in outright defeat—one that the Confederates might be able to turn into a strategic reversal of fortune.

Lincoln's response was characteristic. The foreboding of disaster and the incessant turning over of alternate possibilities for action had made him sick and depressed, but the event itself clarified the choices before him and found him prepared to act decisively. His emotional anguish over McClellan's defeat was real: "I was as nearly inconsolable as I can be and live." But his emotional and intellectual equilibrium were not affected. His response to the distraught telegram McClellan had sent on June 28 mixed reassurances of support with admonitions intended to bring McClellan back to a proper appreciation of the actual situation—which Lincoln did not believe was catastrophic. If the army was in danger of destruction, let McClellan save it "at all events." The government would send reinforcements with all possible speed, but the general must bear in mind that "they cannot reach you to-day, to-morrow, or next day." In the meantime, he seems to imply, McClellan should face up to his difficulties and meet them as best he could. Nor did Lincoln forbear to rebuke McClellan for questioning the president's commitment to provide him with adequate forces. In effect, he dismissed McClellan's fear of military catastrophe by responding as he normally did to McClellan's complaints. That same day he initiated the first in a series of long-term military and civil measures that would enable his forces to resume the offensive. He instructed Secretary of State William Seward to go to New York and begin a backdoor political campaign to induce the state governors to "offer" him a new draft of three hundred thousand volunteers.[3]

Among the strains Lincoln faced during that week was anticipation of the firestorm of criticism he was bound to face when news of the defeat reached the public. For a week after their June 28 exchange, knowledge of McClellan's defeat was restricted to those with access to the War Office telegraph. While Lincoln and Stanton grappled with the consequences of McClellan's disaster, newspapers across the country were printing delayed reports from the front that claimed a decisive victory for McClellan. On June 30 the *Hartford (Connecticut) Courant* headlined: "Good News Expected! Great Military Triumph! Richmond Must Fall." On July 1 a *New York Times* editorial claimed, "Our Army Before Richmond [Is] Successful"; and the Rebel capital would soon be in McClellan's hands.[4] By the most unfortunate of coincidences, most papers would not report the full story of McClellan's defeat until July 4—which one diarist called the "gloomiest" Independence Day in our history.

Newspaper editorialists used words like "revulsion," "misery," and "mortification" to express their sense of outrage and dismay. There was panic selling on the stock exchange, and the value of Federal currency plummeted.[5] The panic even upset the aplomb of General Montgomery C. Meigs, the normally unflappable quartermaster general of the army, the professional who had charge of the army's finances and services of supply. Late on the night of July 4 Meigs rushed out to Lincoln's cottage at the Soldiers' Home, pounded on the door to gain entrance, had the president called out of bed, and demanded that the navy immediately begin evacuating McClellan's men, all accumulated supplies to be destroyed and all horses killed to keep them from falling into Rebel hands. We must imagine Lincoln frowsy in his nightshirt and robe and worn carpet slippers, his coarse hair rumpled, looming over the agitated Meigs, hearing him out—then telling him to go home and go to bed.[6]

The source of Meigs's anxiety was probably General Randolph Marcy, McClellan's chief of staff and also his father-in-law, who had been sent to Washington to defend McClellan's conduct of the campaign and appeal for heavy reinforcements. At a face-to-face meeting with Lincoln on either the fourth or fifth of July, Marcy had declared that the army's condition was so desperate that if the Confederates continued to attack in their "overwhelming numbers" it would be compelled to surrender. Lincoln was furious, not only about McClellan's stubborn refusal to accept the real limitations of possible reinforcement but about his willingness to use the threat of surrender to bully Lincoln into giving him his way. The president angrily rebuked Marcy for even suggesting such a thing was conceivable and sent him back to Virginia forthwith.[7] By the night of July 4, when Meigs spoiled his rest with his tale of ruin, Lincoln was already certain that the crisis on the Peninsula had passed. Dispatches from Virginia reported that the army's rear-guard actions had repelled Lee's latest attacks and enabled McClellan's force to complete its retreat to the new and strongly fortified base at Harrison's Landing on the James River.

LINCOLN RECONCEIVES UNION STRATEGY
JUNE 28–JULY 6, 1862

Experience and assiduous study had given Lincoln a solid grasp of the military problem before him. He was no expert in military science, as he himself was the first to admit. But he was a man of extraordinary intelligence whose life had been one long intensive course of self-education from early childhood on. He had, for example, taught himself to master the principles of Euclidean geometry, as a way of sharpening his skill in logical argument. He had applied himself with the same intensity to military affairs, and by July 1862 he had achieved a solid grasp of the fundamentals and had begun to have confidence in his own judgment.

Lincoln laid out his assessment of the strategic situation in the June 28 letter to Secretary of State Seward to explain the reasoning behind Seward's mission, which was to induce the state governors to raise three hundred thousand new troops. Seward was sixty-one, eight years older than Lincoln. His short stature, beak nose, wizened face, and disorderly shock of gray hair gave him the look of "a wise Macaw." He was a veteran politician of the Whig Party and, after 1854, the Republican Party; had been governor of New York; and from 1849 to 1861 had been a leader of the antislavery forces in the U.S. Senate. He had been Lincoln's chief rival for the Republican presidential nomination but had learned to appreciate the president's principled intelligence and strength of character and had become Lincoln's most reliable ally and closest confidant in the cabinet.[8]

As Lincoln saw it, the Confederates had defeated McClellan by moving more swiftly and efficiently to concentrate their forces for the defense of Richmond. That concentration had been possible because of the slow pace of McClellan's offensive, which allowed the Confederates time to develop their defenses, and gave Stonewall Jackson the opportunity to threaten Washington during his Valley campaign. Lincoln had been forced to withhold troops from McClellan for the defense of Washington; and Jackson, who was much closer to Richmond, had been able to combine with Lee before Lincoln could ship reinforcements to the Peninsula. Lincoln also believed that the sluggish movements of Halleck's armies in the western theater had allowed the Confederates to shift forces from Bragg's army eastward, adding to the concentration of force that would defeat McClellan in the Seven Days Battles. Lincoln was wrong in that particular judgment. But he was correct in his general understanding that Confederate forces in the western theater had recovered their freedom of maneuver and, with it, the potential to stage a counteroffensive that could be coordinated with another by Lee's army in the east.[9]

Lincoln was also beginning to recognize that the failure to achieve a decisive victory in the west was not simply the fault of Halleck's excessively methodical operations. Federal armies simply lacked the manpower required for the tasks of occupying large tracts of enemy territory, securing their extended supply lines, and pursuing a highly mobile enemy through the wide expanses of the western theater. The problem was analogous in Virginia, where Federal forces were spread thin trying to meet the dual objectives of assailing Richmond and protecting Washington. Lincoln wasted neither time nor energy lamenting the facts. As he told McClellan, if the retention of troops in northern Virginia had contributed to the defeat at Richmond, "it is the price we pay for the enemy not being in Washington." The answer to such a dilemma was to greatly increase the military force deployed east and west. The campaign Seward was inaugurating to recruit three hundred thousand new volunteers was intended to provide the material strength required.[10]

Lincoln had also come to believe that there had been a fundamental miscalculation of the political character of the struggle. Like most other Northern leaders, Lincoln had generally assumed that secession was the work of a small but powerful cadre of "ultra" politicians whose demagogy had carried moderate Southerners and the nonslaveholding populace willy-nilly into revolution. The strategy of conciliation assumed that by inflicting a series of costly defeats on Southern armies, capturing a few major cities, and imposing an economic blockade, Federal forces would demonstrate the prohibitive costs of resistance. The core of the South—geographically and socially speaking—would be threatened but not attacked. There would be no massive invasion to cause economic ruin and emotional outrage, and no measures affecting the legitimacy of property in slaves. The intended result was to give moderate and economically rational Southerners and poor Whites every reason to break with the ultras and accept a conciliatory settlement.

The hard fighting of the past year had demonstrated that Southerners had a stronger commitment to secession and a higher tolerance for economic pain and military loss than Lincoln had allowed for. Moreover, a year of Confederate government and military success had reinforced the popular basis of the Davis government. The residual unionism of the upper South, on which Lincoln had counted, had never materialized beyond marginal districts like east Tennessee.

The desire to protect and perpetuate slavery was the prime motive of the rebellion, and Lincoln had seen no sign that any considerable body of Southern opinion was willing to return to a Union whose president was committed to the principle that slavery must be put on the road to "ultimate extinction." Lincoln was not privy to discussions of slavery among the leaders of the Confederacy, but there were representatives of the slaveholding South closer at hand in the Unionists of the Border States. For the first year of his presidency he had labored to persuade Border State leaders to accept the idea of gradual, compensated emancipation. The policy was consonant with his long-held view that slavery must ultimately cease to exist, on grounds both moral and political. In this case his chief motive was strategic: if the Border States voluntarily agreed to the eventual abolition of slavery, the Confederacy would lose the leverage its agents now exerted to pry these states out of the Union. During the first two weeks of March 1862 he had pressed Border State congressmen to accept such a plan and pushed through Congress a bill supporting the project. He urged them to consider that the institution was already doomed by the spirit of the modern age and by the "mere friction of war"—the fact that wherever Federal armies passed, slaves deserted their masters. He did not have to remind them that a tide of anger against the rebellion, a desire to punish the South, was rising even among Northern Democrats. The direction of things was indicated by the passage, in April, of bills abolishing slavery in the District of Columbia and in Federal territories.

Yet by July 1862 none of the Border States—not even Delaware, with fewer than two thousand slaves and no plantations—was willing to accept, even in principle, the idea of emancipation, even if it were to be compensated by Federal funds and spread out over the life of two generations. If that was the response of the Unionist Border States, it would be utterly impossible to persuade the seceded states to accept "ultimate extinction" as a condition of their return to the Union, unless they were subjugated by force. For his part, Lincoln would never abandon the principle of ultimate extinction. It was his deep conviction that slavery had been, and always would be, the chief and perhaps the only source of dissension among Americans. His disappointment at the failure of his own policy of conciliation was offset by the thought that, if he had succeeded in restoring the Union at the cost of perpetuating slavery, the motives for rebellion would have continued to operate, all but guaranteeing another civil war sometime in the future. On moral as well as pragmatic grounds, it was preferable to face up to the problem and deal with it now.[11]

Given the proven military strength and political will of the Confederacy, it was apparent that victory would require a broader and more intense mobilization of the north's military force and political will for a longer, harder war. Such a war would require more than three hundred thousand new volunteers. It required a strategy that directly attacked slavery, which was the root cause of the war and the basis of the South's political and military strength. Such a strategy would also require a restructuring of leadership in the Federal army: a new and more efficient command system, capable of coordinating offensives on a continental scale; and generals personally committed to the new strategy, willing and able to carry it out.

Lincoln's own determination to meet exigencies of a long war was absolute. As he told Seward, "I expect to maintain this contest until successful, or till I die, or am conquered, or my term expires, or Congress or the country forsakes me." He would also declare his intention not to quit the game while he had a single card left to play. What he needed was a general whose determination and commitment matched his own. What he had instead was General McClellan.[12]

Lincoln had "studied him and taken his measure as well as he could." The general had done a superb job training his army and preparing for the campaign, but he moved too cautiously and slowly and, when faced with the necessity of committing his force to battle, "became nervous and oppressed with the responsibility and hesitated to meet the crisis." These were not the qualities required for the longer, harder war Lincoln knew he had to fight.[13] On the other hand, McClellan had real ability as an organizer, trainer, and motivator of volunteer troops; and it was not at all certain that Lincoln could find anyone better to replace him as commander of the Army of the Potomac. As of July 4, 1862, there was no other general in the service who had had comparable experience in the command of so large a body of troops—except for Halleck, whose weaknesses as a field commander were known and who was slated for a different role in the high command. Grant and Buell were already assigned to army commands in the West, and neither had yet proven himself in that role. Brigadier General John Pope had had some success in a minor campaign in Missouri, which led Lincoln to put him in command of the troops defending Washington on June 26; but he had yet to show he could command a large army. General Ambrose Burnside had shown promise in conducting the operations that had seized the North Carolina sounds between February and June 1862, but this had been primarily a naval campaign.

Despite his defeat, McClellan remained extraordinarily popular with his troops; and the officer corps of the Army of the Potomac was for the most part intensely loyal to their commander. Those feelings were an element of strength, enabling him to restore his army's morale and rouse its fighting spirit—if only he would commit himself to action. The dark side of that virtue was the fact that McClellan had fostered a cult of personality in his army and among his officers that would make it extraordinarily difficult—perhaps impossible—for any replacement to command them effectively.

However, the McClellan problem went beyond merely military considerations. During his yearlong tenure in command, McClellan had become the leader of the political opposition to Lincoln and the policies of the Republican administration. Yet paradoxically, his strong support by the Democratic Party made it more difficult for Lincoln to relieve him of command. The North's ability to maintain the war for the Union depended on the backing of the so-called War Democrats, whose loyalty to the Union moved them to serve or support a Republican administration. The general was the very personification of the War Democrat. He had served the Union cause at the highest level by personally organizing its army and fighting its battles. When Lincoln brought McClellan to Washington in July 1861, they had been substantially in agreement on the aims and methods of Union strategy. But over the ensuing year they had become increasingly estranged: partly because of their incompatible personalities, partly because of the inevitable disagreements between the military and the political leadership over the management of army affairs—but primarily because of their profound disagreement about the political character of the war and the policies needed to win it.

Lincoln and McClellan embodied the principles that governed the beliefs and actions of their respective parties, and their conflict defined the primary fault lines in the Unionist cause. These differences were fundamental, rooted in the political battles of the 1850s that had culminated in secession and civil war: Should slavery in the South be perpetuated and permitted to expand into new territories or put on the path to ultimate extinction? And did the Federal government have the power and the right to limit its expansion and regulate it toward extinction?

To understand the process of political and military analysis that drove Lincoln to radicalize Union strategy, we have to look closely at the way his conflict with McClellan developed during the year that began with McClellan's appointment to the high command on July 26, 1861, and ended on July 1, 1862, with the retreat of McClellan's defeated army to Harrison's Landing.

THE INDISPENSABLE MAN:
McCLELLAN AND LINCOLN
JULY 1861–FEBRUARY 1862

George Brinton McClellan was thirty-four years old when, on the day after the Federal rout at Bull Run, Lincoln summoned him to Washington to take command of the forces defending the capital. The two made a striking contrast when they met on July 26: Lincoln exceptionally tall and almost preternaturally lean of face and figure, dressed in a rumpled suit and worn top hat; McClellan a little under average height but built like a fireplug, his handsome face adorned with well-barbered mustache and goatee, his barrel chest proudly forward, trim and trig in his blue and brass. The strong physical contrast was offset by the warmth of their meeting. Lincoln was gratified by the belief that he had found a general fully competent to the task before him, McClellan pleased to have won at last the recognition he deserved—recognition that had been long delayed but which, when it came, had come with astonishing suddenness.

McClellan had long been considered one of the Regular Army's best and brightest. He had ranked second in the highly distinguished West Point Class of 1846, whose fifty-nine graduates produced twenty-two future generals, twelve for the Union and ten for the Confederacy, with Stonewall Jackson heading the latter group. McClellan had served along with then Major Robert E. Lee as an engineer on the staff of General Winfield Scott in the 1847 campaign against Mexico City and was generally recognized as an officer of great energy, ability, and ambition. After the Mexican War he was favored with choice assignments by Secretary of War Jefferson Davis. In 1853 he led one of the army expeditions sent to survey possible routes for a transcontinental railroad, and in 1855–57 he traveled to Europe as the army's official observer of the Crimean War. Nevertheless, like a lot of the army's more energetic junior officers, he found that peacetime service offered little prospect of promotion. He resigned from the army in 1857 to find more interesting, lucrative, and empowering work in the growing civilian economy, where trained engineers and managers were in high demand. He was a great success as an executive of the Illinois Central Railroad. Through his work he forged close ties to Illinois senator Stephen Douglas and to the leaders of the Douglas wing of the Democratic Party, whose distaste for abolitionism he shared. In 1859, after a long courtship, he married Mary Ellen Marcy, the daughter of Major Randolph Marcy of the army engineers. McClellan valued her opinion highly and adopted her deeply religious understanding of history and human destiny. His wartime letters to her shared his innermost thoughts and feelings and reflected his intense desire to earn and maintain her approval of his character and actions.

Despite his marital and business success he missed the army and petitioned several times for reinstatement. In 1859 and 1860 he wrote to his mentor, Quartermaster General Joseph E Johnston, later a senior Confederate general, seeking restoration of his former rank. The application failed, because the army was in a period of fiscal retrenchment and not able to increase the size of the officer corps. McClellan also asked Johnston to recommend him to the organizers of a filibustering enterprise: a private military expedition aimed at overthrowing a Latin American government and acquiring territory suitable for the expansion of slavery. There had been several controversial attempts of that kind in the 1850s, notably by William Walker in Nicaragua in 1855–58, to which the U.S. government had turned a blind eye. But by 1860 the government of President James Buchanan had banned the launching of such expeditions from U.S. soil, because they were liable to exacerbate the political conflict over slavery expansion and endanger relations with foreign governments. It is not clear whether Johnston declined to recommend McClellan because such ventures were illegal, or if the expedition (which would have been highly speculative) failed to get the needed funding. In any case, McClellan remained desk-bound at the Illinois Central. At age thirty-four he was a man both successful and disappointed.[14]

The outbreak of the Civil War finally gave McClellan his chance to return to the army with high rank. Within weeks after Fort Sumter, with the support of Republican governor Dennison of Ohio and General in Chief Winfield Scott, he was commissioned as major general of volunteers and assigned to command the regiments that were being formed in Ohio and Indiana. He proved to be a superb organizer and trainer of volunteer troops, with a flair for publicity and a gift for the grand gesture that makes military service seem glorious to the men in the ranks. On May 26 he received an appeal from a group of political leaders in western Virginia who intended to resist the secession of their state and wanted Federal military support. In relatively short order McClellan assembled an infantry force and organized it for an extended operation in the West Virginia mountains. In a monthlong campaign, McClellan established Union control in this vital border area. At its height McClellan's force did not amount to more than twenty thousand troops, and the Confederate "army" that opposed it was never able to concentrate more than three thousand men in any one place. Nevertheless, McClellan's achievement in clearing and holding West Virginia for the Union was impressive. McClellan and the press trumpeted as major victories the two small skirmishes in which he defeated Confederate forces sent against him; but it was his mastery of organization and logistics that enabled him to complete a successful offensive in that region of high mountains, deep woods, and primitive communications.

The significance of the West Virginia campaign became magnified by the contrast between McClellan's swift and efficient operations and the shameful rout of the army commanded by Irvin McDowell at Bull Run. At Lincoln's call McClellan was suddenly translated from the West Virginia backwater to the nation's capital and the center of the War for the Union. On the four-day train trip from Wheeling to Washington, crowds gathered on every station platform to hail him as the nation's hope. On arrival he was received as the incarnation of military professionalism, which precisely matched his self-conceit. He expected the civilian leadership to defer to his judgment, and for a time it did. Lincoln in particular—his nominal commander in chief—seemed ready to grant him far wider authority over operations and appointments than would ever have been permitted in the hidebound and hierarchical prewar Regular Army. It was astonishing. In the last six months McClellan had gone from unhappy railroad vice president to putative savior of the Republic. The president and General Scott, the cabinet and senators, "give me my way in everything, full swing & unbounded confidence. All tell me that I am responsible for the fate of the Nation." Some men might have been awed by the adulation or oppressed by the weight of expectation that went with it. McClellan let his ego swell till it matched those expectations. He assumed from the first a perfect self-confidence: "It is an immense task that I have on my hands, but I believe I can accomplish it."[15]

The Mexican War had taught him to despise the incompetence of the politically connected amateurs who commanded volunteer regiments. He believed with all his heart that victory for the Union would require that control of everything from preparations to operations be entrusted to professional soldiers like himself. He would come to see his elevation as providential and would interpret his successes and failures as signals of God's intentions toward the American republic: "I feel that God has placed a great work in my hands." He confided to Mary Ellen his sense that "by some strange operation of magic I seem to have become *the* power of the land. I almost think that were I to win some small success now I could become Dictator or anything else that might please me—but nothing of that kind would please me—*therefore* I won't be Dictator." His sense of power is conveyed by his emphasis on "therefore": if he does not assume the dictatorship, it is because it does not please him to do so.[16]

The idea of a military dictatorship was not an idle or passing fancy. Demands for dictatorship would regularly recur whenever the war seemed to take a turn for the worse. It had proponents in both political parties as well as the army and was advocated from time to time by important journals in the national press. The recurrence of the dictatorship theme, and the seriousness with which it was advocated, is a significant measure of the depth and complexity of the political crisis with which Lincoln had to deal; and the possibility of dictatorship would define the stakes in the personal and political conflict between President Lincoln and General McClellan.

We are used to thinking of the president's standing as commander in chief as embracing powers clearly defined by the constitution, and as extensive in scope—indeed, according to some recent interpretations, even "unlimited." But those principles were not at all settled in 1861. Although the Constitution designates the president as commander in chief of the armed forces, at the start of the Civil War there was no clear precedent for how that command should be exercised. In the most recent case, the Mexican War, President Polk had used his power to authorize the invasion of Mexico, approve in a very general way the strategic offensives proposed by his senior generals, and appoint army commanders and several of their senior subordinates. The commanding generals, operating thousands of miles from Washington, were able to conduct operations and even peace negotiations as they saw fit. The present war would take place on home ground, and in a country with excellent rail and telegraphic communications, which meant the president and secretary of war in Washington had the ability to exercise close supervision or control of operations if they chose. But this war would also require the mobilization and operational use of forces on a scale infinitely larger than any previous war. There was certainly good reason to doubt the capacity of any civilian leader to muster and master so large and complex a military machine. Lincoln had no military or executive experience, and even many supporters believed that he lacked the great force of character his task would require.[17]

The most basic premises of Lincoln's warmaking policy were held questionable. There was a considerable body of Northern opinion, not exclusively Democratic, which doubted the constitutionality of his plan to coerce the seceding states or questioned the wisdom and/or morality of trying to pin the Union together with bayonets. In such a setting, with a revolution already commenced, with civil authority fragmented and social violence spreading, the traditional constraints of political imagination are loosed, and radical actions and political transformations of all sorts become conceivable and plausible, even appealing. If one state or group of states could secede, why not others? There were secessionist organizations at work in Missouri and the Border States, in Illinois and Indiana, and even in New York City. In the late summer of 1861 General John C. Fremont, commanding Union forces in the West, had threatened to lead a secession of western states, with himself as dictator. He was resisting an order from Lincoln to rescind a proclamation freeing large numbers of slaves in his district, which was itself a usurpation of presidential authority. Fremont had backed down and Lincoln eventually relieved him from command, but the threat of further secessions and of a military putsch remained.[18]

In his own capital city, Lincoln was confronted with a host of opposition factions and movements whose members not only criticized his conduct of the war but attempted to usurp his authority. The leading men in his cabinet were also faction leaders who used their power and standing to influence Lincoln's policies. The most powerful and ambitious cabinet officers would try to wrest control of military and/or civil policy out of Lincoln's hands. Secretary of State Seward tried the trick with a presumptuous memorandum during the first days of the administration; but when Lincoln quashed the attempt, Seward backed off and became the president's closest colleague. On the other hand, Treasury Secretary Chase never stopped angling for control of the administration.

Chase was an impressive figure, tall and burly, with the high forehead that was supposed to be the sign of great intellect, a founding leader of the Republican Party, a former senator and governor of Ohio, a strong antislavery man who was the cabinet voice of the Radicals. He thought Lincoln weak-minded and vacillating and rather blatantly promoted himself as the president's replacement in the next election.[19]

A more explicit threat of usurpation came from the Radicals in Lincoln's own party. Their chief instrument was the Joint Committee on the Conduct of the War, which used its powers of investigation to intimidate the army and the executive branch, subjecting generals to days of unfriendly inquisition—and getting one brigadier, the unfortunate Charles Stone, thrown into prison on mere suspicion of disloyalty. The temper of the Committee is indicated by the character of its chairman, Senator Zachariah Chandler of Michigan. Chandler was New Hampshire born, but in 1833, at age twenty, he moved to the Michigan frontier, where he opened a general merchandise store. From earliest youth he had detested the very idea of slavery, and his early political activities were devoted to that cause rather than to any specific party. However, in Michigan the Democrats were more closely identified with support of slavery than the Whigs. When Chandler formally entered politics, as successful candidate for mayor of Detroit in 1851, he did so as a Whig; and when the Republicans emerged as an antislavery party in 1854, Chandler became a charter member. He made his bones, so to speak, organizing gangs of antislavery roughnecks to fight it out with the mobs of bully-boys that Democrats sent to intimidate voters at the polls. After serving as mayor of Detroit, he won election to the Senate as a Republican in 1857. There he espoused militantly antislavery views. He disapproved of Lincoln's early efforts to negotiate a peace and his hope of conciliating Southern Unionists. To those "traitorous States" he would offer "no concessions, no compromise," nothing but "strife unto blood before yielding to the demands of traitorous insolence."[20]

Lincoln and his confidential secretaries John Hay and John Nicolay privately referred to Chandler and his colleagues as "the Jacobins," determined to figuratively guillotine those suspected of lacking enthusiasm for the cause. For some Radical leaders, the work of the Joint Committee was merely the prelude to a more revolutionary reorganization of constitutional government. Senator Charles Sumner of Massachusetts believed, and in June 1862 would assert in open debate, that the Constitution vested the power to wage war in Congress, not the president, and that the legislature's war powers were virtually unlimited. Sumner was the intellectual leader of the Radicals, a true Boston Brahmin, a graduate of Boston Latin School and Harvard—a scholar and orator in the classical mode, who had been a leader of the antislavery forces in the Senate since 1851. The Radicals wanted to use the authority implicit in the war powers to annul the constitutional standing of the seceded states, reducing them to territorial status, and to abolish slavery. If successful, their effort would have fundamentally altered the constitutional division of legislative and executive authority.[21]

The confusion and mismanagement that characterized the early days of mobilization, coupled with the embarrassing defeat at Bull Run, magnified doubts about Lincoln's competence to the point where some in Congress and the press were willing to consider the appointment of a professional soldier as "dictator." Powerful faction leaders, including Senator Chandler and Treasury Secretary Chase, supposed that a dictator put in place through their influence would look to them, rather than the president, for advice on policy. Such a dictatorship would be the result not of a coup but of deliberate legislation, which would limit its duration and powers. The dictator's appointment would terminate with the end of hostilities, and his powers would be restricted to "purely military" affairs, leaving civil policy and authority in the hands of the president. It was supposed that this could be done without compromising the republican character of the government—though all historical precedents, from Caesar's Rome to Napoleonic France, suggested the contrary.

The idea appealed for several reasons, apart from the fear that Lincoln was inexperienced or inept. It is worth noting that Confederate leaders were also drawn to the idea of dictatorship, despite the fact that President Davis was a West Point graduate, a combat veteran, and a former secretary of war. Behind such proposals was the assumption that military and political affairs could be treated as distinct and separate realms of activity; and that military measures were best conducted by politically disinterested professionals, without the interference of politicians. In fact it is neither possible nor desirable to separate the operational conduct of war from consideration of political questions, since every war is ultimately political in its causes and objectives—especially a civil war. Nevertheless, military professionalism is of real value in war-fighting, and Lincoln acknowledged this by persistently searching for a general in chief to whom he could entrust the management of military operations. McClellan seemed perfectly cast for the role.

At first it appeared that Lincoln and McClellan agreed on the basic elements of Union strategy. McClellan declared that "military action . . . prompt and irresistible" and in "overwhelming strength" was necessary "to convince all our antagonists, especially those of the governing aristocratic class, of the utter impossibility of resistance." He also shared Lincoln's expressed belief that the shortest and least costly path to reunion required the conciliation of Southern slaveholders.[22]

This apparent agreement masked serious and fundamental differences, which would become more pronounced as the war itself was prolonged and intensified, and it would threaten to fracture the political unity of the Unionist cause. Lincoln's support of conciliation was pragmatic: it seemed to offer the least destructive path to reunion. But he remained convinced that the Union was unsafe so long as slavery was free to expand and states insisted on a right of secession, and he would not accept terms of conciliation that left either question unresolved. In contrast, McClellan described himself as a conservative and "a strong Democrat of the Stephen A. Douglas school." The conflict that developed between them was, in a sense, a continuation of the famous Lincoln-Douglas debates of 1858, which set the terms for the Union's wartime debate over slavery and states' rights.

To understand the significance of McClellan's identification with Douglas, we have to look briefly at the three-sided political struggle among Republicans, Southern Democrats, and "Douglas Democrats" that had raged from 1854 to 1860 and culminated in secession and civil war.

THE CONFLICT OF PRINCIPLES, 1854–1860

The issue that first divided the parties arose in 1854, when the Kansas-Nebraska Bill promoted by Senator Stephen A. Douglas of Illinois broke the terms of prior compromises and opened previously "free" territories to settlement by slaveholders. The question that then divided the major parties, and factions within the parties, was whether or not the Federal government had the power and the right to exclude slavery from the unsettled western territories acquired by the nation through the Louisiana Purchase of 1804 and the Mexican War. The newly formed Republican Party held that the Federal government did have that power under the Constitution; and that it ought to use it to prevent the spread of slavery and the aggrandizement of "the Slave Power"—the Southerners whose dominance of the Democratic Party had given them control of Congress and of the presidency. Among Republicans, antislavery sentiment ranged from abolitionists who detested slavery on moral grounds and wanted it extinguished everywhere to westerners solely interested in preserving the new territories for White men.

Abraham Lincoln became the Republicans' representative man because he was able to articulate a set of common principles on which the whole party could agree. His core principle was the belief that the United States could not continue as a "house divided," half-slave and half-free. Slavery was both morally wrong and radically inconsistent with the democratic principles on which American nationality was founded, and for *that* reason it must be put on the path to ultimate extinction. Preventing the spread of slavery to the western territories was the essential first step toward that goal, and the Federal government had the power to exclude it.

This statement of policy was based on a deeper principle, which would become more crucial during the war as the slavery issue came to the fore. Lincoln insisted that the principle of equality enunciated in the Declaration of Independence was the moral compass of the nation and the implicit promise of the Constitution. Although neither he nor his party was prepared to advocate immediate universal abolition or the granting of full civil rights to Black people, they were committed in principle to freeing Blacks from economic servitude. As Lincoln put it, during his 1858 debate with Senator Douglas, "in the right to eat the bread, without leave of anybody else, which his own hand earns, *he is my equal and the equal of Judge Douglas, and the equal of every living man.*"[23]

The Democrats were divided between a "Southern" wing, comprising slave-state politicians and their Northern allies, and a Northern wing led by Douglas. The Southern faction held that slavery was a beneficent institution, necessary to the maintenance of White supremacy; and that the Federal government had neither the power nor the right to exclude it from territories acquired by and for the whole nation. The Republican claim that slavery was "immoral" was both an insult to Southern honor and an unacceptable form of agitation likely to foment social violence. Extremists within the Southern wing also held that Federal attempts to exclude slavery would violate the Constitution and justify secession.

The Douglas Democrats occupied a middle ground between Southern Democrats and Republicans. Douglas himself represented the interests and ideas of Democrats in the region then known as the Northwest, the states north of the Ohio River formed out of the old Northwest Territory. His constituents favored the Democratic Party's positions on trade, tariffs, and westward expansion and were virulently anti-Negro. But they had no love for slavery as such, and wanted the western territories reserved for White family farmers; and they resented the fact that their party was controlled by the Southern wing, which denied the presidential nomination to the Northwest's favorite son, Stephen A. Douglas.

Douglas's platform was given its definitive shape during his classic debates with Abraham Lincoln, during the Illinois senatorial election campaign of 1858. He denied the Republican premise that either slavery or freedom must become universal. The nation had been half-slave and half-free for generations and could continue so indefinitely if extremists on both sides would cease agitating the issue. He refused to engage the morality of slavery. Such questions were matters of conscience; statesmen must only concern themselves with the law and the public interest. While he did not explicitly endorse the Southern view that slavery was a "positive good" and enslavement the natural and necessary condition of the Negro, he did emphatically endorse the principle of White supremacy on which the defense of slavery was based. In his debates with Lincoln, Douglas specifically rejected the idea that the principles of the Declaration of Independence applied to Negroes. He declared his belief that the American government had been founded "on the White basis . . . by white men, for white men"; and that Negroes or Indians, while they deserved decent treatment, had no claim to civil equality.[24]

However, Douglas broke with the Southern wing of his party on the critical issue of the territories. While he accepted the South's view that the Federal government could not exclude slavery from the territories, he held that the people of the territory could vote to exclude it. The principle was known as "squatter sovereignty," and Douglas adopted it because the people he represented were independent farmers who saw the territories as a land of opportunity and did not want to have to compete with the owners of large, slave-worked plantations. The Southern wing of the party saw Douglas's policy not only as a blow to their economic interests but as an implicit endorsement of the Republican view that slavery was "wrong," morally and/or economically, and ought to be restricted and ultimately extinguished. It therefore did Douglas no good to insist that neither Christian morality nor the principles of the Declaration was at stake in the 1860 election. At its presidential nominating convention the Party split, with a bare majority supporting Douglas and a Southern faction nominating John C. Breckinridge of Kentucky. With the Democrats divided against themselves, Lincoln and the Republicans won the election, and the threat of Republican antislavery measures drove the South into secession.

Douglas had always been a staunch Unionist and opponent of secession, and after the firing on Fort Sumter he would support the use of military force to end the rebellion. Lincoln could not have mustered the required political support or the recruits for the war effort without the backing of Douglas and other "War Democrats." However, despite the fact that secession had carried the Southerners out of the Democratic Party, its ranks still contained a substantial number of so-called Doughfaces, or "Northern men of Southern principles," who wanted to settle the conflict on Southern terms. Moreover, even War Democrats like Douglas still held to the principles Douglas had enunciated in 1858: that the nation had been founded on "the White basis," by and for White men exclusively; and that slavery was both a constitutionally protected institution and the guarantor of White supremacy. They therefore worked for the restoration of a Union in which slavery remained intact; and they wanted the seceded states restored to the Union with their political rights largely intact, so that a reunited Democratic Party could regain control of the government.

With those ends in view, Douglas and his Democratic colleagues in the period between the first secessions and Fort Sumter (January–April 1861) tried to restore the Union by offering the South extremely generous terms of compromise. These included the passage of constitutional amendments guaranteeing the perpetuation of slavery, the opening of some western territories to slavery, and even the restructuring of the government to allow Southern states to veto Federal legislation. Since all of these ideas required the Republicans to abandon the core principles and planks of their platform, the compromises failed. Nevertheless, they indicated the extent to which Democrats might be willing to go to conciliate the South should the strategy of conciliation succeed in bring the Confederate leadership to terms.

McClellan had been close to Douglas during his years as vice president of the Illinois Central Railroad, and he strongly and actively supported Douglas against Lincoln in both the 1858 Senate campaign and the 1860 presidential canvass. As a railroad executive he had also made contacts among a group of financiers in New York City who were also active in the Democratic Party and supporters of Senator Douglas. Chief among them were two men who would become McClellan's political mentors and his link to the Party leadership: Samuel L. M. Barlow, a corporate lawyer who often represented railroad interests, and William Aspinwall, a wealthy merchant and railroad entrepreneur. Through them he became acquainted with August Belmont, the German-born international banker and financier who had been Douglas's most effective fund-raiser. Belmont was the financial bulwark of the wartime Democratic Party. In 1863 he would be elected as its national chairman, and with Barlow's aid he would mastermind the movement that would nominate McClellan for president in 1864.

However, in 1861 neither Belmont nor Barlow was thinking about the presidency. Nor was McClellan himself. In the summer of 1861 the party was in total disarray. Senator Douglas, its leader and chief presidential aspirant, died suddenly of typhoid, on June 3, 1861. Not until May 1862 would the Democrats' congressional caucus be able to formulate the rudiments of a national platform. In the interim Belmont and Barlow and other New York Democrats assumed leading roles in the task of reorganizing their diminished party as a strong and conservative opposition. From their perspective, McClellan was the conservatives' best-placed and most powerful instrument of political influence. They were eager to make use of him, and McClellan had a great deal to gain from their support.[25]

AGENT OF INFLUENCE:
McCLELLAN AS GENERAL IN CHIEF
AUGUST–DECEMBER 1861

McClellan embraced his role as the conservatives' man at the top because he sincerely believed in their principles and because he thought that as general in chief his responsibilities included civil as well as military policy. Throughout his service as military adviser to the president and commander of the army, McClellan would confer and consult with his New York advisers, seeking their guidance about his own course of action and asking them to use the party's newspapers and its congressional delegation to support him against his opponents in the administration. This they were more than willing to do, since it furthered their efforts to rebuild their party as a viable opposition and regain control of Congress and crucial governorships in the next midterm election in November 1862.

McClellan tried to use his position as army commander to make himself the leader of his own powerful conservative faction, and to contest with Chase and Seward and the Joint Committee on the Conduct of the War for the power to direct a weak and incompetent president. He would benefit from the fact that he was also the object of desire for faction leaders in the Republican Congress and for members of the "Team of Rivals" who comprised Lincoln's cabinet. The more ambitious among them saw in the young professional a cat's-paw to diminish or effectively displace Lincoln as commander in chief. At one time or another McClellan would be courted by Radicals like Michigan Senator Zachariah Chandler, of the Joint Committee on the Conduct of the War, and by cabinet officers seeking to control the president's councils, including Treasury Secretary Chase (Radical), Secretary of State Seward (moderate), and Postmaster General Montgomery Blair (conservative).[26]

Although he was willing to court and be courted by the likes of Chase and Seward, McClellan was committed in principle to the conservative cause. The basis of his political ideology was Douglas's premise that the American government had been founded "by white men, for white men" and that Negroes were unfit for citizenship. McClellan thought slavery an anachronistic economic system, with many unsavory features that needed reform; but he thought the "best men" of the South could be trusted to improve the system while preserving White supremacy. McClellan, and the Democratic leaders who supported him, hoped to see the Southern wing of the party, chastened by defeat and diminished in power, reconnected to the national Democracy in a conservative coalition that would once again dominate U.S. politics. The general asked his political mentor Samuel L. M. Barlow to use his influence with the press to discredit the Radicals and "Help me to dodge the nigger— we want nothing to do with him. *I* am fighting to preserve the integrity of the Union & the power of the Govt—on no other issue. To gain that end we cannot afford to raise up the negro question." He believed that conciliation was the only way to restore the Union without compromis- ing the republican character of the American government. To attempt the military subjugation of a free people (the South) would transform the republic into a despotism, and drive the Rebels to a defense so desperate it could never be overcome.[27]

In contrast, Lincoln's commitment to "conciliation" of the South was conditional rather than absolute. He did hold that the Constitution restrained the power of the president and Congress to alter slavery in a state by executive order or simple legislation. He was indeed reluctant to deal with the revolutionary consequences that would follow from large- scale abolition. But the fundamental principle of his political program was the insistence that slavery must be started down the road to eventual extinction; and this, as McClellan rightly believed, was something the South would never accept. If conciliation failed, Lincoln was not only prepared but determined to fight a war of subjugation, to restore the Union and begin the destruction of slavery by force if nothing else would suffice. And while he did not underestimate the difficulty of such a task, he considered it within the realm of possibility, if the North was willing to put out its full strength and bear the costs of total war.[28]

In August 1861, however, these differences were not yet material. Lin- coln immediately brought McClellan into his circle of close advisers and solicited his advice on grand strategy. McClellan presented a compre- hensive plan on August 2 that showed his grasp of the big picture as well as the military details. He was soon more valued than Secretary of War Cameron, and coequal with Lieutenant General Winfield Scott in man- aging army operations. When Scott disagreed with and opposed McClel- lan's views, McClellan began a bureaucratic campaign to discredit Scott and force his relief or retirement. It was easy to deride the pomposity of a proud old general whose nickname, even in younger years, was "Old Fuss and Feathers," and to imply that Scott's expertise was out of date. But McClellan went beyond that ploy with statements that defamed Scott's character and intelligence and questioned his loyalty. On November 1 Winfield Scott, who had been for fifty years the nation's most distinguished military commander, was compelled to accept the indignity of an enforced retirement, and McClellan was appointed to replace him as general in chief.

The press nicknamed him "The Young Napoleon" and photographers demanded he act the part, standing with chest thrust out and right hand tucked into the front of his uniform coat. Accordingly, he trimmed his mustache and goatee in the Imperial style established by Napoleon III, who had become emperor of France through an 1852 coup d'etat. The dark side of being a young Napoleon was that if dictatorship did become necessary as a means of saving the nation, was he not obliged to assume it? But if he did, might he not also become the destroyer of republican institutions? On August 9 he wrote his wife, "I receive letter after letter—have conversation after conversation calling on me to save the nation—alluding to the Presidency, Dictatorship, &c. As I hope one day to be united with you forever in heaven I have no such aspirations—I will never accept the Presidency—I will cheerfully take the Dictatorship & agree to lay down my life when the country is saved." Less than a month after assuming command he imagines himself refusing the offer of the presidency—he was too young for the office in 1862, and the next election was two years away. But he can "cheerfully" accept the proffer of immediate dictatorship—though now the fantasy includes a patriotic suicide, acknowledging the fact that the resort to dictatorship would imperil the future of republican government. "I have no choice," he confided to his wife, "the people call upon me to save the country—I *must* save it & cannot respect anything that stands in the way."[29]

His sense of himself as a superior man, and his unswerving belief that he was uniquely qualified to be the savior of the republic, made it hard for him to bear the constraints of working within Lincoln's circle of advisers and having to explain and justify his actions to men he considered his intellectual inferiors or political enemies. The great outpouring of public support that he enjoyed during his first six months in power was, as he saw it, a kind of symbolic election, by which the people had chosen him during this hour of darkness to vindicate the national cause. In his first official message to Congress Lincoln himself acknowledged that "the nation seemed to give a unanimous concurrence" with McClellan's promotion, and his appointment to command is "in considerable degree the selection of the Country as well as of the Executive."[30] But McClellan's popularity fostered the illusion, abetted by his friends and advisers in the Democratic Party, that there was a kind of moral equivalence between himself and Lincoln; that he represented in some unofficial yet real way the "conservative" views held by a putative majority of Northern people.

McClellan's correspondence offers a unique insight into his state of mind and his way of responding to the political and personal tensions around him. During the nine months he spent in Washington, his official correspondence with Lincoln and other administration figures is on the whole formally correct and duly respectful. But his letters to his wife and to Samuel Barlow are filled with angry fulminations and vicious aspersions on the character and intentions of Lincoln, the cabinet, the Republican Party, and any politician or fellow officer opposed to his policies or interests. The general tenor of these opinions, also shared with close colleagues and officers of his staff, gradually became public. Lieutenant General Scott, the most distinguished soldier of his age, had once been hailed by McClellan as his hero and mentor. But when Scott disagreed with McClellan's plans, or his assessment of enemy strength, he became "that confounded old Genl . . . a perfect imbecile. He understands nothing, appreciates nothing & is ever in my way. . . . I do not know whether he is a *dotard* or a *traitor*! . . . If he cannot be taken out of my path I will . . . resign & let the admn take care of itself."[31]

McClellan's sense of self-worth, which had butted in vain against the constraints of the prewar army and the business world, was suddenly invited to spread itself. The cost of that expansion was also a terrible concentration and isolation of the self, which distorted his personality, his relations with the administration, and ultimately his ability to understand and deal effectively with the strategic problems he faced as a military commander. He felt himself to be at once uniquely and terribly empowered, and uniquely and terribly vulnerable. If he believed himself capable of winning the war in a single campaign, he also had to fear that he might lose it in one campaign. For all his real expertise and immersion in practical affairs, McClellan was living in a military and political fantasy world—of his own devising, abetted by his supporters—in which he was the central figure in a two-front war to save the Union from the Rebels in front and the Radicals in the rear. On August 16 he wrote his wife, "I am here in a terrible place—the enemy have from 3 to 4 times my force—the Presdt is an idiot, the old General [Scott] in his dotage." He was then in Washington, DC, surrounded by a ring of fortifications and the camps of his own army, a hundred thousand strong.[32]

Before he could risk his standing by moving against the enemy in his front he needed to secure himself against the enemies in his rear. He labored and schemed to force Scott into retirement, feeling sure he would succeed him "unless in the mean time I lose a battle—which I do not expect to do." The only way to be certain of that was to avoid battle entirely. But after Scott was gone other enemies appeared to threaten his position—rival generals, Radical senators, hostile cabinet members. For more than eight months after he assumed command he would refuse to lead the Army of the Potomac into battle.[33]

Instead, from his appointment in the summer of 1861 till his departure for the Peninsula in April 1862, McClellan waged a series of political and bureaucratic battles, first to gain exclusive control of military affairs, and then to hold the civil policy of the government to a conservative course. McClellan thought Lincoln was weak-minded: essentially conservative and "sound on the nigger," but susceptible to pressure from the Radicals. McClellan believed that he could dominate the president's councils, draw him away from the Radicals, and win his support for conservative positions espoused by the Democratic Party. Despite his occasional alliances with Chase and Seward, Postmaster General Montgomery Blair, the most conservative Republican in the cabinet, was the only consistent supporter of McClellan and of the conservative program he espoused.[34]

The most immediate obstacle to McClellan's control of military affairs was General Scott. From August to the end of October 1861, McClellan conducted a systematic campaign intended to undermine Scott's authority and drive the "Grand Old Man of the Army" into retirement. McClellan spread rumors about Scott's physical and supposed mental incapacity, ignored or bypassed the old general in issuing military communications, and treated Scott with studied rudeness. When Scott resigned and

McClellan succeeded him as general in chief, Lincoln expressed concern that McClellan was taking on too many tasks: exercising strategic command of all the Union armies while he was also closely engaged in organizing and commanding the huge Army of the Potomac. McClellan confidently replied, "I can do it all." Having struggled to achieve what he thought would be the exclusive control of military affairs, he was not inclined to invite outside assistance, least of all from a president he despised.

McClellan's self-confidence was unjustified. At that stage of the war, with Federal armies still in process of formation, it was probably impossible for any general to succeed in the dual tasks of creating his own huge army from scratch and commanding it in the field, while at the same time developing and ordering the execution of a grand strategy for several large field armies operating across the entire breadth of the nation. The only Civil War general to successfully combine the functions of strategic generalissimo and army commander was Ulysses S. Grant; but when Grant took charge in 1864, the Federal armies were all veteran forces, under commanders with three years of experience behind them. McClellan seems to have been overtaxed by his dual role, and his labors were set back for several weeks in December 1861 and January 1862 when he came down with typhoid.

There was also increasing discord during the fall and winter of 1861–62 among McClellan, the administration, and the Joint Committee on the Conduct of the War. There had been criticism of McClellan's inaction on the Potomac front during September and October; and after McClellan was appointed general in chief, he was also held responsible for the inaction of Halleck's and Buell's armies in the western theater. The political leaders believed it was vital for military operations to begin as soon as possible, preferably in the fall of 1861 before the onset of winter made operations in Virginia impossible. Their reasons were sound. The lack of Federal action was undermining the confidence of American and European financiers in the feasibility of the war for the Union, frustrating the administration's efforts to float loans and raise money to support the armies. Northern public opinion was also discouraged, seeing the lack of action as a sign that effective action was impossible. The longer the Confederacy stood unassailed, the stronger its forces grew, the more credible were its claims to have established its independence, and the better its case for recognition by Britain and France.

McClellan, Halleck, and Buell agreed it would be a grave mistake to take the offensive until their troops were properly trained and their armies properly organized and supplied. There was merit in these objections. It was far more difficult to conduct offensive operations than to stand on the defensive, especially with raw troops and untested systems of command, communication, and supply. The disaster at Bull Run demonstrated the danger in moving prematurely. That lesson was reinforced on October 21, 1861, when a Union brigade was virtually destroyed at Ball's Bluff while conducting a reconnaissance across the Potomac.

However, even if a strategic offensive was not possible in the fall of 1861, there were a number of important tactical objectives close to Washington with which McClellan's forces might well have coped. For example, the Rebels had planted batteries along the lower Potomac which prevented shipping from using the river and subjected Washington to an embarrassing blockade. Given the Union navy's dominance of the waterways, a Federal division could easily have taken and held these outposts. McClellan's refusal to undertake even so limited a mission reflects something more than concern about the rawness of his troops and his army's incomplete organization. He refused to risk even a minor a setback that might strengthen his critics and his enemies.

McClellan was not wrong in seeing his position as vulnerable, although his own inaction was partly responsible. In early December the Joint Committee subjected him to close and, he believed, hostile questioning. His testimony was not made public, which allowed McClellan to try to preempt its bad effects by leaking his own highly inaccurate version to the press. However, the Committee struck back by investigating the conduct of General Charles Stone, the division commander who had ordered the reconnaissance that had ended in disaster at Ball's Bluff. Stone was a close associate of McClellan, shared his commitment to the conciliation of Southern slaveholders, and had ordered his troops to return fugitive slaves to their masters—which was in accordance with both Federal law and current policy, but anathema to the Radicals. The committee would decide that Stone was guilty of sympathy for and perhaps collusion with the enemy, and order his imprisonment without trial. McClellan believed the attack on Stone was the prelude to a move against himself, and he may have been right.[35]

During the fall of 1861 McClellan found an important ally in Edwin M. Stanton, one of the best-known and most successful trial lawyers in the country and a lifelong Democrat. Stanton had served briefly in President Buchanan's cabinet as the secession crisis was breaking and had done his utmost to make Buchanan act firmly in defense of Unionist principles. After Sumter he emerged as a leading War Democrat, respected by both parties and often consulted by members of Lincoln's cabinet, who trusted his loyalty and his judgment. Stanton was forty-eight years old, clean-shaven about the cheeks and mouth but with a full beard along the jawline that flowed down from chin to mid-chest. He glared at the world through round, rimless spectacles: a man of choleric temperament, strong convictions, and violent expression. Samuel Barlow had urged Stanton to help McClellan, who was being dogged by the whole "abolition pack" because of his opposition to their "anti slavery schemes." In August of 1861 he became an intimate of McClellan, with whom he shared party loyalties and principles as well as contempt for the person and politics of Abraham Lincoln, dubbed by Stanton "the original gorilla."[36]

McClellan delighted in that description, which he would use repeatedly in his private correspondence. The pleasure he took in it expressed the most dangerous aspect of McClellan's state of mind, which was his instinctive and unjustified disdain for Lincoln. Some of this was simple snobbery. McClellan's social origins were upper-class, though not aristocratic as Americans understood that term. His father was a well-to-do physician, his mother a daughter of one of Philadelphia's social elite. But his sense of status was shaped by West Point, where Southern officers and cadets defined the category of "gentleman" and drew a strict line between themselves and cadets of insignificant lineage or breeding. McClellan's sense of himself as a gentleman, living by a code of honor superior to ordinary morality, was directly tied to his ideal of the professional soldier—the privilege accorded the man of superior training was as necessary, and as justified, as the privilege accorded the man of superior social standing. His outrage at the appointment of "political" officers blended the professional's disdain for the amateur with the gentleman's disgust for the parvenu. On both scores, Lincoln was unacceptable: a man of low birth and small education, lifted by vile politics above his social and intellectual superiors. McClellan therefore found his subordination to Lincoln nearly intolerable. His attitudes ranged from a patronizing acknowledgment of Lincoln's dim-witted honesty and good intentions to vicious contempt for the President's person, manners, intellect, morals, and patriotism. When Lincoln did something that pleased him, McClellan might offer some condescending praise: "The Presdt is perfectly honest & is really sound on the nigger question. I will answer for it now that things go right with him." More often he dismissed Lincoln as a "well-meaning baboon" or "the *original gorilla*." When Lincoln opposed or criticized McClellan, the general branded him as either a traitor or the witless tool of traitors. This was a dangerous notion for a man who believed he was the country's chosen savior, who could not, in duty, "respect anything that is in the way."[37]

McClellan's manner toward the president was often disrespectful. The gentleman's code laid great stress on the power of the snub to put an inferior in his place or compel an equal to either challenge you or give way. He used it on Lincoln to rebuke the president for his continual interference. On returning to his headquarters one day, he was told the president was awaiting him in the drawing room—and without a word he went upstairs to bed. Lincoln took the rudeness in stride, remarking that he would hold the general's horse if he would only win victories. One of Lincoln's strengths as a commander was his ability to set such petty insults aside. With McClellan, however, that virtue became a flaw: a true gentleman resents an insult, and by bearing this one Lincoln merely confirmed his inferiority in McClellan's eyes.[38]

Lincoln tolerated McClellan's rudeness, intransigence, and disregard of presidential pleas and directives because he still thought McClellan was the general best qualified to command in Virginia. To get the job done Lincoln was willing to use whatever tools were at hand, however problematic. But his pattern of alternately pushing McClellan to act, then settling for an assurance of future action, merely reinforced McClellan's belief that the president was weak-minded, succumbing first to the influence of McClellan's enemies then bowing to the superiority of McClellan himself. That view reinforced McClellan's belief that it was possible for him to gain control of the administration—and necessary for his own sake that he do so.

Far more serious was McClellan's refusal, through December and January, to discuss with Lincoln his plans for the 1862 military campaign. McClellan had outlined a general plan of campaign in a report to the president back on August 2, but the plan was short on specifics, and in the interim changing conditions had rendered it useless. McClellan considered a number of possible plans after becoming general in chief, but these were very tentative and indefinite. He remarked to Secretary Chase that he expected to capture Richmond in February, but he made no preparations for such a move. He had begun considering a plan that called for the navy to rapidly shift his army to a point on the Virginia coast from which he could strike at the line of communication between the Confederate army at Manassas and its base of supply in Richmond. But the plan was unsettled, and his bout of typhoid prevented his developing it from December 20 through January 7. Lacking a definite plan, he was reluctant to consult the president and so invite the suggestions Lincoln was bound to force upon him.

Faced with the inaction of his armies and McClellan's refusal to confer with him, Lincoln chose to force the issue. He called a council of war on January 12, to which he invited cabinet secretaries Chase and Seward and an assistant secretary of war, and for the army Quartermaster General Meigs and Generals Irvin McDowell and William Franklin. Franklin was an engineer, top of his West Point class in 1843, a longtime friend and associate of McClellan, now a senior member of his staff and presumably able to speak for his ailing commander. McDowell was the general who had lost Bull Run, uninspired and uninspiring, a dull man who had risen in the Regular Army thanks to his competence as an artilleryman and the operations of seniority. McClellan regarded him as a rival, an enemy, and a tool of the Radicals. At the meeting, McDowell proposed a direct advance against the Rebel army at Manassas, while Franklin hinted at McClellan's idea for a move by sea. Lincoln asked the generals to consider the possibilities in more detail and return for a second meeting on the thirteenth.

McClellan learned about the meeting through his friend Stanton, and both men recognized the "grand conclave" as a potentially fatal usurpation of McClellan's command prerogatives. McClellan had actually been recovered from his illness for a week—he had been feigning to forestall presidential consultations—and he invited himself to the January 13 meeting.

The conference was held in Lincoln's White House office and attended by most of the civilian and military officers who constituted the Federal high command. In addition to Lincoln and McClellan, General Meigs attended, along with Secretaries Seward, Chase, and Blair representing the cabinet. Secretary of War Cameron was absent—he was being forced to resign and had not yet been replaced. Generals McDowell and Franklin, whose advice on the offensive Lincoln had sought, were also present.

McClellan's demeanor was hostile and sullen throughout the meeting. Each of the generals spoke in turn, laying out the ideas they had earlier presented to the president. McClellan said nothing. When General Meigs attempted to summarize the views of the council, "McClellan replied somewhat coldly . . . 'You are entitled to have any opinion you please!'" He refused to say anything more. He saw himself as alone in a room full of conspirators who consulted in whispers between bouts of inquisition and addressed him with what he thought was "uncalled-for violence of . . . manner"—though Meigs thought the hostility was all on McClellan's side. When Lincoln pressed McClellan for his plans, he refused in terms insulting to the cabinet officers and the president: "[N]o general commanding an army," he said, "would willingly submit his plans to the judgment of such an assembly, in which some were incompetent to form a valuable opinion, and others incapable of keeping a secret." With what seemed deliberate rudeness McClellan added that he would not tell Lincoln his plans because the president would blab them to the *Herald*, a newspaper that shared McClellan's antipathy for antislavery Republicans. The meeting ended without an agreement on future operations.[39]

McClellan's insulting accusation of Lincoln's supposed propensity for blabbing things to the press was the more egregious, considering that the next day McClellan himself would arrange to leak his plans to the *Herald* in order to build public support for his position. He owed that connection to his friend Stanton, who had arranged for McClellan to meet with a reporter named Malcolm Ives. Through Ives, McClellan arranged to plant stories favorable to his interests in the *Herald*. He also asked his father-in-law and chief of staff, General Marcy, to meet in New

York with James Gordon Bennett, publisher of the *Herald*, and confirm McClellan's intention "to keep Mr B. well posted" with the inside story of military affairs.[40]

On his return from the January 13 meeting, McClellan received the welcome news that Stanton had been appointed secretary of war, succeeding Simon Cameron. The two friends had actually helped bring that change about through a dubious bureaucratic ploy. In December, just after McClellan's triumph over General Scott, Cameron had asked them for advice in preparing his annual report, and they had suggested Cameron make a strong statement in support of emancipation and the recruiting of Black troops—policies that neither Stanton nor McClellan actually favored but which they knew were contrary to Lincoln's policy. Cameron's report embarrassed Lincoln; and since there was also ample evidence of Cameron's incompetence as an administrator, Cameron was forced to resign.

For a few weeks McClellan enjoyed the luxury of having a true friend in the president's inner circle. Then Stanton abruptly changed sides. His devotion to the Union was real, and he was fiercely determined to make the Federal war effort efficient and energetic. As secretary of war he was frustrated by McClellan's reluctance to act, when action was politically and militarily imperative. As McClellan's former confidant, he was also aware of the general's desire to control the conduct of the war, and saw him as a rival. Only two months after his appointment he joined Lincoln in criticizing McClellan's prolonged inaction, mocking one mismanaged field exercise as "another damned fizzle." Stanton would become McClellan's chief opponent in the cabinet, and forcing Stanton to resign would be McClellan's chief political project for the rest of his active service. The most outrageous aspect of Stanton's betrayal was his transfer of loyalty from McClellan, an officer and a gentleman, to the man Stanton himself had called "the original gorilla." His sense of victimization was extreme, and expressed in language that reflected McClellan's inflated sense of significance: he wrote his wife that Stanton was "worse than Judas," which made McClellan a kind of Christ.[41]

Through February and into March McClellan persisted in his refusal to take the field, even for such minor operations as clearing Confederate batteries from the lower Potomac or testing Rebel strength at Manassas by a reconnaissance-in-force. His inaction seemed all the more egregious after February 4, when U. S. Grant, of Halleck's command, began the rapid and effective offensive that culminated in the surrender of fifteen thousand Rebel troops at Fort Donelson on February 16.

But in the weeks following the January 13 council, McClellan had developed a new strategic plan whose centerpiece was the movement of his own Army of the Potomac by sea to the Virginia Peninsula. The development and execution of that plan would complicate and intensify the conflict between the civil government and its most powerful military leader.

CHAPTER 2

McCLELLAN'S STRATEGY: IRRESISTIBLE FORCE

FEBRUARY 1–JULY 11, 1862

❧ ❧

WITH ENEMIES FRONT AND REAR AND THE FATE OF THE NATION IN his hands, McClellan believed that he must not risk his person or his reputation for infallibility until he could put his army in position for a decisive victory. He believed that the plan of campaign he developed in February and March 1862 would produce just such a result. Instead of making a frontal attack on the Confederate army, he would force it to retreat, and ultimately to fight him at a disadvantage, by a making a grand turning movement against its eastern flank. The plan went through several versions, all of which featured the movement of his main force by sea while a smaller force remained behind to defend Washington. The first version called for the strike force to land at Urbanna, a town on the Chesapeake Bay shore of Virginia from which McClellan could attack the supply line linking the Rebel army at Manassas to the capital of Richmond. That plan became moot on March 10 when it was discovered that the Confederate commander, General Joseph E. Johnston, had pulled his forces back from Manassas and formed a new defensive line behind the Rappahannock River, some thirty miles closer to Richmond. McClellan then developed a more daring and potentially decisive version of the Urbanna plan. He would carry his army to Fort Monroe on the Peninsula of Virginia, only fifty miles from Richmond—much closer to the city than Johnston's army. A rapid march up the Peninsula would put him at the gates of Richmond, where he could compel Johnston to stand and fight a decisive battle.

The campaigns of Napoleon—still the ideal theoretical model for the modern strategist—had shown that an aristocratic society like the South could be defeated by wrecking the prestige and breaking the morale of the ruling class; and that could most readily be done by defeating its principal army and capturing an important city, preferably the capital. The Napoleonic example was reinforced by more modern conflicts, like Scott's campaign in Mexico and the Crimean War. McClellan would bring overwhelming force to bear on the capital city of Richmond. Because of its importance, both material and symbolic, the Confederates were bound to concentrate the largest possible and best equipped force to defend it. By defeating that force and capturing the capital, McClellan would have demonstrated the impossibility of resisting the Federal armies. If at the same time it could be shown that the North had no disposition whatever to interfere in the master-slave relation, then those Southern leaders not utterly carried away by fanaticism might be induced to make a rational choice for peace.[1]

From Lincoln's perspective, McClellan's plan had two drawbacks. It required the army to continue its inactivity in and around Washington, since the idea was to tempt Johnston to remain in northern Virginia rather than scare him farther south. The more serious objection was that while McClellan's troops were in transit, and even while they were on the Peninsula, Washington would be exposed to attack by the large Rebel force that was supposed to be concentrated around Manassas. McClellan rated that force as between 70,000 and 102,000 men, and the administration accepted McClellan's estimates for want of anything better. Lincoln insisted that before McClellan made his invasion, Rebel forces must be pushed farther from the capital; and that a substantial force must be left behind to defend Washington. Although several commands were involved in the capital's defense, the specific bone of contention was the infantry corps commanded by Gen. Irvin McDowell, the largest and best-trained of these commands.

The argument over how many troops, and which units, should be committed to the defense of Washington began when McClellan first laid out his Urbanna plan in March, and it did not end until McClellan's army ended its retreat from Richmond on July 2. In a sense it would never end, because in his subsequent official reports and press interviews, in his 1864 campaign for the presidency, and long after the war in his memoirs, McClellan, characteristically, would blame his defeat on Stanton and Lincoln for withholding those troops. From the first, discussions of the issue were poisoned by mutual suspicions. McClellan believed that Stanton and the Radicals were conspiring to ruin his campaign and his career by starving his army of troops. Some Radicals, including Zach Chandler, suspected McClellan of a treasonable plot to hand Washington over to the enemy, in order to preserve slavery and return the Democratic Party to power.

McClellan's standing was weakened by the retreat of Johnston's army, of which McClellan had had no inkling because he would not let his army engage in active scouting or large-scale armed reconnaissance. When McClellan finally marched his troops out to "pursue" Johnston, the Rebels were out of reach. He also discovered that the Rebel fortifications, which had seemed so formidable to the errant citizens who reported on them and the observers who had viewed them through telescopes at a great distance, were mostly sham. Logs had been mounted at the embrasures as dummy cannons called Quaker guns. That suggested to many the possibility that the Rebel army had been generally much weaker than McClellan supposed. Republican papers mocked the futility and folly of McClellan's excursion to Manassas, and McClellan called on his friend Barlow to activate the anti-administration New York papers, the *Herald* and the *World*, in McClellan's defense.

To McClellan's chagrin, he returned to Washington on March 11 to find that Lincoln had relieved him of the duties of general in chief. The president denied that the action was intended as a rebuke and said, rather, that it was necessary because McClellan was soon to take the field as commander of the Army of the Potomac, whose operations would absorb all his energy and attention. But it looked to all the world like a demotion and a rebuke. McClellan also saw it as a part of a political intrigue intended "to secure the failure of the approaching campaign."[2]

It was unfortunate that no one tried to follow up the suggestion that Johnston's force had been overrated. A closer inspection of the encampments might have yielded real intelligence on Confederate strength, which was in fact about forty-eight thousand, less than half of McClellan's high estimate. But the failure of intelligence on that score was chronic, rooted in the combination of McClellan's peculiar psychology and the faulty organization of his intelligence staff, and it would affect every decision and action of the Federal high command from the summer of 1861 to the winter of 1862–63.

THE NUMBERS GAME:
McCLELLAN'S INTELLIGENCE SERVICE

McClellan's overestimate of enemy strength was fabulous in scale, and the errors that produced it were systematic. McClellan typically credited the Confederates on his front with two or three times their actual strength. Every military operation McClellan undertook, from his arrival in Washington to the end of the Antietam campaign, would be premised on the belief that the enemy heavily outnumbered him. Because the War Department did not have its own intelligence apparatus, it had no independent means of checking McClellan's estimates.

McClellan's earliest force estimates were based on Confederate newspaper reports and civilian rumors, but he soon put in place an intelligence service commanded by the railroad detective Allan Pinkerton, alias "Major E. J. Allen." Pinkerton was forty-two years old in 1861. He had a full beard, dark and neatly trimmed, and even at army headquarters wore civilian garb: a frock coat, checked shirt, and bowler hat. He was born in Scotland in 1819. As a young man he had been engaged in the Chartist struggle to expand voting rights in Great Britain, and the failure of that movement led him to emigrate to the United States and settle in Chicago in 1842. There he founded the North-Western Police Agency, later known as the Pinkerton National Detective Agency, which soon emerged as a major presence in law enforcement in a nation that lacked professional police at any level. His agency's forte was surveillance, and the use of operatives to infiltrate and break up criminal gangs and expose embezzlers—techniques he would use after the war to break up labor unions. In the 1850s his major clients were midwestern railroad companies, the Illinois Central prominent among them. His railroad work was well known to both Lincoln and McClellan. President-elect Lincoln had used his agents to protect him on his journey to Washington.

Although Pinkerton's methods were effective against rear-area subversives like the pro-Confederate Knights of the Golden Circle and the Baltimore "Blood Tubs," he was out of his depth in the field of military intelligence. His operatives did succeed in infiltrating Confederate offices, obtaining army paperwork, and gathering rumors about Rebel operations; but they did not know how to distinguish units that existed merely on paper from regiments fully manned, equipped, and ready for battle. They could tell McClellan the number of regiments officially credited to Lee's army but not the actual strength of these units. The failure was not entirely their fault—Confederate accounting methods were so slipshod that even an army commander like Lee could not be absolutely certain of the number of troops in his command. Nevertheless, the result was an astounding overestimate of the Rebel forces in Virginia.

Pinkerton's information might have been useful had it been subject to critical analysis by an intelligence staff and supplemented by other forms of intelligence gathering—scouting by cavalry, or the use of large units for a reconnaissance-in-force, the taking and questioning of POWs, and assessment of their state of equipment, health, and training, and so forth. An analysis of the Federal army's own difficulties in raising troops, equipping them, and maintaining regiments at full strength would have suggested how unlikely it was that the Confederates were raising a larger army—given the fact that the North had a larger White population to draw on, and far better resources for transporting and supplying its armies. But since McClellan insisted on being his own chief of intelligence, there was no independent staff review. McClellan also read all intelligence through the distorting lens of his conviction that he and his army were the Republic's sole hope of salvation and must run no risk of defeat. It followed that in estimating the opposition he must always err on the side of caution, basing his moves on the assumption that the enemy force was as large as it could conceivably be. Field reports that suggested the enemy in his front was at less than maximum possible strength were characteristically discounted. He never tested these strength estimates by matching them against the known limitations of Confederate manpower, production, and transportation.[3]

So utterly out of scale were McClellan's estimates that he was suspected of cooking the books to justify his unceasing calls for reinforcement. However, all the evidence suggests that he and his closest advisers genuinely believed their absurd figures. He and his army were the sole reliance of an imperiled republic and the only force capable of over-throwing the rebellion. It was only logical to assume that the Rebels would concentrate every available man to oppose him and destroy the army he commanded.

McCLELLAN'S ARMY AND THE CULT
OF PERSONALITY

In McClellan's view, the fate of the republic absolutely depended on the triumph of the principles and policies he represented; and his fate, in turn, depended on the success of his Army of the Potomac. That army must not be exposed to a serious risk of defeat, since a reverse would be doubly fatal. It would embolden the South to continue the war indefi-nitely; and by discrediting McClellan it would hand the Federal govern-ment over to the Radicals. He therefore abandoned the idea of prompt action in order to build an army that would be invulnerable.

Lincoln was not mistaken in thinking McClellan a master at train-ing raw troops. McClellan's critics mocked the incessant drills and the grand reviews as mere showmanship. But in fact these exercises instilled high morale in the army's units and taught officers and men the difficult tasks of maneuvering brigades and divisions on the battlefield. McClel-lan turned his volunteer gunners into superb artillerymen by combining volunteer with Regular batteries and putting them through long hours of practice.

If he was frustrated in his attempts to gain leverage within the cabinet, McClellan could take great satisfaction in his ability to build the Army of the Potomac into a powerful and efficient military force. But the army McClellan created was also a political instrument.[4]

McClellan tried to maintain direct control over every part of his vast army from his own headquarters, which was manned by staff officers personally chosen for their loyalty as well as their expertise. McClellan's headquarters was a closed circle, an echo chamber filled with follow-ers and acolytes who praised his every decision as masterful but also echoed and amplified his rage at the supposed bad faith of the president, and his fear that enemies in the administration were continually conspiring against him. In the army at large McClellan favored his loyalists and ignored or neglected his critics, which divided the officer corps into pro- and anti-McClellan camps.

His closest colleague was Fitz-John Porter, a close friend from prewar days, who became McClellan's primary counselor on military and political affairs. Porter had graduated from West Point a year ahead of McClellan, had won promotion for gallantry during the Mexican War, and had served as an instructor at West Point. He was often described as the ideal soldier, erect in carriage, handsome, and full-bearded. He would serve on the staff while McClellan was organizing his army, before being promoted to divisional and finally to corps command.

McClellan also did his best to bind the ordinary soldiers to him by a strong and personal bond. He made frequent tours of the camps and presided at drills and reviews, displaying in a thousand ways his interest in his men and concern for their welfare. He frequently addressed them, in person and through general orders and proclamations. The style of these is revealing. McClellan speaks as if no intermediaries exist between the enlisted men and himself as their leader, teacher, and benefactor. Although the training and supply of the army, and the maneuvering of men in battle, was the work of hundreds of staff, division, brigade, and regimental officers, McClellan never used the word "we" when addressing *his* men. He presented himself as a superior intelligence, an all-seeing father who had full control of everything concerning the army. He honored his "boys" by making them worthy of his comradeship. His General Orders No. 1, of February 2, 1862, is characteristic. Explaining the long delay before he would commit them to action, he wrote: "I have long held you back my comrades, at first that from a mass of brave but undisciplined citizens I might cement you into an Army. . . . I have restrained you for another reason also. I wished you to strike when the time arrived for giving the death blow to this accursed rebellion. The task of discipline is completed—I am satisfied with you." The time is near "When I place you in front of the rebels."[5]

More than obedience, McClellan needed the adulation of his soldiers. In his dubious battle with political enemies, the cheers of his men, their hero adulation, was balm to his wounded ego. His letters to his wife are filled with anecdotes of soldiers, singly and in masses, cheering him, praising him as the savior of the nation.[6]

Yet the love he so often professes for his men is sentimental rather than authentic. He rarely visited his wounded in the field hospitals or shared the risks of the battle line. What he loves about his men is their love for him, the way they idolize him as a godlike figure. In a world of enemies, the Army of the Potomac was McClellan's hearth and refuge, a perfect social order created by himself, an extension of his identity. His love for it was self-love—no less real and powerful for that. As an extension or projection of McClellan's identity, the Army of the Potomac could not risk taking the field until it had been made indestructible.

THE PENINSULA CAMPAIGN, APRIL 1—JULY 6, 1862

In his attempt to make his army an irresistible force McClellan turned it into a nearly immovable object. He had spent eight months training and equipping the Army of the Potomac, during which time he had refused to undertake any significant military action. In the first week of April his lead elements landed at Fort Monroe and made contact with the enemy. But McClellan remained risk-averse, refused to advance until success was assured. His method would reduce to futility the brilliant maneuver by which he transferred his army by sea to the Peninsula only fifty miles from Richmond—a good deal closer than General Johnston, whose army was still waiting for McClellan up on the Rappahannock.[7]

In the opening weeks of the campaign sixty thousand to seventy thousand Union troops (with another thirty thousand on the way) faced no more than fifteen thousand Confederates at Yorktown. Johnston's main force of forty-five thousand would take three weeks to reach the scene. Had McClellan struck hard with his whole force and followed up with energy, he would have found Richmond defended by fewer than sixty thousand troops, disorganized and perhaps demoralized by defeat and the hasty withdrawal from northern Virginia. Instead he spent one month besieging Yorktown, and another working his way up the Peninsula. By the time he reached the outskirts of Richmond in early June, Johnston's whole force and substantial reinforcements were waiting to oppose him. After Johnston was wounded in an engagement at Seven Pines on June 1, Robert E. Lee assumed command of the Confederate force. The change pleased McClellan, who thought Lee was "a timid general."[8]

Yet even with this supposed advantage he still hesitated to attack. The rivers were too high, the weather was bad, the roads not suited for the passage of his heavy guns. He needed still more reinforcements before he could put at risk the army and the reputation on which the fate of the republic depended. To order his troops into battle was to pass a point of no return—he would not pass that point without assurance of victory.

During the long months of his slow march to Richmond, McClellan barraged Washington with demands for reinforcement by McDowell's Corps, the largest and best of the commands that had been retained to defend Washington from Confederate Stonewall Jackson's menacing operations in the Shenandoah Valley. Ironically, Lincoln's reluctance to send McDowell was based in part on his acceptance of McClellan's overestimate of Confederate strength—he thought Jackson's command was twice its actual size. To McClellan, however, the denial was deliberate sabotage, proof that Lincoln and his cronies were "traitors who are willing to sacrifice the country & its army for personal spite and personal aims. The people will understand the matter and woe betide the guilty ones." He intensified his contacts with political supporters in the Democratic Party and the New York press, to make them more active in defending him against Lincoln and Stanton. He sent Allan Pinkerton to Washington to spy out the shifting alliances within Lincoln's cabinet, and who might now favor his cause. He cultivated the correspondents attached to his headquarters, some of whom were also political operatives, and he used some of his officers as surrogates in letter-to-the-editor campaigns.[9]

Fitz-John Porter, the McClellan confidant, was the most prominent and active of the surrogates, and he corresponded frequently with Manton Marble of the New York *World*, the semi-official organ of the New York Democratic leadership. On June 20 he alerted Marble that the army faced the prospect of defeat on the Peninsula because "The secy [Stanton] and Prest ignore all calls for aid . . . I wish you would put the question—Does the President (controlled by an incompetent Secy) design to cause defeat here for the purpose of prolonging the war."[10]

Though McClellan may have supposed that his direct connection with Marble and Barlow was not generally known, by the end of June 1862 it was generally assumed that McClellan was the White hope of the New York Democratic Party leadership and shared its views on compromise with the South. On July 1 the *New York Times* characterized a Democratic mass meeting at Cooper Union as a gathering of "The Submission Party," organized by "The Haters of Negroes and Yankees." The writer mockingly claimed they had but three principles: "that they are white men, that they hate black men, and that they have confidence in MCCLELLAN."[11]

Despite his concern about Lee's supposed advantage in numbers, McClellan anticipated success in the battle for which he was preparing, and he had begun thinking about how he might use the prestige of victory against his enemies in the administration and the Radical Republicans in general. A campaign of slow movement and infrequent combat had left him leisure to begin drafting the master plan for the reorganization of national policy. On June 20 he wrote to Lincoln, asking "permission to lay before your Excellency by letter or telegram my views as to the present state of military affairs throughout the whole country." Lincoln said he would welcome those views but thought it unwise to use the telegraph for exchanging so much military information; and since neither he nor McClellan could leave his post of action with battle imminent, perhaps it was best done by letter.[12]

Before McClellan could complete or send that letter, "unforeseen disaster" suddenly overtook the general and his army.

McCLELLAN'S DEFEAT: THE SEVEN DAYS BATTLES
JUNE 25-JULY 1, 1862

McClellan's reluctance to close with the enemy—his refusal of risk, his belief that he was outnumbered—had produced precisely the situation he most feared. Since the Battle of Seven Pines on May 31–June 1, he had done nothing to pressure Lee's army in front of Richmond. Stonewall Jackson had completed his disruptive campaign in the Shenandoah Valley on June 10, having defeated two of the Federal commands sent against him while evading a third. On June 16 Lee sent orders for Jackson to leave the Valley and march for Richmond.

With the addition of Jackson's three divisions Lee had amassed the largest force he would command in battle, roughly 90,000 as against McClellan's 105,000—as close to battlefield equality as he would ever get. Lee then split his force, sending nearly two-thirds of it to fall upon and destroy Porter's V Corps of perhaps 16,000 men, which was north of the Chickahominy River, separated from the rest of McClellan's army. This left only 30,000 Confederates south of that river to face the bulk of McClellan's force. But active feints and diversions—their significance magnified by McClellan's inflated estimate of their numbers—kept McClellan from immediately reinforcing Porter.

The Rebel onset struck him with the force of a realized nightmare. He told Washington, and genuinely believed, that he was being assailed front and flank by overwhelming numbers. Porter's Corps was saved from outright destruction by the fact that Lee's army was not yet properly organized for so large an offensive operation. Confederate attacks on June 26 were poorly coordinated, and Porter was able to retreat to a better defensive position around a hamlet called Gaines' Mill. McClellan sent reinforcements piecemeal, which eventually raised Porter's strength to about 34,000. But the Confederates had 57,000 at hand, and when they finally organized a proper attack late on June 27 they broke Porter's line and forced all Union troops to retreat south of the Chickahominy.

That retreat exposed their base of supply at White House to capture by the Confederates, and it seemed to leave McClellan no choice but to burn his supply dumps and retreat to a new base on the James River, where the navy could reopen the line of supply. To reach safety the Army of the Potomac had to fight a rear-guard action at Savage's Station (June 29), stave off a major Confederate offensive at Glendale (June 30) that threatened to cut the retreating column in two, and fight off a last heavy assault at Malvern Hill (July 1).

Most historians and military analysts have faulted McClellan for failing to respond aggressively to Lee's attack on June 25–27 and for a premature decision to retreat to the James. In his defense, his June 27 decision to retreat to the James and establish a new base of operations actually made good tactical sense, especially considering his gross overestimate of enemy strength. It surprised Lee and delayed his pursuit of the retreating army, and the new base of operations was better in every way than the old one at White House on the York River. However, even the ever-faithful Fitz-John Porter was dismayed by McClellan's decision to retreat, rather than counterattack, after Union troops backed by massed artillery had slaughtered Lee's last frontal assault at Malvern Hill.[13]

McClellan's behavior during the retreat has led some historians to conclude that the sudden reversal of fortune, the emotional stress and physical exhaustion of days of intense activity, produced a psychological breakdown that eventually left him incapable of exercising command. The telegrams he sent to Stanton on June 25 and 28 certainly seem increasingly desperate and even hysterical in tone. Then on June 30, with his rear guard preparing to fight the most critical battle of the campaign at Glendale, McClellan effectively abandoned his army. He rode away without appointing anyone to command the fighting force in his absence, ostensibly to choose a final defensive position on the James—a task that could have been left to his highly competent engineering staff. McClellan's contemporaries found his action either inexplicable or discreditable, and even the most sympathetic of his recent biographers sees it as a "dereliction of duty," brought on by extreme physical and emotional exhaustion.[14]

On the other hand, most of the officers and newspaper correspondents who observed or worked with McClellan thought his manner calm and even self-assured, up to and including the hour in which he rode away from Glendale. His telegram to Stanton on June 25 seems overwrought: he speaks as one faced with imminent defeat by a superior force and declares that "I will do all that a General can do with the splendid Army I have the honor to command & if it is defeated by overwhelming numbers I can at least die with it & share its fate." Yet McClellan's actions were not actually governed by this prophecy of disaster. Porter had repulsed the attack on the twenty-fifth, and McClellan thought enough of his chances to keep him fighting north of the Chickahominy for two more days (June 26–27). During that time he would confer frequently with staff and line commanders, and hold one general council of war at which the retreat was decided upon. Not all of the officers and newspapermen who attended these meetings were "McClellan men," but none reported any signs of panic or desperation in McClellan's manner. It appeared to the reporters that McClellan was eager to counterattack by throwing his whole force into battle and had to be talked out of his daring by more cautious subordinates.[15]

In fact, the council was a charade: he had already given orders for the retreat. He would arrange the same sort of drama after his troops had repulsed Lee's attack at Malvern Hill, playing the fighter for the press when his real purpose was to escape the chaos of a battle he could not control. However, the success of this performance indicates that McClellan *was* in control of his emotions, and thinking intelligently about the way in which his behavior would be presented to the public. He did not know how to fight Robert E. Lee, but he thought he knew how to fight Lincoln and Stanton. Perhaps he had been defeated on the Richmond front, but that could be mended so long as he maintained his strong position in Washington and New York.

Nevertheless, in the telegram he sent on June 28 to Stanton just after the council of war McClellan *does* sound like a man unhinged and enraged by a catastrophic defeat. He stridently denies any personal responsibility for the disaster and accuses Stanton and Lincoln of betraying not only the army but the nation:

> The Government must not & cannot hold me responsible for the result. . . . I again repeat that I am not responsible for this & I say it with all the earnestness of a General who feels in his heart the loss of every brave man who has been needlessly sacrificed today. . . . I know that a few thousand more would have changed this battle from a defeat to a victory—as it is the Govt must not & cannot hold me responsible for the result.
>
> I feel too earnestly tonight—I have seen too many dead & wounded comrades to feel otherwise than that the Govt has not sustained this Army. . . . If I save this Army now I tell you plainly that I owe no thanks to you or any other persons in Washington— you have done your best to sacrifice this Army.[16]

Much of the telegram is an extended rant, and the accusations McClellan makes go well beyond the complaints of ill-treatment in his earlier official correspondence. In effect he accuses the president and secretary of war of something like treason—connivance in the deliberate destruction of their own army. The last sentence ("If I save this Army now . . .") seems to threaten an open break between McClellan and the civilian government. McClellan's language so obviously crossed the line of permissible disagreement that the telegraph officer who received it at the War Department omitted the sentence from the text he passed on to Stanton. The suppression of this sentence would lead to a critical misunderstanding between Lincoln and McClellan when the two men met only a week later, on July 8.[17]

It is possible that, after putting up a brave front for the reporters, McClellan succumbed to an emotional reaction that made him indiscreet. Certainly the rage and sense of grievance he expresses were genuinely felt. However, it is also possible that, like his disingenuous display of combativeness at the council of war, the telegram was a histrionic performance designed to dramatize the contrast between his righteous heroism and the treacherous pusillanimity of the administration. The statement functioned both as a paper record of his claim that Stanton was responsible for the defeat and as a rhetorical device meant to persuade the public that *he* must not be held responsible for this terrible defeat—must not because he is the only one who can save the republic from *both* secessionism and Radicalism.[18]

His belief that he alone could save the Republic also underlies his questionable decision to leave the field of Glendale before the battle was joined. It is certainly true that by June 30 McClellan was physically and emotionally stressed, getting little sleep and suffering from diarrhea, perhaps dysentery. Officers who saw him after he left Glendale said that he looked "used up" and "cut down." Even so, his departure was not marked by any display of anxiety or distress, although the action itself was an "astounding" breach of military custom and practice. Generals Franklin and Heintzelman, two of the corps commanders who were left to fight the battle on their own hook, thought McClellan acted out of confidence in his troop dispositions; and a staff officer who was with McClellan said the army commander believed the task of defending Glendale was "straightforward & plain work" that did not require the master's hand to direct it. McClellan's biographer Stephen Sears sees his behavior as evidence that he had lost "the courage to command," and perhaps his physical courage as well, so that he "deliberately fled the battlefield." Yet McClellan never expressed any embarrassment about his action, and never felt the need to justify it until it became a political football during his presidential campaign in 1864. Although many of his colleagues thought his decision questionable, he was able to retain his reputation for courage among an officer corps that would have treated cowardice with merciless contempt.[19]

McClellan's behavior was not the result of psychological collapse but of a flawed approach to command, and a flawed character as well. He had told his wife, nearly a year earlier, that he must not risk defeat until his political position was unassailable. On the Peninsula, just before the Seven Days, he would write to her: "I feel too that I must not unnecessarily risk my life—for the fate of my army depends upon me and they all know it."[20] But it was not just his physical life that had to be kept out of harm's way. If he was to save the republic from the twin menaces of secessionism and Radicalism, he had to maintain his prestige as the nation's preeminent military genius and his command of the Army of the Potomac. The motives that led him to separate himself from the fighting at Glendale were the same as those that informed his June 28 telegram: to protect himself against an attack from the enemies in his rear, from Lincoln and Stanton and the Radicals. Without his presence, a local defeat would be the fault of the local commanders, as the general defeat was the fault of the administration. It was McClellan's good fortune that Lee's army was too poorly organized to exploit its opportunity at Glendale; and that his corps and division commanders, acting on their own, were able to improvise a successful defense. If any praise is due to McClellan, it is for the coherence and high morale he instilled in his infantry regiments, which enabled them to win the fight despite his absence.

THE ARMY OF THE POTOMAC made a miserable, rain-soaked retreat from Malvern Hill to the encampment McClellan had prepared for it at Harrison's Landing. The mood in the ranks was chiefly one of bewilderment at the swiftness with which preparation for triumph had been turned into desperate retreat. McClellan issued a statement congratulating them on having fought well and maintained their honor, and this jibed with their knowledge that, with the exception of the fight at Gaines' Mill on July 27, they had repulsed every enemy attack. Yet these tactical victories had somehow ended in the essentially shameful fact of their own retreat, with heavy loss of prisoners and equipment. McClellan's claim that they had made a strategic "change of base" rather than a retreat was not entirely credible, although the vast majority of the enlisted men continued to vest full reliance in their beloved commander.

This was a remarkable testimony to McClellan's hold on their emotions, especially since conditions in the Harrison's Landing camp were demoralizing. Over ninety thousand men and at least as many horses, mules, hogs, and cattle were crammed into a space only four miles long by one mile deep. The ground along the James River bank was soggy and marshy, which made setting up tents and finding bedding problematic. Drainage was poor, so the men lived in a fetid stench, swarmed over by lice, which not only spread disease but which the men regarded as a social humiliation. Bad water, bad sanitation, and mosquitoes out of the nearby swamps bred camp fevers and malaria. Everywhere was the dispiriting sight of "the barefooted boys, the sallow men, the threadbare officers and seedy generals, the diarrhea and dysentery, the yellow eyes and malarious faces . . . mud, mist, and rain."[21]

However, with his army safe in its fortified camp, McClellan recovered his aplomb, self-regard, and sense of destiny with remarkable speed. He pitched his headquarters tents on the grounds of the Berkeley Plantation, one of the grandest of the old Virginia estates, showing his respect for gentility by refusing to occupy the elegant great house, built of brick in the Georgian style in 1726. The cheers of his men reassured him of their love and admiration. He set about cleaning up the encampment, resupplying his men, and restoring their morale with the efficiency he always displayed with such tasks. The Confederates could no longer threaten him, and he had reason to think that, despite his defeat, he had actually gained ground on his second front.

It seemed highly significant to him that neither Lincoln nor Stanton had challenged the accusation of deliberate betrayal in his June 28 telegram. Lincoln's response, sent as well on July 28, did not blame McClellan for what he termed a "misfortune" rather than a defeat: "If you have had a drawn battle, or a repulse, it is the price we pay for the enemy not being in Washington. We protected Washington and the enemy concentrated on you." From McClellan's viewpoint, this was an acknowledgment that the withholding of McDowell's troops had caused McClellan's defeat. Instead of rebuking McClellan's insulting accusations, Lincoln mildly chided McClellan for misunderstanding his intentions, and he assured the general that "I feel any misfortune to you and your Army quite as keenly as you feel it yourself." On July 5 Stanton sent McClellan a personal note, in which he tried to revive the friendship they had shared before Stanton joined Lincoln's cabinet. McClellan read these responses as the acts and words of men conscious of their guilt, fearful of having to answer McClellan's charges before the people. As he told his wife, "The Presdt was entirely too smart to give my correspondence to the public—it would have ruined him & Stanton forever."[22]

He also had reason to think that his views enjoyed wide public support. From the start of the Peninsula campaign, McClellan had cultivated the sympathies of newspaper correspondents attached to the army and fed privileged information to papers hostile to the administration. Even Samuel Wilkeson, correspondent for the Republican *Tribune*, affirmed the accusation that "the refusal to reinforce McClellan" had led to defeat, and constituted "a crime against the nation." The Republican *New York Times* also agreed, and in its editorial of July 10 would suggest that if Stanton were fired, McClellan should replace him. An editorial in the independent-conservative *New York Herald* praised "The sagacity which marked [McClellan's] original plan" and excoriated "the criminal folly" of those who questioned, obstructed, or refused to support the campaign. The chief criminals were Stanton, "the abolitionist radicals of Congress," and the "Traitor Journals" of the Republican press. The *Herald* demanded the "reconstruction" of the cabinet for the "prosecution of this war for 'the integrity of the Union,' and not for the extirpation of slavery." These views were, point for point, the same as those in the letter McClellan had prepared for Lincoln.[23]

Thus for McClellan a defeat on one front was balanced by victory, of a sort, on the other. Defeat seemed not to have diminished his importance to the war effort but rather to have enhanced it. Who but McClellan could organize the army's recovery from the disaster caused by the administration's malfeasance? He still even felt himself to be an agent of divine Providence, and was drawn to the notion that there was even something providential in his defeat. He would write his wife on July 10, "I think I begin to see [God's] wise purpose in all this & that the events of the next few days will prove it. If I had succeeded in taking Richmond now the fanatics of the North might have been too powerful & reunion impossible."[24]

When McClellan learned of Lincoln's intended visit to Harrison's Landing on July 7, McClellan was prepared to meet him, not as a general asking pardon for a defeat but as the indispensable man, entitled and indeed obliged to show the president the error of his ways and his willingness to turn his policies in the right direction. He put in final form the comprehensive review of military affairs, which he had proposed to Lincoln on June 20. On July 8 he told his wife that if Lincoln would read his letter and "[act] upon it the country would be saved." He thought the record would show that "I understood the state of affairs long ago, & had my advice been followed we should not have been in our present difficulties."[25]

He could hardly have been more mistaken about the president's attitude and intentions. McClellan was unaware that the telegrapher had censored the most provocative sentence in his June 28 telegram, in which he explicitly accuses Lincoln and Stanton of deliberately betraying their nation's army. Lincoln was not at all abashed by his own role in the campaign. He was coming to judge for himself whether McClellan was capable of prosecuting the war with the intensity, energy, and commitment that his new strategy would require.

DECISION AT HARRISON'S LANDING, JULY 8, 1862

The weather was insufferably hot and humid. McClellan paraded his troops, and Lincoln was surprised and pleased by the numbers of men around the regimental colors, by their physical condition and spirit— loud cheers spread along the ranks as the two leaders rode past. McClellan's efforts at restoring at least the semblance of health and high morale had been effective. After the review, the two men returned to Lincoln's steamer and met under an awning on its deck. The contrast between them was, as always, extreme. Lincoln was uncommonly tall and lanky, his weathered brown face all bones and hollows, shaggy brows lowering over ice-blue eyes, his clothes ill-cut and rumpled. McClellan was stocky and full of face, his dark eyes wary or disdainful in Lincoln's presence, his powerful chest in blue and brass puffed out above the gold sash of his rank.

Their physical difference was matched by their difference of character. McClellan was self-vaunting and egocentric, unable to see the war except in terms that centered on himself. Lincoln was haggard and humorous, with a sense of irony and proportion that allowed him to set his ego aside, to refuse to quarrel over inessential points, over displays of bad manners or verbal tirades like McClellan's June 28 telegram. Still, as his secretary John Hay observed, it soon became clear to his sharper opponents that he preferred his own thought to theirs, and would follow the course of action he thought best in spite of everything.

McClellan was not one of Lincoln's sharper opponents. His self-absorption made him an execrable judge of character: he had thought Lee was a "timid" commander, and he condescended to Lincoln, whom he thought weak-minded and malleable. The first misjudgment had cost him a battle; the second would cost him his command.

Lincoln wanted to know when McClellan would be ready to resume the offensive, and what kind of operations he planned. Instead of answering, McClellan begged leave to submit his ideas in a letter, which he handed across to Lincoln. The president opened and read it right there, and if its contents astonished him he kept his poker face. The letter said nothing about the army's defeat; did not explain why it had been driven from its lines in headlong retreat, with great losses of men and materiel; did not propose a plan for renewing the offensive. It was instead a political manifesto, laying out McClellan's grand design for the future civil and military policy of the country.[26]

It began by asserting that the country desperately needed an authoritative statement of "civil and military policy, covering the whole ground of our national trouble"—implying that Lincoln's yearlong efforts to coordinate military and civil policy were either negligible or wrongheaded. McClellan called for a "conservative" approach to three basic policy issues: the legal and military consequences of secession; the status of slavery; and the division of power between the president and a proposed military "Commander in Chief of the Army."

McClellan first set forth a political theory that explicitly rejected the principles on which Lincoln had based his defense of the Union. It was fundamental to Lincoln's constitutional theory that secession was entirely illegitimate, that there was no "Southern Confederacy" but only a violent and unjustified rebellion against a legally constituted government. McClellan asserted that what had begun as "rebellion," led by a disaffected aristocracy, had become a full-fledged "War," supported by the masses and by the whole civil polity of the seceded states. The Confederacy had thus acquired a kind of natural-law legitimacy, as the consensual government of a "people." By the canons of American democratic theory, it was impermissible for the U.S. government to prosecute "a War looking to the subjugation of the people of any state," because a government capable of fighting such a war would be, by definition, a despotism. Conciliation was therefore the only legitimate way to end the conflict; and to fully conciliate the South the Federal government had to accommodate the peculiar interests and beliefs that were the motives for secession, and forswear all attempts, whether rhetorical or substantial, to undermine or abolish slavery.

He therefore stipulated that as the civil authority of the Federal government was reestablished in Southern territory, Union military officers and magistrates should be required to respect not only the property rights of Rebels and their supporters but their "political rights" as well—that is, their right to elect their own officials and govern themselves. Nor should any oath of loyalty be required of those seeking to exercise their political rights. If put into effect, such a policy would have left Southern voters in conquered territory free to reconstitute the Confederacy in all but name behind Yankee lines, and to withhold allegiance from the national government, thus reducing to absurdity the whole project of restoring the Union by force. However, as McClellan well knew, restoration of an unreconstructed South to the body politic would also restore the Democratic Party's national majority, and put an end not only to abolitionism but to every plank in the Republican platform, from unconditional unionism to the tariff to the banning of slavery from the territories.

McClellan also wanted Lincoln to repudiate the substantial and growing antislavery element in his own party and adopt the conservative and Democratic position espoused by Douglas that Negro slavery must be protected. "Military power should not be allowed to interfere with the relations of servitude." This was necessary to reassure Southerners—and Northern Whites as well—that the government would not revolutionize race relations and imperil White supremacy by a general emancipation of slaves. McClellan piously hoped that "A system of policy thus constitutional and conservative, and pervaded by the influences of Christianity and freedom, would receive the support of almost all truly loyal men, would deeply impress the rebel masses and all foreign nations, and it might be humbly hoped that it would commend itself to the favor of the Almighty." McClellan warned Lincoln that if he took the opposite course, "A declaration of radical views, upon slavery, will rapidly disintegrate our present Armies." Coming from the commander of the nation's most powerful army, in which McClellan had inculcated a cult of loyalty to his person, such a warning had baleful implications.[27]

Finally, McClellan wanted the nation's military forces concentrated in one or two crucial theaters rather than being "dispersed in expeditions, posts of occupation and numerous Armies." While reasonable on its face, this recommendation was really a reiteration of McClellan's perennial demand that his own force be increased at the expense of other theaters. It treated as mismanagement Lincoln's well-considered and largely successful use of amphibious expeditions, and in general suggested that the president had neglected vital matters in the pursuit of ephemera. Assuming the president would acknowledge his errors and limitations, McClellan wanted him to turn over control of military operations to "a Commander in Chief of the Army; one who possesses your confidence, understands your views and who is competent to execute your orders. . . . I do not ask that place for myself. I am willing to serve you in such position as you may assign me." Behind the display of self-abnegation, McClellan was clearly self-nominating for commander in chief, a title constitutionally applied to the president alone.

What was most disconcerting to Lincoln about the "Harrison's Landing letter" was the fact that McClellan delivered it with such self-assurance in the aftermath of defeat. Did the general somehow believe that *defeat* rather than victory would enhance his standing, and make it possible for him to demand a degree of power within or over the administration that he had labored vainly to acquire for the past year?

McClellan left their meeting under the impression that his letter was a triumph in itself, a perfect statement of the proper way to go about winning the war. His first reaction was that Lincoln had been favorably impressed, though he doubted whether the president was capable "of rising to the height of the merits of the question." Two days later he began to have second thoughts: the president's manner when he left "seemed that of a man about to do something of which he was much ashamed." But the encouragement he was receiving from his political allies and newspaper supporters gave him reason to hope: on July 11 he wrote delightedly to his wife, "I have commenced receiving letters from the North urging me to march on Washington & assume the Govt!!" It was an idea to which he would return.[28]

LINCOLN'S REACTION TO McCLELLAN'S letter was swift and decisive. Over a two-week period following his return to Washington he made a series of decisions, which together constituted a transformation of Federal strategy—and a total repudiation of the "conservative" platform espoused by McClellan.

McClellan had urged Lincoln to appoint a single commander to direct all the nation's military operations, supposing himself to be the preeminent candidate for the position. And he had demanded the concentration of all military reserves in the theater under his direct supervision. On July 11 Lincoln ordered General Henry W. Halleck, commander of Federal armies west of the Appalachians, to come to Washington and assume command, under the president, of all Federal armies including McClellan's Army of the Potomac. His first assignment would be to see whether McClellan was willing to renew his advance on Richmond with his available force; and if McClellan refused, to relieve him and withdraw his army to Washington to begin an entirely new campaign.

McClellan had urged Lincoln to commit his government to protecting the institution of slavery and the "political rights" of the Rebels. On July 12, in a private conversation with Secretary of State Seward and Navy Secretary Gideon Welles, Lincoln did the reverse, unequivocally declaring his intention to issue a proclamation, freeing all slaves in the rebellious states; and on July 22 he would present a draft of the proclamation to an astonished cabinet. He did so with full awareness that such a proclamation would effectively repudiate the strategy of conciliation, and commit the Union to an all-out war of subjugation.[29]

CHAPTER 3

PRESIDENT DAVIS'S STRATEGIC OFFENSIVE

JULY 5–AUGUST 14, 1862

LINCOLN'S CRISIS WAS JEFFERSON DAVIS'S OPPORTUNITY. IN JULY 1862, for the first time in the war, it seemed possible for the Confederacy to seize the strategic initiative. In the west, the six-month Union grand offensive had reached the limit of Federal strength and ground to a halt. In Virginia, Lee's victory over McClellan had stymied the Union drive to capture Richmond. All of the major Confederate field armies had disengaged from their Union opponents and recovered their freedom to maneuver and to strike at points of their own choosing. These included Lee's army in Richmond, an army of about fifteen-to-nineteen thousand commanded by General Edmund Kirby Smith in eastern Tennessee, Bragg's thirty-five thousand troops in northern Alabama, and a force of some twenty-five thousand men under Generals Earl Van Dorn and Sterling Price defending northern Mississippi.

Davis had been criticized by a considerable faction of Confederate leaders and newspapers for standing too long on the defensive, allowing the Yankees to invade and occupy Southern territory. That criticism has been echoed by military historians, who have contrasted Davis's supposed predilection for territorial defense with Lee's preference—his perhaps excessive preference—for the offensive. In truth, it was not want of will but want of power that prevented him from carrying the war to the enemy.[1]

Until July 1862 Confederate strategy had been crippled by the conflicting demands of defending its territory and developing offensive capability. The Confederate army had to defend a territory nearly as large as that of the Union, with far less military manpower. The total population of the Northern states was more than twice that of the Confederacy (twenty-two as against nine million). The differential in military manpower was actually greater, because nearly 40 percent of the Southern total were slaves, who could not be used as combatants. The South's ability to mobilize its military strength was also slowed by its limited capacity for manufacturing war materials (weapons, ammunition, uniforms) and the inadequacy of its railroad network. During the opening months of the war, Davis and Lee, who was then acting as the president's chief military adviser, had to divide their limited resources to concentrate field armies for the defense of a northern border that stretched fifteen hundred miles from Virginia to western Missouri. At the same time they had to form garrisons and mobile reserves to defend critical points all around the Confederate coast, from the Carolina sounds to New Orleans. Despite its best efforts, during the first year of hostilities the Confederacy was unable to recruit, arm, and train forces sufficient for those tasks. Thus when Halleck's armies advanced into central and western Tennessee in February and March 1862, Davis had to strip the garrison of New Orleans to reinforce his Army of Tennessee. The reinforcement proved inadequate to defeat Halleck, and its removal allowed a Federal amphibious expedition to capture New Orleans. Similarly, the concentration of Virginia and North Carolina troops in the defense of Richmond left the North Carolina sounds and the coast southward vulnerable to Federal amphibious expeditions.

The conflicting military demands of concentration and peripheral defense were also the central problem of Confederate politics.

As president of the Confederacy, Davis's mission was to establish and defend a new government, whose fundamental principles were the primacy of the states' powers as against those of the national government, and the protection of the property right in slaves from interference by government authority. His foreign policy was summed up in the simple phrase "All we ask is to be left alone." But in the fifteen months that ran from the firing on Fort Sumter in April 1861 to the first weeks of July 1862 Davis had been schooled by the exigencies of war, the loss of major seaports and large territory to invasion, the disruption of the cotton economy and the plantation system. Davis found that in order to maintain the struggle for national independence he had to challenge the strict interpretation of states' rights theory: imposing taxes, demanding the release of state troops for service with the national armies, suspending habeas corpus, reaching past the governors of the states to conscript soldiers directly into the national armies. He would also find himself interfering with the master-slave relation, by requisitioning slaves to work on fortifications.

These policies provoked a reaction from leaders who, for reasons of interest and ideology, advocated a strict construction of the Confederate constitution's states'-rights principles. Some Southern governors, like Georgia's Governor Joe Brown, were concerned about the defense of their own communities and therefore resisted national conscription and refused to release state troops for service with the national field armies. A powerful minority within the Confederate government, led by Vice-President Alexander Stephens of Georgia, resisted every measure of the Richmond government that infringed on the sovereignty of the states, no matter how necessary the measure might be to national defense. In the summer of 1862 Stephens condemned Davis's policies as incipient despotism, every bit as bad as the supposed tyranny of Abraham Lincoln, against which they had rebelled. Stephens declared that he would rather see the Confederacy perish than suffer its government to violate the strictures that limited its powers.[2]

States'-rights fundamentalism also affected the way Confederate leaders thought about military operations. There was a significant minority of opinion that regarded the use of Confederate forces to invade Northern territory as constitutionally illegitimate. Some even questioned whether regiments from one state were obliged to serve beyond its borders, even in defense of another state. A purely defensive policy was consistent with the ideological principle which held that secession was not a revolutionary or hostile act but a necessary measure of self-protection, and with the administration's declared war aim: "All we ask is to be left alone." That principle was most eloquently argued by James D. B. DeBow, a pioneer statistician and social scientist, former head of the U.S. Census Bureau, and editor of *DeBow's Review*, the South's preeminent intellectual journal. "We are not revolutionists," he wrote in May 1862, "we are resisting revolution" to conserve an established order. It follows that "We can never become aggressive; we may absorb, but we can never invade for conquest, any neighboring State." Ideological resistance to invasion was augmented by the misguided pragmatism of politicians who (as Davis complained) "feared to excite the hatred of our enemies, and the few others who clung to the [delusive] hope of aid from our old party-allies at the North."[3]

On the other hand, Davis was also assailed by those who believed he was entirely too enamored of defensive warfare, which had left the South exposed to invasion. The Savannah, Georgia, *Republican* derided Davis's defensive policy as "a blunder, and a most grievous one, entailing increased bloodshed and melancholy devastation." The *Richmond Daily Dispatch*, one of the Confederate capital's own journals, informed Davis that Southern newspapers, the voice of the Southern people, were "unanimous, or nearly so, in favor of an advance into the enemy's territories." Davis had so far rejected that call: "Will the voice of the people again be denied?" The *Charleston (South Carolina) Mercury*, journalistic voice of the city and state whose uncompromising advocacy of states' rights and slavery had driven the South into secession, was unequivocal in demanding a change of policy. Halleck's army must be checked at Corinth and McClellan defeated at Richmond, and then "we trust and believe that we shall have done with the defensive policy, and that two powerful columns will at once be put in motion toward the banks of the Ohio and the Susquehannah."[4]

Davis had to strike a balance between these conflicting principles and the policies they entailed. He approached the problem as a Southern nationalist, not a states'-rights strict constructionist. He accepted in principle the division of powers in the Confederate constitution, but in practice pressed against its limitation of central government powers in order to achieve the ultimate purpose for which the state was founded—national independence. Two measures in particular had driven his own vice president, Alec Stephens, into political opposition: the Conscription Act, which empowered the national government to draft troops in the states, overriding the authority of the governors; and the suspension of habeas corpus, giving the Richmond government power to suppress dissidence, insurrection, and draft resistance in the states—in Stephens's view a despotic overthrow of civil liberty.[5]

It is easy to condemn the shortsightedness of governors like Brown for failing to recognize that the war could not be won, and independence achieved, without victories by the national field armies; and that if the war was lost, local defense was meaningless. However, it must be remembered that the purpose of secession and of the struggle for independence was to preserve slavery and the social order based on that institution. By the summer of 1862 Southern leaders from Davis on down were learning for themselves the truth of Lincoln's warning to the Border State congressmen: that slavery could be destroyed by "the mere friction of war." Wherever Northern armies went, slaves fled to Federal lines or were confiscated from Rebel owners. Already Union forces occupied large swathes of territory in which plantation agriculture predominated: Missouri, west and central Tennessee, Louisiana between New Orleans and Baton Rouge, the Sea Islands of Georgia and South Carolina, the North Carolina sounds, the Virginia Tidewater. Raids from these districts disrupted plantation discipline (and provoked flight by slaves) along the Mississippi River, in northern Mississippi and Alabama, and inland from the beachheads along the Atlantic coast. To retain control of their property, many planters in these districts were collaborating with Union occupiers, which undermined the struggle for Southern independence.[6] The Richmond *Whig*, the most influential of the papers published in the Confederate capital, stated the problem clearly for the Southern public and their elected officials to read. A slaveholding society could not protect itself by a "Fabian," or defensive, strategy. "A slave-holding community . . . is most powerful for offensive war; for while the whites go to war, the slaves carry on the productive industry of the country. But for defensive war, it is the weakest," since the invader, by freeing slaves, destroys "the very elements of subsistence."[7]

In developing a war-winning strategy, Davis and Lee had to take into account the vulnerability of the social system they were defending. Clearly they could not allow the need for local defense to drain their field armies of strength. Neither could they indefinitely expose the plantation system to the friction of war. The only remedy was to win the war for independence in relatively short order. In July 1862 Davis, like Lincoln, had abandoned the hope that a "conservative" approach to war—in this case the refusal to invade Northern territory—might so conciliate the enemy that he would consent to separation. Like Lincoln, Davis recognized that prewar political allies and ideological sympathizers who remained in the enemy's camp could not immediately aid his cause. The only way to break the enemy's political will and rouse a political opposition to his regime was to make the Northern people feel the pain and cost of war. That could only be done by inflicting heavy defeats on his armies and carrying the war into enemy territory. In July 1862 the opportunity to do so was tantalizingly close. Davis and Lee were agreed in principle on the necessity of counteroffensives. They had still to decide what kind of offensives were possible; how limited or ambitious the objectives should be; what the chances were of winning decisive results that might shorten the war, and how much could be risked to make the attempt.

The general framework of their strategic thought has been described as "offensive-defensive." The primary goal of such a strategy is to defend one's society and territory against invasion by an enemy superior in strength. Defensive tactics are used to delay, disrupt, and attenuate the invading force; but the defender maintains a mobile reserve force with which to counterattack the invader. Within that general structure significant choices had to be made about the balance between offense and defense, and the intensity and function of counteroffensive operations.

The American War of Independence offered the model best known to Davis and Lee and was in many ways an appropriate one. The two most successful American generals, Washington and Nathanael Greene, had used defensive measures to weary and attenuate British forces. They had also accepted battle or attacked when they saw a chance to cut off or drive back an advanced force, but avoided the kind of all-or-nothing combat that risked the destruction of their own forces. As Greene said, "We fight, get beat, rise, and fight again." These tactics, coupled with raiding and guerrilla warfare, allowed the Americans to limit the territory the British could occupy and control. They also enabled the Americans to effect opportunistic concentrations against exposed British columns, which led to important victories like Trenton (1776) and Cowpens (1780), and the decisive surrenders of British armies at Saratoga (1777) and Yorktown (1781).[8]

It has been said that the strategy of Washington and Greene was to "win by not losing," emphasizing defense and force protection over offense, prolonging the conflict till the enemy despaired of winning it. Some historians have criticized Davis and/or Lee for being both impatient with defense and overinvested in offensives that chased a chimerical dream of decisive victory. But unlike the thirteen colonies, the Confederacy could not afford an indefinite prolongation of the war. It took eight years for the Continental Army to outlast the British—whose base of supply was on the other side of the ocean—and even then their victory also required the military intervention of France, Holland, and Spain. Small British armies could only occupy a few seaports; they could ravage the countryside, but in a land of small plantations and subsistence farms the damage they did was ephemeral. The Confederacy's enemies were next-door neighbors, and their stake in preserving the Union was more strongly and immediately felt than the British public's stake in its distant colonies. Northern armies were large enough, and close enough to their base of supplies, to occupy considerable territory. Moreover, the slave-based system of plantation agriculture on which the modern South depended was far more vulnerable to catastrophic disruption than the relatively simple agrarian economy of the colonies. A long war might theoretically exhaust the North's taste for conquest, but the strains such a war would impose on Southern society were likely to prove fatal.

Davis's understanding of these issues was clearly set out in a letter sent on July 18 to John Forsyth, a supporter who had written to warn Davis that the public was unhappy with his defensive military policies and puzzled by his unwillingness to take the war to the enemy. Davis answered that it was not want of will but want of power that had prevented him from attacking the North directly, to make the enemy "feel in its most tangible form the evils of war." Because of its relative weakness, the Confederacy had had no choice but to stand on the defensive until the Union's invading columns had been checked. However, once that was achieved, Davis believed that the Confederacy could and should take the offensive in order to reverse the course of the conflict. Two kinds of counteroffensive were possible. One was to make what Davis called "aggressive movements upon detachments of the enemy"—that is, to concentrate forces against an advanced column of Union troops, defeat it and force it to retreat, or even cut it off and destroy it. Although Davis did not say so, this was the method that had been tried unsuccessfully against Grant's army at Shiloh but with great success against McClellan's army in the Seven Days.

The other offensive model was to attempt an "invasion" of Northern territory, which Davis believed was the most effective way to win the war. "My early declared purpose and continued hope was to feed upon the enemy and teach them the blessings of peace by making them feel in its most tangible form the evils of war." The two modes were not exclusive. Before a successful invasion could be mounted it would be necessary to defeat the Federal armies that were pressing against vital points in both the western theater and the eastern. But the Forsyth letter indicates that, in the aftermath of the Seven Days, Davis was reconceiving Confederate strategy in the largest terms; not limiting his plans to the repulse of Federal attacks and the recovery of lost ground, but trying to imagine a war-winning strategy that would directly attack the political will of the Unionists. He would reiterate that theme in his July 5 proclamation congratulating Lee's army on its triumph. It was not enough that they had won a brilliant victory over a superior force. Their ultimate purpose remained: not only to drive the invaders back but to "carry your standards beyond the outer boundaries of the Confederacy, to wring from an unscrupulous foe the recognition of your birthright, community independence." In this respect he was in accord with his chief adviser and victorious army commander, Robert E. Lee.[9]

THE STRATEGIC PARTNERSHIP OF DAVIS AND LEE

Davis was a West Point graduate (Class of 1828) who had served seven years in the Regular Army before resigning to become a planter in Mississippi. He had raised a volunteer regiment for the Mexican War and won distinction as a combat commander. During his tenure as secretary of war (1853–57) he had organized the army's great survey expeditions that explored the West for possible transcontinental railroad routes. As Confederate president he possessed and exercised the powers of commander in chief and took primary responsibility for strategic planning.

His training and experience gave him a confidence in his military expertise that was not entirely justified, and he did not suffer criticism gladly. He was humorless, stiff, and cold in manner; a sufferer from neuralgia and other ailments that shortened his temper. His intelligence was legalistic rather than logical, moralistic rather than ethically astute. He prided himself on his high principles and personal rectitude, assuming a moral height from which opposing opinions seemed crass or discreditable. He had the unfortunate tendency of seeing disagreements, whether on matters of judgment or of principle, as personal slights, aspersions cast on his honor. His correspondence with his generals and other Confederate leaders is peppered with quarrels over relatively minor points of difference, which Davis seems unable to avoid or let pass. Over time, these qualities would poison his working relationship with two of his most senior and experienced field generals, Joseph Johnston and Pierre Beauregard, both of whom shared his tendency to "greatly find quarrel in a straw." On the other hand, Generals Bragg and Hood won Davis's favor by adopting his views and by flattery; and Davis would maintain them in command despite strong evidence of their unfitness.[10]

But Davis had real abilities and virtues as a commander in chief, which came to the fore in the summer of 1862. He had already displayed both good judgment and political courage in pushing vital "national" measures like the Conscription Act, without which the armies would have been inadequate to defend themselves, let alone take the offensive.[11] Then in July he would respond with intelligence, daring, and flexibility to the opportunities that had suddenly opened to him. The quality of his performance was undoubtedly aided by his reliance on his chief military adviser, General Robert E. Lee.

Lee was almost unique in his ability to maintain cordial and collegial relations with Davis, balancing deference and respect with a patient but firm insistence on his own views. It helped that Davis admired Lee's character and military abilities, and trusted him absolutely. At fifty-five, Lee had poise, dignity, and self-command. He was above average in height, with steel-gray hair and a full beard—the gray had overtaken him suddenly during the crisis over Virginia's secession. Something in his manner evoked instant respect and deference from nearly everyone with whom he came in contact.

Davis was one generation removed from the hardscrabble existence of the same Kentucky frontier that produced Lincoln. His status of gentleman was hard and newly won, and therefore vulnerable and in need of defense. Lee inhabited honor as a garment native to him—though he too had had to work to maintain it. His lineage was aristocratic, as Americans understood the term. His father was "Light Horse" Harry Lee, a scion of Virginia's patrician planter class and a hero of the American Revolution. But Light Horse Harry's questionable business dealings had impoverished the family and in some measure disgraced the name. Robert had regained the fortune by marriage to a descendant of Martha Washington, and the honor through hard service in the military, and an uncompromising devotion to the ideals embodied in the Code. Yet "honor" only has meaning if conferred by the particular community to which one is born, which for Lee was Virginia. So when Virginia seceded, Lee went with his state.

He was well versed in the curriculum and theory of war, and had had a uniquely rich and illuminating experience of combat as a staff officer for Winfield Scott in the campaign against Mexico City. He had moved from headquarters to the front lines and was engaged at every level, from the scouting of terrain and enemy positions to the timing and conduct of assaults. Scott's army had been badly outnumbered and was operating on foreign soil with the most tenuous line of supply. Still, Scott had managed to win the battles and the war by creating an army superior to its enemy in discipline and organization, and therefore with superior mobility. He had used that mobility to seize and keep the initiative, not only throwing the enemy off balance but preventing his reorganization. Above all, Scott had won the war because he had been willing to undertake great, almost forbidding risks—risks that lesser military minds regarded as impossible but which his own careful calculation told him his army could overcome. Lee would take that same approach in planning his own operations. McClellan's judgment that Lee was an excessively "timid" commander ranks among the most egregious of McClellan's many intelligence failures. Fortunately for the Confederacy, President Davis's opinion was the only opinion that mattered.[12]

The relationship between Davis and Lee was the antithesis of the antagonism between Lincoln and McClellan. The Confederate president and his general in chief were entirely in agreement on the ultimate political purposes for which the war was being fought: Southern independence and the preservation of the Southern way of life. There was never any question of Lee's loyalty to the national cause or his subordination to the civilian authority. Although Davis was generally more cautious than Lee, he shared his general's belief that a purely defensive strategy was inadequate. He was willing, even eager, to undertake offensives involving real but limited risks, in order to frustrate Federal plans and discourage the Northern public.[13]

There were some moments after Lee's assumption of command when the uncertain boundary between presidential and military authority was tested. The fact that the Army of Northern Virginia operated close to the capital offered many temptations to presidential interference with operations. On one occasion during the Seven Days, when Davis appeared at the front, Lee pointedly asked, "Am I in command here?" and, when Davis acknowledged his authority, ordered him away from the command position. As the war went on, Lee would use various means, direct and indirect, to keep Davis away from the army in the field. In striking the balance between risk and prudence, Lee was more inclined to risk; and there is some evidence that at Gettysburg Lee deliberately obscured or concealed his intentions in order to conduct a more daring campaign than the president favored. In the summer of 1862, however, the two shared a common understanding of the tactical problems they faced, the strategic goals they sought, and the kinds of risk they might have to take to achieve those goals.[14]

The most immediate objective was to reverse the tactical momentum of the war by throwing the Federal armies onto the defensive and forcing them to withdraw from some or all of the territory they had won in the first six months of the year. By shifting the zone of conflict back toward the northern borders, the Confederacy would not only make its economic heartland more secure but also regain access to the resources of their lost counties. Such a tactical success would at least forestall further offensives by the North and buy time for the Confederacy to build its strength.

A successful strategic offensive also had the potential for producing decisive political results, by convincing Maryland and Kentucky to join the other slave states in secession. It might also produce a political revulsion in the North against the Republican administration and its war policy. Davis was very much aware that the North's midterm congressional elections were approaching, and he believed that a series of impressive Southern victories would stimulate the energies and raise the electoral prospects of the "peace party" in the north. A defeat for Republicans at the polls, coupled with Confederate victories on the battlefield, might in turn have a decisive effect on the British and French governments, which were considering whether or not to intervene diplomatically with an offer of mediation that would lead to Confederate independence.

Davis's agents in Europe, and his official representatives to Britain and France, James Mason and John Slidell, reported that both governments were eager to regain access to Southern cotton. However, because they also wished to avoid war with the Americans, they were waiting for signs that the Northern people were turning against the war and willing to give it up.[15]

PLANNING A STRATEGIC OFFENSIVE
JULY 5–AUGUST 5, 1862

The elements of a new offensive strategy developed in stages, over a one-month period—roughly from July 5 to August 5—in response to the shifting tactical alignment of forces both in the western theater and on the Richmond front.

Lee's victory in the Seven Days had saved Richmond and left McClellan's army apparently unable to resume the offensive until it had been reorganized and reinforced. Still, it was impossible for Lee to exploit his victory by continuing to attack. McClellan's army was unassailable—eighty-five thousand strong, in a fortified camp with the U.S. Navy providing artillery support and protecting its supply lines. Lee's army, soon to be renamed the Army of Northern Virginia, had suffered heavy casualties in its week of repeated assaults—twenty thousand killed, wounded, and captured, 22 percent of his initial force of between ninety and ninety-five thousand. The army had been further diminished by lax administration in its regiments, whose officers were liberal to the point of carelessness in granting furloughs and sick leaves. Lee was working hard to tighten the army's discipline and organization and, with Davis's active help, was rebuilding its strength. The situation at Richmond was becoming increasingly desperate, because through the first two or three weeks of July Lee had only fifty-six thousand troops concentrated for action against McClellan, who had eighty-five thousand on hand, with another twenty thousand reinforcements headed his way.

Lee's situation was further complicated by the discovery (July 10) that the Federals were forming a new army in northern Virginia, commanded by Major General John Pope, an energetic general who had been transferred from the western theater. Pope's force was estimated at forty thousand troops, organized from among the disparate commands that had vainly chased after Stonewall Jackson during his Shenandoah Valley campaign. It was a number that was likely to rise, since the Federals were known to be transferring troops from North Carolina and West Virginia to reinforce both Pope and McClellan. In a matter of weeks Pope's force could be raised to fifty-five thousand or more, and if it were to unite with McClellan's one hundred thousand, the odds against Lee would be prohibitive.[16]

Lee was thus faced with a seemingly intractable tactical dilemma. From its position at Harrison's Landing, McClellan's army posed an imminent threat to the capital, and Lee lacked the strength to drive the Federals from that position. Once Pope's army was fully organized and reinforced, it would be able to move against Richmond from the north. If left unchecked it would cut the link by which supplies reached Richmond from the Shenandoah and eventually approach the capital itself. Once his army got close to Richmond, Pope could coordinate with McClellan a combined assault by some 150,000 troops against a Confederate force of less than half that strength. The obvious way to forestall that fatal combination was to attack and destroy Pope's army while it was still well north of Richmond. Unfortunately for Lee and Davis, to destroy a force of that size would require the detachment of at least 30,000 from the Richmond defenses, leaving the capital inadequately protected against an advance by McClellan's 85,000-plus.

Davis and Lee agreed on the necessity of preventing Pope's army from reaching Richmond, and on the need to balance risk with prudence in deciding when to shift troops away from Richmond. However, since Lee's whole theory of war emphasized the necessity of gaining and holding the strategic initiative, to control the timing and direction of operations, he was more willing than Davis to thin the force defending Richmond and rely on McClellan's notorious reluctance to advance to keep the city safe while he was defeating Pope.

Davis was more than willing to consider a possible offensive. Since the spring, pressure for a strike against the North had been mounting from the press, and from political leaders in states invaded by Federal forces. Anger at the losses inflicted by the invaders and the desire for retaliation lent passion to these demands; Lee's victory lent them plausibility. The *Richmond Daily Dispatch* of July 5 urged Davis to "Follow

Up the Victory . . . 'Retaliation' should be now the watchword. Defensive warfare is, under peculiar circumstances, wise, and in our case has been unavoidable. But at the earliest moment the enemy should be made to feel some of the horrors of invasive warfare."[17] However, Davis's daring was tempered by concern for the safety of Richmond. It was a keystone of the war effort, as both a manufacturing center and as the most valued symbol of Confederate nationality. Its loss would shake the morale of the Southern people, and it would be a heavy if not fatal blow to Davis's campaign to win diplomatic recognition and assistance from Britain and France.

Davis was also concerned about the casualties likely to result from an all-out strike against Pope. Twice his armies had concentrated to strike at Federal "detachments" thrust deep into Southern territory. They were defeated at Shiloh and victorious in the Seven Days. But, whether in victory or defeat, their losses had been terrible: 10,700 killed, wounded, or missing at Shiloh, more than 20,000 lost during the Seven Days. Repeated losses on that scale might exhaust the Confederacy's limited manpower. The problem with any offensive in Virginia was the likelihood that a maneuver plan would end in a general engagement. In the western theater, Federal armies with an aggregate strength of about 150,000 men defended a front that stretched more than 400 miles, over varied terrain, from the Mississippi River to Cumberland Gap. There was ample space for a Confederate army on the offensive to maneuver without being forced into an unwanted general engagement. In Virginia the Federals had 150,000 troops concentrated within 100 miles of Richmond, and the area open to offensive operations was constricted to the narrow region between the mountains and the tidewater, which averaged less than 100 miles from east to west. If Lee moved north he would almost certainly have to fight a general engagement, which would inevitably entail serious casualties.[18]

From Lee's perspective, such costs might be justified if by moving against Pope he could so threaten Washington that McClellan's army would be withdrawn from the Peninsula. The zone of conflict would then be shifted from the Richmond suburbs to the approaches to Washington, which would free the productive farms of northern Virginia from Federal occupation. More significantly, Union forces in the theater would be thrown onto the defensive. At the least that would mean a long delay in any new Federal offensive against Richmond; and if Lee could gain and hold the tactical initiative he could control the course of war in the theater, and perhaps even win a decisive engagement. Although the potential results would be of great or even decisive value, Davis was not yet ready to run the risks of such a campaign. He chose a compromise solution. He would hold the bulk of Lee's army in the Richmond defenses but authorize Lee to detach a force of fifteen thousand under Jackson to Gordonsville, where it could observe Pope's movements. However, Jackson lacked the strength to defeat Pope if the latter made a determined advance with his full force. Jackson moved north on July 13 and was in position two days later.

While Davis and Lee were struggling with the problems of the Virginia theater, prospects for a counteroffensive were emerging in the West. Buell's army was marching laterally across Tennessee toward Chattanooga, its supply lines exposed to constant disruption by Rebel cavalry raiders. Buell was an officer of the McClellan type, never one to move with alacrity, and these difficulties slowed his march to a crawl. In the meantime the army commanded by U. S. Grant was forced to stand on the defensive around Corinth, unable to begin its offensive down the Mississippi because its reserves were spread out trying to defend Buell's supply lines.

As a result, none of the Confederate armies in West were being pressured; all were free to maneuver, and their commanders had time to consider measures for countering or reversing the Federal advances. The two most important armies in the theater were the Army of Tennessee, the force that had assailed Grant at Shiloh, thirty-five thousand troops commanded by General Bragg, and a smaller army of nineteen thousand troops in East Tennessee commanded by General Edmund Kirby Smith. Bragg and Smith developed, and set before President Davis, a bold plan for a theater-wide counteroffensive that would culminate in the invasion and "liberation" of Kentucky. Smith's forces would lead the way, striking into Kentucky. Bragg would shift his entire force eastward by rail to Chattanooga, moving much faster than Buell's plodding, harassed columns, then follow Smith into Kentucky. Buell would be forced to turn north to prevent Bragg and Smith from cutting his supply line to Louisville, and the two Rebel armies could combine to defeat him. To prevent Grant's army from interfering, Bragg would transfer to Mississippi the troops under Generals Van Dorn and Price that had been fighting west of the big river.[19]

Events would show that the wisdom of the Bragg/Smith plan was questionable, and its conduct would be riddled with errors of judgment and missed opportunities. However, what concerns us here is the effect of their plans and actions on the strategic design Davis and Lee were developing. Davis was ready to seize the opportunity that had suddenly opened and shift from defense to the strategic offensive. Davis received and approved a general outline of the Bragg/Smith plan on July 13—the same day that Jackson began his movement against Pope—and by July 21 Bragg had laid out his plan in detail. Davis's determination is reflected in the instructions he sent to Bragg and Smith, which enjoined them to "crush" Buell's army in decisive battle before invading and recovering Tennessee and Kentucky. He told them that he hoped to be able to "strike a blow" in Virginia as well, holding McClellan in place with one force while striking at Pope with another. Thus Davis's plans were national in scope.[20]

The prospect of a decisive offensive in the West made necessary some sort of action on the Virginia front, if only to give Federal troops "full employment in this quarter" and prevent reinforcements from going west. The offensive spirit shown by Bragg and Smith, coupled with political developments in northern Virginia, made Davis more willing to authorize the kind of offensive operations Lee was advocating. For months Davis had been noting signs of increasing radicalization in Federal policy. On March 13, 1862, Lincoln had issued an order forbidding army officers from returning fugitive slaves to Rebel owners, reversing an earlier policy under which the government had continued to enforce the Fugitive Slave Law. A month later Congress abolished slavery in the District of Columbia, and on June 19 it passed a law barring slavery from U.S. territories. On July 17 Congress passed the Second Confiscation Act, far more severe than its predecessor; and the tenor of congressional and editorial debate showed strong and growing support for more punitive policies. Federal generals in New Orleans and the Sea Islands had actually begun recruiting "confiscated" slaves for military duty; and though the Lincoln administration disavowed and reversed their actions, Davis correctly read these acts as omens of future policy.

Then, in mid-July, General Pope suddenly emerged as the symbol and most powerful agent of Northern Radicalism. Pope's sudden transfer from the West, and his assumption of the important command in northern Virginia, coincided with passage of the Second Confiscation Act, and Pope immediately put himself forward as the act's most militant enforcer. In a general order, issued on July 18, Pope informed his army that it would "subsist upon the country in which their operations are carried out." To that end, he gave his troops license to confiscate from Virginia civilians anything required for the army's subsistence, including food, draft animals, and (presumably) slaves who might be used as cooks, teamsters, laborers, and so on. The order also declared that civilians would be held responsible for the actions of guerrillas operating in their area. They would be compelled to repair or to pay for any damage to railroads, bridges, or government property, and be subject to punitive confiscation. This was followed on July 23 by a still stronger order that required all civilians in Pope's area to choose between swearing an oath of loyalty and being exiled from the district; and anyone who then violated the oath could be executed, and his family's property confiscated.

Davis and Lee were outraged by Pope's proclamation and protested it as a violation of the laws and usages of civilized war. In his July 28 letter to General Smith, Davis referred to Pope's proceeding as a "reign of terror." He told Lee that Pope "ought to be suppressed if possible," as if he were an outlaw rather than an honorable opponent. Davis went further. On July 31 he issued an executive order that officers captured from Pope's command should be imprisoned as felons and denied the rights accorded prisoners of war. On August 21 he would proclaim that the Federal commanders in New Orleans and the Sea Islands were criminals guilty of fomenting servile insurrection because of their attempts to enlist Blacks. General Lee supported his president, complaining to General Halleck about "the merciless atrocities which now characterize the war against the Confederate States."[21]

Neither Davis nor Lee expected these measures to deter the radical tendency of Union policy. Rather, Davis's protests registered his recognition that the Federal government was not interested in conciliation or a negotiated separation; that the Lincoln administration and its supporters, for the moment dominant in Northern politics, intended to destroy both Confederate independence and the Southern way of life.

That understanding altered Davis's calculation of the balance between prudence and daring. In a war for national survival, necessity is the only prudent measure of risk. Lee had already accepted that principle as the basis of military decision making; Davis was now prepared to meet him on that ground. In his final instructions to General Bragg, sent on August 5, Davis recommended a course of action that would have required Bragg to embrace the risks of heavy and repeated combat in order to achieve decisive victory. He told Bragg to seize any opportunity to strike Buell while his force was in motion, "fight the enemy in detachments," and destroy him in detail. After crushing Buell's army, he should assault and recapture Nashville, which was the keystone of Federal operations in the West. That would compel the Federals under Grant to retreat from Tennessee, and Bragg could make "a complete conquest over the enemy" by destroying that force as well, thus achieving "the liberation of Tennessee and Kentucky."[22]

As it happened, Bragg decided to turn that program on its head, invading Kentucky before attempting to "crush" Buell, and avoiding the decisive battles Davis recommended. Nevertheless, the aggressiveness of Davis's recommendations was a sign of his increased willingness to accept the kind of risks and costs that might enable Lee to destroy Pope, and the plan he recommended to Bragg very closely resembles the program Lee would follow. On July 27 Davis agreed to Lee's proposal that Jackson's command be reinforced to thirty-five thousand, making it large enough to strike Pope's forty-five thousand with some effect. However, the threat to the capital posed by McClellan's army was still so grave that Lee had to keep the larger portion of his army in its defensive positions, and try to hold McClellan in place.

The new plan of operations was only one week old when Federal actions threatened to wreck it. On August 3 McClellan suddenly became active, sending a strong force across the James as if he intended to begin an advance on Petersburg, the junction point for four of the five railroads supplying Richmond from the south. Two days later he sent a strong force west out of Harrison's Landing to occupy Malvern Hill, a strong point from which a new advance on Richmond could be launched. At the same time, Lee's cavalry reported that a Federal corps of sixteen thousand under General Ambrose Burnside had occupied Fredericksburg. With so large a force, Burnside could break through Lee's cavalry screen to threaten Richmond in combination with McClellan. He could also march west to join Pope, bringing the Army of Virginia up to nearly sixty thousand men—double Jackson's augmented force. To forestall that possibility, Jackson elected to strike Pope. On August 9 Jackson engaged one of Pope's three army corps at Cedar Mountain, a high hill some twenty miles east of the Blue Ridge Mountains. Though he gained a tactical victory he could not exploit it, since Pope's army still outnumbered him two to one. When Pope advanced to Cedar Mountain with his united force, Jackson had to retreat to his starting point at Gordonsville. A few days after the battle Pope's army had taken up a strong position at Cedar Mountain, with its front along the Rapidan River—a tributary of the Rappahannock that ran west to east under the southern slope of Cedar Mountain.[23]

It was now apparent to Lee that a merely daring plan of campaign could not save the capital. He would have to send the bulk of his forces against Pope, leaving an inadequate force to defend Richmond against the double threat of Burnside and McClellan. He thought he could rely on McClellan's characteristic reluctance to attack, and perhaps reinforce it by an energetic program of feints and deceptions. To ensure that that most critical aspect of the campaign was properly conducted, and to reassure President Davis that his capital would be well defended, Lee himself would stay behind to command the defense. He would have to leave the equally vital task of destroying Pope to subordinates. On the same day that Jackson engaged Pope, Lee ordered Lieutenant General James Longstreet to take his newly formed army corps, some six divisions, to join Jackson. As the senior officer, Longstreet would command his and Jackson's Corps (more than sixty thousand troops), and Lee gave him general instructions for an operation against Pope.

It would take a week for Longstreet to move all his troops and equipment to Jackson's position, which was something over sixty miles from Richmond via the Virginia Central Railroad. While the move was in progress, Lee's tactical problem was radically simplified by two Federal actions. On August 13 the cavalry reported that Burnside's Corps was moving west to join Pope—not south to threaten Richmond. That same day a deserter from McClellan's army told his interrogators that McClellan was planning to withdraw his troops from Harrison's Landing, presumably to ship them north for a grand concentration of force in northern Virginia. That intelligence would quickly be confirmed as Confederate scouts reported large troop movements from Harrison's Landing to the docks at Fort Monroe.[24]

But Lee did not wait for confirmation of McClellan's withdrawal. It was enough to know that an offensive against Richmond was not under way. Lee immediately ordered an additional infantry division and all his remaining cavalry to join Longstreet and Jackson, and he himself went north to command the united force. The day after Lee left he received word that McClellan's army was abandoning the Peninsula. It would take several weeks for McClellan's force to complete its embarkation and transshipment to Washington and march overland to join Pope. There would be a brief interval in which a rapid concentration of force would allow Lee to take the offensive against Pope. Such an offensive could do more than block Pope's advance. It might wreck or destroy Pope's force. If that were done promptly and thoroughly, Lee might have an opportunity to hit McClellan's force before it was reorganized and defeat it in detail. That in turn might create an opening for an invasion or incursion into northern territory—a sequence similar to the one Davis had suggested to Bragg.

McClellan's withdrawal removed at a stroke the only serious obstacle to a Southern offensive toward Washington and freed Lee's entire field force for the purpose. Lee made no attempt to account for this astonishing turn of events—he simply moved with speed and efficiency to exploit it. In fact, he owed his opportunity to Abraham Lincoln, whose reorganization of Union strategy stumbled over the intractability of the McClellan problem.

PART TWO

THE CONFEDERATE OFFENSIVE

August 1862

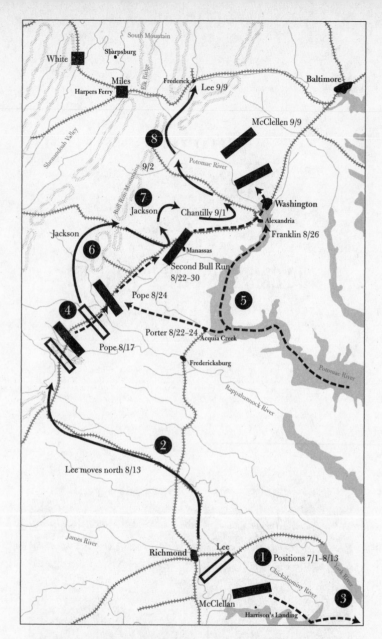

MAP 1: THE VIRGINIA THEATER, JULY 1–SEPT. 9, 1862

1. McClellan at Harrison's Landing, Lee at Richmond, July 1–Aug. 13
2. Lee moves north to join Jackson, Aug. 13
3. McClellan begins retreat from Peninsula, Aug. 14
4. Pope retreats to Rappahannock, Aug. 17–24
5. III and V Corps join Pope, Aug. 22–24; VI Corps at Alexandria, Aug. 26
6. Jackson's flank march to Manassas, Aug. 25–27
7. Battles of Second Bull Run and Chantilly, Aug. 27–Sept. 1
8. Lee invades Maryland, Sept. 1–9

CHAPTER 4

SELF-INFLICTED WOUNDS:
THE UNION HIGH COMMAND

JULY 22–AUGUST 22, 1862

※ ⁂

THE WITHDRAWAL OF THE ARMY OF THE POTOMAC, WHICH OPENED the way for Lee's offensive against Pope, was the perverse result of Lincoln's decision to radicalize and intensify the Union's offensive strategy. The political basis of that strategy would be set by the issuing of a proclamation or executive order freeing all slaves held in territory controlled by the Rebels. That act would signal the end of conciliation and the commitment of Union forces to a war of subjugation. Military operations would be reordered to give effect to this new strategy. Large offensives would have to be mounted on multiple fronts and pressed continually until the Confederacy's capacity for military resistance was destroyed. To sustain such operations Federal forces would have to be hugely augmented, through aggressive recruitment and (eventually) conscription. Army commanders would also have to accept the necessity for such a war of subjugation and be willing to press the offensives that victory required.

Lincoln knew the political and the operational aspects of this strategy were inextricably linked, and the key decisions in each area were nearly simultaneous. On July 11, immediately after his return from Harrison's Landing, Lincoln issued the order that would bring Major General Henry W. Halleck to Washington as general in chief of the armies. The very next day he secretly informed Secretary of State Seward and Navy Secretary Gideon Welles of his decision to issue an emancipation proclamation. He would present a draft of that proclamation to an extraordinary session of the cabinet on July 22, before ordering Halleck, who had just arrived in Washington, to go to Harrison's Landing, assess the state of affairs, and press McClellan to renew his offensive against Richmond. If McClellan refused, Halleck was empowered to relieve him from command. However, although the orders were clear, neither Halleck nor Lincoln was ready to face the political consequences of firing McClellan. The end result was a compromise, which left McClellan in nominal command but withdrew his army piecemeal to northern Virginia—and in the process immobilized half the Union's combat forces in the theater.

EMANCIPATION: THE FIRST DRAFT, JULY 21-22, 1862

The first version of Lincoln's emancipation policy was prepared in secret and without consultation. Lincoln set the stage for its presentation to the cabinet at a meeting on July 21, where he read a series of executive orders that expanded the provisions of the Confiscation Act and authorized the states to enlist Blacks for militia service, not as soldiers but as laborers, cooks, teamsters, and so forth. He also showed them a draft order for colonizing the Blacks freed by these orders in some tropical country. The cabinet was not asked for its opinion on these measures, which did not radically alter existing law or policy. He then called a second extraordinary meeting of the cabinet for July 22, at which he read the draft of a proclamation of general emancipation. Before presenting it, he stated flatly that the question was "settled in his own mind." All he wanted from the cabinet were suggestions how and when to implement the decision.[1]

The measure he then laid out was implicitly revolutionary, but hedged by critical silences and gestures of deference to conservative opinion. The president cited as authority for his action the Confiscation Act of July 17, and his inherent power as commander-in-chief to take all measures needful for the suppression of the rebellion. "[A]s a fit and necessary military measure for effecting this object" he ordered that as of January 1, 1863, "all persons held as slaves within any state or states, wherein constitutional authority of the United States shall not then be practically recognized, submitted to, and maintained, shall then, thenceforward, and forever be free." By this act, all slaves held in states and districts not under Union control were confiscated and declared free, without any civil or judicial proceeding. By making them "forever" free, Lincoln precluded the possibility that postwar action, by courts or legislatures, could restore them to slavery. No distinction was made between loyal slaveholders and Rebels within those districts. This was collective punishment, imposed on all those who submitted to Rebel jurisdiction, whether willingly or not. His assertion of the power to make such a broad and categorical confiscation of property was radical; and its social effects, if realized, would be revolutionary. To ameliorate the latter implication, the lengthy middle paragraph of the draft advocated the colonization of freed slaves outside the United States and compensation for slaves emancipated by the loyal states.[2]

The draft proclamation also stopped short of authorizing the enlistment of Blacks in the combat arms of the military and said nothing about the legal consequences of emancipation for slaves in Confederate territory. Were slaves freed by the proclamation permitted to disobey their masters and/or the laws of the states in which they resided? And if they disobeyed or resisted—or rose in rebellion—were Federal officers permitted or obliged to come to their aid? The possibility of "servile insurrection" was feared in the South but also detested by most Whites in the North.

As originally formulated, the proclamation resembled an ultimatum, which in principle allowed Southern states a little less than six months to end the rebellion and avert the effects of the proclamation. It is highly unlikely that Lincoln expected any appreciable number of states or counties to accept the ultimatum. His failed negotiations with Border State unionists had convinced him that slaveholders were immovable on that issue, and secessionists would never rejoin a union committed in principle to "ultimate extinction." Moreover, he would make no adjustment of the deadline after agreeing to postpone its issuance until a military victory had been won. Even if that victory had been gained (as he hoped) by Pope's army in August, the deadline would have been shortened to something over four months. As it happened, the victory was not won until September 17; and when the Emancipation Proclamation was issued on September 22, the January 1 deadline was retained—allowing the South barely three months to comply.

Thus it seems clear that the Emancipation Proclamation was not an ultimatum at all but a reformulation of war aims implying a change in strategy. Lincoln had abandoned the hope that a quick series of impressive victories could demoralize the South into negotiation. Instead he was now ready to commit the nation to a war of subjugation, aimed at destroying the South's ability to resist and uprooting its fundamental institution. In Lincoln's mind, the Civil War had already passed the point of no return. The Proclamation made compromise impossible and guaranteed that even if the Union were restored it would not be "the Union as it was."

The responses of Lincoln's cabinet officers reflected the persistent divisions among his own party's various factions. They were, as Doris Kearns Goodwin has called them, a "Team of Rivals" representing the major factions and voting blocs that contended for control of the Republican Party.

Montgomery Blair spoke for the conservative and Border State element. Clean-shaven and handsome, with a high, broad forehead, he was a West Point graduate, Class of 1835, and a veteran of the Seminole War who had left the army for a career in law and politics. His father, Francis P. Blair Sr., had been one of Andrew Jackson's chief advisers. Like Jackson, the family owned slaves but was militantly Unionist, and it had helped found the Republican Party. The Blairs were Free-Soilers, opposed to slavery in the territories but also to the idea of general emancipation or any measure that threatened the exclusive political prerogatives of the White race. Blair opposed issuing such a proclamation, on the ground that it might drive the Border States out of the Union and would throw the midterm elections to the Democrats.

Attorney General Bates was also a Border State conservative, at sixty-nine the oldest man in the room. He had been Missouri's favorite son candidate for the 1860 nomination, and Blair had backed him. But Missouri politics had long been marked by violence between pro-slavery and Free-Soil partisans, which made Bates more willing than Blair to hurt the slaveholders—so long as White privilege and exclusivity were maintained. He favored issuing the proclamation, but only if it included the *compulsory* colonization of freed Blacks outside the United States.

Secretary of War Stanton wanted the Proclamation issued at once. Although he had been a Democrat and had shared his party's distaste for abolition and racial equality, since his appointment to the cabinet he had allied himself more and more closely with the Radicals. His intense feud with McClellan undoubtedly strengthened this tendency. Stanton also understood that in an extended conflict the Union would need the additional military manpower that free and freed Black men could provide.

Secretary of State Seward and Navy Secretary Gideon Welles were Lincoln's most loyal and consistent supporters in the cabinet. He had trusted them with the secret of his emancipation plan on July 12, and they had kept it. Welles was a moderate Connecticut Republican noted for his full fluffy beard and a fools-nobody hairpiece. Though he had absolutely no preparation for his job, he proved to be an extraordinarily competent naval administrator and policymaker. He favored the proclamation on practical grounds: if the Union did not make use of the slaves, the South would.

Seward favored the proclamation but strongly advised against issuing it now, after the Union's military defeats. He feared it would appear, not as a measure of liberation, but as our "last *shriek* on the retreat." He also feared that the positive effect of emancipation on British public opinion would be negated if it seemed to be linked with a call for servile insurrection—the English still had raw memories of the Sepoy Mutiny of 1857.

The most surprising and complicated response came from Treasury Secretary Chase. As the cabinet's Radical member he ought to have jumped at the prospect of immediate emancipation. Instead he questioned the president's constitutional authority to act and expressed the fear that a general declaration of "universal emancipation" would lead to "depredation and massacre." Although "I am not myself afraid of the negroes," he thought it better to let military commanders in the field use their authority under martial law to confiscate and emancipate slaves as required for their operations, while using military force to prevent uncontrolled outbreaks. This last idea closely resembled McClellan's advice in the Harrison's Landing letter. So McClellan may have been right in thinking that, in addition to Blair, he had a sometime cabinet ally in Chase.[3]

Lincoln adopted Seward's view that the proclamation should not be issued until a Union victory had been won. Because that could not happen unless Union armies resumed offensive operations in Virginia, Lincoln had already ordered General Halleck east to take charge of military operations, with the hope that under his orders Pope and McClellan would cooperate in a grand offensive against the Confederates defending Richmond. Once again, McClellan proved to be the chief difficulty. Because he would not fight, the general could not execute Lincoln's strategy, but he was also too powerful politically and within the army for Lincoln to fire him outright.[4]

In moving toward a stronger stance on emancipation, Lincoln was reverting to values and positions he had long espoused, acting on a hatred of slavery that was visceral as well as principled. There was also a new strain of anger in the feelings that drove him, a rising sense that vindication of the rule of law, and the principles of justice, required that unjust rebellion be punished, not merely suppressed. On July 26 Lincoln impatiently dismissed the complaints of Border State Unionists that the military government was emancipating slaves in occupied Louisiana. Louisianans had rebelled against the government, although they knew "full well, that I never had a wish to touch the foundations of their society." If they had now to endure a military government, "it is their own fault." If they wanted to be rid of it, "they also know the remedy"— abandon the rebellion. Failing that, "If they can conceive of anything worse . . . within my power, would they not better be looking for it?" What would the Border State men do if they were in his place? "Would you drop the war where it is? Or, would you prosecute it in future, with elder-stalk squirts, charged with rose water? Would you deal lighter blows rather than heavier ones?" "I am a patient man," he told them, "but it may as well be understood, once for all, that I shall not surrender the game leaving any available card unplayed."

Even more to the point was his response to August Belmont, national chairman of the Democratic Party, who had urged Lincoln to adopt a program essentially the same as that laid out in the Harrison's Landing letter. Lincoln's response, on August 31, was brusque. The harm already done to slavery by the war to date was past mending. The only way to prevent further harm was for the South to return to its allegiance, and "The sooner she does so, the smaller will be the amount of that which is past mending." If the rebellion were to continue, then the damage to Southern institutions would become punitive. "This government cannot much longer play a game in which it stakes all, and its enemies stake nothing. Those enemies must understand that they cannot experiment for ten years trying to destroy the government, and if they fail come back into the Union unhurt."[5]

Lincoln's anger was in harmony with the public mood in the North. There was a growing rancor toward Confederate slaveholders for having precipitated an unnecessary and unjust war, causing so much bloodshed and grief, disrupting the prosperous and progressive course of national history. The desire to punish slaveholders by attacking their property interest did not necessarily guarantee support for a general emancipation, but it made Lincoln's new policy politically feasible. However, public opinion also identified General McClellan as the man best suited to press the more vigorous military measures, which made it difficult for Lincoln to remove or even entirely control McClellan's actions.[6]

The complex and (from Lincoln's perspective) contradictory state of public opinion can be read on the editorial pages of the four large New York daily newspapers.

The *Tribune* was edited by Horace Greeley, who had been a major figure in American journalism and literary culture for more than twenty years. Greeley had made the *Tribune* a vehicle for some of the most interesting and creative writers and thinkers of his time, from the feminist Margaret Fuller to Karl Marx; had lent its pages to his own progressive enthusiasms for reform in politics, culture, and education. Democrats and conservatives mocked and castigated him as a sponsor of free love, vegetarianism, and "nigger equality." He was eccentric and mercurial but also a powerful spokesman for the Radicals, and his paper reached beyond New York City to subscribers across the nation.

The *Times* was edited by forty-two-year-old Henry Raymond, who had founded the paper in 1851. Like Lincoln, he had belonged to the Whig Party before 1854, and he was one of the founding members of the Republican Party in New York State. His editorials reflected the views of moderate Republicans.

The *World* was edited by Manton Marble, a professional journalist with no strong political allegiances. Marble had been hired by the leaders of the New York Democratic Party to edit their semi-official newspaper. He was in close contact with Barlow and Belmont and received correspondence from McClellan's confidant Fitz-John Porter. When

McClellan asked Barlow to talk to the press on his behalf, Marble was the first man to be contacted.

The *Herald* rivaled and ultimately outdid the *Tribune* in fame and in national circulation. But where Greeley's paper specialized in high-mindedness, the *Herald* reveled in scandal and sensation. It was the first paper to give front-page coverage to a murder, the first to illustrate its stories with woodcuts. Its publisher, James Gordon Bennett, was nominally independent but politically conservative. His editorials are filled with ugly racial barbs, and he frequently declared that Republican Radicals were more dangerous enemies of the Union, and indeed of civilization, than the Rebels.

Despite their differences, in July 1862 all four papers reflected a rising tide of anger against the South, which was expressed in calls for more energetic military campaigns and "sterner measures" of punishment against recalcitrant Rebels. All four papers agreed that the war effort was failing because the North had not mobilized its full resources, and because the army and the administration had not prosecuted it with sufficient vigor, sternness, and efficiency. All four enthusiastically supported the president's call for three hundred thousand new volunteers, and the *World* even urged Lincoln to consider a draft. They also welcomed the promotion of Halleck to overall command as a sign that military strategy and operations would be more efficient. Most significantly, from Lincoln's point of view, all four papers gave strong support to the punitive measures so far taken against slavery by the administration and the Congress, including the Second Confiscation Act. However, of the four papers only the Radical *Tribune* advocated general emancipation.

The *Herald* called for "action, action, and again action. We have done playing with war, and must now fight in earnest." The *World* demanded: "the preposterous mixture of war and peace principles, the practice of treating the Rebels with both bullets and sugar-plums, is to cease." Moreover, "The study is no longer how to carry on this war with least damage to slavery." If slavery "stands in the way of the effective exercise of the war power, it must just to that extent be put out of the way." However, the *World* was at pains to distinguish confiscation from general emancipation. The latter would violate constitutional principles and the rules of jurisprudence by punishing the innocent with the guilty; wreck the "industrial system" of the whole country; and inaugurate a social and racial revolution that most Anglo-Saxon Americans would find repugnant. It was to *avoid* such a revolution that the *World* advocated a sterner war policy. "The fact is notorious that the prolongation of the war operates almost everywhere to deepen the hatred against slavery" and promote the radical agenda. Therefore, "The interests of true conservatism . . . require the adoption of the sternest war policy."[7]

The *Herald* used less moderate language and was more explicit in asserting that the ultimate goal of Federal policy must be to preserve White supremacy in a restored Union. For Bennett the Radicals were equivalent to Jefferson Davis as enemies of the nation and far worse as enemies of the White race. Their call for abolition, for the enlistment of Black soldiers, and for Negro citizenship was perversely intended to "drag down the white man to the level of the negro, or rather to produce from both, by amalgamation, a mongrel breed inferior to either. . . . Forbid it, God and nature; forbid it, humanity and the interests of civilization." If the government would only strike down these "abolition traitors," all those patriots who have hesitated "to fight for emancipation and amalgamation, will crowd our armies and carry the old flag triumphantly over the last stronghold of the rebellion." Yet the *Herald* also supported the Confiscation Act, and for a while even supported its draconian application by General Pope—a figure who soon became a symbol of Radical excess. Like Marble of the *World*, Bennett wanted to preserve slavery in most of the South to insure White supremacy. But he too believed that only a quick victory could insure that result; and that required a vigorous military campaign, coupled with a punitive but limited confiscation of slaves to demonstrate the ultimate consequence of continued rebellion.[8]

Not surprisingly, both conservative papers saw McClellan as the general best qualified to conduct such a campaign. They blamed McClellan's defeat on Stanton, for his "deliberate" mischief of withholding reinforcements, and defended McClellan's retreat to Harrison's Landing as "a strategic success of magnificent and truly Napoleonic character." What they wanted was a new "War Cabinet": let General Halleck replace Stanton, and General Banks (a former Democrat) take over the Navy Department. Above all, "Reinforce McClellan promptly and *adequately*, and no subsequent blundering by the War Department can defer the fall of the Rebel capital." Only the *Tribune* unequivocally defended Stanton and blamed McClellan for the failure of the Peninsula Campaign.[9]

The radical/conservative split on the question of emancipation was predictable, as was disagreement about the merits of General McClellan. From Lincoln's perspective the most dismaying editorials of the period would have been those of the *New York Times*. As the voice of moderate Republicans it hewed to the party line on emancipation: embraced confiscation as a limited, legal, and necessary war measure but would not abolish slavery in the states where it already existed. Like a good moderate, editor Raymond criticized both "conservatives and radicals" for agitating the slavery question while the war was going on. "The great matter in hand is *fighting*—and fighting only. . . . Let us have war in earnest, and no more debates." The *Times*, like the *Herald* and the *World*, thought McClellan was the man to fight that war. It blamed Stanton for McClellan's failure and not only entertained the idea of a cabinet reshuffle but recommended McClellan as Stanton's replacement! "If Mr. Stanton is to be removed, the country will be reassured, and the public interest greatly promoted, by making Gen. McClellan his successor. Even those who cavil at his leadership in the field, do not question his mastery of the art of war."[10]

Thus despite his defeat in the Seven Days, McClellan still enjoyed very broad support, not only in the army but with the public and in the press. He and his political allies had been extraordinarily effective in persuading much of the public and the press that Stanton and the War Department were to blame for McClellan's defeat—and that McClellan was the man best suited to prosecute the more vigorous war the public now demanded. According to a report in the popular newspaper, *Spirit of the Times*, McClellan sent a brigadier general from his command to New York City to explain his commander's views on national policy to the city's business, political, and journalistic leaders. Under these circumstances any effort to interfere with McClellan's command, or to relieve him, would present extraordinary political difficulties.[11]

HALLECK'S TURN, JULY 23–AUGUST 3, 1862

In the weeks that followed the July 22 cabinet meeting, Lincoln had to maintain a precarious balance among contending policy imperatives. He had to keep secret his plan for emancipation yet somehow prepare the public for its proclamation. Over the next month he would pursue a complex and sometimes devious course of actions and public statements, some designed to placate or disarm conservatives, others trial balloons to signal the shift in policy—at times seemingly self-contradictory, as if the president did not know his own mind.[12]

He could not resolve the ambiguity, and openly commit the nation to his new policy, until his armies had won an important victory in the field. However, there could be no offensive in Virginia unless McClellan moved against Richmond—which he seemed unwilling to do. So Lincoln also had to resolve the McClellan problem without provoking a political controversy that would weaken support for the recruiting drive. Lincoln therefore decided to fob the decision off on General Halleck. He was considered the quintessential military professional: whatever he did with McClellan would be seen as the result of professional judgment, not political rancor.

When Halleck arrived in Washington on July 23 to assume his new duties, he was immediately ordered to visit Harrison's Landing and judge McClellan's situation and state of mind. If he thought McClellan capable of effective action, he might retain him—as a subordinate. If not, he had authority to relieve McClellan of his command.

Halleck was the antithesis of the Young Napoleon: forty-seven years old, pudgy and balding, with goggle eyes and pendulous cheeks. He had not seen combat in the Mexican War. His military experience was entirely in staff work and administration, at which he excelled. He was nicknamed "Old Brains," in tribute to his reputation as an expert in the theory of warfare as a translator of the writings of the Napoleonic strategist Jomini. As commander of Union forces west of the Alleghenies he had presided over the most successful offensives of the war. However, the actual operations were conducted by army commanders Curtis, Pope, Grant, and Buell. Halleck himself was a poor field commander, as he showed in his glacially slow pursuit of the defeated Confederates after Shiloh. Lincoln and Stanton recognized and accepted this limitation, as did those in the press who commented on Halleck's appointment. His new position only required that he do nationally what he had already done in the western theater: activate and coordinate the operations of several armies, each under its own energetic commander.

In reorganizing the Virginia theater, Halleck faced a military choice with political ramifications. There were two armies—John Pope's in northern Virginia and McClellan's in front of Richmond—and three possible lines of operation. He could send most of Pope's army to McClellan by sea; but while those troops were in transit the Rebels could threaten Washington, as Jackson had done a few months earlier. Lincoln would not support this option. Or Halleck could reinforce Pope's command with Burnside's IX Corps, up from North Carolina, and have it march overland to connect with McClellan. That was only feasible if McClellan were willing and able to undertake an offensive against Richmond with his present force. If he merely held his ground the Confederates could concentrate against Pope and destroy his army. The third option was to withdraw McClellan from the Peninsula by sea and unite his force with Pope's in northern Virginia for an overland campaign against Richmond. That would create a window of vulnerability for both armies. If Lee had the numbers with which McClellan credited him, he could either strike McClellan's force while it was embarking or move north and hit Pope before McClellan could join him.

For Halleck, the essential question in his talks with McClellan was whether or not McClellan would declare his willingness to advance against Richmond with the limited reinforcements Lincoln was able to provide. If McClellan balked, Halleck had two options. He could order McClellan's army withdrawn from the Peninsula and transferred corps by corps to Washington to join with Pope's army—or he could relieve McClellan of his command, and replace him with someone willing to mount an offensive from the Harrison's Landing base.[13]

The military problem was complicated by the fact that in the week before Halleck took command, McClellan and Pope had become embroiled in a raging political controversy. In his single month in command of the Army of Virginia, Pope had made himself the military embodiment of the Radical approach to war—and, as such, as obnoxious to McClellan as he was to General Lee and President Davis.

John Pope had great energy, large ambition, and unlimited self-confidence. He was also a blowhard whose ambitions were barefaced and pursued in ways that some thought unscrupulous. He had served ably in the Mexican War and afterward in the conduct of several railroad surveys. Unlike most serving officers he was a vocal political partisan, and had been court-martialed for his open advocacy of the Republican ticket in 1860. As a field general he had campaigned with some success against Confederate guerrillas in Missouri, and had led the army/navy campaign that captured the important Confederate bastion of Island No. 10 in March 1862. His prior service was not adequate preparation for the command of the Army of Virginia. In the west his army of twenty-five thousand had been opposed by fewer than half their number of Confederates and had enjoyed powerful naval support. In Virginia his command would rise from forty-five thousand to seventy-five thousand during the course of the summer, and he would be opposed by a large and powerful field army under the command of the Confederacy's greatest generals, Lee, Jackson, and Longstreet.

McClellan saw Pope as Halleck's protégé, and therefore a rival. He also knew Pope as a partisan Republican who had violated the code of military ethics by giving political speeches during the 1860 presidential campaign. The taint was not diminished by the fact that a court-martial had acquitted Pope. McClellan's political suspicions were confirmed, and his anger aroused, by the orders Pope issued on assuming command of the Army of Virginia (July 14). Pope contrasted the frustrations and failures of McClellan's Virginia campaigns with the achievement of the Western armies, whose troops "have always seen the backs of our enemies . . . whose business it has been to seek the adversary and to beat him when he was found; whose policy has been attack and not defense." He also took a direct shot at McClellan when he asked his troops to "dismiss from your minds certain phrases, which I am sorry to find so much in vogue amongst you . . . of 'taking strong positions and holding them,' of 'lines of retreat,' and of 'bases of supplies.' "[14]

Pope's order of July 18, authorizing his troops to seize their subsistence from the civilians in their zone of operations, transformed the personal into the political. McClellan saw Pope's order in exactly the same light as did Davis and Lee: it was the military expression of the Radical principles just made law by the Second Confiscation Act. McClellan believed he had a sacred duty to oppose Radicalism in every form, lest the republic become a despotism. He therefore declared his intention to defy both the congressional act and the presidential orders giving it effect—and by that act to draw the line between himself and General Pope. "As soon as I receive an official copy of the Presdt's Proclamation [giving effect to the Confiscation Act] I shall issue orders directly opposed to Pope's—then there will be a furious row." He also contemplated with pleasure the like-lihood that Pope would soon be defeated: "Stonewall Jackson is after him, & that paltry young man who wanted to teach me the art of war will in less than a week be in full retreat or badly whipped. He will begin to learn the value of *entrenchments, lines of communication & of retreat*."[15]

When Halleck arrived at Harrison's Landing on July 25 he was, in McClellan's eyes, the emissary of his old enemy Stanton and the sponsor of his new enemy, Pope. McClellan considered Halleck's appointment itself a "slap in the face," part of Stanton's campaign to so insult and humiliate him that he would voluntarily retire. He also resented hav-ing to take orders from "a man whom I know by experience to be my inferior." Still, McClellan could not resign without abdicating his role as savior of the nation. So he swallowed his pride and worked hard to persuade Halleck of the necessity of concentrating all possible force at Harrison's Landing for a new advance on Richmond.[16]

Though they discussed the costs and benefits of operating from Har-rison's Landing and from northern Virginia, for McClellan these talks were simply an extended negotiation for reinforcements. While privately he reckoned that Lee's army mustered 150,000–170,000 troops (which was a gross overestimate), he told Halleck that the enemy had 200,000 troops in and around Richmond, and he needed a reinforcement of 30,000 before he could advance. Halleck said only 20,000 were avail-able. McClellan countered by suggesting that Pope's force be sent to the Peninsula and put under his command. That was ruled out, as before, by Lincoln's requirement that a large force be kept to defend Washington. In the end, Halleck left McClellan with a choice: either begin the offensive against Richmond with the reinforcement of 20,000, or prepare to with-draw from the Peninsula and combine his force with Pope's. In the latter case, Halleck promised that McClellan would command both armies.[17]

While Halleck's chief concern with relieving McClellan was the lack of a suitable replacement, he may also have been influenced by the intense partisan loyalty displayed by many of the army's higher officers, which would have made any replacement difficult and potentially dangerous.

Halleck was accompanied by General Ambrose Burnside, whose troops were being transferred from the North Carolina coast to the Vir-ginia front. Three days prior to their arrival Lincoln had asked Burnside to replace McClellan as commander of the Army of the Potomac. Burnside had refused. That the offer was made indicated the poverty of Halleck's and Lincoln's alternatives. Burnside might have performed competently in command of the amphibious expedition that seized control of the North Carolina sounds, but he had no experience of commanding a large army in a major battle.

Ambrose Burnside, 38, cut an impressive figure, his sturdy six-foot frame topped by a large bald head, whiskers worn in the double-scallop known ever after as "burnsides." He was a strange mixture of ability and incompetence. In the first year of the war it was the ability that stood out, and it would earn him promotion far beyond his talents. He was affable and considered modest because he did not pursue promotion with the hell-bent intensity that marked most of his fellow generals. He was also a loyal friend, and was deeply in McClellan's debt. Burnside had gone bankrupt trying to promote a carbine of his own design, and McClellan had given him a job with the Illinois Central that saved his reputation and restored his finances. His refusal of Lincoln's offer was based on loyalty, well-founded self-doubts, and a genuine belief in McClellan's abilities. His testimony about the state of mind prevailing at McClellan's headquarters is therefore highly credible.

The president had also asked Burnside to make private inquiries among McClellan's staff, and his corps and division commanders, to learn what they thought about their commander's performance and his future plans. Burnside was appalled by their expressions of contempt and hostility toward the civilian government, and by their open discussion of the need for a military takeover. Burnside took the threat seriously and rebuked it: "I don't know what you fellows call this talk, but I call it flat Treason, by God!" Halleck dismissed all this as "staff talk." But the staff was taking its language and its political cues from General McClellan, who had been fulminating for weeks against the administration's "radical and inhuman views," its deliberate and treacherous attempt to "sacrifice" the army. McClellan had told his wife that he found it gratifying to be continually "receiving letters from the North urging me to march on Washington & assume the Govt!!"[18]

McClellan was also receiving frequent visits by important leaders in the Democratic Party, especially New Yorkers like Barlow, Aspinwall, and Fernando Wood. Although the general and his confidant Fitz-John Porter were gratified by these visits, they caused some controversy within the army. Division commander Philip Kearny, one of the best combat generals in the army, wrote his wife that he considered such close contacts with supposedly pro-Southern politicos a sign of disloyalty: "There is either positive treason or at least McClellan or the few with him are devising a game of politics rather than war." Kearny also thought McClellan's conduct of the campaign had been utterly incompetent, and his decision to retreat rather than counterattack after Malvern Hill the result of either "cowardice or treason." Few of his fellow officers went as far as Kearny, but his opinion mattered in army circles. He was the kind of man McClellan himself most admired: a West Point graduate, a cavalryman who had won a reputation for headlong courage in two armies— the French, with which he served in Algiers and against the Austrians in the 1850s, and the American, with which he served on the frontier and in Mexico, where he lost an arm. He was also a gentleman and a millionaire, whose father had helped found the New York Stock Exchange, and he raised and equipped a brigade at his own expense.[19]

Even McClellan's friends were concerned that he was breaching the wall between military and civil authority. General William "Baldy" Smith was an old friend of McClellan's, a member of his staff and later a division commander in VI Corps. He claimed that McClellan had shown him the text of a letter in which he committed himself to a run for the presidency in opposition to the present administration. He also showed Smith the text of his Harrison's Landing letter and ignored Smith's warning that it "looks like treason and will ruin you & all of us."[20]

Buoyed by signs that he enjoyed strong public and political support, and by the weakness of will implied by Halleck's accommodating manner, McClellan ignored the stark alternatives Halleck had offered (advance with your present force or be withdrawn) and continued to press his case for reinforcement. No sooner had Halleck returned to Washington than a dispatch from McClellan arrived, dated July 26, reporting that Lee was being reinforced by troops from the Carolinas and "Beauregard's old army." The latter was Bragg's Army of Tennessee, which was then in Chattanooga preparing to invade Kentucky. When added to McClellan's existing overestimate of the Confederate force, this reinforcement would give Lee a two-to-one advantage. He therefore requested that "*all* the troops of Burnside & Hunter—together with all that can possibly be spared from other points—be sent to me at once." With that additional force—far more than the twenty thousand Halleck declared to be the maximum possible—he would be willing to undertake the required advance on Richmond. But he wanted yet more: "Can you not *possibly* draw 15,000 or 20,000 men from the West to reinforce me temporarily?"[21]

McClellan also tried to woo Halleck into his political camp. On August 1 he wrote again, promising "my full and cordial support in all things" and offering his sympathy for the "unpleasant" political engagements that went with Halleck's position. "If we are permitted to do so [by the politicians], I believe that together we can save this unhappy country and bring this war to a comparatively early termination." He then rehearsed for Halleck's benefit the main points of the Harrison's Landing letter: that the war should be conducted on "civilized" principles, with as much protection to the "constitutional, civil, and personal rights" of rebel civilians as military necessity would allow. Above all, "the question of slavery should not enter into this war . . . we should avoid any proclamation of general emancipation, and should protect inoffensive citizens in the possession of that, as well as other kinds of property. . . . The people of the South should understand that we are not making war upon the institution of slavery." He then went on to condemn "pillaging and outrages"— a catch-phrase used by critics of Pope's military administration.[22]

If he thought Halleck could be persuaded to abandon his own views for McClellan's, he was mistaken. When it became clear that McClellan was unwilling to mount an offensive with his present force, Halleck informed McClellan on August 3 of his intention to withdraw his army. McClellan's reply was proper, but he stated his objections in terms that challenged Halleck's military judgment. Halleck's order "has caused me the greatest pain I ever experienced, for I am convinced that the order to withdraw this Army . . . will prove disastrous in the extreme to our cause—I fear that it will be a fatal blow." Halleck's order now joined him with Stanton and the others on McClellan's enemies list: the man was a "scalawag . . . dull & incompetent." He had "begun to show the cloven hoof" and would "kill himself in less than two weeks."[23]

McCLELLAN'S SECOND FRONT, AUGUST 13–21, 1862

On the surface, McClellan seemed to accept his new role, dutifully carrying out his orders, preparing and superintending the withdrawal of eighty or ninety thousand men with all their equipment. Heintzelman's III Corps and Porter's V Corps began shipping out on August 16. On the twenty-second they disembarked at Alexandria and Aquia Creek, respectively. Heintzelman's troops took the train south from Alexandria to join Pope, while Porter's men had to march cross-country by bad roads and with little guidance from Pope's headquarters. In the meantime the ships steamed back to Virginia to pick up the II and VI Corps. While McClellan's public dealings with Halleck were proper and polite, his private correspondence over the next week (August 13–21) reflected a state of mind disordered by rage and self-pity, in which reasoned analyses of strategy and politics veer into fantasies of victimization and revenge. His obsessions and resentments were mirrored and amplified by a doting staff.

Having imagined a Confederate army that was too powerful to be attacked—and having been, in any case, deprived of the force with which to attack it—McClellan focused his anger and his energy on his political enemies. On this front, too, he exaggerated and misread the character, power, and malice of the forces working against him. He was not wrong in thinking he had enemies, especially in the Radical camp, who were agitating for his removal; nor in thinking that officers like Halleck and Pope were jealous rivals eager to advance themselves at his expense. No, his main misconstruction was of Lincoln's character, intelligence, and motives; and that was so egregious that it bordered on delusional. If the president urged him to action it was with the aim of driving him into the jaws of destruction. If Lincoln sustained him in command, despite his defeat and the enmity of the Radicals, it was only because he was afraid McClellan would expose his malfeasance by releasing their exchange of telegrams on June 28. He also failed to appreciate the fact that the support he enjoyed among moderate and conservative editors and politicians depended on their belief that McClellan was the man to prosecute the war to a speedy end. He had rationalized his defeat in the Seven Days as an event willed by God to frustrate the Radicals: "If I had succeeded in taking Richmond now the fanatics of the North might have been too powerful & reunion impossible." However, he was virtually alone in thinking it was the Radicals who stood to benefit from a quick Union victory. Even his staunchest journalistic supporter, the *New York World*, recognized the need for a speedy victory: "The fact is notorious that the prolongation of the war operates almost everywhere to deepen the hatred against slavery."[24]

At moments McClellan's rage rose to a Lear-like intensity of grievance and vengeful fantasy. He looked forward to the destruction of Pope as an act of Divine Providence, punishing those who had tried to destroy him: "The more I hear of their wickedness the more I am surprised that such a wretched set are permitted to *live* much less to occupy the positions they do." McClellan imagined that he himself would soon have the power to visit punishment upon them: "If I succeed in my coup everything will be changed in this country so far as we are concerned & my enemies will be at my feet. It may go hard with some of them in that event, for I look upon them as the enemies of the country & of the human race." To Samuel Barlow he wrote that "the rascals" were afraid to fire him outright because "[t]hey are aware that I have seen through their villainous schemes." They had conspired to destroy the republic's best army, because they had no real desire to restore the Union—they wanted a "Northern Confederacy," free of the conservative opposition based in the South, in which to realize their abominable Radical agenda. To suppress such a treasonous movement the most forcible means might be necessary. The Radicals feared McClellan because "[If] I succeed my foot will be on their necks." Fitz-John Porter, McClellan's closest confidant, echoed and amplified McClellan's darkest fantasy, writing to a friend, "Would that this army was in Washington to rid us of incumbents ruining our country."[25]

It is hard to say what sort of "coup" McClellan envisioned. Although he often spoke of marching on Washington, he made no plans for a military *putsch*. Even if he had desired one, until the end of August the only force that could have attempted it was with him on the Peninsula. He may well have hoped that his efforts to force Stanton from office were bearing fruit. Newspapers and correspondence from friends in the North, and rumors conveyed by intelligence chief Allan Pinkerton, just back from Washington, would have made that seem quite possible in early August.[26] The real significance of these rants is their revelation that the commander of the nation's largest army was in an extraordinarily dangerous state of mind. He rejoices in the hope that an army of the nation he serves will be destroyed, so that he can be vindicated and restored to power: "I think the result of their machinations [Stanton's and Halleck's] will be that Pope will be badly thrashed within two days & that they will be very glad to turn over the redemption of their affairs to me." McClellan goes as far as to declare that the legitimate heads of the government he has sworn to loyally serve are dolts and traitors, hardly fit to live. He is pleased when supporters write urging him to "change front on Washington" and clean the rascals out, and he imagines a triumphant return to power in which his enemies are forced to beg him for "redemption" from their sins and errors—but he will not save them unless they grant him "full & entire control."[27]

These angry rants were coupled with a campaign—partly open, partly covert—to recover the influence and power he had lost since the Seven Days. At dark moments he seemed intent on simply maintaining command of the Army of the Potomac, but his ultimate goal was to force Stanton's resignation and recover his lost position as the dominant voice on military policy. The campaign was waged through his political supporters in Washington and his allies in the press. Staff officers and senior commanders, notably Fitz-John Porter, acted as his surrogates, transmitting his strategic views and his attacks on the administration to correspondents and editors. McClellan set the agenda by a series of symbolic gestures, to which he drew the attention of the correspondents in his camp. McClellan wanted the public to see Pope and Lincoln as ideological twins. He would then identify himself as the champion of conservative views by rebuking Pope and defying Lincoln. On July 30 he had declared his intention to defy Lincoln's order promulgating the Second Confiscation Act by issuing "orders directly opposed to Pope's." On August 8 he told his wife, "I will issue tomorrow an order giving *my* comments on Mr. Jno [*sic*] Pope—I will strike square in the teeth of all his infamous orders & give directly the reverse instructions to my army."[28]

The conservative press quickly picked up on McClellan's gesture. The *Herald* and the *World*, which had taken a favorable view of Pope's militancy, reversed themselves and attacked him as a Radical. They praised McClellan for both his military skill and his conservatism, and lambasted Stanton as the author of McClellan's defeat because he had refused to send reinforcements. Their polemics produced a wave of anti-Stanton sentiment that transcended party lines. Lincoln had to make a public defense of his secretary of war, but he felt it necessary to minimize the disagreement between Stanton and McClellan and to suggest that their "quarrel" was fomented by the press—which he knew very well it was not.[29]

Then on August 21 Halleck informed McClellan that "Pope & Burnside are very hard pressed." Lee was beginning his initial moves against Pope's position on the Rapidan, and Halleck wanted McClellan to send his remaining troops north as fast as possible and *"come myself as soon as I possibly can!"* McClellan presumed that on his arrival he would assume the command of Pope's army and his own, and he wrote his wife, "I believe I have triumphed!!" He gloated over the embarrassment of the Lincoln administration, forced to recall the man derided as "the 'Quaker,' the 'procrastinator,' the 'coward' & the 'traitor'!" He urged Porter to embark with the greatest possible haste and dashed off a brief note implying that he would soon arrive to take command: "Whatever occurs, hold out till I arrive." He may have given Porter some verbal instructions relating to his assumption of command, to be passed in secret to Burnside.[30]

While the three-way tug-of-war between Halleck, McClellan, and Pope wore on, Lincoln could do nothing to openly advance the strategic and political transformation embodied in the Emancipation Proclamation. Instead, he followed a devious course of action. On August 4 Lincoln declined the offer of two Negro regiments from Indiana, and on August 6 he ordered the disbandment of the unauthorized Black regiments that had been raised by General David Hunter in the Sea Islands. Then on August 16 Lincoln secretly authorized Hunter's replacement, General Saxton, to enlist and arm five thousand freed slaves for service as garrison troops. The public statements he made during that summer obscured his commitment to emancipation. On August 14—while McClellan's troops were beginning their evacuation of the Peninsula—Lincoln met with a "Deputation of Negroes," to persuade them to sign on to his plan of colonizing free Blacks somewhere in tropical America. He declared, tersely and coldly, that the racial difference between White and Black was deeper "than exists between almost any other two races," and that the health of both races required their permanent separation. For Blacks to seek equality within the United States, rather than a separate national life elsewhere, was to take "an extremely selfish view of the case." Taken at face value, it was a morally purblind and reprehensible performance, and suggested he was still committed to his old and long-discredited obsession with colonization. Yet the man who gave that speech on August 14 had a draft of the Emancipation Proclamation finished and ready for issuance. Perhaps it was merely a political ploy, intended to placate all those popular and factional elements who feared that emancipation would send waves of free Blacks into the North to take jobs and threaten White supremacy. It certainly showed sympathy and deference for the position taken at the July 22 meeting by Attorney General Bates, that emancipation be followed by the compulsory colonization of Blacks in some tropical country.[31]

The outrage of Radicals at this performance was predictable, and to some extent deliberately provoked by Lincoln, who needed strong pressure from his left to offset the demands of conservatives on his right. On August 20 Horace Greeley published an open letter to Lincoln, chiding the president for failing to enforce the antislavery provisions of the Confiscation Act with sufficient rigor. Like McClellan, Greeley thought Lincoln lacked a firm policy on slavery, but the policy he wanted was radical rather than conservative: "On the face of this wide earth, Mr. President, there is not one disinterested, determined, intelligent champion of the Union cause who does not feel that all attempts to put down the Rebellion and at the same time uphold its inciting cause are preposterous and futile."[32]

Lincoln had already reached the same conclusion, but his response to Greeley appeared to evade or postpone the necessity of embracing emancipation. The first principle of his policy was "to save the Union . . . the shortest way under the Constitution."

> My paramount objective in this struggle *is* to save the Union, and is *not* either to save or to destroy slavery. If I could save the union without freeing *any* slave I would do it; and if I could save it by freeing *all* the slaves I would do it; and if I could save it by freeing some and leaving others alone I would also do that. What I do about slavery and the colored race, I do because I believe it helps

to save the Union; and what I forbear, I forbear because I do *not* believe it would help save the Union.[33]

In fact, he had already decided that the Union could not be saved unless he did something to put slavery on the path to ultimate extinction. But he was helpless to act until someone—Pope, Halleck, or McClellan— won a military victory.

CHAPTER 5

BOTH ENDS AGAINST THE MIDDLE: THE CAMPAIGN OF SECOND BULL RUN

AUGUST 15–SEPTEMBER 1, 1862

JOHN POPE AND HIS SOLDIERS WERE CAUGHT IN AN IRONIC TWIST. For most of the month of August 1862 Confederate President Davis and General Lee on one side, and General McClellan on the other, were equally eager to see John Pope defeated and discredited. Behind that irony was a tangle of military and political conflicts with the potential to wreck the war for the Union.

The cleanest thread in the knot was the determination of Davis and Lee to smash Pope's army before McClellan's troops could reinforce it. While their main purpose was to shift the cockpit of war to northern Virginia and throw the Federals onto the defensive, they were also moved by the desire to rebuke the Radical political program Pope had openly espoused.[1]

On the Federal side matters were more complex. For Lincoln and Stanton, Pope represented a potential replacement for McClellan. They saw him as the kind of general the new strategy required: one who was offense-minded and in tune with the administration's hard-war line. General in Chief Halleck partly shared their investment in Pope, who had been his protégé. But Halleck was more bureaucrat than general. His willingness to run the risks of military decision making was hedged by his need to protect the prestige that had won him his high position. He preferred to foist the responsibility for dangerous decisions onto subordinates, reserving the right to blame them for any setbacks. That same self-protective caution affected his decision not to relieve McClellan but to temporarily disempower him by transferring his corps piecemeal to northern Virginia. By so doing he believed he had demonstrated his power over McClellan without entirely estranging McClellan's political and military partisans. He also left himself an alternative if Pope should fail.

From McClellan's perspective Pope was an enemy whose destruction was (at the moment) more desirable than the defeat of Lee's army. McClellan's was a two-front war, and in August the Washington front was the more critical. McClellan had already decided that an early and decisive victory for Federal forces would benefit the Radicals. If Pope won that victory, McClellan would no longer be indispensable to the Lincoln administration, and his dismissal would leave Radicalism in total control of the war effort. Victory and a restored Union would become impossible, because the South would never submit to an openly abolitionist regime. However, if Pope were defeated, Halleck and Lincoln would have no choice but to recall McClellan to command. Such a result might give McClellan the leverage he needed to reestablish his primacy in the government's military councils, to reduce Halleck to subordination, and to force Stanton's dismissal from the cabinet.

LEE'S STRATEGIC DESIGN, AUGUST 1862

With McClellan's army in the limbo of transshipment to Alexandria and Aquia Creek, Lee was free to move against Pope. In mid-August Pope's Army of Virginia, now some fifty-five thousand strong, was posted near the Cedar Mountain battlefield on the north bank of the Rapidan River. Stonewall Jackson's Confederate force had been blocking Pope's advance by holding a position south of the Rapidan at Gordonsville, some seventy miles north and west of Richmond. Gordonsville was a critical transportation hub, where the railroad from the Federal base at Alexandria crossed the Virginia Central, the line connecting Richmond with the Shenandoah Valley, the Confederate capital's major source of food supplies. Pope's campaign had been intended to cut that supply line as a prelude to the drive against Richmond.

When Lee arrived at Gordonsville with Longstreet's command, his force was roughly equal to Pope's, and he immediately took the offensive. On August 17 he tried to get around Pope's left, or eastern, flank by pushing troops across a ford of the Rapidan. The move was delayed by high water, and Pope adroitly avoided it by retreating some fifteen miles north, to the far side of the Rappahannock River. This put his army in a more defensible position, where it was better placed to receive the approaching reinforcements. Over the next three days Pope would be joined by elements of the IX Corps, marching cross-country from Fredericksburg, and McClellan's III Corps (under Heintzelman), which came by train from Alexandria. Porter's V Corps, marching overland from Aquia Creek, took longer to join up, but by August 24 Pope had about sixty-five thousand troops in hand behind the defensive moat of the Rappahannock, facing fifty-five thousand Confederates.

Lee still held to the strategic objectives that had led him to leave the Richmond front: to shift the theater of operations away from Richmond, to recover the productive region of northern Virginia, and to forestall the opening of a new Federal offensive. To achieve those objectives he had to maintain the initiative, force Pope to retreat, inflict a defeat heavy enough to render Pope's army ineffective, and do it all before the rest of McClellan's army arrived. Pope's numbers and the strength of the river line precluded anything like a direct approach. He therefore planned a grand "turning" movement, a strike at Pope's communications that would force him into a long and difficult retreat. A retreating army would be vulnerable to disruption if properly attacked, so it was conceivable that Pope's army could be decisively defeated before its junction with the rest of McClellan's force. To achieve this Lee would divide his already outnumbered army in half, sending Stonewall Jackson with twenty-five thousand infantry and nearly all his cavalry on a wide swing to the west and north behind the screen of the Bull Run Mountains, then east through Thoroughfare Gap to come in behind Pope's front and seize his supply base at Manassas Junction. Longstreet's troops would fire artillery and stage limited attacks against the Rappahannock line to hold Pope in place until Jackson could strike. When Pope retreated or turned to deal with Jackson, Lee and Longstreet would follow Jackson's route around the hills and through the gap. Then the reunited army would pursue and attack the Federal army while it was still disorganized by its retreat.[2]

By dividing his army in the face of superior numbers, Lee was taking the most extreme risks, which only the prospect of strategic victory could justify. While Jackson was making his flank march Pope had the option of throwing most of his sixty-five thousand men against Longstreet's twenty-eight thousand on the Rappahannock. Or if Jackson reached the rear of Pope's army, the Federal general could send a strong detachment to block Longstreet at Thoroughfare Gap, then turn on Jackson's twenty-five thousand with nearly his whole force.

IT IS HARD TO BE entirely certain of Lee's intentions. Unlike McClellan, who paraded his strategic genius in lengthy position papers, Lee wrote sparingly about his plans and hardly at all about his theories of war. Difference in personality partly accounts for this, but equally significant is the fact that mutual mistrust led McClellan to belabor Lincoln and Halleck with the polemics of military professionalism, and leak his ideas to the press to build public support for his positions. Lee and Davis had hashed out their differences face-to-face and were now in substantial agreement on most critical strategic questions. One side effect of this mutual understanding is that the documentary record of Lee's and Davis's strategic planning and decision making is thin. The same is true of the records of Lee's operational planning. Lee's command system depended on close contact and mutual understanding among Lee, his wing commanders Jackson and Longstreet, and his cavalry chief, J. E. B. ("Jeb") Stuart. The objectives and general design of a given operation were usually presented and worked out in face-to-face meetings. Once his plan was well understood, Lee trusted his subordinates to use their own discretion and initiative to achieve its objectives.

Historians have therefore had to deduce Lee's strategic thinking by correlating his actions with the scanty written record. The traditional view sees Lee as a genius in both theater and battlefield tactics, and the campaign against Pope as a masterpiece executed according to a brilliant plan. A revisionist view, developed by military historians Grady

McWhiney, Alan Nolan, Russell Weigley, and others, sees Lee as a general imbued with a Napoleonic concept of decisive battle, which led him to stage costly attacks that entailed casualty rates the South could not afford. The revisionists also fault Lee as a strategic thinker whose understanding of larger issues was limited by his intense personal investment in the defense of Virginia and his distaste for politics. A more balanced view emerges from historian Joseph Harsh's close studies of Confederate strategic thinking in 1862. Harsh sees Lee's determination to seize the initiative through a strategic offensive as a rational response to the strategic threat posed by the concentration of Federal armies in northern Virginia, and not as merely the expression of a combative temperament. His analysis of Lee's dispatches shows that Lee's plans developed in stages, responsive to the changing strength and position of Pope's army; and allowed for the possibility of a maneuver campaign that would force Pope to retreat without bringing on a general engagement.[3]

However, the benefits of a pure maneuver campaign would be as limited as the risks. The premise of Lee's move against Pope was the conviction that Confederate forces in Virginia were inadequate to check an advance by the united forces of McClellan and Pope. The only way to forestall such a campaign, or reduce the odds of its success, was for Lee to seriously damage or destroy Pope's force before McClellan's arrived. The strategic dilemma did not absolutely require Lee to accept battle and seek decisive victory if his maneuvers failed to bring about a favorable situation. But it did impel him to follow a plan that would make a decisive battle possible. Although battle entailed the risk of heavy casualties, if Pope's army could be caught at a disadvantage, attacked while its elements were disorganized by a hurried retreat, Lee might cripple the Federal army and force it to undergo a lengthy reorganization. While that army stood on the defensive northern Virginia was safe, and Lee was free to strike other blows that might further derange the Union war effort.[4]

SINCE IT WAS APPARENT that any new offensive would require an increase of force, between August 21 and 24 Lee sent several dispatches to Davis urging that more troops be sent to him from Richmond. Lee's dispatch of the twenty-fourth has seemed to some historians an effort to prod or pressure a reluctant president to endorse a high-risk campaign: instead of *asking* Davis for reinforcement, he informed the president that he would order five brigades now at Richmond to come north, unless Davis explicitly countermanded the order. In fact, Davis was not at all reluctant. Two weeks earlier he *had* hesitated to accept the risks entailed by Lee's plan to strike Pope, and Lee had not only labored to persuade him but may have fudged his account of troop strengths to reassure the president about the strength of Richmond's defenses. Even so, these were disagreements about the size, timing, and feasibility of operations, not about the strategic problem before them. Whatever doubts Davis had had, they had seemingly been resolved. He abandoned his earlier insistence that thirty thousand troops be left at Richmond and offered to send Lee twice the number of troops he had requested. They would not arrive in time for the fight against Pope, but knowing they were on the way gave Lee a wider margin of risk when considering battle.[5]

Lee prepared for action by completing the reorganization of the army's command system that he had begun just after the Seven Days. Several ineffective division commanders had been replaced. The old organization, in which fifteen or so division commanders reported to army headquarters, had been replaced by a structure in which two wing commanders were responsible for the divisions grouped under them. In Jackson and Longstreet, Lee had a complementary pair of battle-tested subordinates—Jackson superb at independent action, Longstreet an aggressive and competent combat commander.

Longstreet, born in South Carolina and raised in Georgia, the son of a plantation owner, graduated near the bottom of the West Point Class of 1842 and won promotions for gallantry as an infantry commander in the Mexican War. He was not an ardent secessionist but resigned his commission as major in the Regular Army when Georgia left the Union. His reputation in the army led Jefferson Davis to commission him as one of the Confederacy's first cadre of brigadier generals, which gave him the advantage of seniority in the Southern military system for the rest of the war. During the Seven Days he had been in effective command of half the army; and though Lee was dissatisfied with the coordination of his attacks at Glendale, he valued Longstreet's aggressiveness. Lee judged correctly that with more experience and a better-organized army behind him, Longstreet would prove a capable corps commander. His nickname was "Old Pete," and Lee called him "My Old War Horse"—names suggesting the solidity and reliability that were his best characteristics.

Thomas J. "Stonewall" Jackson was a unique character and an eccentric military genius. His uniforms were worn and rumpled, his shaggy black beard often unkempt, and he often sucked fresh lemons as he rode. His most striking feature were pale blue eyes that had earned him the nickname "Old Blue Light." Their glare expressed his fierce combativeness and a commitment to his cause that could be merciless to friend as well as foe. Jackson was a ferocious disciplinarian who did not hesitate to rebuke general officers and arrest them even for minor infractions.

In 1862 he was thirty-eight years old, the orphaned son of a farmer from western Virginia, raised by relatives who owned a mill in the hill country. He won admission to West Point in 1842 and graduated in 1846, in the same class as George McClellan. In Mexico his gallantry earned him more promotions than any officer in the army. In 1851 he took leave from the army to accept a professorship at Virginia Military Institute in the Shenandoah Valley, and he made his home there for the rest of his life. Jackson was an extremely pious and devoted Christian, a member of the Presbyterian Church, and Christianity shaped his complex relation to slavery. He had no ties to the plantation South and was not among those who advocated slavery as a positive good for both races. However, his reading of Scripture convinced him that slavery had divine sanction, and he therefore accepted it. As a Christian he also felt he had a duty to enlighten and educate the slaves in his charge. Jackson violated the legal and ethical codes of the slave states by teaching Negroes to read and write—first as a young schoolteacher in the hills, and later as the owner of six slaves acquired through his first marriage.

In 1861 Jackson left his professorship and his Regular commission to serve Virginia after his state's secession. As a longtime inhabitant of the Shenandoah Valley he was chosen to command Confederate troops in that region, and his familiarity with the people and the terrain of the Valley and the western mountains would enable him to conceive and conduct his brilliant Valley campaign from March through May of 1862. With an army of fifteen thousand troops he had marched up and down the Valley, forcing Lincoln to withhold reinforcements from McClellan on the Peninsula, defeating in detail three different Federal armies that piled into the Valley from different directions in an effort to corner him. The campaign earned Jackson international fame, but he followed with a fumbling performance in the Seven Days—perhaps because he was physically and mentally exhausted by his efforts in the Valley. As with Longstreet, Lee appreciated Jackson's potential, and he would favor Jackson for any mission requiring action independent of Lee's own command.

Lee consolidated his cavalry in a single division of three brigades under a superb leader, Jeb Stuart. His West Point nickname of "Beauty" was a sarcasm that referred to Stuart's homeliness, which in 1862 was concealed behind a luxuriant full beard. He had graduated in 1854 and seen some active service on the Indian frontier, but his most notable pre-war exploit was serving in the force commanded by Robert E. Lee that captured John Brown during his raid on Harpers Ferry in 1859. Stuart had led a cavalry brigade on the Peninsula and performed a notable and gallant exploit in riding all around McClellan's army, brushing aside the scattered cavalry units sent against him. He was a skilled organizer of cavalry, an arm that requires more extensive training than infantry and is more difficult to manage and maintain. Cavalry have to act with dash and vigor, and Stuart modeled the kind of élan required with his cavalier dress of plumed hat and scarlet-lined cloak. The primary duties of his cavalry were scouting and screening, and at these tasks Stuart excelled. He knew how to get information and how to make intelligent use of it. In the coming campaigns he would generally give Lee better information about enemy movements than any Union general could procure, and his aggressive patrols would keep Yankee cavalry in check and screen the army's movements.

The week spent sparring with Pope gave this new organization a useful shakedown. Lee's army was far more mobile, as Jackson's infantry would show by marching 120 miles in two days. The Federals could not yet match the quality of Stuart's cavalry, which was also more familiar with the terrain. By using those advantages Lee expected to set the terms of any engagement, attacking Pope under conditions that would minimize the federal advantage in numbers and artillery. Jackson's end run and surprise descent on Manassas should shock Pope, and induce him to retreat in some haste. If Lee and Longstreet could swiftly reunite their forces, they would be in position to attack an army strung out along its line of retreat.

The plan of campaign was brilliant and daring. The secret of its success was not the perfect execution of a brilliant plan but rather the flexibility with which Lee and his generals responded to the unanticipated consequences of their maneuvers. Although Lee was not able to attack Pope's retreating army as he had planned, his maneuvers would succeed in creating a confusion so complete that the bewildered Pope made a catastrophic botch of the ultimate battle.[6]

LEE'S OFFENSIVE, AUGUST 25-29, 1862

Pope's scouts actually spotted Jackson's march around their flank on August 26, but Pope and his officers were unable to make use of the information. At first they ignored the report because it came from Major General Franz Sigel's infantry wing. Sigel had been a professional soldier in the German state of Baden. He had participated in the liberal revolution of 1848 and fled to the United States after its suppression. As a veteran soldier and a leader of the German American community he had won a general's commission early in the war. He had seen extensive action in Missouri, sometimes successful and sometimes not, but overall he had earned a reputation for being skittish in the face of the enemy. Halleck, who had commanded him out west, remarked that Sigel "will do nothing but run: never did anything else." True to form, Sigel let Jackson pass unmolested, then retreated without orders, which opened the path for Lee and Longstreet to follow in Jackson's wake without being discovered. Pope did not learn where Jackson was until his corps materialized out of Thoroughfare Gap, swooped down on Pope's undefended base at Manassas Junction on August 27, and cut his communication with Washington.

Jackson's Confederates looted the supply dumps for food, shoes, uniforms, and ammunition, then burned what they could not carry off and destroyed the railroad yards and the trains. Jackson then moved his wing to a strong defensive position on a wooded ridge seven miles northwest of Manassas. His divisions used several different routes to reach the position, a maneuver designed to keep Pope guessing as to where they were going and what they intended to do.

Pope responded more quickly than Lee expected. He marched his army north—not in retreat, but as an offensive maneuver to trap and destroy Jackson's force. He was not in time to prevent Jackson's capture of Manassas, but now Pope's army was between Jackson's force and Lee's. Pope believed he could turn disaster into victory by hitting Jackson's twenty-five thousand with overwhelming force while it was still isolated. If he had managed the movement properly he might well have succeeded. However, his scouts completely lost track of Jackson's command—it was as if twenty-five thousand men, with horses, wagons, and artillery in due proportion, had simply vanished. Pope marched his troops hither and yon in the stifling August heat for more than twenty-four hours, searching in vain for Jackson. He might never have found him had Jackson not wanted to be found and have Pope concentrate against him. At that point Jackson wanted to hold Pope in place till Lee and Longstreet could come up to damage or destroy him in battle, although his situation was precarious. Longstreet's troops were just breaking through the cavalry outposts that held the Bull Run Mountain gaps, fifteen miles away, while Pope had nearly all of his army in or around Manassas Junction, from which it could move against Jackson. With the force in hand Pope outnumbered Jackson two to one. A successful attack on Jackson on August 29 was not out of the question, if properly and promptly organized.

Thus Lee's maneuver had failed to achieve its prime objective, which was to catch Pope on the retreat and beat him in detail. But Pope, having avoided the planned disaster, gave Lee the chance to improvise a different one by committing a cascading series of almost unfathomable errors. Some were tactical, while most were products of the deeply flawed organization and command system in the Army of Virginia. In his concentration on the blundering effort to find and destroy Jackson's wing, Pope lost sight of Lee and Longstreet. Because Pope had dispersed his cavalry, he had no force capable of penetrating the Confederate cavalry screen, and no way of learning how swiftly Lee and Longstreet were approaching the battlefield. What little information did get through was misconstrued by Pope's inexperienced staff.

Nor was there effective coordination between army headquarters and the staffs of the different corps under Pope's command. The three corps originally assigned to him had never worked together, and what little combat experience they had was misfortunate—they had been harassed, frustrated, and beaten by Jackson back in May and June during the Valley campaign. Of the three corps commanders, Sigel was, as noted, battle-shy; Major General Nathaniel Banks owed his rank to political influence rather than competence; and McDowell was disliked and distrusted by his own troops. To this ill-assorted mix had been added part of Burnside's IX Corps and the corps of Heintzelman and Porter from the Army of the Potomac—officers and men aggrieved by their separation from McClellan, and generals who had been taught to think of Pope as an enemy.

Pope's defects of personality made the situation worse. Although Confederate maneuvers had obviously bewildered him, he refused to compromise his pose of aggressive self-assurance. He issued confused and contradictory orders in a bullying tone. Beneath the guff he was uncertain whether he faced disaster or golden opportunity. He was anxious for Halleck to send reinforcements forward as soon as possible. Yet he also felt it necessary to appear confident of victory, lest his reputation in Washington be diminished. This added to Halleck's confusion about the real state of affairs at the front and complicated his efforts to bring McClellan's newly arriving troops into play.

Pope assumed that Jackson was still as isolated and exposed to entrapment on August 29 as he had been on August 27–28. He had failed to discover, let alone block, Lee's and Longstreet's movement to Thoroughfare Gap. So on August 29, while Longstreet moved unnoticed toward Pope's left flank, Pope sent his infantry against Jackson in frontal assaults. The Confederate position was probably too strong to be taken that way even if the assaults had been well coordinated—which they were not. The valor of the Federal infantry strained but could not break the Confederate line.

By evening the tactical situation was transformed. Longstreet's wing of twenty-five or thirty thousand men was in position, a huge threat hovering over Pope's left flank. While Lee's initial impulse was to attack, Longstreet advised against it, and Lee assented. His experience during the Seven Days showed that under prevailing conditions infantry assaults were likely to suffer heavy casualties. It would be less costly, and far more effective, to let Pope persist in his frontal assaults, then strike when the Federals were repulsed and falling back.

Porter tried to tell Pope of the danger to his left, but Pope mistrusted him as the partisan of his rival McClellan, and believed on no evidence that Longstreet must still be a day's march away. Pope therefore prepared for another day of frontal assaults on Jackson. He also wired Halleck in Washington, claiming that he had won a great victory—but asking that reinforcements be sent immediately.

HALLECK VS. McCLELLAN VS. STANTON
WASHINGTON, AUGUST 25-29, 1862

The crisis exposed Halleck's weaknesses as a commanding general. It was already clear, to Halleck himself and to the administration that employed him, that he was not a good field general. His strength was supposed to lie in the ability to manage and coordinate the operations of several independent field armies across a wide geographical theater. But the multiple threats posed by the Confederate offensives of Bragg, Van Dorn, and Lee, and the severity of the crisis in Virginia, overtaxed his abilities and shook his confidence. He became increasingly reluctant to take responsibility for critical decisions, and desperately anxious for McClellan to leave the Peninsula and assume personal command of the forces in and around Washington. Yet he balked at giving McClellan actual command of operations in the theater, for reasons that were personal and political as well as military. He was well aware of Stanton's hatred of McClellan and had no stomach for crossing Stanton. Nor was it in his interest to do so, since McClellan was his chief rival for control of military affairs.

McClellan understood the crisis in terms very different from those that troubled Halleck. Lee's threat to Pope presented McClellan with a perfect chance to regain command of the Virginia theater and win the Washington half of his two-front war. He had spent the first three weeks of August raging impotently against Halleck, Stanton, and Lincoln, fantasizing about a political "coup" that would restore him to power and allow him to wreak God's own vengeance on those he considered "the enemies of the country & of the human race." Now, with his "considerable military family" at hand and Halleck shaking in his boots, he was in position to do just that. To his wife he gloated, "They"—meaning Pope, Halleck and the administration—"will suffer a terrible defeat" if they go on as at present, but "I *know* that with God's help I can save them." However, he would only save them if they restored him to command of the forces now in the field. If they insisted on treating him as a subordinate he would cavil at his orders, ask them to consider and reconsider all possible objections, and obey only when all resources of correspondence were exhausted.[7]

McClellan had arrived at Aquia Creek on August 23 and immediately asked Halleck to clarify his command status. He wanted to know whether Halleck would keep his promise to put McClellan in command of all field forces once his army was joined with Pope's. Halleck avoided giving a definitive answer. Instead, on August 26 he asked McClellan to go to Alexandria to expedite the forward movement of Franklin's VI Corps. That corps had landed on August 25, and Halleck had ordered Franklin to prepare for an immediate march to Manassas to join Pope. But when McClellan got to Alexandria he countermanded those orders without explanation. He would subsequently justify his decision on two grounds: that Franklin lacked sufficient draft animals and wagons to move his artillery and supplies; and that the lack of cavalry to scout the road to Manassas made it too dangerous for Franklin to advance without the support of the II Corps, which had not yet disembarked. The next day, August 27, Jackson's Corps struck Manassas and cut Pope off from Washington. There is no knowing whether an advance by VI Corps on the twenty-sixth would have checked Jackson, but it would certainly have complicated his mission. At the very least it would have given Halleck's headquarters timely notice of the strength and position of Jackson's force.[8]

Jackson's occupation of Manassas had broken communication with Pope's army for two days, and Halleck—who believed the chronic overestimate of Confederate strength—was afraid the Army of Virginia might now be surrounded by a superior force. On August 27 Halleck urgently ordered McClellan to send Franklin forward, if possible to reopen communication with Pope, but at least to define the tactical situation by a reconnaissance-in-force. McClellan ordered Franklin to prepare to march at once—which was not the same thing as having him march at once. While Franklin marched in place, McClellan harassed Halleck with telegrams warning against a premature advance. He proposed waiting until Sumner's II Corps could add its strength to Franklin's, which would delay any movement for two or three days. When a telegram from Pope finally got through asking for reinforcements, McClellan took another step backwards. "The great object," he told Halleck, was not to aid Pope but "to collect the whole Army in Washington ready to defend the works." Franklin and Sumner should be held back for the defense of Washington. He also quarreled with Halleck about who was to blame for the success of Jackson's raid.[9]

This barrage of argument and advice, implying a dire threat against Washington, weakened Halleck's resistance to McClellan's demand for "authority." It did not help that Pope's communications alternated confident bluster with appeals for aid. Halleck had no wish to make decisions in such a crisis. On the evening of August 27, Halleck rather lamely conceded: "As you must be aware, more than three-quarters of my time is taken up with the raising of new troops and matters in the West. I have no time for details." He therefore left it to McClellan as "ranking general in the field [to do] as you deem best."[10] This was still not the formal investment as field commander McClellan had sought, so the contest continued. On August 28 McClellan promised to send Franklin forward as soon as "a reasonable amount of artillery is at hand." But he shortly reversed himself, advising Halleck that "[n]either Franklin's nor Sumner's Corps are now in condition to move & fight a battle—it would be a sacrifice to send them out now."[11] Rather, he wanted Halleck to order Pope to abandon the field and retreat to the safety of the Washington defenses, where he would come under McClellan's command. At 3:30 PM Halleck countered: "Not a moment must be lost in pushing as large a force as possible towards Manassas."[12] McClellan explained that this was impossible. Halleck now showed annoyance: "There must be no further delay in moving Franklin's corps." McClellan promised that Franklin would march at 6:00 AM the next day but also warned Halleck that Lee and 120,000 men "intend advancing on the forts near Arlington and Chain Bridge, with a view of attacking Washington and Baltimore." He proposed blowing up Chain Bridge to prevent its seizure by the Rebels. The threat was absurdly chimerical, but if it had been true, it would have required Halleck to bring Pope's army back to Washington as quickly as possible, where it would come under McClellan's command.[13]

Halleck dismissed the supposed threat to Chain Bridge and again insisted that Franklin be sent forward. So on August 29 McClellan finally ordered Franklin to march and (with an eye to the paper record) made a show of ardor: "Let it not be said that any part of the Army of the Potomac failed in its duty to General Pope." Franklin was an engineer by training, with the engineer's occupational preference for slow, cautious movement—a tendency so marked that even McClellan complained about it. Franklin moved his corps only as far as Annandale, seven miles from his starting point, where he stopped, again on McClellan's order. Another exchange with Halleck ensued. The VI Corps lacked artillery and ammunition. Did Halleck *really* "wish the movement of Franklin's corps to continue?" Halleck did! He wanted him at least to go far enough to find the enemy. But McClellan found even these simple and direct instructions questionable. At 1:00 PM he asked Halleck whether or not the order naming him "ranking general" had empowered him to "do as seems best to me with all the troops in this vicinity, including Franklin who I really think ought not under present circumstances to advance beyond Annandale." Again he was pushing Halleck to decide whether to let McClellan take charge or to assume for himself the burden of mastering the crisis. The result was an impasse: McClellan would not let Franklin move to Pope's aid, and Halleck would not commit himself to putting McClellan in field command.[14]

President Lincoln and the leading members of his cabinet were privy to many, if not all, of these exchanges, and found them alarming. Lincoln was disturbed by McClellan's self-serving prophecies of doom, which made him the "chief alarmist and grand marplot of the Army," and by his constant harping on "what is his real position and command," which suggested that personal advancement was of greater concern to him than the fate of Pope's army. He was also dismayed by McClellan's response to his August 29 inquiry on the state of affairs. McClellan had said that only two choices remained: "[t]o concentrate all our forces" to relieve Pope or "[t]o leave Pope to get out of his scrape & at once use all our means to make the Capital perfectly safe. No middle course will now answer." He had promised to obey whatever orders Lincoln might give, but "I wish to know what my orders & authority are—I ask for nothing, but will obey whatever orders you give." To Lincoln it was perfectly clear that McClellan was angling for command of the field army, and he was appalled by the seeming callousness of the proposal to "leave Pope to get out of his scrape." Stanton's response was more overtly hostile. While the battle was still in progress, he leaked to the press his intention to hold McClellan responsible if Pope were defeated.[15]

By the evening of August 29, the balance in this internecine struggle had shifted against McClellan—which led Halleck to reassert himself. On the twenty-eighth Stanton had sent Halleck a memorandum pointedly inquiring whether McClellan had moved with proper celerity in obeying the order to withdraw from the Peninsula and forward troops to Pope. Halleck's response to Stanton (August 29) gave the secretary all the ammunition he could want for relieving McClellan. From the time he was first ordered to withdraw from the Peninsula down to the time of that evening's last dispatch, McClellan had "not obeyed [his orders] with the promptness I expected and the national safety, in my opinion, required." The brief was supported with summaries of the telegraphic exchanges between the two generals. With Stanton behind him, Halleck's orders to McClellan now took a more peremptory tone. After learning that McClellan had once again ordered Franklin to halt his march at Annandale he fired off an angry dispatch: "This is all contrary to my orders; investigate and report the facts of this disobedience. That corps must push forward, as I directed . . . and open our communication with Manassas." This time McClellan obeyed.[16]

It was too bad that Halleck had not got the courage of his convictions two days sooner. On August 28 and 29, while Halleck and McClellan and Franklin were dithering, VI Corps infantry could actually hear gunfire from Manassas, where Pope's infantry were fighting and dying in their vain effort to break Jackson's line. Franklin's corps would finally begin their advance on the thirtieth, but their leading elements had not yet reached the Bull Run bridge when they met the first fugitives from Pope's disaster.

SECOND BULL RUN, AUGUST 30–SEPTEMBER 1

The immediate military effect of the Washington imbroglio was to prevent the reinforcement of Pope by the VI Corps. But lack of these troops should not have been critical. For despite everything, by the night of August 29–30 Pope had succeeded in concentrating most of his army in front of Jackson. His supply train, guarded by Banks's corps, was safe, and he had reopened rail communications with Alexandria and Washington. He had on hand sixty-two thousand troops against Lee's army, whose nominal strength of fifty-five thousand was probably lessened by the straggling that attended their long, hard flank march. Pope's artillery outgunned his opponents in number of pieces and firepower. The head of a reinforcing column of troops from McClellan's army was at Fairfax Courthouse, only twenty miles from Manassas. If Pope had organized the troops on hand properly for defense they could certainly have held their ground or made good an orderly retreat to Centreville, where ample supplies and reinforcement awaited.

However, Pope was still convinced that he had Jackson cornered, and that Lee and Longstreet were a long day's march away. He ordered another round of frontal assaults on Jackson, and to give them weight he ordered Porter's V Corps to leave its position defending the army's southern flank and join the attack. This left Longstreet free to strike at will.

The fact that Longstreet was on the scene, positioned to crush Pope's flank, is one measure of the difference between McClellan's approach to impending battle and Robert E. Lee's. McClellan refused to risk his VI Corps by sending it to Pope's assistance. Between his caution and Franklin's own deliberate movements it took three days for the VI Corps to move twenty-five miles—and even then it failed to reach the battlefield. In contrast, Lee had boldly risked Jackson's wing in order to achieve his tactical objectives. Jackson had demanded, and his troops had executed, forced marches covering eighty miles over a two-day period. Longstreet's wing had followed at a similar pace; and on August 28, fearing that Jackson's wing might be in trouble, it covered the last twenty miles in half a day. Thanks to Pope's ignorance of their presence, they were able to rest and recover on the twenty-ninth before being called upon to attack on the thirtieth.

Lee wanted Longstreet to strike quickly, but the latter advised waiting until the Federals were thoroughly entangled with Jackson. When he judged that V Corps was fully engaged he ordered his artillery to rake Porter's lines. When the V Corps wavered Longstreet's infantry advanced, some divisions rolling up Porter's line, others sweeping out to the right to get behind the Federal army and cut off its retreat. Jackson's wing, which had been hard-pressed, counterattacked as the Federal assault troops pulled back. Hit from the front and flank, Pope's army lost all cohesion, and large masses of disorganized troops went streaming to the rear. Yet the army was not entirely routed. Stubborn stands and counterattacks by well-led regiments and brigades checked the Confederate assault columns. A rear-guard stand at dusk on the Henry House Hill allowed almost the entire army to escape to the far side of Bull Run. Still, the Federals suffered heavy losses, some sixteen thousand out of an engaged force of sixty-two thousand. Perhaps a third of these were captured—although there were no mass surrenders of brigades or divisions, which would have indicated general demoralization.

THUS BY A MIXTURE of good planning, hard marching, brilliant opportunism and Federal incompetence, Lee had achieved several of his primary objectives. He had shifted the zone of warfare from Richmond to Washington and driven Federal forces out of northern Virginia. He had also created an opportunity for the kind of victory that might substantially damage the North's ability to wage war. Pope's army was beaten, disorganized, and in retreat. Now if he could pursue and strike it in force while it was in that condition he might effectively destroy a Federal field army, with incalculable effects on the course of the war.

Nevertheless, it would be difficult to mount such a pursuit. Lee's own losses were not inconsiderable—nine thousand out of fifty thousand engaged. Pope's army was regrouping around Centreville on the far side of Bull Run, and was finally being reinforced by elements of McClellan's VI and II Corps. For Lee to make a frontal attack across Bull Run would be costly, even if successful. Pope also had a short line of retreat to Alexandria and the safety of the Washington forts. If Lee wanted to strike again, he had to act quickly.

Lee therefore decided to repeat, on a smaller scale, the turning movement that had produced the victory at Second Bull Run. This one was aimed at cutting Pope's line of retreat, which ran east on the Warrenton Turnpike through Fairfax Courthouse to Alexandria. Once again Stuart's cavalry and Jackson's wing would lead, crossing Bull Run upstream and marching north to reach the Little River Turnpike, a road that ran back south through the village of Chantilly to Fairfax Court House, a forced march of more than twenty miles. Longstreet's wing would demonstrate to distract Pope's attention, then follow in Jackson's footsteps.

The maneuver failed to produce the desired result. Lee ordered Jackson to march on August 31, while the wounded were still being brought in from the previous day's fighting. Though the distance to be covered was far less than that achieved by Jackson's "foot cavalry" on August 25-26, his men were now worn down by long marches capped by three days of intense combat. Aside from their physical weariness, many had literally been marched out of their shoes. Rain slowed the march by softening the roads to mud. Stuart's cavalry also threw away whatever chance Jackson had to surprise the enemy by raiding into the Union rear on the night of August 31. Meanwhile, Pope's troops had rallied in some old entrenchments around Centreville, and had been joined by fresh troops from the II, VI, and IX Corps.

Forewarned of Jackson's approach, Pope pulled two divisions out of line and sent them to Chantilly, where they collided with Jackson's advance in a raging thunderstorm on the night of September 1. Though the Union troops were not under unified command, they were led by aggressive and competent generals, Isaac Stevens and Philip Kearny, the one-armed general who had criticized both McClellan's dilatory tactics on the Peninsula and his political associations. Stevens and Kearny sent their battle lines forward through the downpour, the flash of infantry volleys and cannon fire echoed and exaggerated in the stormy sky. Stevens was killed at the head of his division, Kearny rode into Rebel lines in the darkness and was shot dead out of the saddle, but their counterattacks stopped Jackson, as Pope's troops withdrew to Fairfax.

On September 2 Lee tried yet again to turn the flank of the Federal army and force it to retreat under pressure. But Stuart's cavalry could find no vulnerability in Pope's position. Before Lee could attempt anything further, a demoralized Pope ordered his army to withdraw to the fortified lines of Alexandria and Washington—a move that was completed before the Confederates could interfere.

———

THE ESCAPE OF POPE'S ARMY confronted Lee with a strategic conundrum. The objectives for which he began his counteroffensive had been achieved. The seat of war had been shifted from the suburbs of the Confederacy's capital to its northern frontier. Most of northern Virginia had been liberated and its productive potential restored to the Confederacy. Southern victories had enhanced the Confederacy's chances for foreign recognition and roused the spirits of a populace that had been discouraged by the setbacks suffered in the winter and spring. Battlefield defeat had disorganized Federal armies and presumably depressed Northern morale. It would take some time for the Federal armies to reorganize for a resumption of the offensive. While it did, Lee could stand on the defensive, resupplying and recruiting his hard-used army.

Yet if Lee gave the Federals time to reorganize, the offensive would certainly be resumed, this time by the united armies of Pope and McClellan—with tens of thousands of new recruits added by Lincoln's last call for volunteers. That huge force might be ready to march in a month, and would have perhaps three months to campaign before winter closed things down. The only way to forestall that advance—and the only way to exploit the advantages gained at Second Bull Run—was to continue his own offensive. But his army lacked the numbers, artillery, and supplies to directly attack the Washington fortifications. If he wanted to press the offensive, he would have to attack indirectly, menacing some vital point in order to draw the Union army away from its invulnerable fortifications.

The day after his last fling at Pope he set in motion the invasion of Maryland.

One day earlier, George McClellan had been reappointed to the command of the field armies in northern Virginia.

CHAPTER 6

McCLELLAN'S VICTORY

AUGUST 30–SEPTEMBER 3, 1862

❦

AUGUST 30 WAS A DAY OF DISCOURAGEMENT AND HUMILIATION FOR General McClellan. Halleck had taken from him the last elements of the Army of the Potomac, the corps of Franklin and Sumner, sent forward to reinforce Pope. He was a general without an army, denied even the privilege of merely accompanying his men "to share their fate on the field of battle." The latest dispatches from Pope claimed success in the fighting on August 29 and anticipated a major victory on the thirtieth. It appeared that McClellan's aid would not be required to save the capital, and that Halleck and Stanton were prepared to relieve him.[1]

Behind the scenes, Stanton was at work on a coup that, if successful, would finish McClellan's career. Stanton had already told the president that "after all these battles, there should be one Court Martial, if never any more. He said that nothing but foul play could lose us this battle & that it rested with McClellan and his friends." His correspondence with Halleck had put the General-in-chief on record, declaring that McClellan had failed to obey his orders. Stanton then drafted a formal petition for the cabinet to sign, which called for "the immediate removal of George B. McClellan from the command of any army in the United States." Coming from men who were both his official councilors and leaders of the constituent factions of Lincoln's own party, such a declaration would have weight. Chase circulated it among the cabinet, urging all members to add their signatures. Chase had been suspected of flirting with a McClellan alliance in the past, but the general's recent behavior had turned him into a determined enemy.

The petition charged McClellan with incompetence, as evidenced by the failure of his campaigns and their heavy losses, "And also because by recent disobedience to superior orders and inactivity he has twice imperiled the army commanded by General Pope, and while he continues to command will daily hazard the fate of our armies and our national existence." The petition concluded with an implicit challenge to the president's judgment: "We are unwilling to be accessory to the waste of national resources, the protraction of the war, the destruction of our armies, and the imperiling of the Union which we believe must result from the continuance of George B McClellan in command." Stanton and Chase planned to surprise Lincoln by presenting their protest at the next cabinet meeting, on September 2.[2]

There was wide though not unanimous agreement in the cabinet that McClellan was excessively cautious in the field and had deliberately thwarted the reinforcement of Pope. Stanton and Chase, with Seward the most powerful men in the cabinet, believed he was guilty of actions and sentiments akin to treason. Attorney General Bates condemned "a criminal tardiness, a fatuous apathy, a captious, bickering rivalry, among our commanders who seem so taken up with their quick-made dignity, that they overlook the lives of their people & the necessities of their country." Seward would not join in promoting the petition out of loyalty to Lincoln, but he planned to absent himself from the September 1 cabinet meeting—which suggested his acceptance, if not approval, of the movement. Navy secretary Welles agreed with the criticism of McClellan but refused to sign because he thought the petition violated the cabinet's proper role, by seeking to "control" rather than to advise the president. Only Postmaster General Blair, the most conservative member of the cabinet, disagreed with the petitioners' judgment of McClellan. He was never approached for a signature and knew nothing of the plot.[3]

Stanton had launched his conspiracy on August 30, while Pope was still issuing confident bulletins promising victory. Twenty-four hours later the situation was transformed. The first definitive reports of Pope's disaster reached the capital on the night of the thirtieth, and once again the Union high command was thrown into confusion. It was uncertain whether Pope's army was still capable of self-defense, or if Washington itself was in danger. Halleck broke under the pressure, writing to McClellan: "I beg of you to assist me in this crisis with your ability and experience. I am utterly tired out."[4]

For McClellan the reversal of fortune was so stunning and swift as to seem providential. At 9:30 that morning he had written to his wife lamenting the humiliating and powerless position in which he found himself. He was planning to write to William Aspinwall, his New York political supporter, "so that my friends in New York may know" that he bore no responsibility for the catastrophe. A little more than twelve hours later he had Halleck's telegram begging for assistance. McClellan had said he would not deign to rescue the administration again unless they conceded "control." True to his word, he refused to help unless Halleck restored him to command: "I am ready to afford you every assistance in my power, but you will readily perceive how difficult an undefined position such as I now hold must be." He proposed a meeting for the morning of August 31, "alone, either at your house or the office." But Halleck would not take responsibility for reappointing the object of Stanton's hatred. He postponed the meeting till the next day (September 1), and asked Lincoln to attend and make the final decision.[5]

For Lincoln the question of McClellan's command was fraught with political as well as military problems. For months he had been at pains to deny, evade, or minimize the conflict between McClellan and Stanton, which threatened to split the bipartisan coalition that had so far sustained the war for the Union. Now he would have to side with either the secretary or the general, and make the choice in the midst of a crisis of apparent military collapse and divisive political recrimination. Rumors of the power struggle between McClellan and Stanton, and deliberate leaks by the participants and their partisans, created a poisonous atmosphere in a city made anxious by the approach of the Rebel army and the lack of news from Pope. Captain Charles Francis Adams, Jr., whose First Massachusetts cavalry regiment had been hastily shipped north from the Sea Islands, was appalled at the state of mind prevailing in the capital. Adams belonged to one of the first families of American politics, and at twenty-seven he already knew Washington's culture from the inside. His great-grandfather John Adams and grandfather John Quincy Adams had been presidents of the United States; his father was a leading Republican currently serving as Lincoln's ambassador to Great Britain. "Our rulers seem to me to be crazy," young Adams wrote his father. "The air of this city seems thick with treachery; our army seems in danger of utter demoralization. . . . Everything is ripe for a terrible panic, the end of which I cannot even imagine."[6]

The cabinet and especially Stanton had invested its hopes in John Pope, and preferred to blame McClellan for Pope's defeat. But Pope had utterly discredited himself with all but his most partisan supporters. He had not only lost his battle, the dispatches he had sent during the action were so far out of touch with reality as to suggest abysmal incompetence or deliberate falsification. ("As big a liar as John Pope" was already a cant phrase in the capital.) Pope had also exacerbated the political divisions within the officer corps by charging McClellan, and the Potomac generals assigned to Pope's army, with deliberate sabotage of his operations: "Everybody in this army considers [McClellan] responsible for the failure to send forward Sumner and Franklin and Cox or anybody else."[7] To give color to these charges he had arrested Generals Fitz-John Porter, William Franklin, and Charles Griffin. The *New York Tribune*, responding to leaks from Stanton's aides, blamed McClellan for the defeat at Manassas and accused the general and his acolytes of actions akin to treason.[8] A reporter for the popular *Spirit of the Times* decried the public's "infatuation" with McClellan, a "false prophet" whose support came from advocates of "Southern rights" and pro-slavery filibusters, "a military adept, and he cannot plan . . . a soldier and he cannot fight."[9] On the other side, McClellan's officers were filling Washington with dark rumors of Stanton's jealousy and malfeasance, and the opposition press was defending McClellan and urging his reappointment to command.[10]

The drift of public opinion favored McClellan. Even the staunchly Republican Adams was persuaded that McClellan, not the administration, was in the right. Adams was getting inside information from officers on McClellan's staff, who saw Lincoln's cabinet as the seat of "treason." Adams was too shrewd to take these claims at face value, but he was convinced that the war effort required a single controlling hand to reconcile the army and the War Department, and for that role he declared, "I still believe in McClellan."[11]

FROM LINCOLN'S PERSPECTIVE, the worst part of all this was that ("treason" aside) there was some truth in what each side was saying about the other. Lincoln knew that Pope was a failure, and that the army would not willingly fight another battle under his command. McClellan was the obvious choice to replace him: he was the senior officer by rank and experience, had the confidence of the Army of the Potomac, and was justly renowned for his skill in organizing and raising the morale of an army. But Lincoln shared the cabinet's belief that McClellan had "wanted [Pope] to fail," an "unpardonable" breach of faith, even if its motive was personal jealousy rather than political disloyalty. Halleck informed him that McClellan's officers serving under Pope had indeed been bad-mouthing their commander, thus undermining morale.[12]

Still, the prime necessity was to maintain the army's will and capacity for fighting the enemy, and at the moment that required the dismissal of Pope and McClellan's reappointment to command of the troops. The first necessity was to reorganize the army and prepare it for battle. McClellan had the skills to do that, and more importantly the officers and men who comprised the army were eager for him to be restored to command. As Lincoln told John Hay, "There is no man in the army who can man these fortifications and lick these troops into shape half as well as he. . . . If he can't fight himself, he excels in making others ready to fight."[13]

Lincoln was willing to give McClellan command of the forces now gathering in the Washington defenses and charge him with the task of reorganizing and preparing them to renew the fight. However, he was not yet ready to give McClellan command of the army in the field. Lincoln was not yet aware of Stanton's petition, but he expected that his cabinet, which would meet on September 2, would oppose even this limited empowerment of McClellan. To offset the suspicions of those who accused McClellan of sabotaging Pope, and perhaps to reassure himself of McClellan's loyalty, Lincoln asked the general to write directly to Fitz-John Porter and other former colleagues, asking them to be more supportive of Pope while the latter remained in command. McClellan did just that on the evening of September 1, asking "for my sake and that of the country & of the old Army of the Potomac that you and all my friends will lend the fullest & most cordial support to Genl Pope. . . . The destinies of our country and the honor of our arms are at stake, & all depends now upon the cheerful cooperation of all in the field." While the letter may have satisfied Lincoln's demand, it put Porter and his colleagues in an uncomfortable position by implying that hitherto their support had been less than complete. Since Porter was facing court-martial for having disobeyed Pope's orders, that implication was damaging. His response was to tell McClellan, "You may rest assured that all your friends, as well as every other lover of his country, will ever give, as they have given, to General Pope their cordial cooperation. . . . Our killed, wounded, and enfeebled troops attest our devoted duty."[14]

The cabinet meeting was even more difficult than Lincoln expected. Navy Secretary Welles believed that the majority of his colleagues came to the meeting with "a fixed determination to remove, and if possible to disgrace, McClellan. Chase frankly stated he desired it, that he deliberately believed McClellan ought to be shot." Lincoln's announcement that McClellan had been put in command of the Washington defenses was countered by Stanton's petition, whose recommendations were supported by all those present except Blair. Lincoln said he was "distressed . . . exceedingly to find himself differing on such a point from the Secretary of War and the Secretary of the Treasury." Still, he defended his decision: McClellan might be "deficient" in the qualities that make a good field general, but "there is no better organizer" of troops, and "he had beyond any officer the confidence of the army." Moreover, his new command was limited to the defense of Washington. The choice of a new field commander had not yet been made, and Lincoln was willing to consider other candidates for that position.[15]

The cabinet was unable to recommend a viable alternative. Chase suggested Generals Hooker, Sumner, and Burnside. Hooker had not commanded anything larger than a division, and Sumner had already been promoted beyond his level of competence. Burnside had been offered the command and had turned it down out of loyalty to McClellan. No one there thought Halleck could do the job, but Lincoln was willing to give him a try. On September 3, the day after McClellan assumed command of all forces in and around Washington, the president asked Stanton to prepare an order for Halleck to organize a field army "for active operations." Halleck simply passed the buck to McClellan.

On September 5 came word that Lee's army had crossed the Potomac and was invading Maryland. The choice of a field commander could no longer be delayed. Lincoln made one last attempt to get Burnside to accept the active command, while McClellan remained in Washington. When Burnside again refused, there was no option but to hand the field command to McClellan.[16]

A QUESTION OF CHARACTER

Lincoln appreciated the fact that McClellan had been "working like a beaver" to reorganize the army, but he still had doubts about McClellan's generalship. His extreme reluctance to engage and his exaggerated response to enemy threats that had often proved illusory suggested that he lacked the nerve to fight a battle when it was necessary to do so. Lincoln also had doubts about McClellan's character. His behavior during the Second Battle of Bull Run led Lincoln to question whether McClellan's first loyalty was to the Union cause or to his own and/or his party's interest.

The controversy over McClellan's motives and actions was intense among his contemporaries, and historians have continued the debate. In a strictly military view, McClellan's objections to Franklin's move were unreasonable and inadequate, and his refusal to obey orders inexcusable. Even if McClellan's presumptions had been true—that Jackson was blocking the road with a numerically superior force—an advance toward Manassas by VI Corps was a sound and even necessary tactical move, which might have relieved Pope by threatening to take Jackson in the rear. McClellan's fear of a Confederate attack on Washington via the Chain Bridge was preposterous.

However, responsibility for the disaster at Manassas was not McClellan's alone. Halleck failed to exercise his authority as army commander. If his orders to McClellan had been as firm on August 27–28 as they were on the evening of the twenty-ninth, Franklin's Corps might have intervened sooner. Pope's handling of the battle was utterly incompetent. Even without VI Corps, Pope had more men on the field than Lee. His army was certainly large enough to hold its ground, and if he had stood on the defensive Lee might well have hesitated to attack. If Pope's own assaults had not been so utterly misconceived and mismanaged, his army would not have been driven from the field after their repulse.

There is no question that McClellan's response to Pope's crisis and Halleck's orders was obstructive rather than cooperative. The real questions concern his motives. His critics believe he deliberately delayed the sending of reinforcements to Pope's army, hoping his rival's defeat would lead to his own restoration to command. His worst critics at the time saw him as a crypto-Confederate and accused him of treason. Navy Secretary Gideon Welles had a more balanced view of McClellan than Chase or Stanton, but even he was troubled. Welles did not for a moment "entertain the thought that he is unfaithful," let alone Chase's view that he was "imbecile, a coward, a traitor." He thought McClellan's reluctance to fight was partly a matter of personality, but also worried it might reflect a deeper problem: "I sometimes fear his heart is not earnest in the cause." He believed McClellan had allowed his antipathy for Pope to override his duty to support him. His insistence on seeing a moral equivalence between secessionism and abolitionism had blinded him to the true political character of the war. Welles had been appalled by McClellan's assertion that "[h]e detested . . . both South Carolina and Massachusetts, and should rejoice to see both States extinguished"—this at a time when Massachusetts men were fighting and dying in McClellan's own army.[17]

Welles was right in seeing McClellan's motives as a combination of personality and politics. The general was incapable of seeing the war, or any of its events, from any perspective but his own. The Union could only be properly saved if McClellan saved it. For that reason he had abandoned his own army on the battlefield of Glendale, leaving his men to get out of their scrape as best they could. His care during the crisis of Second Bull Run was for himself, and for the force immediately under his command, and what happened to Pope and his army was of secondary importance.[18]

McCLELLAN'S EGOCENTRICITY WAS not merely a personal pathology but the functional equivalent of a strategic theory. His approach to every strategic or tactical problem began with the assumption that the fate of the republic depended on his achieving and maintaining personal supremacy in the making of policy. His willingness to run the risks inherent in battle was constrained by his need to defend his political position against attack by Stanton and the Radicals in his rear. So long as Stanton remained in power he had little to gain by risking a decisive engagement with Lee's army: a defeat would ruin him, a victory would only strengthen the Stanton-Lincoln regime.

On the other hand, Lee's victory at Second Bull Run was effectively a victory for McClellan in his struggle against Stanton, and his first impulse was to exploit that victory. He consulted with his staff and other supporters about the feasibility of issuing an ultimatum to Lincoln: McClellan would refuse to save Maryland from invasion unless Lincoln agreed to purge Stanton from the cabinet. Burnside, fresh from having refused Lincoln's proffer of the command, spent till three in the morning talking him out of it, explaining how wrong it would be to create a political crisis while Lee was in Maryland. McClellan finally agreed to withhold his ultimatum, but as the campaign went forward his officers and political supporters would intensify their campaign to give McClellan greater control over civil and military policy.[19]

THROUGH THE CONFUSION and alarm of the previous week, Lincoln had maintained his focus on the strategic essentials. His secretary John Hay declared, "It is due in great measure to his indomitable will, that army movements have been characterized by such energy and celerity for the last few days." The Confederate army must be fought if it was to be damaged or destroyed, and if Lee was on the offensive, so much the better—battle was inevitable. All that was wanted was a general who would commit to the attempt all the forces Lincoln could give him. Since McClellan was all Lincoln had, he would bow to necessity and get what use he could out of the man. As he told John Hay, "we must use what tools we have." Perhaps McClellan might be "aroused to doing something, by the sort of snubbing he got last week."[20]

During the time when he was considering whether or not to restore McClellan to command, Lincoln penned a meditation on the divine will. He shared with nearly all his countrymen, including General McClellan, a conviction that the course of human events was shaped by divine intelligence and intention. But as Lincoln understood things, the God of history was no respecter of either persons or nations, and His methods were dark and seldom pleasant.

> In great contests each party claims to act in accordance with the will of God. Both *may* be, and one *must* be wrong. . . . I am almost ready to say that this is probably true—that God wills this contest, and wills that it shall not end yet. By His mere quiet power, on the minds of the now contestants, He could have either *saved* or *destroyed* the Union without a human contest. Yet the contest began. And having begun He could give the final victory to either side any day. Yet the contest proceeds.

The appropriate response to such a God was a kind of heroic humility, which acknowledged the limits of human power and the necessity of using whatever power one had to define a just objective and work to achieve it. God's purpose might well be "something different from the purpose of either party—and yet human instrumentalities, working just as they do, are of the best adaptation to effect his purposes." It was in that spirit that he resigned himself to using McClellan as the instrument of his policy, despite the latter's weaknesses as a field general, despite his "unpardonable" sabotaging of Pope, despite the danger that his army might be more loyal to their general than to the republic.[21]

McClellan's view of divine providence was simpler and more self-serving. Though he used the formulas of Christian humility, he read the disaster to his nation's government and its army as divine vindication of his own actions and his beliefs, confirmation of his standing as the agent of divine providence for the salvation of the republic. The defeat of the army led by Pope and McDowell was "a signal act of retributive justice"—God's work, not the result of his own action or inaction: "I have done nothing towards this." God has been "trying me in the fire," but now that he was in command, "I believe that God will give us the victory." "Again I have been called upon to save the country—the case is desperate, but with God's help I will try unselfishly to do my best & if he wills it accomplish the salvation of the nation. . . . I know that the interests at stake are so great as to justify his interference—not for me, but for the innocent thousands, millions rather, who have been plunged in misery by no fault of theirs."[22]

Within the week McClellan would enjoy a piece of luck so outrageous and unearned that he might be pardoned for thinking himself favored by providence.

PART THREE

THE INVASION of MARYLAND

September 2-15, 1862

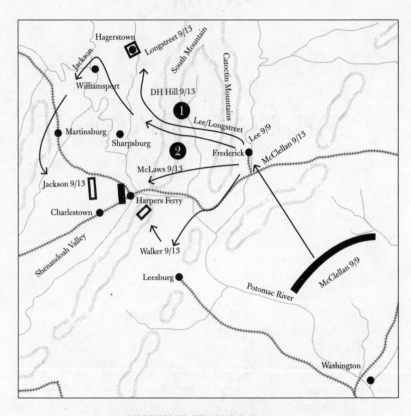

MAP 2: LEE DIVIDES HIS ARMY, SEPT. 9–13

1. Battle of South Mountain (Turner's Gap), Sept. 14
2. Battle of Crampton's Gap, Sept. 14

CHAPTER 7

LEE DECIDES ON INVASION

SEPTEMBER 2–9, 1862

❧

I N THE HISTORY BOOKS THE SECOND BATTLE OF BULL RUN USUALLY figures as the culmination of an offensive that carried the seat of war from Richmond to northern Virginia. For Lee himself the successful campaign against Pope was merely a phase in a larger strategic offensive. The last elements of Pope's rear guard withdrew to the Washington defenses on September 2, and the decision to invade Maryland was made that evening, with the initial movements ordered on September 3. The Army of Northern Virginia made a leisurely march northward to Leesburg, Virginia, where Lee would reorganize his forces for the invasion of Maryland. Thus Lee "opened the chapter on his next campaign less than six hours after closing the old one."[1] He did so while suffering the painful effects of injuries to his arms, suffered when his horse spooked and threw him to the ground. Both arms were in splints, so he could not use the reins to control his horse, and would have to travel in an ambulance for nearly two weeks.

The defeat of Pope's army left the initiative in his hands, but his options for exploiting the opportunity were limited. He could stand on the defensive, allowing his army to recover its strength and supplies and gathering reinforcements. However, if he did so he would have to pull his army back to the Rappahannock River, because the region just south of the Potomac had been stripped of food and fodder by the two armies and was exposed to forays by the superior Union forces accumulating in the DC area. Such a retreat would sacrifice much of the territory won by his campaign, and diminish the political impact of his victory at home, in the North, and abroad. In a few weeks the Union armies would have recovered their morale, repaired their organization, and replenished their ranks, and would be ready to begin another offensive with superiority in men, guns, and resources. To forestall such an offensive, he had to keep the Federals on the defensive, maintaining the initiative by offensive operations of his own. He lacked the troop strength and heavy artillery to attack Washington directly, and his army was too small to surround and besiege the city. The only alternative was to threaten some vital point beyond Washington and compel the Federal army to come out and defend it. That left him with the choice of marching away from Washington, to drive the Federals out of their posts in the northern Shenandoah Valley, or crossing the Potomac into central or western Maryland.[2]

The speed with which Lee made such a critical decision suggests that he had anticipated the situation he now faced. On September 2 he marched the main body of his army to Leesburg, in a gap of the Bull Run Mountains some twenty miles northwest of Chantilly. From Leesburg his army could either move against Federal forces in the northern Shenandoah Valley and Harpers Ferry or ford the Potomac well upstream from Washington and invade Maryland. By the evening of September 3 he had decided on the latter operation, and wrote to inform President Davis and briefly explain his reasoning. He began by stating his belief that "The present seems the most propitious time, since the commencement of the war, for the Confederate Army to enter Maryland." The crucial point was this: "[We] cannot afford to be idle, and though weaker than our opponents in men and military equipments, must endeavor to harass, if we cannot destroy them." However, he did not ask, nor did Davis offer, explicit approval for his operations; and that pattern would persist throughout the campaign.[3]

Some historians have seen Lee as having presented Davis with accomplished facts, in order to preempt anticipated objections. Lee certainly wanted to determine the pace and course of operations without presidential interference. When Davis declared his intention to visit the army in the field, Lee discouraged him. However, there is nothing in the written record, or in Davis's behavior after August 21, to suggest that Davis was reluctant to grant Lee authority to determine the objectives and pace of military operations. Despite Davis's earlier concern for the defenses of Richmond, when Lee asked reinforcement for his strike against Pope, Davis sent almost double the number asked for, and stripped the Richmond garrison of its best troops in order to do so. His response to the demands of Lee's plan of invasion would also be proactive rather than reluctant. It makes more sense to see Lee's swift and autonomous decision making as a reflection of the mutual trust between Davis and Lee and the closely shared understanding of strategic imperatives they had developed during their long and close association while Lee was Davis's chief military adviser.

The harmony of views between Davis and Lee was consonant with the public mood, as reflected in Southern newspapers. Calls for an end to defensive warfare and for retaliation on the Northern invaders had been accelerating since May. Lee's success against Pope, and early bulletins from Bragg's invasion of Tennessee, transformed the call into a demand. The *Richmond Whig* condemned defensive warfare as a "humbug" and demanded that Lee "concentrate a force sufficient to strike them to the heart, and deliver the whole continent from bondage." The *Charleston Mercury* demanded that "Our victorious troops in Virginia, reduced though they be in numbers, must be led promptly into Maryland, before the enemy can rally," to win a victory and raze Washington to the ground. The *Jackson Mississippian* mirrored Davis's own analysis by astutely noting that the upcoming elections in the North offered an opportunity for Southern armies to overthrow Republican rule. Kentucky was ripe for liberation, and "Maryland would rise with a wild shout of exhultation when they hear the clarion notes of restored freedom and see 'the gathering of the clans' in their sister states. . . . Let us then . . . *conquer a peace* before the year ends. *Forward*, FORWARD, FORWARD."[4]

In his July 18 letter to Forsyth, Davis had projected an invasion of Northern territory as the logical and necessary culmination of a war-winning strategy. Only by carrying the war to the enemy and defeating him on his home ground could the Confederacy break the political will that sustained the Unionist war effort, and do so before the strain of war inflicted critical or even fatal structural damage on Southern society. Invasion might succeed by simply inflicting punitive damage on Northern farms and factories, comparable to that suffered by the invaded South. Yet Davis also saw invasion as the means by which the Border States of

Maryland and Kentucky might be detached from the Unionist cause—a shift that would profoundly alter the balance of forces and resources. Nevertheless, before a successful invasion could be mounted, Southern armies would have to inflict crushing defeats on the "detachments" (that is, field armies) that had invaded Southern territory and seized the critical positions of Corinth, Nashville, and the Virginia Peninsula.[5]

It was with that strategic design in mind that Davis and Lee had approved Bragg and Smith's proposal to "crush" Buell's army in Tennessee and then invade Kentucky. Davis's instructions to Bragg showed that he not only accepted the risk of a general engagement, he positively urged Bragg to make the defeat of Buell the precondition for his invasion. When the withdrawal of McClellan's troops from the Peninsula made a similar strike possible in Virginia, Davis accepted Lee's plan to "suppress" Pope's detachment. It was impossible to know in advance what kind of opportunities might open up as a result of Pope's defeat, but Davis and Lee had agreed going in that it would be desirable to exploit any victory by continuing operations in northern Virginia. It was necessary to keep Federal forces on the defensive to forestall a new advance on Richmond, and to prevent the sending of reinforcements to the western theater by keeping the enemy occupied in Virginia. Lee's plan to continue the offensive by an invasion of Maryland was perfectly consistent with these objectives, and with the strategy Davis had already urged on Bragg. Davis trusted Lee's judgment that invasion was necessary and success feasible, and left to his general the development of an operational plan. He also backed that plan without reservation, forwarding all the reinforcements he could muster.

STRATEGIC AIMS OF THE INVASION

In the campaign that followed, Davis would have to play the role of strategic commander without the benefit of Lee's advice. Close consultation was simply impossible with Lee commanding a field army more than a hundred miles from the capital. Although Lee was certainly aware that his offensive was strategically connected to Bragg's in Tennessee and Kentucky, only Davis was in a position to see each operation in relation to the other. His orders to Bragg and Lee were nearly simultaneous. He received and approved Lee's preliminary invasion plan on September 3 and gave his approval to Bragg's plans on September 4. However, once these operations were launched, Davis could do nothing to control or coordinate the actions of his field commanders. It was more by coincidence than by order that Bragg moved out from Chattanooga on September 5, the same day that Lee crossed into Maryland.[6]

What Davis could do was formulate the political objectives of the two invasions and develop means for achieving those objectives. The most critical was to attack the political fault lines in the Unionist camp. Davis and Lee believed that the Unionist sentiment of the Border States was weak, and balanced by strong cultural affinities and economic interests with the slave states. The Confederate Congress had made the accession of Maryland in particular a war aim, and Davis had instructed his diplomats in England and France to insist that any mediated peace settlement allow Marylanders to decide by plebiscite whether they still wished to stay in the Union. The appearance on their soil of a victorious Confederate army might produce a political overturn that would carry these states into the Confederacy or, failing that, at least produce an uprising of Southern sympathizers behind Yankee lines.

Lee and Davis also hoped to take advantage of the fact that midterm congressional and gubernatorial elections would be held in two months. A coherent opposition to the Lincoln regime was finally emerging, uniting conservatives of various schools against the increasing "radicalism" of the Republicans. It was perhaps premature to characterize this movement as a peace party, but its leaders certainly favored a settlement that accommodated the slavery interest, and compromises like those that had been offered in 1861 by Senators John Crittenden and Stephen Douglas, which conceded to the South a form of political autonomy within the Union. A successful invasion of Northern soil, demonstrating the Lincoln government's inability to protect its own territory, let alone conquer the South, coupled with an appeal to conservatives, might produce a powerful revulsion at the polls that would substantially weaken political support for the war effort.

Davis also hoped that a Confederate victory on Northern soil would encourage Britain and France to recognize Confederate independence, and intervene on its behalf with financial and military aid and an offer— backed by force—of mediation. Lee may have shared the hope, but did not believe the Europeans would intervene until the Confederacy had made victory certain using its own unaided power. Davis's hope was actually closer to fulfillment than he realized: the British government was going to begin actively considering intervention shortly after Lee's army crossed the Potomac. There had been a brief flurry of interventionist activity in Britain in December 1861, after a Union naval vessel had stopped a British ship on the high seas and seized the Confederate emissaries Mason and Slidell—which ended when Lincoln repudiated the seizure and released the two men. A second wave of interventionist sentiment had risen in Parliament in mid-July, following a false report that the Seven Days Battles had ended with the surrender of McClellan's army—thwarted when more accurate reports were received. But news of Lee's triumph at Second Bull Run, following so closely on the heels of McClellan's defeat, had convinced the British cabinet that the proper circumstances for intervention might be developing.

The politics of intervention were complicated. There was a general conviction among leaders in the British and French governments that the attempt to restore the Union by force was doomed to ultimate failure, and that the Confederacy was already qualified as a nation-state by all the canons of international law and custom. That belief was shared even by those (like Chancellor of the Exchequer William Gladstone and French foreign minister Edouard Thouvenel) who were sympathetic to the Union cause. Both countries were also suffering economic hardship because of the Federal blockade, which cut them off from the supply of American cotton on which their industries depended. The breakup of the Union might benefit the British by weakening a potential maritime Great Power rival; it would certainly aid Napoleon III's project of turning Mexico into a French client state. Both powers therefore looked forward to the moment when, by diplomatic intervention, they might bring the war to an end and recover their access to Southern ports. However, both powers had to be concerned about the European balance of power, and the threat of war in their own regions. France was heavily engaged in the Italian struggle for national unification, which had already embroiled it in one war with Austria and might well require another. France and Britain were also concerned about the ambitions of Prussia, which under Bismarck was emerging as a power to rival France on the Continent, and was preparing war against Denmark—a move threatening Britain's access to the Baltic.

These varied considerations put two constraints on those interested in intervention: neither Britain nor France could risk acting alone; and neither could afford a war against the American North, which would draw naval and military forces away from Europe (and in the French case, Mexico). The French would wait on a British commitment to act. The British ministry would watch for clear signs that the North was willing to accept mediation without going to war. It was possible that a series of decisive victories by Confederate armies would make Southern independence a fait accompli, which could be safely recognized. However, a more likely and certain sign would be an electoral victory for anti-administration forces in the November midterm elections. Mason and Slidell made their pitch for early recognition on the ground that that would encourage Northern opposition to the war and produce the electoral victory the British were waiting for. The Europeans preferred that recognition wait on the election. From either perspective, it was clear that the most critical element of Lee's proposed campaign was its potential effect on the fall elections.[7]

Lee's operational plan was shaped as much by political as by purely military considerations, and his ideas on the subject matched Davis's point for point. He knew that the redemption of Maryland had been a Confederate war aim from the start of the conflict, and that Davis was particularly eager to attempt it. In his September 3 dispatch Lee advised Davis, "If it is ever desired to give material aid to Maryland, and afford her an opportunity to throw off the oppression to which she is now subject, this would seem the most favorable." To that end, Lee requested (September 4 and 7) that E. Louis Lowe, a former governor of Maryland, accompany his expedition, to advise him on the political questions that might arise, and perhaps to develop contacts with potential allies. In fact, Davis had already decided to send Lowe to the front—another sign of their common understanding, and perhaps prior agreement, on strategic means and ends.[8]

Lee continued to think through the political potential of his invasion, and one of his first acts on entering Maryland would be to formulate a systematic program of political action to augment the effect of his operations. He would set forth his ideas in a dispatch to Davis sent on September 8 from Frederick, the initial point of concentration for Lee's invading force. Although the general had never before infringed on President Davis's area of responsibility, this dispatch was exclusively political, and offered detailed and assertive advice on the political dimension of their strategy. He believed the military advantage he now enjoyed would allow Davis to negotiate from a position of strength a final political settlement of the conflict. "The present position of affairs, in my opinion, places it in the power of the Government of the Confederate States to propose with propriety to that of the United States the recognition of our independence." Such a proposal, made while Lee's army was operating on Northern soil, "could in no way be regarded as suing for peace but, being made when it is in our power to inflict injury upon our adversary, would show conclusively to the world that our sole object is the establishment of our independence and the attainment of an honorable peace." If the Lincoln administration rejected such a proposal, it would prove to the country "that the responsibility of the continuance of the war does not rest upon us, but that the party in power in the United States elect to prosecute it for purposes of their own." The events of the previous six months proved that the attempt to resist secession had led to devastating losses, "without advancing the objects which our enemies proposed to themselves in the beginning of the contest." Lee specifically took notice of the upcoming midterm elections. If at that time there was a large Confederate army firmly planted on Union soil, threatening the capital and raiding Pennsylvania, there might be a revulsion of feeling against Lincoln and the war party. In such a context, "The proposal of peace would enable the people of the United States to determine at their coming elections whether they will support those who favor a prolongation of the war, or those who wish to bring it to a termination, which can but be productive of good to both parties without affecting the honor of either."[9]

That same day, Lee would issue a proclamation, calling on Marylanders to rise and cast off the tyranny that had been imposed on them by Yankee force. His language was politically astute, striking a nice balance between the conservative adherence to states'-rights' legalism and the essentially revolutionary call for an overthrow of the existing state government. He listed their grievances for them—their capital occupied "by armed strangers," newspapers suppressed, citizens subjected to arbitrary arrest and imprisonment. "Our army has come among you, and is prepared to assist you with the power of its arms in regaining the rights of which you have been despoiled." However, if Marylanders declined this offer, the Confederate army would respect their exercise of states' rights: "while the Southern people will rejoice to welcome you to your natural position among them, they will only welcome you when you come of your own free will." While Lee did not believe that a "general rising" in the state was likely, he did believe his proclamation might rouse the Southern sympathies of individual Marylanders, and persuade them to either join the Confederate army on its march or supply its desperate wants of food and clothing. Such a movement would be a serious blow to the material strength of the Yankees and would weaken their moral hold on Maryland and other Border States.[10]

Once again Lee's proposals anticipated the thoughts and actions of President Davis. On September 12, Lee would receive a dispatch from Davis indicating his intent to issue a similar proclamation; their messages had crossed in the mail, a not uncommon occurrence. Lee would apologize for seeming to preempt his president's actions, but the embarrassment was slight. Davis's own proclamation indicated that he had been thinking along the same lines, but it was broader in scope than Lee's—more like a political manifesto—and was addressed not only to Lee for use in Maryland but to Bragg and Smith for use in Kentucky.

Davis began by explaining and justifying the Confederacy's reasons for invading the North. The act was neither malicious nor vengeful but a regrettable necessity forced upon a reluctant Confederacy by Federal aggression. He reminded Northerners that the Confederacy fought only in self-defense, not for territorial gain; and that his government was willing to guarantee by treaty the free navigation of the Mississippi. These were issues of particular concern to the states of the Old Northwest, and by including these assurances Davis was suggesting the terms of a potential peace settlement. Davis then appealed to Northern citizens in terms that echoed Lee's September 8 dispatch. He hoped they would prevail on their government to respond to the peace overtures Davis's government had already made.

However, instead of Lee's suggested offer of new peace negotiations, Davis issued a challenge with revolutionary implications. The laws of war entitled Southern armies to respond in kind to the depredations committed by the North's invading forces, and to punish "those who persist in their refusal to make peace." This was, in effect, the mirror image of Pope's decrees, which had also threatened punishment for Southerners who refused to swear allegiance to the Union. To escape Confederate retribution, the Northern people would have to convince their government to end the war, presumably by using the ordinary civil means of petition and election. However, should such efforts fail, Davis invited the people of individual states to "secure immunity" by making "a separate treaty of peace which this Government will ever be ready to conclude on the most just and liberal basis." This last appeal was implicitly a call for revolution in the North. The treaty-making power belongs exclusively to the Federal government. By inviting individual states to sign treaties of peace, Davis was proposing an assertion of state sovereignty not far removed from actual secession; and he threatened those states that refused to rebel with a ravaging akin to that which the South had been suffering.[11]

This was Davis's finest moment as a strategist. He had heeded the suggestions for offensive action suggested by Bragg and Lee, and to the extent possible coordinated their operations. With his generals he had developed what Lincoln had been trying in vain to achieve: simultaneous offensives by the three main field armies spanning the breadth of the Confederacy. Moreover, he had linked these invasions to a coherent political program, which attacked the structures of state power that constituted the Union. The result was a development of Confederate strategy that mirrored the evolution of Union strategy, toward intensified and more punitive military operations and a more radical assault on the enemy's social and political order. Driven by the demands of a war that put at risk the survival of their nations, both presidents were doing things that would make reconciliation more difficult and make the Civil War a "total" war, a "remorseless revolutionary conflict."

ACROSS THE ATLANTIC, political developments also appeared to favor the Confederacy, though Davis had no way of knowing this. Because of the blockade it could take months for communications to pass between Davis and his European emissaries, and even without the blockade there was a lag of nearly two weeks between events in America and the receipt of the news in London. England got the news of Pope's defeat and McClellan's reappointment on September 10, five days after Lee's army had crossed the Potomac into Maryland. The British cabinet had been deeply impressed by Lee's victories, especially Second Bull Run, and were aware that the Confederates intended to press their advantage. Anticipating further Confederate successes and a corresponding loss of Northern morale, Foreign Minister Lord John Russell and Prime Minister Lord Palmerston believed it was time to begin preparing for the inevitable moment of intervention. Russell opened the conversation on September 11, and Palmerston stated the policy options openly in a letter to Russell on September 14. If the Confederates were able to follow Second Bull Run with a victory on Northern soil it might be time for England and France to "address the contending parties and recommend an arrangement upon the basis of separation."[12]

LEE'S OPERATIONAL PLAN

The overall purpose of Lee's plan was, as he told Davis, to "harass, if not destroy" the Federal field army defending Washington. Obviously, the destruction of that army was the most desirable outcome, but Lee was not overinvested in the idea of a Napoleonic battle of annihilation. The plan he developed was flexible and offered several different ways of achieving the desired political objectives.

Lee's offensive options were limited by the disparity of strength between the armies. His Army of Northern Virginia was outnumbered and outgunned by the Federal forces in Washington, which may have numbered 120,000 all told. However, the only fresh veteran units available to the Federals were the II and VI Corps from McClellan's army, the XII Corps of Pope's command, and two divisions of Burnside's IX Corps that had missed Second Bull Run—about 55,000 troops. They could be augmented by elements of Pope's army, and by the newly recruited regiments that had arrived in the capital, but these units were of doubtful value. The Federal corps that had fought under Pope had suffered debilitating losses of men and matériel, and Lee believed they were seriously "weakened and demoralized." The newly recruited regiments were untrained and likely to prove liabilities on the battlefield.

Lee believed he could immediately field an army of between 65,000 and 72,000 men, quite large enough to deal with a Federal army of these ill-sorted elements. His own army would have a distinct advantage in both morale, as a result of its recent victories, and organization, since Lee's reformed command structure had been tested and perfected in the last campaign. The events of the past month showed that a well-led, veteran, and high-morale force could defeat a larger Federal army deficient in those categories.[13]

While a direct assault on Washington was beyond Lee's capabilities, Lee could threaten so many vital and politically sensitive areas by moving into Maryland that Federal commanders would be compelled to leave their fortifications and move against him before their forces were fully reorganized.

To provoke a premature Federal advance, Lee would first seize Frederick, Maryland, only fifty miles west of Washington. His reasons were political as well as military. The town was centrally located in the mainland portion of the state, convenient to Baltimore and its environs, where pro-Confederate sympathies were strongest. It was therefore the best position from which to instigate a popular uprising in the state, to attract recruits, and to obtain supplies. Because of its proximity to Washington, its occupation by the Army of Northern Virginia constituted a damaging demonstration of the Lincoln administration's weakness. It was also a deliberate provocation to the Union military, a challenge to battle on their doorstep that might goad them into advancing before their army had recovered from its defeats. If the Federals accepted, Lee felt confident of winning a general engagement. If the North declined his gambit, Lee would shift his forces away to the west, behind the high, extended ridges that ran north from the Potomac into Pennsylvania. The passes through these elongated ridges were narrow and easily defended against a Federal advance. These ridges were also, in effect, northern extensions of those that bounded the Shenandoah Valley on the south side of the Potomac. A Confederate army positioned behind them would enjoy direct access to the Valley's agricultural resources, and the Valley itself provided a mountain-sheltered route for military supplies carried north from Richmond via the Virginia Central Railroad and the Valley's excellent road system.

Before he could use the Valley as a supply line, Lee had to drive away the large Federal garrison that held the town of Harpers Ferry at the northern outlet of the Valley. This outpost, and the associated positions at Winchester and Martinsburg, were sustained by lines of communication that ran eastward through the Maryland panhandle and southern Pennsylvania. It was an impediment that should be relatively easy to remove. When the Confederate army interposed between Harpers Ferry and Washington, the outpost would be isolated, and its garrison would have no choice but to withdraw or be destroyed. With Harpers Ferry in hand, and a protected supply line running through the Valley, Lee's army would be able to maintain itself in western Maryland for an extended period of time. Basing itself in Hagerstown, it could harass the Federals by raids into Pennsylvania, compelling Lincoln to defend his capital and its hinterland instead of marshaling a new offensive against Richmond. If the Federal army moved to attack him west of the mountains, it would be acting at a greater distance from its own base in Washington, and in its attempts to strike across the mountain barrier would expose itself to defeat by the kind of rapid maneuvers at which the Army of Northern Virginia excelled. Under these circumstances Lee would have a good chance of inflicting a decisive defeat or even destroying the opposing army. Otherwise Lee could use Hagerstown as the base for a deeper invasion of the North, following the route he would later take in the Gettysburg campaign: north to Harrisburg to cut the Pennsylvania Railroad, the North's main west-to-east railroad line, then south to threaten Baltimore and Washington from the rear, maneuvering so as to confuse and divide the pursuing Federals and defeat them in detail.[14]

Fortunately for Lee, while decisive battle was desirable, it was not essential to a successful campaign. By simply prolonging his presence in Maryland, he would dramatically demonstrate the Confederacy's ability to stymie Federal efforts at invasion and subjugation, and do so at a moment when such a demonstration could have powerful and perhaps lasting political effects.

WHILE HIS ARMY TOOK its brief rest at Leesburg, Lee assessed its strengths and weaknesses and reorganized its elements for the campaign he had in mind. The commands of Jackson and Longstreet were roughly equivalent to army corps. This clarified the chain of command

and, over time, would enable the component divisions to perfect their teamwork. Just after Second Bull Run, Lee received three new divisions, commanded by Generals D. H. Hill, Lafayette McLaws, and Richard Anderson, which had been sent from Richmond by President Davis in response to an earlier request. Lee chose not to assign these divisions to Jackson or Longstreet for the moment but to treat them as independent commands reporting to his own headquarters. He could use them as a general reserve or assign one or more of them to either Longstreet or Jackson as circumstances might require. Lee also ordered the movements of Stuart's cavalry division.[15]

Although he was heavily outnumbered by Federal forces in the theater, Lee considered his army strong enough in numbers and in morale for the campaign he was planning. "The only two subjects that give me any uneasiness are my supplies of ammunition and subsistence." The army lacked "much of the material of war, is feeble in transportation, the animals being much reduced, and the men poorly provided with clothes, and in thousands of instances, are destitute of shoes." However, he had reason to think that the army could get supplies of flour, meat, and forage from the farms of western Maryland. Since he expected the Federals shortly to abandon the Shenandoah, he asked Davis to send ammunition, especially for the artillery, via Winchester. He also expressed concern about the army's lack of discipline, especially the tendency of troops to straggle or otherwise absent themselves from their commands, and their tendency to pillage the country they passed through. In response, he instituted a beefed-up provost guard system to deal with stragglers, but its efforts would prove inadequate.[16]

Every unit was to reduce its transportation needs to the bare minimum, taking only enough livestock and wagons to haul basic subsistence and ammunition. All horses and mules freed by this process were to be turned over to the army quartermaster for redistribution. The artillery presented special problems. A powerful artillery was essential to success on the battlefield, and on paper the Army of Northern Virginia possessed an ample supply: some three hundred guns in seventy-four batteries. However, the quality of these units was extraordinarily uneven. The Confederacy had not been able to develop a large-scale manufacturing capacity, so its artillery was a mishmash of modern guns and antiques, warehouse stock that had moldered in Southern arsenals, captured Federal guns, and a few British pieces run through the blockade. Lee subjected his artillery to triage, cannibalizing equipment and redistributing the sound draft animals to bring his best batteries closer to the mark, at the cost of leaving other batteries behind. Even though this part of the plan was not fully carried out, in part because these volunteer units were political as well as military entities, and state pride forbade their surrendering equipment and the right to fight to units from other states, the net effect was to increase the efficiency and mobility of his artillery.[17]

The unit pride that prevented Lee from completely reorganizing his artillery was otherwise his army's greatest strength. Although he faulted their lack of discipline in the camp and on the march, Lee rightly regarded his soldiers as superb combat troops. As combat veterans the soldiers knew what to expect on the battlefield and were unlikely to panic or break without good cause. Although conscription had been in effect for four months, these men were still volunteers. Whatever their reasons for enlisting—for adventure, to be part of a great community engagement, to vindicate Southern rights, to defend their homes from invasion—they now identified community, pride, and patriotism with their units. Those who would make the march were also, for the most part, men who had proved their devotion by sticking to the flag through grueling marches and terrible combat. More than 60 percent of the regiments in Lee's army had already participated in three or more general engagements. More significantly, most of the brigades and divisions were composed of units that had served together through the Richmond and Second Bull Run campaigns. Their officers were familiar with each other and with each other's troops, an invaluable kind of experience that made for efficient communication and liaison on the battlefield. The corps organizations were of more recent vintage, but most of Longstreet's and Jackson's divisions had made at least one campaign together.[18]

However, the actual troop strength of the Army of Northern Virginia at the start of the Maryland campaign is difficult to assess. Historians have estimated Lee's initial force at anywhere from 50,000 to 75,500. The latter estimate is based on Confederate records, so it is possible that Lee had a similar estimate in mind. However, Confederate paperwork was notoriously incomplete and inaccurate. Moreover, Lee himself could not have had a clear or accurate knowledge of his army's numerical strength, since he had not yet instituted the most basic of accounting systems, which requires unit commanders to report their strength up the chain of command. Nonetheless, he did know that he had a huge number of regiments under his command. With the accession of the divisions from Richmond, the Army of Northern Virginia contained 205 regiments—fully a third of the units then under arms in the Confederacy. If Lee supposed these to be at anything near half their authorized strength, he might have estimated his army's strength as near the 75,500 figure.[19]

There are also reasons to doubt the high estimate of Lee's force. The report Lee made after the Battle of Antietam asserted that he had fewer than 40,000 in that engagement, which occurred only two weeks after the start of the campaign. Only about 3,000 men were lost in the battles and skirmishes leading up to Antietam. If Lee's initial force had been 75,500, then his army would have lost 32,000 men, or 43 percent of its strength, to nonbattle causes (mostly straggling and desertion) in less than two weeks' time. With such a rate of loss, officers would have seen their commands melt away before their eyes; it suggests a degree of demoralization that no officer observed at the time. Yet most of the reports made after the campaign suggest that the extent of straggling was not generally realized until the battle was about to start, with some officers failing to note its effects till the army was back in Virginia. Lee himself would later remark that straggling had reduced by a third the force he was able to field at Antietam. If that estimate is correct, then his army probably mustered 65,000 to 70,000 at the start of the campaign.[20]

Whatever the actual numbers, the salient fact is that Lee began his campaign without knowing his army's exact strength—and most probably with an exaggerated idea of its numbers. As the campaign went forward, it would also become apparent that he had overestimated his soldiers' physical endurance and failed to properly anticipate the consequences of their lack of food, clothing, and especially shoes.[21]

Although the troops were not informed of the army's plan of operations, they were aware that an invasion of enemy territory was in the works. For most of the army's veterans that news would have been a boost to morale. Some units were thought to have objected on ideological grounds to fighting for any purpose but homeland defense, but this does not appear to have affected any significant number of regiments. However, there was a good deal of reluctance felt by troops who had been marching and fighting almost without letup for the past month. The vast majority of these stayed with their units, but many would fall out by the way because of physical and mental exhaustion.[22]

THE INVASION BEGINS, september 4–10, 1862

Lee's initial moves were provocative. On September 4 General D. H. Hill crossed the Potomac at Point of Rocks, to break the B&O Railroad line, disrupt Federal communications between Washington and Harpers Ferry, and make a reconnaissance in force toward Frederick. If the implied threat of Hill's movement did not force the abandonment of Harpers Ferry, the concentration of Lee's whole army north of the Potomac would do the trick.[23] On September 5 Jackson's command crossed the Potomac at White's Ford, only twenty miles from Washington, while Stuart's cavalry crossed lower down and aggressively probed Federal positions. On the sixth Jackson occupied Frederick and Longstreet's Corps forded the Potomac and marched to join him.

The current was swift where Jackson crossed, and in one Georgia Regiment "to keep from washing down four men would get in line up and down the river and hold on to each other for support." This "kind of dammed up the water" behind their line, and guaranteed them all a good soaking. They savored the cooling effect on what turned into a hot, dry, dusty daylong march.[24]

Despite eighty-degree heat, the march up to Frederick was otherwise a pleasant one, and the troops were in high spirits, anticipating better and more plentiful food supplies to be gathered from Maryland's rich farms and happy to be hitting the Yankees where it hurt. Frederick itself was a prosperous and pretty market town of redbrick and white clapboard houses set among trees and broad fields.

By holding Frederick, Lee put his army at the center of the region's road network and cut the B&O Railroad at Monocacy Junction south of town. From Frederick he could then threaten movements against the northwestern defenses of Washington, raid into Pennsylvania, or bluff an advance on Baltimore, whose pro-secession population might be ripe for an uprising. With the belligerent and impulsive Pope in command, Lee could hope that the Federals would move to counter his offensive before their battered army was fully prepared, allowing Lee to fight them on his own chosen ground. If that failed he would also have an open route for retreat across the mountains to Hagerstown, where he hoped to establish a long-term presence.

The prosperous civilians of Frederick thought the Rebel army were "the dirtiest men I ever saw . . . a most ragged, lean, and hungry set of wolves." One observer compared them to a barbarian horde, a resemblance reinforced by the presence of a large number of Negroes, serving as teamsters or ambulance aides or officers' servants, dressed in rags but often armed with "rifles, muskets, sabers, bowie-knives or dirks." The vast majority of soldiers were clothed in homespun garments, made of various combinations of cotton, linen, and/or wool, haphazardly dyed in shades of gray, or the varied browns and ochers produced by the use of butternuts, a variety of white walnut, in the dye-stuff. Some wore the natty-looking French kepi, a leather-billed cap that could be given a rakish tilt; but most wore "slouch" hats, broad-brimmed and high-crowned, stained by sweat and battered by weather. Those who had had the luck to raid the Yankee depots at Manassas had shoes or boots to wear. A great many started out barefoot, and many more would march their footgear to pieces over the next week. Their equipment was patchwork as well. Wagon trains and artillery batteries were pieced out with vehicles and guns captured from the enemy, many still bearing the "U.S." marking.

The infantry would get a few days' rest at Frederick and have an opportunity to gather supplies while it waited to see how the Federals would respond. The Twenty-second Georgia rejoiced in the opportunity to wash their clothes in the Monocacy River, "to drown some of the lice of which we had plenty. We had not washed our clothes for about a month, and the bugs were getting unbearable." The problem was not exclusive to the Georgians. A local doctor noted "the penetrating ammoniacal smell," a compound of piss and sweat both horse and human, which pervaded the air wherever the Rebels camped, and announced their coming if the wind was behind them. "A dirtier, filthier, more unsavory set of human beings never *strolled* through a town—marching it could not be called." However, the doctor was mistaken in thinking their informal marching style a sign of indiscipline. As veterans they had learned to prefer the loose and natural stride to the measured pacing of the drill ground; and their discipline was generally good, as reflected in their obedience to the orders that forbade looting or seizing goods without at least offering payment—in Confederate currency. The troops understood that the purpose of their invasion was to win the hearts and minds of Marylanders for the Confederacy. Even the Frederick doctor who sneered at their rags admitted, "They all believe in *themselves* as well as in their generals, and are terribly in earnest."[25]

To keep the enemy confused as to his purposes and movements, Lee ordered Stuart to scout and skirmish actively in two directions: toward Washington, to keep close tabs on Federal advances; and toward Baltimore, to threaten that city and compel the Yankees to divide their attention and their forces. Lee himself needed the rest to recuperate from the injury to his hands and arms. He used the interval (September 7–8) to complete his reports to Davis and issue his proclamation inviting Marylanders to rise in revolt.[26]

It soon became apparent that their hopes for a revolutionary uprising in Maryland were misplaced. Confederate sympathizers freely visited the camp, many of them relatives of Marylanders already serving in the Army of Northern Virginia. However, these were mainly from Baltimore and the Eastern Shore, where Southern sympathies were strongest. Unionist sentiment became stronger as one moved west from Baltimore—in Frederick, forty miles from Baltimore, the majority were either pro-Union or indifferent to the Southern cause. There would be no substantial accession of recruits from the state. Barely two hundred enlisted while the army was in Frederick.

The expectation of enjoying ample supplies of foodstuffs and clothing was also disappointed. There was not sufficient livestock to supply either draft animals or meat in the quantities required by the army. The grain harvest was not far advanced, and the millers demanded payment in U.S. currency for turning what grain there was into flour. Instead of bread or hardtack, the troops ate cooked grain and uncooked or even unripe corn. The result was that they began to suffer from diet-related diarrhea, in addition to the bowel problems endemic to all Civil War armies from drinking polluted water and living and eating in unsanitary conditions. For troops already worn down by hard marching and harder fighting, this was physically disabling. Even at this early and easy stage of the campaign in Maryland, Lee was newly concerned about further straggling, though Lee attributed it to "cowardice" rather than debility.[27]

On September 9 other misjudgments became apparent. Contrary to both expectations and all military logic, the Federal garrisons at Harpers Ferry and Martinsburg had not been withdrawn. As long as Federals held Harpers Ferry, the Valley supply line was closed. Lee had originally counted on that line for the resupply of ammunition and military equipment he would need once fighting began. Now he realized he would also have to draw on the Valley for foodstuff and livestock. So rather than linger in his exposed position at Frederick, Lee decided to fall back on his alternative plan to retreat west of the Catoctin Mountains and establish a base of operations from which he could "harass, if not destroy" the Federal army.[28]

The new plan made it imperative to open the Valley supply route by driving out or capturing the large Federal garrisons that held Harpers Ferry and Martinsburg. Their continued presence there was a serious tactical problem and something of an astonishment. When Lee's army crossed the Potomac it had cut the line of supply linking these garrisons to Washington, and if Lee sent a force of any size into western Maryland they could be completely isolated and compelled to flee or surrender. By all the canons of military science the troops there should already have been withdrawn.

In fact, the canons of military science had nothing to do with the case. The garrisons were immobilized by the confusion or incompetence of their commanders, by the tangled webs of bureaucracy, and by the continuing fuss over lines of authority between Halleck and McClellan.

The Harpers Ferry garrison was not attached to the field army but to the Military Department of Maryland and Southern Pennsylvania, a purely administrative entity whose commander was General John Wool, a superannuated veteran of the War of 1812. Wool was out of touch with the garrison, his office in Baltimore was more than a hundred miles away, and he wanted to pass responsibility for the post to General McClellan. McClellan, too, wanted the garrisons placed under his command, partly for the usual reason—he was "outnumbered" and needed every available man—but also because in its present position it was uselessly imperiled. Halleck refused his request for no discernible reason and threw the responsibility for ordering an evacuation back on Wool, relying on his nonexistent "experience and local knowledge." Wool was unwilling to take that responsibility and passed the decision down to the garrison commander, Colonel D. S. Miles—an incompetent who had been sent to rusticate at Harpers Ferry after a disgraceful performance at First Bull Run. While Miles would not take responsibility for abandoning the post without positive orders, he also failed to take the necessary measures for making the place defensible. It would take nearly a week for McClellan to pry command of the garrison away from Halleck—from the sixth to the eleventh of September—and by then it was too late for Miles to do anything but hunker down.[29]

The Martinsburg garrison, commanded by Brigadier General Julius White, was the larger of the two, but it seems to have been an administrative orphan. His command was far out on a limb, holding an indefensible position in the West Virginia foothills, ostensibly protecting the B&O Railroad line west of Harpers Ferry. While Halleck, Wool, and McClellan fussed over Harpers Ferry, White was left without instructions, and he, too, chose to stay where he was.

This tangled web of blunder and misfeasance would doom the garrison to hapless defeat. But it also threatened to derange Lee's whole plan of campaign, and confronted him with an extremely complex tactical problem. In trying to solve it he would expose his army to destruction.

LEE DIVIDES HIS ARMY, SEPTEMBER 10–13, 1862

The combined garrisons of Martinsburg and Harpers Ferry mustered nearly thirteen thousand Union soldiers. The force sent against them would have to be at least twice as strong. Stonewall Jackson was the obvious choice to lead the expedition. Jackson excelled in independent operations and had the most thorough knowledge of the Harpers Ferry terrain. Lee met with him on the evening of September 9 to work out the details.[30]

The operation was designed to surround and capture the Federal force in Harpers Ferry, not simply to drive it away. The peculiar character of the terrain would complicate the maneuvers required to assault it. Harpers Ferry sat at the northern entry to the Shenandoah Valley, among the high, wooded ridges of western Virginia. The town was sited on a triangular peninsula formed by the confluence of the Shenandoah and Potomac rivers, with the Shenandoah Valley opening out to the west. A ridge named Bolivar Heights ran across the base of the peninsula, and a trench line there defended the town from troops attacking out of the Valley. The town was overlooked by two other ridge lines. Southward on the other side of the Shenandoah River was Loudon Heights and northeastward, on the other side of the Potomac, was a high bluff called Maryland Heights. If an enemy were to capture these heights, their artillery would dominate the entire peninsula and the garrison would have to surrender. Colonel Miles posted a brigade and artillery on Maryland Heights, but Loudon Heights was weakly held.

To surround Harpers Ferry and force its surrender, Confederate troops had to put a large infantry force west of the town to attack Bolivar Heights, and at the same time seize both Loudon and Maryland Heights. However, because of the high mountains, deep rivers, and bad roads of the region there was no single route by which a united Confederate army could reach its objectives. Infantry could only attack the town by getting into the Shenandoah Valley west of Bolivar Heights, but to get there from Frederick, Jackson's troops would have to march past Harpers Ferry on the opposite bank of the Potomac, pass through the little crossroad town of Sharpsburg, cross the Potomac at Shepherdstown Ford five or six miles upstream from Harpers Ferry, then work their way down through the hills. En route Jackson would have to detach a large force under the command of General Lafayette McLaws to capture Maryland Heights, which could only be approached from the north. To complicate matters, Loudon Heights could only be approached from the east, on the Virginia side of the Potomac. It would therefore be necessary for Lee to further divide Jackson's force, sending J. G. Walker's infantry division with some cavalry back into Virginia to march on Loudon Heights from that side. Once they separated, Jackson, McLaws, and Walker would be unable to communicate with each other until all three arrived at Harpers Ferry. It would therefore be impossible for Jackson to control and coordinate their movements or compensate for setbacks or delays they might suffer. All three columns were supposed to converge on and take Harpers Ferry by September 12.

While Lee and Jackson were conferring, General Longstreet arrived. He was initially opposed to the idea of dividing the army, preferring the more cautious plan of advancing against Harpers Ferry as a united force. Lee rejected this idea, for reasons that remain conjectural. However, Lee modified his plan in accord with Longstreet's suggestions. Lee's original plan called for Walker's Division and a cavalry brigade, about five thousand troops, to cross the Potomac back into Virginia, then march west to seize Loudon Heights. Jackson was to march west through the gaps of South Mountain with his own three divisions, about twenty thousand men, followed by McLaws's Division of about seven thousand, which was supposed to peel off and capture Maryland Heights. At Longstreet's urging Lee strengthened McLaws's column with the three brigades of R. H. Anderson's Division, raising the strength of his detachment to seven thousand. This addition raised to about thirty-seven thousand the troops committed to seizing Harpers Ferry—more than half of Lee's total force of between sixty-five thousand and seventy thousand of all arms. In the meantime Longstreet's command, reduced to three infantry divisions and screened by Stuart's cavalry (about twenty-six thousand total), would fall back on Boonsboro, near one of the gaps in the Catoctin Mountains, where it could offer earlier resistance to any Federal advance out of Washington and secure control of Hagerstown. This was consistent with his overriding desire to retain the offensive initiative: even as he moved to secure his supply line he would be establishing the base for his next offensive.[31]

LEE'S DECISION WAS probably made before he learned from the Baltimore papers of McClellan's assumption of command, but when it came the news would have reassured him. He believed he could count on McClellan to undertake an extended period of reorganization, to be followed by the most cautious of advances. Meanwhile, with his supply line cleared by the capture of Harpers Ferry, Lee would reunite his army either in Boonsboro or Hagerstown. From that point, his campaign would take on the desired form. Catoctin Mountain and South Mountain would be a defensive bulwark between his army and McClellan's. He would be in an ideal position to harass the Federals by raiding into Pennsylvania or to strike for a decision by marching in force against Harrisburg and seeking a general engagement.

The maneuver plan was extraordinarily complex and risky. Its success required the coordination of three converging columns, operating on separate lines, unable to communicate with or support each other. The timetable was also aggressive: Lee expected Jackson to have

Harpers Ferry in hand by September 12, less than three days after he marched out of Frederick. The plan made no allowance for the appearance of unanticipated difficulties that might slow the rate of march or require a change of route. Its success also depended on the dangerous assumption that enemy responses would conform to Lee's expectations. Until Harpers Ferry surrendered or was abandoned, the separate elements of Lee's army would be far apart. Lee had taken similar risks in the campaign against Pope, but then he had played for the chance to destroy the main force arrayed against him. Here the objective was the capture of an outpost, which could have been taken by the safer (albeit slower) means suggested by Longstreet. If the garrisons of Martinsburg and Harpers Ferry chose to fight rather than flee, Lee's timetable would fall apart. If McClellan was not as slow to advance as Lee expected—if Lincoln's goading or some unforeseeable turn of events led him to move with unwonted energy—he might catch Lee's army while it was still divided and defeat it in detail.

The directives that would set the several columns of the army in motion were written out on September 9 in Special Order No. 191, and copies were sent by mounted courier to President Davis and to the commanders of those divisions not yet incorporated with the commands of Jackson and Longstreet. Two copies were directed to General D. H. Hill, one from Lee's headquarters and another from Jackson's. Protocol demanded the latter, because Hill had been temporarily attached to Jackson's command. The copy sent by Jackson never reached Hill. It was lost by the courier, along with three cigars, in a field outside of Frederick. The courier never reported the loss and Hill did not miss it, since he received the original from Lee's headquarters.[32]

ALL OF THE CONFEDERATE COLUMNS, with the exception of Walker's, would move west by the same route, the well-engineered National Road that ran twenty-five miles west from Frederick through Turner's Gap in South Mountain to Boonsboro. But Jackson's command moved slowly. His troops had been nicknamed "foot cavalry" for the speed with which they covered great distances, but they were worn out from months of such marches, and the macadam and packed-stone road was agony to march on with the broken shoes or bare feet most were reduced to. Jackson halted at Boonsboro so that his scouts could reconnoiter the route he planned to follow. For all of September 10 and part of the eleventh the rest of the army was queued up along the road behind Jackson or waiting in Frederick until he cleared the way.

Boonsboro was a small town, a way station on the National Road, a few taverns and stores along the highway. Skirmishes with Union patrols revealed that the Sharpsburg–Shepherdstown road was watched, and Jackson received reports indicating that the Martinsburg garrison (about six thousand men) was still holding its ground. Jackson therefore altered his line of march to cross the Potomac upstream at Williamsport, ten miles farther from Harpers Ferry than Shepherdstown, so he could cross unopposed and close off the Martinsburg garrison's escape route to the west. Instead of marching a bit over twenty miles to reach an *abandoned* Martinsburg, as Lee had planned, Jackson's troops would now have to march thirty-five miles, then deploy for action against the garrison. Jackson pressed ahead on the eleventh and by evening had most of his command across the river and within two hours' march of Martinsburg— with absolutely no chance of reaching Harpers Ferry on the twelfth, let alone capturing the place. Moreover, his men were exhausted, and he had lost heavily in stragglers.

Lee was aware that the physical strength of his men had been seriously worn by months of campaigning, hundreds of miles of hard marching, and heavy combat. Jackson's command, which had the longest line of march to Harpers Ferry, had already done more forced marches than the rest of the army. Lee therefore directed Jackson to limit his rate of march to three miles an hour and allow frequent rests. But these measures were inadequate. Jackson had to cover a considerable distance in a limited time, and while he may have slowed his usual rate of march he could not come near meeting his schedule without extending the hours of march from predawn to postdusk. His men were desperately hungry, poorly supplied by their commissary, and unable to find any quantity of decent food by foraging. Soldiers with blistered and bleeding feet who could not keep up fell out by the roadside. Most would struggle to rejoin their commands, but many gave up and went back to Virginia, where the sandy roads were gentler and the rations more reliable. Other men fell out because they were racked with diarrhea and dysentery, which left them too weak to catch up. One of Jackson's brigadiers was bitter about the fact that "[o]ur men march and fight without provisions, living on green corn. . . . Jackson would kill up an army the way he marches and the bad management in the subsistence Dept." Jackson's command may have lost nearly a third of its numbers just marching to Harpers Ferry.[33]

The regiments that fell back to Boonsboro with Lee and Longstreet on September 11 would similarly leak stragglers all the way. Lee's troop strength—which was, to begin with, less than he supposed—was diminishing every day. This wing consisted of two divisions of Longstreet's command plus D. H. Hill's Division, accompanied by the army's reserve artillery and the large wagon trains that carried its supplies and ammunition. Lee also disposed of the cavalry concentrated under Stuart's direct command, which lingered in and around Frederick to screen the army's movements. On September 11 Longstreet's divisions, with the army's artillery and supply wagon train, completed their march to Boonsboro, while Hill's Division lingered as a rear guard in the vicinity of Turner's Gap, where the National Road from Frederick crossed the high ridge of South Mountain. Shortly after their arrival, Lee received reports that a Federal force of unknown strength was marching down from the north, threatening to occupy Hagerstown some fifteen miles north of Boonsboro. The report was probably an exaggerated account of the militia and home-guard units then forming to resist any incursion into southern Pennsylvania, but Lee was concerned by it.

Hagerstown played a significant role in Lee's new plans. It was one of the larger towns in the region, well stocked with provisions, clothing, and shoes. It had good road connections in every direction and was also the southern railhead for a line that ran north into Pennsylvania, which made it an ideal base for future offensives into the north. Lee also wanted Hagerstown as a place, well beyond McClellan's reach, in which to park his army's large train of supply wagons and its reserve artillery. He therefore sent a reluctant Longstreet to secure Hagerstown, and divided his command yet again, leaving only D. H. Hill's Division to defend the South Mountain gaps and the army's headquarters and base of supply at Boonsboro.[34]

While Jackson was marching to Williamsport and Lee to Boonsboro, the columns led by Walker and McLaws had made little progress. Walker had crossed back into Virginia on the tenth, but his men were so worn-out that he decided to let them rest all the next day before moving on Loudon Heights on September 12.

On that day McLaws's command, consisting of his own division and R. H. Anderson's, was preparing to cross South Mountain at Crampton's Gap, which was twelve miles south of Turner's Gap. His was the most crucial assignment: to make Harpers Ferry untenable by seizing Maryland Heights, the high bluff that rose at the southern tip of a long ridge called Elk Mountain. But McLaws had no experience in independent command. The terrain before him was difficult and unfamiliar, held by an enemy whose strength and position were unknown, and the army had not provided him with scouts who knew the area or cavalry sufficient to clarify the situation. McLaws had not only to organize an assault on a position of unknown form and strength, in his approach he had to prevent the garrison from breaking out and escaping to the north. He therefore spread his command in a broad line, spanning Pleasant Valley and straddling Elk Mountain as it advanced. The difficult terrain and the need to maintain the cohesion of his line slowed his advance, so that his lead brigade did not locate the Federal force on Maryland Heights until the evening of the twelfth. Since that force appeared to be sizable, and holding a strong position, McLaws could do nothing until he had concentrated most of his command against it.

Meanwhile, unbeknownst to any of the Confederate commanders, on the night of September 11–12, General White had decided to escape Jackson's impending assault by abandoning Martinsburg and retreating to join Miles's command at Harpers Ferry, some fifteen miles south. Thus on the twelfth of September there were nearly thirteen thousand Federal troops concentrated in Harpers Ferry, twice as many as McLaws and Walker expected to meet; and they were preparing to fight, not flee. Because the three prongs of the Confederate advance had no way of communicating with each other, none could call on any of the others for support in case of attack. Under an enterprising commander, a force of that size could have held McLaws at bay, crushed Walker's Division, and made its escape before Jackson could even reach the scene. It was Jackson's good luck that the Union commanders, White and Miles, were not at all enterprising, and that Miles (who had primary responsibility for the Union defense) was barely competent.

On September 12 the three independent Confederate columns were converging, more or less simultaneously, on their objectives. Walker's Division seized undefended Loudon Heights on the evening of September 12. McLaws's advancing troops discovered that Colonel Miles had entrusted the defense of Maryland Heights to an inadequate infantry force under an incompetent commander. McLaws would attack and carry the position the next morning. Meanwhile Jackson's command was marching over the hills from Martinsburg and would soon begin deploying across the face of Bolivar Heights. The Union garrison was now trapped in the town of Harpers Ferry, and once Walker and McLaws got their guns in position the town would be exposed to devastating fire from high ground on two sides.

However, although the capture of Harpers Ferry was ultimately assured, the operation was already a full day behind schedule and far from complete. It would take another day to bring up the guns and put the town under fire, and there was no telling how long the garrison might hold out before surrendering. Then there would be further delay while the victors dealt with their large haul of POWs, distributed the captured food, uniforms, and ammunition they so badly needed, and recovered from days of hard marching and the strain of combat. Until all that was done, Lee's army would remain badly split: more than half of it around Harpers Ferry, the rest divided among Turner's Gap, Boonsboro, and Hagerstown. In these circumstances the army's safety depended on Stuart's cavalry screen, and on General McClellan staying true to type, advancing slowly and cautiously, reluctant to press hard.

McClellan's initial movements justified Lee's belief that the Union advance was in fact extremely deliberate. The Federal cavalry never seriously tested Stuart's screen, and McClellan's advance guard did not retake Frederick until September 13, by which time Jackson was at Harpers Ferry and all of Lee's infantry was west of Catoctin Mountain.

Then, on September 13, Lee's campaign encountered bad luck so egregious that it would have nullified even the most perfect tactical plans. A pair of Union infantrymen, preparing to bivouac outside of Frederick, found under a tree an envelope containing three cigars and a piece of paper—which, when opened, proved to be the lost copy of Lee's General Order 191. The finding of that lost order gave McClellan detailed information on Lee's plans and exposed the dangerous division of his army. It compromised Lee's plan of campaign and encouraged the cautious McClellan to dare the offensive that culminated at Antietam.

CHAPTER 8

McCLELLAN TAKES THE OFFENSIVE

SEPTEMBER 2–14, 1862

❦

THE ASSUMPTIONS THAT LED LEE TO DIVIDE HIS COMMAND WERE reasonable but erroneous. Lee misjudged the temper of the Union army, which was not demoralized by Pope's defeat, and also the speed and effectiveness with which McClellan would reorganize his divisions and prepare a field army for operations.

In the brief period between his restoration to command and Lee's crossing of the Potomac, McClellan had justified Lincoln's belief in his peculiar skills. His revival of the army's morale began with his assumption of command on September 2. With his staff behind him he rode out from Alexandria toward Centreville and crossed paths with Generals Pope and McDowell. Although neither had yet been formally relieved of command, they were leaving an army that regarded them with distrust and dislike. McClellan dismissed them with a salute and rode on. Staff officers rode ahead announcing his second coming to the Army of the Potomac, and the columns of tired and discouraged troops erupted in cheers and rejoicing. As one officer remembered,

> Shout upon shout went out into the stillness of the night; and as it was taken up along the road and repeated by regiment, bri- gade, division and corps, we could hear the roar dying away in the distance. The effect of this man's presence upon the Army of the Potomac—in sunshine or rain, in darkness or daylight, in vic-

tory or defeat—was electrical, and too wonderful to make it worth while attempting to give a reason for it.[1]

It was indeed a magical moment, remembered as such by the soldiers as well as McClellan himself. The men recognized his jaunty figure as the embodiment of a soldierly ideal to which he himself had taught them to aspire.

The soldiers' feeling for McClellan and their familiarity with army routine made the task of restoring order much easier than it had been after First Bull Run. But there was more at work than McClellan's charisma. Washington now had ample facilities for bivouacking and resupplying the men. McClellan had long ago established an effective system of provost guards to round up stragglers, and the veteran regiments had their own well-used means of restoring discipline and establishing well-ordered encampments. The turnabout in army morale also registered the fact that their recent defeat had not been as demoralizing as the Union leadership feared or Lee hoped. Most of these men were veterans who had learned how to estimate the merits of their own performance. Their sense of Second Bull Run was that they had fought well but that their generals had misled them. They appreciated McClellan's virtues but did not hero-worship him. Those who had served on the Peninsula knew him to be capable of failure and understood that he had limitations. Still, with McClellan in charge they would not have to fear the kind of high-risk blunders of which Pope was guilty; and they knew he would do his best to see that they were kept healthy, well fed, and even well rested.

McClellan would also have to figure out how to make immediate use of the half-trained newly recruited regiments that had been arriving in the capital for the past two months. Anticipating this problem even before he left the Peninsula, he had already requested and received authority to assign these new regiments to existing veteran brigades without regard to their state affiliation. The idea was that the veteran outfits would teach the rookies by example and experienced brigade commanders would know how to make use of raw troops. State governors resisted the change because it limited their power to influence the appointment of brigade level officers. For once, professional wisdom overrode politics.[2]

On September 5, as the Confederates were crossing the Potomac, McClellan was ordered to assemble a large field army and assume command of its active operations. The task presented serious difficulties. Only three army corps (II, VI, and XII) were relatively fresh, having missed Pope's debacle. McClellan would have to augment this force by culling from the defeated troops gathered in Washington. He would also have to integrate units, general officers, and staffs from Pope's army and his own. The personal and political antipathies that had divided Pope's loyalists from McClellan's acolytes were now augmented by grievances born of the recent defeat: the suspicion in Pope's army that McClellan had deliberately allowed them to be beaten; the anger among McClellanites that Pope had wasted their lives and their valor and blamed their generals for his own ineptitude. Among the rank and file, McClellan's veterans showed disdain for the lackluster record of Pope's men, who resented the aspersion of their courage.

McClellan's integration of the Armies of the Potomac and Virginia was part reorganization, part purge. He kept Porter, Sumner, Franklin, and Heintzelman in command of the corps they had led on the Peninsula (V, II, VI, and III), though Heintzelman's Corps was too badly damaged to take the field. Pope's Corps commanders, McDowell, Sigel, and Banks, were relieved, and the politically powerful Banks was mollified by appointment to command of the Washington garrison.

Franklin and Porter were longtime friends and supporters of McClellan. Both were well tried by combat on the Peninsula. Franklin had shown competence in command of VI Corps, though he did not move his units with energy or speed. Porter was the best of the corps commanders in large-scale combat. His V Corps had borne the brunt of the fighting throughout the Seven Days, and for part of the time during McClellan's absence Porter had effectively commanded the whole army. It was not certain that all of his corps could take the field, because it had taken heavy losses at Second Bull Run; but McClellan relied heavily on Porter's advice and would insist that Porter and the division of Regular Army units from his V Corps go with him into the field.

Major General Edwin Vose Sumner commanded II Corps, the strongest in the army: nearly eighteen thousand veteran troops under experienced division and brigade commanders. Sumner was brave to a fault but as a corps commander utterly out of his depth. Born in 1797, at sixty-five he was the oldest man to serve as a field general in the Civil War, and his understanding of tactics, which may never have been acute, was long out of date. His nickname was "Old Bull Head," which aptly describes his courage and his intellectual limitations. His virtues had been well displayed on the Peninsula. At Seven Pines and again during the Seven Days he had saved the army from disaster by marching to the sound of the guns, orders and obstacles be damned. The problem was that once engaged he had no judgment, no grasp of the situation beyond what his eyes could see, no understanding of how the action in front of him related to the battle or campaign as a whole.[3]

McClellan promoted Major General Joseph Hooker to command McDowell's Corps, now renumbered I Corps. "Fighting Joe" Hooker was forty-eight, fair, floridly handsome, and clean-shaven, with a reputation for bravery, unscrupulous ambition, and a rakehell social life. He had graduated from West Point in 1837 and had prewar combat experience against the Seminoles and in Mexico, but he had left the army in the 1850s for an unsuccessful fling at farming in California. Lincoln commissioned him as brigadier general right after Bull Run, and McClellan put him in command of a division in the III Corps. Hooker earned his nickname during the Peninsula campaign, as he led his division with dash and efficiency in several major engagements. While his courage and competence as a combat general were never questioned, Hooker had a well-earned reputation as a striver and schemer for personal advancement. Although he was not a Radical in politics, he had developed a close relationship with Secretary Chase, who would become his backer in his quest for army command.

Sigel's and Banks's troops became the Army of the Potomac's XI and XII Corps. The former would remain in the Washington defenses when the army took the field. The latter would be temporarily led by Brigadier General Alpheus Williams, the senior division commander, until a major general could be found to fill the appointment. Williams was fifty-two, and his most striking physical characteristic were the magnificent mustachios that swept out nearly a foot to either side above his grizzled chin-beard. His only prewar experience was in the Michigan state militia, but he had actually performed quite well as a division commander.

General Burnside retained command of IX Corps. Two of his divisions under Brigadier General Jesse Reno had suffered in Pope's defeat. Reno had graduated with McClellan in the Class of 1846 and had remained an artillery officer in the Regulars until the Civil War. He had led a brigade and later a division in Burnside's North Carolina campaign, where he proved his competence in small-scale actions. At Second Bull Run he had handled his two divisions well under the impossible conditions produced by Pope's incompetence and managed their retreat without letting them become disorganized.

Burnside also gained two fresh divisions. One had served in his North Carolina campaign, and the other was the "Kanawha Division," which had operated independently in West Virginia under the command of Brigadier General Jacob Cox. Cox was thirty-four, another amateur soldier who had proved he could learn on the job. He had studied for the ministry at Oberlin, a college noted for its radical experimentation with both religious doctrine and social reform, and became a committed abolitionist. Instead of the ministry, Cox pursued a career in law and politics, served as a militia officer, and became a Republican political leader in the state of Ohio. He served efficiently under McClellan in West Virginia and won a general's star, and, despite his politics, McClellan had entrusted him with important field commands. Nevertheless, he had no experience in the command of large forces in combat.[4]

McClellan also tried to remedy the misuse of cavalry that had marked his own operations as well as Pope's. He regrouped regiments that had been scattered among various division and corps commands in a unified division under Brigadier General Alfred Pleasonton and sent them out to probe Lee's position at Frederick. Pleasonton was one of McClellan's inner circle of friends and supporters, an experienced cavalry officer who had served in that arm on the frontier and in Mexico after graduating from West Point in 1844. The new organization would eventually allow the Union cavalry to develop into a powerful military instrument, even if, for the present, it was unable to pierce Jeb Stuart's cavalry screen. McClellan's military intelligence was therefore as bad as ever. On September 7 Pleasonton reported that Lee had thirty thousand men at Frederick and another sixty thousand sweeping north and east to capture Baltimore, and that General Bragg with another forty thousand was rumored to be in the Shenandoah. The next day Pleasonton reported, on the basis of unreliable civilian observations, that Lee had a hundred thousand troops and was about to invade Pennsylvania.[5]

While Lee's entire force cannot have been larger than seventy-two thousand and Bragg's army was in east Tennessee, preparing to invade Kentucky, Lee's invasion fostered the illusion of a triumphant Confederate grand army riding the crest of victory. The result was panic among civilians throughout the northeast. The governors of Pennsylvania and Maryland called out the militia and stridently demanded protection from Washington. Pennsylvania Governor Curtin appealed directly to McClellan, bypassing the War Department. McClellan reassured the governor that if the Rebels did menace his state, "I shall act with all possible vigor."[6]

McClellan did move promptly, albeit cautiously, into the field. With only fifty-five thousand troops available for immediate service, he had good reason to be cautious. His field force was indeed outnumbered by the Confederates—though not as badly as Pleasonton led him to believe. An equivalent number of troops remained behind in the Washington fortifications, including his own III and V Corps, and the XI Corps.[7]

McClellan spread four army corps in an arc across the western approaches to Washington: Franklin's VI Corps on the left, closest to the Potomac; Sumner's II and the XII Corps from Pope's army in the center; and Burnside's IX Corps holding the right, or northern, flank, the critical post if Lee should move on Baltimore. On September 10, Federal cavalry, with infantry backing, probed Confederate positions in front of Frederick, and McClellan learned that Lee's troops were pulling out of the town—most retreating westward, and some units apparently returning to Virginia. The administration wanted him to take the offensive and at least force Lee to retreat across the Potomac. But McClellan refused to advance beyond Frederick unless the Harpers Ferry garrison was put under his command and the V Corps added to his field force. These requests for reinforcement were perfectly justified if McClellan was to meet Lee's army on equal terms. Although Lee had far fewer than the 100,000 troops with which McClellan credited him, it would require a force of 75,000 or more to mount an offensive campaign against the Army of Northern Virginia. Even so, Lincoln and Stanton's mistrust of McClellan, and Halleck's jealousy of his command privileges, made them reluctant to meet McClellan's demands.

AN ATMOSPHERE THICK WITH TREASON:
THE WASHINGTON FRONT
SEPTEMBER 3-11, 1862

The mistrust was mutual. To McClellan the menace of Lee's army at Frederick was again of less immediate concern than the malevolence of his enemies in Washington. He believed that Pope's disaster and his sudden recall to command were signs of a reversal in the tide of his political fortunes. His reputation as the nation's chief military reliance, its Great White Hope, was confirmed. The menace of Lee's invasion had made the administration feel its dependence on his military genius. His first impulse after being restored to command was to use the opportunity to finally stage his palace coup: he would refuse to save Lincoln unless the president agreed to purge Stanton from the cabinet. While Burnside had talked him out of making a move so blatantly political, in the days following McClellan's assumption of command his officers and political supporters intensified their campaign to win for McClellan greater control over civil and military policy.[8]

McClellan's headquarters had become a protective bubble, almost impenetrable by people whose ideas differed from McClellan's, let alone by actual critics. A perimeter defense manned by aides restricted access to the commanding general, admitting his military supporters, friendly journalists, and political allies, denying entrance not only to agents of the administration but even to military officers whose views or presence he had no use for. His inner circle of staff officers had been purged of potential critics and lukewarm supporters, and his circle of military confidants was small, and due for further contraction. His chief of staff, General Marcy, was also his father-in-law. Colonel Thomas Key may have been the most influential of his senior staff—critics considered him McClellan's "evil genius," for advice that maximized the general's ties to conservative Democrats.[9] Among the corps and division commanders, Franklin was a strong and loyal ally, and Fitz-John Porter, as we have seen, his most trusted confidant. At the moment Generals Burnside of IX Corps and William "Baldy" Smith, now division commander in VI Corps, were considered friends and allies. But Burnside had spoken against McClellan's ultimatum against Stanton, and Smith had expressed reservations about McClellan's political connections, and both would soon find themselves outcast from the general's circle. In the daily life of his headquarters, whether established in some large house or in tents in the field, wherever McClellan turned he heard his own opinions praised and repeated, felt his own angers and grievances as emotions shared and affirmed by all with whom he came in contact. He lived in a hall of mirrors. As he told his wife on September 7, "I have now the entire confidence of the Govt," by which he meant Lincoln, "& the love of the army . . . my enemies are crushed, silent & disarmed—if I defeat the rebels I shall be master of the situation."[10]

Public opinion did appear to be moving in his direction. James Gordon Bennett's *New York Herald* hailed McClellan's reappointment as the start of a "New Order of Things." The repulse of the Rebel invasion was now certain, and the country could rest assured that the war policy of Lincoln's administration would take a conservative direction. Bennett praised Lincoln's "firmness" in sustaining McClellan, which was "a death blow to the meddling radicals" and the "howling dervishes of abolitionism."[11] Manton Marble of the *World* was no less pleased, though his praise of McClellan was tempered. "We congratulate the nation!" he wrote on McClellan's restoration to command. "He may not have the genius of a Napoleon" but he is preferable to the "pseudo-Napoleons" lately in command, and in his hands "the capital is safe" and the army assured of prudent use. Marble then went on to strenuously condemn Stanton and the Radicals for their "slurs on Gen. McClellan and his mode of conducting the war." History would record with "amazement and shame" that such scoundrels should ever have been heeded. "The President, the army, the whole country stand aghast at the results of the system into which [Lincoln] deviated under pressure of the radicals against General McClellan."[12] Even the Republican *New York Times* took a favorable view of his ascension. Only Greeley's *Tribune* warned the president "not to lean upon broken reeds, nor to pamper incompetency, nor rely upon imbecility, in the execution of its decrees." The people would not forgive the president if he grew timid about "hurting, despoiling, or even exterminating Southern traitors, or of offending their secret coadjutors in the North."[13]

All of the actors in this political drama—Lincoln and McClellan, the cabinet and the army staff, the congressmen and newspaper editors and party notables—moved in an atmosphere still "thick with treason," or with accusations of treason, which under the circumstances were nearly as dangerous to republican government as treason itself. With a civil war raging, political hysteria rising, and the enemy at the gates of the capital, the expectation of treason might drive patriots to actions that verged on revolution. The proposal made on September 2 by Chase and Stanton, that McClellan receive "summary justice"—Chase said he should be shot—would have been akin to the guillotining of generals by the Jacobins during the French Revolution's Reign of Terror. When McClellan fulminated against the traitors and fools in the government, and fantasized about assuming the dictatorship or marching on Washington, his staff officers and senior generals, and his political backers, inevitably began thinking about when and even how such an action should be attempted, and a Napoleonic overturn of the American republic became imaginable.

Rumors were rife that a military *putsch* was in the offing. On September 13, George Templeton Strong, a wealthy New York Republican, noted in his diary, "A new and most alarming kind of talk" among the more pro-Southern Democrats in the City, to the effect that McClellan was planning to confer with former colleagues turned Confederate generals, to arrange a compromise peace which the military would then "enforce" on the two governments. On September 10 Senator Henry Wilson of Massachusetts, chairman of the Committee on Military Affairs, told Navy Secretary Welles that McClellan's staff were conspiring "for a revolution and the establishment of a provisional government." Welles dismissed Wilson as an alarmist but was deeply troubled that McClellan had made his army into a political power base whose values and purposes were at odds with those of the elected administration, "a spirit more factious and personal than patriotic." Welles believed McClellan meant to "use [the army] for his own purposes—an informant who had been privy to one of McClellan's early conferences with S. L. M. Barlow recalled McClellan saying that he "would pursue a line of policy of his own, regardless of the Administration, its wishes and objects." Lincoln himself agreed that there had indeed "been a design, a purpose in breaking down Pope, without regard of consequences to the country. It is shocking to see and know this; but there is no remedy at present, McClellan has the army with him."[14]

The most explicit threat of a military coup was passed to reporter

Nathaniel Paige of the *New York Tribune* by Colonel Thomas Key, the so-called evil genius of McClellan's staff. On September 11, as the army was bivouacking near Frederick, Key told Paige that some of his colleagues were planning to "change front on Washington" to compel the government to abjure its "abolitionist" sentiments, and thus open the way to a negotiated peace, which might recognize some form of Southern independence. These officers were, said Key, "fighting for a boundary line and not for the Union." Key swore that McClellan knew nothing of this and would have rebuked it if he had known. However, instead of informing McClellan, Key was leaking this information to a reporter for a paper that was Radical in sentiment and so hostile to McClellan that it had recently accused him of imbecility and disloyalty. Key might have been acting in good faith, seeking to warn the administration of its danger while still protecting McClellan's standing. He also might have been attempting to pressure the administration to follow McClellan's lead or face a military uprising.[15]

Horace Greeley evidently heard the threat and took it seriously. On September 12 and 13 the *Tribune* published a pair of editorials warning of "a conspiracy between the chiefs of the Rebel and Union armies to subvert the Republic and establish a Pro-slavery despotism on its ruins." Greeley took note of the proclamations made by Lee and Davis, which called for an uprising of Southern sympathizers in support of the Confederate invasion. "Our army has come among you, and is prepared to assist you with the power of its arms in regaining the rights of which you have been despoiled." He linked this appeal with another issued by Confederate agents in Canada, which suggested that what the Davis government now sought was not separation and independence but an actual *conquest* of the North—a reestablishment of the Union on a pro-slavery basis. Lee's invasion was presumably the first step in this conquest. Greeley accused the *Herald*, along with its audience of "Northern men with Southern principles," of assisting this project by fomenting "a Military conspiracy culminating in a dictatorship." The *Herald* and its claque had repeatedly called for "Gen. McClellan to disperse [Congress] with the bayonet, after the fashion of Cromwell and Bonaparte" if it did not "legislate according to the Pro-slavery programme." Now they were seizing the opportunity of Lee's invasion to resume their "diabolical work."[16]

The Cromwell reference was apropos. On September 11 a New York *Herald* editorial was urging McClellan not only to "insist upon the modification and reconstruction of the cabinet, in order to have it purged of the radical taint which may again infuse its poison over the whole," but to demand on his own account "indemnity for the past and security for the future." The latter implied some formal acknowledgment by the administration that it had been guilty of mistreating McClellan in the past, and a guarantee that his present elevation to command would not be rescinded. The *Herald* insisted such an assertion of personal power was justified, because "[t]he safety of the country is entrusted to him," and he is therefore entitled to destroy the "insidious enemy" in his rear, which threatens to disrupt his plan of campaign.[17]

Stephen Sears, whose studies of McClellan's career are both thorough and highly critical, has concluded, "It cannot be imagined that George McClellan would have lent himself to a military coup." However, there is ample evidence that McClellan's closest colleagues were actively imagining that very thing, and that the atmosphere of McClellan's headquarters allowed the possibility of a coup to be freely entertained. Even if the call to "change front on Washington" did not reflect McClellan's actual plans, it reflected beliefs and desires he had often expressed. Those who openly discussed the matter certainly did so in McClellan's interest, and if not on his instructions then almost certainly with his knowledge. In a time of crisis and an atmosphere of treason, with aggrieved officers and armed men thronging the capital, it was a dangerous suggestion to make.[18]

THE LOST ORDER, SEPTEMBER 11–13, 1862

Military victory offered McClellan a clearer, cleaner, and more certain path to power than a coup at Washington: "if I defeat the rebels I shall be master of the situation." Still, he could not defeat Lee's army by standing on the defensive in the Washington suburbs while Confederates ravaged the countryside and raided into Pennsylvania. Some kind of counteroffensive had to be undertaken. It would be extraordinarily risky to confront Lee's "superior" force in a general engagement, but he could count *himself* victorious if he merely compelled Lee to abandon his invasion and retreat to Virginia. If he kept his forces well concentrated and properly positioned they could repel any attack Lee might make and impose losses serious enough to force a Confederate withdrawal, while not risking a decisive battle. Even a campaign of maneuver might induce Lee to retire without a fight—he could not stay indefinitely north of the Potomac with a concentrated Army of the Potomac dogging his heels. So despite the weakness of his force, of which he was painfully aware, and Lee's strength (which he grossly overrated), McClellan was more than willing to "act with all possible vigor."[19]

While Lee remained at Frederick, McClellan was uncertain whether to prepare for an opportunistic advance or a desperate defense. When he learned (on September 10) that Lee's forces had pulled out of Frederick, and that part of Lee's army (Walker's Division) had returned to Virginia, McClellan ordered his entire force to advance and called for reinforcements that would allow him to pursue and strike an enemy that might be on the retreat. On September 11, he wrote Halleck that he was opposed by a "gigantic rebel army" of 120,000 men, and though he was willing to confront that army with his own inferior force he was doubtful of the outcome and feared that "if we should be defeated the consequences to the country would be disastrous in the extreme." He therefore renewed his request for the Harpers Ferry garrison and at least one of the three army corps currently reorganizing in Washington.[20]

The Confederate army was moving west and away from Washington, clearly designing to pick off the garrison at Harpers Ferry. Such a move could either indicate a general withdrawal into Virginia via the upstream fords of the Potomac or be a mere preliminary to the renewal of offensive action out of western Maryland. As he advanced toward Frederick, McClellan was still expecting Lee to turn and attack him. He told his wife that he expected "to fight a great battle," but it would be a defensive one: "I do not think the secesh will catch me very badly." To Halleck he wrote that he thought himself safe unless attacked by "overwhelming" force; and when Halleck urged him to beware of an attack on Washington, McClellan answered that a defeat to his army would be far more dangerous to the nation than the loss of the capital. Aside from exposing the fact that McClellan still identified the national cause exclusively with his own fate and that of his army, these dispatches indicate that, as late as September 11, McClellan thought defensive operations more likely than an offensive.[21]

However, on that most eventful day McClellan received word that Lincoln had acceded to his requests: Harpers Ferry was now under his command (too late for that to do any good), and two divisions of V Corps led by the loyal Fitz-John Porter were marching to join him at Frederick. No other reinforcement could have been so gratifying to McClellan. Porter was his staunchest ally, and in sending him forward Halleck was also setting aside the charges that had been filed against Porter by John Pope.

McClellan also received reports (mainly from civilian sources) that seemed to indicate Lee might be planning to retreat into Virginia. They confirmed the news that Lee's main body had gone west, passing over both Catoctin Mountain and the longer, higher ridge of South Mountain, to Boonsboro; that some troops had already returned to Virginia (this was Walker's Division, marching on Harpers Ferry); and that a large column (it was Jackson's) had recrossed the Potomac well upstream from Harpers Ferry. It was possible that Lee's army was "skedaddling," as he wrote to Mary Ellen. It was certain that Lee's army was divided, but the proportions were unknown, and the fact that Lee had risked such division was an indication of his army's superior strength.

Nevertheless, McClellan for once seemed determined to strike a blow. Buoyed by these reports, by reinforcements, and by the evidence they gave of his power with the administration, McClellan began to consider an offensive that would rescue Harpers Ferry and "catch" Lee's army before its elements could recombine or recross the Potomac. On September 13 McClellan ordered Pleasonton's cavalry, with a division of Burnside's IX Corps infantry behind it, to break through the Confederate cavalry defending the passes through Catoctin Mountain and find out where and how Lee's army was positioned.

Those operations were already under way when a dispatch arrived at his headquarters from General Alpheus Williams, temporarily commanding the XII Corps. An enlisted man, Corporal Barton Mitchell of the Twenty-seventh Indiana, had found an envelope lying on the ground that contained three cigars and a copy of Special Order No. 191, issued by General Lee on September 9, which laid out in detail the planned movements of Lee's divided army over the past five days.

The finding of this lost order was a turning point in the campaign and an event so unlikely, and so charged with ironies, that it has become historical legend. It was an unearned intelligence coup for McClellan, whose generalship was marked by abysmal incompetence in gathering and handling intelligence. It was a catastrophic piece of bad luck for Lee, which wrecked his plan of campaign and gave the cautious and slow-moving McClellan the confidence to assume the offensive and advance with greater energy and determination than he had ever shown.

McClellan got his hands on the orders late in the morning of September 13 and instantly recognized the opportunity they afforded to catch and defeat Lee's army. He dashed off a dispatch to Lincoln at noon in which he boldly declared, "I have all the plans of the Rebels and will catch them in their own trap if my men are equal to the emergency. I now feel I can count on them as of old." He told the president that the army was already in motion "as rapidly as possible." It is evidence of his exalted self-confidence that he would promise so much to a president who always demanded more speed and harder fighting than McClellan was willing to deliver. When General John Gibbon, commander of I Corps' "Iron Brigade," stopped in at headquarters later that afternoon, McClellan told him that Lee had committed a serious blunder in dividing his army and that with that information, "if I cannot whip Bobbie Lee, I will be willing to go home." If Gibbon and his comrades would give him two days' hard marching he would "pitch into [Lee's] centre" while his army's wings were divided, the way Napoleon I had beaten the Austrians at Castiglione in 1796.[22]

In his conversation with Gibbon, in his telegram to Halleck, and in the orders he later issued to Franklin, McClellan declared his intention to achieve a "decisive" result. That word "decisive" seems to imply an intention to seek a Napoleonic triumph, in which the opposing army is virtually destroyed and the war effectively won. Gibbon certainly understood it that way: after speaking to McClellan, Gibbon told his men that they would soon get the Rebels "in such a tight place they could never get out."[23]

But McClellan had a different understanding of what, under the circumstances, would count as decisive victory. It is telling that he used the Battle of Castiglione as an analogy to his current operation. In that campaign Napoleon's army, besieging Mantua, was outnumbered by Austrian forces advancing to the city's relief. Napoleon maneuvered deftly to keep the Austrian forces divided, then concentrated a superior force to defeat the largest relief column at Castiglione. However, the result was neither tactically nor strategically decisive. Castiglione merely compelled one Austrian relief column to retreat. The siege would continue for six months, during which Napoleon had to fight seven more general engagements to repel Austrian relief operations.

From McClellan's perspective, any action that compelled Lee's invading column to retreat from Maryland would be "decisive," because it would confirm his standing as the indispensable man and enable him to become "master of the situation" in the ongoing struggle to control Lincoln's administration. If he could confront Lee at Boonsboro before Jackson could complete his conquest of Harpers Ferry, he would compel Lee to choose between fighting McClellan's superior force and a withdrawal to Virginia. Knowing what he himself would do in Lee's place, McClellan was drawn to the thought that Lee would retreat—hence his supposition that he might have to "catch" Lee before he got away.

McClellan would still have to guard against Lee's boldness. The lost order was four days old, and in that time Lee might well have altered his plans. Intelligence had indicated there were large enemy forces at Martinsburg—were these new troops, or was this merely belated news of Jackson's Corps? If the latter, were they en route to Harpers Ferry or poised to rejoin Lee? To the cautious McClellan it was inconceivable that Lee would have so divided his army unless he had indeed disposed of superior forces. The 120,000 estimate he reported to Halleck had no basis in any report from scouts or informants, and it significantly, perhaps purposely, exaggerated the estimate of 100,000 reported by Pleasonton. However, even at Pleasonton's estimate, McClellan's total strength of about 75,000 was weaker than Lee's. According to the lost order at least half of Lee's army was concentrated at Boonsboro, twenty miles away by the National Road from Frederick. To assail it, McClellan's troops might have to first fight their way through the passes of Catoctin Mountain, and then through the steeper, narrower passes of South Mountain, ideally suited to defense. Moreover, McClellan could not throw his whole force against Boonsboro. He had to send a large detachment to the relief of Harpers Ferry, using a separate and parallel route of march twelve miles to the south. That would leave him fewer than sixty thousand to oppose Lee's estimated fifty-plus thousand in a strong defensive position. If Lee's force held out, Jackson might be able to rejoin him. Their united force would considerably outnumber McClellan's, who would then have to choose between defeat by superior forces or ignominious retreat—neither of which would make him "master of the situation" in Washington.[24]

McClellan's dispatches to Halleck reflected his ambivalence. At 8:45 PM on the thirteenth he assured Halleck that the whole of Lee's army was before him and added: "Will soon have decisive battle." Three hours later, his detailed report was far more circumspect. Although he enjoyed the advantage of knowing how Lee's force was divided, "they outnumber me when united." He was moving to relieve Harpers Ferry and expected "a severe engagement tomorrow" but warned Halleck that "we may be too late." It was vital that Halleck understand that, though he did not "undervalue" the safety of Washington, "upon the success of this Army the fate of the nation depends." It was a restatement of the fundamental premise of McClellan's strategy: that the Army of the Potomac must not risk a serious defeat. If he had earlier oversold his prospects of triumph to Lincoln, he was now underselling them to Halleck.[25]

McClellan's operational orders reflected a sort of judicious daring. For his own reasons he knew he had to take the offensive, and so for the first time he showed a willingness to meet Lincoln's requirement that field commanders use their available force, whatever the risk, to achieve necessary military goals. His plan was to attack a detachment under Lee that he believed was not much weaker than the numbers he could bring against it. He would advance more boldly, with greater speed and urgency than ever, yet still at a measured pace that would keep his forces concentrated for mutual support.[26]

His army would advance in two columns. McClellan himself would command the main force, which would follow the National Road from Frederick to Boonsboro, crossing South Mountain at Turner's Gap. The cavalry would lead, backed by the Kanawha Division commanded by Brigadier General Jacob Cox, recently attached to IX Corps. The rest of IX Corps would follow, with Hooker's I Corps coming up behind it.

McClellan assigned Burnside to command this advance force (between 25,000 and 28,000), while McClellan brought up the XII, II and V Corps (30,000). With luck this force might catch Longstreet's wing with its elements divided and defeat it in detail. Failing that, McClellan would at least hold Lee's strength in front of Boonsboro and prevent his interference with the relief of Harpers Ferry.

In a strategic sense, the relief of Harpers Ferry was the most critical aspect of the operation. If it succeeded it would save 13,000 troops from capture while also potentially giving McClellan the chance for a substantial, perhaps even a decisive, military victory over the separate components of Lee's army. Conversely, if the relief failed and Jackson seized Harpers Ferry, Lee might be able to reunite his army and confront the Federal army with what McClellan believed were superior numbers. The relief column was entrusted to Major General William Franklin, his old friend and supporter, who commanded two divisions of the VI Corps (13,000) camped just south of Frederick, and a division transferred from IV Corps (6,500), commanded by Brigadier General Darius Couch, which was still some distance behind. McClellan wanted Franklin to cross Catoctin Mountain south of the National Road, then strike for Crampton's Gap in South Mountain. If his corps broke through the gap, Franklin could then turn south to attack McLaws's command, which, as the lost order showed, was the only part of Jackson's Corps north of the Potomac.[27]

Although McClellan was committing his whole force to the offensive, he also hedged against the risks he was assuming by enjoining Burnside and Franklin to advance with caution. His orders to Burnside were given orally, but the written orders to Franklin indicate the balance between boldness and anxiety that shaped his tactics. He told Franklin he intended to "cut the enemy in two & beat him in detail" by striking Boonsboro quickly and in strength. No considerations "should for a moment interfere with the decisive results I hope to gain." A degree of urgency was suggested by McClellan's unwonted demand that they march at daybreak—a more energetic commander might have had them march that evening, even though a night march is more difficult and risky. Nor did McClellan demand that they push their commands forward by forced marches. Instead, McClellan warned Franklin to keep his troops well concentrated, "prevent straggling & bring every available man into action" lest the Confederates surprise him with one of those rapid concentrations at which Lee and Jackson were so adept.[28]

The ambiguity in these orders is significant. McClellan knew that Franklin was characteristically slow in conducting operations—so much so that McClellan had complained to his wife about it, and considered relieving him of command. Knowing that, McClellan still did not urge Franklin to move with speed but rather encouraged caution and circumspection. The pace of Burnside's column was similarly regulated to allow its elements to close up for mutual support.

McClellan, moving more aggressively than ever before, had to take what advantage he could of the situation exposed by the lost order. Nevertheless, his aggressive intent was modulated by the fundamental principle that forbade endangering the safety of his own force. He could not catch Lee at a disadvantage at Boonsboro, or break the encirclement of Harpers Ferry, without ordering the advance elements of his command to rush forward and engage the enemy before the main body of the army could come up. But to do that was to expose those detachments to defeat or destruction, and McClellan saw no need to run that risk. If he could confront Lee's divided force with his own army mostly united, Lee would be compelled to retreat—and that would be victory enough to solidify McClellan's standing as hero of the hour.

LEE ON THE DEFENSIVE, SEPTEMBER 12-14, 1862

On September 13, Lee was with Longstreet at Hagerstown, tired out by the long journey from Frederick, still suffering from the fall that had disabled him. He had had some notice that McClellan's army was on the move. On the twelfth, Stuart had informed Lee that Federal troops had occupied Frederick and that he was surprised by McClellan's relatively rapid advance. The very next day, Stuart reported that Federal cavalry, with infantry support, had broken through the units he had posted on Catoctin Mountain to screen Lee's withdrawal from Federal observation. Still, Catoctin Mountain was only the first of the two ridgelines that stood between McClellan's army at Frederick and Lee's at Boonsboro, and the Federal force that had broken through was not large enough to defeat the defense D. H. Hill's Division could offer at South Mountain. Lee therefore judged the threat of a large-scale attack was not imminent.

Then at eight that evening, Lee received shocking news. By a coincidence almost as outrageous as the finding of the lost order, a Maryland civilian and Confederate sympathizer had been at McClellan's headquarters when the dispatch was being read. Although the civilian did not know what the dispatch contained, McClellan's enthusiastic outcry, "Now I know what to do!," and the flurry of orders that followed, suggested the find was significant. The civilian rode away and made contact with Confederate cavalry. By five in the evening the news had reached Stuart. Whether or not Stuart guessed that McClellan had seen a copy of Lee's General Order No. 191, the civilian's report suggested that McClellan had discovered the division of Lee's army and was moving to exploit it. The burden of Stuart's message was confirmed by a report from D. H. Hill, that the valley below Turner's Gap was filled with the campfires of Federal infantry, indicating that McClellan's main body was moving against Boonsboro.

Lee's campaign was now in extreme peril. The vanguard of McClellan's army was approaching Turner's Gap, less than ten miles from Boonsboro, in a force large enough to overwhelm Hill's single division defending the center of Lee's far-flung army. The nearest reinforcement for Hill was the infantry of Longstreet's Corps, which was some twenty miles away at Hagerstown. On the map it looked possible for McClellan to smash through Hill's defense, then turn north to attack Longstreet's heavily outnumbered divisions and threaten the army's artillery reserve and supply train. At the same time, the VI Corps might break through Crampton's Gap to relieve Harpers Ferry. If it did, McClellan's army would be in position to cut the Valley route that supplied Lee's army, and to interpose itself between that army and Richmond; and that would compel Lee to either assault the Army of the Potomac head-on or make a desperate march through the West Virginia mountains to get around McClellan's flank.[29]

All through the evening of September 13 and late into the night, Lee was intensely engaged in building a clear picture of the tactical situation and developing plans to deal with it. Not only did he need current intelligence on the enemy's movements, he also needed to find out where the several elements of Jackson's wing were located and how far they had advanced toward the capture of Harpers Ferry. He had had no reports from Jackson for two days. His requests for information, and the responses, were delayed to the pace of mounted couriers riding over the thirty miles of roads and river fords to Jackson, over twenty or more miles of mountain road to Stuart. As reports came in he had to translate the emerging intelligence into plans of action, and orders, for defending the two most vulnerable points on his line: Turner's Gap, and McLaws's position on Maryland Heights.

It was still possible to avoid catastrophe if prompt action was taken to delay McClellan's advance. McClellan would have to attack through the South Mountain gaps, which were ideally suited to defense. D. H. Hill's Division, with support from Stuart, was positioned to defend the northern gaps on the roads to Boonsboro. They would have to hold off McClellan's main body long enough for Longstreet's infantry to come to their support. With his northern elements reunited at Boonsboro, Lee could fight a delaying action that would enable Jackson to complete the conquest of Harpers Ferry. Should things go badly, Longstreet's Corps would still have a line of retreat to Virginia, via Sharpsburg and the fords at Shepherdstown.

Lee therefore ordered Hill to defend the South Mountain gaps to the last extremity, and Longstreet to join Hill by a forced march from Hagerstown. Jeb Stuart and two of his three brigades were still in the Turner's Gap area, and Lee wanted them to stay there and assist in prolonging Hill's defense. But Lee's orders were badly worded—perhaps the result of physical exhaustion, the lingering effects of his injuries, and the strain of sudden crisis in the dark of a long day. Stuart thought Lee wanted him to defend Crampton's Gap, and he rode off southward with his whole command—except for one regiment, the Fifth Virginia, left behind by mistake.

Since the outcome of this defensive operation was most uncertain, Lee also thought it prudent to get the army's slow-moving wagon train, with its reserves of ammunition and equipment, out of harm's way. He ordered the trains and the army's artillery reserve back to Virginia via the six-mile road that ran south from Hagerstown to Williamsport.

Lee was also gravely concerned about the threat posed to McLaws's Division by VI Corps' advance on Crampton's Gap. He had had no

reports from McLaws for two days and did not know whether he had succeeded in capturing Maryland Heights or was still embattled on his front
and unaware of the threat approaching from his rear. So far as Lee knew,
the only defense in Crampton's Gap was Munford's cavalry brigade: a
few hundred troopers with short-range carbines facing thirteen thousand infantry with heavy guns. If Franklin crashed through the cavalry
screen he could wheel south through Pleasant Valley and hit McLaws's
position on Maryland Heights from the rear. If Harpers Ferry was still
holding out, McLaws would be isolated and trapped between the garrison and Franklin's corps.

Lee did what little he could to aid a command with which he was
completely out of touch. He sent several dispatches to McLaws, warning
of the approaching danger and suggesting possible lines of retreat, by
which McLaws could evade Franklin and rejoin the army at Boonsboro
or Sharpsburg; but he cautioned that his suggestions were subordinate
to whatever orders McLaws might in the meantime receive from Jackson.

McLAWS'S SITUATION WAS less dangerous than Lee feared, but still precarious. On the morning of September 13, McLaws's assault brigades
had advanced against the Federal defense line on Maryland Heights.
Instead of a strong and well-entrenched force of infantry and artillery,
they found a scratch force of 1,600 Federals, most of whom belonged
to the 126th New York, whose men had only been in uniform for three
weeks and had barely learned the manual of arms. The position did hold a
powerful artillery battery of three heavy rifled guns and four short-range
smoothbores—but they had been posted to fire on enemies approaching
via the river valley, and could not be used to defend against an attack
from the north. This inadequate and badly conceived defense was the
responsibility of Colonel Miles, who had been advised to strongly fortify Maryland Heights and had done nothing about it. When the Confederates charged, the New Yorkers broke and ran, spreading disorder
among the troops behind them. The veteran thirty-second Ohio tried to
hold the line, but it soon fired away all of its ammunition. Colonel Ford,
who commanded the outpost, sent to Miles for reinforcements, to which
Miles responded, "You can't have another damned man. . . . If you can't

hold it, leave it." Ford spiked his guns and rolled them down the slope, then led his survivors across a pontoon bridge and into Harpers Ferry.[30]

The loss of Maryland Heights cut off the garrison's route of escape to the north and was sufficient in itself to make Harpers Ferry untenable once McLaws planted his artillery on the heights. Miles was also hemmed in on the southeast by Walker's Division, which had seized Loudon Heights, and Jackson's twenty thousand were approaching from the northwest, threatening to envelop the garrison. Miles concentrated his entire force in a perimeter around the town of Harpers Ferry and established a defensive line on Bolivar Heights. But the position was so tight that every part of it could be swept by Walker's and McLaws's guns. Miles did nothing to disrupt Jackson's deployment, which would bring overwhelming strength to bear against Bolivar Heights.

Nevertheless, despite Miles's incompetent defensive measures, McLaws's command was still in some peril. The original garrison of Harpers Ferry was larger than Lee or his generals had anticipated, and the arrival of General White's command from Martinsburg had raised their number to nearly thirteen thousand. A force of that size, if it had determined leadership, could hold out for days, despite the advantages of number and position enjoyed by the Confederates. Colonel Miles was not a very determined leader, but even he believed that the garrison could hold out for one more day. On the night of the thirteenth he sent a staff officer, Captain Russell, through enemy lines with a message to McClellan, describing his situation and warning that if relief did not reach him first he would have to surrender on September 15.

If Franklin broke through Crampton's Gap on the fourteenth, and moved swiftly against Maryland Heights, McLaws's command might well be trapped between the hammer and the anvil.

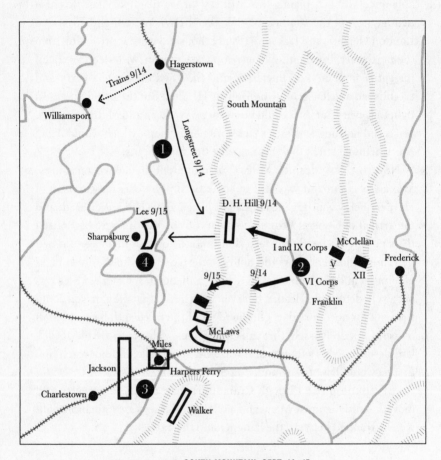

MAP 3: SOUTH MOUNTAIN, SEPT. 14–15

1. Longstreet reinforces D. H. Hill at Turner's Gap; C.S. trains withdraw
2. U.S. IX and I Corps attack Turner's Gap; VI Corps attacks Crampton's Gap
3. Colonel Miles (U.S.) surrenders Sept. 15
4. Lee (C.S.) takes position at Sharpsburg

CHAPTER 9

THE BATTLES OF SOUTH MOUNTAIN

SEPTEMBER 14, 1862

❦

THE ARMIES FOUGHT THREE BATTLES ON SEPTEMBER 14. EACH was tactically separate from the rest, but they were, in effect, phases of a single far-flung engagement in which Lee resisted McClellan's attempt to exploit the opportunity created by the finding of the Lost Order.[1]

The long, rugged ridge of South Mountain separated the opposing armies. It could be crossed by troops with artillery at two points. The northernmost was Turner's Gap, where the National Road linking Frederick with Boonsboro crossed the mountain; and adjacent to Turner's were smaller gaps crossed by country roads, the most important being Fox's Gap, one mile south. McClellan's main force would follow this route to confront Lee's detachment of the Army of Northern Virginia. Twelve miles south as the crow flies, but almost twice that by road, was Crampton's Gap, where another road crossed the mountain into Pleasant Valley. For an army north of the Potomac this offered the most direct route to Maryland Heights, and it was the route by which VI Corps was marching to effect the relief of Harpers Ferry.

At Harpers Ferry itself, the morning of the fourteenth saw the Confederates completing their encirclement of the garrison. Walker's Division (five thousand) occupied Loudon Heights, southeast of town on the far side of the Shenandoah River. McLaws's command was in possession of Maryland Heights on the north bank of the Potomac, and his men were swinging axes and shovels to hack a path for their artillery through the woody thickets along the ridgeline of Elk Mountain. When their guns were in position they would be able to sweep every part of the Union lines. Jackson's command (twenty thousand) was completing its march from Martinsburg, emerging from the hills and marching across the open ground in front of Bolivar Heights south of the town. Although every element necessary to force the surrender of the post was on the scene, it would take Jackson all day to put his forces in position to make victory certain. His troops had to deploy and begin its advance against Bolivar Heights, working itself forward to a position close enough to allow Jackson's artillery to support an infantry assault. A. P. Hill's Light Division would have to push its way through the woods along the Shenandoah River, seeking a position from which it could assail Bolivar Heights from the flank. Jackson was also having great difficulty establishing effective communication with the commands of Walker and McLaws. The peculiar terrain around Harpers Ferry, which had made it necessary for the three columns to move independently, made it impossible for them to establish direct contact. Walker was separated from Jackson by the Shenandoah River and the open country at the foot of Loudon Heights. McLaws was cut off from both Jackson and Walker by the Potomac River—the only bridge in his sector led straight to the Union lines at Harpers Ferry.

McLaws was almost completely isolated, in a position vulnerable to attack by Federal forces moving through Crampton's Gap. His communication with Jackson was tenuous. There was no physical contact between the commands and they could only communicate by using signal flags. Lee could offer him no material aid, and although he sent several dispatches offering advice, he would not give McLaws any orders. McLaws had been apprised of the danger from Crampton's Gap, but he was deeply absorbed in his primary mission of bringing his artillery onto Maryland Heights. He had sent only two small infantry brigades to hold Crampton's Gap, and they had been joined during the night by two brigades of Stuart's cavalry that had ridden down from Turner's Gap.

TURNER'S GAP, DAWN TO 2:00 PM

Lee's immediate concern on September 14 was to prevent McClellan from smashing through D. H. Hill's Division at Turner's Gap and striking Longstreet's Divisions before they could be concentrated for the defense of Boonsboro. If that defense failed he would have to make a hasty retreat to Virginia, to save his army's supply train and artillery reserve and prevent the destruction of Longstreet's divisions.

Although McClellan credited Lee with fifty thousand troops concentrated at Boonsboro, he probably had fewer than half that number. Longstreet's and D. H. Hill's commands might have mustered twenty-six thousand men at the start of the campaign, but by the fourteenth, straggling had reduced their strength dramatically. Hill had no more than eight thousand of all arms, Longstreet fifteen thousand or fewer because he had to detach several regiments to guard the army's trains and artillery as they withdrew toward Williamsport. Moreover, on the morning of September 14 the elements of the defending force were still divided. Longstreet's troops had been marching all night from Hagerstown and would have to make a forced march from Boonsboro to reach the gaps by 1:00 PM, losing strength to straggling as they came. Three of Hill's brigades had bivouacked near Boonsboro and would not reach Turner's Gap until noon. At daybreak on the fourteenth the only forces in place to defend the gaps were two brigades of Hill's Division and a single cavalry regiment, about 2,300 men. They faced an immediate assault by the infantry of Cox's Kanawha Division and Pleasonton's cavalry, about 8,000 strong. Fortunately for Hill, the Union IX Corps would not break camp until 10:30 AM, and its infantry would not begin to arrive until noon, by which time the rest of Hill's units would be at hand and Longstreet's troops would be approaching the gaps from the west. Hooker's Corps had a much longer march—fourteen miles from Monocacy Junction—and would not reach the field until well after noon.

Major General Daniel H. Hill was noted equally for his piety and a sarcastic manner that did not endear him to his superiors. He was forty years old, West Point Class of 1842; had distinguished himself in combat during the Mexican War, then resigned his commission in 1849 to teach mathematics at Washington College, Davidson College, and the North Carolina Military Institute. As a colonel of North Carolina troops in June 1861 he had won the first post-Sumter skirmish of the war, at Big Bethel, Virginia, and was immediately promoted to brigadier general. He was promoted to major general during the Peninsula campaign, where he proved to be one of the abler division commanders. Though his difficult personality would eventually lead Lee to transfer him out of the Army of Northern Virginia, both Lee and Longstreet thought he had the tactical skill and aggressive instincts needed for the desperate defense of Turner's Gap.

The main route through Turner's Gap was easy to defend. At the crest, the National Road ran through a narrow passage between high, wooded hills. With fieldworks across the low ground and riflemen on the slopes, Colquitt's Brigade of about 1,000 infantry and a battery could hold its ground against a much larger force. However, one mile north and one mile south of Turner's there were other gaps, reached by roads branching off the National Road. Fox's Gap to the south was the larger of these, a saddle half a mile wide, separated from Turner's Gap by a steep wooded ridge. There was another, smaller set of gaps to the north, but the terrain there was more rugged and heavily wooded, and the gaps harder to approach. D. H. Hill lacked the strength to cover all three gaps, so he used his lone cavalry regiment to screen the northern gap and sent Brigadier General Samuel Garland's Brigade to cover Fox's Gap.

Federal General Jacob Cox brought his Kanawha Division forward early in the morning, assessed the strength of the Turner's Gap position, and decided to turn it by striking through Fox's Gap. His lead brigade, three thousand men with an artillery battery, peeled off the National Road and trudged up through the woods to the cleared ground at the top of the pass. Among the regiments led by brigade commander Colonel Eliakim Scammon was the Twenty-third Ohio, commanded by Lieutenant Colonel Rutherford B. Hayes, which included a platoon led by Sergeant William McKinley. Hayes would be wounded that day, McKinley would pass unscathed, but both would survive to be elected president of the United States.

Scammon made contact with Garland's line and deployed his brigade into line. He outnumbered Garland three to one. The Federals opened up with shell fire and musketry, then advanced in a line that outflanked Garland left and right. The Twelfth North Carolina, a rookie regiment, broke and ran, and Garland was killed trying to hold the rest of the brigade together. By 10:00 AM Fox's Gap had been cleared.

Cox might have been able to drive the rest of D. H. Hill's troops off South Mountain if he had followed up this success. His second brigade, commanded by Colonel George Crook, was right behind Scammon's. It could have passed through, swung to the right, taken the defenders of Turner's Gap in the rear, and forced them to retreat. However, Cox did not know what kind of strength the Rebels had on his front. Heavy rifle fire from skirmishers in the woods ahead suggested the presence of a large force. Cox was also far in advance of the rest of IX Corps, isolated for the moment and without support. He therefore decided to hold until the rest of IX Corps came up.

Brigadier General Jesse Reno was in command of IX Corps. He did not have the proper rank for corps command but was an experienced officer who had commanded two divisions of the corps at Second Bull Run. His orders were now coming from General Burnside, who had been commanding IX and I Corps as a "wing" of the army since September 7. Burnside delayed Reno's advance until midmorning to allow I Corps to close up. It was not until 10:30 AM that IX Corps broke camp and began its march up the National Road, with Willcox's Division in the lead followed by the divisions of Sturgis and Rodman. Perhaps an hour behind Rodman were the advance elements of I Corps, which had marched at daybreak from its encampment south of Frederick.

As the day's fighting began, McClellan was still at his headquarters in Frederick, more than fifteen miles from Turner's Gap. At 9:00 AM Captain Russell, the messenger sent by Colonel Miles, reached him after an all-night ride, with the warning that Harpers Ferry would only be able to hold out for one more day. McClellan sent three couriers to carry his reply, urging Miles to hold out to the last extremity and assuring him relief was on the way. However, McClellan did not pass Miles's warning to Franklin or enjoin him to meet the emergency by moving faster and striking harder. And none of his messengers got through to Miles. McClellan then mounted up and rode forward to confer with Burnside, whose field headquarters were just off the National Road where it begins its rise toward Turner's Gap. General Reno's IX Corps headquarters were probably nearby.

The day was hot, temperature only in the midseventies but the air humid and heavy. Federal soldiers wore uniforms of blue wool, more durable than Southern homespun, but heavier and hotter, especially on a day when high humidity stifled the evaporation of sweat. All the corps in the northern axis of advance were queued up along a single highway, the National Road that ran from Frederick to Boonsboro. This slowed the pace of their advance and deployment. Every brigade had to wait for the one ahead of it to deploy before it could follow and go into action. They were also hindered by the terrain, which was hilly and covered with woods and thickets. The Confederates complicated things by the active use of skirmishers—small parties of riflemen spread out in advance of their main line—not only in Fox's Gap but on the hillside north of the National Road as well, where a lone cavalry regiment disputed the paths by which troops could circle behind the Turner's Gap defenses.

At noon General Orlando Willcox's Division arrived at IX Corps headquarters. Reno ordered the division to leave the National Road and go to Cox's support in Fox's Gap. Willcox's two brigades followed the rough path that Cox's Division had used earlier, but before they reached the gap they had to leave the path and move through the woods to take position at the right of Cox's line, and that disrupted their organization and slowed their movement.

At the same time, on the Confederate side the remaining three brigades of D. H. Hill's Division had finally reached Turner's Gap after a six-mile hike from Boonsboro. Hill had only Colquitt's Brigade blocking the main road through Turner's Gap, but its position at the narrowest point of the gap was extremely strong. Hill sent Rodes's Brigade to defend the small gaps one mile north of Turner's, which had been thinly held by a single regiment of cavalry. The other two brigades were sent through the woods to the south, with orders to attack and drive the Federals out of Fox's Gap. Brigadier General Roswell Ripley, who was to lead the attack, had just reached the scene and was unfamiliar with the Federal positions and blinded by the woods. The attack he ordered was disjointed, some units getting in among the Union lines and taking heavy losses while others failed even to find the enemy. Cox's and Willcox's troops easily beat back the assault.

However, the noise of that failed Confederate attack was heard at headquarters, and made Burnside worry that more strength was needed

to drive through Fox's Gap. At about 2:00 PM Burnside sent Reno with
the rest of IX Corps up the narrow track to prepare a heavy offensive,
just as Hooker's lead elements came marching up after a long hike from
Frederick. The I Corps troops roused at the sight of McClellan himself, sitting his big black horse by the roadside as they hit the upslope to
Turner's Gap. McClellan turned the moment into grand theater, with
himself as the central figure—not merely a hero but an object of worship.
A Massachusetts soldier remembered:

> It seemed as if an intermission had been declared in order that a
> reception might be tendered to the commander-in-chief. A great
> crowd continually surrounded him, and the most extravagant
> demonstrations were indulged in. Hundreds even hugged the
> horse's legs and caressed his head and mane. While the troops
> were thus surging by, the general continually pointed his finger to
> the gap . . . through which our path lay. It was like a great scene in
> a play, with the roar of the guns for an accompaniment.[2]

Burnside, with McClellan's advice, would direct the battle for the
gaps. IX Corps would soon be heavily engaged on the left at Fox's Gap. A
direct attack up the National Road was inadvisable, because the narrow-
ness of the pass would constrict the Federal battle line and funnel it right
into the guns of the defenders. Burnside therefore ordered Hooker to
swing most of his corps off to the right, and advance through the woods
to another smaller pass that broke the ridgeline a mile or so north of
Turner's Gap. The Confederates would have to stretch out their defenses
to block IX Corps at Fox's Gap and Hooker's I Corps at the northern
gap. The strength of their battle line would be attenuated, and it would
break when I and IX Corps attacked in concert.

The difficulty of moving through mountainous and heavily forested
terrain meant that these Federal maneuvers took a great deal of time.
If Burnside had not waited for Hooker but had attacked with IX Corps
alone between noon and 2: PM, he might well have driven D. H. Hill's outnumbered brigades out of the gaps. After the rout of Garland's Brigade,
Hill had fewer than seven thousand troops facing about fifteen thousand
Federals. But it was extraordinarily difficult for Burnside's officers to
establish the strength of the enemy in their front, because of the heavy

woods and the Rebels' effective use of skirmishers. Caution was justified by the best available intelligence, which indicated that half of Lee's army was no farther off than Boonsboro and might well have moved eastward in the days since the lost order was issued.

But the delay in the Federal attack insured the result they feared. At 2:00 PM the last of D. H. Hill's brigades reached Turner's Gap. Behind them were Longstreet's divisions, turning onto the National Road after a fourteen-mile march from Boonsboro. Despite his splinted arms, General Lee mounted his horse and had his aide lead him to the roadside to encourage the troops by his presence. Drayton's Division passed, followed by the division of Brigadier General John Bell Hood.

Hood had earned a reputation as the hardest-hitting offensive general in the Army of Northern Virginia. West Point–trained, tall, blond and powerfully built, his reputedly handsome features were masked by a full beard that reached to his chest. The slight downward droop of his fierce eyes gave him the look of a mournful lion. He had made his name at Gaines' Mill at the start of the Seven Days, when he led his Texas Brigade in a bayonet charge that broke the Union center and forced Porter's V Corps to begin the retreat that would end at Harrison's Landing. From that day "Hood's Texas Brigade" were rated the shock troops of the army, a reputation they vindicated at Second Bull Run when they led the charge that broke Pope's flank. They were westerners in an eastern army—and Texans to boot—frontiersmen bearing the pride of their section among strangers in the metropolis. This day Hood himself was in arrest for a minor breach of discipline. As his old Texas Brigade passed the men called out to Lee, "Give us Hood!" Lee answered, "You shall have him," and released the general from arrest in time for Hood to lead his men into action.

Though Longstreet was now the senior general on the scene, he left direction of the field to D. H. Hill, who was more familiar with the terrain and troop deployments. Hill had sent Rodes's Division to defend the gaps north of Turner's against Hooker's impending assault. He split Drayton's Division as it came up, sending half south to Fox's Gap and the rest to join Rodes; then did the same with Hood's Division, sending two of his brigades to Fox's Gap and the third to the northern flank. It would be close to 4:00 PM when they arrived, just ahead of the Federal attack.

CRAMPTON'S GAP, DAWN TO 4:00 PM

McClellan had ordered General Franklin to march at dawn on the fourteenth, break through Crampton's Gap, and relieve Harpers Ferry. Franklin's Corps was roused early in the morning and took the road at about the time Cox was making his first attack at Fox's Gap. The VI Corps had fourteen miles to march before it reached Burkittsville, at the base of the Crampton's Gap road. Slocum's division led the march and did not reach the town till noon. Yet by one of those ironies characteristic of the Antietam campaign, the delay actually improved Franklin's odds of achieving his objective.

Jeb Stuart had concentrated all but one of his available cavalry units at Crampton's Gap, on the correct assumption that a Federal drive against McLaws's rear posed the most significant danger to Confederate operations. As a result, he was confused and concerned to see the morning pass without any sign of a Federal offensive toward Burkittsville. Stuart assumed that Union forces were using a different route to effect the relief of Harpers Ferry: most likely the twisting road and railroad right-of-way that followed the north bank of the Potomac—eight miles south by air line, twice that far by road. Stuart therefore withdrew Hampton's Brigade, the largest component of his force, back through Crampton's Gap into Pleasant Valley, then rode south to the river road. He left behind a half-strength brigade to aid the two infantry brigades stationed in the gap by McLaws. Stuart told McLaws what he was doing, and in the late morning McLaws ordered an additional brigade to join the defense at the gap—"Cobb's Legion," another under-strength unit, which had been raised and was commanded by Brigadier General Howell Cobb, a former U. S. Treasury Secretary and one of the Confederacy's Founding Fathers. Then McLaws returned to his main task, trying to speed the placement of artillery on Maryland Heights to support Jackson's attack.

Slocum's Federal division arrived at Burkittsville at noon and found the town lightly held by Confederate infantry. The division deployed a heavy skirmish line and advanced, and the Rebels retreated into the gap. Slocum followed them cautiously, since he did not know the strength of the enemy ahead of him. Franklin's second division under General William "Baldy" Smith was some distance behind Slocum, and Franklin held it back as a reserve. Couch's Division had been camped far to the rear of the other divisions, and Franklin seems not to have had any idea when it might catch up. That left him with only two divisions, thirteen thousand troops, to face whatever force Lee and Jackson might have behind South Mountain. He had no way of knowing whether any of Longstreet's men had come south to block Crampton's Gap; nor did he know what was happening at Harpers Ferry, and whether some, most, or all of McLaws's command was waiting for him.

It was 2:00 PM when Slocum's division finally reached the top of Crampton's Gap. At the same time, twelve miles north, Burnside's IX and I Corps were just beginning to move into position for their assault against three Confederate divisions. Slocum had about 7,000 troops facing no more than 2,200 Confederates, and Slocum was an experienced combat leader who knew the value of prompt and energetic movement. He deployed his division in line of battle overlapping the Confederates on both flanks, raked their position with artillery, then sent the infantry forward. The Confederate regiments tried to stand their ground but they were outflanked and overwhelmed. After a short and sharp struggle, they broke down from the gap into Pleasant Valley, with Slocum's Brigades on their heels. The fugitives met Cobb's Legion on the road, and tried to rally around them, but this line, too, was outflanked and driven back to Elk Mountain. McLaws got word of the disaster and pulled as many units as he could spare off Maryland Heights and formed them for defense at the northern end of the ridge. Slocum had lost 531 men, the Confederates about 900, half of them prisoners.[3]

Two hours after Slocum's attack Franklin had two divisions in firm possession of Crampton's Gap and three hours of daylight in which to use them. Baldy Smith's Division had not had to fight that day, and Slocum's Division was probably fit for further service. Franklin's orders called for him to turn south and strike for Maryland Heights, but he was also to keep an eye out to the north. Opportunity might beckon there, to strike the Lee-Longstreet force in its southern flank; but if Lee was able to send aid to McLaws it would come from the north, and hit Franklin from the rear if he turned south. Franklin was out on a limb, uncertain of McLaws's strength and of Lee's intentions. Couch's Division had not yet caught up. No advice came from McClellan. So instead of advancing,

Franklin consolidated his defenses in the pass and waited for Couch to come up.

Historians of the campaign have criticized Franklin for not trying to complete his mission to relieve Harpers Ferry on September 14. However, it is unlikely that a continued offensive by the two divisions he had on hand would have broken through McLaws's defense on Elk Mountain and reached Harpers Ferry in time to prevent its surrender. There were only three hours of daylight remaining. Both of Franklin's divisions had made a long march that day, and Slocum's men had fought a wearing battle. The ridged and wooded terrain of Elk Mountain would have slowed even an unopposed advance along its eight-mile length, and McLaws had five thousand infantry in line to defend it.

But if the chances of an actual breakthrough were doubtful, the sounds of a continued offensive might have told Harpers Ferry that help was near, and encouraged the garrison commanders to make a stronger defense.

HARPERS FERRY, 2:00 PM TO DUSK

All that day, while the troops of Longstreet, D. H. Hill, and McLaws struggled to hold the South Mountain gaps, Jackson's Corps was completing its approach to Bolivar Heights, pushing twenty thousand infantry forward to cover the emplacement of artillery. The menace of its inexorable advance was augmented by the gunfire from Walker's Division on Loudon Heights and McLaws's gunners on Maryland Heights, which raked the town's defenses and the rear of the Bolivar Heights line.

In front of Bolivar Heights, Jackson's infantry established advanced positions right up against the thick abatis that protected the Federal line—a barrier of interlocked brush and small trees. At the same time Archer's Brigade of A. P. Hill's Division had worked down through the woods along the Shenandoah River and lined itself up to hit Bolivar Heights from the flank. However, before the infantry could storm the Heights, engineers would have to cut paths through the abatis, while the artillery would have to beat down the defenders' guns. The result was that no infantry attack could be mounted until the following day,

September 15, three full days after the date Lee had expected Harpers Ferry to be in his hands.

Nevertheless, the positions attained by Jackson's infantry and artillery made the defense of Harpers Ferry absolutely hopeless. Bolivar Heights was the only high ground from which the town could be defended, and Jackson's troops and guns would be able to hit it front, flank, and rear at first light. At nightfall Jackson sent a courier to Lee: "Through God's blessing, the advance, which commenced this evening, has been successful thus far, and I look to Him for complete success to-morrow."[4]

TURNER'S GAP, 4:00 PM TO DARK

The Federal assault on D. H. Hill's attenuated line began at 4:00 PM, just as Franklin's assault at Crampton's Gap was winding down. Hooker's I Corps was in position on the right, ready to attack the northern flank of the Confederate line. If he could break that line or even throw it back, his corps could threaten or cut the National Road and compel the Confederates to retreat from South Mountain in great haste. Hooker maneuvered his divisions effectively, forcing Hill to spread his units more thinly. Then, at the given word, the corps' three divisions surged forward, thirteen thousand infantry against about half that many Confederates.

Simultaneously, over on the Union left, Brigadier General Jesse Reno led the IX Corps in a frontal assault against the Fox's Gap line. The Federals, crossing open ground, ecountered stubborn resistance as Confederate Brigadier General John Bell Hood aided the defense with two veteran brigades and his own superb skill as a combat commander. Reno's battle lines struggled uphill against heavy fire, and Reno himself was shot from his horse with a mortal wound. Cox of the Kanawha Division was the senior officer on the scene, and he assumed command despite the fact that his division had only recently, and provisionally, been assigned to the corps. The fighting here became a furious extended stalemate, battle lines so broken by woods and thickets that command and control was problematic. Individual Union and Confederate regiments staged lone-wolf attacks, thinking to seize some local advantage, only to be cut off and cut up and driven back.

Hooker made much better progress on the right. By 5:20 PM Brigadier

General Randolph Marcy, McClellan's chief of staff, reported opposition melting away in front of I Corps. Even so, it was impossible for the victorious Federals to simply sweep through the northern gaps and cut the National Road. Pockets of resistance and the rocky thickety terrain made an organized advance difficult. As the sun sank, General Burnside thought a new assault was needed to finally break the Rebel line. He ordered Brigadier General John Gibbon's "Iron Brigade" to charge straight up the National Road and storm the defensive position where Colquitt's Brigade had been dug in for two days.

Gibbon's brigade had seen its first combat only two weeks before, but it had already earned a reputation as one of the best fighting commands in the army. Gibbon was Philadelphia-born but raised in North Carolina, an 1847 graduate of West Point who had missed seeing action in the Mexican War and spent fifteen years in the thankless task of commanding artillery units in the peacetime army. He had fought his battery well at First Bull Run, won his general's stars and command of four rookie regiments, the Second, Sixth, and Seventh Wisconsin and the Nineteenth Indiana, to which his own Regular Army artillery battery was added. Western troops were reputed to be undisciplined, but Gibbon had the right touch and the men were apt pupils. Like Hood's Texas Brigade on the Confederate side, the Iron Brigade were westerners in an eastern army and felt they had something to prove about the soldierly virtues of people in their part of the country. They marked their difference by wearing, instead of the standard issue kepi, a distinctive bell-crowned black hat, one brim pinned up with a black cockade—an assertion of pride, which made them conspicuous while they strove to justify the assertion. The brigade's baptism of fire had come against Stonewall Jackson's troops less than a month before, in the prelude to Second Bull Run. In that first fight, and in the army's disastrous defeat on August 29-30, the brigade had held its ground despite heavy casualties and the demoralization of the troops around it.

However, their present assignment was hopeless. They had to attack on a narrow front, straight into the rifles and artillery of well-entrenched Confederates. Their valor and skill only served to carry them closer to their goal than an average outfit would have got, at the cost of heavier losses—over 250 men. Unlike the average brigade, they were not demoralized by the setback but angry and eager to get even.

But the Iron Brigade's attack was unnecessary. Hooker's sweep had compromised the Confederate defensive line. At nightfall Lee ordered D. H. Hill and Longstreet to pull their men off South Mountain that night and form them up for a retreat.

THE RESISTANCE OF LONGSTREET's and D. H. Hill's divisions had succeeded in delaying the advance of McClellan's main force for one full day, inflicting 1,800 casualties in the process. By keeping Union troops at bay until nightfall, they had contributed to the uncertainty that had led Franklin to halt his advance at Crampton's Gap and postpone his advance to relieve Harpers Ferry till next morning.

However, Lee had no knowledge of what was happening at Crampton's Gap or at Harpers Ferry. He only knew that the northern wing of his army had suffered a serious defeat, and he was doubtful whether it could stave off a determined advance by McClellan's much larger force. The Confederates had 2,300 troops either killed, wounded, or missing, and many other men had straggled on the way to the fight or been separated from their units during the battle. The three divisions in this part of Lee's army would not be fit to stand and fight for a day or so, which meant they could not make more than a token stand at Boonsboro. Lee feared that if Franklin was advancing against McLaws with the same energy and force McClellan had shown at Turner's Gap, McLaws's hold on Maryland Heights would be compromised, and the siege of Harpers Ferry doomed to failure. In these circumstances, he thought it was imperative to save McLaws's command from being surrounded and destroyed. So at 8:00 PM (and again at 11:15), Lee sent orders for McLaws to withdraw his command northward to Sharpsburg, where it would join the troops retreating from Turner's Gap.[5]

It seemed evident to Lee that the Maryland campaign had failed, and that the forces north of the Potomac would have to retreat to Virginia to reunite with Jackson's command in the northern Shenandoah Valley. The army's wagon train and reserve artillery were already crossing the Potomac near Williamsport, which was more than fifteen miles west of Boonsboro, but Lee was concerned enough about their safety to send part of Georgia Brigade for additional protection. The units defeated at Turner's Gap were stumbling down the road to Boonsboro in the dark.

Walking wounded mixed with files of weary riflemen, and ambulances carrying stretcher cases were scattered through the marching columns, as were artillery batteries—guns, caissons, and limber chests. Regimental officers built campfires off the road and stood calling out their unit names, hoping to draw in companies that had become separated in the retreat through the woods.

Hood's infantry was behind them as a rear guard, with Brigadier General Fitzhugh Lee's newly arrived cavalry brigade watching the side road down from Fox's Gap. All of these commands would fall back through Boonsboro to Sharpsburg, a small town on Antietam Creek that offered a short line of retreat across the Potomac to Virginia via Shepherdstown and Boteler's Ford.

HARPERS FERRY, NIGHT

Inside Harpers Ferry, Colonel Miles and General White accepted the hopelessness of their situation. The military code of honor, and the common practice of Civil War armies, did not require Miles to fight to the last like Travis at the Alamo. On the contrary, commanders trapped in an obviously indefensible position were expected to surrender to avoid "the useless effusion of blood." Miles was obliged to wait until Jackson opened fire and formed his troops for the assault, but once Jackson had demonstrated his readiness to storm Bolivar Heights, Miles was free to send out the white flag.

One of Miles's subordinates was unwilling to go along with the program. Colonel Benjamin "Grimes" Davis, commanding the Eighth New York cavalry, wanted to break out and save his command from capture, and after dark he went to Colonel Miles's headquarters in town to ask for permission. Miles refused, insisting he needed every man for the defense, despite the obvious fact that he intended to surrender the next day. Davis had his own ideas of duty and honor, and the courage to back them against any opposition. He was a veteran Indian fighter, thirty years old, Alabama-born and Mississippi-raised, the only West Pointer from the Deep South to reject the claims of kin and section and stay with Old Flag. He told Miles he saw neither honor nor military use in surrendering his outfit, when it could readily escape the trap and rejoin the main army for its impending showdown with the Rebels. Davis put his case in terms strong enough to provoke a heated argument, which he ended by informing Miles that no matter what the post commander said, he was going. Miles gave in.[6]

The argument was overheard by the commanders of the other cavalry units in camp, who decided to join his attempt at a breakout. After dark, Davis led about 1,300 troopers over the pontoon bridge below Maryland Heights, the planking covered with hay to muffle the clump of hooves. Local guides directed the horsemen onto a winding path through the woods that followed the river under the western scarp of the Heights. Davis was prepared to cut his way through with saber and pistol, but McLaws had only a small infantry squad guarding this road. Davis's advance guard captured it, and his command rode on unmolested.

About ten miles north of their crossing, the flatlands of the Antietam Creek valley opened out on their left. They crossed the creek and picked their way north along country lanes that skirted the town of Sharpsburg. In the dark, Confederate troops and wagon trains were moving in bunches here and there along all the roads running down from Hagerstown in the north and Boonsboro to the northeast. With skill and luck, Davis's pickup brigade avoided colliding with any of these units as it rode north. Davis reckoned that all of Lee's army was between him and McClellan's forces on the far side of South Mountain, so he kept riding north in order to pass around the Confederates' northern flank. Just before first light, thirty-five miles from his crossing, he reached the road that ran between Hagerstown and the Williamsport fords—the road by which the wagon trains of Lee's army were retreating from Hagerstown. Out of the predawn mist came a forty-wagon ordnance train bearing the ammunition reserves of Longstreet's Corps. Davis hailed the lead wagons in fluent Alabaman and ordered them to follow him. He led them north while the Twelfth Illinois of his command held off the Confederate train guards, who belatedly discovered that their charges had gone astray. At 9:00 AM Davis brought his four regiments and the wagon train to safety in Greencastle, Pennsylvania. He reported his arrival to the governor of the state, who passed the message to Stanton: the wagons captured, but Harpers Ferry certain to surrender that morning.[7]

CHAPTER 10

THE FORCES GATHER

SEPTEMBER 15-16, 1862

〽️

Mcclellan has been roundly criticized by historians for his cautious handling of the opportunity presented by the finding of the lost order. He certainly failed to act as promptly and energetically as he could have. If McClellan had ordered Burnside and Franklin to march on the night of the thirteenth instead of the following morning, Franklin might have relieved Harpers Ferry, and McClellan's column might have been able to attack and destroy Longstreet's Divisions while they were marching up from Boonsboro. It could be argued, however, that McClellan's caution was reasonable given his estimate of enemy strength, even if it is hard for historians who know how wrong McClellan was to accept that judgment.

As a matter of general principle, McClellan ought to have ordered the forward movement sooner and demanded more aggressive action by his front-line commanders. However, a swifter stronger offensive would probably not have produced the decisive results that historians have envisioned. Night marches were especially wearing on troops and tended to produce more than the usual amount of straggling. If Franklin had made his fourteen-mile march to Crampton's Gap at night, he would have arrived at about 9:00 AM with his force diminished in numbers and physical stamina—to find J. E. B. Stuart's two brigades of cavalry still in place, supporting McLaws's infantry. Franklin's troops would then have had a harder, longer, and costlier fight to clear Crampton's Gap, and he would have faced the formidable task of storming the length of Elk Mountain with a weakened and weary force. By 4:00 PM on the fourteenth the Harpers Ferry position was already indefensible, Colonel Miles had decided to surrender, and it is unlikely that an earlier start and a more aggressive drive by Franklin could have prevented Harpers Ferry's fall.

The case is similar for McClellan's northern column. An early-morning breakthrough at Turner's Gap would not have forced Longstreet to stand, fight, and be destroyed. Rather, it simply would have convinced Lee that he could not delay McClellan long enough for Jackson to rejoin him. He would have had little choice but to withdraw Longstreet's infantry divisions via the Williamsport fords, following the wagon train and reserve artillery that were already withdrawing from Hagerstown. There was a risk that Hill's Division would be badly mauled fighting as the rear guard, but the bulk of Lee's detachment had plenty of time and space to make good its retreat.

Instead, the caution with which McClellan moved actually increased his odds of "bagging" Lee's army. It tempted Lee to stay in the danger zone, in the hope that he could reunite his army in time to win the victory his strategy demanded. The process by which Lee succumbed to that temptation is a strange blend of tactical acumen, misunderstanding, and outrageous fortune.[1]

SHARPSBURG
SEPTEMBER 15, 1862, MIDNIGHT TO NOON

Lee spent a sleepless night, riding in his ambulance from Boonsboro to Sharpsburg ahead of Longstreet's retreat—an interminable stream of the ambulance trains, walking wounded, stragglers, and refugees from units wrecked or disorganized in the fighting. He issued a series of orders to ensure an orderly retreat to Virginia, among them several dispatches advising McLaws to make a prompt withdrawal northward from Maryland Heights, keeping Elk Mountain between his men and the enemy troops in Pleasant Valley, so that he might rejoin the main army at Sharpsburg,

Then, at 8:00 AM on September 15, Jackson's dispatch, sent from Harpers Ferry the evening before, finally caught up with Lee. Jackson's assurance that Harpers Ferry would fall that same day transformed the tactical situation. It might now be possible for Lee to reunite his army at Sharpsburg before McClellan could concentrate against him. Still, the conditions of battle would not be those he had hoped to create. Lee's original plan called for his whole army to be concentrated west of South Mountain, rested, resupplied, and poised for rapid maneuver, to strike McClellan's columns as they emerged from the narrow passes and tried to deploy in the Antietam valley. Now the units of Jackson's force would have to scramble to get to Sharpsburg on time, while Lee would have to concede the initiative to McClellan and improvise a defensive battle plan. Still, the chief purpose of the campaign had been to inflict the most damaging blow possible on the morale and political solidarity of the North, and the only way to do that now was to meet McClellan's army in battle and defeat it.

Orders went out to Longstreet and Hill to halt and take a defensive position at Sharpsburg, to McLaws and Jackson to come north and join them as soon after the surrender as possible. Then Lee rode out in his ambulance to survey the ground on which he would fight.

Sharpsburg was a small country town, a dozen square blocks of wood-frame houses on a plateau of rolling ground west of Antietam Creek. It was a junction where the roads from Hagerstown to the north and Boonsboro to the northeast met the roads running west to the Potomac crossings and south to the Harpers Ferry pontoon bridge. It was an obvious point of concentration for the troops retreating from Turner's Gap and Hagerstown and for troops marching north from Harpers Ferry. It also offered a short and easy retreat via the Shepherdstown fords in case of defeat. The plateau was not sharply or steeply elevated above the valley of Antietam Creek, but it offered substantial advantages for an army on the defensive. There were only a few points by which an enemy approaching from the east could cross the creek, and most of these could be swept by artillery. The plateau was high enough to allow the defenders to see and fire on attacking columns as they advanced, and it was broken by thick woodlots, small rises of ground and sunken roads that offered the defenders concealment and protection from enemy fire.

Lee and his engineers sketched a compact arc of infantry and artillery positions, and as Longstreet's troops reached Sharpsburg they took their designated places in the line. By 11:00 AM all of Hill's and Longstreet's troops were in position and had been joined by Colquitt's Brigade and other units recalled from their duty of guarding fords or wagon trains. When stragglers from Hagerstown and Turner's Gap came in, Lee would have between fifteen and eighteen thousand troops in line and—more significantly—over a hundred artillery pieces.

Although that line was thin and the reserves minimal, the position was a very strong one for the defense. Its right, or southern, flank was anchored on a high, steep ridge that overlooked the southernmost bridge over the Antietam. It appeared that this flank could only be turned by a frontal assault in overwhelming strength, something not likely to occur in the near term. The main line of defense ran north along a ridge of high ground, from which gunners could cover a Federal crossing by the Middle Bridge. The end of the ridge was marked by the Roulette Farm, and here the Confederate line was "refused," or turned at a right angle, to defend against a Federal sweep around the northern flank.

Although there was no continuous ridgeline on this front, the ground still offered advantage to the defense. The cavalry division of Fitzhugh Lee held Nicodemus Hill, which was at the extreme left of the line, and close enough to the Potomac River to block an end run around that flank. "Fitz" Lee was a nephew of Robert E. Lee, a recently promoted Brigadier General at age twenty-seven, rated as one of Stuart's most skilled subordinates.

Midway between Nicodemus Hill and the Roulette Farm was another hillock on which stood a little wooden church of the Dunker religious sect. This high ground was the central strongpoint of the north-facing Confederate line, and Lee posted several batteries of the reserve artillery force here to augment the defense's firepower. The guns were commanded by Colonel Stephen D. Lee, a slender, dark-bearded twenty-nine-year-old South Carolinian whose abilities would eventually earn him command of an army.

The infantry line north of the Dunker Church was about two-thirds of a mile forward of Colonel Lee's guns. It was anchored on the left in a long woodlot, known as the West Woods, and on the right by the smaller East Woods. Between these two woods was a broad swath of open ground, forming a natural corridor down which the Yankee attack was likely to come. The Hagerstown Pike ran down along the west side of this corridor, and much of the ground east of the pike was taken up by a large cornfield enclosed by a "worm fence": a zigzag structure of long wooden rails laid between wooden crosspieces. A Federal column attacking down the pike would have to run a gauntlet of flank fire from the two woods, and frontal fire from infantry in the cornfield and the artillery posted at the church.

The Dunker Church could also be attacked by a force advancing down the Smoketown Road, a country lane that slanted down from the northeast to meet the Hagerstown Pike in front of it. But this road ran right through the East Woods, which would have to be cleared before an assault could be mounted from this direction.

The Confederate position as a whole formed a four-mile arc, running from the Rohrbach, or Lower, Bridge at the southern end to Nicodemus Hill at the northwestern extremity. The setup gave Lee the advantage of moving his reserves and shifting his troops along interior lines—shorter routes than those McClellan would have to use to go around the outside of the arc. While this tactical advantage offset somewhat the weakness of Lee's infantry force, his chief reliance was in Jackson's speed and McClellan's sloth.[2]

At noon he received word from Jackson that Harpers Ferry was being surrendered.

HARPERS FERRY, DAWN TO NOON

Jackson had opened his batteries as soon as targets could be discerned through the light morning mist. Plunging fire from Maryland Heights hit the Federal infantry line that defended the town side of the pontoon bridge. Bolivar Heights was raked from the rear by Walker's guns on Loudon Heights and heavy bombardment on the front and flank from Jackson's artillery. Federal gunners replied sporadically and ineffectively, but mostly huddled in their entrenchments along with the infantry. Below Bolivar Heights Jackson's infantry was slowly clawing its way through the abatis. But the artillery dominated the field, and after two hours of bombardment Colonel Miles concluded that honor had been served. A rider with a white flag showed himself on the ridgeline and the ceasefire call ran left and right along Jackson's front. Some of his artillerymen decided to unload their pieces by firing a last shot at the

Yankees. One of these exploded next to Colonel Miles, ripping a deep wound in his leg. He was carried to a hospital, where he would die the next day. In his stead, General White, who had abnegated his rank to subordinate himself to Miles, surrendered the post.

The Union troops were disgusted and humiliated rather than demoralized by their situation. Most felt they had not been beaten in a fair fight but let down by the military nincompoops who had commanded them. They passed disparaging remarks about the ragged, filthy, and hungry Rebel soldiers who looted their camps. Then General Jackson rode by in his scruffy rumpled uniform: "Boys," said one Federal soldier, "he isn't much to look at, but if we'd had him we wouldn't have been caught in this trap."[3]

However, Jackson and his men still had a great deal of work to do if the Rebels were going to realize the fruits of the victory. There were 11,300 Federal soldiers who had to be paraded, disarmed, counted, and lined up to sign the parole papers that would forbid their fighting or aiding their own army in any way until they were properly exchanged for Confederate prisoners or parolees. Soldiers on both sides were, in general, scrupulous in observing the terms of their parole.

Then the surrendered troops had to be mustered under guard, supplied with rations, and marched off without interfering with Confederate operations. While that was going on Confederate units had to be detailed to occupy the town and to secure the captured supplies to prevent or at least limit the spontaneous looting that always broke out whenever these chronically underfed and ill-clothed troops seized a Federal depot. The captured matériel—clothes and shoes, weapons and ammunition, food and forage—had to be sorted and piled, and Jackson's officers had to organize a system for distributing the goods where they were most needed. Thousands of men needed new footgear or replacement for worn-out clothing, regiments armed with smoothbore muskets (or not armed at all) had to be reequipped with Yankee rifles. Everyone was ravenously hungry. The army had been on field rations since early August, a lean diet even when the rations were delivered, which they often were not. The green fruit and uncooked corn they had eaten in Maryland had not slaked their hunger and had played havoc with their bowels.

Jackson sent a dispatch to notify Lee of his triumph and to ask whether Lee wished him to rush as many troops as possible immediately to Sharpsburg. Assuming Lee did want that reinforcement, Jackson proposed leaving A. P. Hill's Light Division behind to finish paroling the prisoners. Hill's units had undertaken the hardest part of the siege operation, and most of Jackson's two hundred casualties had come from Hill's command. This was the dispatch Lee received at noon, some three hours after it was sent. He did not hesitate long. Although no copy survives of his response to Jackson, he evidently ordered Jackson to send all divisions but A. P. Hill's to Sharpsburg as soon as possible. The two remaining divisions of Jackson's Corps could march straight north and cross the Potomac by either the Shepherdstown or Boteler's Ford. Walker's Division would have to pass around or through Harpers Ferry to follow them. McLaws, however, was still in an awkward position, with the Federal VI Corps blocking the direct northern route through Pleasant Valley. He would have to disengage from those Federal troops and find another route to Sharpsburg. If these elements marched that afternoon, Lee thought they could be in Sharpsburg by nightfall. Since McClellan did not appear to be mounting a vigorous pursuit, Lee anticipated having most of his army concentrated to face McClellan in battle on September 16.[4]

LEE WAS RIGHT about the slow pace of McClellan's advance, but he overestimated the speed and efficiency with which Jackson's Divisions would move to his aid. The work of managing the surrender and resupplying his divisions proved tedious and time-consuming. It took most of the day before the divisions of Lawton and J. R. Jones disengaged from their fighting positions, resupplied with food and ordnance, and took the road northward. The weather was stiflingly hot and humid, and the men were dead tired. As part of Jackson's command they had marched farther and harder than any units in the army. In addition to the two long flank marches they had made during the Second Bull Run campaign a month earlier, they had just completed a march of some seventy-five miles from Frederick to Harpers Ferry, crossing several high ridges and fording the Potomac in the process. They had been either marching or fighting every day since September 11. To get to Sharpsburg at daybreak on the sixteenth, they would have to make a grueling sixteen-mile night march that would leave them worn-out and weakened by straggling.

The commands of Walker and McLaws were also ordered to Sharpsburg on the fifteenth. They too had to dismantle their fighting positions on the heights, march down to the town for resupply, then work their way through the streets crowded by supply wagons, quartermaster details, and other units coming in for supply, to find their way north. McLaws's command could not begin its movement until he was certain that the Federal corps in Pleasant Valley was not planning to assault his defense line on Elk Mountain. He had to disengage carefully, pull back along the rough terrain atop the ridge, then cross the pontoon bridge into Harpers Ferry before turning north behind Walker. As a result the divisions of Walker, Anderson, and McLaws would not be ready to march north till the morning of September 16. The only units from Harpers Ferry that arrived in time to take up fighting positions on the fifteenth were Stuart's two cavalry brigades, which had missed the action at Crampton's Gap.

On that same afternoon, McClellan's infantry appeared in strength on the high ground east of Antietam Creek. Instead of having all but one of his divisions in line, as he had hoped, Lee had barely half of his army with him. Moreover, whether he knew it or not, the army itself had lost so heavily to straggling that its total strength was less than two-thirds what it had been at the start of the campaign. He ordered Longstreet to keep his skirmishers active, harassing the Union brigades as they took position. Longstreet had his artillery keep up sporadic but persistent firing, making great display of the number of batteries ranged all along the line. Longstreet had over a hundred guns, the normal complement for a much larger force than the eighteen thousand or so gathered around Sharpsburg, and they created an exaggerated impression of strength.

McCLELLAN TRIUMPHANT

SEPTEMBER 15, MIDNIGHT TO 4:00 PM

McClellan knew he had won an important victory on September 14, but as dark closed down he was uncertain of its dimensions and consequences. At 9:40 PM he telegraphed Halleck, briefly characterizing the storming of Turners and Fox's gaps. "It has been a glorious victory," he concluded, but "I cannot yet tell whether the enemy will retreat during the night or appear in increased force in the morning." It was possible that the gaps had been defended by a mere detachment and that the main body of Lee's northern wing, which McClellan rated at forty to fifty thousand, was concentrating at Boonsboro for a counterstroke.[5]

He was up early on the morning of the fifteenth but remained at headquarters, where he could receive reports from Hooker, who was leading the advance force at Turner's Gap, and from Franklin's detachment at Crampton's Gap. At 8:00 AM he was able to telegraph Halleck that Franklin had carried Crampton's Gap "after a severe engagement," and that the enemy on his own front had "disappeared during the night" and seemed to be retreating. He had ordered Franklin to pursue but did "not yet know where [the enemy] will next be found." He clearly believed that the forces he had engaged on the fourteenth were "The Corps of D. H. Hill and Longstreet." What is not clear is whether he literally supposed Hill's command was a full army corps, or was using the term generically to refer to a substantial body of troops. It certainly would have been consistent with his estimate of Lee's Boonsboro wing to rate Hill's Division at double its actual strength.

Further reports from Hooker allowed him to telegraph Halleck at 8:30 AM that Lee's force was in full retreat, "making for Shepherdstown in a perfect panic, & that Genl Lee last night stated publicly that he must admit they had been shockingly whipped." It was information with no better authority than "some citizens from Boonsboro," but McClellan was prepared to believe it. Shortly after this he received a report from one of his young staff officers, the dashing but not yet legendary Captain George Armstrong Custer, that Lee himself had been wounded in the action and D. H. Hill killed. The confusion was likely due to a civilian's having seen Lee riding in an ambulance, because of the earlier injury to his hands; and there was a dead general, but it was Brigade Commander Garland, not D. H. Hill. Custer also reported a civilian's statement that Lee had estimated his loss on the fourteenth as fifteen thousand troops. This was evidence of "a glorious & complete victory," and McClellan was issuing orders for "hurrying everything forward to . . . press their retreat to the utmost."[6]

For once, McClellan did seem actually to be hurrying. He ordered Hooker to lead the pursuit toward Boonsboro, with XII Corps following, and Burnside to clear IX Corps from the road so that fresh units from the II and V Corps could pass. After sending his last telegrams at

10:00 AM, McClellan would ride forward himself and discover that Burnside's troops were just breaking camp, delaying the relief column. He impatiently ordered Burnside out of the way, and in his annoyance began entertaining doubts about his old friend's military abilities.

At this point, McClellan was so enthusiastic about his prospects that he took time to send a personal telegram to Winfield Scott, informing his old commander that he had defeated a large enemy force, "occupying a strong mountain pass," which was now "routed and retreating in disorder" with himself in close pursuit. He also wanted Scott to know that this "signal victory" had been won over an army with "R E Lee in command"—Lee, who had always been Scott's favorite. To his wife he wrote, "If I can believe one tenth of what is reported, God has seldom given an army a greater victory than this."

In fact, a substantial discount was warranted. Actual Confederate losses at South Mountain were about 2,300 out of 18,000 engaged, a rate of nearly 15 percent—a very serious loss to the northern wing of Lee's army, which reduced its effective strength to approximately 15,000. If Lee had actually had the 40,000-plus troops with which McClellan credited him, a loss of 15,000 (upwards of 33 percent) would have been catastrophic. The passes through South Mountain would have been carpeted with bodies and the haul of prisoners in the thousands. McClellan could see for himself that this was not the case as he rode through the pass on the Boonsboro pike.[7]

It was risky to have exaggerated the scale of his victory as he had done. John Pope boasted of triumph, then saw himself discredited when Lee sprang his surprise assault on August 30; and, by McClellan's estimate, Lee still had at least 35,000 troops, enough to cause problems for McClellan's Corps as they filed through the gaps. Nevertheless, as he rode down from the hills on the road to Boonsboro he had reason to hope that he had indeed just fought and won the crucial battle of the campaign. Lee's wing was evidently in full retreat, and, with Franklin poised to relieve Harpers Ferry, it seemed likely that Lee would have to abandon his invasion and return to Virginia. If that happened, McClellan would have met the fundamental requirement of his mission: to thwart the invasion of Maryland. He would have achieved that victory without running the risks or bearing the costs of a general engagement. By exaggerating the destruction inflicted on the enemy he magnified that achievement into something approaching a Napoleonic victory and anticipated the demand Lincoln was sure to make—that the enemy be destroyed or crippled by the defeat.

However, by early afternoon his situation began to seem more problematic. McClellan had been waiting to hear what progress Franklin was making in his attack against McLaws's position on Elk Mountain. Shortly before noon he received a dispatch from Franklin, sent at 8:50 AM, reporting that firing could no longer be heard from Harpers Ferry, an indication that the post had surrendered. Franklin had not advanced against the Rebel troops in Elk Mountain and Pleasant Valley, and he wanted reinforcements. At about the same time, a report from Captain Custer indicated that Lee's force was no longer retreating. It was drawn up in line of battle on high ground west of Antietam Creek, in front of the town of Sharpsburg. The line was "a perfect one about a mile and a half long. . . . Longstreet is in command and has forty cannon that we know of." Custer was on higher ground east of the creek, from which most of the Antietam valley was visible. When General Hooker reached the same vantage point he thought the enemy force might be thirty to fifty thousand strong, with a hundred artillery pieces. He was right about the guns, but the haze of that hot and humid midday obscured his survey of the infantry positions, so that his estimate more than doubled Lee's actual strength.[8]

It now appeared to McClellan that Lee's army was not as demoralized as had been reported. If Hooker and Custer were right, it held a strong position, which it could defend until Jackson's Corps, freed by the surrender of Harpers Ferry, could rejoin. With his army reunited, Lee could return to the offensive and attempt to complete what McClellan assumed was his strategic design for the conquest of Maryland. The "signal victory" at South Mountain would be valueless if McClellan could not compel Lee to retreat. But that would require another battle, most likely a general engagement to which the main force of the army would have to be committed.

That being the case, it would be best if McClellan could attack Lee's detachment before Jackson's troops rejoined. However, bringing his whole force to bear was not a simple task. Hooker had only two divisions fronting Sharpsburg. Before he could consider attacking the supposed thirty thousand to fifty thousand Confederates at Sharpsburg, McClellan had to assemble and properly organize a force of at least equal and preferably much greater strength. By McClellan's own calculation, he had some thirty-eight thousand infantry in I and II Corps and Sykes's Division who could reach the Antietam by early afternoon, in time to fight a battle. The XII Corps was still at Turner's Gap and could not reach the Antietam till nightfall.

Burnside's IX Corps, with about thirteen thousand infantry, was not far behind Hooker's units—but at 3:45 PM McClellan felt compelled to divert its march. Now that the Rebels held Harpers Ferry, Jackson could throw most of his force into Pleasant Valley, smash through Franklin's VI Corps, and threaten to take McClellan's main force in the flank and rear, as he had done to Pope at Second Bull Run. Since McClellan credited Jackson with twice his actual force, such a menace seemed plausible. So McClellan ordered Burnside and IX Corps south to Rohrersville, at the northern end of Pleasant Valley, where it could go to Franklin's aid if needed. McClellan would later reconsider that assignment and order Burnside to rejoin the main body, but IX Corps did not reach the hills above the Antietam until nightfall, too late to join in an attack.

McClellan rode ahead to join Hooker on the heights east of Antietam Creek. It was late afternoon on a parching hot day. Hooker's troops were establishing positions on the slopes dropping down to the creek, and Confederate artillery was actively bombarding them. When McClellan's large entourage emerged on the skyline, some of the fire was sent their way, so the general sent his staff to cover and made his telescopic survey of the enemy positions with a single aide. Heat haze, rolling terrain, and the large woodlots around Sharpsburg made it difficult to ascertain the exact size and positioning of the Rebel troops. However, from his vantage point McClellan could see that Lee's forces were posted in strong positions on high ground west of the creek. There were three bridges across Antietam Creek, two of which were well covered by Confederate gunners. The Lower Bridge seemed to mark the southern flank of Lee's position. There were high, steep, wooded hills immediately above it on the western bank, which made this an exceptionally strong defensive position. Federal troops advancing across the Middle Bridge would have to attack frontally across open ground against infantry and artillery on higher ground or in protected positions. It seemed a better idea to turn the Confederate position by crossing a strong force at the Upper Bridge and attacking Lee's northern flank. However, with only forty thousand troops at hand McClellan did not have enough to hold Lee in front and at the same time swing a large force over the Upper Bridge to strike the flank.[9]

In fact, on the afternoon of September 15 Lee had fewer than half the troops with which McClellan credited him. McClellan and his colleagues were fooled, in part, because of their misguided assumptions about enemy strength, by the faulty system of intelligence gathering that supported those assumptions, and by the boldness of Lee's decision to stand at Sharpsburg with such a small force. But they were also deceived by what they saw accurately enough: the number of regimental flags visible along the enemy line, and the number of guns firing from Rebel positions. Lee's infantry regiments had been radically depleted by straggling, illness, and battle losses, but each still carried its flags, and Federal observers counting them from a distance could not tell whether they mustered fifty rifles or five hundred. Every brigade and division was assigned a certain number of artillery batteries, and these had not been reduced by straggling or battle loss. The divisions lined up across the Antietam still had their full complement of artillery, and Longstreet was advertising their presence by a program of active firing, which contributed to the impression that a solid corps of several divisions was making its stand and inviting attack.

McClellan therefore decided to postpone any offensive action until the following day, September 16, when he expected to have nearly his entire force concentrated against Sharpsburg.

BY FAILING TO ATTACK on September 15, McClellan lost an opportunity to ravage a major part of Lee's army. The irony is that by declining to attack on that day, he also increased his chances for winning a major, perhaps even a decisive, victory.

McClellan had forty thousand troops at hand against the eighteen thousand under Lee and Longstreet. An all-out attack would likely have broken or compromised Lee's defensive line and compelled his army to retreat—although such an outcome was far from certain, given the strength of Lee's position and the quality of the force under his command. However, it is highly unlikely that an assault would have led to the destruction of that part of Lee's army. An attack in sufficient strength could not have been launched until late in the day, by troops tired from long marches and (for I and IX Corps) a day of hard fighting. The Army of the Potomac had no doctrine for pursuit, and neither cavalry nor infantry was prepared for it. Lee would most probably have been able to save most of his infantry and artillery. It would have been a blow to Confederate prestige and to army morale for Lee's force to have been driven from the field, though the capture of Harpers Ferry would have been some compensation. Nevertheless, such a defeat would not have "destroyed Lee's army." The eighteen thousand troops at risk represented about one-third of Lee's present force but less than 15 percent of the Army of Northern Virginia's reserve troop strength in the Virginia theater—enough of a reserve to enable Lee to reconstitute his army and effectively resist a Federal offensive.

The opportunity lost through McClellan's unreasonable caution was restored by Lee's unreasonable daring. Seeing the apparent hesitancy with which McClellan moved against him, Lee was tempted to risk Longstreet's force for the chance to recover the initiative, reunite his army, defeat McClellan in battle, and complete the strategic design inherent in the invasion of Maryland. He held his eighteen thousand in place, spreading his depleted infantry to cover a position fit for an army, using his artillery aggressively, to bluff McClellan into delaying his attack.

But once again, McClellan's unreasonable caution would lead him to miss his opportunity—and Lee's unreasonable daring would hand it right back.

McCLELLAN HESITATES, SEPTEMBER 16, 1862

On the morning of September 16, McClellan had almost all his force concentrated within easy supporting distance of the Antietam Creek position. Lee's army was still divided, with most of Jackson's wing at Harpers Ferry, seventeen miles away by the shortest marching route. Whether this position gave McClellan a tactical advantage or put his army in danger depended on the size of the two Confederate forces. Jackson's was the wild card. From Harpers Ferry it could either march to join Lee, strike through Pleasant Valley to attack McClellan's flank and communications, or attempt some combination of these two maneuvers. If Lee's force was weak enough, an attack by McClellan's available force might drive it from the field before Jackson could come to its aid; but if it was strong enough to hold its ground, Jackson's arrival, especially if it took the form of a powerful flank attack, might catch McClellan's army between anvil and hammer, as Pope had been caught. But how strong an attack could Jackson mount through Pleasant Valley? And how large a force would McClellan need to protect his flank? The answer to that last question would determine how much of his army McClellan could use against Lee on the sixteenth.

If McClellan's estimates were accurate, on the fifteenth Lee and Longstreet had at least thirty thousand troops at Sharpsburg and Jackson between forty and fifty thousand at Harpers Ferry. McClellan thought he had about forty-five thousand troops immediately at hand with which to attack Lee. The army's artillery reserve, with its batteries of powerful long-range guns, would come up early in the morning, and by noon would be positioned along the ridgeline east of Antietam Creek, firing to suppress the Rebel guns across the valley.[10] There were also another fifteen thousand infantry marching down through the passes, but they would not reach the battlefield until late afternoon or early evening, too late to be useful in a general assault. Before McClellan could safely commit his main force to attack Lee, he had to ascertain where Jackson's forces were, and how they were moving. Given McClellan's estimate of Jackson's strength, it was conceivable that overnight Jackson had sent Lee enough reinforcement to match McClellan's forty-five thousand, while retaining enough strength at Harpers Ferry to attack Franklin's nineteen thousand with superior forces.

In reality, only two of Jackson's infantry divisions would reach Lee on September 16, footsore and weary after a night march, raising Confederate strength to about twenty-seven thousand. But that reinforcement merely doubled the stakes Lee had at risk. McClellan would have five of his six army corps concentrated on the high ground east of Antietam Creek, an effective strength of about sixty thousand augmented by an artillery arm that far outgunned and outranged its Confederate counterpart. Franklin's VI Corps was still guarding Pleasant Valley but could have been called up in time to provide a defensive reserve. An all-out assault on the sixteenth would have had excellent chances of success, and the victors would have had a long, late-summer day in which to pursue a retreating enemy.

IT HAD RAINED during the night, and the heat of the new day brought up a heavy fog that cloaked the Confederate positions at Sharpsburg, frustrating McClellan's attempts to inspect the Confederate lines through his telescope. The fog cleared after 9:00 AM, but the day remained hazy. From McClellan's position it was impossible to tell whether Jackson was on the scene or still moving up over the road from Shepherdstown or Boteler's Ford. To clarify the situation, McClellan had to probe the enemy positions by making limited attacks. But it was useless to probe the positions fronting Antietam Creek, where attackers had to cross open ground against lines well supplied with artillery.

The best option was to move against Lee's northern flank, where the Rebel positions looked weaker and scattered woodlots would give the attackers cover in the advance and shelter in case of a reverse. However, to approach that flank, Federal troops had to cross the Antietam upstream and act separately from the rest of the army, where they could be cut off and destroyed by a Confederate concentration. So the force sent had to be large enough to stave off an attack by fifteen or twenty thousand Confederates.

After spending the morning considering his options, McClellan ordered Hooker to take I Corps, "cross the river . . . and attack the enemy on his left flank." Hooker was not entirely happy with the assignment. His own survey of the Rebel positions on the fifteenth led him to believe Lee had at least thirty thousand on the scene, while his corps had, by his own estimate, only twelve or thirteen thousand with which "to attack the whole rebel army." After giving his orders, he rode to McClellan's headquarters to state his concerns. He was afraid "the rebels would eat me up" if McClellan did not divert Lee's strength and attention by making "another attack . . . on the enemy's right" or stand ready to send reinforcements "promptly" to his aid. McClellan reassured him that any call for reinforcements would be met and that any forces sent would be under Hooker's command. This was not only a proper command arrangement for such an operation, it was a sop to Hooker's notorious ambition for higher command. It implied that in conducting this operation he would not be subordinate to any of the other corps commanders, all of whom were senior to Hooker.

However, McClellan would give no orders for diversionary attacks against other parts of the Confederate line. Nor did he move any of the available II Corps divisions into positions from which they might have reinforced Hooker on September 16. Despite the fact that Hooker's operation was originally styled an attack, it was in effect a reconnaissance-in-force, aimed at both establishing the location and strength of Lee's northern flank and discovering whether Jackson's reinforcement had arrived. With that information in hand, McClellan would know whether any part of VI Corps could be recalled from its watch on Pleasant Valley to augment the offensive against Sharpsburg.[11]

Hooker got his orders just after 1:00 PM, but his advance was slow to develop. It took time for Hooker to give his orders, for his brigadiers to get their troops into marching order, cross the Antietam via the upper bridge and an adjacent ford, then deploy and begin the advance toward the enemy some four miles farther on. It was after 4:00 PM when his lead division made contact with the Confederate skirmish lines. Hooker pushed his divisions ahead until stiffening resistance revealed the Rebels' main line of resistance in the woodlots and fields flanking the Hagerstown Pike. Hooker halted, established a defensive position for the night, and called for reinforcements. He had established that the Rebels' northern flank ran along relatively higher ground for a mile and a quarter, from Nicodemus Hill on the east, through a large woodlot (the "West Woods"), across the north-south Hagerstown Pike to the Roulette Farm buildings a quarter mile west of the Pike. There was a half-mile gap between Nicodemus Hill and the Potomac River, but even with reinforcement Hooker's line could not be extended far enough to turn that flank. Hooker could offer no information as to whether or not Jackson's Corps was on the scene.

By the close of day on the sixteenth, reports from Franklin had given McClellan some assurance that there was no sign of a Confederate attack northward through Pleasant Valley. While that suggested that Jackson had sent most of his troops to Sharpsburg, it was less worrying to have Jackson in front than looming as a menace to his flank and rear. He therefore ordered Franklin to march at dawn and join him on the Antietam with his two VI Corps divisions. However, he remained concerned enough about a flank attack out of Harpers Ferry to order Couch's newly arrived division to move south through Pleasant Valley, to develop any Rebel movement there and if possible seize Maryland Heights. He would also caution Burnside, whose IX Corps would form his left flank on the Antietam, to keep an eye out for a Confederate flanking column coming up from Harpers Ferry.

The delay further enabled McClellan to concentrate nearly his entire field force for the confrontation with Lee. The XII Corps, which arrived late in the evening, could be sent to support Hooker on the far side of the Antietam without weakening the main body. Franklin's two divisions would arrive in the morning to form (with V Corps) a powerful reserve behind Sumner's II Corps. Most importantly, McClellan and his staff would have time to properly position the powerful batteries of the army's artillery reserve. In a clash between infantry armies of equal strength, artillery superiority could give the Army of the Potomac a crucial tactical edge. The basic principle was Napoleonic, and it was the core of McClellan's tactical doctrine. In the Peninsula campaign he had planned to defeat an enemy of equal or superior infantry strength by deploying the huge heavy guns of the army's siege train. While there were no siege guns with the artillery reserve at Antietam, the guns its batteries did deploy were twenty-pounder Parrott rifles and thirty-two-pounder howitzers, the heaviest field pieces used during the war, superior in range and in the weight and explosive power of their shot to anything in Lee's artillery train. From the high ground east of the creek, where engineers had carefully emplaced them, their shell fire could hit anything on the battlefield that appeared in their line of sight.

Still, by postponing action until September 17 and allowing Jackson to reinforce Lee, McClellan lessened his chances of winning a decisive tactical victory, the kind that had seemed possible on September 13 as he studied General Order No. 191. As McClellan saw it, that opportunity had vanished when Lee escaped the pursuit after South Mountain and took his stand at Antietam. Nor was such a victory a strategic necessity.

He had been restored to command at a moment of strategic crisis, with the army in disarray, the government deranged by the machinations of the Radicals, and the people demoralized. Here also was a large victorious Rebel army invading Northern territory, threatening to detach Maryland from the Union, while menacing Northern cities like Harrisburg, Baltimore, and Philadelphia. To bring this strategic crisis to a successful end and vindicate his status as the indispensable man, all he had to do was fight hard enough to compel Lee to retreat. That being the case, it was not only unnecessary but also unwise for him to run the risks entailed by any attempt to win a Napoleonic victory—for example, by hurling his available force at Lee on September 16. By delaying action he believed he minimized the odds that he might suffer a disastrous defeat. His army was concentrated so it could not be attacked in detail, and positioned so that it could not be easily or speedily outflanked. His artillery advantage made it possible for him to conduct a successful attack on Lee's infantry line, and he had also hedged against the risk of a repulse by occupying a very strong defensive position. His high ground was higher than Lee's and packed with artillery. McClellan would also have a substantial infantry reserve posted behind the center of his line, from which it could either exploit a breakthrough or backstop a retreat.

All of McClellan's actions and refusals of action on September 16 were reasonable and prudent, given his assumptions about the strength and position of the enemy before him. The reality was that McClellan wasted September 16 maneuvering against phantoms. Jackson never intended to mount an offensive through Pleasant Valley, and lacked the strength to do so. His weary divisions had taken much longer to reach Sharpsburg, and arrived in far less strength, than either Lee or McClellan had expected. The divisions of Lawton and D. R. Jones had arrived at 6:00 AM but added only eight thousand troops to the nineteen thousand already in position there. Even without VI Corps, McClellan had more than sixty thousand troops against Lee's twenty-seven thousand—a force more than ample for the tactics McClellan had in mind. He enjoyed the same two-to-one superiority he had had on September 15, but now he had two-thirds of Lee's army in his grasp and hours of daylight in which to attack and pursue.

By failing to attack, McClellan missed his best opportunity to inflict a decisive defeat on Lee's army at little cost to his own. His hesitation allowed Walker's and McLaws's Divisions to reach Sharpsburg before the fighting began, raising Lee's force to roughly thirty-six thousand— only half of the seventy-two thousand McClellan would bring to the field, but still enough for Lee's purposes.

PART FOUR

THE BATTLE of ANTIETAM

September 16–18, 1862

CHAPTER 11

PREPARATION FOR BATTLE

THE NIGHT OF SEPTEMBER 16–17, 1862

To HISTORIANS ARMED WITH HINDSIGHT AND A GOOD MAP IT IS easy to see how McClellan could have ravaged or even destroyed the Army of Northern Virginia on either the sixteenth or the seventeenth of September. McClellan's refusal to attempt such a battle on September 16 can legitimately be blamed on his habitual excess of caution and his egregious overestimate of enemy strength. Yet the most puzzling aspect of his decision making is not his hesitation to attack on the sixteenth but his determination to attack the very next day. He cannot have doubted that the force at Sharpsburg would be reinforced on the sixteenth and would therefore be stronger when he finally moved against it. He still believed that Lee's army, when united, would be at least equal if not superior in strength to his own. Nevertheless, when he telegraphed Halleck of his intention to attack "as soon as the situation of the enemy is developed," he made no mention of fearful odds, made no attempt to hedge his responsibility for the ensuing result. This was not the McClellan of the Peninsula campaign, forever putting off the day of battle until his "outnumbered" army could be reinforced, his mood wildly swinging between predictions of triumph and hysterical prophecies of defeat for which he *must not* be blamed.[1]

THE TELEGRAM MCCLELLAN sent retired General in Chief Winfield Scott the day after South Mountain opens a window into his new state of mind. The old warrior had long been a figure of powerful but unresolved significance in McClellan's life: his commander, his hero, his mentor during the war with Mexico, when McClellan and Robert E. Lee were engineer officers on Scott's staff. It was widely known that in 1861 Scott had thought Lee the man best qualified to command the Federal armies, just as he had rated Lee the best and bravest of his staff officers in Mexico. When McClellan came to Washington, Scott was at first his patron, then his critic, then the obstacle blocking his path to control of military policy, and finally an enemy he had driven from command by a systematic campaign of intrigue and defamation. Yet even in the midst of the labor and anxiety of a military crisis, McClellan wanted Scott to know that he had routed and driven from the field an army command that had "R E Lee in command." The Battle of South Mountain had a personal significance for McClellan that was nearly as vital as its potential strategic consequences. Scott must see, and acknowledge, that he had been wrong to prefer Lee, wrong to doubt McClellan, wrong to oppose him in the President's councils.[2]

That victory also armored McClellan against the malice of his political enemies: Stanton, the Committee on the Conduct of the War, and the Radical press. Despite his protestations of contempt for his persecutors, he had taken to heart their insulting characterization of him as "the 'Quaker,' the 'procrastinator,' the 'coward' & the 'traitor'!"[3] What gave those taunts their stinging power was McClellan's own uncertainty about his ability to fight and win battles. His victory at Seven Pines during the Peninsula campaign was defensive and unplanned, and since then he had known nothing but defeats. The fight at South Mountain was the first major battle he had planned, initiated, and won.

Lee's decision to challenge battle at Antietam all but nullified the effect of South Mountain as both strategic victory and personal vindication. It was therefore necessary, as he wrote to his wife, to show "I can fight battles and win them." As he would note in his official report, under the canons and customs of the military profession a general who brought his army face-to-face with an enemy was expected to give battle, suspect if he declined it. The point was driven home by two telegrams that reached him late on the fifteenth and on the afternoon of the sixteenth. The first was from President Lincoln: "God bless you, and all with you. Destroy the rebel army, if possible." McClellan resented the message, which ignored his claim of a major victory and repeated the president's nagging demand for greater efforts, more complete victories. The second reply was from Scott, and instead of acknowledging McClellan's bettering of Scott's erstwhile favorite, this telegram echoed Lincoln's judgment that McClellan's task was unfinished: "Bravo! . . . Twice more and it's done."[4]

So McClellan had to fight and win a new battle to vindicate his character and military genius, and preserve the power of the only man capable of saving the nation from the dual menace of Southern secession and Radical despotism. That meant he had to accept a standup fight against an enemy whose overall strength was at least equal to his own. However, for all the old familiar reasons, it remained vital that in undertaking the risks of the offensive he minimize the possibility of suffering a serious defeat—the kind that might wreck the army that was the republic's best reliance and allow his enemies to fire the indispensable man. His decision to attack on the seventeenth was (for him) one of unprecedented boldness; but his execution of that decision would be constrained by his need to ensure absolutely against serious defeat.

QUESTIONABLE JUDGMENTS WERE also being made on the other side of Antietam Creek. Lee had been too sanguine about the speed with which Jackson's force could join him at Sharpsburg, so for the whole of September 16 he had faced McClellan with a force less than half as large. His assumption that McClellan would not immediately attack in force proved correct, but his army's situation on September 17 would be only fractionally better than it had been the day before. All of his labor and daring since September 14 had only succeeded in putting his army in an extremely dangerous position, faced with an enemy twice its strength, with its back to a river crossed by two difficult fords. To achieve a meaningful victory, Lee had not only to defend his lines but to drive the larger army back and force it to retreat behind South Mountain. If at the end of the day McClellan simply held his very strong position on the high ground east of the creek, Lee would have little choice but to retreat to Virginia. It has been said, and is certainly true, that Lee understood McClellan's weaknesses as a battlefield tactician, and believed he could exploit these to win a victory. But that seems a slim reed on which to rest the fate of an army and, potentially, a nation.

Still, the possibility exists that Lee was unaware just how far his original force had been diminished by combat and straggling. Postbattle reports by Lee and some of his subordinates assert that the Army of Northern Virginia had lost a third of its original strength to straggling, combat, and other causes, and that it had fewer than 40,000 troops available for action. However, A. P. Hill's Division (2,500–3,000) was still at Harpers Ferry paroling captured Federals and would not reach the battlefield till late in the afternoon. For most of the day Lee's force was probably no larger than 37,000 and may have been as small as 35,000— which is to say it was no more than half the size of McClellan's effective force of 72,000-plus.[5]

Lee's troops were not only weak in numbers, their physical strength had been compromised by weeks of hard marching and a bad or inadequate diet, in addition to the ordinary debilitating effects of bad sanitation and polluted drinking water. A substantial fraction of Jackson's command had been lost to straggling on the march up from Harpers Ferry, and few of the troops in line had had any rest. Even those from Longstreet's and D. H. Hill's commands, who had been camped around Sharpsburg since the fifteenth, still felt the effects of their hard fight and retreat from South Mountain, and many of them had spent the past twenty-four hours skirmishing with Hooker's and Richardson's advance elements. The men were also suffering from hunger. Most had had nothing to eat for days beyond what they could forage or scrounge on the march. The reminiscences of Private W. B. Judkins, of the Twenty-second Georgia, reveal the degree to which hunger colored the soldiers' experience of the campaign. Judkins spends far more time writing about raids on civilian orchards and chicken coops than about combat. On the march up from Harpers Ferry with the rest of R. H. Anderson's Division, Judkins risked arrest by the provost guard to raid a farmyard: climbed a stone fence and crammed his pockets and his mouth with grapes and a fruit unknown to him that turned out to be unripe gooseberries, which bit his tongue "like eating needles"—then hadn't the strength to climb back over the fence. The flesh was weak, but the spirit willing. Although he was arrested for straggling, he evaded the provost guard and rejoined his regiment.[6] Most of Lee's men had been subsisting on unripe or uncooked corn and unripe fruit, which gave them the "gripes" and the "squitters." Diarrhea and dysentery were endemic in the Rebel camps. After the fighting their abandoned battlelines could be traced in rows of loose and bloody feces.[7]

Nevertheless, from Lee's perspective, there were good precedents for accepting battle against such odds. Frederick the Great had beaten Austrian armies of twice his force at Leuthen and Rossbach during the Seven Years' War. Winfield Scott was operating at the end of an extremely tenuous supply line when he attacked and defeated a numerically superior Mexican army that was fighting in defense of its capital city. Lee himself had already triumphed over superior forces in the Seven Days and at Second Bull Run, and at Chancellorsville in May 1863 he would win a stunning victory against odds comparable to those he faced at Antietam. However, in each of these remarkable triumphs, the victor seized and held the initiative against an enemy that was badly organized and caught at a disadvantage. At Antietam Lee was compelled to stand on the defensive, allow McClellan to determine the pace and place of action—and watch for his chance to turn the tables.

He was willing to risk an attack, despite the disadvantages of his position, because the strategic calculus that had led him to invade Maryland in the first place had not changed. His own earlier victories, and Bragg's offensive into Kentucky, had reversed the momentum of military operations, and produced a political crisis in the North. A victory now, even if it did not destroy McClellan's army, might have a decisive effect on the Union's midterm elections. (Unlike Davis, Lee doubted the British or French would aid the Confederacy, so the hope of intervention played no part in his decision.) McClellan might enjoy an advantage in troop and artillery strength, but as Lee saw it, these advantages were offset by the relative inexperience of many units and their commanders. From Lee's perspective, even McClellan's veteran troops were experienced mostly in defeat. McClellan's corps and division commanders were drawn from two different armies and had not developed the kind of instinctive teamwork that now characterized the Army of Northern Virginia. Lee also saw McClellan as a weak combat commander. He had no great gift for battle tactics; nor had he shown that he had the moral courage to stand and fight when assailed, as he had been in the Seven Days. By his excessive caution, his refusal to move until every risk had been minimized, McClellan revealed his fear of losing control of the action.

In contrast, Lee understood and accepted the fact that battle is chaos. The strategist does what he can to create a situation in which victory is likely and the gains of battle are commensurate with the risks. But battle is the violent collision of two highly complex human systems, driven by different impulses, organized in different ways, with different strengths and solidarities. The outcome may turn on actions far down the chain of command, surprising local successes that boost the morale of one side and demoralize the other, shifts in momentum that produce a series of disruptive effects. Lee, like Napoleon, was a connoisseur of this chaos. He believed that his own skill as a commander, the experience and intelligence of his chief subordinates, the efficiency of his command system, and the superior morale of his troops would allow him to ride that chaos; and that the weaknesses of McClellan, his generals, and his army made them liable to a loss of control, a cascade of failures leading to defeat.

Lee would use the advantages conferred by the terrain and his interior lines of communication to punish McClellan's assault columns, and watch for the opportunity to deliver the kind of counterblow that had wrecked the organization and morale of his opponents during the Seven Days and at Second Bull Run. He did not need to annihilate McClellan's army in order to win a politically decisive victory. All he had to do was compel McClellan to retreat and leave the Army of Northern Virginia free to base itself in western Maryland and threaten a deeper invasion.

CONFEDERATE PREPARATIONS

Lee had decided to fight at Sharpsburg on the fifteenth and had spent the sixteenth laying out and manning the positions he intended to defend. His defensive line was a four-mile arc, running roughly northwest to south. In this position, the army could protect its line of supply and possible retreat, which ran west from Sharpsburg to the Shepherdstown Ford. The ford itself was held by cavalry and part of the army's artillery reserve under Colonel William Pendleton, and Lee was able to draw guns and supplies from Pendleton's command during the action.[8]

The main line of resistance followed the contour of a plateau that rose by a shallow grade above the Antietam river bottom. The reconnaissance by Hooker's Corps on September 16 had warned Lee to expect a heavy attack from the north. He therefore assigned command of this sector to Stonewall Jackson and sent him heavy reinforcement during the night. Since speed and efficiency of movement were primary concerns, the divisions assigned to Jackson were drawn not only from his own corps but from nearby elements of Longstreet's Corps and the general reserve. This arrangement displays very clearly the efficiency and flexibility of command structures in the Army of Northern Virginia. With veteran generals in command at corps, division, and brigade level, Lee could mix and match unit assignments freely, without any notable breakdowns in communication or mutuality of support. This is in stark contrast to McClellan's army, where organizational rigidity and inexperience at the higher command levels would complicate and cripple operations.

In Jackson's sector, the north-facing section of the arc was anchored on the Nicodemus Heights, which took their name from the owner of the nearest farm. The high ground here was held by two brigades of Stuart's cavalry and the guns of Stuart's horse artillery. At the start of the action, Early's Brigade of infantry was stationed here as additional protection, because the position was critical to the defense. Stuart's guns were in position to pour enfilading fire into the Yankee infantry under Hooker, whose attack was expected early on the seventeenth. The key position on this part of the field was the high ground just east of a small clapboard church belonging to the Dunkers, a German Baptist sect with a pacifist creed. The Dunker Church sat at the junction of the south-running Hagerstown Pike and the Smoketown Road, which slanted in from the northeast. It was the height of land here, and if the Federals seized it their artillery could enfilade all the defensive lines north of Sharpsburg, making Lee's position untenable.

The terrain favored the defense. The direct line of approach to the church was a corridor of open ground some four hundred to five hundred yards wide, which ran between two large woodlots, both initially held by Confederate troops. The East Woods was some three hundred yards northeast of the church, covering the Smoketown Road. On the opposite side of the corridor the much larger West Woods jutted three hundred yards forward of the church along the western side of the Hagerstown Pike, then angled out to the west. Between the woodlots the approach was obstructed by a large cornfield, owned by a man named Miller, which filled most of the ground between the pike and the East Woods and was perhaps a quarter of a mile deep. Infantry thrashing its way through the rows of stiff man-high stalks would ultimately come up against a fence-rail breastwork sheltering Confederate riflemen. Two brigades of Ewell's Division, commanded by General Lawton in place of the wounded Richard Ewell, held the cornfield line and the southern end of the East Woods. As a reserve for the right of his line, Lawton could call on a backup brigade, which was positioned due east of the Dunker Church near the Roulette Farm. The Dunker Church position had also been given strong artillery support by the addition of Colonel Stephen D. Lee's reserve batteries to the divisional and brigade artillery.

To the left of the Dunker Church, the West Woods was full of Confederate infantry, with J. R. Jones's Division in the front line and two of Lawton's Brigades in reserve. Deeper in the West Woods, at its southern end, Hood's Division provided a general reserve that could be used anywhere along the northern front. Counting all the artillery and reserve elements, Jackson had more than ten thousand troops with which to defend the northern sector—perhaps as many as thirteen thousand if Stuart's two brigades are taken into account. However, Confederate cavalry were lightly armed for scouting, screening, skirmishing, and raiding, with pistols and carbines or short-barreled rifle-musket—inadequate for a standup fight against infantry armed with rifle and bayonet. But Stuart's troopers could offer some protection to his artillery batteries, and under the right circumstances it might be able to confuse and divert the Federals by striking at the rear of Hooker's force.

Jackson could also draw on the army's general reserve, the divisions of McLaws (three thousand) and R. H. Anderson (four thousand), which were concentrated behind the town of Sharpsburg. These troops were under Lee's personal command, and he would throw them into action when and where the exigencies of battle required. They had arrived less than two hours before the battle began. They were dog-tired after two days of marching and a week of short rations, and their nominal strength was diminished by stragglers who had fallen out on the march up from Harpers Ferry.

From the right flank of Jackson's front the Confederate line turned south. The hinge was marked by the Mumma Farm buildings—and at dawn by a pillar of smoke that rose from those buildings, burned by order of Confederate brigadier Roswell Ripley, who feared they could be used to shelter Federal sharpshooters, who could seriously disrupt the defense by picking off officers and artillerymen. Four brigades of D. H. Hill's Division (5,800) held a line that slanted southeastward from the farm, across the road that ran from the Middle Bridge to Sharpsburg, down to the bank of the Antietam. Though the flanks of this line were on relatively higher ground, the longer section just south of the Roulette Farm followed the angular crescent shape of a country road that had been cut and/or worn a yard or more below ground level. This "Sunken Road" formed a natural trench from which infantry could fight with some advantage. The ground in front of the Sunken Road rolled up in a shallow slope to form a low, smooth ridge, which would protect Federal troops approaching the Sunken Road from the north. However, as soon as the attackers topped that roll of ground they could be hit by massed fire from the entrenched Rebels, and staggered just as they prepared to make their charge across the quarter-mile of open ground. Because that low ridge also offered some protection from Federal artillery, the Sunken Road line was an extremely strong defensive position.

The same could not be said of the extended front that covered the road up from the Middle Bridge. The roadblock was held by G. B. Anderson's Brigade of Hill's Division. Half a mile behind it, two units totaling about a thousand men covered the front of Sharpsburg and initially provided some backup for G. B. Anderson. These units were a brigade of six hundred men commanded by G. T. "Tige" Anderson and some four hundred infantry under Brigadier General Nathan "Shanks" Evans—part of an infantry division nominally belonging to Longstreet's command.

South of Sharpsburg, the main defensive line still followed the edge of the plateau that surrounded the town. The line of the high ground here was held by five infantry brigades of the division commanded by Major General David R. Jones, with a cavalry brigade guarding the extreme right flank. A sixth infantry brigade, commanded by Brigadier General Robert Toombs, was posted a mile or more to the east, holding the hill that looked down on the Lower Bridge of the Antietam, with skirmishers defending the high western bank of the Antietam southward to Snavely's Ford.

Toombs was a wealthy Georgia planter, lawyer, and career politician, a big, bluff, opinionated man with a chin beard, beetling black brows, and an intimidating scowl. He had been a preeminent figure in Southern politics since the Mexican War and had nearly been selected over Jefferson Davis as provisional president of the Confederacy; had been the Confederacy's first secretary of state, but resigned from the cabinet to lead his own brigade on the battlefield. Like many militant politicos and amateur soldiers of that time, he expressed disdain for West Point professionals, for what he supposed was their fussy insistence on troop discipline and well-regulated maneuvers. Unlike most of his type he had some skill as a troop commander.

Toombs's position was extremely strong—if reinforced it could have served as an anchor for the southern end of Lee's line. However, Lee's force was so thin on the ground that it seemed prudent to use Toombs's lone brigade as an outpost, to delay and disrupt a Federal move against the southern flank—after which it would have to fall back on the rest of the division on the plateau south of Sharpsburg. It was critical to the defense that this southern sector remain in Confederate control, to keep open the road to Boteler's Ford—the route by which A. P. Hill's Light Division was marching to reinforce Lee. In the fields just east of the Hagerstown Pike, John Walker's infantry division (four thousand) was posted. It was the closest reinforcement to Toombs, but Lee considered Walker's command part of his general reserve, and he was prepared to put it on the pike and rush it north if (as he expected) the heavy blow fell there.

The infantry force that held the four-mile arc of Lee's defense line was outnumbered by Federal infantry two to one, but this disparity was offset by an ample supply of artillery. The Army of Northern Virginia had 221 guns on the field, as against McClellan's 300. Thirty of the Union pieces were twenty-pounder Parrott guns, heavy pieces that outranged anything in the Confederate train, ideally suited to knocking out Confederate batteries. However, in the coming battle the lighter field batteries would prove more useful. These were the guns that went into action with or just behind the infantry, and their primary function was as infantry killers. Once the fighting came to close quarters, these weapons would provide the decisive margin of firepower. Since all the Confederate guns were in this category, the Union's overall numerical advantage was effectively less than three to two; and at the point of contact the Confederates would often have the advantage—their infantry were positioned with their guns, while the Federals had to bring their pieces forward under fire.

McCLELLAN PLANS HIS BATTLE

McClellan's tasks in preparing for battle were more complex and difficult than Lee's. He had to plan and execute an offensive battle, on problematic terrain, with an army whose commanders and major units had little experience in working together. Moreover, he was up against an aggressive and skillful enemy. Although he had commanded Federal armies for more than a year and led them in two offensive campaigns, McClellan had never both planned and directed a large-scale general engagement. In all the major battles of the Peninsula campaign, from Seven Pines through the Seven Days, the Confederates had taken the tactical offensive. McClellan's forces had responded reflexively, and McClellan himself had not exercised tactical control of the engagements. Burnside and Hooker had ordered the maneuvers that won the Battle of South Mountain. Antietam was therefore the first general engagement that McClellan planned and conducted from start to finish.

To appreciate the tactical problem as McClellan understood it, we first need to consider his estimate of the size of the Rebel force on September 17. In his "Final Report" on the battle, McClellan would state that Lee had had 97,445 troops at Antietam, against his own 87,164. Neither figure corresponds to reality. As always, his faulty methods of intelligence gathering and analysis produced a wild exaggeration of enemy strength. He also overestimated the size of his own force by using a faulty accounting method, which counted all the troops officially credited to a command (the "aggregate present") whether or not they were actually "present for action." Confederates tended to err in the opposite direction, by failing to include in their strength reports the large number of noncombatants attached to each combat unit, who provided essential support services as teamsters, cooks, medical aids, officers' servants, and ammunition carriers. During the invasion of Maryland many of these services were performed by Black slaves, whose presence did not register in accounts limited to White manpower.[9]

However, these figures are useful as an indication that McClellan rated the *relative* strength of the two armies roughly equal. The slight superiority he attributes to Lee is insignificant when set against McClellan's claim that he had been outnumbered two to one on the Peninsula. There is also good reason to think that McClellan actually thought he had a slight superiority in troop strength. Since September 5, McClellan had been deliberately exaggerating the estimates of enemy strength reported by his cavalry chief, Brigadier General Alfred Pleasonton. The latter had initially estimated Lee's strength as 110,000, then reduced it to about 100,000. McClellan had told Halleck that Lee had 120,000, an inflation rate of between 10 and 20 percent. If we apply a 15 percent mendacity discount to his estimate of Lee's strength, Confederate numbers are reduced to about 83,000 against 87,000 Federals—and McClellan's willingness to fight becomes more understandable. McClellan's battle plan is best understood if we see it as designed to cope with an enemy of nearly, but not quite, equal strength.[10]

Again, these numbers only have meaning as an indication of how McClellan rated the *relative* strength of the two armies. By the best estimates available, the Army of the Potomac's actual strength on September 17 was about 72,500 men. For the sake of clarity, all future references to Union troop strength are based on this estimate.[11]

McClellan's tactics were formulated on the afternoon and evening of September 16, but the thinking that produced his plan remains hidden. There is no evidence that he sought a significant amount of advice from his staff, or from Fitz-John Porter. Nor did he consult with his corps commanders, to explain his rationale and objectives or to address any questions they might have about when and how they were to put their troops in action. He did meet with Burnside on the evening of September 16, but the instructions he gave him were far from precise. His other corps commanders received no written orders, only verbal instructions transmitted through staff officers. This lack of documentation creates serious problems for the historian trying to figure out what McClellan intended to do on September 17, and how he planned to do it. It seems also to have left his generals in some doubt as to what exactly he expected of them.[12]

It was only after the battle that McClellan would compose a general description of his plan, and he produced two different versions, a "Preliminary Report," dated October 15, and the aforementioned "Final Report," dated August 4, 1863. The "Final" is highly suspect. It was obviously intended to rationalize the maneuvers that actually occurred during the battle, and to respond to criticisms. The "Preliminary Report" gives a far more credible picture of his battle plan. It was written shortly after the close of active operations, and the tactical plan it lays out makes sense when correlated with McClellan's prebattle troop dispositions.

McClellan's forces were grouped in three maneuver elements. Hooker's I Corps was across the Antietam, fronting Lee's northern flank; and on the night of the sixteenth McClellan ordered the just-arrived XII Corps to cross the river and join Hooker, bringing his total force to perhaps 20,000 infantry. On the opposite flank, Burnside's IX Corps (13,000) was bivouacked on the ridges overlooking the Lower Bridge. In the center, facing the Middle Bridge, McClellan had massed the II Corps as a mobile reserve. At nearly 18,000 veteran troops, this was his largest and strongest unit. It was backed by the two divisions of Porter's V Corps and Pleasanton's cavalry division. The two divisions of Franklin's VI Corps would join Porter early on the morning of the seventeenth, and with V Corps would form the army's general reserve. McClellan thus kept more than 45,000 of his 72,500 troops under his direct command fronting the Middle Bridge and the direct road to Sharpsburg.

The description of the battle plan in McClellan's "Preliminary Report" is marked by an ambiguity of language that reflects the hesitancy and uncertainty of the general's intent. He says, "The design was to make the main attack upon the enemy's left [that is, on Hooker's front]—at least to create a diversion in favor of the main attack, with the hope of something more by [Burnside's] assailing the enemy's right—and as soon as one or both of the flank movements were fully successful, to attack their center with any reserve I might then have on hand." McClellan seems not to have decided at the outset whether Hooker's was to be the main attack, or a diversion in favor of the main attack, which would presumably come from the center.[13] He was hedging his commitment to the offensive and would wait to see how Hooker's attack fared before deciding whether to use his mobile reserve to reinforce Hooker or to attack Lee's center and/or right. The last part of the "Preliminary Report" gives a clearer idea of the sequence of attacks McClellan envisioned: first Hooker would attack Lee's northern flank, then Burnside would move against the southern end of the Rebel line. If those attacks "succeeded" in breaking the Rebel line or diverting troops from Lee's center, McClellan would "attack their center" with the forces massed in his own center. However, McClellan also allowed for the possibility that he might have to send forces from his reserve to aid Hooker and/or Burnside—either to exploit a success or to backstop a repulse. In that case, his ability to attack the Confederate center would be limited by "any reserve I might then have on hand."[14]

THE DISPROPORTIONATE MASSING of infantry in the center is an indication that McClellan considered this the critical sector—either the springboard of triumphant assault or the bulwark of a final defense. That view is supported by the fact that he also chose to concentrate his cavalry at the center of his line. The horsemen, with their added force and mobility, would have been better employed on the flanks of the army, especially the southern, where they could have guarded Burnside's advance against a flank attack by troops out of Harpers Ferry. The only reason for keeping them in the center would have been to exploit an infantry breakthrough at that point—a classic Napoleonic tactic, though one for which Federal cavalry, at this point in the war, was unsuited.

The units massing above the Middle Bridge were those McClellan considered the best in the army: the II, V, and VI Corps that had fought under his command on the Peninsula. The V and VI Corps were each reduced to two divisions and 12,500 troops, but the troops were veterans. The corps commanders, Porter and Franklin. were friends and loyalists who owed their promotions to McClellan. They were also experienced combat commanders. Porter may have been the best combat general of his rank in the Army of the Potomac, since he had played the leading role in the operations that saved McClellan's army during the Seven Days. Now, however, he was under a cloud, falsely accused by Pope of having caused the defeat at Second Bull Run by disobedience of orders. His future depended on McClellan's success in the forthcoming battle, and through most of the action, McClellan would keep him close at hand as confidant and chief adviser.

Major General Edwin V. Sumner commanded the II Corps, at eighteen thousand men the largest unit in the Army of the Potomac. Its power lay in quality as well as mass. Its soldiers were veterans of the Peninsula campaign who had fought with skill and courage in most of its major battles. Its division commanders were combat-tested, and rated with the best in the army; so were most of its brigadiers, whether their commissions were Regular Army or strictly Volunteer. If properly used, II Corps had the combat power to deliver a decisive blow. But McClellan could not trust "Old Bull Head" Sumner to use it properly. The old man was brave to rashness, but hapless at maneuvering any force larger than a brigade. Sumner also had the highest seniority among the corps commanders, which meant that he would automatically take charge of any detached force with which he became connected. McClellan tried to insure himself against Sumner's blundering by keeping the old man and II Corps directly under his own command in the army's center.

The heavy guns of the army's artillery reserve—the batteries commanded by Weed, von Kleiser, and Taft—were posted south of the Middle Bridge on a steep ridge overlooking Antietam Creek, which served as a protective moat. From this position the twenty-pounder rifled Parrott guns had the range to hit nearly any point on the battlefield, and they were immune to counterbattery fire because Confederate guns could not reach them. However, their accuracy was hardly pinpoint, and the explosive power of the shells then in use was not sufficient to destroy well-designed artillery or infantry entrenchments. McClellan had postponed fighting until these guns were in position, because he believed their firepower offset the disadvantage inherent in having to assume the offensive against an enemy of nearly equal strength. These guns could play havoc with infantry or artillery posted on open ground, like that around the Dunker Church. However, there were inherent limits to the effectiveness of these guns: there was a lot of "dead ground" on the battlefield, a sunken road and low rolls of land behind which infantry could shelter, and woodlots whose trees blocked the gunners' line of sight and diluted the effect of shell fire on infantry posted there.

Even with these drawbacks, the concentration of strength at the Union center gave McClellan insurance in case Hooker and Burnside should meet with disaster. It seemed quite possible to McClellan that Lee was strong enough to defeat Hooker's attack without substantially weakening the Confederate center. Hooker's force, isolated beyond Antietam, might then be exposed to destruction by one of Jackson's furious assaults. In that case McClellan would have to dissipate his reserve by sending substantial reinforcements to support Hooker. Then, in his own words, his ability to strike a decisive blow at the Rebel center would be diminished to the remnant strength of "any reserve I might then have on hand." Even if that remnant was inadequate to smash the Rebel center, it would shield the army's vitals from a Confederate counterattack. For McClellan's purposes, it was victory enough if his army held its ground, blocking Lee's path of invasion and leaving the Confederates no option but retreat into Virginia.[15]

The center-weighted alignment had a further advantage, at once political and psychological. By holding the preponderance of his force in the center, under his immediate control, McClellan reserved to himself the maximum authority and flexibility in conducting the battle. He alone could decide whether and when to unleash the reserved power of fifty thousand troops, nearly two-thirds of his total force. He alone was in a position to decide whether to take more risk, by throwing more troops into Hooker's and Burnside's attacks, or to minimize that risk by either withholding his reserves or using them defensively.

But the supposed "flexibility" of the plan masked a fundamental flaw: McClellan had not decided where and how to strike the decisive blow. His tactical dispositions allowed him to postpone the critical choices, but they drastically slowed the speed with which he could respond to battlefield developments. The geography of the battlefield severely limited McClellan's options for using the high concentration of strength at the Union center. Although II Corps was nominally available to reinforce Hooker, it would take nearly an hour and a half for its units to march from the center to Hooker's front. They had to march nearly two miles upstream, cross the Antietam by the Upper Bridge, then march cross-lots for several miles to connect with Hooker's flank.

The alternative to such a roundabout move was for the center units to cross the Middle Bridge and make an all-or-nothing frontal assault against the center of the Confederate line—a dangerous move, considering that the enemy was believed to be of equal strength. McClellan's plan clearly indicates that such an attack would only occur if Hooker and Burnside had already "succeeded."

McClellan's orders to Burnside were in keeping with the ambiguity of his commitment to the offensive. McClellan told Burnside he would have to "attack the enemy's right on the following morning."[16] However, because no time was specified for the attack, Burnside not unreasonably assumed that only a diversion was required. IX Corps was the weakest of McClellan's three attack elements, mustering only thirteen thousand troops, and it could only come to grips with the enemy by fighting its way through two well-defended crossing points: the Rohrbach, or Lower, Bridge, a bottleneck only twelve feet wide completely dominated by a high, steep-sided hill on the western side; and an unmarked ford some miles below the bridge. Moreover, McClellan also assigned IX Corps a defensive task: to guard the army's southern flank against a possible attack by a strong Confederate column from Harpers Ferry. This, too, was an indication that IX Corps was not expected to stage an all-out assault.

MCCLELLAN NOT ONLY limited the forces he entrusted to his assault commanders, he did not fully inform them of the tactical plan for the battle they were about to fight. His refusal may have reflected, and been intended to conceal, his indecision about where and how to strike his heaviest blows. It is also possible that he refused to discuss his plans with his subordinates, and declined to issue written orders, so that no one—neither his colleagues nor his rivals—would know whether his plans had been well- or ill-conceived. His defensive position had to be impregnable on *both* fronts. But what was good for McClellan was not helpful to the men who had to fight his battle. No corps commander, with the possible exception of Hooker in the earliest stage of the battle, had either the authority or the information that would allow him to take intelligent initiatives. McClellan would try to control the entire operation from his headquarters, working even distant units by the word of command. As a result, the army's ability to respond to changing conditions would be slowed to the speed of mounted couriers riding to and from headquarters, where McClellan, beset by uncertainties, would ponder and decide.[17]

The bad effects of that policy were compounded by the fact that the least experienced corps commanders were given the most critical independent roles. Hooker had only been promoted from divisional to corps command on September 6, taking over a corps that had not only served in a different army (Pope's) but whose commanders and constituent units were entirely unknown to him or to the members of his staff. He had led that corps in one engagement, at South Mountain, as Burnside's subordinate. Now he was asked to command two army corps in the most complex, critical, and dangerous assignment of the battle.

He would get no help from General Joseph Mansfield, the commander of XII Corps, which had been assigned to Hooker's support. Mansfield was fifty-nine years old, an army engineer and career staff officer with almost no experience leading troops in combat. McClellan had snatched Mansfield out of his proper sphere because he was desperate to replace Banks, a militia officer who owed his general's star to politics and had performed poorly in the field. However, Mansfield did not catch up with the army to assume the command until forty-eight hours before the battle. XII Corps therefore went into action under a man who had no combat experience and no familiarity with the organization or the men he had to command. He was unable to consult with Hooker on the role his corps was expected to play, and Hooker's orders were too general to be of much use. When the fighting started, Mansfield's responses would be doubtful and uncertain.

Burnside's command experience was both extensive and limited. He had commanded his corps for most of the year, conducting a successful joint operation with the navy to clear and hold the North Carolina sounds, but this had not entailed any large-scale engagements. Part of his corps had fought at Second Bull Run, but under the command of General Reno. The only large engagement Burnside had ever directed was South Mountain. Again, he had had little to do with the battlefield action, where Reno once again led IX Corps, until he was killed and succeeded by Cox. Now Burnside's limitations as a field commander were augmented by his sense of grievance at being demoted and devalued by his erstwhile friend and idol McClellan. At the start of the Mary-

Confederate dead on Hagerstown Pike (Library of Congress)

land campaign, McClellan had elevated Burnside to the status of wing commander, with authority over Hooker's I Corps as well as his own IX Corps; and Burnside believed he had justified that promotion by winning the battle at South Mountain. However, now, to his chagrin, he found that Hooker's Corps had been taken from him and shifted to the opposite end of the line, and that Hooker was now a wing commander in his own right, with authority over I and XII Corps.[18]

Burnside in a crisis, whether emotional or military, lacked the intelligence and flexibility of mind to make rational adjustments to his plans or expectations. McClellan had made him a wing commander, and he was damned if he would accept any lesser role. However, when Burnside insisted that Cox command the corps in the upcoming action, Cox protested. Although he was the senior division commander under Burnside, his Kanawha Division was not formally a part of IX Corps. It was a fragment left over from the abortive Federal campaign against Jackson in the Shenandoah, back in April 1862. Cox and his staff (which was too small for the job) were therefore unfamiliar with the division and brigade commanders. Reno's staff might have compensated for these deficiencies, but they had been allowed to leave the army to escort their general's corpse back to Washington, a noble gesture but hardly responsive to the needs of an army in the field. As a result an already sclerotic channel of communication between McClellan and IX Corps now became even more problematic. When McClellan sent Burnside an order, Burnside would ponder its import and pass it on to Cox. Figuratively speaking, the headquarters of Burnside and Cox were now a pair of stools, between which orders and responsibilities could fall and be lost.

The most critical consequence of this inane arrangement was the failure of IX Corps staff to scout the terrain on the corps front. The infantry had been posted behind a ridgeline well back from the bridge, because the fields closer to the bridge were exposed to harassing fire by Rebel artillery. If IX Corps' attack was to be timely and effective, its officers needed to know the lay of the land they had to cross, especially the land along the riverbank. The bridge itself was more of a bottleneck than a proper avenue of attack, twelve feet wide and overlooked by a steep hillside. Infantry trying to charge across it could have been shot like sardines in a can. Had it been defended in the kind of strength McClellan expected, IX Corps could not have done more than conduct a firefight across the stream, which was thought to be too deep near the bridge to be crossed on foot. However, there were a number of fords downstream, Snavely's being the closest, by which troops could have crossed to outflank the bridge defenses. McClellan's engineers informed Burnside that the ford existed, but neither he nor Cox ordered a reconnaissance to find out exactly where it was. That search would not be made until the troops went into action, and hours would be lost while local farmers were questioned as to its whereabouts. If IX Corps staff had done its job properly the ford would have been discovered on the night of the sixteenth, and a IX Corps attack, if promptly delivered, might have seriously threatened or broken Lee's southern flank.

Yet despite all that McClellan got wrong—his false estimate of enemy strength, his obfuscated command structure, and his ill-conceived troop placement—if his plan had been properly executed it would have subjected Lee's defense to unbearable pressure. Lee's force was far from the 65,000 McClellan imagined, and on the morning of September 17 mustered no more than 36,000, and perhaps as few as 31,000, troops. McClellan had 60,000 troops immediately at hand, with another 12,500 from

VI Corps on the march from Pleasant Valley and likely to arrive before midmorning. With that disparity of force, a sequence of strong attacks, made promptly one after the other—first on the northern flank, then on the southern—would have forced Lee to strip his center to the bare bones, making it vulnerable to a Federal breakthrough. However, the key words are "strong and coordinated." Given the general advantages of the defense, the strength of Lee's position, and his army's advantage in command organization, McClellan would have to press his attacks with energy and power, committing much, if not all, of his reserve to the effort; and his attacks would have to be coordinated and mutually supporting, to offset Lee's ability to shift his units (especially his artillery) along interior lines.

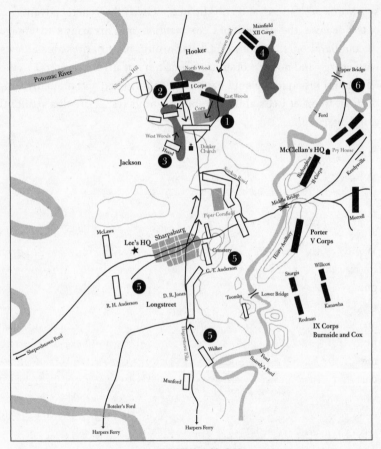

MAP 4: ANTIETAM, 6:30–7:30 AM

1 and 2: U.S. I Corps attacks through cornfield and West Woods

3. 7:30 AM, Hood's C.S. Division retakes the cornfield

4. 7:30 AM, U.S. XII Corps approaches

5. 8:00–9:00 AM, G. T. Anderson's Brigade, McLaws's (C.S.) and Walker's Divisions move to reinforce Jackson

6. U.S. divisions of Sedgwick and French, under Sumner, move to support Hooker

CHAPTER 12

THE BATTLE OF ANTIETAM: HOOKER'S FIGHT

6:00–9:00 AM

❧⚜❧

IT RAINED HARD DURING THE NIGHT, THEN CLEARED OFF AT SUN-rise, a little after 6:00 AM. A spatter of skirmisher fire could be heard along Hooker's front, especially under the dripping leaves in the East Woods where infantry from Meade's division had been tangling all night with Confederates from Trimble's Brigade. Then the long-range guns east of the Antietam tuned up, dropping 20-pound shells into the trees—scaring the infantry but doing little real harm. The sun at low angle threw the shadow of the East Woods across the open ground between the woods. The infantry in Jackson's front line—J. R. Jones's men in the West Woods and Lawton's skirmishers drawn up in Miller's cornfield—saw the dark mass of blue-coated infantry tramping forward into the shadow, steel sparking across the front where their bayonets caught the light. Fighting Joe Hooker had told McClellan he would attack at first light, and he kept his word.

As a division commander on the Peninsula and at Second Bull Run, Hooker had maneuvered three brigades of infantry with energy and skill, leading from the firing line to encourage his men by heroic example and to maintain control of his units amid the stress and confusion of battle. A good corps commander needed those skills, and others besides. Instead of the division commander's three brigades, he had to maneuver three divisions, eleven or twelve infantry brigades, and an artillery reserve. He had to envision and control the action of troops beyond his line of sight, manage the distribution and concentration of far more firepower, and intelligently relate his own actions to the overall plan of action laid down by army headquarters. It was difficult enough for a general experienced in divisional command to quickly grasp and master the technique of corps command. Hooker had led I Corps for less than two weeks, and in its only major combat had been subordinate to Burnside. Now McClellan had assigned him the semi-independent command of a two-corps wing, which made him responsible for coordinating the action of five divisions across a mile-wide battlefront.[1]

Hooker handled the assignment like a corps commander, not a wing commander. He reconnoitered I Corps' front, chose his objective, and half an hour before sunrise his aides delivered the orders that would organize his own three divisions for an assault. Not until all that was done did an aide carry to General Mansfield the order to bring XII Corps forward to "support" I Corps' attack. By the time the order was delivered, however, I Corps was already heavily engaged. Mansfield needed more guidance than that. He was nearly sixty years old, had only commanded his corps for forty-eight hours, and had not exercised field command for fifteen years. Hooker should have conferred with him well before dawn, to make certain Mansfield understood the lay of the land, the planned course of the operation, and XII Corps' role in it. Lacking such preparation, Mansfield understood the order to support Hooker's attack only in the most general terms. He was also unsure about how, where, and when Hooker wanted his support. XII Corps was therefore slow to assemble and hesitant coming forward. It would take an hour or more to bring Mansfield's ten thousand troops into action. Until then, Hooker's three divisions—fourteen thousand men (including artillery) but only nine thousand infantry—would have to fight a Confederate force of comparable strength.[2]

NORTHERN FRONT, 5:30-7:30 AM

Hooker had chosen the proper objective for I Corps' attack, the patch of high ground marked by the little weatherbeaten Dunker Church. The open ground between the two woods and the line of the Hagerstown Pike pointed the obvious path to the target, and Hooker organized his divisions for a frontal assault right down that alley, two in front and one as backup. The brigade commanded by Brigadier General James Ricketts would lead. Ricketts had commanded artillery in the Regular Army since 1839, but when the war broke out the shortage of trained professionals led to his transfer to the infantry and promotion to brigadier general. He formed his three brigades in line of battle behind the East Woods, then advanced—Duryee's Brigade on the right of the line swinging around the end of the woods and striking straight for Miller's cornfield, while the other two brigades were slowed by having to pass through the East Woods.

Hooker's other lead brigade was commanded by Brigadier General Abner Doubleday, a plodding old Regular who did *not* invent baseball, whatever the legends may say. His division was camped astride the Hagerstown Pike. Hooker formed its brigades in columns and ordered it to advance up the pike behind and to the right or west of Ricketts's lead brigade, supporting the attack through the cornfield and defending Ricketts's flank against Rebel infantry in the West Wood.

Behind Doubleday and Ricketts the brigade led by Brigadier General George Meade would advance as the corps reserve. Grizzled, crusty, and goggle-eyed, Meade was a rising star in the army, an 1835 graduate of West Point who had made an excellent record as an engineer and as a combat officer in Mexico and the Seminole War. Governor Curtin of Pennsylvania made Meade a protégé and got him a brigade command early in the war. Meade earned the place in combat on the Peninsula, where his brigade belonged to Porter's V Corps. He had been transferred to I Corps to improve its quality, and he was doing that. Within a few months he would rise to command an army corps, and in less than a year he would lead the Army of the Potomac against Lee at Gettysburg.

Intently focused on his line of attack, Hooker failed to take account of the threat from beyond the corridor. As his infantry pressed forward it was hit from the right flank by Jeb Stuart's cannons on Nicodemus Hill, more than half a mile to the west. At that distance solid roundshot and explosive shells ripped gaps in the marching columns, destroyed artillery pieces or the limber chests of ammunition, killed horses and men. Hooker was not prepared to deal with a threat from that direction. Until he could bring up guns from his corps reserve and align them to fire against Stuart's batteries, his men had no defense against the Confederate shell fire. As the Union troops approached the northern edge of the Miller cornfield, they were also hit by fire from the batteries posted around the Dunker Church, which included the artillery of Lawton's Division and Colonel S. D. Lee's detachment from the army reserve.

Duryee's brigade were the first Union troops into the corridor, 1,100 infantry wheeling to their left around the northwest corner of the East Woods and tramping forward in double line of battle toward the cornfield. The steady walking pace of their advance was set by the regimental drummers, a steady repetitive ratta-pan *pan*. When the drum-rattle quickens the step picks up, but following the cadence keeps the fighting line intact even when bullets and shells begin to whirr past.

The other brigades of their division were lagging, pushing through the woods on their left. Well behind and to the west of Duryee, the lead unit of Doubleday's division, the "Iron Brigade," commanded by Brigadier General John Gibbon, was marching down the Hagerstown Pike in a double column. Union officers on horseback could see amid the tall stalks of standing corn the dull gleam of morning sun reflected on the rifle barrels of Rebel infantry.

At the northern edge of the cornfield Duryee's Federals halted, two lines of riflemen one behind the other. The rattabang and smoke blast of their volley were instantly answered from the southern side of the cornfield, and the noise and smoke solidified as both sides blazed away, the piercing tenor of musketry punctuated by blasts from S. D. Lee's artillery alongside the Dunker Church.

The basis of battlefield tactics in the Civil War is the clash of troops formed in opposing lines of battle, the infantry in each regiment massed shoulder to shoulder in two lines. For soldiers armed with single-shot rifle muskets, this was the only way to concentrate infantry firepower. Once within rifle range of the enemy—say one hundred yards—infantry on both sides would begin firing, the attackers loading and firing as they advanced across the open ground, their pace slowed by the need to prime, load, ram, and fire the muzzle-loaded rifle musket.

In theory, once the attacking force has damaged or shaken the defense by fire, it has to charge with the bayonet and break the opposing line by physical force. In practice, however, bayonet charges on Civil War battlefields were rarely carried to completion. The only way to get volunteer troops to commit themselves to a bayonet charge was to forbid them to load or to cap their weapons. If attacking troops were allowed to return fire, that is generally what they would do. Civil War engagements tended to bog down in inconclusive firefights, fading out as ammunition was exhausted. It required dynamic and intelligent leadership at the regimental level, and high morale in the troops, to break such a standoff and get the attack moving forward again. Then the defenders, seeing the mass that rises against them and sensing the thinness of their own line, hearing the weakness of their own defensive fire, may break to the rear. But in this war the advantage was usually with the defense. Because the attackers advance shoulder to shoulder, the individuals in the mass feel the volume and accuracy of defensive fire, registered as noise and fury but also by the sound of bullet impacts on their neighbors in the line, the dull thud of a body blow or the sharp crack of bone-break, and they sense the weakening of their line as comrades fall right and left. At some point they may reach a kind of dead-line, beyond which it is impossible for them to move. Then, depending on circumstances, they may back away, or break and run to the rear—or come to a stand and begin firing again at much closer range.

There again the attackers would be at a disadvantage. The firepower of a Civil War brigade is not just its rifle strength but the power of its associated battery, the little four- and six-pounder Napoleons. The weakness of the offense is that as you close with the enemy you leave your own guns behind, and your ranks actually mask or block the fire of your artillery support, while the enemy's cannons are firing point-blank. Against infantry more than five or six hundred yards away the gunners use solid shot and explosive shells. As the distance narrows they switch to case shot, each case a hollow iron ball filled with an explosive charge and more than a hundred bullets, that fire in a forward spread when the shell explodes. At four hundred yards the gunners switch to canister, the deadliest weapon against infantry—a thin-walled can packed with up to 120 bullets, sometimes more than one can to a charge, equivalent to the fire of a battalion in line but far more concentrated, like the blast of a monstrous shotgun into the ranks.[3]

The Army of the Potomac was superior in number of artillery pieces, and the Army of Northern Virginia had no match for the long-range batteries ranked on the hills east of the creek. However, at the point of contact, where Hooker's wing clashed with Jackson's, the Confederates had the advantage. Hooker had to shift four of his nine reserve batteries to counter the shelling from Stuart's guns on Nicodemus Hill, instead of using them to support his infantry attack. The long-range fire from east of the Antietam could not entirely compensate for the lack of pieces closer to the battle line. Big shells from the twenty-pounder Parrott guns exploded in the West Woods, smashing tree limbs down on the Rebel infantry. Division commander J. R. Jones was knocked out by concussion from an exploding shell and carried to the rear, command passing to Brigadier General William Starke. Shell fire also damaged and discomfited S. D. Lee's Confederate batteries sited in the open around the church, blowing up ammunition-filled limber chests, killing horses and men. But the bombardment lacked the accuracy and destructive power to knock out Lee's batteries, and the guns of J. R. Jones's and Hood's Divisions were sheltered by the West Woods.[4]

Direct artillery support for Duryee's attack was limited to two four-gun batteries from the divisional reserve, which trotted into position and unlimbered in a field by an orchard a hundred yards behind the infantry. S. D. Lee's guns shifted from antipersonnel to counterbattery fire, in an attempt to knock out the Federal guns with explosive shell. The Union guns responded in kind. Then, on order, they changed from shell to canister, firing musket-ball blasts that scythed the corn in swathes and exposed the Rebels' fence-rail breastwork at the southern edge of the field, where a brigade of Confederate infantry commanded by a Colonel Douglass was waiting. Duryee's order, echoed by his regimental commanders, sent the double line tramping through the cornstalk wreckage with lowered bayonets. In front of them Douglass's Confederates rose up and began firing right in their faces, and bullets also began striking them from the left flank, fired by units of Trimble's Brigade that had been skirmishing with Union troops in the East Woods. These troops were just beginning to be pressured by the Federal brigades of Hartsuff and Christian, which were still working their way south through the East Woods.

Duryee's lines came to a stand some 250 yards from the Rebel breastwork and instead of breaking stood there firing as fast as rifle-muskets could be loaded for some uncalculated but astonishing length of time. Finally, with a third of his men down and Confederate troops edging up through the woods to fire into his flank, Duryee ordered a retreat. His brigade backed off in good order, returning fire as it went.

As Duryee's brigade came back out of the cornfield the Iron Brigade, in their distinctive black hats with the black cockade, leading Doubleday's Division, came trotting down the Hagerstown Pike. Right behind Gibbon's men were the four New York Regiments and Second U.S. Sharpshooters of Colonel Walter Phelps's New York brigade. These two brigades were headed straight down the corridor between the two Woods, toward the cornfield and the Dunker Church. Doubleday's third brigade, commanded by Brigadier General Marsena Patrick, was to protect the right flank of the assault brigades by attacking southward into the West Woods and clearing it of Confederates.

Doubleday was fortunate to have three highly competent brigadiers, because the fighting on his front would be at close quarters and subject to changes so rapid that only skilled officers operating close to the action could respond effectively. General Patrick was fifty-one, with a bald head and a grizzled full beard that flared outward. He had graduated from West Point in 1835, and served in the Seminole and Mexican wars, but was one of those ambitious and intelligent Regulars who had left the army in the 1850s to prosper in the railroad business. Colonel Phelps was a thirty-year-old citizen-soldier about whom little is known. Politics was probably responsible for his original appointment as colonel of the Twenty-second New York, but he learned quickly on the job and would be maintained in brigade command throughout the war. The most able of the three was John Gibbon, and in the coming fight he would display the skill and courage that would lead him to higher rank, as a division and later a corps commander.

Gibbon's Iron Brigade had quick-marched down the pike for over a mile under punishing artillery fire from Stuart's guns on Nicodemus Heights. They were angry rather than demoralized, and eager to pay the enemy back.

The Iron Brigade fronted the cornfield, with Phelps's Brigade hastening up to form a line on its left. Gibbon started forward into the cornfield, the Second and Sixth Wisconsin forming his first line, followed by one section of guns from the brigade artillery, behind them the Seventh Wisconsin and Nineteenth Indiana and the second section of guns. As the Black Hats pressed forward they were hit from the flank by volleys of rifle fire from Rebel troops in the West Woods. To meet that threat Gibbon ordered his second-line regiments and gun section to wheel right and protect the brigade's advance by attacking the Confederates in the woods.[5]

The flanking fire came from the Confederacy's legendary "Stonewall Brigade," the Fourth, Fifth, Twenty-seventh, and Thirty-third Virginia.[6] This was the brigade whose determined stand at First Bull Run earned General Jackson his nickname. Since then it had endured the ferocious forced marches and hard battles of Jackson's Valley campaign, the Seven Days, Cedar Mountain, and Second Bull Run. Its numbers were depleted to less than half its normal strength, but it was still a formidable force. Its commander, Colonel Andrew Jackson Grigsby, was a veteran and a hard fighter. But as Gibbon's regiments advanced against them from the eastern face of the woods, the lead elements of Patrick's Federal brigade came in from the northern end to threaten their flank. Patrick also had to divide his own force to deal with Rebels deeper in the woods who were threatening *his* right flank, but two of his regiments joined with Gibbon's Seventh Wisconsin and Nineteenth Indiana to push the Rebels back toward the southern end of the woods.

Meanwhile, in the cornfield, Phelps had pushed his brigade forward to support Gibbon's advance. The Eighty-fourth New York came up to extend the left, or eastward, end of Gibbon's line, with the rest of the New Yorkers just behind in reserve. As Phelps's reserve line marched south along the edge of the West Woods, they also took fire from that flank. Phelps sent the Second U.S. Sharpshooters toward the wood to counter. As the Union troops came out of the cornfield they were also hit with heavy rifle and artillery fire from the Confederate infantry and artillery defending the high ground around the Dunker Church. There the battle line halted and, as before, Union and Confederate units stood and faced each other across the open ground below the church. Double lines of riflemen loaded, rammed, aimed, and fired, deafened by long ripping bangs of rifle fire, blinded by the gray clouds of gunsmoke that accumulated and settled over the front, blotting out the lines so that the commanders had to fight their units more by ear than by sight. The hunters, farmers, and backwoodsmen of the Sixth Wisconsin with their black hats were steady under that fire. Alongside them stood the Eighty-fourth

New York—originally a militia regiment, the Fourteenth Brooklyn, a k a the Brooklyn Chasseurs. They had been outfitted as zouaves, in the uniform worn by the French army's tough Arab auxiliaries, short blue jackets and red pants that ballooned over white puttees. But they had earned their laurels at Bull Run, where they had repeatedly charged the hill held by the Stonewall Brigade—charged so hard that the Stonewalls dubbed them "those red-legged devils."[7]

Confederate gunners blasted canister into the cloud, and it was answered by the battery that Gibbon ran up onto a small rise behind his firing line. Gibbon's line was being raked by oblique fire from Starke's Brigade in the West Woods, despite the efforts of Phelps's sharpshooters to suppress them. To deal with it he would have to wheel his two front-line regiments forty-five degrees to their right—which would expose their flank to Confederate General Lawton's Georgia Brigade in front of the church. Gibbon and Phelps organized a nearly seamless maneuver. As Gibbon's two Wisconsin regiments swung west, the reserve line of Phelps's New Yorkers stepped forward to bear the brunt of fire from the Dunker Church. The firefight here rose to a pitch of frenzy, the firing constant as rear ranks passed loaded rifles forward. "Men and officers of New York and Wisconsin are fused into a common mass, in the frantic struggle to shoot fast. . . . Every body tears cartridges, loads, passes guns, or shoots. Men are falling in their places or running back into the corn." To a Southern war correspondent at Lee's headquarters, it sounded "like the rolling of a thousand distant drums."[8]

Directly to the east of them, the five regiments of Hartsuff's Brigade finally came out of the East Woods into the cornfield and joined the firing line—without Hartsuff, who had been seriously wounded and replaced by one of his regimental commanders. This was a mixed brigade of New York, Maine, Pennsylvania, and Massachusetts regiments. Among the latter was the Twelfth, the Webster Regiment, so-called because its first commander was the son of Daniel Webster, the legendary Bay State senator and statesman. There were many upper-class Bostonians in the Twelfth, which gave the regiment a kid-glove aura. They were also deeply imbued with abolitionist sentiments—disliked McClellan's politics and liked to get his goat by singing "John Brown's Body" whenever he reviewed them. A regiment had to be good at soldiering to sustain that kind of attitude.

They were in a very bad spot, exposed to direct fire from Colonel Lee's guns in front of the Dunker Church. Blasts of canister ripped into the turf with a sound like a knife through a melon rind. "Just in front of us a house was burning, and the fire and smoke, flashing of muskets and whizzing of bullets, yells of men, etc., were perfectly horrible." But their fire kept the Confederate gunners from raking the Iron Brigade as it wheeled to its right to attack the Rebel line in the West Woods.[9]

Gibbon sent his two Wisconsin regiments forward against Starke's Louisianans, and with Phelps's Second Sharpshooters they assailed the West Woods position from the east. As they did, Patrick's Federal troops and Gibbon's other two regiments pressed down through the trees from the north, catching Starke's men in a crossfire. With bullets hitting them from two sides they broke ranks and went to the rear. General Starke was shot three times and died before he could reach an aid station. Command of Major General J. R. Jones's Division passed down to the senior colonel, Grigsby of the Stonewall Brigade—but by now the division was probably no larger than an understrength brigade.

To Confederate General Lawton, commanding at the Dunker Church, it seemed that Federal pressure on his line was mounting to the crisis point. The artillery batteries posted around the church were being blasted by McClellan's long-range guns, firing from beyond the Antietam. The troops holding his left in the West Woods were pulling back, and beyond the East Woods to his right Federal troops seemed to be massing against Ripley's Brigade. The firing in his front was terrific, a deafening continuous roar of rifle and cannon fire. It appeared that the Federals in front of the East Woods were edging forward, perhaps preparing to storm the Dunker Church position.

Lawton had only one brigade still unengaged, the notorious Louisiana Tigers. The Tigers were raised in New Orleans, where the color line dissolved into a spectrum of tones and class lines were drawn in language and lineage. They were a mixed crew of Creoles and Cajuns, Anglos and waterfront Irish, with a reputation for bad discipline, looting, and wild fighting. They were rated a brigade, but their total strength on this day amounted to little more than that of a regiment. Their commander was forty-two-year-old General Harry Hays, a Tennessee-born Louisiana lawyer who had been a volunteer officer in the Mexican War, a "political general" who proved an able battlefield commander. Lawton ordered Hays to counterattack the Yankees who seemed to be advancing out of the East Woods, then sent riders to ask help from General Hood, whose division was in reserve at the southern end of the West Woods.

The target of Hays's attack was Hartsuff's brigade, on the east end of the Union battle line. If they were menacing the Dunker Church it was not because anyone had ordered it. Hartsuff himself had been shot and carried from the field, and his successor Colonel Coulter thought his men were just holding the line in front of the East Woods. The infantry may have been moving up on instinct, blinded by the smoke of their firing, edging forward step-by-step each time they loaded and aimed, trying to get out of the smoke so they could see better how to shoot. Into this steady but indeterminate advance the Louisiana Tigers charged with a yell. For a brief moment there was close-range firing, Algiers and the French Quarter against Boston and Cambridge—then the Federals backed away, still fighting, till they got the woods around them, where they again stood firm. At that point, Christian's Brigade, which had gone astray in its march through the East Woods, joined the firing line—albeit without Colonel Christian, who had taken to his heels. The Federals were in an ideal position, protected by woods, while the Tigers and the other Confederate units that had tailed onto their charge were out in the open. One Union soldier thought, "Never did I see more rebs to fire at than at that moment presented themselves."

The Federals cut loose, the Tigers' charge stumbled against their fire and broke, and Hays's men scurried back across the field to Lawton's line. The Webster Regiment had lost two-thirds of its men, Hays lost 61 percent, and the lines stayed where they were. A corporal in the Twelfth Massachusetts stated the case for both when he wrote, "It was a hot time for us, and most all of our Regt. were used up in a very short time."[10]

On the western side of the cornfield the same pattern held. Gibbon's Iron Brigade, aided by two of Patrick's Regiments, made their push against the West Woods and drove back the brigades of Grigsby and Starke. But the losses they took doing it brought them to a stand, while the Confederates rallied and held.

It was 7:00 AM, and the fighting had been going on for a little more than an hour. Hooker's two lead divisions, under Ricketts and Doubleday, and the two divisions that formed Jackson's front-line defense, had each fought the other to a standstill at horrendous cost. Now Meade's Union division was coming up to throw more weight into the drive against the Dunker Church. On the Confederate side Hood's Division, summoned by Lawton, came rushing up the Hagerstown Pike and formed its battle lines behind Lawton's front.[11]

HOOD'S COUNTERATTACK, 7:30–8:00 AM

Hood was known as a heads-down fighter, but his assessment of the situation in front of him, as given to an aide sent by General Jackson, was clearheaded. His division would have to make a spoiling attack to disrupt the Federal offensive against the Dunker Church, but unless reinforcements could be brought forward the position was likely to fall. Hood sent that appeal to Jackson, who reached out to D. H. Hill, whose division held the next section of the line to the right of the Dunker Church.

Meanwhile Hood brought his men into line, facing northward against the Federals, who were in line across the cornfield, from the West Woods to the East. The Texas Brigade, with which Hood had earned his reputation as a fighting general, would lead the attack, with Evander Law's Brigade in support. The Iron Brigade, on the western end of the Federal line, was facing west against the Rebels in the West Woods, exposing their flank to Hood. The Texas Brigade opened the attack by firing a massed volley that hit the Sixth Wisconsin "like a scythe running through our line." Hood then ordered the division forward. The Texans led the charge, their battle cry the long-drawn keen of the "Rebel Yell," with Law's men and some from other brigades following. Momentum had turned against the Federals. However, rather than retreat back across the cornfield, parts of the Federal line broke to left and right, toward the sheltering woods. The survivors from Ricketts's division, Hartsuff's and Christian's brigades, faded back into the East Woods. Gibbon's Iron Brigade backed off fighting into the West Woods.

Hood's assault force split in pursuit, most of the Texans and some of Law's men swinging toward the West Woods, while the rest slanted off to the right, firing into Ricketts's troops as they left the field. Inflamed by the excitement of the charge and the sight of Federal troops breaking in front of them, Law's regiments rushed through a corner of the East Woods, and in the open fields beyond saw Meade's division advancing to take Ricketts's place in the line. Law's troops kept firing and advancing. The Second and Eleventh Mississippi Regiments led the charge against the Pennsylvania Reserve Division, and when the Federal retreat left a battery without infantry support they charged it, despite double-shotted canister blasts. They took some of the guns, but left their dead lying in long ranks. There were too few left to hold the position.

On the left of the Mississippians, the wild men of the First Texas dashed off at an eccentric angle, beyond the control of the brigade commander. In the northwest corner of the cornfield, they ran up against a solid line of Pennsylvania Reserves, which outnumbered and outflanked them. The Texans' upper bodies were hidden by a bank of gunsmoke, but the Pennsylvanians aimed for their legs, then cut loose with converging fire from their extended line, heavy volleys of musketry supplemented by canister from guns run right up to the edge of the cornfield. The Texans broke and those who could went back the way they had come—80 percent of the regiment were left as casualties on the field. But Law's attack had hit Meade's division hard enough to stop it at the northern boundary of the cornfield.

The fight in front of the West Woods was fiercer still, where the Iron Brigade was trading volleys with three sof Hood's Texas regiments, the Eighteenth Georgia and the Hampton Legion—a high-toned South Carolina outfit recruited and equipped by General Wade Hampton, a wealthy planter and political leader, who was fighting elsewhere on the field at the head of one of Stuart's cavalry brigades. Rallied elements from Starke's Louisiana Brigade were also returning to the fight in the West Woods itself, threatening the Iron Brigade's flank from the south. The Confederate firing line was protected by the fence that lined the Hagerstown Pike, and the Iron Brigade was hit hard—Bloomington and Vincennes, Portage and Fond du Lac on one side, San Antonio and Nacogdoches, Charleston and Columbia on the other. "The musketry became incessant," one Texan wrote, "and rolled out in tremendous volleys, the artillery thundered, shells exploding men yelling and hurrahing."[12] But the Iron Brigade's own battery was up by the Miller Farm, northward up the pike, where it had a clear angle of fire into Hood's flank. Seeing that the guns were off target, Gibbon himself rode to the battery and sighted its pieces. First single, then double, charges of canister ripped the Confederate firing line from end to end, literally tearing men apart, leaving the dead in rows along the fence.

THE TACTICAL PATTERN of this initial engagement would hold for most of the battle. An infantry attack begins, supported at the start by its own artillery, and with the energy of its initial impetus confronts the enemy line and drives it back. But as the attack goes forward it is attenuated by the friction of the battlefield, the derangement of troop organization by loss of commanders and passage over difficult terrain, and the steady drain of rifle strength to fatigue and enemy fire. Every step takes the attackers farther from their own artillery and closer to the enemy's guns, firing charges of canister. In the end they run up against a strong and steady defensive line, or fresh reserves advancing to the fight. They come to a stand, waver, and then pull back, either on the run with broken ranks or steadily, face to the enemy. Then it is the enemy's turn to change the momentum of the fight: the infantry charges, its ranks are winnowed by fire and disorganized by terrain and blinding smoke, it reaches the far side of the cornfield or the wood and is brought up short by the opponent's artillery and advancing reserves—who take their turn following up the retreating foe, with the same result as before.

The process is best described as a meat grinder, in which the front-line units of offense and defense wear each other out without producing a decisive result. Hooker's assaults on the northern front of Lee's position had not been able to break the meat-grinder pattern, to generate the momentum that would push the Confederates back from the line of resistance. The fault was partly Hooker's. There was little coordination between Ricketts's attack in the cornfield and Doubleday's advance against the West Woods. Lack of coordination was fatal on this part of the field, because the Confederate reserves were strong and posted within near supporting distance of each other. The infantry Lee had sent to Jackson on the night of the sixteenth had given the Confederates something like parity in the numbers of infantry immediately available.

The artillery reinforcement he sent gave the Confederates effective superiority over Hooker's gunners firing in support of infantry, since Hooker had to divert nearly half his artillery reserve to counter Stuart's guns on Nicodemus Hill. The long-range fire from the east side of the Antietam had damaged the Confederate batteries near the church but had little effect on Rebel infantry. I Corps had lost a third of its infantry strength and was out of the fight until its units could be rallied and regrouped. Meade's division was less damaged than Ricketts's or Doubleday's, but it had been hit hard in its brief struggle with Hood's Division.[13]

Despite all that, Hooker's troops had hit the Rebel lines with such power and determination that they had forced Jackson to call up all of his reserves and throw them into the meat grinder. By 9:00 AM both Hooker's I Corps and Jackson's three divisions were wrecked. Half of the men in Lawton's Division were casualties, Lawton and one of his brigadiers wounded, another brigadier dead. Casualties were also heavy in J. R. Jones's Division—Jones wounded and his replacement (General Starke) killed. When Hood was asked where his own division was, he replied, "Dead on the field." In fact, some 60 percent of Hood's force were casualties.

The best hope for breaking such a pattern lies in the use of reserves. A strong force held out of the meat grinder till attacker and/or defender has exhausted his strength, then thrown against a vulnerable point at the right moment, can turn the momentum of battle. McClellan understood the principle well enough, which was why he had built up such a large infantry reserve at the center of his position. But these reserves were too far from Hooker to provide timely reinforcement. It would take an hour and a half for troops from the center to make the roundabout march over the Upper Bridge. Hooker had a powerful reserve closer at hand in Mansfield's XII Corps. If Hooker had brought XII Corps forward in time to support his initial wave of attacks, he could have used it, in combination with Meade's Division, to exploit the failure of the Confederate counterattacks. But his orders to Mansfield had been vague, and Mansfield lacked the field experience that might have enabled him to act effectively on his own initiative. So at 7:30, with Hood falling back, XII Corps was just beginning to arrive at the front.

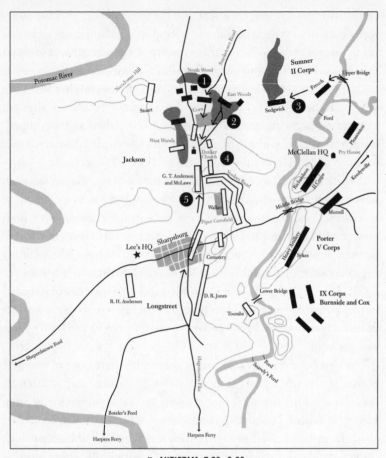

MAP 5: ANTIETAM, 7:30–9:00 AM

1. I Corps (U.S.) reorganizing
2. U.S. XII drives Hood (C.S.) back across cornfield, but is repulsed at Dunker Church
3. Sumner (U.S. II Corps) with Sedgwick's and French's Divisions
4. D. H. Hill's (C.S.) counterattack fails
5. C.S. reinforcements approach Dunker Church

XII CORPS ATTACKS, 7:30–9:00 AM

The history of XII Corps had been a tale of unending misfortune. Its nucleus was the force commanded by General Nathaniel Banks, which had been defeated by Stonewall Jackson and run out of the Shenandoah during Jackson's Valley campaign in April and May of 1862. It had been defeated again at Cedar Mountain on August 9–10 and shared the ignominy of Pope's defeat at Second Bull Run, although it was guarding the wagon train and had missed the actual fighting. It was a second-rate outfit, as compared with those who had fought on the Peninsula, but its soldiers were better than their record showed, and its two divisions had competent and experienced leaders. Brigadier General Alpheus Williams was a militia officer, not a professional, but he had held an active command for more than a year and had temporarily commanded XII Corps on its march up from Washington. George S. Greene was one of the oldest field generals in either army, still vigorous at sixty-one, his most striking feature a magnificent set of gray whiskers—thick mustachios flaring to the sides over a spade-shaped beard, in the style of a sixteenth-century monarch. Although he was a West Point graduate (Class of 1823), he had known only garrison service before resigning in 1836 to pursue a career in civil engineering. His first experience of combat command had come only two months earlier, but he proved to be a skilled and aggressive tactician. At Cedar Mountain his brigade had beaten back attacks by three times their number.

Mansfield had roused his troops early and formed his two divisions in two long columns for the march. Among the litter left in their night camp were decks of playing cards, sets of dice, and salacious or sensational literature in paper covers. Civil War soldiers usually divested themselves of the impedimenta of sin and vice on the day of battle, in case they should be called before their Maker.

But Mansfield was uncertain when to move and where to take them, so the men marched a few hundred yards and halted, waiting for instructions that never came. Some units broke ranks to boil coffee and breakfast on hardtack and salt pork while the sound of battle southward rose to a steady roar and clouds of gunsmoke began to pile up beyond the trees. With stops and starts it took them an hour and a half to march the single mile from their bivouac, until their lead elements finally approached the eastern end of the Miller Farm, gateway to the fighting in the cornfield and the East Woods. Between 7:00 and 7:30 Mansfield rode ahead to meet with Hooker at the Miller farmstead and receive his instructions. At this point in the action, Hooker was more concerned about checking Hood's counterattack across the cornfield than renewing the assault on the Dunker Church. He ordered Mansfield to send one division to support the troops fighting in the cornfield, and the other to check the Rebels in the East Woods.

But XII Corps was not yet ready to go into action. Mansfield had marched them to the front in column, with units closed up on each other, a formation that made it easier to control troops on the march. However, it was a bad formation for troops under fire, providing a massed target for artillery—and Confederate batteries began hitting the lead division as soon as it came in sight of the East Woods. Mansfield's veteran division commanders, Brigadier Generals Williams and Greene, therefore reformed the troops in a more open order. But when Mansfield returned he put his regiments back in column, overriding the objections of Williams and Greene. Mansfield was focused on the problem of moving his troops into position and getting them into action swiftly, and he was worried about maintaining control of his units during the approach. He had reason for concern. His corps had more than its share of untried rookie regiments, much larger than the veteran regiments whose ranks had been thinned in months of marching and fighting, but inadequately trained in battlefield maneuvers. In his preoccupation with speed Mansfield had simply formed his column by the numbers (that is, First Brigade of the First Division was first in line). As a result, the corps was led by a brigade consisting of three of these big, awkward, hard-to-maneuver units—the 124th, 125th, and 128th Pennsylvania.

Mansfield split his divisions. Greene's troops were put in line and marched to confront the Rebel troops along the northeastern face of the East Woods, and the open ground east of the woods. Williams's Division was to march west and form a support line across the rear of the I Corps troop fighting in the northern part of the cornfield. Mansfield decided to accompany his First Brigade, with its big rookie regiments, which had to pass around a northward projection of the East Woods to reach its desired position. The tactical situation here was confusing. Hood's attackers were pulling back into the woods, impressed by the mass of the dark blue regiments, but they left plenty of skirmishers behind to harass the advancing Federals. But Mansfield had been told to look for Federal units here as well, troops he was supposed to support—who might be retreating before an unseen Confederate advance.

Mansfield was trying to get the 128th Pennsylvania into position when he saw the Tenth Maine of his command firing into the East Woods. He rode over to stop them, thinking they were firing into their own men. The officers of the Tenth disagreed, so Mansfield rode out ahead of their line to see for himself. "Yes, yes, you're right," he told his riflemen, who just then heard the hard double thump of two bullets hitting home. One struck Mansfield's horse and the other took him square in the chest. He dismounted carefully, led his horse to the rear, then dropped to the ground. An ambulance took him to a field hospital for surgery and death. Command of XII Corps would pass to Alpheus Williams, but it was not at all certain that he could coordinate the efforts of two divisions so widely separated.

Nearly two hours after Duryee's attack began the battle, the Federal offensive on Jackson's front was stymied.

LEE'S HEADQUARTERS, 7:30-9:00 AM

Lee was monitoring the action from Cemetery Hill, a bulge of high ground east of Sharpsburg. He had still not recovered from the injury to his hands, but to command effectively he had to be able to move freely throughout his army's position, so an aide was assigned to help him mount his horse, Traveller, and to lead the mount by the bridle wherever Lee needed to go. Longstreet joined him at an early hour—he was nominally in command of all units not assigned to Jackson's front, but today all troops were at the disposal of the commanding general.

Their position was not at all a safe one. McClellan's long-range guns kept the place under intermittent shellfire, and the single battery posted to defend Cemetery Hill lacked the range for effective counter-battery fire. From here Lee could catch glimpses of troop movement on Jackson's front, but the rise and fall of sound was probably a better guide to the ebb and flow of the fighting—that, and the sight of disorganized troops streaming southward down the Hagerstown Pike. Lee was annoyed:

"The infantry, sir, are straggling, they are straggling." This was a misconception and an injustice. The refugees were men whose units had been broken by fire in charge or countercharge.

An hour or so after the start of fighting—about the time Hood's Division was making its assault through the cornfield—D. H. Hill trotted his horse into the cemetery. He reported Jackson's request for additional troops and asked permission to take his whole division to Jackson's aid. Hill commanded five brigades. One of these (Ripley's) had been detailed to support the Dunker Church line before the battle began. Three of D. H. Hill's brigades were posted in an arc-shaped position, set in the natural trench of a sunken road, looking north toward the Roulette Farm buildings. This was a vital and potentially vulnerable position, the hinge of the Confederate line where it swung south to defend the front of Sharpsburg. Hill's remaining brigade, commanded by G. B. Anderson, was stretched across the road that ran from the Middle Bridge to Sharpsburg's central street, and constituted the first line of defense against an assault on Lee's center.

Lee had other units he could draw on, but with his resources so limited any commitment of reserves to one sector constrained his ability to fight in another. David R. Jones's Division held the line of the Sharpsburg plateau across the front of the town itself and southward; but this was Lee's last line of defense against Federal columns attacking via the Middle or Lower Bridges, and it seemed advisable to hold them in place. The mobile reserve for the center and left of his line were the divisions of R. H. Anderson and McLaws, which had arrived during the night after a long, hard march. They were posted behind the town of Sharpsburg. Walker's Division was in reserve at the extreme southern end of Lee's infantry line, posted to support Toombs's Brigade in defending the Lower Bridge. Before deciding which reserves to use, Lee needed to make a more direct observation of the embattled front.

With Lee's horse led by the bridle, the generals and their staffs rode to the west side of Sharpsburg, to a high point in the ridgeline that was the apex of the Sharpsburg plateau. From here they could see Federal columns (probably XII Corps) marching toward Jackson's front, and D. H. Hill's battle line stretched out south and east from the Sunken Road position across the front of the plateau. As they were making their observations a shell from a Union battery cut through the group, amputating the two front legs of Hill's horse as it passed and creating the grotesque spectacle of Hill too entangled to dismount from the horse, which was still alive with its rump in the air and its chest on the ground. The men laughed: one who was there insisted the laughter was at Hill, not the horse, as they all loved horses.[14]

With Jackson's position in peril, and a Federal corps moving against the Dunker Church line, there was no time to wait for the more distant reserves to be brought forward. Lee therefore allowed D. H. Hill to send the brigades of Colquitt and Garland out of the Sunken Road to Jackson's aid. Lee would also draw the brigade of G. T. "Tige" Anderson from D. R. Jones's Division and send that north as well. Hill rode off to the front to take personal leadership of the brigades moving to Jackson's support. Shortly thereafter he sent a rider to Lee with the encouraging word that if Lee could send him reinforcement he would "have the battle won by eleven o'clock."[15]

But the word from Jackson himself was more dire: fresh Federal troops, coming in on the heels of Hood's repulse, were threatening to break the line around the Dunker Church. Lee trusted Jackson's estimate absolutely. He therefore decided to take McLaws's Division from the army reserve behind Sharpsburg and commit it to Jackson's front. He also made the more interesting decision to summon John Walker's Division from the far southern end of his battle line and throw it into action on the opposite flank. R. H. Anderson's Division was much closer to Jackson, bivouacked alongside McLaws's Division west of Sharpsburg. By reaching for Walker, Lee lengthened the time till the reinforcement could reach Jackson. But with Hill's brigades stripped from the army's center, Lee needed some reserve to counter a Federal attack in that area, and R. H. Anderson's was the force best positioned for that purpose.

However, by moving Walker's Division, Lee also substantially weakened the force that was holding the lower crossing of the Antietam. So far the Federals had made no threats whatever against the Lower Bridge, but the day was just beginning—it was not yet 8:00 AM. Lee may have decided to run that risk in the belief that Jackson was in dire straits. But he may also have had in mind the possibility that, given an ample reserve, Jackson might not only check Hooker's assault but mount a decisive counterattack.

Lee himself rode northward up the pike toward the Dunker Church, the aide still leading his horse, to be closer to the critical field of action and get a clearer sense of actual conditions close to the front. Shortly before 9:00 AM he was met by a battle-grimed and deeply anxious Colonel S. D. Lee, the artillery commander whose guns Lee had assigned to the defense of the Dunker Church. Colonel Lee had a message from Hood for General Lee, given just after the repulse of Hood's attack by Meade's Division and the Iron Brigade. "Unless reinforcements were sent at once the day was lost." Shortly thereafter both men saw the first of McLaws's Brigades quick-marching up the Hagerstown Pike.[16]

The outcome of Hooker's and Jackson's fight now hinged on the arrival of reinforcements rushing into the meatgrinder. D. H. Hill's, McLaws's and Walker's Divisions were marching up from the south, the Union XII Corps was coming into line alongside I Corps—and McClellan was preparing to order two of Sumner's Divisions across the Antietam to add their weight to Hooker's drive.

MCCLELLAN'S HEADQUARTERS, 7:00–8:40 AM

General McClellan had ridden forward at dawn from his main headquarters, which were established in the little hamlet of Keedysville, two miles east of the Middle Bridge. He would view the battlefield from a forward command post at the Pry house, a two-story Georgian-style brick house on the bluffs overlooking the bridge, where Fitz-John Porter had set up V Corps' headquarters. Several easy chairs and some tables had been brought out of the farmhouse and set in the front yard for the use of the general and his staff, but McClellan spent much of his time watching the action on Hooker's front through a telescope mounted on a tripod. In planning his battle he had not shared his thoughts and intentions with his colleagues, and as the action unfolded he concealed his reactions by keeping even his own staff at a distance. Only Fitz-John Porter stood near him, communicating "to the commander by nods, signs, or in words so low-toned and brief that the nearest bystanders had but little benefit with them."[17]

McClellan had received no reports from Hooker. He probably expected none. It was possible to communicate brief messages over some distance by signal flag, but heat haze and gunsmoke limited the usefulness of the semaphore. Clearer and more detailed messages were best carried by horseback messengers, whose intelligence or orders would be out of date by the time they were delivered, which was why McClellan had directed Hooker to act as a semi-independent wing commander. Hooker himself was immersed in the fighting, too busy managing the rapidly shifting flux of events to make sense of them for McClellan. But what McClellan saw led him to conclude that Hooker's attack was succeeding. Perhaps he had glimpsed the Iron Brigade's advance in the cornfield, or Hays's Brigade breaking back across that dark and bloody ground after its repulse. Perhaps it was only the long, dark column of Mansfield's Corps marching across open ground on its way to the front. "All goes well," he told Fitz-John Porter. "Hooker is driving them."

At around 7:30 AM in the cornfield Hood was mounting his spoiling attack, while in the Sharpsburg cemetery, D. H. Hill was meeting with Lee.

The proper and necessary next move was to augment and support Hooker by putting some of the army's reserves into action. If Hooker's assault had forced Lee to weaken his center, McClellan might have been able to stage a successful drive across the Middle Bridge. He had two of his best combat divisions, Richardson's veterans from II Corps and Sykes's Regular Army brigades from V Corps, in position to cross the Middle Bridge, with Pleasonton's cavalry for a reserve and all that heavy artillery on the heights above. But McClellan had seen no sign of troop movements away from the center, and since he rated Lee's army as at least equal to his own, he feared a premature assault here would be bloodily repulsed. Fear of Lee's strength in the center also constrained his willingness to use units of his reserve elsewhere on the battle line. Franklin's VI Corps had not yet arrived from Pleasant Valley, and would not be available until after 9:00 AM. So all McClellan had in hand for his center were the three divisions of Sumner's II Corps, two divisions of Porter's V Corps, and Pleasonton's cavalry division.

He therefore decided to reinforce Hooker by sending him two of Sumner's divisions, commanded by Sedgwick and French, while retaining Richardson's division and all of V Corps to defend his own center. He also ordered Burnside to make ready for his move against the Lower Bridge.

There were several things wrong with these decisions, and with the way they were executed. By hedging his investment in Hooker's advance he had greatly reduced the chances that Hooker could achieve anything decisive against Jackson. Sumner could only reach Hooker by a round-about march, north to the Upper Bridge, then south and west across the fields and woodlots to the fighting front. It would take Sumner nearly two hours to get there. Sumner's reinforcement, of perhaps eleven thousand men, would be largely offset by the reinforcements Lee was sending, by a shorter and more direct route, to Jackson's aid—the divisions of McLaws and Walker and D. H. Hill's two brigades, perhaps nine thousand strong.

To make matters worse, the move was badly handled. McClellan had kept Sumner under his eye because he was rightly mistrustful of the old man's competence in independent command. In his original orders, McClellan had assured Hooker that all forces sent to his sector would be placed under his command, and he probably intended Sumner to place himself under Hooker's orders once he arrived at the front. Although Sumner was vastly senior to Hooker, it would not have violated protocol for Sumner to defer to the commander of the forces already engaged in battle. However, there is nothing in the record to indicate that McClellan told Sumner to place himself under Hooker's command, nor any indication that McClellan notified Hooker that Sumner was on the way. As a result, there was no liaison between the staffs of Hooker and Sumner, no process for advising Sumner how best to approach the field or how Hooker wanted his force deployed. For his part, Sumner neglected to have his staff reconnoiter the ground to be crossed or the enemy positions that might threaten his line of advance. These errors of omission, compounded by Sumner's incompetence as a field general, would cap Sumner's march with a catastrophic blunder some two hours after it began.

McClellan's excessive concern for the safety of his center may also have been responsible for his mishandling of Burnside's part of the operation. McClellan's battle plan had called for an attack by Burnside's Corps against the Lower Bridge and the southern flank of Lee's position. If this was to be a diversion in aid of Hooker, the time to make it was early in the day—if not simultaneously with Hooker's attack then certainly within an hour or two. At 7:00 AM McClellan sent a dispatch rider to put Burnside on alert for a move against the Lower Bridge, but he did not order an immediate advance, nor specify a time for Burnside to move. He would not commit IX Corps to action until VI Corps arrived to replenish the army's reserve.

The consequence was that every move on this front would be plagued by hesitancy and delay. Burnside received McClellan's message but, since he was still pretending to be a wing commander, did nothing but pass the order on to Cox. Since no time of advance was specified, neither man saw any urgency about the matter. So IX Corps stayed in its nighttime position behind the sheltering ridge, at some distance from the bridge—which meant a further delay of effective action when the order to advance finally came.[18]

By failing to threaten an immediate attack against Lee's center and right, McClellan left Lee free to reinforce Jackson with troops from his general reserve and strip the defense of his southern flank to the bare bones.

NORTHERN FRONT, 8:00–9:00 AM

In the wake of Hood's assault, Jackson had reordered the defensive line in front of the Dunker Church. Ripley's Brigade, which D. H. Hill had loaned to Jackson at the start of the day, was shifted west and formed in line of battle across the southern end of the cornfield, replacing the shattered remnants of Lawton's Division that had defended the position. Early's Brigade had been brought in from the left flank, where it had been protecting Stuart's guns, and now formed line on Ripley's left, defending the southern end of the West Woods. That part of Hood's Division which had been fighting against the Iron Brigade along the Hagerstown Pike had been pulled back to form a reserve behind Ripley. What was left of the other half of Hood's Division still held out in the northern end of the East Woods.

On the Union side, some of I Corps still maintained a defensive line fronting the West Woods and across the Pike north of the cornfield. But most of the units that had been fighting for the past two hours were in the rear reorganizing, and none were fit to resume the offensive. Williams's division of XII had been moving up to take their place in line when Mansfield was shot. At that point the division's advance was thrown into confusion. The rookie 128th Pennsylvania, which Mansfield had been trying to square away, was milling in confusion in the northeast corner of the cornfield—its numbers so large that it effectively blocked the next brigade from advancing. For a horrible interval, XII Corps was paralyzed with shellfire and case-shot blasting its ranks.

Finally Williams and his brigadiers took control and got the division moving forward into the corn. To its left and rear, Greene's Division came forward against the northeastern face of the East Woods, pressuring the remnants of Hood's Division that held out there. The crossing of the cornfield was a passage through horror. The corn was trampled, and dead men lay in crisscrossed windrows to mark where battle lines had stood to take and give fire. Wounded men tried to crawl aside, or snatched at the legs of the advancing infantry, cried out for aid, for water, for God, for a bullet to put them out of intolerable suffering.

However, by this time the first wave of Confederate reinforcements was arriving, the brigades of Colquitt and Garland led by D. H. Hill himself. As always, the presence of a ready reserve created the possibility not only of repulsing the assault but of turning the momentum of battle back against the attacker. It was probably at this moment that Hill sent Lee his enthusiastic assertion that with a bit more reinforcement, he would "have the battle won by eleven o'clock."

Colquitt's Georgia regiments arrived first, and Hill put them in to buttress Ripley's defensive line. Williams's lead brigade in the cornfield was brought to a stand by fire from the infantry line in front of the Dunker Church, and by its supporting artillery. The Federals refused to back off farther than the northern side of the field, and once again there was an intense firefight in the cornfield, where the stalks by now had been cut to the nubs and the furrows were thickly strewn with dead and wounded men. At the height of the action, Hill's other brigade, North Carolina Regiments officially Garland's but commanded by Colonel McRae, came up double-quick from the rear. Hill formed them for a charge and ordered them forward into the cornfield.

But Garland's Brigade was in no condition for such an assignment. Its ranks had been decimated at South Mountain, where it had been driven from the field and seen its commander killed. Its regiments also had a significant number of conscripted troops, the first fruits of Jefferson Davis's military draft. Such units had the same kinds of problems maneuvering and fighting on the battlefield that afflicted the big rookie regiments in XII Corps, although the Confederate army mitigated the problem by mixing the conscripts into established units rather than using them to form new regiments. Colonel McRae led his brigade forward, slanting across the cornfield from southeast to northwest corner, and as they forged ahead someone saw what appeared to be a whole Federal brigade massing to hit them in the right flank and rear. The North Carolinians remembered South Mountain all too well. At the cry "We're flanked" the brigade dissolved and ran back the way it came. Some of its elements fled through the East Woods, carrying away with them units that had been supporting Hood's survivors in their firefight with Greene's Division of XII Corps. The last of Hood's units joined the retreat, and Greene's Brigades swept into the East Woods and around its eastern edge. They hit Colquitt's Brigade with fire and drove it from the field as well.

By 8:45 AM Hill was trying to rally his men behind Ripley and Colquitt's defensive line, and Hooker was helping Williams reorganize XII Corps for a concerted drive to capture the Dunker Church position. The Confederate defense was down to D. H. Hill's shaken brigades and Colonel S. D. Lee's artillerymen, holding the Federal infantry off with blasts of canister. Greene's drive had actually forced the Confederates to reorient the defense in front of the church. At the start of the battle the Confederate defense line ran west to east across the southern boundary of the cornfield. That line had been turned by Greene's conquest, so the Confederate defense was now aligned facing northeast from the church. Greene's Brigades had swept through the East Woods and on to a piece of rising ground beyond it, from which divisional artillery firing at short range could pound S. D. Lee's cannoneers at the church.

Then Hooker was shot, with a sharpshooter's bullet through the foot, and he was carried to the rear half-unconscious from loss of blood. Command of the field should probably have passed to General Meade, the senior division commander on the scene. But with Hooker's wounding, Meade had also succeeded to command of I Corps, and he had all he could do to rally and reorganize its exhausted brigades. Alpheus Williams was the senior officer on the current battlefront—a brigadier general who had briefly acted as XII Corps commander while they waited for Mansfield's arrival. In the course of an hour, he had succeeded first to corps command and then, in effect, to Hooker's wing command. He was out of his depth and faced with responsibilities beyond his pay grade.

The Dunker Church (LIBRARY OF CONGRESS)

The quickest way to communicate with McClellan was by semaphore. At about 9:00 AM signal flags flashed the message that Mansfield was "dangerously" and Hooker "severely" wounded. Williams added that "Genl Sumner is advancing," with the implication that Sumner would soon be in command, though we do not know whether he viewed that possibility with relief or apprehension. Finally he informed McClellan, "We hold the field at present. . . . Please give us all the aid you can." Whatever plan there had been for a drive against the Dunker Church was put on hold when Hooker fell.[19]

McCLELLAN'S HEADQUARTERS, 9:00–10:00 AM

McClellan was now faced with a double crisis. It appeared that the attack by Hooker's wing could achieve nothing more without substantial reinforcement, but there was little McClellan could provide. The two divisions led by Sumner, dispatched an hour and a half earlier, would just be reaching the battlefront at 9:00 AM. McClellan still declined to aid his assault force by making a diversionary attack across the Middle Bridge with V Corps, despite the fact that Franklin's VI Corps divisions were beginning to arrive from Pleasant Valley. Nevertheless, he now felt able to release Richardson's division to rejoin Sumner's command. Richardson would take a shorter route to the action, crossing his infantry at Pry's Ford about midway between the Middle and Upper bridges. Even so, Richardson could not rejoin II Corps until 10:30 AM. His three artillery batteries had to use the more roundabout route via the Upper Bridge—which carried them into the Dunker Church zone of battle, where they would be coopted for the support of XII Corps, leaving Richardson without artillery suited to the close support of his infantry.

The other crisis was the certainty that with Hooker and Mansfield down, Sumner would assume command of the right wing and responsibility for organizing a new offensive by II and XII Corps and whatever elements of I Corps were fit to join in. McClellan rightly considered Sumner unfit for a large and independent command, and he had tried to prevent such an outcome by keeping Sumner under his eye, and issuing orders that gave Hooker control of all units sent across the Antietam. He might have remedied the situation by riding to the scene himself, as Lee had done earlier. Instead, he chose to stay at the Pry house and let events play out as they would on the other side of the river.

After some further thought, McClellan also decided it might be time to bring Burnside's Corps into play. While Richardson's command was moving out, McClellan dispatched an aide to Burnside with orders for him to advance his corps and seize the Lower Bridge over the Antietam. Once Burnside had carried the bridge, McClellan would order a supporting attack across the Middle Bridge, which would enable Burnside to press in on Lee's right or southern flank. Burnside got the order at 10:00 AM and, still performing his "wing commander" charade, passed the order to Cox. IX Corps had barely started moving when the battle across the Antietam reached a new crisis.[20]

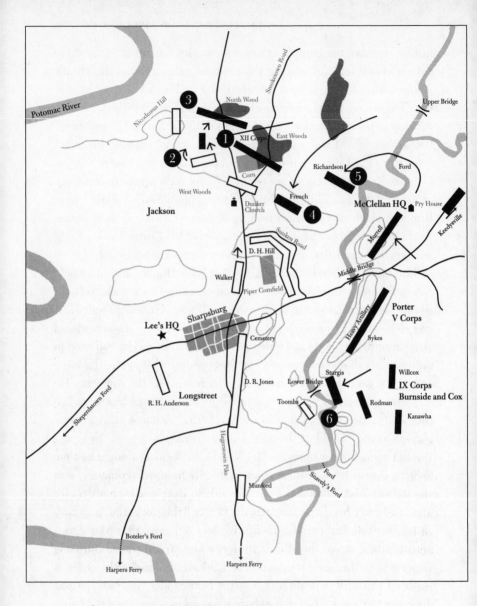

MAP 6: ANTIETAM, 9:30–10:00 AM

1. Sedwick's Division (U.S.) crosses face of West Woods
2. G. T. Anderson's Brigade and McLaws's Division (C.S.) smash Sedgwick
3. Sedwick's Division driven off
4. French's Division (U.S. II Corps) attacks Sunken Road
5. Richardson's Division (U.S. II Corps) approaches
6. IX Corps (U.S.): Sturgis's Division and Crook's Brigade repulsed at Lower Bridge

CHAPTER 13

THE BATTLE OF ANTIETAM: SUMNER'S FIGHT

9:00 AM–NOON

GENERAL SUMNER'S ARRIVAL AT THE NORTHERN FRONT GUARANTEED that the assault there would be renewed. Sumner's one virtue was his willingness to fight. Here, in the absence of other abilities, it would lead to tragedy.

He rode up the road from the Upper Bridge at the head of his lead division, commanded by Brigadier General John Sedgwick, with Brigadier General William H. French's division twenty minutes behind. On the way he met the ambulance carrying the wounded Hooker. The latter had passed out and therefore could give Sumner no guidance, but the sight of him told Sumner he was now in charge on this front. He also had a brief meeting with General Ricketts, who was the only one of Hooker's division commanders in this part of the field, and whose account of the corps' condition convinced Sumner that Hooker's command was "dispersed and routed." Accepting this at face value, Sumner made no attempt to contact those units of I Corps that were reorganizing around the North Woods, or the two brigades, commanded by Patrick and Gibbon, that were still skirmishing with the enemy in front of the West Woods. Sumner also assumed that XII Corps was used up—which was far from the case.[1]

Sumner led Sedgwick's troops into the meadows behind the East Woods and rode ahead to confer with Brigadier General Alpheus Williams, the senior officer at the front. Williams tried to explain the situation to him, outlining the picture he had formed of Confederate strength and the position of their units, indicating the readiness of his own two divisions to continue the assault. Sumner either did not attend or could not comprehend what Williams was telling him. From where he stood he could see Confederates around the Dunker Church exchanging fire with Williams's skirmishers to the east, and gunsmoke rising from the northeast corner of the West Woods where the 125th Pennsylvania was skirmishing with the Rebel's last reserve brigade, headed by General Jubal Early. It appeared to him that the Rebel line ran from that corner of the woods down to the road junction by the church. For some reason, Sumner also decided that the northern flank of that line was "in the air," and that he could turn it by marching Sedgwick's three brigades around the end of the Rebel line and swooping down on them from the north.[2]

Sumner's idea was to march Sedgwick's Division past what he thought was the end of the Rebel flank, execute a ponderous left wheel to face south, then advance and sweep the Confederate line from north to south. But the Rebel flank was not unprotected. Survivors of the Stonewall Brigade and other commands that had fought in the West Woods were still there, led by Colonel Grigsby, and so was Early's relatively fresh brigade. Early was not being strongly pressured by the 125th Pennsylvania and could easily shift troops to reinforce Grigsby along the northern rim of the woods. As Sumner's troops marched past, these troops could fire into their flank. Federal troops rounding the northern end of the West Woods would also be marching straight into the fire of Stuart's horse artillery on Nicodemus Heights. Moreover, the Confederates were about to receive heavy reinforcement. As Sedgwick's men began their advance, the lead elements of Tige Anderson's Brigade were approaching the Dunker Church, with McLaws's Division close behind.

Not only was Sumner's understanding of the tactical situation entirely erroneous, but the tactics by which he planned to exploit it were badly conceived. Sumner formed the division's three brigades in three long double lines, a formation suitable for a frontal attack but one which made the brigades virtually defenseless against an attack from the flank. Sumner's chosen line of march would take Sedgwick's Division across the northern face of the West Woods. When they crossed it, Confederate riflemen firing from the shelter of the woods would be able to rake those lines from end to end.[3] To cap these blunders, Sumner decided to march at the head of Sedgwick's Division, to lead the assault like the gallant soldier he was. For the commander of a corps or, as he now was, of a three-corps wing of the army, Sumner's proper place was in the rear, where he could coordinate the movements of supporting troops in response to battlefield events. One can imagine a skilled corps commander in his position developing a combined attack against the West Woods and Dunker Church by his own two divisions and XII Corps. But once Sumner had chosen his course he plunged down it with tunnel vision. He not only neglected to make use of XII Corps, he lost contact with French's Division of his own corps.

Stonewall Jackson, on the other hand, had a far more accurate understanding of the tactical position than Sumner, and an intelligent plan for exploiting it.

THE WEST WOOD, 9:00–10:00 AM

The original Confederate line had run from West Woods to East Woods across the southern edge of the cornfield and the meadows facing north from the church. The brigades that had held that line, and the reserves that had come to their aid, had not only been wrecked in the charges and countercharges, but their defense had been radically reshaped. The survivors of Grigsby's Stonewall Brigade, and other remnants of Jones's Division, still held on in the northern part of the West Woods, opposing Patrick's Brigade to the north, the last of I Corps' units still in action. Early's Brigade was deeper in the trees, skirmishing with the 125th Pennsylvania in the northeastern quadrant of the woods. But Confederate troops outside the West Woods had retreated to the south, where a new north-facing line was being established about five hundred yards south of the church and the road junction, at the point where the Sunken Road met the Hagerstown Pike. This new line was held by the rallied remnants of Colquitt's and Garland's Brigades, who tied in on the right with D. H. Hill's two remaining brigades in the Sunken Road—a naturally strong position that could anchor the right end of Jackson's line. But between Colquitt's position and Early's there was an eight-hundred-yard gap in the line defended only by S. D. Lee's batteries, with a light infantry screen. If the next Federal attack struck simultaneously against the West Woods and this gap, the army's northern flank might be compromised.[4]

Jackson's military doctrine rated a bold offense as the best defense. It was vital to retain control of the West Woods. It provided the best position for defending the army's north-facing flank; and from its eastern edge, which ran for nearly half a mile alongside the Hagerstown Pike, Confederate riflemen could put flanking fire on Federal troops attacking out of the East Woods area toward the Dunker Church. Those defensive advantages could also be turned into offensive potential. The West Woods position projected nearly a mile north of that new line below the Dunker Church. When the Federals moved against that line, a large force massed in the West Woods might be able to strike their flank, perhaps with decisive results. Such a move would have been perfectly consonant with Lee's strategic objective, which was not simply to hold his ground but to force McClellan to retreat and make it possible to extend the invasion of Maryland.

Jackson therefore sent the first-arriving reinforcements to secure the West Woods, reserving only the last of McLaws's units to fill the gap between Early and Colquitt's flank. The brigade of Tige Anderson was directed into the West Woods, to join Early's Brigade for an assault on the 125th Pennsylvania. On Anderson's heels came the first of McLaws's Brigades, dog-tired after a grueling day and night march that had only got them to Sharpsburg at 4:00 AM. They had had barely four hours to boil coffee or catch a rest when Lee's summons sent them trotting north. Jackson sent Barksdale's Mississippians and Kershaw's South Carolina Regiments deep into the woods, then had them peel off to their right to strike the 125th Pennsylvania's line from the flank and secure the whole of West Woods extending north of the church. The Union's rookie regiment was nearly as large as a Confederate brigade, and its line cut across a large quadrant of the woods. Its men were willing enough to stand, but officers and men lacked the kind of experience that would have enabled them to fight effectively in wooded terrain where they could not see much of the enemy or of their comrades. The attack of Early and Tige Anderson shook them, and the flank attack by Barksdale and Kershaw broke them and sent them streaming back toward the East Woods with Kershaw's men in pursuit. Sedgwick's Division was just then passing to the north, and two of his regiments (their commanders acting on their own) with an artillery battery peeled off to come to the Pennsylvanians' aid. Their fire checked Kershaw and allowed the rookies to reorganize as they pulled back.

In the meantime, Jackson was also taking measures to bolster his defenses. To solidify the right side of his position, he sent Cobb's Legion, the smallest of McLaws's brigades, to fill the gap between the Dunker Church and the flank of Colquitt's Brigade. To thwart Sumner's flanking maneuver against his left, he ordered Semmes's Brigade (McLaws's Division) to pass around the western side of the woods and form a line to block any attempt to turn the West Woods position. He also ordered Barksdale and Early to break off their fight with the 125th and move toward the northern end of the forest, where they could oppose Sumner's column.

Barksdale, Early, and the other Confederate commanders on this line had no tactical plan but were expected to respond to Federal movements as they occurred. They considered the most likely line of attack a frontal assault from the north. What they received instead was an unimaginable opportunity, the gift of Sumner's mismanagement. The brigades of Barksdale and Early were barely in position when Sumner's three-line column appeared, marching as if on parade across the open ground north of the West Woods and into a smaller and more open woodlot that projected northward from the main woods. Incredibly, the Federals ignored the Confederate battle line among the trees to their left and continued to march across the face of the Confederate position, offering their unprotected flanks to the ambush.

The disaster to Sedgwick's Division unfolded in full view of the Federals of Patrick's and Gibbon's Brigades, who were watching helplessly from their positions north of the West Woods. Confederate riflemen concealed in the woods fired volley after volley, sweeping each of the three double lines from end to end. Sedgwick's Division contained some of the best veteran regiments in the army, but they were helpless to defend themselves. In their present alignment, six men—the file closers of each brigade's double line of battle—faced the woods from which some 1,400 Confederate infantrymen were firing, and as the rest of McLaws's troops came up, the number rose to over 4,000.[5] There was no time for the regiments closest to the woods to change formation and facing—to wheel ninety degrees to the left while being raked by close-range infantry fire. The regiments further away could not maneuver because their ranks were disordered and their line of fire masked by troops from the broken units fleeing directly away from the Confederate line. Only the regiments farthest from the point of contact were able to wheel around, hold their ranks, and offer some opposition to the Confederates—who advanced firing out of the woods to complete the rout. Division commander Sedgwick was wounded and more than a third of his 5,500 veteran infantrymen were killed, wounded, or captured. Old Sumner, his white hair flying, rode through the shambles trying to rally his men, then let himself be carried away by the rout. Rebel infantry surged out of the woods to follow up their success but were stopped by those I Corps infantry and artillery units that had remained on the line.

Sumner was shaken by disaster of a kind and scale he had never experienced. His semaphore stations relayed to McClellan his belief that his entire wing was dissolving—"Our troops are giving way"—and that heavy reinforcement was needed. The disaster, however, was limited to Sedgwick's division. There were still plenty of Federal units on the scene, ready and able to resume the offensive—units whose presence Sumner had ignored in his rigid focus on the attack by Sedgwick's division, and continued to ignore in his obsession with Sedgwick's disaster. Sumner now asked Alpheus Williams to send XII Corps into action, to check Confederate exploitation of the rout, and sent riders in search of French's division, out of contact with Sumner's headquarters since they had crossed the Antietam. It would turn out that French had already gone into action, without reference to Sumner, and was engaging D. H. Hill's infantry in the Sunken Road.

McCLELLAN'S HEADQUARTERS, 9:30–10:00 AM

McClellan now had a critical decision to make. Franklin's VI Corps was finally at hand, and together with V Corps and Pleasonton's cavalry McClellan had a force of some 38,000 troops massed in his center. The army reserve, which he had diminished by sending II Corps to Hooker's aid, was now largely reconstituted. His tactical plan had envisioned the possibility of using that central reserve for a "main attack" on the center of Lee's line—if Hooker's attack on the northern flank had succeeded in drawing off the Confederate reserves. On the other hand, his plan also allowed for the use of that reserve to support Hooker, either to exploit a breakthrough or support him if his attack failed and he needed reinforcement to repel a Rebel counterblow. McClellan now had to choose between those alternatives.

The signals sent by Sumner indicated that there was indeed a crisis across the Antietam, and that Sumner thought reinforcements were needed to avert a complete debacle. As far as McClellan knew, Sumner's "Our troops are giving way" applied to all the units that had been sent to the right wing: I Corps, XII Corps, and both Sedgwick's and French's divisions of II Corps. Richardson's division had already been dispatched to Sumner's aid, though it would not arrive until 10:30 AM. McClellan could only provide additional reinforcement by sending all or part of V or VI Corps, and to do so would make a "main attack" against Lee's center impossible.

In fact, the conditions McClellan had set for a main attack against Lee's center now actually existed, though McClellan could not see them. Lee had weakened the center and right of his line and committed most of his reserves to reinforce Jackson. Parts of two divisions (D. H. Hill's and D. R. Jones's) now held the rim of the Sharpsburg plateau north and south of the Boonsboro Road—the road that led from the Middle Bridge straight through the town. R. H. Anderson's Division of about four thousand men was concentrated to the north of the town, ready to send reinforcements to either Jackson or D. H. Hill, or to check a Federal advance across the Middle Bridge. Most of David R. Jones's Division was in a defensive line along the high ground in front and to the south of Sharpsburg. In this position it could either defend the Middle Bridge approach or provide a last line of defense against a Federal attack across the Lower Bridge. That last was now a potentially dangerous possibility, because the departure of Walker's Division had left a single Georgia Brigade, commanded by the political magnifico Robert Toombs, to defend the bridge and the fords below it. Once the Federals pushed Toombs aside, there was nothing to stop them in the three-quarters of a mile that lay between the Lower Bridge and D. R. Jones's line. Jones's four-thousand-man division would be in serious trouble if McClellan were to strike simultaneously and in force across both the Middle and Lower bridges—especially so if the continuing assault against Jackson and Hill forced Lee to commit R. H. Anderson's men to the north.

The opportunity for such a three-pronged assault was real. Unbeknownst to McClellan, elements of the XII and II Corps were preparing to mount a new offensive against the northern end of the Rebel line. At 10:00 AM McClellan had 25,000 infantry (V and VI Corps) and 4,800 cavalry massing east of the Middle Bridge, 38,000 troops against the 9,000 in the divisions of R. H. Anderson and D. R. Jones.[6] Even if he rated the force opposite at twice its actual strength, McClellan still had enough local superiority to strike a potentially decisive blow. He had just sent a courier to Burnside with orders to get his attack moving—a move that might at least draw more Confederate strength from the center, and at best allow Burnside to add his 13,000 troops to an assault on the Sharpsburg plateau. Had McClellan attempted an attack across the Middle Bridge he might have cracked Lee's defense in front of Sharpsburg. A breakthrough there would have given McClellan control of the road junctions linking all of Jackson's force to the north to the Shepherdstown Road—the army's primary escape route. Half of the Army of Northern Virginia would have been threatened with entrapment against the unfordable Potomac River. Even if the rest of the army managed, by last-ditch fighting, to keep the route open, Jackson's command would have to make a demoralizing and potentially disastrous daylight retreat.

True to his character and his sense of priorities, McClellan chose the defensive course. He ordered Franklin to march his two divisions around by Pry's Ford to come to Sumner's aid. While it was on the march, VI Corps would be unavailable to exploit the opportunities created by Lee's depletion of his reserve, and by the strenuous offensive which was now being mounted against the Dunker Church and Sunken Road. McClellan also sent a couple of testy dispatches to Burnside, demanding that he hurry his assault on the Lower Bridge. But that operation was not to be part of a concerted attack on Lee's center and right—it is hard to know what McClellan expected of it, beyond the application of pressure to the far end of Lee's line. Although the situation was not yet irreversible, the departure of VI Corps probably signaled McClellan's decision not to commit the army to an all-out offensive, but to limit his objectives to the gaining of useful terrain and the maintenance of an unbroken line. His once-ample reserve was now reduced to the two divisions of V Corps and Pleasonton's cavalry.

THE SUNKEN ROAD, 9:30–10:30 AM

While McClellan was depleting his reserve to fend off what he supposed was a debacle on his right flank, the troops under Sumner's nominal command were mounting a new offensive. Sumner himself had nothing to do with it. It was the result of individual initiative by the division commanders on the scene, responding instinctively and (in some cases) intelligently to the tactical situation in front of them. All Sumner did was call on Williams, the acting commander of XII Corps, to come to his aid, which Williams answered by advancing his own division to threaten a move against the Confederates defending the open ground between the West and East Woods. South of Williams's position, in the East Woods, General George S. Greene's Division fronted the Dunker Church, with the eastern rim of the West Woods behind it, defended by the brigades of Tige Anderson and Kershaw. The Confederates here had driven the 125th Pennsylvania out of the woods, and they tried to exploit their victory by charging across the open ground north of the church to drive Greene's Division back. While the Union troops beat off the first assault and held their position, they could not counter because they were short of ammunition.

While that was going on, Brigadier General William French's Division of II Corps suddenly appeared on Greene's left flank. French was forty-seven, a veteran of twenty-five years' service in the Regular Army, and he owed his command of the division to his solid performance in combat as a brigade commander on the Peninsula. As French came up in the rear of XII Corps he heard the sound of firing to the south, where Greene's Division was fighting. He had lost contact with Sumner and was too far behind to see Sedgwick's Brigade turn off to march due west toward impending disaster. On his own responsibility and initiative, and without notification to either Sumner or Williams, he decided to go to Greene's support and turned his division south. His line of march would bring him in on the left, or eastern, flank of Greene's position. His three brigades, each in double line of battle and deployed one behind the other, tramped forward for two miles, over open fields that rolled south in a series of shallow dips and low rises. When the lead brigade topped the last rise it came suddenly face-to-face with D. H. Hill's infantry in the Sunken Road.

The Rebels were ready for them, ordered to hold fire until they could clearly see the cartridge-boxes on the Yankees' belts. French's lead brigade was about sixty yards away when they cut loose a volley that "brought down the enemy as grain falls before the reaper." For the Federals, "The effect was appalling. The entire front line, with few exceptions, went down in the consuming blast." In five minutes the brigade lost 450 men out of the 1,400 it took into action. The lead brigade fell back, most of the men still in ranks though there were plenty who bolted back over the roll of ground, seeking shelter beyond it. The fugitives disrupted the advance of the next brigade, especially that of the rookie Fourteenth Connecticut; but the brigade and the regiment rallied, formed firing lines, and began volleying back at the Rebels down in the Sunken Road, some firing "with precision and deliberation" while others—unwilling or afraid to run but not equal to the test of combat—"shut their eyes, and fired up in the air."[7]

There were about 2,500 Confederates sheltered by the road embankment, as if in a natural entrenchment. French had about 5,500 troops, but as soon as they topped that roll of ground they were exposed to heavy rifle fire from Rebel infantry sheltered by the embankment and artillery fire from Confederate batteries on the plateau above them. French was unable to bring his own divisional artillery into action—gunners and horses would have been shot down as soon as they topped the rise— and McClellan's heavy guns could not hit the Sunken Road with any consistency. Confederate fire power prevented the Federals from storming the position with the bayonet. The lead brigade of Union infantry marched into killing range, only eighty yards from the Rebels, and stood its ground out in the open in a prolonged firefight; then fell back to the ridge crest behind them, lay down, and resumed firing. When Rodes tried to follow up their retreat with a counterattack, Federal infantry fire decimated them and drove them back. The firefight became permanent. French would send one brigade forward at a time, and when it was used up pulled the survivors back and sent the next brigade forward. They kept it up for nearly an hour and a half, "a savage continual thunder"—an incredible duration for so intense a firefight, under conditions so unfavorable to the attackers.[8]

Meanwhile on the Dunker Church/cornfield front, Kershaw's Confederates made one more try at driving Greene's Division from its position. The old general with the spectacular whiskers had prepared his division for both strong defense and an aggressive counterattack. Greene brought his artillery right up to the firing line and kept his infantry level with "the axle-trees of the guns." He had them hold fire till the Confederates were within seventy yards—within the absolute killing ground—then cut loose with volleys of rifle fire and blasts of canister. Kershaw's men suffered heavy losses, broke, and ran back toward the church. Greene immediately ordered his men to fix bayonets and follow. Kershaw's retreating troops masked the head-on fire of the defending infantry and artillery, and fire from the flanks was too weak to check the Federal charge. Greene's line of battle, four regiments abreast, crossed the open ground and swept around the Dunker Church and on into the adjacent section of the West Woods. The Federals had finally captured, and for the moment held, the high ground that had been the morning's first objective.

Greene's position was precarious. Both his flanks were exposed. His right flank was separated from Alpheus Williams's Division by the length of the cornfield; while east of Greene's left flank, and separated from it by some hundreds of yards, French's Division fought on, taking terrible casualties without breaking. Now Confederate John Walker's Division was arriving on the scene after its long march from the southern flank and was forming up against Greene's center and left. If Jackson could somehow disengage some of McLaws's units from the northern front of the woods, he might throw them against Greene's right and break it.

On the other hand, if Williams's Division could advance to Greene's support, aided by rallied elements of I Corps; and if some part of French's Division could connect with Greene's left, then Greene's lodgment might become a wedge driven into the Confederate line and Federal artillery on the Dunker Church rise could sweep the Confederate rear. It would soon be possible for French to shift closer to Greene's position, because Richardson's division was coming up on French's left to augment the attack on the Sunken Road. But Sumner lacked the intelligence to organize and Williams the authority to order a tactical maneuver involving four divisions from two different corps. Instead the division commanders fought on without guidance, doing the best they could with their limited knowledge of the larger tactical situation. French's advance against the Sunken Road was made without reference to Greene's movements, and when Richardson's division came up it went into action on French's left. At 10:30 AM three Union divisions were pressing the attack along a discontinuous line that ran from the Dunker Church to the eastern end of the Sunken Road, with no one exercising overall command of their movements.

AT ABOUT THE SAME TIME, at the far southern end of the Federal position, Burnside and Cox were finally beginning their attack on the Lower Bridge, defended by the Confederate infantry of Toombs's Brigade. Burnside had got the order from McClellan at 10:00 AM and passed it to Cox, who then ordered two of his four divisions forward. The Kanawha Division, now under the command of Colonel Scammon, was ordered to move directly against the bridge, while Rodman's division was to march south and cross by the ford they would find downstream. However, the engineers from McClellan's staff who had informed Burnside of the ford's existence had not told him exactly where it was. No one on the staff of IX Corps had thought to seek it out the night before or in the early hours of the morning. The staff in question was Burnside's, but because he was pretending to be a wing commander, most of his staff had been loaned to Cox, and it was absorbed by the tasks of helping him form a new corps headquarters. So instead of crossing the Antietam and sweeping north to hit Toombs's defensive line in the flank, Rodman's division spent more than two hours marching up and down, while the division staff tried to find a local farmer who could tell them where to find the ford.

While that was going on, Scammon was making a dismal failure of the attack on the bridge. In fairness it should be noted that Scammon was a colonel, with some experience in brigade command, forced to assume division command when Cox took over the corps. He was also attacking an extremely strong position. The Confederate defenders of Toombs's Brigade were on a high, steep, and wooded hill that overlooked the bridge, with skirmishers spread out in sheltered positions along the creek banks. Toombs was fantastically outnumbered. He had seven or eight hundred infantry in line against IX Corps' thirteen thousand. However, until the Federals found that missing ford, they could not bring more than a fraction of that force to bear on Toombs's position. The only way to attack Toombs directly was by having an infantry column charge across the stone bridge, which was only twelve feet wide—a column of men three abreast and dozens of ranks deep charging into the teeth of Confederate rifle fire, which could sweep the column from front to rear.

Neither Scammon himself nor his assault commander (Colonel George Crook) had taken care to scout the approach to the bridge. So Crook's command got lost in the woods and wandered north, finally reaching the creek some 350 yards north of the bridge. Instead of regrouping and trying again, Crook's Brigade formed a firing line in the willows and shrubbery and started a firefight with the Rebels on the other side. This might have provided useful supporting fire if another column had tried for the bridge, but Scammon could not manage to assemble such a force. After a few abortive attempts to wade the creek, the rest of his men also settled down for a firefight. Over the next hour they would exhaust their ammunition and, according to their officers, their physical energy, without achieving anything at all. Behind them the men of Burnside's other two divisions, led by Generals Sturgis and Willcox, waited complacently for some change in the situation.

LEE'S HEADQUARTERS, 10:00 AM

Command and control were more efficient on the Confederate side. Lee registered the strength of the Federal pressure between the Dunker Church and the Sunken Road. Walker's Division was already arriving to support the Dunker Church position, but the Sunken Road seemed vulnerable. The embattled section of the Sunken Road was shaped like a very shallow and inverted letter *V*, its left leg running west-east, its right leg slanting slightly to the south and west. The left end of the line was held by the remnants of both Colquitt's and Garland's Brigades, as well as the Cobb Legion from McLaws's Division, but most of the left leg of the *V* was held by Robert Rodes's five Alabama regiments. On their right was G. B. Anderson's North Carolina Brigade, shortly to be reinforced by Wright's Brigade (Georgia) of R. H. Anderson's Division. The road embankment offered some protection to infantry in it, but it was not high enough to offer full-body cover, especially since the Federal infantry were on slightly higher ground. At the point of the *V* where the defending brigades touched flanks, the embankment was nearly level with the road. Losses to French's fire mounted steadily. The dead and wounded accumulated at the feet of the men who stood in the lane, shooting or waiting to shoot. Generals and field officers were killed or wounded as they walked upright behind the firing line to encourage their men. Brigadier General George Anderson of the North Carolina Brigade was wounded and his successor instantly killed by a shot in the head at the moment of assuming command.

At some time after 10:00 and before 10:30 AM, Lee ordered the last of his infantry reserves, R. H. Anderson's Division, perhaps four thousand troops, to support the Sunken Road line from positions behind and above it on the rising ground that led to the Sharpsburg plateau. Lee also ordered up reserve batteries to support this movement. From this line Anderson's infantry and the gunners could shoot over the heads of the troops in the Sunken Road, doubling the effective firepower of the Sunken Lane line. Unfortunately for Anderson, the position also left them exposed to shell fire from the long-range guns on the other side of the Antietam; and French's men, frustrated at their seeming inability to hurt the infantry in the Sunken Road, raised their sights to shoot at Anderson's men. The Twenty-second Georgia of Wright's Brigade had formed its firing line in an apple orchard, where the Yankee bullets thumped into tree trunks as well as bodies, and for Private Judkins and his starving comrades the bounty of apples "shot off the trees" nearly canceled the effects of danger, wounds, and death.

> The company that was there was in the thick of the fight there in the apple orchard and cornfield. The ground was covered with apples where we fought, shot off the trees. . . . I was slightly wounded there by a Belgium ball or shell hitting a rock in the road and bursting, a piece of it went into my arm. I was in a great deal of danger, carrying off wounded. We got quite a lot of apple butter

and preserves out of a house at Sharpsburg, it was nice with our hardtack and tough beef.[9]

But the combined fire of French's infantry and the Federal artillery was heavy and began to take its toll in the enlisted ranks and among the officers. Division commander R. H. Anderson himself went down with a bullet in his ankle, and command passed to his senior brigadier, General Roger Pryor, another ultrasecessionist politician-turned-soldier. Pryor ordered Brigadier General Ambrose "Rans" Wright to lead his Georgia Brigade down to the Sunken Road, across the cornfield owned by a farmer named Piper. At the head of his brigade, Wright rode his horse into the corn. The horse was shot, Wright stepped away from the animal as it collapsed and was leading his line on foot when another Yankee bullet brought him down, wounded and out of action. But Wright's Georgians dashed forward into the Sunken Road to join the defense on the right end of the lane as the rest of Hill's infantry closed up to the left.

The intervention of R. H. Anderson's Division shifted the balance of forces in and around the Sunken Road. French had initially brought 5,500 Federals against 2,500 Confederates. Anderson's 4,000 gave the Confederates a numerical as well as a positional advantage, and their presence might have turned the tide if not for the arrival (at about 10:30 AM) of Brigadier General Israel Richardson's division of the II Corps.

SUNKEN ROAD II: RICHARDSON'S FIGHT
10:30 AM-NOON

Richardson might have been the best combat commander among the army's current cadre of division leaders. He had graduated from West Point in 1841, served against the Seminoles, and distinguished himself in the war with Mexico where he won two brevet promotions for gallantry. He earned two nicknames: "Fighting Dick," for his battlefield prowess, and "Greasy Dick," for his roughneck manner and style of dress, modeled on his hero Zachary Taylor, "Old Rough-and-Ready," the crusty old Indian fighter who had commanded the American army in northern Mexico during the Mexican American War. As a division commander

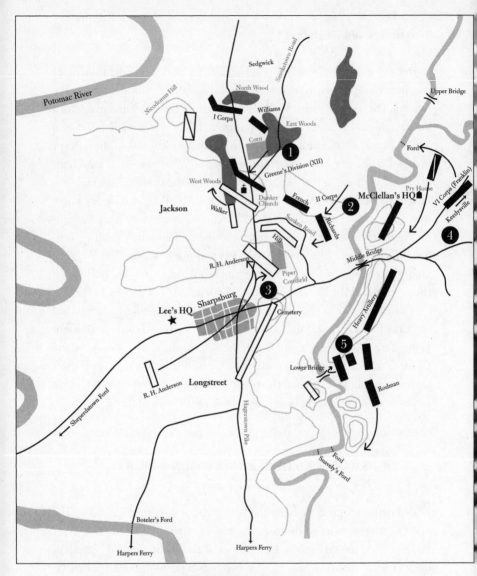

MAP 7: ANTIETAM, 10:30 AM–NOON

1. Greene's Division (U.S. XII Corps) captures Dunker Church
2. Richardson's Division joins French's Division (U.S. II Corps) vs. Sunken Road
3. R. H. Anderson's Division (C.S.) moves to support Hill's Division in Sunken Road
4. U.S. VI Corps (Franklin) arrives, sent to aid Sumner
5. U.S. IX Corps: Sturgis repulsed at Lower Bridge; Rodman seeks a ford

on the Peninsula, Richardson had fought with determination and skill at Seven Pines and through the Seven Days. The three brigades that made up his division were among the best in the army, four thousand infantrymen in veteran units that had fought all through the Peninsula Campaign.

First on the field was the Irish Brigade, commanded by Brigadier General Thomas Meagher. Richardson was not well pleased with Meagher's battlefield performance—he had a tendency to be absent or in hospital when battle was in the offing—but the brigade Meagher had created was a redoubtable fighting force. Thomas Meagher was an authentic Irish rebel who had escaped from the British penal colony in Tasmania and became a leader of the Irish American community. In the northern states the Irish were widely regarded as an inferior and unwanted "race," only slightly preferable to Blacks, and subject to comparable discrimination in employment and housing. The critical difference was that the Irish could vote, and because they were also White the Irish, like poor Whites in the South, could pride themselves on the difference of color, and aspire to eventual civil and social equality. The Irish in general, and the New York Irish in particular, were staunch Democrats, because the party welcomed them as voters and gave them a share of the patronage. They were also violently antipathetic to the Republican Party, which they saw as essentially "Yankee," anti-immigrant, anti-Catholic, and antislavery. Democratic leaders played up fears that emancipation would bring cheap Negro labor north, to drive the Irish from their foothold at the bottom of the economic ladder and deprive them of their racial distinction.

It was a remarkable achievement, then, that Meagher was able to recruit and organize three Union regiments among the New York City Irish—the Sixty-third, Eighty-eighth, and Sixty-ninth, the latter known to glory as the "Fighting Sixty-ninth." To reward him, and ensure his services in further recruitment, Lincoln made him a brigadier general and banded his three regiments in the Irish Brigade. Its ethnic character was so firmly established that it survived the addition of the Twenty-ninth Massachusetts, a thoroughly Yankee outfit, to bring it up to authorized strength. On the Peninsula, the Irish Brigade earned a reputation for dash and gallantry. As representatives of an oppressed nation marked by a long history of defiant rebellion, they had a character to live up to. As members of a despised race, they had something to prove. This was a motivation for heroism they would share with African American soldiers, when these eventually joined the Federal army—a likeness the Irish would dismiss with hatred and contempt.

Behind the Irish came the brigade of Brigadier General John Caldwell, an adequate brigade commander blessed with some extraordinary subordinates. His command was made up of veteran regiments, including the Eighty-first Pennsylvania, the Seventh New York, the Fifth New Hampshire and the combined Sixty-first/Sixty-fourth New York. The Seventh New York was known as a kid-glove militia regiment, because in peacetime its officers were drawn from the top of New York society; but it had been one of the first to reach Washington in April 1861 and had fought well in every major engagement since First Bull Run. The Fifth New Hampshire was led by red-bearded Colonel Edward Cross, who had been by turns a newspaper editor, an Arizona pioneer, an army scout on the frontier, and a volunteer in the army of Benito Juárez, the Mexican revolutionary and reform president. Cross was a fierce disciplinarian and fighter and instilled those virtues in his regiment. He wore a red bandanna over his balding head instead of a hat, the better to be seen by his men, ignoring the fact that it also made a fine target for Rebel sharpshooters.

The Sixty-first/Sixty-fourth New York combined the remnants of two regiments reduced by battle losses on the Peninsula. The Sixty-first was from the City and the Sixty-fourth from upstate, a partnership of urban mechanics, clerks, and roughs, with "apple-knockers" from the orchard country around Elmira. They were commanded by Colonel Francis C. Barlow (city) and Lieutenant Colonel Nelson Miles (upstate), two of the best combat officers in the army. Both were civilians who learned their new trade quickly and well, and both would end the war commanding infantry divisions. Barlow was twenty-eight, a slender and boyish-looking aristocrat, Brooklyn-born but Harvard-educated. Miles was twenty-three, a farmer's son whose education was earned in night school and included deep reading in military science and history. After the war, Barlow would return to civilian life as a lawyer, but Miles would join the Regulars, make his name in the Plains Indian wars, and retire in 1903 with three stars as general in chief of the armies.

Last in the column was Colonel John R. Brooke's Brigade, made up of regiments from Delaware, New York, and Pennsylvania. Brooke was also a gifted military amateur. He had entered the service as captain in a three-months regiment, would rise to brigadier general, and after the war win a commission in the Regular Army. Of his units, all but the Delaware regiment were veterans of the Peninsula campaign and had been heavily engaged at Seven Pines and through most of the battles of the Seven Days. They would form the division reserve in the fight for the Sunken Road.

Richardson's intention was to join French's attack on the Sunken Road by bringing his division in on French's left. The onset of Richardson's troops could not be instantaneous. Each brigade in turn had to change formation from marching column to line of battle, move into place, then advance. Meagher's Irish Brigade could march right up alongside French's men, but Caldwell's Brigade would have to slant off to its left, then turn and march forward to come up on Meagher's left.

Meagher's Brigade was the first to make the transition from column to battle line. The brigade's distinctive colors, a golden Irish harp on a field of green, were displayed alongside the national colors. On Meagher's order they fixed bayonets and marched up over the rise of ground and into an immediate storm of rifle-musket fire from the Sunken Road, canister and case-shot from the batteries on the rising ground behind it. French's battle line, shrinking under the steady rain of musketry, shifted to let them come up on their left. The firefight, which was already at an almost intolerable pitch of noise, redoubled. The men in the firing line were drowned in the acrid gunsmoke that piled up around them in the hot, windless air, nearly deafened by the ear-splitting, unending crash of rifle fire from their own comrades, the background roar of the enemy's musketry punctuated by explosions of case-shot, and over and over the dull thump and bone-crack of bullets hitting the men left and right where they stood in ranks almost shoulder to shoulder. Meagher ordered the Sixty-third and Sixty-ninth to charge and carry the road at the point of the bayonet, and the double lines surged forward—then stopped and began firing again, now at murderously close range.

The intensity of the action distorted the time sense of those engaged. Some experienced an extreme compression, as if the events of an hour passed in a flash, while for others fifteen minutes of action seemed like hours. Meagher rode back to find Richardson and beg for Caldwell to come up on his left and join the attack. Right after rejoining his men, however, he had to leave the field when his horse was killed and he was injured in the fall.

It took Caldwell perhaps half an hour to move past Meagher's rear, form up, and advance on his left. Colonel Barlow, commanding Caldwell's lead regiment, found the Irish Brigade already hotly engaged when he brought his own men into position. Barlow's Sixty-first/Sixty-fourth New York found itself on a spur of rising ground that overlooked the right leg of the Sunken Road position, from which G. B. Anderson's North Carolinians and Wright's Georgians were shooting it out with Meagher's Irishmen. Now was the time for Caldwell to bring the rest of the brigade into line, hit the Rebels with enfilading fire, followed by an oblique attack that would take their line in flank and sweep it end to end.

But no such order was given. Caldwell's approach to command was passive. Having put his men more or less in position, he set up his headquarters behind a haystack and awaited further orders from Richardson. It is not clear just how long the Irish Brigade were left to fight alone. Colonel Barlow, whose regiment was closest to the action, spent what he thought was about fifteen minutes as a frustrated spectator of the fighting. Colonel Kelly of the Eighty-eighth New York, who took command of the Irish Brigade when Meagher was disabled, said he did not know "exactly how long we were in action, but we were long enough there to lose, in killed and wounded, one-third of our men."[10]

By now it was probably close to noon. The fighting had been raging for hours along a relatively static battle line, from Greene's foothold around the Dunker Church across the northern face of the Sunken Road. The firing position of Federal units were marked by rows of dead men, shot down in line of battle. The intensity of rifle and artillery fire was nearly intolerable; troops on both sides had their nerves strained to the breaking point.

It was Richardson who made the crisis break in favor of the Union. He had been preoccupied with the process of bringing Brooke's Brigade into position and the quest for artillery support. His own divisional artillery had been diverted to the support of Greene's division at the far right of the fighting line. McClellan's long-range guns were not precision weapons under the best of circumstances, and here their line of sight was marred by clouds of gunsmoke rising from the firefight, by dust and heat haze. While they raked the Confederate batteries supporting the Sunken

Road line, with such ferocity that one Confederate officer thought he had gone to "artillery hell," they were still unable to completely suppress the Rebel gunnery and did only limited damaged to the troops of R. H. Anderson's Division in the cornfield behind the road. Richardson managed to locate an unengaged Rhode Island battery and bring it forward, but its guns had no effect on the infantry in the Sunken Road. He also scrounged up an uncommitted Regular battery, but it was quickly put out of action by Confederate counter-battery fire.

When Richardson learned that Caldwell's men were not yet in action he rode over to the position, dismounted, and went stalking down the brigade line on foot looking for Caldwell. Told that the brigadier was somewhere in the rear, Richardson cried, "Damn the field officers!" He then ran along the line, sword in hand, down past the Fifth New Hampshire, Eighty-first Pennsylvania, and Seventh New York till he got to Barlow and the Sixty-first/Sixty-fourth New York, ordering everyone up for an advance.

While Caldwell's Brigade was gathering itself, the Irish Brigade was preparing to withdraw. The brigade had suffered 60 percent casualties, mostly in the two front-line regiments (Sixty-third and Sixty-ninth New York), and it was out of ammunition. But as Irishmen they still had something to prove. In an act of stunning bravado they ceased fire, and as if on parade ordered arms, reformed their battle lines into columns of fours, about-faced, and marched to the rear at a steady pace, flags flying—all of this while still under fire by Rebel infantry and artillery. However, as Colonel Barlow gratefully noted, their firefight had significantly reduced the numbers of Rebel infantry in the right leg of the Sunken Road line.

Richardson now ordered Barlow to lead Caldwell's Regiments forward against the exposed flank of Wright's Georgia Brigade below them in the lane. He himself ran back along the rear of the fighting line to summon Brooke's and Meagher's men to join in a frontal attack.

Meanwhile, down in the Sunken Road, Brigadier General Robert Rodes had recognized the weakening of his line and the intensifying threat from the Federal infantry on his front and right flank. Rodes was thirty-three, an 1848 graduate of the Virginia Military Institute whose only prewar service was as a professor at VMI and a civil engineer. However, he had shown an aptitude for combat command at First Bull Run and Seven Pines and had been appointed to command of his Alabama infantry brigade after Pope's defeat at Second Bull Run. Rodes needed reinforcements to deal with the impending threat to his line, so he dashed back across the Piper cornfield to where Brigadier General Roger Pryor, commanding in place of the wounded R. H. Anderson, had positioned the three still uncommitted brigades of Anderson's Division. These brigades had been so worn down by battle loss and straggling that the entire force probably amounted to fewer than 2,100 infantry.

Pryor ordered the brigades forward, directing them toward the imperiled right half of Rodes's position. But Pryor was an amateur, not a West Pointer like R. H. Anderson, and he lost control of the movement. The Virginians of Pryor's Brigade bulled into the rear of G. B. Anderson's North Carolinians, disrupting both units. Featherston's Mississippi Brigade, commanded by Colonel Carnot Posey, charged straight across the Sunken Road to try to come to grips with the Federal firing line. It ran into a storm of bullets so intense that, as several observers reported, the brigade seemed simply to vanish. Pryor's third brigade never made it to the road.[11]

While these Confederate troops were in motion, Caldwell's brigade made its charge against the right flank of the Sunken Road, and Richardson sent Brooke's brigade forward in a frontal attack against the same section of the line. The flank attack was led by Colonel Barlow and the Sixty-first/Sixty-fourth New York. A remnant of the Irish Brigade had been delayed in its retreat and was still on the field. Barlow linked his right flank with the Irishmen as he swept forward, while the other regiments of Caldwell's brigade dashed forward and attached themselves to Barlow's left, extending his line till it crossed the T at the end of the Confederate line. Struck from the front, flank, and rear, the infantry of Wright's and G. B. Anderson's Brigades tried to retreat back along the Sunken Road, and as they jammed their way down the lane they disrupted the troops who were still facing front and shooting it out with French's Federals. As this was happening, French's Division made its move against the left leg of the Sunken Road line. Rodes was on the spot, trying to reorient his men to repel Richardson's flank attack while still holding off French. In the confusion generated by the intrusion of Pryor's reinforcements, Rodes's order to change facing was misunderstood as an order to retreat. The Confederate line crumpled from end to end, with many units dropping their guns in surrender while others broke and fled west and south across the cornfield toward the high ground around Sharpsburg.

The Sunken Road, which had been a bulwark, now became a death trap for the Southern infantry. Troops fleeing from Barlow's flank attack crowded back down the road, jamming into the ranks of their comrades who were still firing toward their front. "The slaughter was terrible!" a soldier in Wright's Georgia Brigade remembered. "When ordered to retreat I could scarcely extricate myself from the dead and wounded around me." The only choice was "to run or surrender," and once started many officers and men kept running till they had left the field entirely. An officer in the Fifth New Hampshire saw so many dead Rebels lying in the road "that they formed a line which one might have walked upon as far as I could see . . . they lay just as they had been killed apparently, amid the blood which was soaking the earth."[12]

The stubborn valor of French's and Richardson's men and the disciplined energy of Richardson's offensive had achieved a remarkable feat of arms. Against a Confederate infantry force not much weaker in numbers, fighting from a strong defensive position and backed by artillery, they had maintained an intense firefight for more than two hours. They had had only marginal support from their own artillery. McClellan's long-range guns had little impact on the fight, and all of the II Corps artillery had been diverted to the support of XII Corps in the Dunker Church/East Woods sector. Despite those disadvantages, the two II Corps divisions had stormed the Sunken Road line and driven the defenders off in disorder.[13]

Richardson was up on the front line, coordinating the advancing elements of French's division as well as his own troops. With Caldwell somewhere in the rear, Colonel Barlow was effectively in command of the brigade. He managed the difficult task of reorienting its advance from its sidewise sweep of the Sunken Road to reform its line facing the fleeing Rebels and their defensive line on the Sharpsburg plateau. Two of French's regiments were on his right, and Richardson ordered Brooke's Brigade forward to support a new attack, exploiting the apparent rout of the Sunken Road defenders. Although both of the II Corps divisions had been fighting for hours and had taken heavy casualties, they were elated by their success and the sight of enemies in flight. With Richardson in command they were swiftly forming up for an attempt to storm the high ground and break Lee's main line of defense north of Sharpsburg.

That line of defense was extremely thin. The defeated elements of D. H. Hill's and R. H. Anderson's Divisions were rallying, but at the moment the Confederate defense consisted mainly of artillery. Most of the guns belonged to the divisions that had been fighting here, but Lee and Longstreet were also rushing batteries from elsewhere, to offset with firepower the Federals' advantage in infantry strength. Many of these additional batteries had already been in action on Jackson's front. Some had returned to the reserve area to replenish ammunition and were then redirected to the new line. Others were pulled directly from Jackson's supporting lines. Events were showing that Lee's infantry could make only limited use of the internal lines of communication around Sharpsburg. Once committed to action, infantry was either too exhausted or disorganized by combat, or too entangled with enemy forces, to be freely and speedily shifted to a new sector. However, artillery remained mobile as long as there were horses to pull the guns and limbers. Lee's army was not much inferior to McClellan's in the number of guns it had dedicated to killing infantry. Moreover, Lee's guns were deployed closer to the fighting line than McClellan's, and pushed forward with far more daring and aggression. Now their fire checked the Federal advance in the Piper cornfield while Jackson was mounting a counterattack against Greene's XII Corps division at the Dunker Church.[14]

CONFEDERATE COUNTERATTACK
AT THE DUNKER CHURCH, 1:00–2:00 PM

For the past hour and more, while the fighting at the Sunken Road had been static, Greene had been holding on in his isolated position around the church, without guidance or material support from his superiors, Sumner and Williams. His left flank was vulnerable because there was a gap between it and French's Division, covered by a few unsupported artillery batteries positioned back near the East Woods. Because Greene had not been informed about the rout of Sedgwick's Division, now more than two hours past, Greene still supposed Sedgwick was protecting his right by engaging Confederate forces in the West Woods. When an aide from Sumner's staff finally brought the news of Sedgwick's disaster, it was too late for Greene to respond effectively. Rebel troops from Walker's Division had moved through the West Woods to strike his front and right flank, hitting from the very direction from which Greene expected Sedgwick's troops to arrive. Greene tried to make an orderly retreat, but the pullback across the open ground east and north of the church was hasty and disordered, and Walker's Rebels came on in pursuit, hoping to regain the East Woods. The Rebels were defeated by the same kind of force that had checked Richardson: a line of batteries brought forward from reserve positions. As Walker recoiled, the lead elements of Franklin's VI Corps began arriving to solidify the Union defense—and create the potential for yet another counterstrike.

While most of Walker's Division was attacking Greene's right flank a small composite brigade of regiments from McLaws's and Walker's Divisions, under the command of a Colonel Cooke, had attacked into the gap between Greene and French, assailed and captured the batteries defending it. Longstreet, who had come forward to oversee this maneuver, alertly recognized that Cooke's advance had created an opportunity to reverse the defeat at the Sunken Road. He sent an aide to Cooke, ordering him to pull his four regiments out of the fight with Greene, reorient them ninety degrees, and lead them in an attack against the exposed right flank of French's division. This maneuver, like Barlow's after the taking of the Sunken Road, was extremely difficult for a unit already closely engaged. Cooke's strike was beaten back when French matched the Rebel maneuver, wheeling two regiments around to face Cooke. But the threat posed by Cooke's flank attack, announced by the roar of musketry and the keen of the Rebel yell as Cooke's men charged, when added to the frontal fire from Lee's artillery line, brought Richardson's attack up short.[15]

Now it was the Confederates' turn to try to exploit a wavering among the attackers. But with no fresh infantry reserves left in Lee's army, the counter was made by rallied regiments from D. H. Hill's and R. H. Anderson's Divisions, backed by those infantry-killing batteries that hit the Federals in the cornfield with charges of canister. Again the turn of battle depended on regimental and company officers. Colonel Barlow held the Union front line together. Colonel Cross of the Fifth

Confederate dead in Sunken Road (NATIONAL PARK SERVICE)

New Hampshire, spotted a Rebel column circling to hit the brigade from the left flank. The former Indian fighter wheeled his regiment to face it, calling for his men to "Put on the war paint!" Cross and his men blacked their faces with gunpowder soot, the colonel conspicuous and piratical-looking with his red beard and his head bound in its red bandanna, and they beat back the flank attack.

As General Richardson saw it, the chief thing preventing him from storming the Confederate line was his lack of artillery. He sent a request to McClellan for one section of rifled cannons with the range and weight of metal to hurt the Confederate guns and distract them from their killing of infantry. McClellan refused. Richardson was still determined to attack, convinced that the chance for a decisive breakthrough existed on his front. But he would have to attack with his infantry alone, holding back his one battery of short-range cannon until the fight was at closer quarters. He went to the battery to give Captain Graham his orders and help him get his guns into a position more protected from Confederate shell fire. While he was doing that, a case-shot exploded nearby, and a big lead ball from the shell struck him in the leg. The wound was serious. Richardson was carried off, eliminating the only general in that part of the field with the skill, energy, and drive to organize an offensive. At about the same time, his brigade-level counterpart, Colonel Barlow, fell victim to the heavy fire sweeping the Piper cornfield. Barlow would survive his wound, but Richardson would die of infection six weeks later. With these two out of action the Federal drive hung fire.

The situation on the field was once again in a state of chaotic equilibrium, the battle lines still in place but troop morale and tactical position made fluid by intense combat and rapidly changing events. It would require the effective intervention of new reserves to tip the balance one way or the other.

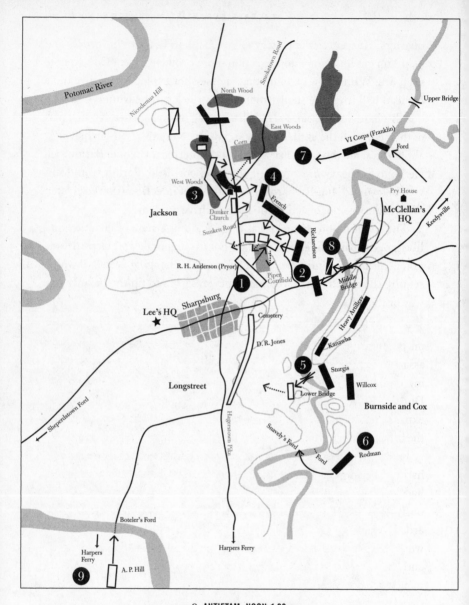

MAP 8: ANTIETAM, NOON–1:00 PM

1. C.S.: Pryor (R. H. Anderson's Division reinforces Sunken Road
2. U.S.: Richardson's flank attack breaks Sunken Road line, Rebels retreat
3. C.S.: Walker and McLaws force Greene to abandon Dunker Church
4. U.S.: French repels Longstreet's flank attack
5. U.S.: Ferrero's Brigade (IX Corps) storms Lower Bridge
6. U.S.: Rodman's Division (IX Corps) crosses at Snavely's Ford, forcing Toombs's (C.S.) retreat
7. U.S.: VI Corps reinforces right wing
8. U.S.: Pleasonton's cavalry and Buchanan's Brigade (V Corps) cross Middle Bridge
9. C.S.: A. P. Hill's Division approaches from Harpers Ferry

CHAPTER 14

THE BATTLE OF ANTIETAM: THE EDGE OF DISASTER

NOON TO EVENING

❧

By THROWING THREE-QUARTERS OF HIS FORCE INTO THE FIGHT on Jackson's front, Lee had repulsed McClellan's poorly coordinated assault and neutralized three of his army corps. After the Federal storming of the Sunken Road and the retreat of Greene's division from the Dunker Church, there was a lull in the fighting on this front, and Jackson expressed his certainty that "they have done their worst" on this part of the field and that "there is now no danger of the line being broken."[1]

Jackson was right in thinking that the Federal attack in his sector had broken down. The Federal units engaged on the northern front had lost 28 percent of their strength, and six divisions had been seriously disorganized by their repulse. The divisions of French and Richardson were, for the moment, elated by their victory; but exhaustion would soon overtake them—they had been fighting intensely for hours and had taken heavy losses. The Federals had also lost two corps commanders, one of whom was also the wing commander, two of their best division commanders, and four brigadier generals. However, the Union still had a preponderance of strength that could be used on other fronts. McClellan had used a little less than half of his 72,500-man force so far, and his casualties (perhaps 10,000) amounted to only 14 percent of his command. In contrast, Lee had begun the day with fewer than 35,000 troops. Three-quarters of those men had already been committed to action, and upwards of 9,000 had become casualties—35 percent of his available strength. That total did not take into account the large number of men who were temporarily separated from their units—whether lost in the confusion of battle, frightened and in flight, or straggling. Casualty rates that approached or exceeded 30 percent usually rendered the units involved too weak in numbers and morale for offensive operations, and might well make them unfit for further action. The army's command organization had also been impaired by the death or disabling of three division commanders and four brigadiers, and J. R. Jones's Division was now commanded by a colonel.[2]

The situation in the center, where Longstreet was in immediate command, seemed especially dire. The infantry divisions that had held the battle line in the Sunken Road had been driven back in some disorder, and for the moment the defense here consisted of artillery with only minimal infantry support. In this moment of crisis and extreme vulnerability rank temporarily went by the boards. D. H. Hill picked up a musket and fought alongside his rallied infantry, while Longstreet took charge of an artillery battery.

The real danger to Lee's position, however, lay southward from the Sunken Road. By throwing all of his reserve infantry into action north of Sharpsburg, Lee had thinned the rest of his line to the breaking point. The only infantry units not yet engaged were the brigades of D. R. Jones's Division, supplemented by one cavalry brigade and some detached infantry from other commands—between four and five thousand troops. They were committed to the defense of two vital sectors: the road that led from the Middle Bridge to Sharpsburg; and the high ground south of Sharpsburg, which protected the road that ran west to the Shepherdstown and Boteler's fords—the road by which A. P. Hill would be marching his desperately needed reinforcement. The Sharpsburg section of this line was exposed to a direct assault by the two V Corps divisions and the cavalry McClellan had massed above the Middle Bridge. The southern section could not be attacked until IX Corps had forced the crossing of the Lower Bridge. But Toombs's Brigade of eight hundred men, defending the position, was heavily outnumbered and certain to be brushed aside whenever Burnside and Cox organized a serious attack. Once IX Corps was across, the Federals would have strength enough to overlap and outflank D. R. Jones's line and threaten to cut Lee's line of retreat to the Potomac fords. On this part of the field McClellan now enjoyed a vast preponderance of strength: seventeen thousand in V Corps and the cavalry near the Middle Bridge, thirteen thousand under Burnside and Cox at the Lower Bridge, against no more than five thousand Confederates.

MIDDAY CRISIS, NOON–2:30 PM

McClellan, however, could not see any of that from his Pry house headquarters. From the messages he had been receiving he could not be certain whether he was on the verge of "a great defeat or a most glorious victory." He would use just those words in a telegram to General in Chief Halleck, sent at 1:25 PM—then scratch them out, and substitute a pious wish that God favor him with victory. But his doubts were real.

Since seven in the morning, he had been a distant spectator of the terrible combat that raged on the approaches to the Dunker Church, and he had had to send all of II Corps to reinforce Hooker's wing. At 10:00 AM, Sumner had told him that almost the entire right wing of the army had been defeated and disorganized, forcing him to send Franklin's VI Corps to that part of the field—not to mount an attack, but to prevent the right wing from being driven off the field by a Confederate counterattack. Under his gaze, the divisions of French and Richardson had locked in the prolonged firefight in front of the Sunken Road, so intense that McClellan thought their struggle the most "magnificent" he had ever seen. A reporter who was near him described the distant view of "riderless horses and scattering men, clouds of dirt from solid shot and exploding shells, long dark lines of infantry swaying to and fro, with columns of smoke rising from their muskets, red flashes and white puffs from the batteries—with the sun shining brightly on all this scene of tumult."[3]

Nevertheless, McClellan would not aid them by further weakening his reserves. All he did was send Pleasonton's cavalry and a few artillery batteries across the Middle Bridge at noon, to stage a small and ineffective diversion. Meanwhile Burnside was making no progress in his attempts to carry the Lower Bridge and threaten Lee's right flank; and because he could not get past Toombs's isolated brigade, the weakness of Lee's southern flank could not be detected.

McClellan could not see enough of the battlefield to judge the state of things on Sumner's front. He stood in the front yard of the Pry house, on the brink of the ridge that overlooked the Middle Bridge, watching the action through a telescope mounted on a staff. He saw the Confederate line in the Sunken Road collapse and blue-coated infantry surge into the cornfield beyond it—then recoil. But the gunsmoke that kept piling up around the Dunker Church and the East Woods obscured the exchange of charge and countercharge between Walker's Confederate division and the Federals of Greene's division.

Aides dispatched by Sumner and Franklin galloped out of the battle smoke to deliver reports and pleas for reinforcement and to offer conflicting advice about what McClellan ought to do next. Back into the smoke went officers from McClellan's own staff, with responses to Sumner and Franklin, and renewed requests for information on the state of the field. It took anywhere from thirty minutes to an hour and a half for a message to go one way; and since conditions on the battle line were constantly changing, by the time answers were received the generals were dealing with a different set of questions.

Then, between 12:30 and 2:00 PM, a series of such exchanges transformed McClellan's conception of the course of battle. The exact sequence and timing of the messages cannot be reconstructed, but their drift can be read in the account given long afterward by James H. Wilson, then serving as a lieutenant on McClellan's staff. Wilson was twenty-five, a member of West Point's last prewar graduating class. He was trained as an engineer, like most of the academy's best and brightest, but experience would prove he had military aptitude beyond his undergraduate specialty. He had already mastered the varied and demanding tasks of the general staff officer, which ranged from clerical work to acting as his general's vicar, observing and reporting on distant events, not only delivering messages but interpreting their intent. As the commander's representative, a staff lieutenant might well find himself giving orders to gray-haired generals of vast seniority—a role that required tact as well as intelligence and self-confidence. Young Wilson affected a mustache and chin beard that made him look older than he was.

While Richardson and French were driving the Rebels out of the Sunken Road, McClellan sent Wilson riding to Sumner's headquarters with orders for him to hold the positions he had seized "at all hazards." The orders, which took Wilson a half-hour to deliver, reflected McClellan's uncertainty about the state of affairs on the right wing. To Wilson's dismay, Sumner was unable to grasp the meaning of his orders. He seemed to think McClellan wanted him to attack. No matter what Wilson said, Sumner repeated his demand that Wilson inform McClellan that he could not attack, because his demoralized troops were liable to rout and might not be able to rally this side of the Antietam.[4]

Sumner's confusion may have been the result of a disagreement that had erupted between himself and General Franklin, who was now on the field with both of his infantry divisions. Franklin's reading of the battlefield led him to believe that the tide had turned sharply against the Confederates and that a prompt and strongly supported offensive on this part of the field might well produce a decisive result. The evidence of Confederate vulnerability must have been substantial, because Franklin had a well-earned reputation for slowness and caution in making and executing operational decisions. Franklin had sent a dispatch advocating an attack directly to McClellan, which probably reached the Pry house after Wilson's departure. Sumner must have gotten it into his head that Wilson was bringing the attack order that Franklin had requested, and nothing that Wilson said could get past that assumption. So back went Wilson, to repeat Sumner's words to McClellan.

Wilson was an extremely able and ambitious young officer, confident in his military judgment—justifiably so, according to General Grant, who would see him promoted to divisional, corps, and independent command before the war was done. He also read the situation here as one of opportunity rather than menace. On his way back to McClellan he accosted George Smalley, the *Tribune* reporter who had been covering the action on this part of the field, who agreed that the Rebel line here was reeling and that a strong push could break it.[5] Wilson asked Smalley to ride to Hooker's headquarters and beg Fighting Joe to resume command of the right wing—even if he had to do so from an ambulance. Hooker could replace the demoralized and incompetent Sumner, and his troops would rally to his return and support Franklin's fresh troops in a climactic assault on the Rebel line. Wilson was risking a charge of mutiny, and Smalley of conspiracy, and both were ludicrously out of line. But they had seen the field, and their judgment supported the more substantial recommendation made by Franklin.

Franklin and Wilson had seen what McClellan could not: that the crisis that might have led to the rout of his right wing was past, and the victory in the Sunken Road had reversed the momentum of battle. The arrival of Franklin's first division had checked the Rebel attack, which had driven Greene's division back from the Dunker Church. The Confederates here would have to regroup before renewing their attacks, and while they did so, the battered brigades of I and XII Corps were reforming their ranks—already capable of holding their ground, which would free Smith's division for offensive operations. In the meantime, Franklin's second division had arrived, giving Franklin some twelve thousand fresh infantrymen for an offensive. Franklin had also seen, at close range, the triumphant conclusion to the attack on the Sunken Road, and marked the enthusiasm that carried Richardson's men beyond the road in pursuit. Many of Richardson's and French's units were probably capable of joining an assault, their battle-weariness and losses offset by the elation of their sudden triumph and the sight of Rebel infantry fleeing the Sunken Road. However, that ardor had to be used before it cooled.

The situation now, just after 1:00 PM, was actually more promising than Franklin knew. For defensive reasons, McClellan had augmented the force fronting Sharpsburg. Pleasonton's horse artillery proved inadequate to deal with the Confederate gunners, so McClellan sent part of the artillery from Sykes's Division across, with a small brigade of Regular Army infantry under Lieutenant Colonel Robert Buchanan—not to attack, but to protect the guns. When complete, this would put a combined infantry/cavalry force of more than five thousand men in position to attack Sharpsburg directly. Meanwhile, down at the far southern end of the battlefield, IX Corps had finally forced its way across the Antietam, and was at last in position to throw its full weight against Lee's southern flank.

BURNSIDE'S BRIDGE, 1:00–2:30 PM

McClellan had wanted Burnside's diversion to draw off Confederate troops from the active front, and while Richardson and French fought for the Sunken Road, McClellan had been sending regular hurry-up messages to Burnside, to no appreciable effect. After Crook's assault against the Lower Bridge misfired, a brigade from Sturgis's Division made an attempt to cross the bridge. After it failed, the division commanders reverted to passivity, awaiting new orders, while Rodman's division continued its sun-bedazzled search for the lost ford. Finally, shortly after noon, McClellan sent a senior staff officer, Colonel Sackett, with orders for Burnside to carry the crossing at all costs. Burnside passed the order to Cox, who summoned General Samuel Sturgis, who passed it to the commander of his second brigade, Edward Ferrero—a militia officer in peacetime who had made his fortune as the operator of fashionable dance clubs in New York.

Ferrero chose two regiments to make the assault, the Fifty-first Pennsylvania and Fifty-first New York, commanded respectively by Colonels John Hartranft and Robert Potter. Both were lawyers in civilian life, who became highly competent combat officers and would ultimately be promoted to divisional command, in Potter's case over the head of Ferrero, his erstwhile brigadier. The stone bridge was a potential bottleneck and death trap, completely exposed to rifle fire from Confederates posted on the steep wooded hills overlooking the far side. Artillery could do nothing to suppress that fire. The only hope was for Hartranft to mass his regiment in column of fours and run like hell across the bridge, letting the dead and wounded fall as they would; then deploy into line and advance uphill while Potter's regiment ran the gauntlet behind them to join the attack.

That is what they did. The Pennsylvanians and New Yorkers made their run across the "Bridge of Death," took their losses, deployed in the brush, and began climbing the steep slope toward Toombs's infantry.

Confederate resistance on the hilltop flurried and faded away. At almost the same moment that Hartranft attacked the bridge, General Rodman's division finally discovered Snavely's Ford, less than half a mile south of the bridge, and forced a crossing against the thin infantry screen Toombs had posted there. With his flank turned and three thousand Federals threatening to cut him off, Toombs had no choice but to fall back on D. R. Jones's defense line. By 1:30 PM Burnside had three brigades across the river, with another three immediately available to cross the bridge and form up for a concerted drive against the Rebel lines south of Sharpsburg.

Thus, when Wilson returned to headquarters after his encounters with Sumner and Smalley, he found McClellan encouraged by the combination of Franklin's dispatch and the good news from Burnside's front.

For the first time, and after unconscionable delay, McClellan's infantry was in position to engage the entire length of the Confederate line: on the right the rallied elements of I and XII Corps held the North and East woods, and Richardson and French the Sunken Road, with VI Corps in reserve. Pleasonton's cavalry, backed by artillery and Buchanan's Regulars from V Corps, were established across the Middle Bridge, opening the approach for an attack into Sharpsburg; and now IX Corps was across the Lower Bridge, and preparing to advance against the southern, or right, flank of Lee's position, which was "in the air"—open to a sweep around its far southern end.

Back went Wilson with new orders for Sumner, to let Franklin attack and give him all the support his other commands could manage. Burnside was also ordered to press the attack on the other end of the line, and McClellan promised to support his attack by a strong demonstration against Sharpsburg by Pleasonton and Sykes.

Wilson rode back to Sumner in record time—but Old Bull Head was immovable. He could not see the field as Franklin saw it, could not see that I and XII Corps units were rallying and reforming, could not see the significance of the Confederate break at the Sunken Road. All he could see was Sedgwick's ruin, in which he had been physically immersed, an experience so overwhelming that it seemed to him to have wrecked the entire right wing. He told Wilson to go back and tell McClellan, "I have no command . . . my command, Banks' command and Hooker's command are all cut up and demoralized." Franklin's corps was the only unit capable of self-defense, and it had to be reserved as the right wing's last resort.

Wilson would carry this message back to McClellan, and while he was in transit there would be no attack. By now it was well after 2:00 PM. Richardson's and French's men had pulled back from the Sunken Road to positions more sheltered from artillery fire, rested a bit, and resupplied with ammunition. Their physical strength and armament improved, but the wild energy that might have carried them up the slope to Sharpsburg had lapsed with the sudden relief from battle stress. On the Confederate side the chaos produced by the rout from the Sunken Road was steadily diminishing. The routed troops were rallying and reforming their ranks. Their morale was resilient enough that officers were able to improvise new formations using individuals from different units. The Federals still enjoyed a powerful advantage in numbers, but the intangible elements that had given the Union army the opportunity for a decisive stroke were steadily dissipating while its commanders debated their course of action.

McClellan's response to Wilson's latest report was characteristic. Instead of reaffirming the order to attack, he reconsidered the impulse that had led him to issue it. Perhaps Sumner was right and Franklin mistaken. The core of his military doctrine was to ensure against the possibility of defeat before assuming the risks inherent in attempting to win a victory. He mistrusted the chaos and fluidity of battle, in which events could take uncontrolled direction.[6] He believed the issue was still very much in doubt. His overestimate of Lee's numbers made it plausible to fear a heavy counterattack against the Union right wing, which, if Sumner was correct, might drive half the army from the field in abject rout. McClellan decided to ride to Sumner's headquarters and judge for himself the feasibility of a new attack on that front. His ultimate decision was foreshadowed by the fact that he left his headquarters without giving orders to Pleasonton, Sykes, or Porter to prepare supporting attacks in the Middle Bridge sector. He sent no additional orders or information to Burnside, whose troops under Cox's command were slowly assembling in their hard-won bridgehead and preparing—still preparing—to advance.

LEE'S HEADQUARTERS, NOON–2:30 PM

However erroneous his estimate of Lee's capabilities, McClellan was accurate in assessing his opponent's intentions. Lee's response to the crisis, like McClellan's, was characteristic. He embraced the chaos and fluidity of battle, confident in his own ability to read the play of forces, and in the ability of his corps and division commanders to execute his orders with initiative, energy, and good judgment. He also believed that his soldiers were markedly superior to those of the enemy in both combat skills and morale. As he rode north to confer with General Jackson, he passed one of those improvised formations composed of men who had been rallied after being separated from their home units. He hailed them, urging them to prove "that the *stragglers* of the Army of Northern Virginia, are *better than the best troops of the enemy*." He may have intended the speech as a buck-me-up for the troops, but his subsequent actions suggest that he believed what he said.[7]

Lee had sent the preponderance of his infantry strength to Jackson's front. With his center thin to breaking and his right threatened, the obvious next move was to borrow what force Jackson could spare to buttress Longstreet's line facing the Sunken Road and D. R. Jones's at the Middle Bridge. Instead, Lee would use his strongest concentration of force to strike what he deemed the weakest part of the Federal line, the flank held by the defeated troops of I and XII Corps. At some time between 1:30 and 2:00 PM—while Lieutenant Wilson was riding back and forth between McClellan and Sumner—Lee met with Jackson and ordered him to pull together a striking force and swing it wide to the north in an attempt to either turn McClellan's right flank or break it by assault.

Lee's plan seems quixotic. Its likelihood of success was slim, given the large disparity of numbers on this part of the field. For his assault force, Jackson would have fewer than ten thousand men of all arms. The task of turning or smashing the Federal flank was assigned to Jeb Stuart, who would lead a mixed force of something over four thousand cavalry, infantry, and guns—the cavalry predominating, which meant the force had less firepower than the equivalent number of infantry. Jackson would support Stuart with a column of five thousand infantry, gathered in the West Wood. When Stuart was in position to attack, Jackson would order his infantry forward, and the sound of their rifles would be Stuart's cue to assault. Jackson was well aware that the Federals in his front represented elements of three army corps, and that even with their numbers reduced by combat losses they significantly outnumbered his own available force. The rallied elements of I and XII had between ten thousand and twelve thousand infantry in line, with an ample supply of artillery; and they were backed by Smith's Division of VI Corps, with six thousand fresh men. However, like Lee, Jackson assumed that these troops had been demoralized by the repulse of their attack and by the counterattacks that had driven them back to their start lines. That idea seems to have been widespread among the Confederate high command. At about the time that Jackson was assembling his force, Longstreet met with General John Walker to propose an attack by Walker's Division against the Federal line in the East Woods. He called it off when informed of Lee's decision to make the attack on Jackson's front, but he clearly shared Lee's sense that the Federals were badly shaken and that a sudden stroke might reverse the momentum of the fight.

There was more to this belief than the legendary Sothron sense of superiority to all things Yankee. In both the Seven Days and Second Bull Run campaigns, Lee's army had succeeded in attacking a Federal army, superior in numbers and materiel, and driving it from the field in full and even abject retreat. At South Mountain it had held at bay a vastly superior force, then retreated in good order. On this day, it had held its lines against heavy assaults by an army that outnumbered it two to one. On the right a single brigade had held off an army corps for three hours. And on the north, in Jackson's sector, it had driven the Federal right wing back to its start line. Though D. H. Hill's and R. H. Anderson's Divisions had been driven from the Sunken Road, they had apparently fought the Yankees to a standstill—at least, they were not attempting to advance from the captured position. That hesitancy was itself proof of a kind that Federal troops lacked the skill, the leadership, and the morale to make the kind of attacks that won battles. Confederate generals understood that part of that failure could be blamed on the caution, perhaps the faintheartedness, of Federal generals. But it was not unreasonable to think that perhaps that caution reflected the generals' lack of confidence in their own troops. Lincoln certainly thought McClellan mistrusted the quality of his force. One of the strongest criticisms he would level at McClellan was that by failing to demand that his army march and fight as hard as the Rebels, he implied a belief that his men *as men* were inferior to their enemies.[8]

Although Lee's plan for Jackson's flank attack was daring, it was not irrational. At the very least, Jackson's attack might serve to distract the Federal command, force it to divert attention and resources to the northern flank, and thereby weaken or forestall an attack against Sharpsburg. Lee also anticipated the arrival of A. P. Hill's Light Division, which had been on the march from Harpers Ferry since 6:30 AM. An attack by Jackson at the northern end of the line would divert strength and attention away from Hill's line of approach.

Finally—if Jackson did no more than mount a serious threat to the safety of the Federal wing, his attack might so unhinge McClellan that he would pull his army back across the Antietam. The flank attack by Longstreet and Jackson at Gaines' Mill at the start of the Seven Days had broken McClellan's will to stand and fight and started him on the long retreat to Harrison's Landing. Jackson's flank march against Pope, and Longstreet's flank attack at Second Bull Run, had done the same to Pope's army. It would be success enough if the threat of a similar strike here did no more than force McClellan to abandon the attack. Lee's army could then regroup and resupply, and consider whether to retreat in safety or continue the campaign. If McClellan could be frightened as badly as he had been on the Peninsula, he might even retreat behind the mountains, and that would enable Lee to achieve the goal of his campaign: a durable position for his army in western Maryland from which to menace and raid the cities and railroads of Pennsylvania.

At 2:30 PM, Lee's confidence was augmented by the appearance at his headquarters of Major General A. P. Hill, who had ridden in advance of his column to report that four of his five brigades were now less than two hours from the field. When they arrived Lee would be able to strike at both ends of the Federal line.

McCLELLAN'S HEADQUARTERS, 2:00-4:00 PM

While Jackson was gathering his assault force and giving Stuart his orders, McClellan had ridden to Sumner's headquarters to look at the ground and the troops and make his choice between Franklin's urging to attack and Sumner's insistence that his wing could do little more than defend itself. His ride to the front would have taken him through the backwash of the Sunken Road assaults and the fighting around the East Woods, past windrows of dead shot down in ranks, past hundreds of his wounded, dead, and dying soldiers, past stragglers and disorganized gangs of men from broken units—evidence supportive of Sumner's brief. If Franklin was right, here was a chance to win a substantial, perhaps decisive, tactical victory. But were the odds good enough to justify the risks involved, when if Sumner was correct a repulse might wreck most of four army corps? McClellan's strategy assumed that the Army of the Potomac, with himself in command, was the only power in the land capable of saving the Republic from the twin menaces of secession and Radicalism. It was (in his view) irresponsible to risk the army's safety and his own reputation on the wild chances of a chaotic combat like this one.

By the time he reached Sumner's headquarters, between 2:30 and 3:00 PM, McClellan's interest in the offensive had cooled. As Franklin recalled it, the gist of their discussion was that the right wing had probably done all it could, and McClellan "was afraid to risk the day by an attack there on the right at that time." Franklin loyally deferred to his leader's judgment, but he was clearly disappointed. McClellan backed his judgment by ordering two brigades from his carefully hoarded infantry reserve to march to Sumner's support. Then he rode back to his headquarters, arriving there between 3:30 and 4:00 PM, in time to face a new crisis.[9]

BURNSIDE'S FIGHT, 3:00–5:30 PM

In McClellan's absence, IX Corps had been making slow progress in carrying out his order to press the attack against the Confederate line south of Sharpsburg. After Rodman's and Sturgis's divisions had secured the crossings at Snavely's Ford and the Lower Bridge, it had taken nearly two hours for the other two divisions, with their artillery, to cross the single span of the bridge and deploy in line of battle facing northwest. In judging the efficiency of this performance it should be noted that IX Corps divisions contained two brigades each, rather than three; yet it took them twice as long to deploy as Sumner's three divisions, which were larger and had more, and more difficult, ground to cover when they went into action.

Nevertheless, despite all the delays and the lost opportunities of the daylong struggle, it was still possible for the Union army to achieve a tactically decisive breakthrough south of Sharpsburg and into the town itself. The meat-grinder fighting north of the town had absorbed and used up the offensive capacity of three-quarters of Lee's available force—twenty-five thousand of the thirty-five thousand with which he had begun the day's fighting. What remained of Jackson's offensive capability was already committed to the attempt to turn McClellan's northern flank. To defend the line from the front of Sharpsburg south to the junction of the Harpers Ferry and Boteler's Ford roads, all that remained were between three and four thousand infantry, mostly from David R. Jones's Division. Three small brigades held the line that straddled the Boonsboro Road, which ran up to Sharpsburg from the Middle Bridge.

The strongpoint here was Cemetery Hill, southeast of the town. The brigades of Drayton and Kemper extended this line along the crest of the plateau south of Sharpsburg for perhaps six hundred yards. Beyond Kemper's right flank the next six hundred yards of the line was held by detached regiments and batteries, but the Federal approach to this weak defense was obstructed by Toombs's Brigade, skirmishing as it withdrew after its defense of the Lower Bridge. The only infantry reinforcements Jones could hope to receive would come from A. P. Hill's Light Division, which at 3:00 PM was still nearly an hour and a half away. To compensate for the lack of infantry, Lee once again deployed his highly mobile field artillery. S. D. Lee's gunners had already fought in support of the northern flank around Dunker Church and the Sunken Road offensive. Now he was sent with his twelve surviving guns to the extreme southern flank of the army, to hold the line beyond Kemper's flank with artillery unsupported by infantry.

Against this attenuated and improvised defense, the Federals could immediately deploy between 9,500 and 10,000 infantry and more than 4,000 cavalry, with ample artillery support. Burnside and Cox would advance uphill against the Confederates defending the Boteler Ford road and the southeast side of Sharpsburg, with the divisions of Rodman and Willcox, each augmented by a brigade of the Kanawha Division as a reserve. Behind this array Sturgis's division formed a corps reserve of 2,500–3,000 men, still resting and resupplying with ammunition after its storming of the bridge. Willcox would make the main attack toward Sharpsburg and Cemetery Hill, with Rodman advancing in concert to protect his left flank.

As Willcox advanced, his right would come in contact with the forces that McClellan had earlier sent across the Middle Bridge: Buchanan's small brigade of Regular infantry and Pleasonton's 4,500 cavalrymen. The attack here would have the support not only of divisional artillery but of the heavy guns east of the Antietam, which could hit the Rebels in front of Sharpsburg with line-of-sight fire over what was, for them, short range. However, the potential assault force on this front was limited to Buchanan's Brigade of fewer than 2,300 infantry. Cavalry was considered to be unsuited for the kind of frontal attack that would be required, and McClellan had depleted the V Corps infantry reserve when he ordered 2,000 men under General Morrell to go to Sumner's aid. McClellan still had 4,000 infantry east of Antietam Creek, but he would be extremely reluctant to commit this last reserve to action.[10]

Nevertheless, even without that last 4,000, Union forces outnumbered Confederates in this sector by nearly three to one. However, there was no commanding intelligence on the scene willing or able to put all of those forces into play. McClellan had not yet returned from his conference with Sumner and Franklin, and he had left no instructions allowing, let alone commanding, Porter to send any part of V Corps to Burnside's support. Like Hooker and Mansfield, Sumner and Greene, French and Richardson, Burnside and Cox would conduct their operations without physical support or command guidance from army headquarters.

At 3:00 PM IX Corps' attack swept into the open, Willcox's Division in advance and Rodman's in echelon behind it. They could be seen from McClellan's headquarters at the Pry house, and the staff officers and reporters admired the magnificent spectacle of rows and rows of infantry in line of battle, the sun glinting on their brass and steel, advancing steadily under brilliant flags against D. R. Jones's Division on the Sharpsburg plateau.

Rodman had the dual task of supporting Willcox and guarding the IX Corps left flank, a difficult assignment requiring a tactical expertise that he lacked. Isaac Peace Rodman had been a merchant and political leader before the war—a Quaker, whose decision to fight for his country had been spiritually wrenching. He of course had no prewar militia experience, but as a leading citizen he was able to recruit a regiment and earn its colonelcy. His effective service with Burnside in the North Carolina campaign earned him promotion to brigadier general. However, his only experience of divisional command had come three days earlier in the engagement at South Mountain. When he received his orders, IX Corps headquarters assumed that the primary threat to the corps flank would come from the reserves Lee was supposed to have behind Sharpsburg. Any Confederate counterattack would therefore be launched from the line Willcox was approaching head-on. Rodman sent all of his First Brigade and half of his Second to attack the Confederate troops on Willcox's left—the Second threatening the line held by the brigades of Toombs and Kemper, while the First Brigade, commanded by Colonel Fairchild, slanted off to the right, to attack Drayton's Brigade defending the south side of Sharpsburg.

Rodman detailed only two regiments to watch the left (southern) flank and posted them off to the left and well behind his advancing battle lines. One of these was the Sixteenth Connecticut, a large rookie regiment whose numbers made them comparable in strength to two worn-down veteran regiments. The other was the Fourth Rhode Island, a long-serving outfit that had had little experience of major combat. They were not posted in defensible terrain, had no special orders, and were not assigned an experienced senior officer to direct their operations. They were just lined up facing west toward the Boteler's Ford road, with their flanks in the air: 940 green infantrymen watching the rising dust that concealed the 2,500 veteran soldiers of A. P. Hill's Light Division, footsore from their forced march but possessing high morale and incomparable battle experience.

Officers manning the signal station above McClellan's headquarters also noticed the heavy cloud of dust on the Boteler's Ford road, which indicated that Confederate reinforcements from Harpers Ferry were approaching the battlefield. Word was sent to Rodman by way of McClellan, Burnside, and Cox to guard against an attack by forces moving east via the Boteler's Ford road. The message never reached Rodman.[11]

In the meantime, Willcox's men went into action. His right flank brigade, under Colonel Christ, moved frontally against the strong Confederate position on Cemetery Hill. The Rebel gunners there were being blasted by the long-range guns from across the Antietam, but they reserved their fire for infantry and imposed heavy losses. Willcox's other brigade charged on the left and outflanked the Cemetery Hill position, while Lieutenant Colonel Buchanan, on his own initiative, sent part of his Regular brigade forward on Christ's right. There was not enough Confederate infantry here in Evans's and Jenkins's Brigades to hold the line against these multiple thrusts. The guns were pulled off Cemetery Hill back into the streets of Sharpsburg. Captain Hiram Dryer of the Regulars was able to get into the east end of town, and he came out again to report that the Rebels here had barely two regiments and a battery capable of defending the critical center of the Confederate position. Even without calling on the reserves from across the Antietam, with Buchanan's infantry and Pleasonton's cavalry there were almost five thousand additional troops just behind the battle front, and the rest of Sykes's division was poised at the bridge. If these had joined the attack they could have seized the town, but neither Pleasonton nor Sykes would move without orders from Porter or McClellan.[12]

At about this same time—that is, 4:00 PM—Fairchild's brigade of Rodman's division charged the line held by Drayton's Brigade south of Sharpsburg, broke it, and turned north to threaten the town from the south side. The Confederate line in front of Sharpsburg was cracking, the streets of the little town were clogged with disorganized troops, with wagons and artillery trying to escape entrapment. Some of Fairchild's men got in among the buildings on the south side of town and began shooting up the retreat.

Meanwhile the situation of Rodman's other brigade, commanded by Colonel Harland, was growing problematic. To protect the left flank of Fairchild's attacking column, two regiments of Harland's brigade had advanced against the part of the Confederate line held by Kemper and Toombs, with Ewing's brigade from the Kanawha Division in support. Fairchild's brigade was making its successful assault on Drayton, and Harland's lead regiments were already engaged with Toombs and Kemper, when Rodman became aware that Confederate units of undetermined size were not only approaching from the west on the Boteler Road but preparing to swing around and strike his open left flank. His units were not well positioned to meet the threat, with only two regiments posted on the flank and his entire reserve following Harland's line of attack. Rodman had to alert his flank guard, then get hold of Ewing and tell him to redirect his advance south and west. He was galloping across the fields to do just that when a Rebel sharpshooter drilled him through the chest. He was carried from the field, mortally wounded, and the division was left effectively leaderless.

A. P. HILL'S FLANK ATTACK

A. P. Hill was prepared to strike as soon as his vanguard reached the battlefield. At thirty-seven, Hill had earned the respect and confidence of both Robert E. Lee and Stonewall Jackson. He had graduated West Point in 1847, a year after McClellan—the two had been rivals for the hand of Mary Ellen Marcy, and McClellan had won. "Little Powell" was forty-seven, below average height, heavily bearded—a veteran of the

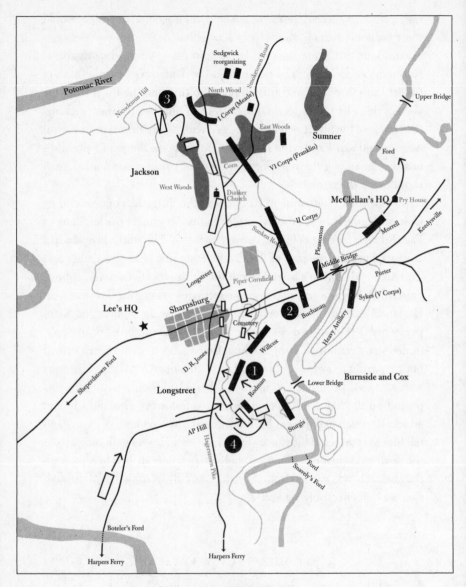

MAP 9: ANTIETAM, 3:00–5:00 PM

1. U.S.: IX Corps advances vs. D. R. Jones's Division (C.S.), 3–4:30 PM
2. Buchanan's Brigade (U.S. V Corps) advances into Sharpsburg
3. C.S.: Stuart's attack on U.S. I Corps repulsed
4. C.S.: A. P. Hill's flank attack forces IX Corps to retreat

Mexican and Seminole wars who had resigned an active commission in 1861 to serve the Confederacy. He won promotion to the rank of major general and division command early in the Peninsula Campaign, and had proved to be one of the best division commanders in the army. He had named his present command the Light Division, to borrow the aura and the élan of the famed British light infantry division that had fought in the Napoleonic Wars. Technically his brigades were not "light infantry," which in European armies were specially armed and trained for skirmishing and scouting. But they lived up to their name by making long marches with more than usual speed, by the efficiency and quickness with which they maneuvered on the battlefield, and by the power with which they made their assaults.

Jackson considered Hill's the best of his divisions, and when possible reserved them for the most vital and arduous missions. Jackson had marched the division hard during his advance on Harpers Ferry, because he planned to use it for his final assault. He had left Hill behind, partly to rest his command, but also because he trusted Hill to wind up affairs at Harpers Ferry and bring his division north with all possible speed, and have it ready for instant action.

Hill did not disappoint Jackson. He had brought his command up from Harpers Ferry by a sixteen-mile march that began at 6:30 AM, pushing the pace as hard as he could in the heavy heat and glaring sun, balancing the need for speed against the necessity of preserving his men's strength. He had ridden ahead to confer with Lee at 2:30 PM and had been apprised of the army's precarious position and of the powerful Federal attack that was building against the southern end of the line. He was therefore quick to recognize the alignment of the Federal forces attacking Jones's Division, and to exploit the opportunity offered by their weakly defended southern flank.

Hill sent his first brigade into action as soon as it reached the junction of the Boteler's Ford and Harpers Ferry roads, at 4:20 PM. This was Gregg's Brigade of South Carolina infantry, and at seven to eight hundred men it was the largest in the division. Gregg's Regiments deployed rapidly on a roll of higher ground. Half of them advanced against the leftmost elements of Harland's brigade, the IX Corps unit that was advancing toward the Rebel line south of Sharpsburg. The other half swept past Harland's flanks to attack the hapless rookies of the Sixteenth Connecticut. Gregg's veteran infantry took advantage of the stone walls that separated the cornfields and orchards on this part of the field to work their way around and behind the rookies' west-facing firing line.

The rookies were brave enough to stand and fire, checking Gregg's first onset. But the regiment's training had been negligible, and when their officers tried to shift their alignment to counter Gregg's attempt to flank them the troops became confused and disordered. Unable to maneuver, and with bullets hitting them from front and flank, they broke and ran for the rear. Behind them the inexperienced Fourth Rhode Island was also thrown into confusion by Gregg's attack. In the smoke and confusion its officers were uncertain whether the troops in front were friend or foe—many of Gregg's men were wearing blue uniforms looted from the stores at Harpers Ferry. The Fourth Rhode Island broke as well, and the flank of Rodman's division was compromised.[13]

The rest of A. P. Hill's units deployed with speed and efficiency. The brigades of Branch and Archer swept past Gregg's left, then turned north to strike the flank of Harland's Brigade, which had been pressing the attack against the line held by Toombs and Kemper. When Harland's men pulled back, they exposed the flank and rear of Fairchild's Brigade to infantry attack. Fairchild's units had suffered 63 percent casualties in their attack on Drayton, so they had no choice but to retreat, and when they did they uncovered the left flank of Willcox's division.

The situation south and east of Sharpsburg was now in flux. Union infantry in this sector still outnumbered the Confederates, but the momentum had shifted from IX Corps to the Light Division. Confederate infantry were able to press their attack against superior numbers because—with IX Corps batteries pulling back or masked by retreating troops—they now enjoyed a local superiority in artillery firepower, thanks again to the guns Lee had shifted to support his weakened flank. The mobility of Lee's artillery reserve was proving an effective counter for those long-range but immobile heavy guns on which McClellan relied. In addition, the Federals' heavy guns were running so low on ammunition that they had to cease their supporting fires for Willcox's infantry in front of Sharpsburg.

General Cox rode forward to take charge in this crisis. He directed Ewing's brigade, which had been Rodman's reserve, to confront the Rebel brigades (Pender and Archer) that had broken Harland's Brigade.

In the meantime Pender's and Brockenbrough's Brigades of the Light Division had peeled off to Gregg's right, and gone into line facing north against the flank and rear of Ewing's Brigade. Behind Ewing, there were only scattered regiments and rallied remnants to resist a flank attack—and Sturgis's two brigades back by the bridge, still somehow unready to take the field. By 5:00 PM, then, Cox had no choice but to recall Willcox from the attack on Sharpsburg and pull everyone back to the Lower Bridge.

MCCLELLAN'S HEADQUARTERS, 4:00–5:30 PM

The emergency on Burnside's flank was not immediately registered at army headquarters. McClellan had returned to the Pry house at about 4:00 PM, after the conference with Sumner and Franklin, and was confronted by what had seemed to be the chief crisis of the day's action.[14]

Behind him, a crescendo of artillery fire from the north announced that Jackson was assailing the right flank of his army. This seemed to confirm Sumner's fears of a powerful Rebel counterattack against his supposedly shattered divisions, and to justify his own decision to hold VI Corps on the defensive and dispatch two of Morrell's V Corps brigades for additional support. At the same time, McClellan received warning of A. P. Hill's approach from the observers in his high signal station.

McClellan could not know that the huge uproar of artillery on his right flank was almost entirely produced by his own gunners. As soon as the heads of Stuart's attack columns emerged from the woods below Nicodemus Hill, I Corps artillery hit them with a heavy barrage of shell fire. It did not take long for Stuart and Jackson to conclude that Federal troops on this flank had rallied and were standing firm. Jackson called off the flank attack, and, because his troop strength was so reduced by casualties, he also decided to pull Stuart's command off Nicodemus Hill and tie it in with his line in the West Woods. This was a dubious move: if the Federals discovered it and decided to seize the Hill, the whole northern flank would be compromised. Federal artillery firing from Nicodemus Hill could sweep the left flank and rear of Jackson's line and force him to retreat. Luckily for Jackson, the Union troops stayed on the defensive.

While the noise of Jackson's aborted attack still sounded from the right, observations from the Pry house yard indicated that Burnside's assault was succeeding. Willcox's Division and Fairchild's Brigade could be seen sweeping forward against the Confederate line. At about this same time Captain Dryer arrived at headquarters with his report that the Rebels had hardly any organized forces left to defend the town of Sharpsburg, and to suggest that an immediate attack in force would break the Rebel line.[15]

For the first time that day, McClellan was in the right position from which to act directly upon the battlefield. It appeared the moment had come to strike a decisive blow, and McClellan seemed ready to seize it. The crucial orders came from Fitz-John Porter, presumably, though not certainly, at McClellan's behest. At 5:00 PM Porter informed General Sykes that "Burnside is driving the enemy" and instructed Sykes to order Buchanan's Regulars to join the assault and also "drive them." If successful, the joint attack by Willcox and Buchanan would give Union troops possession of Sharpsburg, the nexus of the roads and lanes that linked the wings of Lee's army to the center. It would create a breach in the center of Lee's line, exposing his artillery reserve and trains to destruction, threatening his army's line of retreat to the Shepherdstown Ford.[16]

However, even as he licensed the offensive, McClellan withheld the force that would have made its success certain. Porter would commit only the small brigade already in position across the Middle Bridge. He did not release the rest of Sykes's Division or the remaining brigade of Morrell's Division, which now constituted the army's general reserve.

A short time later the question of an attack by Sykes became moot. Before Porter's order could be executed, headquarters got word of A. P. Hill's onset and the sudden emergency on IX Corps' front. The effects of Hill's assault could be observed from the Pry house yard—blue infantry falling back from the Confederate line along the high ground south of Sharpsburg, the slippage proceeding from left to right as the effect of Hill's flank attack was felt down the line. There was no word from Sumner or Franklin about the outcome of the flank attack Stuart had attempted. The tactical situation, as McClellan perceived it, was fluid and confusing. It seemed clear that Lee had mounted a major strike against Burnside's flank, and perhaps against I Corps as well. But Franklin's advice, along with Dryer's testimony, suggested that Lee had weakened other parts of his line to do so. Thus even with much of IX

Corps apparently in retreat, McClellan still had the option of launching an attack against Sharpsburg, to break or threaten the "hinge" on which Hill's advance swung—the juncture between Hill's left and Lee's center. Sykes had one brigade of 2,300 men already in action there, and another of similar strength in reserve—a potential attack force of 4,500 infantry for the heavy work of taking the town, with Pleasonton's 4,500 cavalry to support the flanks.

But to mount such an attack at such a moment was extremely risky. Since McClellan had credited Lee with nearly double his actual strength, he thought it likely that the Confederates still possessed a substantial reserve. He probably believed A. P. Hill's column was twice its actual strength. How else explain the fact that, after suffering heavy losses, Lee was mounting simultaneous offenses against *both* Federal flanks? McClellan had already rejected Franklin's assertion that Lee's north-facing line was weakened and vulnerable to attack. The weakness Dryer had seen on the Sharpsburg front might have been merely a temporary disorder among front-line troops, easily remedied by Lee's supposed reserve. In that case, with much of IX Corps disorganized by retreat, a severe check to a new offensive—and all offensives so far had been severely checked—followed by a Rebel counterattack out of Sharpsburg, might unhinge the whole center of the Army of the Potomac. McClellan's hoarded infantry reserve had been largely depleted. Of the forty-eight thousand men he had held in reserve that morning, only five thousand men in two V Corps brigades, one from Sykes's Division and one from Morrell's, remained on the heights above the Middle Bridge. Morell's other two brigades had been ordered to reinforce Sumner and were half a mile down the road.

The safer alternative was to stand on the defensive, rally IX Corps, and use the remaining reserves to hold their ground against the counterattacks apparently developing against both of the army's flanks. The decision was made after a brief exchange between McClellan and Porter. Reporter George Smalley, who was on the scene, thought McClellan's face grew "darker with anxious thought" as he glanced at Sykes's infantry drawn up below the Pry house before turning to Porter. In response to the question implied in that glance, "Porter slowly shakes his head, and one may believe that the same thought is passing through the minds of both generals. . . . 'They [V Corps] are the only reserves of the army.

They cannot be spared.' " However, General George Sykes, the usually stolid commander of Porter's Regular Army division, remembered
Porter's statement as stronger, defining the crisis in much larger, almost
apocalyptic terms: "Remember, General . . . I command the last reserve
of the last Army of the Republic." McClellan then rejected the idea of
using his reserves in an assault against Sharpsburg. Instead he recalled
the two brigades of V Corps that had been sent to aid Sumner, to reinforce his center. McClellan also sent word to Burnside that he "must hold
his ground till dark at any cost," but that no infantry could be spared
from the reserve to reinforce him.[17]

McClellan's response to this final crisis has been the subject of controversy, among his contemporaries and with historians as well. The
decisions he made are clear enough. What is at issue is the reasoning
behind those decisions, and the motives that shaped them. These have
significance beyond their obvious effects on the tactical conduct of the
battle, because they raise questions about McClellan's character and
state of mind, and about his larger strategic goals—that is, his way of
conceiving the relationship between his military struggle with secession
and his political struggle to wrench control of civil and military policy
from Lincoln, Stanton, and the Radicals.

Smalley would seem to be a more reliable witness than Sykes. His
account was written just after the battle and published in the *Tribune*
two days later. In contrast, Sykes's recollection was offered more than
twenty years later, in 1885, in an interview with editors preparing an
article on the battle for *Century* magazine. Yet Sykes's version has been
persuasive to many modern historians, because it so accurately reflects
McClellan's way of thinking, and the state of mind prevailing inside the
defensive bubble maintained by his aides, his staff, and his inner circle
of confidants. But either formulation was profoundly out of touch with
reality. V Corps was hardly the last reserve of McClellan's army—not
with VI Corps uncommitted and two fresh divisions marching up to
join the army that evening. Moreover, McClellan's was hardly the "last
army of the Republic." Aside from the armies of the Cumberland and
the Tennessee, and the smaller field armies in Louisiana and Missouri,
there were two army corps and a host of recruits in the Washington fortifications. There was only one perspective from which the Army of the
Potomac could be called "the last army of the Republic": the perspective

unique to McClellan and his circle of advisers and confidants. These not only considered the Young Napoleon the one man capable of saving the nation from both secession and Radicalism, but they saw his army as the only institution strong and loyal enough to support the general's campaign to control the administration. From that perspective, any significant check to the Army of the Potomac might indeed have apocalyptic consequences, imperiling the survival of the Republic.

That was the possibility that weighed on McClellan and Porter as they mounted their horses and rode off to the left to find Burnside and get his assessment of the crisis on his front. Before they had ridden very far they were met by a messenger from Burnside. According to McClellan, Burnside said that if he were not supported his corps might be driven back across the Antietam; Burnside would later deny making so dire a prediction. Neither man's word can be trusted implicitly, however, since they had been increasingly at odds with one another since McClellan deprived Burnside of his wing command. By the time they wrote their official reports, each was defending himself against accusations by the other. Even so, Burnside must have given a grim report of his situation and made a strong plea for reinforcement. According to Smalley, who rode along with McClellan and Porter, McClellan told Burnside's courier that the army's resources were exhausted: "I can do nothing more. I have no infantry." As the courier started away, McClellan recalled him. McClellan had already ordered Burnside to hold his ground "at all costs." He now reinforced that command with an emotional injunction: "Tell [Burnside] if he *cannot* hold his ground, then [he must hold] the bridge, to the last man!—always the bridge! If the bridge is lost, all is lost."[18]

It is hard to imagine what possible debacle on IX Corps' front could have led to a defeat of "all is lost" dimensions. Did McClellan fear a massive attack against his southern flank and center, like the flank attack of Longstreet's Corps at Second Bull Run that drove Pope's army in ruin from the field? Setting aside the fact that Lee had nothing like the troop strength with which McClellan credited him, before A. P. Hill's attack could reach the Federals' vital center east of the creek it would have to fight its way through the woods and hillocks that lay between the rim of the Sharpsburg plateau and the Lower Bridge—terrain well suited to defense. Beyond these positions was the creek itself, which could only be crossed at two points, the Lower Bridge and Snavely's Ford. Captain Dryer's report showed there was no danger of a Confederate attack via the Middle Bridge. Unless Burnside's corps simply and almost instantly dissolved, there was no conceivable danger to McClellan's core position east of the Antietam. However, if Burnside's corps, like the corps of Hooker, Mansfield, and Sumner, was substantially wrecked, McClellan might well be compelled to pull all his troops back across the Antietam, or even (at the worst) retreat behind the shield of South Mountain. Either of those outcomes would count as a defeat, so damaging to McClellan's prestige that his enemies might well succeed in removing him from command. Since he was the only man who could save the Republic, all would then indeed be lost.

In similar circumstances, during the Seven Days, the prospect of personal and political ruin had driven McClellan to a kind of hysteria, expressed in the strident and accusatory telegrams he dispatched to Washington. It is conceivable that his emotional state here was similarly labile. On the other hand, both before and immediately following this outburst, McClellan displayed coolness and self-possession. After dismissing Burnside's courier and turning his horse back toward headquarters, he almost immediately recovered his aplomb. This suggests that McClellan's "all is lost" outcry was neither a sincere response to a crisis nor a display of emotional imbalance, but rather a histrionic display, an act played out for calculated effect on his officers and men, and on reporter George Smalley. By exaggerating the dimensions of the crisis he also magnified his own heroic stature in meeting that crisis, demanding of weaker men the most desperate of defenses, and inspiring them to achieve it. On a more mundane level, he would also have been dramatizing the genuineness of his belief that the enemy before him was indeed in great if not superior strength. This was the justification for all of the tactical decisions he had made so far, and it established the context in which the next decisions would be made.

BY THE TIME HE reached the Pry house, at about 5:30 PM, it was clear that IX Corps was not in danger of destruction. As the gunfire sputtered and died out, McClellan continued on to Franklin's headquarters to assess the state of things on his right flank. There he learned that

Burnside Bridge, as Confederate defenders saw it (NATIONAL PARK SERVICE)

Jackson's and Stuart's counterattack against the Union right had been easily repulsed. He also found that Franklin was still firmly convinced that Lee's army was shaken and vulnerable to a well-planned offensive. Franklin proposed using the VI Corps in a dawn attack to seize Nicodemus Hill, with the rallied elements of I and XII Corps advancing in support. Once he had planted artillery on that high ground he could sweep the Confederates' northern line with fire, enabling a general offensive against Lee's flank.

The opportunity here was better than Franklin knew. At the time of his conference with McClellan, Nicodemus Hill was completely undefended. The position was critical to both attack and defense on the northern end of the battlefront. From the hill, Confederate artillery had raked Union troops attacking the West Woods. Jackson had pulled Stuart's command off the hill only after his failed flanking maneuver, because his divisions were so thinned by their losses that they could not extend their lines to include the hill. By evening there were no Confederate troops on Nicodemus Hill, and there was little Jackson could do about it. After dark he had Stuart send out a company-size reconnaissance, which found that the Federals had not yet seized the position. Fifty men were then left to defend a position that had been held at dawn by some 5,500 cavalry, infantry, and gunners.

It was unfortunate, and utterly characteristic of McClellan's command system, that Franklin did not order a reconnaissance to Nicodemus Hill. If he had, he could have accomplished the first stage of his planned assault without firing a shot. But Franklin had already shown more than his usual energy and aggressiveness by urging McClellan to attack in the morning. His views altered McClellan's understanding of the day's events. Burnside's rout and Sumner's dire dispatches suggested that the army had come perilously close to defeat—but those crises had apparently passed. Franklin's advice suggested that the enemy had also been heavily damaged, and that the balance of results was actually favorable to the Army of the Potomac.

McClellan felt encouraged enough to give tentative approval to Franklin's plan of attack before returning to his own headquarters at Keedysville for the night. However, he had much to think about before committing his battered army to a renewed offensive on September 18. Burnside's and Hooker's corps, and Sedgwick's division, had been driven from the field—did they have the morale to rally and throw themselves into an assault the very next day? Richardson's and French's divisions had been victorious, but their losses had been fearful—did they have the strength and will to make another such attack? He had four relatively fresh veteran divisions in V and VI Corps, and two new divisions marching to join them. Would they have strength enough to break the Confederate line if he committed them to action tomorrow?

The answer to that question depended on the condition of Lee's army. Had it been hurt as badly as his own? Was the weakness reported by Lieutenant Wilson and Captain Dryer real; or were they mistaken, and was the Confederate army still before him in unbroken strength?

McClellan had a long night ahead of him, hours in which to weigh the alternatives, to consider and reconsider the risks of further offensive action.[19]

CHAPTER 15

THE DAY WHEN NOTHING HAPPENED

SEPTEMBER 18, 1862

❦❦

BY EARLY EVENING THE FIGHTING HAD ENDED. THE SUN AS IT SET appeared swollen and blood-red. Except for scattered spats between infantry patrols, the gunfire dwindled to silence. Then you could hear rising from the fields between and behind the lines the cries and moans and shrieks of more than 17,000 wounded men, and smell beneath the fading bitterness of gunsmoke the rising stench of 3,600 men and hundreds of horses and mules lying dead on the ground and beginning to rot in the heat. "[G]roans and cries for water could be heard the whole night. We could not help them." There would be no flag of truce put out, under which the wounded lying between the lines could be found and carried to an aid station. According to military protocol, to ask for a flag of truce was to acknowledge defeat and implicitly agree to discontinue the engagement. Both sides believed that, despite the daylong fight and the terrible casualties, the issue had not been settled. The fighting would continue in the morning. Search parties had to sneak around in the dark, bearing lanterns or candles, risking a bullet to recover the wounded and the bodies of dead comrades, who were also their friends, neighbors, kinfolk.[1]

This was the atmosphere in which Lee and McClellan, along with their army staffs and field commanders, met to assess the day's achievements and decide what to do the following day—attack, hold their ground, or retreat.

Their choices were characteristic. The battle so far had produced a tactical stalemate. Lee chose to hold his ground and embrace the risks and opportunities of continued battle, hoping to make the stalemate break in his favor. McClellan would refuse those risks and stand on the defensive. Neither choice was justified by the real balance of forces on the battlefield. At the beginning of the fight, McClellan had opposed 72,500 troops to Lee's 35,000, to which A. P. Hill's Division added perhaps 3,000—a Union advantage approaching two to one. Battle losses had reduced Lee's available force to about 27,000 men, while McClellan's losses (about 13,000) would be largely offset by the arrival of two fresh divisions. That reinforcement would give McClellan an advantage approaching three to one. To transform stalemate into decisive victory, Lee would have had to strike with sufficient force to compel McClellan to retreat. Yet, given the sheer mass of the Federal army, and the nature of the terrain, that was an impossibility. McClellan could simply stay put, and Lee would have to retreat. By holding his ground and toying with the idea of a counterattack, Lee would expose his army to further loss and possible destruction without a reasonable chance of victory. McClellan's bad judgment was the mirror image of Lee's: he would fail to recognize and make use of his advantage in numbers, allowing Lee to stand his ground unmolested all day on the eighteenth and to retreat with impunity that night.

The net result of their decisions was that, in a tactical sense, nothing happened on September 18. Nevertheless, their decisions had strategic consequences, affecting both the future of military operations and the political actions that would transform the character and conduct of the war.

UNFINISHED BUSINESS:
LEE PLANS TO CONTINUE THE BATTLE

Lee's decision to hold his ground on the eighteenth has been praised as an act of daring, which minimized the impact of defeat on the army and the Southern public. According to this view, Lee required the entire Army of Northern Virginia to display the same bravado shown by the Irish Brigade when it formed in parade-ground ranks before marching off to replenish its ammunition, and for the same purpose: to maintain its own pride and overawe the enemy. The only justification for the decision was Lee's assumption, based on experience, that McClellan would be reluctant to fight. For Lee's critics, the success of the gamble does not obviate the question whether or not this was an appropriate purpose for which to risk the army. They see this decision as reflecting his excessive commitment to the offensive, which over time would drain his army's and his country's limited manpower resources. Lee himself never fully explained the grounds for his decision. His reasoning can only be guessed from the little he did say, and the actions he took.[2]

AFTER SUNSET, THE ARMY'S senior officers made their way to the tent in which Lee had his headquarters, to report to their commander. There were fires and lanterns in the tented encampment, but the red glow of a nearby burning farmhouse colored the atmosphere. Lee and his small staff sat at a camp table in the open air, and as they arrived the corps and division commanders came up to make their reports, then stepped back to add themselves to the growing circle around the army commander.

Lee's manner was, as always, calm and assured, and he seemed to expect words of encouragement as he asked each general, "How is it on your part of the line?" The responses he got were uniformly grim. As artilleryman S. D. Lee remembered it, each reported heavy losses and lines thinned to the danger point. The normally ferocious General Hood seemed "visibly shaken" as he reported the destruction of his division as a fighting force: "They are lying on the field where you sent them." Longstreet arrived late, and Lee's greeting indicated the kind of report he was looking for: "[H]ere's my old war-horse! Let us hear what he has to say." But Longstreet reported that his front was held by "little better than a good skirmish line." These reports should have left Lee in no doubt that his army was in poor condition and substantially weaker than it had been on September 17.[3]

Nevertheless, he seems not even to have considered retreating on the night of the seventeenth. He took a few minutes to digest, in silence, these reports of loss and near disaster. Then he calmly issued orders to prepare for another day of battle. Although his exact words were not recorded, their effect and his intentions were clear: "Gentlemen, we will not cross the Potomac to-night. You will go to your respective commands, strengthen your forces . . . collect your stragglers and get them up. . . . If McClellan wants to fight in the morning I will give him battle again."[4]

Nothing in his demeanor or his actions suggests that he feared his army might be overmatched if it stayed to fight another round. At 6:30 PM, he composed a report of the day's action for President Davis, inaccurate in some particular details. He describes the end result as a limited success for Confederate arms: his troops had been hard-pressed by Hooker's assault on their left, less so by Burnside's attack on their right, but at the end of the day they had recovered nearly all the lost ground and maintained their position. He makes no mention of the heavy battle losses suffered by the army or the weakness due to straggling, and gives no estimate of the size or combat power of his remaining force, although he had lost more than twelve thousand killed, wounded, or captured, about a third of his initial strength. Historian Joseph Harsh, whose study of Lee's headquarters is the most detailed we have, is uncertain whether Lee believed his army was in good shape for a fight or was merely putting a good face on things for President Davis.[5]

His actions suggest that he thought his army fit to continue the fight. After their conference, he sent his generals back to their commands with orders to strengthen their lines, gather in stragglers, and prepare for battle. He may have discounted his generals' reports—in the emotional reflux of intense combat officers commonly overestimated their losses. During the night, men who had gotten separated from their units and were counted among the dead would return to the ranks; and stragglers who had fallen out on the forced march from Harpers Ferry were coming into camp. One of Lee's aides estimated that as many as five thousand rifles might have returned to the battle line. It is also possible, even likely, that Lee never had a clear idea of the numerical strength of his army. Like McClellan, he may have supposed his twelve thousand casualties came from a force significantly larger than the thirty-nine thousand who had actually fought on September 17.[6]

There was also good tactical justification for standing pat. Even if he had believed his army was overmatched, it would have been extremely difficult to make an organized and orderly general retreat in the immediate aftermath of battle. Front-line commands were still partly entangled with the enemy. All had suffered considerable disorganization during the fighting, and it would take hours for dislocated troops to rejoin their commands. A day's delay would allow the safe removal of many wounded men who would otherwise be left behind and lost to the army. With these considerations in view, it is easier to understand Lee's willingness to risk an attack on the eighteenth and to see his defiant stance as a bluff.

However, Lee did not see his options as limited to a defensive bluff. When by midmorning it appeared that McClellan was not about to attack, Lee decided to take the offensive himself. Around 10:00 AM he rode to Jackson's headquarters to propose a heavy assault against McClellan's right flank. The previous day's action had showed that the Confederates' mobile artillery was capable of swift concentration and that its firepower could yield decisive results. Lee proposed to send Jackson fifty guns, commanded by Colonel S. D. Lee, whose rapid movement and skilled gunnery had saved each flank of the army in turn. If Colonel Lee's guns could suppress the Federal artillery of I Corps, it might be possible for Jackson and Stuart to succeed in their second attempt to break or turn McClellan's right flank.[7]

It is hard to know exactly what Lee intended or hoped to achieve. The maneuver could have been justified as a spoiling attack designed to impress McClellan with the danger of resuming the offensive on the eighteenth, thereby making it easier for Lee's army to retreat in good order that night. But nothing in the conversations among Lee, Jackson, and S. D. Lee indicates so limited a mission. It is more likely that the proposed attack was Lee's last bid for battlefield victory. He hoped that Jackson's assault would so threaten McClellan's flank that the Federal general would take fright, as he had in the Seven Days, and retreat to or beyond the South Mountain passes.[8]

The fact that Lee would contemplate such an offensive suggests that he had not fully grasped the character and outcome of the previous day's fighting. While Lee's contempt for McClellan was justified by experience, he should have had a better appreciation of the morale and combat effectiveness of McClellan's soldiers. It was irrational to suppose that the troops who had shown such skill, persistence, and courage battling for the Dunker Church and storming the Sunken Road could be driven from their positions with fifty guns and a few thousand infantry. Confederate generals were perhaps too prone to believe Confederate propaganda, which denigrated the Yankees' commitment to their cause and dismissed them as store clerks and mercenaries. Lee's orders also suggest that he was out of touch with the precise condition of his own army, and the extent of its losses both to straggling and to combat. However, from the beginning of this campaign Lee had grossly overestimated the strength and capabilities of his command. That overestimate had led him to divide his army and disperse its strength, and send it on those long marches over mountain and river that would exhaust the men and cause the straggling that would deprive him of a third of his infantry.[9]

The result was an army that had reached the limit of its offensive capacity. Jackson and S. D. Lee both examined the Federal lines through field glasses, and Jackson, without indicating his own attitude, pressed Colonel Lee for his opinion whether he could "crush the Federal right with fifty guns." The colonel's answer was that "it cannot be done with fifty guns and the troops you have near here." No amount of artillery could compensate for the lack of infantry. On Jackson's order, Colonel Lee reported their conversation to General Lee, and he noted that "a shade [came] over General Lee's face." He had been forced to recognize that no offensive action on his part could reverse the verdict of the seventeenth. As Colonel Porter Alexander had said, he could get no more from this ground than a battlefield stalemate. That being the case, he had no recourse but to call off the campaign and retreat to Virginia.[10]

Orders went out to keep up a strong front that day and prepare the army for a retreat that night.

McCLELLAN: "IT IS ALL IN [GOD'S] HANDS, WHERE I AM CONTENT TO LEAVE IT"

On the other side of Antietam Creek, McClellan's refusal to attack on the eighteenth raises far more serious questions about his judgment and motives than the errors of planning and execution that marred his tactical command the day before. These can be explained as the mistakes of a general with no experience in conducting an offensive general engagement, who was also handicapped by a false estimate of enemy strength. The fact remains that he initiated the combat, and did so in hopes of winning a victory by forcing Lee to retreat into Virginia. His decision not to continue fighting on the eighteenth is more puzzling, and would prove far more troubling to McClellan's contemporaries than the indecisive result of the fighting the day before.

McClellan returned to his headquarters in Keedysville at nightfall. The very large, peak-topped white tents in which he and his staff lived and worked gleamed among the small clapboard houses of the little town. McClellan's conference with Franklin earlier that evening had seemingly convinced him that a new offensive was feasible. Before midnight he sent off an urgent dispatch to Halleck requesting a resupply of ammunition for his twenty-pounder Parrott guns, essential support for any offensive. According to Colonel Strother of his staff, he sketched out a preliminary plan of attack, based on Franklin's proposal. At daybreak Franklin would use his two VI Corps divisions to storm Nicodemus Hill and plant batteries there to sweep the left flank of the Confederate line. I Corps, commanded by General George G. Meade in place of the wounded Hooker, would support this attack by advancing against Confederate positions in the West Woods and adjacent fields. McClellan also ordered Couch's Division to march up from Pleasant Valley to provide a reserve for Franklin and Meade. In conjunction with Franklin's attack, Burnside's IX Corps would assault the Confederate right, presumably as a diversion. Porter's two V Corps divisions would remain massed in the center, to be joined at an early hour by Humphreys's Division of V Corps, marching up from Washington. Some or all of V Corps could then be used for an attack across the Middle Bridge or to reinforce Franklin or Burnside as needed.[11]

Strother went to bed happy in the assumption that the army would attack at dawn and win a great victory. His expectations were widely if not universally shared. Lieutenant Wilson agreed that an offensive against Lee's left would lead to victory. General Sykes believed the reports of his officers who had seen the thinness of the Confederate line in front of Sharpsburg. Both thought McClellan had missed splendid opportunities during the day, but such errors were inescapable in the confusion of battle. They thought McClellan might do better now that he had time to make a plan and could draw on the knowledge of the enemy gained in fourteen hours of close engagement.

George Smalley, the *Tribune* correspondent, concurred in that judgment. He had been with McClellan for most of the day, had visited the crucial northern front just after the capture of the Sunken Road, and had drafted a long article giving a fairly complete account of the fighting. At nightfall he mounted his horse and set out on an all-night ride to the telegraph office in Frederick, where the story he filed would give Washington its first real news of the battle, and Smalley's assessment of the army's prospects. Smalley had personally observed some of the most critical turns in the battle, and his report made it clear that opportunities had been missed. Nevertheless, he thought that if McClellan followed through on his plan to attack again on the eighteenth, "there is every reason why McClellan should win."[12]

Of course there were also reasons why McClellan might *not* win. During a night of what he described as "anxious deliberations," McClellan was bound to come up with a list of cautions and caveats, shared with a group of advisers whose views were far less sanguine than those of Franklin, Wilson, and Strother. General Meade, who had replaced Hooker, thought I Corps was fit and ready "[t]o resist an attack in our present strong position," but "I do not think their *morale* is as good for an offensive . . . movement." Sumner told McClellan that Sedgwick's Division was "a good deal scattered and demoralized" and "not . . . in proper condition to attack the enemy vigorously the next day." He also expressed doubts about the condition of French's and Richardson's Divisions. These divisions had suffered casualty rates of 35 percent and 29 percent, respectively—much higher than the losses in I Corps, which Meade thought unable to take the offensive. Sedgwick and Richardson, Sumner's most aggressive division commanders, were wounded and out of action, as were many of the brigade and regimental commanders whose skill and courage had enabled them to carry the Sunken Road.[13]

The situation in IX Corps was also uncertain. By objective measures, their casualties had been relatively light. Rodman's Division was wrecked, with casualties at 41 percent of its engaged strength; and Sturgis's Division had suffered serious losses (20 percent) which still fell well short of the rates in I, II, and XII Corps. But the divisions of Scammon and Willcox had been pulled back before the Rebel counterattack could hit them, and their losses were relatively light—15 percent and 8 percent, respectively. The problem in IX Corps was not strength but spirit. McClellan believed that the large number of "new troops" in IX Corps had been "driven back and their *morale* impaired." General Burnside's morale was also questionable.

After dark, Burnside rode to the Keedysville headquarters to ask for reinforcement by Morell's Division of V Corps. Burnside would later claim that he reported his corps in good condition and only wanted Morell to lend strength to any projected attack. According to McClellan, Burnside needed reinforcement simply to hold his present lines. Both accounts were offered much later, at a time when the two generals were defending themselves against the dangerous scrutiny of the Joint Committee on the Conduct of the War. While neither can be taken at face value, McClellan's is the more credible. Burnside could not have been seeking support for a morning attack, since McClellan had not yet decided to make one. Moreover, there is little doubt that Burnside had been shaken by his corps' repulse, and the request for reinforcement would have added credibility to his excuse that superior enemy force had caused his defeat. When McClellan refused to send Morell, Burnside begged him to visit IX Corps' position early the next morning to judge the situation for himself, and McClellan agreed.

Burnside's visit probably reinforced McClellan's inevitable second thoughts about renewing the offensive at an early hour. Although the divisions of Humphreys and Couch were coming to reinforce him, McClellan thought they would not arrive till late in the morning. After their long marches, there was no telling whether they would be fit for immediate action. Moreover, the ammunition resupply for his heavy artillery could not reach Keedysville till late afternoon.

With this in mind, McClellan temporarily suspended Franklin's attack order. During the small hours of the morning, Colonel Strother was awakened by the sudden stirring of staff officers and was dismayed to hear the order given to hold and "not to attack without further orders." He tried to go back to sleep but was goaded to wakefulness by the premonition that the army was about to "lose the fruits of a victory already achieved."[14]

In fact, McClellan had not definitely abandoned the idea, but he saw difficulties that had to be dealt with first. McClellan's state of mind that morning, and his understanding of his army's situation, is suggested by the telegrams he dispatched at 8:00 AM to General in Chief Halleck and to his wife. Both messages claimed significant but limited success and projected a continuation of the fighting, but in oddly ambiguous terms that suggested both issues were still in doubt. The telegram to Halleck describes an intense and extended combat, largely successful for Union arms but not yet resolved: the army had suffered heavy losses, especially in general officers, but "We held all we gained except a portion of the extreme left," where Burnside had been forced to retreat. He asked that reinforcement be sent "by the most expeditious route." He reported, "The battle will probably be renewed today," but did not say which side would do the renewing. To his wife, he wrote more vauntingly of his own performance in the "desperate" and "terrible" fourteen-hour battle "against the entire rebel army," a phrase that for McClellan implies a superior force. "Those in whose judgment I rely tell me that I fought the battle splendidly & that it was a 'masterpiece of art.'" Yet he candidly admits that the results of the masterpiece were modest: "The general result was in our favor, that is to say we gained a great deal of ground & held it. It was a success, but whether a decided victory depends on what occurs today." At that time he was inclined to do nothing himself to force such a result. "I hope that God has given us a great success. It is all in his hands, where I am content to leave it."[15]

However, the same motives that had driven him to attack Lee on the seventeenth were still operative. As he would later write in his "Final Report," "I am aware of the fact that under ordinary circumstances a general is expected to risk a battle if he has a reasonable prospect of success."[16] That expectation would be heightened for McClellan, who was facing an invading army on Northern soil—who had been summoned from exile to save the nation by repelling or destroying the invader. The odds against McClellan were no greater on the eighteenth than they had been on the seventeenth, and even by his eccentric mathematics they were probably better. McClellan assumed he had originally faced a force roughly equal to his own, and he calculated that casualties had been equivalent on both sides. Couch's and Humphreys's Union troops would nearly replace, in number if not quality, the men lost in action on the seventeenth. Lee had received his last reinforcements when A. P. Hill came storming up the road from Boteler's Ford, and his army was therefore bound to be numerically weaker than McClellan's. But while the odds of battle were better, they were not nearly favorable enough to make success a certainty. If, as McClellan assumed, Lee's initial force had been equal to McClellan's, then the loss of twelve thousand did not put Lee at a decisive numerical disadvantage, so long as he stood on the defensive.

There was also some truth in the claim McClellan had telegraphed to Halleck, that his army had made and held substantial gains. They were not quite as substantial as he said, but they had bettered his position for an offensive. All of his infantry and cavalry, with the exception of Morell's Division and the new reinforcements, were across the Antietam. It would be much easier for them to act in concert, and to maintain a continuous line of battle, than it had been the day before.

On the other hand, his report to Halleck was misleading in its tale of success. The army had not, in fact, held all its gains except for a "portion" on Burnside's front. Hooker's two corps had seized the West Woods and Dunker Church but had been driven back nearly to their start lines. The only permanent conquest by I and XII Corps was the southern tip of the East Woods, from which Rebel skirmishers had been driven. Burnside's Corps had swept nearly to the streets of Sharpsburg, and had then been driven back into a compact bridgehead west of the Lower Bridge. The Confederates had conceded the ground west of the Middle Bridge without a fight but had repulsed the Federal attempt to advance from that point against Sharpsburg. The only substantial gain was the capture of the Sunken Road by French and Richardson, but no attempt was made, or even contemplated, to use it as the springboard for an assault on the Rebels' main line. These minimal gains had been purchased at an exorbitant cost in lives, which seemed to attest to the defensive power of the Confederate army. Despite its heavy casualties, Lee's army had still been able to launch counterattacks against both Union flanks at the end of that long and bloody day.

Although losses had been heavy on both sides, the cost in combat effectiveness was greater on the Union side. The reports of Meade and Sumner, and McClellan's own judgment, rated all of I, II, and XII Corps unfit for offensive action, though they remained capable of defending their positions. The status of IX Corps was doubtful, and the newly arriving V Corps division commanded by A. A. Humphreys consisted of rookie regiments, not yet fit for offensive combat. That left McClellan with no more than thirty-two thousand infantry fit to make an assault. On the other hand Lee, because he was the defender, would probably be able to use all of his available strength—which by McClellan's estimate, and with allowance for yesterday's losses, must still amount to nearly fifty thousand of all arms. By this measure the odds against a successful attack were heavier than they had been on September 17.

Of course, Lee's actual force, even with returning stragglers, was no larger than thirty thousand, and might have been as small as twenty-seven thousand. However, a force of that size, with ample artillery and on ground favorable to the defense, was not likely to be swept from the field by a force only slightly larger. The decisive victory some historians have seen as within McClellan's grasp on September 18 was only possible if McClellan were willing to use almost all of his available force, including the battered divisions of Meade and Ricketts, Williams and Greene, French and Richardson. Under other army commanders, but with conditions no less taxing than those that pertained at Antietam, these same brigades and divisions would display their ability to sustain intense combat for two or three days in a row. But even if McClellan had been willing to use these troops, he was unlikely to carry the day unless he managed to coordinate their assaults. This he had never been able to do, and his tactical doctrine required him to commit his forces piecemeal, holding back his reserves until the enemy's strength had been fully developed—by which time it was too late to turn a repulse into a victory. Those tactics in turn were dictated by his strategy, which forbade the taking of military risks until his political position was secured.

So before beginning a second offensive battle against Lee's army, McClellan wanted to have all his reinforcements in hand to ensure protection for his center when Franklin and Burnside attacked from the flanks. At 7:00 AM on the eighteenth, Humphreys had arrived from Washington with the vanguard of his division, which had been force-marched for more than seventy miles in three days. Humphreys believed he would have nearly all his men (at least six thousand) at hand within a few hours—he was hell on stragglers, who were either arrested for punishment or prodded to their feet by his provost guards. His regiments were almost entirely made up of new recruits, of doubtful value in an assault but a strong reinforcement to the army's defensive reserve. By 10:00 AM, they were in position behind Morell's Division on the heights east of the Middle Bridge.

Couch's Division, however, was still marching in from Pleasant Valley and would not be able to join Franklin's command west of the Antietam until noon. McClellan therefore sent Franklin a written order at 10:00 AM suspending his attack until further notice. At the same time, he acceded to Burnside's request for Morell's division. At 11:00 AM Humphreys' rookies replaced Morell's veterans as the army's defensive reserve, and by noon Morell had crossed the Lower Bridge to join Burnside's command in the woods at some distance from the southern face of Lee's defensive position. By that time Couch was moving into position with Franklin's command west of the Antietam, and all of the elements for a renewed offensive were in place—except the heavy artillery ammunition.

Although the attack order to Franklin was only suspended, not canceled, there were indications that McClellan was growing more reluctant to resume the offensive. He had sent Morell's fresh division to bolster Burnside's force, but Burnside never received orders to prepare an attack. After the battle, McClellan would shift the onus for aborting the offensive to Burnside. In his "Final Report," he described the transfer of Morell's division to Burnside as a purely defensive move: a response to Burnside's fear that if his corps "were attacked again that morning, he would not be able to make a very vigorous resistance" and would need Morell to cover his withdrawal to the east side of the Antietam. In their official reports McClellan and Porter both claimed that Burnside actually did withdraw his corps back across the Lower Bridge, leaving Morell alone to hold the bridgehead. This amounted to a serious charge against Burnside, who had no orders to withdraw. But the charge was false. Burnside declared that he had obeyed the order "from the commanding general to hold the bridge and the heights above at any cost, [and] this position was maintained till the enemy retreated, on the morning of the nineteenth." He had only used Morell's division to relieve his advanced line on the night of the eighteenth.[17]

The early afternoon was passed in preparation and procrastination. McClellan finally authorized a request for a truce so that each army might bring in the wounded and bury the dead that lay between the lines. Implicit in that request was an indefinite postponement of any offensive moves by McClellan's army, since it would take hours to complete the work, and it would require a formal exchange of notes to end the truce.

When the shooting stopped, the wounded who could still crawl began to drag themselves along the ground toward the nearest troops, in desperate need and not caring whether they were friend or enemy, giving to the field "a singular crawling effect." Details of soldiers from both armies now mingled between the lines, scouring the ditches and woodlots and cornfields for the wounded and dead. To one Confederate, "It seemed very curious to see the men on both sides come together and talk to each other when the day before we were fireing at each other." The wounded who were recovered were delivered to the horrors of the field hospitals, pervaded by the "smell of death" from rotting piles of amputated limbs and the stench from voided bowels. The surgeons were "literally covered from head to foot with the blood of the sufferers," as they bound wounds and amputated limbs with unwashed instruments and hands so steeped in blood that their fingernails softened. Assisting the Union surgeons was a corps of wound dressers and nurses, including women recruited for the task by Clara Barton, later the founder of the American Red Cross. Dead men, horses, and mules were scattered everywhere, between and behind the lines, and "In the midst of all this carrion our troops sat cooking, eating, jabbering, and smoking; sleeping among the corpses so that but for the color of the skin it was difficult to distinguish the living from the dead." Among the many shocks of the Civil War battlefield was the discovery that dead White men turned black as Negroes as their bodies began to decompose.[18]

Then in midafternoon the days of cumulating heat finally produced a late-summer thunderstorm, with lightning flashes like amplified muzzle-flashes of a nighttime cannonade. A downpour drenched the battlefield. By the time the storm passed it seemed too late to accomplish anything. At 5:45 PM McClellan finally sent Franklin an order to attack—the next day, "at an early hour in the morning."[19]

LEE RETREATS
NIGHT AND MORNING, SEPTEMBER 18–19

General Lee would spare him the agony of actually deciding to execute that order. In the early afternoon he made arrangements for the retreat, and after waiting out the thunderstorm his plan was put in motion. First the wagon train and artillery took the roads to the fords, with them the ambulances carrying the wounded. There was not enough transport for the badly wounded, so many of those who could not walk were left behind, to be cared for by the enemy. The trains were supposed to have crossed the river by nine in the evening, to allow the infantry to leave its lines and complete the river crossing under cover of darkness. However, the traffic was too heavy for the narrow roads and two difficult fords. Longstreet's infantry abandoned its line at 9:00 PM on the eighteenth but did not cross the Potomac till 2:00 AM on the nineteenth. Jackson's infantry did not reach the fords till daybreak, when there was nothing between Jackson and McClellan's army but a squadron of cavalry and a single cannon, posted on the hill west of Sharpsburg where Lee had had his headquarters. But they were not molested, and by 10:00 AM the last units of the Army of Northern Virginia had put Maryland behind them.[20]

By the time McClellan's skirmishers began their work of feeling out the Confederate positions, there was nothing in front of them but dead men, dead horses, and a few aid stations filled with wounded who could not be moved. As the troops moved forward they crossed rows of bloody, watery feces that marked the positions held by the dysentery-riddled Rebel infantry. At 10:30 AM McClellan would wire Halleck that "Pleasonton is driving the enemy across the river." Like the accusation against Burnside, this was a falsehood, intended to create the impression that McClellan had whipped Lee out of his lines and driven him back to Virginia. In fact, Pleasonton did nothing but pick up a few stragglers on the road to the fords. Lee had made good his escape with minimal losses. For McClellan that was sufficient: "Our victory was complete. The enemy is driven back to Virginia. Maryland and Pennsylvania are now safe."[21]

Fitz-John Porter's V Corps followed up Pleasonton's pursuit to the Potomac fords, which they found apparently undefended. Brigadier General Charles Griffin crossed at Boteler's Ford and snatched four artillery pieces that had lagged behind the retreat. Porter was a better combat general than his commander, and he sent an additional brigade to join Griffin. His idea was to hold a bridgehead from which a pursuit of Lee's fleeing army might be launched. But the move was tentative, and army headquarters not at all eager for an immediate advance into Virginia.

In fact, Lee's army was not in flight. Lee had posted two small brigades and an artillery battery, under Brigadier General William Pendleton, as a rear guard on the high ground well back from the ford. When Pendleton reported the loss of his guns and the presence of Federals across the river, Lee ordered Jackson to drive the Federals back. Jackson detailed the task to A. P. Hill's Division. On September 20 Hill's five brigades attacked. A rookie regiment, the 118th Pennsylvania, bolted at the first fire and lost a third of its 730 men. Porter withdrew the rest of his troops, leaving Lee in control of the Shepherdstown crossings. However, on that same day the XII Corps reoccupied Maryland Heights. That rendered Harpers Ferry untenable for the Confederates, and in a day or so, when the Rebels had withdrawn, the Union army would "recapture" the place.

McClellan was not looking for a fight. Once he was assured that Lee's army had gone back to Virginia, he was content to declare mission accomplished. He was now free to focus his attention and energy on that vital second front in Washington. Antietam was a vindication of his character as a soldier and a man. In a long letter to Mary Ellen, written on September 20, he expressed his relief: "Thank Heaven for one thing— my military reputation is cleared—I have shown that I can fight battles & *win* them!" He also believed that because of his victory, "my enemies are pretty effectively killed by this time."[22]

In this, too, he was mistaken.

PART FIVE

THE REVOLUTIONARY CRISIS

September 22–November 7, 1862

CHAPTER 16

LINCOLN'S REVOLUTION

SEPTEMBER 17–OCTOBER 1, 1862

❧

SEPTEMBER 17 HAD BEEN THE COSTLIEST DAY OF COMBAT IN AMERican history, leaving twenty-five thousand Americans dead or wounded. That Lee's army had retreated meant that the battle was a tactical victory for the Union. But the sound and fury, the immense cost in death, suffering, and grief, had not resolved the strategic crisis that began in the aftermath of the Seven Days. Hardly anyone was entirely happy with the result apart from George McClellan and his supporters. Lincoln had still not effected the strategic transformation envisioned in early July: the shift from a strategy of conciliation to a war of subjugation, in which restoration of the Union was linked to general emancipation—a shift that required the permanent sidelining of General McClellan. Victory at Antietam fulfilled one condition for issuing an emancipation proclamation, but that same victory also seemed to aggrandize McClellan, who opposed emancipation and was willing to use his power to thwart Lincoln's policies.

MISSION ACCOMPLISHED: McCLELLAN'S
HEADQUARTERS, SEPTEMBER 20–24, 1862

McClellan had cleared his front by defeating Robert E. Lee and saving Maryland from invasion. The rebuff suffered by Porter's troops at Shepherdstown was of no consequence, since McClellan had no intention of taking the offensive until he had recuperated, resupplied, and reinforced his army. The setback was more than balanced by XII Corps' seizure of Maryland Heights, a prelude to the repossession of Harpers Ferry that would be consummated two days later.

After September 20 McClellan's military posture was passive, and though scouts and spies reported various Rebel movements, no serious effort was made to find out where Lee's army was, or in what force. As late as the twenty-fourth of September, McClellan was unable to do more than surmise that Lee still held his main army in position to oppose a crossing of the Potomac. His chief military preoccupation was the telegraphic argument with Halleck over whether the army was being properly and promptly resupplied. There was some truth to his contention that the army needed resupply, and some real difficulty in achieving that when the forces were so far from their Washington base, without adequate rail links. But the argument was also an engagement in his ongoing war against Stanton.

IT WAS TIME to move decisively against the foe in his rear: his future would be "determined this week." Through various friends, agents, and intermediaries in the capital he had insisted that Stanton must resign and Halleck "give way to me as Comdr in Chief." (Presumably he meant general in chief.) "The only safety for the country & for me is to get rid of both of them." The national interest and his personal fate were thus equated. He believed it was "now time for the country to come to my help, & remove these difficulties from my path." Twice he had succeeded in "saving the country." Now if his "countrymen" refused to meet his demands, "they must pardon me if I decline the thankless avocation of serving them." What he now demanded of the people, and the government, was license to run the war with a free hand: "If I continue in its service I have at least the right to demand a guarantee that I shall not be interfered with." This amounted to a demand for the kind of dictatorship that had been dangled before him since July 1861: exclusive control of war policy, without presidential or congressional interference.[1]

He believed that support for such an overturn was building. He had had a letter from Montgomery Blair, his ally in the cabinet, that assured him the President rejoiced in his victory, not least because it had vindi-cated McClellan, for whom (Blair said) Lincoln felt a genuine friendship. The governors of the Northern states were meeting in Altoona, Pennsyl-vania, to consider the state of affairs and the direction of administration policy, and make strong recommendations to Lincoln on the conduct of the war. McClellan believed that his supporters among the governors would use the occasion to "enable me to take my stand," and support his demand "that Stanton shall be removed" and Halleck replaced by McClellan. The conference had been called by Governor Andrew Cur-tin of Pennsylvania, a Republican but also a long-time friend and ally of McClellan. Curtin was one of the most active and enterprising of the war-time governors, who raised 300,000 troops for the Union army, and sent them forward with the best training and equipment he could procure. He had met McClellan during the latter's railroad-official days, had been impressed by his efficiency and professionalism, and had asked McClel-lan to take command of the state's troops at the outbreak of war. He had publicly supported the general in the controversies of the past year, and during the Confederate invasion had frequently sought McClellan's aid and advice. Other attendees would include Governor Tod of Ohio and D. G. Rose, representing Governor Morton of Indiana. Like Curtin, Tod and Martin were moderate or conservative Republicans, and had been opposed to a policy of general emancipation. Dennison was also a McClel-lan supporter, who had outbid Curtin for McClellan's services in 1861.[2]

McClellan's officers were aware of the potential significance of the conference, and hoped it might produce a more effective war policy, based on a rapprochement between the victor of Antietam and a moderate Republican president. General Jacob Cox, commander of the Kanawha Division, was not a member of McClellan's inner circle. However, he had been a major figure in Ohio Republican politics before the war, and was in close contact with Ohio's Governor Dennison during the governors' conference. The two men deplored the estrangement between McClellan and Lincoln and believed that the two held comparable views on slavery, preferring gradual abolition to Radical ideas that were "imprudent and extreme." Cox reached out to Colonel Thomas Key, thought by many Radicals to be McClellan's "evil genius," and was reassured on this score. Cox advised Key that if McClellan "would only rebuff all political intriguers and put more aggressive energy into his military operations," there would be no quarrel with the administration, and "his career might be a success for the country as well as for himself."[3]

But McClellan wanted more than a rapprochement. He wanted to force Lincoln to concede control of war policy, so that McClellan could substitute the "conservative" or Democratic program for the policy of Lincoln and his party. Through his personal advancement, the political opposition would gain control of public affairs. He believed that his battlefield triumph had restored his standing with the public as the republic's preeminent military leader. There was enough adulation in the Democratic press, as McClellan read things, to more than offset the carping of Republican journals over Lee's escape. *Harper's Weekly*, the popular illustrated magazine which called itself "A Journal of Civilization," praised him in terms that perfectly mirrored his own self-image:

> *Once* more we hail thee, Chief! The nation's heart,
> Faint and desponding, stricken to the dust,
> Turns back to thee with the old hopeful trust,
> And childlike confidence, and love. Thou art
> Our chosen Leader. We have watched thee well,
> And marked how thou hast borne the taunts and sneers
> Of those whose envious falsehoods harmless fell
> About thine head; how, unmoved by their jeers,
> Thou hast toiled on with patient fortitude,
> Winning from all the Legions under thee
> A love which is almost idolatry;
> Thy one sole aim thy Country's greatest good.
> Press on, young Chieftain, foremost in the van!
> The Hour of need has come—be thou the Man![4]

Democratic Party leaders and activists began showing up at McClellan's headquarters, as they had done during a similar lull on the Peninsula. General William "Baldy" Smith recalled that after one of these visits McClellan called him aside and told him that Fernando Wood and the other Democratic leaders had renewed an offer made to him on the Peninsula early in the summer: to support him for the presidency in 1864 if he would issue a statement laying out his own prescription for how and for what purposes the war should be conducted. Smith was an old friend, a fellow engineer who had graduated West Point one year before McClellan and served with him in Mexico. He had been an effective brigade commander on the Peninsula and had been promoted to division command in VI Corps, led by McClellan's close protégé William Franklin. Months before, Smith had warned McClellan against that kind of political confrontation with the president. Now he thought McClellan was feeling him out to see where his loyalties lay in what promised to be a dangerous political conflict. Smith response was to say nothing, and ask for a transfer out of the Army of the Potomac.[5]

Despite the reassurances he had received from Colonel Key, General Cox found some of the headquarters talk disturbing and vaguely conspiratorial, suggesting "disloyal influences at work." Some days after the battle McClellan invited his senior officers to a religious service and social gathering at the Keedysville headquarters. The prayer service was offered in the open, in a space framed by the big tents that housed the general and his staff. At the reception afterward, Cox noted the presence of a number of civilians, one of whom singled Cox out for what at first appeared a casual conversation. John Garrett, president of the Baltimore and Ohio Railroad, praised McClellan in terms that drew Cox's loyal assent. The civilian then accused "the politicians in Washington [of] wickedly trying to sacrifice the general, and added, whispering the words emphatically in my ear, 'But you military men have that matter in your own hands, you have but to tell the administration what they must do, and they will not dare to disregard it!'" This "roused" Cox, with its implication that the army should turn against the elected government. Garrett seemed shocked, and "mumbled something about having taken me for an acquaintance of his, and moved away among the company." Cox later saw the man in close conversation with Fitz-John Porter, seemingly questioning him about who Cox was and where his sympathies might lie.[6]

MCCLELLAN SOON DISCOVERED that his position was not as impregnable as, in his view, it ought to have been. It seemed that Antietam was not regarded as self-evident proof of McClellan's indispensability. Although the press had hailed the news of McClellan's victory as a triumph, praise for his achievement was almost immediately leavened with criticism for the inaction that allowed Lee's army to escape. Even among McClellan's officers there was dismay at his failure to act. Franklin loyally set aside his own disappointment and admitted he was "not sorry" his attack order was rescinded, because so many veteran formations had been used up by the fighting. But others remained troubled, and their opinions were picked up by the reporters who came swarming out to the battlefield.[7]

Reporter George Smalley of the *New York Tribune* set the terms for the journalistic coverage of the battle. He had ridden to Frederick on the night of the seventeenth to telegraph his story to the *Tribune*. The telegrapher sent it to the War Department by mistake, and gave Stanton and Lincoln their first information about the fight. Stanton had forwarded the dispatch to New York, and it appeared in the *Tribune* on September 19. Smalley's extensive, detailed, and vivid story of the fighting was the first published account of the battle, and its fair-minded treatment of McClellan gave it broad credibility despite its appearance in a Radical journal. Although Smalley detailed some of the tactical errors that marred McClellan's performance, he presented the battle as a great and hard-won victory. He also stated his belief that an even greater triumph could be expected when, not if, the battle was renewed next day. By the time the dispatch was published both the War Department and the public knew that McClellan had not attacked on September 18, and that by the nineteenth Lee was safe across the Potomac. Thus Smalley's account justified the *Tribune* editorial assertion that September 18 was a "fatal Thursday" because McClellan had refused to attack and destroy the Rebel army. Greeley's front-page headline treated McClellan's claims of victory with contemptuous sarcasm: "Retreat of the Rebels . . . They Run Away in the Night Again . . . Stonewall Jackson Dead Again."[8]

Democratic newspapers affirmed the judgment that an opportunity had been wasted, though they blamed Stanton rather than McClellan. But the charge lacked force. McClellan, not Stanton, had been the man on the scene. He had pinned the elusive and dangerous Rebel army in a vulnerable position, with the whole Army of the Potomac in its front and a wide river with few crossing points at its back. That situation was obvious to everyone, from officers and men at the front, to the high command in Washington, to the civilian reader scanning the sketch-maps published by the newspapers. Under such circumstances it was to be expected that some attempt should be made to beat Lee from his lines and drive his army into the river.

More ominous was the fact that since September 15 McClellan had received no communications from the president—neither of congratulation nor complaint. His last word from Lincoln was the injunction following South Mountain to "destroy the enemy if possible." On September 21 he wrote Mary Ellen that he expected such ingratitude and dismissed it; but Lincoln's silence rankled, and he thought it a sign that new "persecutions" might be in store. He therefore sent a confidential agent to Washington, to make inquiries and even to "shadow" the president, to find out how his struggle with Stanton was playing out. That agent was Allan Pinkerton, nominally chief of intelligence for the Army of the Potomac, who would bring to this task the same powers of analysis that led him to overestimate Lee's army by some 200–300 percent.

Pinkerton's shadowing of the president seems not to have gone unnoticed. On September 22 Lincoln invited the chief of intelligence to his office for a chat. The president questioned him closely about the fighting and conditions at the front, but he assured Pinkerton he was not looking to find fault with anything McClellan had done; nor, as Pinkerton reported to his chief, was Lincoln fishing around "for the purpose of seeking aught against you." Lincoln expressed his sense of profound gratitude, of a debt greater than could be repaid, for the great victories at South Mountain and Antietam. It was just that he wished to inform himself of some matters "which he supposed, from the pressure on your mind, you had not advised him on or that you considered was of minor importance, not sufficiently worthy of [presidential] notice." Lincoln pressed Pinkerton closely about what McClellan had been doing to pursue or pressure the enemy since his victory on the seventeenth, and charmed the master detective into revealing how little had been done. Pinkerton went away filled with reassurance for his employer: "He expressed himself as highly pleased and gratified with all you had done," even "commending your caution."[9]

Lincoln was laying it on thick for the gullible Pinkerton, who was disarmed by his belief that the president was not very intelligent. Lincoln's real evaluation of McClellan's performance was expressed shortly after he ushered Pinkerton out of his office and crossed the hall to join a special session of the full cabinet. He had called this meeting to show them the text of a Preliminary Emancipation Proclamation, which he would sign and issue that afternoon. He told his colleagues, "The action of the army against the rebels has not been quite what I should best have liked." He had wanted and expected Lee's army to be destroyed. However, "they have been driven out of Maryland," and that was victory enough to meet the conditions he had set for issuing a proclamation emancipating slaves in Rebel-held territory.

LINCOLN'S PROCLAMATION
SEPTEMBER 22–24, 1862

Lincoln presented this final draft just as he had presented the first back on July 22, as a settled decision, made by himself. The cabinet's views were welcome but their consent was neither courted nor required. He might have explained his decision by reminding them of Seward's political advice, which he had accepted, to delay the Emancipation Proclamation until a victory had been won. Instead he characterized his decision in religious terms. He had (he said) "made a vow, a covenant, that if God gave us the victory in the approaching battle, he would consider it an indication of divine will and that it was his duty to move forward in the matter of emancipation. It might be thought strange that he had in this way submitted the disposal of matters when the way was not clear in his mind what he should do. God had decided this question in favor of the slaves." It was not at all unusual for Americans of that time to prayerfully beg signs of God's will, but it was unusual for Lincoln. His closest aide, John Hay, was not aware that Lincoln experienced a spiritual crisis during the week preceding Antietam, although he had been thinking intensely about emancipation and making significant revisions in his original draft. The revised document was revolutionary in its assumption of power and its potential effects, and Lincoln may have wanted more authority for his presumption than mere political calculation.[10]

Lincoln had used the three months delay to make the Proclamation more radical. The most revolutionary aspect of the Proclamation was still its assertion and expansion of presidential powers in wartime. At the start of the war it had not been clear what kind of authority was actually conferred by the constitutional designation of the president as "commander-in-chief of the armed forces." Congress had challenged Lincoln's authority to control war policy and even military appointments, and army officers had treated Lincoln's orders as if they were merely advisory. Now Lincoln was asserting that as commander in chief, he had the power to confiscate en masse the property of citizens inhabiting rebellious districts, without judicial or criminal proceeding to determine their *personal* affiliation (or lack thereof) with rebellion. At a stroke of the pen some $3.5 billion in property was legally annihilated—this at a time when national GDP was less than $4.5 billion, and national wealth (the total value of all property) was about $16 billion. In purely economic terms, this was an expropriation of property on a scale approaching that of Henry VIII's seizures of church properties during the Reformation, exceeded only by the nationalization of factories and farms after the Bolshevik Revolution.[11]

The new draft was also more radical in its challenge to the legal and social premises of White supremacy. The original draft had sought to alleviate racial fears by stressing the necessity for a program of colonization, to remove most if not all freed slaves from American territory. In the final draft, colonization is mentioned as a worthwhile project but not greatly stressed. Instead the legal language was strengthened to guarantee that any slaves freed by the Proclamation could not be reenslaved by any postwar court decision.

Two codicils, which were not in the first draft, had especially radical implications. One of these enjoined Blacks freed by the act "to abstain from all violence, unless in necessary self-defense." This was intended to mollify those in the North and especially in England who feared that general emancipation would be the signal for a "servile insurrection." However, as conservatives were quick to note, by suggesting that Blacks *could* use violence for self-defense, the Proclamation attacked the fundamental principle of plantation law and discipline, which not only forbade the slave to resist punishment or even abuse by a legal master, but also prohibited an appeal to either the civil or the criminal court. That principle was most clearly stated by Justice Thomas Ruffin, of the North Carolina Supreme Court, in a precedent-setting 1829 case. "The slave, to remain a slave, must be made sensible, that there is no appeal from his master; that his power is in no instance, usurped; but is conferred by the laws of man at least, if not by the law of God." By conferring a right of self-defense on the slave—a right whose exercise civil law could test and justify—Lincoln had negated the fundamental law of slavery.

A second and more obviously radical addition was the declaration that slaves freed by the Proclamation "will be received into the armed service of the United States." The Proclamation thus granted Blacks the civil right to join in the common defense—a right that *none* of the free states then recognized. By extending that right to African Americans through the use of Federal power, Lincoln fundamentally altered the civil status of Blacks in the north, setting a precedent and stimulating a political movement for equal citizenship. From a military perspective, this was the most significant element of the proclamation. Ultimately it would bring 180,000 African Americans into the ranks. Black troops would provide roughly 9 percent of the two million total Union armies enlistments, and their actual contribution was significantly greater, since these enlistments were concentrated in the last two years of the war, when the total strength of the Union armies varied between 700,000 and one million men.[12]

The Preliminary Proclamation had the form of an ultimatum: its provisions would not take effect if Southern leaders ended the rebellion by January 1, 1863. The conservative *New York Herald*, which was opposed to emancipation in principle, actually supported the Preliminary Proclamation in the hope that its menace would bring the South to the negotiating table.[13] But Lincoln did not expect the mere threat of emancipation to induce Southern leaders to sue for peace and reunion. The January 1 deadline had been laid down in the first version of the Proclamation, and presented to the cabinet on July 22, when the South would have had nearly six months to consider acquiescence. Three months later the deadline was unchanged, which gave the South only three months to respond. Lincoln understood very clearly that the Proclamation would harden the South's will to resist, and that the war could not in future be prosecuted as anything but a war of subjugation and a "remorseless revolutionary conflict." For that reason it was accompanied by other draconian measures. On September 24, two days after issuing the Proclamation, the president authorized suspension of the writ of habeas corpus anywhere in the country, which allowed the arrest and detention of those accused of being Confederate agents or sympathizers, and the suppression of newspapers for "sedition."

The cabinet meeting on September 22, and the actions that followed, transformed the politics of the Union war effort. It remained to be seen whether the military leadership was prepared to fight a war of subjugation. Lincoln and his closest advisers were most deeply concerned about how General McClellan would respond to this radical turn in policy. His opposition to emancipation and subjugation were of long standing and well known. His political support was also so formidable that for weeks the administration had been fending off demands in Congress and the press for purging Stanton from the cabinet.

Lincoln and his circle of advisers were also aware that officers close to McClellan, and leaders of the Democratic opposition, had discussed the desirability of somehow using McClellan's control of the army to force a change in the personnel and policies of the administration. Generals Burnside and Halleck had heard that kind of talk from McClellan's staff when they visited Harrison's Landing in late July, and though neither made a formal report, they must have discussed the experience with colleagues. Rumors of plots and counterplots were rife in Washington; as Charles Francis Adams had said, the atmosphere was "thick with treason." A very explicit threat had been communicated to *Tribune* reporter Nathaniel Paige by Colonel Thomas Key back on September 11: that high officers of the Army of the Potomac were planning to "change front on Washington," take control of the government, and negotiate a settlement favorable to Southern independence. On the twelfth and thirteenth the *Tribune* had published a pair of editorials that warned of "a conspiracy between the chiefs of the Rebel and Union armies to subvert the Republic and establish a Pro-slavery despotism on its ruins" and accused the *Herald* of urging "Gen. McClellan to disperse [Congress] with the bayonet, after the fashion of Cromwell and Bonaparte."[14]

Lincoln's confidential secretary, John Hay, believed that there was indeed a "McClellan conspiracy" within the military, which deliberately thwarted presidential policies and aimed to discredit and ultimately displace the administration—though McClellan himself might not be its conscious agent. Lincoln considered McClellan's refusal to aid Pope an "unpardonable" breach of faith but was uncertain whether his motives were political or driven by ambition and personal pique. Within the cabinet, only Montgomery Blair thought McClellan both loyal and capable. Otherwise, opinion ranged from Stanton and Chase's conviction that

McClellan was a conscious traitor to Welles's more temperate view that he was merely selfish and ineffective. By any of these interpretations, McClellan was untrustworthy.[15]

The administration's suspicions came to a head on September 25. On that day Interior Secretary Caleb Smith received a report from Judge Advocate Levi Turner, of Halleck's staff, on a conversation he had had with a colleague, Major John Key. Turner had expressed "his surprise that McClellan had not followed up the victory last week by pursuing the Rebels." Key had replied that to do so would have been against "the policy" of the army command, which was "to compel the opposing forces to adopt a compromise by stringing out the struggle till both were exhausted." Then military leaders would assert themselves and demand a negotiated settlement. Thus "it would have been impolitic and injudicious to have destroyed the Rebel army, for that would have ended the contest without any compromise." Major Key presumably knew whereof he spoke, since he was the brother of Colonel Thomas Key, of McClellan's staff—the same man who, on September 11, had warned, and perhaps implicitly threatened, *Tribune* reporter Nathaniel Paige with his talk of a military coup. Within twenty-four hours Judge Turner's story was known to both Navy Secretary Welles and to President Lincoln himself. After discussing the matter with John Hay on the evening of the twenty-fifth, Lincoln ordered the case investigated, "and if any such language had been used, [the officer's] head should go off." But when Hay sought to frame the episode as part of "the McClellan conspiracy," Lincoln ended the discussion. "He merely said that McC. was doing nothing to make himself either respected or feared." It is not clear whether Lincoln refused to credit the reality of conspiracy, or for political reasons refused to acknowledge its existence—since to do so would provoke a direct and dangerous confrontation between the civil and military authorities.[16]

However, the Key affair, which played out on September 26–27, may have tilted the balance of suspicion against McClellan. Lincoln had reason to think that what Key had said reflected views expressed at McClellan's headquarters, and Key and Turner were summoned to Lincoln's office on the twenty-sixth. Turner told the president that he had "asked the question why we did not bag them after the battle at Sharpsburg." Major Key had answered that "that was not the game, that we should tire the rebels out, and ourselves, that that was the only way the Union could be preserved, we [North and South] come together fraternally, and slavery be saved." Lincoln personally cross-examined both men and concluded: "In my view it is wholly inadmissible for any gentleman holding a military commission from the United States to utter such sentiments as Major Key is . . . proved to have done." Key was summarily dismissed from the service, not just for his own misdeeds but as "an example and a warning" to "a class of officers in the army, not very inconsiderable in numbers, who were playing a game to not beat the enemy when they could, on some peculiar notion as to the proper way of saving the Union."[17]

It is most unlikely that McClellan was playing the game described by Major Key. The idea assumes that McClellan had the skill and courage to toy with Lee's army, feeling assured that he was too strong to be defeated. How, then, to account for Major Key's statement? It was far too dangerous a thing to say unless Key thought it both true and worth saying. Perhaps it did reflect a thread of opinion among the staff about the way the war was going or ought to go. Or it may have been Key's way of rationalizing a series of otherwise egregious military errors by his admired chief.

What is significant in all of this is the fact that McClellan's past behavior, his obstructionism and displays of rancor, his public and private expressions of contempt for the administration, made plausible the belief that McClellan was playing a double game, pretending to seek victory when in fact his purpose was to postpone decisive action until he had won political control of the administration; or to deliberately seek stalemate rather than victory, so that in mutual exhaustion North and South would reconcile on terms of compromise favorable to slavery and "Southern rights." How else explain his pattern of skillfully maneuvering to create opportunities, then refusing to use all of the forces at his disposal to exploit them? For Lincoln that question was unavoidable, and the choice of answers was stark. Either McClellan's motives were disloyal, or he was a military incompetent; and either of these possibilities constituted good grounds for relieving him of command.

However, to fire him now would vitiate the good political effects of the victory and provoke a military crisis while public opinion was still disordered by the Emancipation Proclamation and the suspension of habeas corpus—all on the eve of the midterm elections. Although there was some disappointment, even in Democratic papers, that McClellan had failed to trap and destroy Lee's army, the victory enhanced the general's standing with the army and the country. Antietam had, at least, checked what had seemed an unending series of defeats inflicted by Lee and Jackson. The general was still an idol to most of his army and to the Democratic opposition, and McClellan still had support among moderates and conservatives in Lincoln's own party. Evidence of the latter was on display at the Altoona governors' conference, where Republicans Curtin of Pennsylvania and Tod of Ohio joined Democrat Augustus Bradford of Maryland to block a resolution sponsored by Radical governors to condemn McClellan's leadership and call for his removal.[18]

So to weaken McClellan's position, Lincoln and John Hay began feeding criticism of the general's performance to Republican journals. One of Lincoln's favorite criticisms of McClellan—that he was "an auger too dull to take hold"—started popping up (without attribution) in the *Tribune*.[19] Lincoln also authorized John Hay to begin a secret journalistic campaign to expose McClellan's flaws as a general, thus preparing the public mind for a possible removal. Hay's method was one Lincoln had often used against opponents in the path: he satirized the general, deflating him by ridicule.

In an article first published anonymously in the *Missouri Republican* on September 30, Hay began by giving McClellan his due for having rallied the army after Pope's defeat, and by denying the "outrageous slanders of treachery, cowardice" leveled against the general. However, his record of hesitation and failure can only be explained by "an inherent vice of mind . . . which makes him *never ready to act*." Having beaten Lee at Antietam, "while all the world looked on and cried, 'Bravo! God bless you, General!.' he sat absolutely motionless on the field of battle, not sending out a picket or firing a gun till the beaten and routed enemy had safely crossed the Potomac." To cap his critique, Hay mockingly compares McClellan to Stonewall Jackson—the "chivalrous and accomplished soldier" contrasted with "the shaggy, unkempt fanatic." Jackson's rapid marches and audacious attacks had violated every precept of military science, while McClellan's operations have "never once offended against the masters who have written of war." Yet what had been the result? "[O]ut of Jackson's audacious follies and aimless blundering energy has grown success and honor to rebel arms, while our careful and scientific strategy has landed us, after a year's hard fighting, at the place where we began."[20]

On the day Hay's article appeared, the president decided to visit McClellan's army at Sharpsburg, to see and judge for himself the condition and temper of the army and to learn what he could about McClellan's plans and state of mind. When one considers the context of the visit, the disaffection of the officer corps revealed by the Key case, and the rumors of a planned "countermarch" on Washington, it might have seemed dangerous to go unarmed into McClellan's camp. It did not seem so to Lincoln. His judgment of McClellan's weakness as a commander was set, his suspicions of McClellan's motives strengthened by the Key affair. But he did not think McClellan capable of actually staging a coup, and refused to act as if such a thing were possible.

Had Lincoln been aware of the discussions at McClellan's headquarters that preceded his visit, he might have rated the dangers higher.

"LARGE PROMISE OF A FEARFUL REVOLUTION": McCLELLAN'S HEADQUARTERS
SEPTEMBER 24–OCTOBER 1, 1862

McClellan first learned of the president's Emancipation Proclamation on September 24, to be followed shortly by word of the suspension of habeas corpus. The manner of discovery must have been almost as galling as the matter. Just the day before Pinkerton had reported on his meeting with Lincoln and conveyed the president's assurances of his esteem and support. Now it was obvious that Lincoln had deliberately hoodwinked Pinkerton to surprise McClellan with this radical turn in policy. These two presidential proclamations represented Lincoln's final and complete repudiation of the principles McClellan had laid down for his guidance in the Harrison's Landing letter. McClellan had demanded assurance that slavery would be left alone—Lincoln had opted for general emancipation. McClellan had demanded strict limits on military actions against the rights and property of Confederate civilians—Lincoln had not only expropriated Southern property en masse, he had extended the military power of arrest and confiscation into the North. This political

372 | THE REVOLUTIONARY CRISIS

defeat was far more decisive than the military reverse he had inflicted on Lee.

The results of the war governor's conference in Altoona were also disappointing. McClellan's allies had defended him against attacks by Governors Andrew of Massachusetts and Sprague of Rhode Island— Sprague had actually called Antietam a "defeat," because Lee had out-maneuvered McClellan. But the Conference also approved the Emancipation Proclamation and sent a delegation to the White House to make a public gesture of their endorsement.[21]

McClellan was outraged but at a loss how to respond. In a letter of September 25 he told his wife that "the continuation of Stanton & Halleck in office render it almost impossible for me to retain my commission & self respect at the same time. I cannot make up my mind to fight for such an accursed doctrine as that of servile insurrection. It is too infamous. Stanton is as great a villain as ever & Halleck as great a fool—he has no brains whatever!" But he could not bring himself to resign in protest. The Army of the Potomac was his creature, his family, his base of support, his instrument of power. If he left it, he would be helpless to affect the course of events. Was it possible to retain his command and still oppose the president's policy?

McClellan discussed possible responses to the proclamation with his closest confidants on September 24. The tenor of their discussion may be indicated in a letter of that date sent by a *Herald* reporter to publisher James Gordon Bennett. The reporter had spoken with a number of officers, presumably at headquarters, who told him, "The sentiment throughout the whole army seems to be in favor of a change of dynasty." If these men were indeed typical of the Potomac officer corps, "there is large promise of a fearful revolution . . . that will startle the Country and give us a Military Dictator."[22] McClellan's own response was more controlled and tactically cautious. On September 26, he wrote to William Aspinwall, his close friend and political ally, asking him to sound out the Democratic Party leadership in New York City to see whether they would support him if he were to openly oppose the two proclamations. The tone of this letter sets it apart from the rest of his correspondence with Aspinwall, which had always been very personal and informal. This letter has the rhetorical tone of a political manifesto:

I am very anxious to know how you and men like you regard the recent Proclamations of the Presdt inaugurating servile war, emancipating the slaves, & at one stroke of the pen changing our free institutions into a despotism—for such I regard the natural effect of the last Proclamation suspending Habeas Corpus throughout the land.

I shall probably be in this vicinity [Sharpsburg] for some days &, if you regard the matter as gravely as I do, would be glad to communicate with you.[23]

McClellan charges Lincoln with the gravest of political offenses, akin to treason: the wish to overthrow constitutional government and establish a despotism. On that score, Lincoln's policy is morally and politically equivalent to Southern secession. Indeed, Lincoln's policy may represent the greater menace: a successful secession would leave the constitution intact in the North, while the triumph of Lincoln's policy would destroy republican government North and South. How should such a threat be answered? The ordinary procedures of civil government are inadequate in such a crisis. Lincoln had responded to secession by going to war, and stretching the constitution to conduct it. Perhaps Aspinwall could suggest ways of using civil procedures to defeat Lincoln's radical initiatives. But at the moment Lincoln and his party controlled Congress; litigation before the Supreme Court was slow and uncertain, and Lincoln had already defied the Court's injunction against arresting secessionist legislators in Maryland. To defeat Lincoln's reach for despotism, exceptional measures might be justified. The classical models of Roman history, familiar to McClellan, Aspinwall, and all educated men, offered examples of great men who had overthrown the existing government and assumed temporary dictatorship in order to save liberty and republican government.

In his moments of rage and frustration, McClellan had thought about using the army, his "military family," as an instrument for bringing power to bear on the policies and indeed the political structure of the administration. He and his officers had talked loosely of a countermarch on Washington. But to attempt something of that kind was not only to risk political and military disaster but to go against the grain of national tradition, to violate the sacred principles of constitutional government that McClellan genuinely revered. Perhaps something short of that would suffice: a statement representing the army's opinion of the proclamations and its desires for future policy, a sort of "Grand Remonstrance," like the petition of grievances with which Parliament challenged the authority of King Charles I—but originating in the army rather than the Congress. However, such a statement issued from army headquarters would be seen as a military challenge to the supremacy of the civil government. McClellan was not prepared to make so radical a move without considering the range of possible alternatives, with their attendant risks and the consequences.

The dangers of opposition were brought home by another letter from Postmaster General Montgomery Blair, the lone dissenter at the September 22 meeting and McClellan's only ally in the cabinet. The Blair family led the conservative faction in Lincoln's party, and they supported McClellan not only as a conservative counter to Stanton and Chase in the making of war policy but also as an ally in helping them preserve what Blair would later call "this exclusive right of government in the white race." On September 27, Blair secretly wrote to McClellan, warning him of the damage the Key affair had done to his standing with Lincoln and urging him to "clarify" his views on slavery, which Blair supposed were not unlike his own: disapproving the institution on moral and political grounds, wishing its gradual disappearance, but opposed to sudden or wholesale abolition. This was followed by another letter three days later from Francis P. Blair Sr., a political elder whose prestige dated from his service in Andrew Jackson's presidency, urging McClellan to accept the Proclamation as a necessary war measure. Such a public gesture was, in Blair's view, the only way to end those "attacks from the rear" that threatened McClellan's command. However, to make matters more complicated, McClellan was also receiving mail from conservative Democrats who were not interested in the kind of compromise advocated by the Blairs. These men asked McClellan to clarify his views on the Proclamation, with the expectation that he would join them in resisting or reversing it.[24]

McClellan therefore extended his consultations beyond the circle of close confidants that included his staff and Fitz-John Porter. On or about September 27 he summoned Generals Burnside, Cox, and Cochrane to a meeting to ask their advice about "the course he should pursue respecting the Proclamation." The three officers approached the meeting warily: they were all Republicans and known supporters of the Lincoln administration, and well aware that McClellan was considering an open breach with the president over the Emancipation Proclamation.

They met privately after dark in his big headquarters tent, with no aides present. McClellan tried to put them at ease by declaring that he wanted their advice precisely because they were "friends of the administration"—and not identified with the Radicals. He said frankly that he knew in advance that they "would oppose any hostile demonstration on his part." He wanted them to know that he had no desire to make such a demonstration. Rather, he had been "urged to put himself in open opposition to it by politicians not only, but by army officers who were near to him. He named no names, but intimated that they were of rank and influence which gave weight to their advice."

As Cox remembered it, the three generals first asked his opinion about the issue addressed by the Emancipation Proclamation: the continued existence of slavery. For them, as Republicans, this was the critical question: whether McClellan finally accepted the principle that slavery must be put in the way of ultimate extinction. McClellan's answer was equivocal. He agreed that the institution must eventually be extinguished, but said that it was somehow better for that to happen piecemeal, as the army advanced, rather than by systematic change. However, he was convinced "that the Proclamation was premature, and that it indicated a change in the President's attitude which he attributed to radical influences at Washington."

Cox and his colleagues immediately, and without prior consultation, told him "that any declaration on his part against the Proclamation would be a fatal error . . . that any public utterance by him in his official character criticizing the civil policy of the administration would be properly regarded as a usurpation." That told McClellan that the Republicans in his army would reject any open opposition to the president; and if the mere expression of hostile views was "usurpation," then any physical manifestation of opposition, let alone a march on Washington, was clearly forbidden.

Nonetheless, McClellan pressed the question by posing it in the form of a denial. He "intimated" that he agreed with their view that open criticism was akin to usurpation, but said that the idea was continually being "thrust at him by others." As an example of this, he told the three generals "that people had assured him that the army was so devoted to him that they would as one man enforce any decision he should make as to any part of the war policy." He was, in effect, asking whether these Republican generals thought the army would follow him if he were to come out in opposition to the government or its policy. Cox responded:

> that those who made such assurances were his worst enemies, and in my judgment knew much less of the army than they pretended; that our volunteer soldiers were citizens as well as soldiers, and were citizens more than soldiers; and that greatly as I knew them to be attached to him, I believed not a corporal's guard would stand by his side if he were to depart from the strict subordination of the military to the civil authority.

McClellan answered "that he heartily believed both that it was true and that it ought to be so"—a curious way to put the case, which left the suggestion that neither proposition was entirely valid. However, he was still concerned about "an agitation in the camp on the subject, and intrigues of the sort [he] had mentioned." Did they not think it well for him to issue an order reminding the army "that whatever might be their rights as citizens, they must as soldiers beware of any organized effort to meddle with the functions of the civil government"? The question suggested a broader agitation against the Proclamation than actually existed. Cox, Burnside, and Cochrane agreed that this was a good idea.[25]

Although talk about dictatorship persisted among the staff and in the press, McClellan himself made no further allusions to it in private correspondence and took no action to achieve it. Nevertheless, he was not ready to abandon the idea of taking a public stance in opposition to the Proclamation, thereby making himself the symbolic center of opposition to the administration. He made no answer to the appeals of Montgomery and Francis Blair Sr. for a reconciliation with Lincoln. Instead, Fitz-John Porter, acting on McClellan's behalf and probably at his request, reopened his correspondence with Bennett of the *Herald* and Marble of the *World*. What had been a campaign against Secretary Stanton was now an effort to discredit the whole administration. For the moment the *Herald* accepted the Proclamation on the presumption that it was an ultimatum that the South, following Lee's defeat at Antietam, might accept. But the *World* had immediately rejected it as proof Lincoln had been "coerced by the insanity of the radicals" into a violation of his pledge that "this was not to be a war of subjugation." Confederate leaders "will make of this proclamation a moral weapon . . . [and] strengthen the determination of the rebels to fight to the very last."[26]

On September 30, Porter wrote to Marble, justifying McClellan's reasons for not pursuing Lee after Antietam, blaming Stanton and Halleck for the inefficiency and malfeasance that slowed the army's resupply. All of these points would be reflected in the *World*'s coverage of army affairs over the next two months. Porter then characterized the army's reaction to the president's Proclamation, which was "ridiculed" and "caused disgust, discontent, and expressions of disloyalty to the views of the administration amounting, I have heard, to insubordination." In fact, while many enlisted men were opposed to the measure, the only part of the army in which such extreme views were prevalent was McClellan's headquarters.[27]

Porter went on to provide Marble with a full account of what we might call McClellan's platform. Radical policy should be repudiated. Instead, "We must show by a conservative reign that there is no intention to oppress [the South]." Such a "reign" would conciliate the South, and see "the opinion of [its] people softened, the poor enlightened and a new reign established and before summer returns, peace reigns all over the country." The dictatorial connotations of the word "reign" are given substance by Porter's insistence that to achieve all this, "[t]here must be a conservative political policy, a military General-in-Chief who is honest" and who insists on "exclusion of politics from the military sphere"— by which he meant that the civil executive and Congress would have to give McClellan a free hand: "But it must be done under McClellan's mind—not the present chief."[28] The identity of the "present chief" is a little ambiguous. Porter seems to be talking about Halleck, the present general in chief who must give way to McClellan. But Porter also took aim at the commander in chief, condemning Lincoln as "a political coward . . . who holds in his hands the lives of thousands and trifles with them," undoing their hard-won gains by issuing his "absurd proclamation."[29]

Porter does not explain how a McClellan "reign" would produce peace within the year. McClellan's earlier statements suggest that he would have continued to follow the "conciliation" strategy that had prevailed at the outset of the conflict. He would seek to win a decisive battle at Richmond, which would convince Southern leaders that the cost of continued rebellion would be prohibitive. He would offer carrot-and-stick inducements for the South to accept a restoration of the Union, by limiting emancipation to the terms of the Confiscation Act. Only the slaves of active Rebels would be freed, and then only if they were still in arms when the districts they inhabited were actually occupied by Federal troops. The threat of confiscation in this form would give slave owners in the deep South a motive for accepting an early peace, before Northern armies could invade their districts. Implicit in this program was the necessity of reaching some type of compromise settlement of the central issues of the war, the supposed state's "right of secession" and the future of slavery. McClellan offered no specific proposals but was on record as supporting the compromises offered by Democratic senator John Crittenden of Kentucky, with the support of Stephen A. Douglas, in the weeks before the firing on Fort Sumter. Their proposals included constitutional amendments precluding abolition by the central government; permitting slavery in any new territories acquired southward of the old Missouri Compromise line; and perhaps the recognition of Southern autonomy within the Union—for example, by giving its states the power to veto Federal legislation.[30]

In effect, Porter's letter was a response to the urging of New York's Democratic leaders that McClellan declare his positions on the critical political questions facing the nation and the party. McClellan could not make such a statement himself without transgressing his subordination to the civil authority. With this in hand, men of influence like Belmont, Barlow, Aspinwall, and Wood could organize Democratic support for his present continuation in command and advancement to general in chief and for, in the longer term, his presidential candidacy in 1864.

The day after Porter posted his letter to the *World*, Lincoln arrived at Sharpsburg to meet with McClellan.

CHAPTER 17

THE GENERAL AND THE PRESIDENT

OCTOBER 1–NOVEMBER 7, 1862

🙚 🙚

LINCOLN WOULD TELL JOHN HAY THAT HE WENT TO SHARPSBURG on October 1 to "get [McClellan] to move," and that it was only afterward that "I began to fear that he was playing false—that he did not want to hurt the enemy." However, accounts of his visit suggest he brought that suspicion with him. On October 2 Lincoln told Ozias Hatch, a Republican politico and an old friend, that what they saw around them was not the Army of the Potomac: "So it is called, but that is a mistake; it is only McClellan's bodyguard."[1]

Lincoln was accompanied by an entourage, which McClellan and his colleagues contemptuously characterized as a gaggle of Midwestern politicians and political generals. Perhaps that entourage was *Lincoln's* bodyguard. But the presence among them of General John A. McClernand was a sign that Lincoln was already moving to counter McClellan's power as the most prominent and powerful military representative of the Northern Democrats.[2]

McClernand had been a leader of the Democratic Party in Illinois, like McClellan a staunch supporter of Stephen A. Douglas. Lincoln had commissioned him as brigadier general in 1861, along with other prominent Democratic militia officers, to coopt key leaders of the opposition and create a broad Unionist coalition. Lincoln understood McClernand and the Midwestern Democrats he represented. He had spent a political lifetime battling them on the hustings and dealing with them in the legislature, he spoke their language and understood their concerns, and between them enmity was balanced by mutual respect. McClernand and his fellow westerners had a history of bitter intraparty battles with their Southern counterparts and were inclined to want the South punished for its misdeeds. This was not at all the case with McClellan and his backers among the New York financial elite, whose interests and pre-war allegiances made them more willing to conciliate the Cotton South. Lincoln and McClernand were then negotiating a deal, under which McClernand would use his popularity with Democratic voters to stage a massive recruiting drive in Illinois and Indiana in exchange for a major general's commission and promise of an independent command within Grant's theater. This was a bad idea militarily. But it was a political coup of considerable importance to have McClernand promoting the war among his constituents *after* the issuance of the Emancipation Procla-mation. It discredited the claim, made by McClellan and his New York backers, that emancipation would "dissolve our present armies" and wreck the war effort. It diminished or at least offset McClellan's standing as the chief military representative of the Democratic opposition, and aligned a substantial body of War Democrats behind the president and his policy.[3]

LINCOLN ARRIVED BY TRAIN at Harpers Ferry, and with McClellan and their entourages they viewed the battered town from the picturesque vantage points of Maryland and Loudon Heights. Then they rode north to the Antietam battlefield, where the dead men were all buried and the dead livestock buried or burned, for a review of the troops. The weather was splendid, a fine early autumn day in the hills of western Mary-land. But McClellan and many of his officers found Lincoln's attitude chilly and even hostile. Some thought he behaved with studied rude-ness toward McClellan, and even toward the troops assembled for his review—riding "along the lines at a quick trot, taking little notice of the troops. . . . Not a word of approval, not even a smile of approbation." On the other hand, generals like Alpheus Williams of XII Corps, who were not part of McClellan's circle, found Lincoln affable and easy to talk with. Lincoln spent the night and most of October 3 with Burnside and Cox, who thought the president took real pleasure in reviewing the troops and found him appreciative of the army's sacrifice and achievement at Antietam.

There is no necessary contradiction between these accounts. Lincoln was a consummate actor when he needed to be, and it may be that on this occasion he was making an open display of his annoyance with McClellan and his followers, and of his willingness to befriend and favor those who supported him.

McClellan's officers met Lincoln with suspicion and dislike. Brigadier General John Reynolds, a highly regarded division commander, thought Lincoln was a disgrace to his role, "grinning out of the windows [of his coach] like a baboon." Fitz-John Porter had written Marble that presidential visits of this kind always presaged some "injury" to McClellan, the army, or the cause, and he feared this one would produce a new and obnoxious "proclamation or war order." In this instance, as McClellan told his wife, "I incline to think that the real purpose of his visit is to push me into a premature advance into Virginia." General Meade also saw the president as a threat to McClellan's good management of the army, but he thought Antietam would make Lincoln think twice "before he interferes with McClellan."[4]

On October 3, the president and his general met in McClellan's tent, out of the bright sun of the warm fall day. They sat on opposite sides of a camp table, and their conversation was private. McClellan seems to have imagined that he himself was behaving with impeccable politeness, but he flattered himself in his ability to conceal his mood or his feelings. Lincoln was an astute and sensitive reader of people, able to gauge individuals by their look and posture, and crowds by their tone or manner. He was certainly aware of the general hostility toward him among McClellan's officers. He probably found McClellan watchful, suspicious, and slightly sullen—unwilling to speak until the president revealed his agenda.

To soften the mood, Lincoln began by flattering McClellan ("told me he was convinced I was the best general in the country, etc., etc.") and assuring him that "he does feel very kindly towards me personally." However, he had indeed come to press on McClellan his always unwelcome advice, that timely action was a necessity, not only for the national cause but for McClellan's own future as a military commander. Lincoln did so in language that he thought was direct and unequivocal. There were at least two months of good campaigning weather before winter set in, and Lincoln wanted McClellan to use the time to press Lee back hard—to drive him back toward Richmond and if possible destroy his army in battle.

As usual, McClellan heard only what he wished to hear. In a letter to his wife he repeated Lincoln's compliments and declared his belief that he had persuaded the president "of the great difficulty of the task we had accomplished" and of the obstacles to an immediate offensive.

The following day, October 4, McClellan rode east with Lincoln and his party to the South Mountain passes where the army had fought on September 14. As they parted, William Aspinwall met them, riding up the road from Washington. However, the coincidence was unfortunate for McClellan, because it so clearly exposed the fact that he was in close consultation with the political opposition. McClellan was nevertheless glad to see Aspinwall, as he had been eagerly awaiting word on what party leaders like Barlow and Belmont thought he should do in response to the Emancipation Proclamation. The urgency of their advice was marked by the fact that Aspinwall had come to deliver it personally.[5]

The party's advice was not at all what McClellan expected. As McClellan wrote Mary Ellen, "Mr. Aspinwall is decidedly of the opinion that it is my duty to submit to the Presdt's proclamation & quietly continue doing my duty as a soldier. I presume he is right. . . . I shall surely give his view full consideration." Like Burnside and Cox, Aspinwall and his colleagues believed that any form of opposition by McClellan to the president's decree would be perceived as a military "usurpation." A political party that planned to campaign as the defender of constitutionalism against a quasi-despotic Radical regime could not afford to be associated with so unconstitutional an act. While Democrats had toyed with the idea of a McClellan dictatorship, they had supposed it would be achieved by presidential acquiescence. As politicians, they knew better than McClellan's staff how little public support a *putsch* would have, how much democratic ire it would arouse. Why run such risks when the party's prospects in the fall election, especially in New York, were looking so splendid? Indeed, if the New Yorkers had their way, McClellan would be reconciled with Stanton—who was, as they saw it, an old Buchanan Democrat and potential ally.[6]

Aspinwall also agreed with Lincoln that McClellan should make an early start to the next offensive campaign. Bennett of the New York *Herald* believed he was supporting McClellan's views and interests when, in a series of editorials that began on the eve of Antietam, he called for the general to follow up his victory by destroying Lee's army or driving it all the way back to Richmond. Even Marble of the *World* editorialized that for conservative principles to triumph, the army must move vigorously and suppress the rebellion in relatively short order. Only abolitionists preferred a slow military advance that would give the Blacks time to rise in rebellion. In other words, the longer the war, the stronger the Radicals. McClellan now gave up, in principle, his insistence that it was the Radicals who would benefit by a speedy end to the conflict. On October 5, he wrote to Mary Ellen that Aspinwall "is no doubt correct." But the next day, when Halleck transmitted Lincoln's order "that you cross the Potomac and give battle to the enemy," McClellan reverted to his habitual response, that he could not move until he was properly supplied, and when he did move it would not be on the line recommended by Halleck and Lincoln.[7]

Instead of advancing, and despite the advice he had received from nearly every side—from the Blairs, from Aspinwall, from Generals Burnside, Cox, Cochrane and Smith—McClellan decided he must have his say about the Emancipation Proclamation. He prepared a general order on the subject, which, he believed, carefully avoided explicit opposition to the president while still giving an indication of his disapproval. The order on "the President's proclamation of September 22d," issued October 7, said nothing about the subject of the Proclamation—the word "emancipation" is not mentioned. Nevertheless, something in its character makes it necessary for McClellan to lecture officers and men on the "fundamental rule of our political system," the subordination of the military to the civil authority. The president is the "proper and only" source of orders respecting the policies used to suppress the rebellion and the objects for which the army fights. He warns his men that any speech that goes "beyond temperate and respectful expressions of opinion" will impair the "discipline & efficiency" of the army. However, there was a touch of electioneering implicit in his egregious reminder that "[t]he remedy for political error if any are committed is to be found only in the action of the people at the polls."[8]

Although McClellan's order went beyond what Aspinwall had recommended, the party leaders in New York did not object, because its effects were generally positive. The order was not only hailed by Democratic journals, it was approved even by the *Tribune*. Jacob Cox thought it was "an honest effort on his part to break through the toils which intriguers had spread for him." Lincoln might have thought otherwise. Although McClellan's order was formally supportive of the civil authority, it was also a subtle and rhetorically effective gesture of opposition. Lincoln was not likely to have missed the implicit appeal for voters in the upcoming elections to show their disapproval of emancipation. However, for Lincoln the most disturbing aspect of McClellan's order was that it was accompanied by his refusal to obey the president's order to cross the river and attack the enemy. It was at this point that Lincoln "began to fear that he was playing false—that he did not want to hurt the enemy," and so persisted in "delaying on little pretexts of wanting this and that." Still, Lincoln hesitated to remove him for political reasons. The firing of so popular a general after he had won so notable a victory would raise a storm of questions about the administration's motives and hurt Republican prospects in the midterm elections, now less than a month away.

McClellan was also under pressure from nearly every Northern constituency to prosecute the war with great energy. For different reasons, the Radical *Tribune*, the moderate *Times*, the conservative *Herald* and even the partisan *World* agreed in demanding swifter and more efficient action from the armies—the Radicals wanting secession and slavery destroyed in short order, the conservatives hoping that a swift victory by McClellan would bring the South to accept a compromise peace preserving slavery.[9] McClellan was in a bind that he was helpless to break, caught between his profound reluctance to take the offensive and his growing awareness that the demand for action was a rising tide that could not be checked. His response to such pressure was to withdraw into the bubble provided by his staff, where, surrounded by their approval, he would stubbornly resist all calls for action, in a mood that was increasingly sullen and filled with foreboding of disaster—either military defeat if he moved or relief from command if he did not.

The military costs of McClellan's inactivity would be dramatically demonstrated during three days, October 10–13, when General Lee unleashed Stuart's cavalry for a spectacular raid that took him up into Pennsylvania and all around McClellan's army. But the real costs of

McClellan's persistent inaction were still hidden behind the hills that overlooked the Shepherdstown Ford.

CONFEDERATE DEFEAT AND REVIVAL
SEPTEMBER 21–OCTOBER 10, 1862

For two days after his retreat to Virginia, General Lee had refused to accept that Antietam was anything worse than a temporary check. He believed his army could resume the offensive after a brief rest, the recovery of stragglers, and resupply with food, forage, and ammunition. He therefore concentrated his army well back from the Potomac, in the hills that looked down on Martinsburg and the northern end of the Shenandoah Valley. From this position he could check any Federal attempt to cross at Shepherdstown. He could not prevent the Federals from retaking Harpers Ferry, but he did not mind if McClellan shifted his forces and his attention downstream. Lee had positioned his army where it could resume the offensive by moving north through Martinsburg and crossing the Potomac at Williamsport upstream from Shepherdstown. That movement would turn the right flank of McClellan's army, whose elements were ranged along the north bank of the Potomac from Shepherdstown to Harpers Ferry. The Federals would have to retreat to save their line of supply, which was currently tied to the railhead at Hagerstown, about eight miles north of the Shepherdstown Ford. Lee could strike directly for Hagerstown, catch them at a disadvantage, and—with Federal midterm elections only weeks away—win a strategic victory on Northern soil.[10]

It was not until September 21 that Lee began to acknowledge his army's inability to resume the offensive. His report to President Davis detailed the army's weakened state, which Lee attributed mostly to straggling. He had failed to win at Antietam because "[a] great many men belonging to the army never entered Maryland at all; many returned after getting there, while others who crossed the river remained aloof." His tone suggests widespread malingering and evasion of service, and the remedies he asks are a stiffening of the penalties and more rigorous enforcement against straggling and other breaches of military discipline. He does not mention the most probable causes for the nonbattle losses: the physical exhaustion and illness produced by repeated forced marches and inadequate diet. He did implement the kind of census of troop strength that ought to have been put in place in July. It brought him the unwelcome news that even with the recovery of some thousands of stragglers, the Army of Northern Virginia mustered no more than thirty-six thousand men, in poor physical condition and with their morale impaired.[11]

Under these conditions, resumption of the offensive was impossible. Lee would have to concede the initiative to McClellan. He could only try to prevent McClellan's using his advantage by putting up a threatening front along the upper Potomac, "to threaten a passage into Maryland, [and] to occupy the enemy on this frontier." If McClellan showed an aggressive inclination, Lee hoped to entice the Federal army "into the Valley, where I can attack them to advantage." The Valley was familiar terrain to Lee and Jackson, its narrow width would make it harder for the larger Federal army to outflank the weaker Confederates, and a Yankee advance up the Valley would actually carry the Federals away from Richmond. But Lee could no longer hope to impose conditions of battle on his enemies. On September 25, he informed Davis that his plan for a second invasion of Maryland was now impossible: "I would not hesitate to make it even with our diminished numbers, did the army exhibit its former temper and condition; but, as far as I am able to judge, the hazard would be great and a reverse disastrous. I am, therefore, led to pause."[12]

WHILE DAVIS AND LEE were coping with the results of Lee's failed invasion, the western elements of Davis's grand offensive had also been baffled. Davis's instructions had urged Bragg to "crush" Buell's army before moving into Kentucky. Bragg had maneuvered instead, and, by the beginning of October, Buell had connected his field army with the large force of recruits and reinforcements that had been holding Louisville. On October 3, Van Dorn and Price suffered a bloody repulse at Corinth that put an end to the Confederate counteroffensive in the Mississippi valley theater. Kentuckians refused to rally to the Confederate cause, and Buell took the offensive with an army twice as large as Bragg's and Smith's combined force. On October 8, part of Bragg's army blundered into most of Buell's at Perryville, Kentucky, and was beaten. Rather than try to "crush Buell," as Davis wished, Bragg abandoned the invasion and began a long and painful march back to the Tennessee mountains, dropping stragglers all the way. Although Buell let him get away without attempting pursuit, it was clear that Davis's strategic offensive had failed, and the Confederacy was back on the strategic defensive.[13]

The best way to defend a position is to discourage the enemy from attacking it by taking, or threatening to take, the offensive. Lee kept his army concentrated around Martinsburg, where it threatened an invasion of Maryland that it lacked the strength to execute. However, McClellan made no effort to test Lee's strength or to harass his army while it was rebuilding. Apart from the force that reoccupied Harpers Ferry on September 22, McClellan kept his troops north of the Potomac. His passivity allowed Lee to refresh and resupply his army with impunity. In the weeks immediately following Antietam, the Federal army had rebuilt its strength far faster than Lee could rebuild his. In the last week of September Lee had added 16,000 men to his ranks, raising his force to 52,000. By bringing most of the reserve forces up from Washington, McClellan was able to increase his force from 70,000 to well over 100,000. However, McClellan's buildup peaked at 120,000 in October, while Lee's accelerated. Toward the end of October, Lee reported 64,000 men present for duty, and by the start of November he would have 85,000 in hand—a force nearly as large as that which had assailed McClellan in the Seven Days. On September 26 McClellan outnumbered Lee two to one; by November the disparity was three to two, and the Confederate army was more experienced, better organized, healthier, and in higher morale. Lee's offensive had failed, but his army was now stronger for the defensive than it had ever been.

To keep McClellan off-balance and fearful of his flanks, Lee on October 10 launched Jeb Stuart and 1,500 cavalry on their three-day raid. Stuart crossed upstream from Williamsport and rode all the way around McClellan's army, south through Frederick, and back to Virginia by the downstream fords. The raid did little actual damage to Federal supply lines, but it revived civilian panic and embarrassed McClellan, who was supposed to have whipped the Rebels out of Maryland. It also may be said to have goaded McClellan into further inactivity.

Stuart's raid exacerbated the mistrust of McClellan among his critics in the press, Congress, and the cabinet. It was the second time the Rebel cavalryman had literally ridden circles around McClellan's army—the first being just before the Seven Days. Taken with his refusal to advance, Stuart's exploit suggested that the general had learned nothing from past experience. Navy Secretary Welles summed up the emerging consensus in Washington: that McClellan's persistent and "fatuous inaction" was producing a crisis of public confidence. "The country groans." Moreover, suspicion of McClellan's motives was growing among the administration's supporters: "Many believe him to be acting on the army programme avowed by Key." Democratic journals defended McClellan, but both sides implicitly accepted George Smalley's account of the battle and his conclusion that McClellan had missed a chance to destroy or severely damage Lee's army. McClellan's own "Preliminary Report" did little to alter that verdict.[14]

LINCOLN SOLVES THE McCLELLAN PROBLEM
OCTOBER 13–NOVEMBER 7, 1862

Lincoln would later say two very different things about his attitude toward McClellan after their meeting at Sharpsburg. He would tell John Hay that McClellan's refusal to obey the order to advance on October 6 had convinced him that McClellan was playing false and could not be trusted to defeat the Confederate army. He would also claim that he had been willing to leave McClellan in command if the general would advance before the onset of winter and move swiftly enough to cut Lee's communication with Richmond. However, Lincoln's way of dealing with McClellan during this period suggests that he had in fact come to the end of his patience and was determined to replace him immediately after the midterm election.

On October 13 Lincoln sent McClellan a lengthy letter laying out the plan of campaign he expected McClellan to follow. Although the letter echoed themes and concerns that were by now familiar, the tone of this letter differed sharply from any of their earlier exchanges. Hitherto Lincoln had presented himself as McClellan's friend and supporter, larding his advice and softening any criticism with flattery and assurances of personal regard. Now he began in the voice of a displeased parent, chiding an unheedful son: "You remember my speaking to you of what I called your over-cautiousness." He followed by questioning McClellan's soldierly pride, and perhaps his manhood. "Are you not over-cautious when you assume you cannot do what the enemy is constantly doing? Should you not claim to be at least his equal in prowess, and act upon the claim?" There was nothing new in his insistence that McClellan move sooner rather than later, that he not ignore "the question of *time*, which cannot and must not be ignored." But there was a hint of sarcasm in the reminder: "I certainly should be pleased for you to have the Railroad from Harpers Ferry to Winchester, but it wastes the remainder of the autumn to give it to you." He proposed a line of operations that was sound enough—it was one McClellan would actually adopt. However, Lincoln urges it in a peculiar style, lecturing McClellan on the basic principles of military science and the simple propositions of Euclidean geometry. Thus he reminds McClellan that "one of the standard maxims of war, as you know, is 'to operate upon the enemy's communications . . . without exposing your own.' You seem to act as if this applies *against* you, but cannot apply in your *favor*." He explains that McClellan can move "by the chord-line, or on the inside arc" of the figurative circle that enclosed the theater of operations. And he adds another taunt of McClellan's manhood: "It is all easy if our troops march as well as the enemy; and it is unmanly to say they cannot do it." Then, to make responsibility for any failure clear, he closes, "This letter is in no sense an order."[15]

The letter is, first of all, a lawyer's brief, which establishes a paper record showing that Lincoln's removal of McClellan was based not on political differences but on McClellan's failure to carry out a simple and feasible plan of campaign. It is also an exercise in psychological warfare. After so long an acquaintance with McClellan, Lincoln must have known how galling it would be for a man with his sense of social superiority and professional pride to be instructed on tactics and Euclidean geometry by a self-taught frontier lawyer. He almost seems to be goading McClellan into some rash outburst or an angry resignation. The letter also shows that Lincoln's slow-burning anger at McClellan's insults, obstruction-ism, and opposition could no longer be dissembled. It flashed out again on October 26, after McClellan excused his continued immobility by pleading the need for new horses to replace the worn-out beasts the army has been using. Lincoln snapped back, "Will you pardon me for asking

390 | THE REVOLUTIONARY CRISIS

what the horses of your army have done since the battle of Antietam that fatigue anything?" To McClellan's very reasonable request that drafted men be used to bring veteran regiments back to strength rather than used to form new regiments, Lincoln replied, "Is it your purpose not to go into action again until the men now being drafted in the States are incorporated into the old regiments?"[16]

McClellan finally began his advance from Harpers Ferry on November 2. Lincoln would later say that he considered this advance a final test of McClellan's usefulness as a commander, and that if he failed to get between Lee and Richmond Lincoln would relieve him. But the test was one he knew McClellan could not meet. It had taken McClellan more than a week, from October 26 to November 2, to get his army across the Potomac, which gave Lee plenty of time to anticipate the Federal line of advance.

It seems far more likely that Lincoln had already decided to relieve McClellan as soon as it was politically feasible to do so—that is, as soon as the midterm election was settled one way or the other. He was convinced that military operations would continue to be inconclusive without a radical change in the way his armies were commanded. Lincoln had already begun discussing candidates for McClellan's replacement before McClellan even began his advance. He was also planning to fire General Buell, who had let Bragg's army escape without pursuit after its defeat at Perryville. Lincoln would condemn Buell in the same terms he used for McClellan: that he had failed to march as the enemy marches, and fight as he fights.[17]

The last act played out in predictable fashion. Lee answered McClellan's slow-moving offensive by once again splitting his army. He took Longstreet's Corps south and east through Chester Gap, beat McClellan to the critical road junction at Culpeper Court House, and took up a strong defensive position behind the Hazel River. He left Jackson with 40,000 troops at Winchester, a force strong enough to smash through the cavalry guarding the mountain gaps and strike McClellan from the rear, much as Pope had been struck. On November 6 McClellan had 114,000 troops well concentrated in front of Longstreet, and if he had acted with vigor and speed he might have turned the tables on Lee—using one of his infantry corps to reinforce the cavalry at the gaps and hitting Longstreet with nearly double numbers. Instead he stopped to consider the possible mischief Jackson might do.

The next day, a cold November 7 with snow and freezing rain, the order arrived from Washington relieving him of his command and appointing Burnside in his place. It was the third time Burnside had been offered the command, and this time he accepted. After their bitter disagreement over Burnside's command responsibilities and the behavior of IX Corps at Antietam, loyalty to McClellan was no longer an obstacle.

McClellan was not entirely surprised by his relief, and he accepted it passively. On some unconscious level, he may not have been sorry to be relieved of the responsibility of army command—a responsibility heavy enough in its own right, but in his case redoubled by the conviction that he had to fight powerful enemies front and back, with the fate of the republic hinging on his failure or success. The French army officers attached as observers to his headquarters marveled that he did not try to maintain his power by turning his army against the government, as both Napoleons had done. It was a thought McClellan had often entertained in the past. Perhaps his conversations with Aspinwall had convinced him that the American public would not support such a coup; perhaps a decision so bold was simply beyond him.

On November 10 there was one last review, the troops in ranks, as McClellan cantered along the line on his black horse, trailed by his staff. The words of his last order were true to the feelings he had for his men: "In parting from you I cannot express the love and gratitude I bear for you. As an Army you have grown up under my care. In you I have never found doubt or coldness." With adulation and virtual obeisance they had more than met his deep need for total approval and acceptance, and most there would not have begrudged his claim to have been a father to them. There were tearful eyes, and some anger, among the many who had learned soldiering under McClellan's guidance, and respected or even loved him for his careful treatment of them.

The next day, when McClellan boarded the train that would carry him back to Washington, bereft soldiers mobbed the station and uncoupled his car, mutinously urging him to disobey orders and remain with them. Though moved nearly to tears by this last display of the love his boys bore him, McClellan ordered the car rehitched and rode north to "await further orders." He would get none from President Lincoln, but others would take his future in hand. The night before, in New York City, a grand rally had been held to celebrate the Democratic victories in the midterm election. Amid the jubilation, a speaker called for the nomination of General George B. McClellan as Democratic candidate for the presidency of the United States, and the crowd roared its agreement.[18]

CHAPTER 18

DUBIOUS BATTLE:
EVERYTHING CHANGED, NOTHING SETTLED

Two days after Lincoln issued the preliminary Emancipation Proclamation, the president, the cabinet and some associates gathered to hear a congratulatory serenade. Afterward, Secretaries Chase and Bates and several other "old fogies," as young John Hay called them, prolonged the festivities in Secretary Chase's luxuriously furnished parlor. To Hay, "[t]hey all seemed to feel a sort of new and exhilarated life; they breathed freer," as if the Proclamation had freed them along with the slaves. Good wine loosened their tongues as well. "They gleefully and merrily called each other abolitionists," tipsily savoring the pleasure of adopting "that horrible name." It suddenly occurred to Chase that secession had been the "most wonderful" case of the "insanity of a class that the world had ever seen." If the South had stayed in the Union it might have enjoyed its peculiar institution for "many years to come"— abolition as such had little support in the North, and no serious political party espoused it. But by seceding the South had "madly placed [slavery] in the very path of destruction."[1]

Chase had a good point. Southern leaders had chosen to risk the survival of their society and way of life on the chances of war—which is to say, on the outcome of ventures like the Antietam campaign, in which the fate of a nation may hinge on orders lost and found, on coincidences so improbable no novelist would permit them, on an interplay of acumen and miscalculation so intricate that the two can hardly be distinguished. Like the war of which the Antietam campaign was a part, the premises on which the campaign was based, and the decisions that shaped it, were explicable and even justifiable on rational grounds. Nevertheless, once strategic decisions had set the armies in motion, events slipped beyond rational control, and the campaign developed as a tragicomedy of errors.

The Antietam campaign was the product of parallel decision making by the political and military leadership of the Union and the Confederacy, in response to the manifest failure of the strategies each party had been pursuing for the first year and a half of the struggle. Abraham Lincoln undertook a radical transformation of Union strategy, based on a profound understanding of the political and social forces that had caused and shaped the conflict and a critical appreciation of the inadequacies of his own armies' material strength and tactical deployment. Jefferson Davis and his generals recognized that General Lee's victory in the Seven Days Battles, coupled with the mismanagement of Union operations in the West, had given the Confederacy a unique opportunity to reverse the momentum of the conflict by staging a strategic grand offensive. Both strategies were based on sound assessments of the strategic situation, and of the strengths and weaknesses of the opposing forces.

However, in the ensuing campaign the quality of decision making seemed to have no relation at all to the outcome of events. Lincoln is renowned for his ability to manage the "Team of Rivals" that constituted his government, but in 1862 his strategic transformation was nearly wrecked by his inability to get his cabinet officers and his generals to cooperate with him or with each other; while Jefferson Davis, notorious for his inability to get along with his generals, for once maintained seamless cooperation with his commanders. Robert E. Lee's virtues as a commander—the daring that enabled him to seize the initiative, his skill at maneuver—led to the near-fatal division of his army that was exposed by the lost order. It also drove him to seek a battle on September 17 that could only end in stalemate and retreat. The caution that was McClellan's chief defect as a commander actually proved an advantage, because it tempted Lee to stand and fight a battle McClellan could not lose—though he came close. In the fighting at Antietam, Lee's tactical skill barely enabled the Army of Northern Virginia to hold its ground, while McClellan's tactical incompetence wasted his army's strength in piecemeal and half-strength attacks. Yet, in the end victory went to the side with the weaker tactical commander and the less effective coordination of civil-military leadership. The Union won at Antietam because it had the bigger battalions—it could better afford the costs of McClellan's ineptitude than the Confederates the costs of Lee's genius.

Viewed from a strictly military viewpoint, the Battle of Antietam was largely indecisive—full of sound and fury, exorbitant in its human costs, but making very little difference in the tactical positions and military strength of the rival armies. The Confederate invasion of Maryland was defeated and Lee's army compelled to retreat to Virginia. However, many of the other important objectives of the Confederate summer offensive had been achieved. The combined operation against Richmond by Pope and McClellan was broken up and the seat of war transferred to northern Virginia. The Southern public was not at all discouraged by the setback to Lee's army but rather gloried in its successes at Second Bull Run and Harpers Ferry and its repulse of a superior Northern army at Sharpsburg. Most significantly, the defeat did not diminish the war-making power of the Confederacy or the Army of Northern Virginia. Seven weeks after the battle, Lee's army had more than doubled its strength and was more fit for operations, offensive or defensive, than it had been since before the Second Bull Run campaign.[2]

Nevertheless, the indecisive battle did produce a decisive political result. Antietam was victory enough to allow Lincoln to issue the Emancipation Proclamation. Even his disappointment with the extent of that victory was useful, since it strengthened his determination to fire McClellan. The Proclamation profoundly altered the character of the war by linking restoration of the Union with the destruction of slavery. The prospects for a compromise settlement, always doubtful, were now eliminated, since a Union victory would entail destruction of the social fabric of the South. The Union would now fight a war of subjugation, the South a war of social survival, and the conflict would become something like "total war."[3]

Events would show that the South lacked the matériel and manpower resources, the institutional strength and the political culture to win that kind of war—just as the weakness of Lee's army had prevented his winning the Battle of Antietam. But that outcome was not inevitable, and in the fall of 1862 there was every reason to think a Southern victory was still possible.

"NOT WITHOUT HAPPY RESULTS": THE CONFEDERATE PERSPECTIVE

While the Confederacy's strategic offensive in the summer of 1862 was ended by the tactical defeats of Van Dorn at Corinth on October 3, Bragg at Perryville on October 8, and Lee at Antietam on September 17, the strategic achievement was actually quite substantial. Federal armies, which had been on the offensive since January, were not only thrown onto the defensive, but they had to fight to hold or recover territory they thought securely occupied. The planned Federal offensives against Vicksburg, Chattanooga, and Richmond were thwarted and delayed for six or seven months; and when they began, in November and December 1862, they would be sharply checked in northern Mississippi, at Stones River in Tennessee, and at Fredericksburg, Virginia. Davis's offensive thus bought the Confederacy a good deal of much-needed time in which to build up its armies; and the longer his forces kept the Union armies stymied, the better his case for recognition by the British and French.

Confederate gains were especially marked in Virginia. The offensive by Lee's army, which began on August 14, had recovered much of northern Virginia. Despite defeat at Antietam, Lee was able to keep McClellan from crossing the Potomac for two months. Although he eventually had to give ground, he was able to maintain Confederate control of the Shenandoah Valley and to prevent the Army of the Potomac from advancing any farther south than the Rapidan/Rappahannock River line, forty miles south of Washington and sixty miles from Richmond. He had succeeded in his major aim of shifting the seat of conflict from Richmond to northern Virginia, and he would keep it there for the next two years.

Events over the next two years would show that the Confederacy could not afford to repeatedly suffer casualties on the scale Lee's army suffered at Antietam. Its pool of White military manpower was less than half that of the Northern states, and its commitment to slavery forbade the use of Blacks as combat troops. But in the fall of 1862 the Confederacy had experienced less than a year of intensive combat, and the losses so far suffered were more than made up for in conscription and new enlistments—the latter stimulated by the glory Lee's army won in its summer of victories. Although Northern resources were ultimately far greater than the South's, in the months after Antietam the strengthening of Lee's army proportionately outpaced McClellan's reinforcement. By November 2 Lee's force was up to more than eighty thousand, reducing the odds against it to three to two, and the men were in far better physical shape than they had been during the summer.

The Confederacy's most significant loss at Antietam, and in the associated battles of the western armies, was the chance to exploit a unique conjunction of military opportunity and Northern political vulnerability. The North's midterm elections were the most crucial feature of the strategic situation. Discontent with Lincoln's conduct of the war was rife in both political parties, discouraging Republicans and encouraging Democrats. The latter had overcome the ideological and organizational disarray resulting from the loss of its Southern wing and the death of its strongest leader, Stephen Douglas. The Democratic Party was prepared to contest the midterm elections on a platform condemning Lincoln and his party for changing the war for the Union into an abolitionist jihad against slavery, and for mismanaging military operations—as demonstrated by the administration's persecution and ultimate betrayal of General McClellan. Implicit in Democratic attacks on the president and his policy was the belief that the strategy of conciliation could still succeed in bringing the South back into the Union, with compromises insuring the safety of slavery.

The electoral outcome would determine whether or not Lincoln and his party would continue to control the making of war policy, to insist on an unconditional restoration of the Union, and to further its anti-slavery policies—confiscation, exclusion from new territories, ultimate extinction. The elections were also a critical consideration for the British government as it considered whether or not to intervene with an offer of mediation. Prime Minister Lord Palmerston and Foreign Secretary Lord Russell were unwilling to act so long as it seemed likely that the North would go to war rather than accept British interference in American affairs. However, the electoral victory of a party committed to peace and conciliation would have indicated that the North was ready to accept a negotiated end to the fighting.[4]

In evaluating the quality of Lee's and Davis's decision making during the Maryland campaign, we have to bear in mind their awareness that the opportunities before them were not likely to recur. The military advantages of force strength, position, and momentum might conceivably be recovered at some later time, although at great cost in blood and treasure. As it happened, in May and June of 1863, Lee would succeed in creating the conditions that enabled him to mount a second invasion of the North, which ended at Gettysburg. But this second invasion had to proceed without the support of offensives in the western theater; and there were no national elections to amplify the impact of a Confederate success. Lincoln's power to control the Union war effort would not face an electoral challenge again until 1864, when the president had to stand for reelection after a summer of heavy casualties and inconclusive fighting. The political stakes were higher in 1864, and Lincoln's vulnerability at least as great as in 1862; but Confederate armies could do little to exploit that vulnerability, because they no longer had the strength to mount the kind of offensives they had staged in 1862.

Given these circumstances, Davis's decision to launch a strategic offensive, and to urge his commanders to embrace the risks of battle, seems justified. The specific elements of the grand offensive were initially proposed by the field commanders. Davis recognized the larger potential of their initiatives, authorized and to the extent possible coordinated and supported their operations while properly leaving operational details to his field commanders. The plan of campaign he recommended to Bragg was better than the plan Bragg chose to follow; and his unquestioning acceptance of Lee's decision to invade Maryland was based on both an appreciation of Lee's expertise and the knowledge that Lee shared his understanding of the Confederacy's strategic necessities. The contrast with Federal decision making is striking and significant: Lincoln made the crucial decisions alone, taking limited advice from his cabinet, receiving little help or guidance from General in Chief Halleck, and treating his field commanders with well-deserved mistrust. In the summer of 1862 the Davis administration acted with far greater harmony and efficiency than Lincoln and his celebrated "Team of Rivals."[5]

Still, Lee's operational decisions have been criticized for unnecessarily exposing his army to destruction by a much superior Federal force. Lee can certainly be faulted for overestimating the numbers and physical condition of his infantry, and for a plan of campaign that required such extensive and rapid marches that his force was depleted by massive straggling. He also erred in basing his maneuvers on assumptions about what McClellan *would* do, and neglecting to make adequate allowance for what a Union army on its own ground was capable of doing. Lee was also wrong about the quality of the opposing infantry, which was not at all deficient in morale, and nearly broke Lee's line despite the tactical ineptitude of their commander.

However, Lee's most questionable operational decisions must be judged in light of the unique opportunity it was his mission to exploit. From a purely tactical perspective, it was a mistake for Lee to march the whole army to Frederick before having cleared his supply line by capturing Harpers Ferry. The Federal decision to hold out there deranged Lee's plan and forced the division of his army that gave McClellan his great opportunity. Lee learned the tactical lesson, and when he invaded the North in June 1863, he made sure to clear Harpers Ferry early on. But the invasion of Maryland was not a purely tactical exercise. It was part of a military and political strategy whose first objective was to pry Maryland away from the Union, or at least draw its youth into Confederate ranks. Frederick was the only post from which such a political operation could be mounted: central to the mainland part of the state, and as close as Lee could get to the pro-Confederate communities in and around Baltimore. This project turned out to be futile, but there was no way to be certain of that until it had been tried.

Lee's decision to stand and fight on September 17 instead of retreating on the sixteenth can also be questioned on tactical grounds, since he exposed his army to heavy damage, if not destruction by a superior force, under circumstances that made anything better than tactical stalemate and retreat highly unlikely. In Lee's defense, it should be remembered that Braxton Bragg's refusal to risk a general engagement with Buell's larger army was criticized at the time by Bragg's colleagues, and since then by historians, as the waste of a hard-won opportunity. Though it spared the Confederacy a high casualty list, Bragg's retreat seriously damaged his army's morale, while the critical reaction of his subordinates permanently damaged the command structure of the Army of Tennessee. In contrast, the public standing of Lee and his army soared after Antietam, and the morale of the Army of Northern Virginia swiftly revived.[6]

In war, risk is proportional to necessity. The Confederacy could not win a long war, and in September 1862 it had a unique chance to win the war outright. Lee was therefore bound to try by every possible means to achieve his objective. Given McClellan's past performance, and Lee's confidence in the combat proficiency of his own army—and given as well the fact that to "win" Lee had only to induce McClellan to retreat—his willingness to risk his army at Antietam was justified in principle, and not simply by the fact that his army escaped destruction.

As a strategic exercise, the invasion of Maryland and Kentucky also had a political component. President Davis combined armed force with a strong propaganda campaign and the use of high-prestige political figures in an attempt to stir a popular uprising against the states' Unionist governments. This political program failed completely. No rebellion and few recruits were forthcoming. Kentuckians and Marylanders even begrudged the supplies of food and forage their "liberators" required. However, Davis would build on the experience to develop more effective methods of political warfare. Kentucky and Maryland would not rally to the cry of states' rights, but it was conceivable that all of Northern society could be split by an appeal to White supremacy. Over the next two years the Confederate government would support and encourage various subversive, or "Copperhead," movements in the Midwestern states, whose activities ranged from running opposition candidates, to draft obstruction, to abortive conspiracies of sabotage and rebellion. These efforts would culminate in the 1864 presidential campaign, in which the Democrats mounted a serious threat to Lincoln and his war policies, on a platform written by its "Peace" faction and influenced by the work of Confederate agents.

In this, the Confederacy was aided by the Emancipation Proclamation, which produced a racial backlash among important constituencies in the North. However, that reaction was not strong enough to unseat Lincoln, while the positive effects of emancipation ultimately made a decisive contribution to the Union war effort.

END OF THE BEGINNING: THE UNION PERSPECTIVE

The transformation of Union strategy in the summer of 1862 began with Lincoln's decision to emancipate all slaves held in Confederate territory by presidential proclamation. Although Lincoln's opposition to slavery was essentially moral, his decision was based on the recognition that the strategy of limited war and political conciliation had failed; that the Union could not be restored until the South's will and ability to resist had been thoroughly broken. Such a war would be long and extremely costly, and could only be won by combining intensified military operations with an attack on slavery, which was the basis of the Southern economy and social structure. Lincoln was also convinced that no permanent restoration of the Union was possible so long as slavery existed as a permanent element of social organization in the Southern states. Even if the strategy of conciliation succeeded in bringing the Southern states back into the Union, that victory would be meaningless if it left the institution of slavery intact. The old and inescapable conflict of values and institutions would remain, and the threat of secession and social violence passed on to later generations. The costs of a continued war could not be justified, unless the root cause of the war was removed for all time. To achieve that aim Lincoln was willing to accept the costs of a war of subjugation, and risk the social and political disruptions that would result from emancipation.

That political decision required a transformation of the scope, intensity, and duration of military operations. Lincoln would have to vastly increase the military manpower already enlisted. He would also have to find generals willing to both accept the change in Federal war aims and commit to the longer, harder war they entailed. That would require, at the very least, a restructuring of the army's command, beginning with the appointment of Major General Henry W. Halleck as general in chief, with orders to energize the offensive operations of the main field armies, commanded by Generals Grant, Buell, and McClellan.

Though Lincoln's understanding of strategic necessity was impeccable, he botched the military part of the program. The tactical situation in July 1862 required McClellan to renew his offensive against Richmond, to prevent the Confederates from concentrating against Pope's army, which was moving toward Richmond through northern Virginia. When

McClellan balked at the order to advance, Lincoln should have removed him from command at once. Instead he "strategized," passing the decision to Halleck—who lacked the moral courage and decisiveness to act. Halleck and Lincoln chose to evade a confrontation with McClellan and his partisans by shifting the Army of the Potomac piecemeal to reinforce Pope. They thus immobilized more than half the federal troops in the Virginia theater, and freed Lee and Davis to use all their combat-ready units in a counteroffensive that nearly wrecked the Union war effort.

As a result of this blunder, Lincoln had to begin his radical transformation of the Union war effort amid a military crisis. Instead of preparing the public for the proclamation he had shown the cabinet on July 22, he had to spend weeks defending his Secretary of War against scurrilous charges emanating from the headquarters of the Army of the Potomac. After Pope's defeat at Second Bull Run, his plans were further disrupted by the need to reorganize an army wracked by the mutual hostility of its commanding generals, so it could confront an enemy that was threatening invasion. Instead of eliminating the McClellan problem that had dogged his policy for a year, he was compelled to restore McClellan to command, over the violent objections of Chase and Stanton, two of the strongest men in his cabinet.

The decisions Lincoln made during this period were the political equivalent of Lee's decision to fight at Antietam. The two were well matched. To paraphrase Lincoln, neither man was willing to leave the game while any card remained unplayed. Lincoln, like Lee, risked what he could not afford to lose, to gain objectives that were, as he saw them, essential to winning the war. His reappointment of McClellan, after Pope's disaster, outraged nearly all of his cabinet and the most powerful leaders of his party in Congress. His issuance of the Emancipation Proclamation, and the subsequent firing of McClellan, threatened to split the coalition of War Democrats, moderate and Radical Republicans that sustained his administration and the war effort, at a time when his own prestige and public standing were at a low point. Lincoln also ran the risk of an open breach with General McClellan, at a moment when the general's prestige was enhanced by victory, while his civilian partisans were calling for a "dictatorship" and his staff muttering threats of a military coup. Even if those threats were just talk, a public declaration by McClellan that he opposed the president's policy would have created a constitutional crisis and undermined the president's authority as commander in chief while the nation was in the midst of revolution and civil war.

Like Lee, Lincoln judged his opponents accurately enough to escape actual defeat. Though Republicans suffered dismaying losses in the fall elections, they retained their majorities in the House and Senate, and Lincoln's astute handling of War Democrats like John McClernand succeeded in holding his coalition together. In dealing with McClellan, he balanced John Hay's fears of a "McClellan conspiracy" against his own sense of the general's risk-averse character, and called the turn correctly. Despite the urgings of his staff, McClellan backed away from his plan to publicly oppose the Proclamation, and when faced with removal from command chose to obey orders rather than march on Washington. There would be no military coup, and the crisis of presidential authority was resolved.

From this experience Lincoln was both strengthened and schooled on how to deal with generals who thought control of war policy should be conceded to military professionals. During the winter of 1862–63, General Hooker, who was successfully politicking to replace Burnside as commander of the Army of the Potomac, blustered that the administration was adrift and the country needed a dictator to pull things together. Instead of ignoring such talk, as he had done with McClellan, Lincoln openly challenged Hooker: "I have heard, in such a way as to believe it, of your recently saying that both the Army and the Government needed a Dictator. Of course it was not *for* this, but in spite of it, that I have given you the command. Only those generals who gain successes, can set up dictators. What I now ask of you is military success, and I will risk the dictatorship."[7] Hooker was abashed, and never spoke in such terms again.

IN A STRICTLY MILITARY SENSE, McClellan's relief did serious, albeit temporary, harm to the Union cause. Even those in the army aware of his excessive caution and failure to seize opportunities appreciated his skill as an organizer and strategist. His army's movement by sea to the approaches of Richmond in April 1862 was a brilliant stroke, comparable to MacArthur's at Inchon—except that where MacArthur followed through by striking the enemy, McClellan hesitated and temporized until all his advantages were lost. Still, his operations in Maryland showed that he had some capacity to learn from experience. McClellan's performance in Maryland was an improvement over his campaign on the Peninsula. He acted with greater decision and combativeness than he had hitherto shown, although his handling of military intelligence was still incompetent, as were his battlefield tactics. The thoughtful Charles Francis Adams Jr., who had no sympathy for McClellan's politics, regretted McClellan's removal because "[w]e believed in him, not as a brilliant commander, but as a prudent one and one who was gradually learning how to handle our immense army, and now a new man must learn . . . by his own mistakes and in the blood of the army."[8]

McClellan's replacement, General Ambrose Burnside, would prove the validity of Adams's judgment by leading the army into a futile and unnecessary bloodbath at Fredericksburg, nearly destroying its morale and physical health by abysmal mismanagement. His errors, however, were purely military and entirely obvious, and his removal relatively prompt and politically unproblematic. In the last analysis, Burnside's blunders were less damaging to the Union war effort, and less dangerous to the political health of the republic, than McClellan's continual machinations.

McClellan's removal was unquestionably a political act, but also in the largest sense a strategic necessity. McClellan's incessant, incorrigible pursuit of power was the basis of a crippling internal division at the highest levels of strategy and policymaking, and also an implicit threat to the constitutional order. The case of Major Key was so damaging to McClellan because the "game" Key described was such a plausible explanation for McClellan's failure to even attempt the destruction of Lee's army when he had the chance. Historian Ethan Rafuse, whose study of McClellan's politics is both thorough and sympathetic, concludes that "the decisions that prevented McClellan from taking full advantage of the opportunity to destroy Lee's army, which his conduct of operations had created, were also the consequence of the fact that such an outcome, although desirable, was not critical to McClellan's strategic vision in September 1862. [He believed] it was enough that he had saved the North from the consequences of political folly and placed himself in position to carry out the next step in restoring the ascendancy of reason in the Union war effort." The ascendancy of reason of course required his own ascent to a dominant position within the administration.[9]

In the end, no amount of field experience could overcome the fundamental defect in McClellan's approach to war: his conviction that every operation had to contend not only with the enemy in front but with enemies in the rear. Every critical calculation he made in the field was calibrated not only for its effect on the Rebel army but for its possible impact on McClellan's quest for power in Washington. He considered Radicalism to be as dangerous to the preservation of the republic as a successful Southern secession. No military victory was worth winning if it redounded to the benefit of a Radical regime. That was why he both considered his defeat on the Peninsula "providential" and refused to renew the Battle of Antietam on September 18. He had already won victory enough to demonstrate his indispensability and advance his campaign against Lincoln's Radical advisers. Why risk that standing by attacking Lee's army, when a more decisive triumph would merely benefit a Radical administration? Better to see whether the work of his supporters in Washington succeeded in getting Stanton turned out, or the midterm elections produced a "conservative" triumph. No general who thought that way would ever defeat Robert E. Lee, whose concentration on military necessity was ruthless and uncompromised.

Whatever the balance between his virtues and defects as a field general, McClellan was an untrustworthy instrument of civil and military policy, especially for a democratic government in the midst of civil war, faced with revolutions both actual and potential. He persistently resisted or disobeyed his government's demands for consultation on strategy and operations, for truthful action reports, and for the execution of important orders and legal edicts. Through agents like Fitz-John Porter and others, he waged a political campaign aimed at undermining the authority of the president and secretary of war, his superiors in the constitutional chain of command. This was, as one historian has written, "at the least a violation of his soldier's duty under the articles of war and at worst an attempt at military usurpation."[10] He certainly tolerated, and probably encouraged, the loose talk about a countermarch on Washington that Burnside and Cox deemed treasonous. It was at his instigation that Fitz-John Porter wrote to the press, accusing Stanton of incompetence, official malfeasance, and actions akin to treason. Thus McClellan and Porter were guilty of violating Section One, Articles Five and Six of the Articles of War—the congressional act that defined military law from 1776 to 1920. Article Five states:

> Any officer or soldier who shall use contemptuous or disrespectful words against the President of the United States, against the Vice-President thereof, against Congress of the United States, or against the Chief Magistrate or Legislature of any of the United States, in which he may be quartered, if a commissioned officer, shall be cashiered, or otherwise be punished, as a courts-martial shall direct; if a non-commissioned officer or soldier, he shall suffer such punishment as shall be inflicted on him by the sentence of a court-martial.

McClellan's efforts to defame and discredit Generals Scott and Halleck, when they were general in chief, seems an obvious violation of Article Six, which states that "Any officer or soldier, who shall behave himself with contempt or disrespect toward his commanding officer, shall be punished, according to the nature of his offense, by the judgement of a court-martial." Porter *was* tried by court-martial, but not for the violations of which he was guilty; rather, for false charges of disobedience to General Pope, trumped up by Stanton as political revenge against the "McClellan clique."[11]

The conflict between Lincoln and McClellan was not simply about the forms and protocols of civil-military relations. They differed fundamentally on the purposes for which the war was to be fought, and on the strategy for fighting it. McClellan adhered to the principles and methods of the "conciliation" strategy that had prevailed at the start of the war. In the fall of 1862 he still hoped that a combination of rapid and symbolically significant victories by the North, coupled with the proffer of compromises designed to assure the protection of slavery where it existed, would induce Southerners to seek a negotiated settlement of the conflict. By the summer of 1862, Lincoln had become convinced that the South could not be conciliated and would not return to the Union until it had been thoroughly and unambiguously defeated, and its means of resistance destroyed. He also believed that a general emancipation of Confederate slaves was necessary, both as a means to defeating Southern armies and as a step toward the "ultimate extinction" of an institution that was incompatible with democracy and national unity. He therefore embraced a strategy that made a compromise peace virtually impossible.

Before considering the virtues and weaknesses of Lincoln's strategy, we need to ask whether McClellan's offered a viable alternative. The answer is almost certainly that it did not. It is barely possible that if McClellan had won a decisive victory and captured Richmond in June 1862, some Confederate leaders—though never Jefferson Davis—might have been open to negotiating for peace with a conciliatory Union government. However, it is far more likely that the struggle would have continued. The Confederacy would still have had large armies in the field and an as yet untapped reserve of military manpower. The loss of Richmond would have been a blow to Confederate morale, to armaments production, and to international prestige; but the South would suffer greater losses over the next three years and remain committed to the struggle for independence. There is no evidence whatever that in the fall and winter of 1862 any considerable body of Southern opinion was open to the kind of settlement McClellan and the "conservatives" contemplated. President Davis, the Confederate Congress, Southern governors and generals might disagree about the military policies of their government, but they remained unanimous in their support of the struggle for independence. That support would not even begin to crack until 1864, in the face of massive military defeats and the Federal invasion of the deep South; and even then, the Southern "Peace" movement remained marginal. It is hard to imagine the South, in 1862, accepting a return to the Union on terms that did not grant the South some special form of autonomy or leave open the question whether they might secede in the future; it is impossible to imagine Northerners accepting such a compromise, unless *they* had suffered a decisive and irretrievable military defeat. Though McClellan sincerely maintained that his purpose was to restore the Union as it was, his program could not have succeeded. If there had ever been a chance that the Civil War could be ended by compromise, which is doubtful, by the summer of 1862 that chance was long gone.

Lincoln believed the Emancipation Proclamation was the act by which history would judge him and his administration, and as a matter of moral principle he was content that that be so. However, in its original context, the Emancipation Proclamation was justified as a "war measure,"

and its effectiveness must first be judged by considering its strategic consequences: its effect on military operations, and on the political will of
Unionists to fight a much longer war; and its effect on the Confederacy's
morale and material strength, and its prospects for foreign intervention.

The Proclamation was initially greeted with a wave of approval in
Northern newspapers across much of the political spectrum. However,
as Lincoln told Vice President Hamlin, "while commendation in newspapers and by distinguished individuals is all that a vain man could wish,
the stocks have declined, and troops come forward more slowly than
ever. . . . The North responds to the proclamation sufficiently in breath;
but breath alone kills no rebels." Lincoln expected a backlash at the polls
and in the press from Democrats, and from Border State politicians in
both parties—and was not disappointed. It is worth noting that Lincoln
could have evaded the political costs of this backlash by withholding the
Proclamation till after the election. That he did not do so gives the lie
to McClellan's accusation of "despotism." By issuing the Proclamation
in September, Lincoln enabled voters to express their opposition at the
polls. That opposition was serious, but Lincoln's party was able to hold
its majorities in the House and Senate and retain critical governorships.
It is not clear to what extent the midterm revival of the Democratic Party
represented a reaction against the Emancipation Proclamation, a general disapproval of the administration's conduct of the war, or merely the
usual reversion of voters to normal party affiliations in a nonpresidential
canvass. In any case, the outcome did not seriously weaken Lincoln's
ability to control the course of policy.[12]

In the longer term, by promising to eliminate slavery the Proclamation exposed the underlying problem of race in America—the contradiction between a political state based on the presumption of civic equality
and a culture deeply imbued with the values of White supremacy. The
Democratic opposition would exploit this contradiction, decrying with
increasing vehemence the transformation of a war for the Union into an
abolitionist crusade. The influence of the Copperhead faction within the
Democratic Party would increase, until by the summer of 1864 it would
be in position to write the platform on which General McClellan would
oppose Lincoln for the presidency. McClellan would reject the platform
plank that called for an armistice as prelude to peace negotiations, on
the grounds that this would amount to unilateral abandonment of the

struggle. He nevertheless accepted those planks that called for rescinding the Proclamation, and a peace settlement that would preserve slavery. The 1864 canvass would be nicknamed the "Miscegenation Election" because of the virulence of the Democratic attack on Lincoln's supposed espousal of "nigger equality." The strength of the racialist reaction provoked by the Proclamation may be indicated by the 40 percent of the popular vote that went to McClellan, despite the military victories that promised an early and successful end to the conflict. Yet in the last analysis, fear of "nigger equality" did not substantially weaken the Union war effort or deprive Lincoln of the public support he needed to maintain the conflict; while the Emancipation Proclamation, with crippling effect, split the South along its main fault lines, the color line between slave and free and the class line between planter and farmer.[13]

The Proclamation's effect on the diplomatic front has been exaggerated. It did not deter the British and French governments from continuing to actively consider diplomatic interventions favorable to the Confederacy. The prevalence of antislavery sentiment among various elements of the British and French public played a minor role in government decision making. Liberal opinion in both countries already favored the Union, and the proclamation merely added an element of moral authority to their polemics. But within both countries there was also a strong base of political and even popular support for the Confederacy, and considerable opposition to the Emancipation Proclamation on racial grounds. Russell and Palmerston, and the pro-Southern press, condemned it as a call for "servile insurrection," and stirred the public against the measure by invoking memories of the Sepoy Mutiny of 1857, with its attendant horrors of racial rape and massacre.

What ultimately prevented the British and French from intervening was their fear of becoming embroiled in an American war at a moment when European war seemed quite possible, and while French resources were being committed to the project of turning Mexico into an imperial client state. It was Lee's defeat at Antietam and the failure of anti-administration forces to win a substantial victory at the polls, not the Emancipation Proclamation, that led the British ministry to abandon its plan to intervene in September 1862. The British continued to support the Confederacy by encouraging bankers to lend it money, hiring blockade-runners to carry its trade, and building warships for the

Confederate navy, which attacked and destroyed American merchant and whaling ships on every ocean. The Palmerston government's self-serving decision to stay out of the conflict did not become definitive until September 1863—following major Union triumphs at Vicksburg and Gettysburg—when Lord Russell intervened to prevent the sale of two armored warships to the Confederacy. If the North had lost those battles or if McClellan had won the 1864 election, the Proclamation would not have deterred recognition of the Confederacy by the British and French.[14]

The Proclamation did contribute substantially to the Union's military victory. It undermined the Southern economy and social order by drawing large numbers of slaves away from their plantations. It also contributed directly to Union military strength by allowing the recruitment of Black men into the army and navy. African Americans finally had a concrete political and economic interest in the preservation of the Union. Black leaders and communities in the North, who had been politically marginalized during the first two years of war, became increasingly important elements in the making of war policy. In the South, slaves were assured that a victory for the Union would at least put an end to their enslavement, where a conciliatory peace would have perpetuated slavery under Unionist auspices. They therefore gave trust, loyalty, and service to Federal invaders. While the Proclamation abjured "servile insurrection," and Federal agents made no overt attempts to foment one, its effect was to produce a slow-motion slave insurrection on the largest scale—masses of slaves leaving their home plantations to seek freedom within Union army lines. By detaching slaves from masters, the Proclamation undermined and eventually destroyed the South's system of production.[15]

As McClellan and other conservatives predicted, the Proclamation did intensify Southerners' commitment to the cause of independence, because it threatened both the property interest in slaves and the social interest in preserving White supremacy. However, it also exacerbated the conflict of interests between large planters and small farmers. The planting interest was preponderant in Confederate politics, and planters sought to protect plantation discipline by sponsoring laws that exempted owners and their overseers from the draft—the so-called Twenty Negro

Law. The exemption was resented by nonslaveholding farmers, who were drafted to fight a war for "other men's Negroes," leaving their own farms to be weakly tended by wives, minor children, and aged parents. As Northern armies advanced and slaves availed themselves of the Proclamation's promise of freedom, poorer Whites found themselves torn between their obligation of military service and their wish to go home and protect their families—a contributing cause of the rising rates of desertion that debilitated Southern armies in 1864–65. Nevertheless, until the end of the war President Davis and other Confederate leaders were able to thwart movements for peace or reunion by playing the race card, identifying the Union with "nigger equality" and the Confederacy with the defense of White supremacy.[16]

The most substantial military effect of the Proclamation was its enabling of Black military enlistments. During the last two years of the conflict, nearly 180,000 African Americans served in the Union army—most of them drawn from the Confederate states. In the last year of fighting more than 10 percent of the troops in Federal uniform were Black; and they entered service at a time when White enlistments were falling off. Their contribution to the Union's military manpower was decisive: it is difficult to see how the war could have been won without their addition to the armed forces. Although excluded from the army with which Sherman marched through Georgia, they provided several combat divisions for the Armies of the Potomac, the James, and the Cumberland. They also provided the garrisons required to defend the extended supply lines of advancing armies, and made it possible to control large swathes of territory in Mississippi and Alabama and along the coasts of South Carolina and Florida. The enlistment of Blacks may also have contributed to the notable lack of that "servile insurrection" feared by conservatives by channeling the militancy and anger of former slaves into military service.[17]

The military enlistment clause of the Proclamation also gave a limited but highly significant impetus to the movement for extending full civil rights across the color line. By authorizing enlistment in the national army, the Proclamation conferred a fundamental civil right, an attribute of citizenship from which Blacks had long been excluded even in the free states; and it did so by fiat of the national government. The difference it made was significant and potentially transformative. It created, armed, and empowered a new consciousness among African Americans. Frederick Douglass said it best: "Once let the black man get upon his person the brass letters, U.S., let him get an eagle on his button, and a musket on his shoulder and bullets in his pockets, and there is no power on earth which can deny that he has earned the right to citizenship in the United States."[18]

The change also affected racial politics at the highest level. Before, the Civil War had been essentially a White man's war, and Lincoln, as Frederick Douglass said, exclusively a White man's president. Now Black Americans owned a share of the war, and because of that the president would have to concern himself with their interests and even their opinions. African American political leaders like Frederick Douglass, who had been ignored or treated dismissively by the administration, now became vital and influential members of the Unionist coalition. The change can be measured by the difference between Lincoln's speech to African American leaders on September 14, 1862, and a letter he wrote on August 26, 1863. In 1862 he had urged Black leaders to accept colonization outside the United States, on the grounds that the "physical difference" between the races made it impossible for Blacks to live in the same country without detriment to both races. Less than a year later he would contrast the patriotism of Black soldiers with the carping criticism and implied disloyalty of his White opposition. "You say you will not fight to free negroes. Some of them seem willing to fight for you," and when victory finally comes, "there will be some black men who can remember that, with silent tongue, and clenched teeth, and steady eye, and well-poised bayonet, they have helped mankind on to this great consummation; while, I fear, there will be some white ones, unable to forget that, with malignant heart, and deceitful speech, they have strove to hinder it. . . . But negroes, like other people, act upon motives. . . . If they stake their lives for us, they must be prompted by the strongest motive—even the promise of freedom. And the promise being made, must be kept."[19]

In the long perspective of national history, the Proclamation marks a revolutionary turn in the pervasive struggle between America's democratic ideology and the culture of White supremacy, although, as the historian Eric Foner has shown, the revolution it inaugurated would be left "unfinished" when Reconstruction ended in 1880. While the Proclamation did make the destruction of slavery a war aim equivalent to restoration of the Union, and pointed the way toward its abolition by constitutional amendment, neither the Proclamation nor the Thirteenth, Fourteenth, and Fifteenth Amendments were able to turn America into a multiracial democracy or prevent the failure of Reconstruction and the eventual imposition of Jim Crow laws throughout the former Confederacy. Even in the former free states, to which Blacks were now free to migrate, the acquisition of civil rights was a slow and painful process. The blood price of the Civil War, the 620,000 dead soldiers and uncounted "collateral damage," ought to have purchased more justice than that.

Nevertheless, the Emancipation Proclamation did make Union victory more likely, and it linked that victory to a program that would inevitably abolish an institution that had been an integral part of American society for 240 years. The restoration of the Union would be attended with a transformation of Southern society that was profound and revolutionary, even though it did not make the South into a biracial democracy. Even the limited rights and political power achieved by Southern Blacks altered in fundamental ways the social forms and the psychology of race relations in the region.

Some of those transforming effects were felt beyond the South. The "slavery question" had been one of the central problems of American politics from the founding of the republic, and since 1820 it had been the dominant theme of political controversy. But the moral, social, and economic complexities of the South's "peculiar institution" had partly obscured the deeper underlying question of race: large masses of people hated slavery on moral grounds, or resented the economic and social privilege of planters, while still despising Black people and wishing to exclude them from civil life. By abolishing slavery, Lincoln's Proclamation, and the constitutional amendments that followed from it, stripped away the questions peculiar to chattel slavery and exposed the more fundamental issue of race. For the next century and more, Americans would have to grapple with the contradiction between the values and principles of democracy, on the one hand, and their belief in White supremacy, on the other.

———

ULTIMATELY, THEN, THE Emancipation Proclamation and the strategic program that went with it would lead to Union victory. But only with the benefit of hindsight does Antietam mark the turning point of the Civil War. The Proclamation's military benefits would not be felt for many months, its political effect was problematic, and its influence on diplomacy helpful but not decisive.

After the crises of the summer—after the Confederate offensives were checked at Antietam, Corinth, and Perryville; after emancipation was proclaimed and habeas corpus suspended; after the fall elections ended without a complete reversal of Lincoln's political fortunes—after all that. nothing was really settled. All that had been accomplished by the Battle of Antietam and the Emancipation Proclamation was to explode the illusions and the hope of compromise that had hitherto limited the violence and social disruption of the conflict, and push the Civil War past the point of no return. The crucial battles were still to be fought, and the ultimate result was still very much in doubt.

CHRONOLOGY

FROM THE PENINSULA CAMPAIGN TO ANTIETAM

APRIL 1–NOVEMBER 7, 1862

APRIL 1. In Virginia, McClellan begins shipping the Army of the Potomac from Washington to Fort Monroe on the Peninsula, between the York and James rivers. From there he plans to advance and capture the Confederate capital, Richmond. In western Tennessee, a Union army commanded by Gen. Grant holds an advanced position at Pittsburg Landing after its successful offensive against Forts Henry and Donelson. Another Union force, under Gen. Buell, is marching down from Nashville to join Grant.

APRIL 2. Gen. A. S. Johnston, commanding Confederate forces in northern Mississippi, concentrates his forces for a surprise attack on Grant.

APRIL 3. President Lincoln is upset by the discovery that McClellan has left fewer than twenty thousand troops to defend Washington. He refuses to allow McDowell's Corps to leave for the Peninsula, which upsets McClellan. The Senate abolishes slavery in the District of Columbia, a sign that pressure for antislavery action is rising.

APRIL 4. On the Peninsula, McClellan advances slowly against Rebel lines at Yorktown. In Tennessee, Johnston's Rebel army is moving to attack Grant.

APRIL 5. McClellan decides he can only take Yorktown by a regular siege, although he heavily outnumbers the defenders.

APRIL 6. Siege of Yorktown continues. The main Rebel army in Virginia, led by Gen. Joseph Johnston, begins to move south to reinforce Richmond and Yorktown. In Tennessee, Gen. A. S. Johnston's army attacks Grant's camps around the little Shiloh Church. The Rebels drive the Federals into the river, but Grant rallies his men and they hold on.

APRIL 7. Siege of Yorktown continues. In Tennessee, Buell joins forces with Grant and they drive the Rebel army from the field. The Battle of Shiloh is the bloodiest so far: 13,000 Federal and 10,900 Southern casualties.

APRIL 9. Siege of Yorktown continues. At President Davis's request, Confederate Senate orders the conscription of White males, which troubles states' rights fundamentalists.

APRIL 10. Siege of Yorktown continues. President Lincoln approves a joint congressional resolution calling for the gradual and compensated emancipation of slaves.

APRIL 11. Siege of Yorktown continues. Gen. Halleck arrives at Pittsburg Landing, Tennessee, to take command of the armies of Grant and Buell.

APRIL 12-28. Siege of Yorktown continues. Halleck takes his time getting organized before moving against the Confederate army now concentrated in Corinth, Mississippi, thirty miles from the Shiloh battlefield.

APRIL 29. Siege of Yorktown continues. Halleck begins his slow advance to Corinth, making not much more than a mile a day.

APRIL 30-MAY 2. Siege of Yorktown continues. Halleck's advance plods on.

MAY 3. Confederate troops evacuate Yorktown, before McClellan can attack and overwhelm them. But they have delayed the Federal advance for a month.

MAY 4. McClellan's troops enter Yorktown and pursue retreating Confederates.

MAY 5. McClellan's troops defeat an outnumbered Confederate rear guard at Williamsburg. In the west, Halleck's army plods on.

MAY 6. McClellan occupies Williamsburg. Away to the north and west, in the Shenandoah Valley, Stonewall Jackson is about to begin his Valley campaign, which will seem to threaten Washington—and thereby drive a wedge between McClellan, who wanted McDowell's Corps on the Peninsula, and Lincoln, who wanted it to fend off Jackson.

MAY 8. Jackson wins a skirmish at the town of McDowell, Virginia. Halleck's army is almost at Corinth.

MAY 9-22. On the Peninsula, the Confederate army retreats and forms a defensive position behind the Chickahominy River, fewer than ten miles from Richmond. McClellan follows up the retreat without much aggression. In the Valley, Jackson outmaneuvers Federal forces under Banks and sets them up for the kill. Halleck lays "siege" to Corinth.

MAY 23-24. Jackson captures Front Royal, Virginia, cutting Banks's supply line and forcing him into hasty retreat. Lincoln and Stanton order their scattered forces in northern Virginia to close on Jackson, who moves with greater speed and cunning.

MAY 25-29. Jackson routs Banks's force at Winchester and advances toward Harpers Ferry. Until his threat is eliminated, McClellan will get no more reinforcements. Since he outnumbers the Confederate force at Richmond by almost two to one, he doesn't need reinforcement—but McClellan refuses to believe it.

MAY 30. In the west, the Confederate army—outnumbered more than two to one by Halleck's force—abandons Corinth. In Virginia, most of McClellan's army crosses the Chickahominy River and advances toward Richmond.

MAY 31-JUNE 1. The Confederate army led by Gen. Joseph Johnston attacks McClellan's advance units. In the Battle of Seven Pines the Confederates are defeated. Johnston is wounded and replaced by Gen. Robert E. Lee. McClellan does not follow up his success. He postpones an attack on Richmond pending the arrival of reinforcements and leaves his army in a vulnerable position, with only V Corps north of the Chickahominy to protect his supply line.

JUNE 2-7. In the Valley, Jackson's Rebel force escapes from Union forces converging from three different directions.

JUNE 8. Jackson defeats two separate Union forces on the same day, in battles at Cross Keys and Port Republic, Virginia.

JUNE 10. The army commanded by Gen. Buell begins its eastward trek from Corinth, Mississippi—its objective is Chattanooga, Tennessee, some three hundred miles east.

JUNE 12–15. At Richmond, Rebel cavalry leader J. E. B. Stuart begins a reconnaissance/raid that will completely circle McClellan's army.

JUNE 17. Gen. Lee plans to concentrate Confederate forces for a daring attack on McClellan. He orders Jackson's force to leave the Valley and join him at Richmond. In the west, Gen. Braxton Bragg assumes command of the army opposing Halleck in northern Mississippi.

JUNE 19. Lincoln signs into law a bill prohibiting slavery in the western territories administered by the Federal government.

JUNE 21. Confederate President Davis outlines his strategic thinking in a letter to his wife: Lee must defeat McClellan in Virginia, and there must be a counteroffensive in the west to recover Tennessee.

JUNE 23. Lee confers with his generals and lays out the plan for his attack on McClellan. With a third of his force, he will hold the lines south of the Chickahominy against the bulk of McClellan's troops. Two-thirds of his army, including Jackson's force, will concentrate against and destroy the single Union corps north of the Chickahominy, breaking McClellan's supply line and forcing him to retreat.

JUNE 24. McClellan remains passive while Lee's troops move into attacking position.

JUNE 25. The Seven Days Battles begin with a halfhearted Federal attack at Oak Hill south of the Chickahominy.

JUNE 26. Lee's offensive begins with an attack on the Union V Corps at Mechanicsville, north of the Chickahominy. But the attack is poorly coordinated, and the Union troops withdraw in good order. In Washington, Lincoln appoints Gen. John Pope to command the Union forces in northern Virginia.

JUNE 27. Lee's offensive continues with an all-out attack on V Corps at Gaines' Mill. The Union lines are broken after hard fighting, but poor coordination again allows the Federals to escape destruction. But V Corps has to retreat south of the Chickahominy; McClellan's supply line is cut, and he decides that the army will have to retreat through the swamps to a new base of operations on the James River. In northern Virginia, Pope took up his new command.

JUNE 28. McClellan's army begins its retreat. McClellan sends a distraught telegram to Washington, accusing Lincoln and Stanton of having "done your best to sacrifice this army." Lincoln is unruffled by the crisis and the accusation. He tells McClellan to save the army and assures him of support. He also prepares to issue a call for three hundred thousand new volunteers—the first step in a drastic revision of Union strategy.

JUNE 29. Lee shifts forces south of the Chickahominy to pursue McClellan and try to cut into and destroy his retreating columns. At Savage's Station, Union rear guards repel the Southern attack.

JUNE 30. Lee mounts a heavy assault against Federal troops at Glendale. McClellan leaves his army before the battle, ostensibly to look for a final defensive position, and he fails to appoint anyone to command in his stead. The Union army repels the attack, despite the absence of a commanding general.

JULY 1. Union troops take up a strong position on Malvern Hill. Lee makes a last attempt to destroy McClellan's army but suffers a bloody defeat. Although his field commanders urge McClellan to counterattack, McClellan orders the retreat to continue. The Seven Days Battles have cost the Union more than fifteen thousand casualties and huge amounts of equipment. The Confederates have lost about twenty thousand.

JULY 2. McClellan's army fortifies its new base, at Harrison's Landing on the James River. News of his defeat begins to appear in the north, creating public alarm. Republican papers blame McClellan for the defeat; Democratic papers blame Lincoln and Stanton.

JULY 6. Buell's army is at Decatur, Alabama, a little more than halfway to Chattanooga.

JULY 8. Lincoln arrives at Harrison's Landing to confer with McClellan. Instead of responding to the president's request for a renewal of the offensive, McClellan hands him the "Harrison's Landing letter": a political manifesto urging Lincoln to abjure all thoughts of emancipation, adopt a "conservative" approach to policy in general, and put control of military affairs in McClellan's hands. Lincoln says nothing, but McClellan's power play seems to crystallize his thinking about a new strategic direction.

JULY 10. Lincoln returns to Washington. In northern Virginia, Pope issues his controversial orders threatening punishment to civilians who cooperate with Rebel forces.

JULY 11. Lincoln's first step toward a new strategy: he orders Gen. Halleck to Washington to assume the post of general in chief, which McClellan had coveted.

JULY 12. In a private conversation with Secretaries Seward and Welles, Lincoln reveals his intention to issue an emancipation proclamation. He thereby rejected McClellan's core demand and prepared to commit the nation to a new strategy: one that abandoned hope of a compromise peace and resolved on total war.

JULY 13. In Richmond, Lee faces a double threat: from McClellan's eighty-five thousand at Harrison's Landing and from Pope's Army of Virginia (forty-five thousand) moving down from northern Virginia. He sends Jackson, with twenty-five thousand men, to check Pope. Generals Bragg and Kirby Smith, commanding the two main armies in the Confederate west, propose a plan for a two-pronged invasion of Tennessee and Kentucky, which will force Buell's army to retreat and perhaps recover both states for the Confederacy. Davis approves the plan. It is the first step in developing a grand counter-offensive, involving Lee's army in Virginia, Bragg's and Smith's in Tennessee/Kentucky, and an army led by Gen. Van Dorn in northern Mississippi.

JULY 14. Pope issues a bombastic order, implicitly critical of McClellan. The latter now regards Pope as a tool of the Radical Republicans, and a personal enemy. In Washington, Lincoln asks Congress to approve compensation for any state deciding to emancipate the slaves within its borders.

JULY 17. Congress passes the Second Confiscation Act, which allows seizure of Rebel property, including slaves—who would be emancipated. It also authorizes the president to colonize freed Blacks outside the United States. Lincoln signs the bill, after forcing Congress to soften some of its terms.

JULY 22. Lincoln surprises his cabinet by presenting a preliminary draft of the Emancipation Proclamation. He accepts Seward's advice to delay issuance until the Union has won a battlefield victory.

JULY 23. In Washington, Gen. Halleck assumes the post of general in chief. His first task is to visit McClellan and induce him to take the offensive. If McClellan refuses, Halleck is empowered to relieve him. In the west, Bragg's army begins movement, by road, train, and steamboat, from Tupelo to Chattanooga—the jump-off point for its invasion of Tennessee. Meanwhile Kirby Smith assembles a force of about nineteen thousand for his part of the invasion plan. But action on the Virginia front is suspended: Lee cannot take the offensive against Pope as long as McClellan remains at Harrison's Landing, threatening Richmond.

JULY 25–27. Halleck visits Harrison's Landing, accompanied by Gen. Burnside, and confers with McClellan. Halleck offers McClellan a choice: advance against Richmond, or withdraw his forces from the Peninsula and ship them north to join with Pope. McClellan's opposition to the Lincoln government intensifies. He is gratified to receive "letters from the North urging me to march on Washington & assume the Govt!!" Burnside reports antigovernment sentiments among McClellan's officers that seem downright treasonous.

JULY 31. Confederate President Davis responds to Pope's "infamous" confiscation orders by proposing to treat Pope's officers as "felons."

AUGUST 2. Pope's army advances against Jackson's command near Orange Court House, some eighty miles northwest of Richmond.

AUGUST 3. McClellan has refused to resume the offensive. Halleck therefore orders him to begin shipping his troops north. McClellan protests.

AUGUST 9. In northern Virginia, Jackson's Confederates attack part of Pope's army at Cedar Mountain. Although Jackson wins, the threat of an advance by Pope puts the defense of Richmond in peril.

AUGUST 13. Lee decides to risk the safety of Richmond by shifting most of his army north to strike Pope. Unknown to Lee, McClellan has issued orders to begin the withdrawal from the Peninsula.

AUGUST 14. Clear signs that McClellan is withdrawing allow Lee to turn against Pope with his whole force. Lincoln meets with a delegation of free Negroes. In one of his least creditable performances, he urges them to support colonization and does not mention his plan to issue an emancipation proclamation. In eastern Tennessee, Kirby Smith's Rebel army strikes through Cumberland Gap to begin its invasion of Kentucky. The Confederate grand offensive has begun.

AUGUST 17–19. Menaced by Lee's army, Pope retreats behind the Rappahannock River. Horace Greeley publishes an editorial, "The Prayer of Twenty Millions," demanding emancipation. McClellan and his partisans in the press conduct a campaign against both Secretary of War Stanton and Gen. Pope—McClellan gleefully anticipates the latter's defeat.

AUGUST 21. Bragg's army reaches Chattanooga and prepares to join the offensive already begun by Kirby Smith.

AUGUST 22. Lincoln answers Greeley's appeal, saying that his primary object is to save the Union, and whatever he does or does not do about slavery must serve that goal. Lee's troops skirmish with Pope's along the Rappahannock, while McClellan comes north with the last of his troops, the VI and II Corps.

AUGUST 24. Lee adopts a bold plan to destroy Pope's army. Jackson, with half Lee's infantry and the cavalry, swings wide to the west behind the screen of Bull Run Mountain. He is to go around Pope's flank, come in behind the Union army, and seize Pope's supply base at Manassas Junction. The plan is for Longstreet and Lee to follow Jackson and strike Pope as he retreats.

AUGUST 25. Jackson marches north while Lee holds Pope in place along the Rappahannock.

AUGUST 26. Confederate cavalry strike through Bull Run Gap and capture the rail junction at Manassas, cutting communication between Pope and his base, Alexandria, Virginia. The Federal VI Corps, from McClellan's army, lands at Alexandria; II Corps is boarding ships at Fort Monroe.

AUGUST 27. Jackson's entire corps, twenty-five thousand strong, storm into Manassas and capture Pope's supply depot. Pope sees both peril and opportunity: Jackson has cut his communication with Washington; but Jackson is also isolated. Pope orders his troops back to Manassas to overwhelm Jackson before Lee can come to his aid. Meanwhile Lee, with Longstreet's Corps, begins to march north following Jackson's route. In Washington, Halleck admits he is overwhelmed by his tasks and begs McClellan to order Franklin to go to Pope's aid. McClellan demurs: the "great object" was not to aid Pope but to protect Washington. Franklin stays put.

AUGUST 28. In Tennessee, Bragg's army begins its offensive against Buell's army. In Virginia, Jackson withdraws from Manassas and takes a defensive position in the hills west of the town to await Lee. Pope's scouts search for Jackson in vain. Jackson has to draw attention to himself by attacking a small Union force at Groveton—he wants to distract Pope and keep him from blocking Lee's advance through the mountain gaps. In Washington, McClellan informs Halleck that Franklin can't move until he has more artillery. When Halleck becomes testy, McClellan promises that Franklin will march at 6:00 AM.

AUGUST 29. Second Battle of Bull Run begins with Pope's troops attacking Jackson to no avail. Meanwhile Lee and Longstreet evade Federal notice and take position threatening Pope's left flank. In Washington, McClellan orders Franklin to advance: "Let it not be said that any part of the Army of the Potomac failed in its duty to General Pope." Franklin goes seven miles, then halts.

AUGUST 30. Second Battle of Bull Run ends in Confederate victory, as Longstreet's flank attack routs Pope's army. As promised, Franklin marches for Manassas in the morning, but gets no farther than Centreville, some seven miles from the fighting. Out west in Kentucky, Kirby Smith defeats a hastily assembled Federal force at Richmond.

AUGUST 31. Pope's disorganized army rests at Centerville on the Washington side of Bull Run Creek and is reinforced by VI Corps. Lee plans to complete their destruction by sending Jackson and Stuart to cross the creek upstream and strike the Federal flank.

SEPT. 1. Jackson's flank attack is repelled in the Battle of Chantilly. Pope's army begins retreating to Washington.

SEPT. 2. Lincoln reappoints McClellan to command the Federal forces around Washington, over the strenuous objections of his cabinet. Despite his own belief that McClellan deliberately allowed Pope to be defeated, and his mistrust of McClellan's willingness to fight, he believes McClellan is the only man who can reorganize the Army of the Potomac.

SEPT. 3. Lee decides to continue his offensive by invading Maryland. He moves his army to Leesburg, Virginia, and reorganizes it for the offensive.

SEPT. 4. Lee's cavalry begins fording the Potomac River to screen the main army's advance on Frederick, Maryland.

SEPT. 5. McClellan assumes command of the field army to oppose Lee's invasion. In the west, Gov. Morton of Indiana and other civilian leaders called up militia to counter Kirby-Smith's invading force.

Bragg's army reaches Sparta, Tennessee. The invading column has outflanked Buell's army, which will have to abandon its drive on Chattanooga and march north to confront Bragg.

SEPT. 6. Stonewall Jackson's infantry corps occupies Frederick. Longstreet's Corps crosses the Potomac to join them.

SEPT. 7. Confederate forces are concentrated in and around Frederick, hoping to lure the Federal army into combat before it has fully recovered from Second Bull Run. McClellan tentatively advances toward Frederick, but positions his troops for the defense of Washington. In Tennessee, Bragg bypasses the Federal forces in Nashville and heads for Kentucky. Davis sends Bragg and Lee the text of a proclamation to the people of Kentucky and Maryland, appealing to them to join the Confederacy.

SEPT. 8. Lee is disappointed with Marylanders' response to his invasion. He also learns that the Federal garrison is holding on to Harpers Ferry, at the northern end of the Shenandoah Valley, blocking the route by which Lee expects to draw supplies.

SEPT. 9. Lee decides to withdraw westward from Frederick, and to divide his army into three detachments: one led by Gen. Jackson and Gen. McLaws to envelop Harpers Ferry from the west and north, another led by Gen. Walker to attack the town from the southeast, and the third under Longstreet to seize Boonsboro and Hagerstown as a base of future operations. A copy of his order is dropped and lost in a field near Frederick.

SEPT. 10. The three Confederate columns begin their long marches, abandoning Frederick. McClellan learns of their retreat and cautiously advances.

SEPT. 11. Lee and Longstreet's column seizes Hagerstown. Jackson, McLaws, and Walker continue their march, but Jackson has to march farther upstream before he can cross the Potomac. Lee's timetable for seizing Harpers Ferry is badly behind schedule. Col. Thomas Key tells a *Tribune* reporter that members of McClellan's staff have been contemplating a seizure of the government. This leak is part of an intensified campaign to force Lincoln to fire Stanton and give McClellan control of war policy. In England, the British government makes plans to intervene in the American war, if Lee's invasion succeeds.

SEPT. 12. McClellan's advance elements reoccupy Frederick. The detachments of Walker and McLaws are just approaching their objectives, the heights overlooking Harpers Ferry from northeast and southeast; Jackson is slowly closing in from the north and west.

SEPT. 13. Federal troops concentrate in and around Frederick. Two infantrymen find a copy of Lee's "lost order," and McClellan learns that the elements of Lee's army are widely separated. If he moves fast he can defeat each element in detail or at least compel Lee to retreat. He orders Gen. Franklin with VI Corps to march at dawn, cross the mountains at Crampton's Gap, and relieve Harpers Ferry. With the rest of the army, McClellan will cross the mountains at Turner's Gap to attack the detachment under Lee and Longstreet at Boonsboro. Lee learns of McClellan's discovery that night and plans to resist the Federal advance. But he is out of touch with the forces sent against Harpers Ferry—which are finally in position to attack the Federal garrison.

SEPT. 14. Action on three fronts in Maryland: the forces under Jackson, McLaws, and Walker begin the attack on Harpers Ferry, and by nightfall the garrison commander (Col. Miles) is convinced he will have to surrender. Meanwhile, Franklin's relief column, after a slow approach march, fights its way through Crampton's Gap—then halts. To the north, McClellan's column inflicts a severe defeat on the Confederate forces holding Turner's Gap. As the Rebel troops withdraw, Lee makes plans to abandon the invasion and retreat to Virginia. In Kentucky, Kirby Smith's column threatens Cincinnati, while Bragg's army threatens the Federal post of Munfordville, Kentucky.

SEPT. 15. Harpers Ferry surrenders. Lee now decides to stand and fight in a strong position around the town of Sharpsburg, Maryland, west of Antietam Creek. He orders Jackson to complete his work at Harpers Ferry and send his units to Sharpsburg posthaste. McClellan's troops file down through the mountains and begin to take positions east of Antietam Creek.

SEPT. 16. Lee and McClellan slowly assemble their forces. McClellan is unaware that he substantially outnumbers Lee, so he postpones an attack until the rest of his army comes up. In Kentucky, Bragg's advance guard attacks the Federal garrison at Munfordville and is repulsed.

SEPT. 17. The Battle of Antietam is fought. McClellan stages a series of separate, uncoordinated assaults. Lee's army, outnumbered two to one, is able to shift reserves to barely check each assault. Disaster is only averted late in the day, when A. P. Hill's Light Division—the last units to arrive from Harpers Ferry—routs the IX Corps with a flank attack. In the bloodiest single day of Civil War combat, McClellan loses 12,500 men and Lee 13,700—nearly a third of his force. In Kentucky, Bragg's army surrounds Munfordville and forces its surrender.

SEPT. 18. Lee holds his ground despite his heavy losses, and McClellan refuses to renew the attack despite receiving reinforcements. But the invasion of Maryland has failed, and that night Lee's army begins its retreat to Virginia. In Kentucky, Bragg's army holds Munfordville and prepares to fight Buell's army, which is approaching from the south.

SEPT. 19. McClellan's troops follow up Lee's retreat, and some units cross the Potomac at Shepherdstown to harass the Confederate rear guard. In northern Mississippi, a Confederate force under Gen. Price attacks Federal troops at Iuka to prevent the sending of reinforcements to Buell.

SEPT. 20. McClellan sends two divisions across the Potomac, but they are driven back by A. P. Hill's Division. He makes no further attempt to pursue the defeated Rebels. In Washington, Lincoln drafts the Preliminary Emancipation Proclamation.

SEPT. 21. In Kentucky, Bragg inexplicably abandons Munfordville and marches northeast to join forces with Kirby Smith at Bardstown, Kentucky. Buell's army is able to march to Louisville, where reinforcements await.

SEPT. 22. Lincoln issues the Preliminary Emancipation Proclamation, committing the nation to a new policy linking restoration of the Union to the destruction of slavery. The act marks his final repudiation of McClellan's policies and requires a new strategy of total war, which McClellan is unwilling and unable to execute.

SEPT. 24. To give effect to his new "hard war" policy, Lincoln suspends the privilege of habeas corpus and orders military trials for those who aid the Rebels by discouraging enlistments and other acts of disloyalty. McClellan receives news of the two decrees and considers how to oppose or resist them.

SEPT. 25. In Kentucky, Buell's army arrives in Louisville, bypassing Bragg's force at Bardstown.

SEPT. 26. McClellan writes to one of his political mentors, expressing his wish to oppose Lincoln's "despotic" decrees and asking the advice and support of Democratic Party leaders.

SEPT. 27. In Richmond, the Confederate Congress passes the Second Conscription Act, drafting men thirty-five to forty-five years old—a sign of the South's depleted manpower. In Washington, Lincoln confronts Maj. John Key for asserting that McClellan's officers are conspiring to prolong Confederate resistance in order to make peace on Southern terms. Key is cashiered as an example to deter "the McClellan conspiracy."

OCT. 1-2. Lincoln visits McClellan at his encampment near Sharpsburg to urge him to take the offensive and assess the state of the army. His suspicions are reflected in the remark that the Army of the Potomac is merely "McClellan's bodyguard."

OCT. 3. In Mississippi, the Confederate army commanded by Gen. Van Dorn attacks the Union force at Corinth—the westernmost prong of the Confederate grand offensive.

OCT. 4. The Battle of Corinth ends in Confederate defeat, with 2,500 casualties against a Union loss of 1,700. In Kentucky, Bragg's troops occupy the state capital of Frankfort. Lincoln concludes his visit to the army and returns to Washington.

OCT. 6. Lincoln demands that McClellan cross the Potomac and take the offensive against Lee. McClellan refuses. In Kentucky, Bragg retreats to Harrodsburg and Buell advances to Bardstown.

OCT. 8. Part of Buell's army fights part of Bragg's at Perryville, Kentucky. The Confederates are defeated and Bragg retreats.

OCT. 9. In Virginia, J. E. B. Stuart's Rebel cavalry begin an extended raid behind McClellan's lines.

OCT. 10. Bragg and Kirby Smith retreat toward East Tennessee, effectively ending the Confederate grand offensive.

OCT. 11. Stuart's cavalry raids Chambersburg, Pennsylvania.

OCT. 12. Stuart recrosses the Potomac and rejoins Lee.

OCT. 13. Lincoln chides McClellan for being too cautious and assuming his army cannot do "what the enemy is constantly doing."

OCT. 14. Early elections in Iowa, Ohio, Indiana, and Pennsylvania suggest Democrats will do well in the midterm canvass.

OCT. 22. Bragg and Kirby Smith retreat safely into east Tennessee after a lethargic pursuit by Buell.

OCT. 24. Lincoln relieves Buell of his command and replaces him with Gen. Rosecrans, the victor in the Battle of Corinth.

OCT. 25. Lincoln testily rebukes McClellan for his lack of action.

OCT. 26. The Army of the Potomac finally crosses the river; Lee's army pulls back into the Shenandoah Valley.

OCT. 28. McClellan begins a slow-developing offensive southward from Harpers Ferry.

NOV. 4. In the midterm elections, Democrats make substantial gains in Congress and win key governorships.

NOV. 5. With the election over, Lincoln is free to remove McClellan from command. He writes the orders for his relief.

NOV. 6. Lee reorganizes his army into two corps, commanded by Jackson and Longstreet, who are both promoted to lieutenant general.

NOV. 7. McClellan is relieved of his command. Though some officers urge him to resist the order, he turns the army over to his replacement, Gen. Burnside.

NOV. 10. In an emotional scene, McClellan says farewell to his army and takes the train for Washington.

ANTIETAM ORDER OF BATTLE

ARMY OF THE POTOMAC

Maj. Gen. George B. McClellan, Commanding

I CORPS: MAJ. GEN. JOSEPH HOOKER

First Division: Brig. Gen. Abner Doubleday
First Brigade: Col. Walter Phelps Jr.
Second Brigade: Lt. Col. J. William Hoffmann
Third Brigade: Brig. Gen. Marsena Patrick
Fourth Brigade ("Iron Brigade"): Brig. Gen. John Gibbon

Second Division: Brig. Gen. James B. Ricketts
First Brigade: Brig. Gen. Abram Duryee
Second Brigade: Col. William Christian
Third Brigade: Brig. Gen. George Hartsuff

Third Division: Brig. Gen. George G. Meade
First Brigade: Brig. Gen. Truman Seymour
Second Brigade: Col. Albert Magilton
Third Brigade: Lt. Col. Robert Anderson

II CORPS: MAJ. GEN. EDWIN V. SUMNER

First Division: Maj. Gen. Israel B. Richardson
First Brigade: Brig. Gen. John C. Caldwell
Second Brigade ("Irish Brigade"): Brig. Gen. Thomas F. Meagher
Third Brigade: Col. John R. Brooke

Second Division: Brig. Maj. Gen. John Sedgwick
First Brigade: Brig. Gen. Willis Gorman
Second Brigade: Brig. Gen. Oliver O. Howard
Third Brigade: Brig. Gen. N. J. T. Dana

Third Division: Brig. Gen. William H. French
First Brigade: Brig. Gen. Nathan Kimball
Second Brigade: Col. Dwight Morris
Third Brigade: Brig. Gen. Max Weber

V CORPS: MAJ. GEN. FITZ-JOHN PORTER

First Division: Maj. Gen. George W. Morell
First Brigade: Col. James Barnes
Second Brigade: Brig. Gen. Charles Griffin
Third Brigade: Col. T. B. W. Stockton

Second Division: Brig. Gen. George Sykes
First Brigade: Lt. Col. Robert Buchanan
Second Brigade: Maj. Charles S. Lovell
Third Brigade: Col. Gouverneur K. Warren

Third Division: Brig. Gen. Andrew A. Humphreys
First Brigade: Brig. Gen. Erastus B. Tyler
Second Brigade: Col. Peter Allabach

VI CORPS: MAJ. GEN. WILLIAM B. FRANKLIN

First Division: Maj. Gen. Henry W. Slocum
First Brigade: Col. Alfred T. A. Torbert
Second Brigade: Col. Joseph J. Bartlett
Third Brigade: Brig. Gen. John Newton

Second Division: Maj. Gen. William F. Smith
First Brigade: Brig. Gen. Winfield S. Hancock
Second Brigade: Brig. Gen. W. T. H. Brooks
Third Brigade: Col. William H. Irwin

First Division of IV Corps, attached: Maj. Gen. Darius N. Couch
First Brigade: Brig. Gen. Charles Devens Jr.
Second Brigade: Brig. Gen. Albion W. Howe
Third Brigade: Brig. Gen. John Cochrane

IX CORPS: MAJ. GEN. AMBROSE E. BURNSIDE, BRIG. GEN. JACOB D. COX

First Division: Brig. Gen. Orlando B. Willcox
First Brigade: Col. Benjamin Christ
Second Brigade: Col. Thomas Welsh

Second Division: Brig. Gen. Samuel D. Sturgis
First Brigade: Brig. Gen. James Nagle
Second Brigade: Brig. Gen. Edward Ferrero

Third Division: Brig. Gen. Isaac P. Rodman
First Brigade: Col. Harrison Fairchild
Second Brigade: Col. Edward Harland

Kanawha Division: Col. Eliakim P. Scammon
First Brigade: Col. Hugh Ewing
Second Brigade: Col. George Crook

XII CORPS: MAJ. GEN. JOSEPH K. F. MANSFIELD

First Division: Brig. Gen. Alpheus S. Williams
First Brigade: Brig. Gen. Samuel Crawford
Third Brigade: Brig. Gen. George Gordon

Second Division: Brig. Gen. George S. Greene
First Brigade: Lt. Col. Hector Tyndale
Second Brigade: Col. Henry J. Stainrook
Third Brigade: Col. William B. Goodrich

CAVALRY DIVISION: BRIG. GEN. ALFRED PLEASONTON

First Brigade: Maj. Charles Whiting
Second Brigade: Col. John Farnsworth

Third Brigade: Col. Richard Rush
Fourth Brigade: Col. Andrew McReynolds
Fifth Brigade: Col. Benjamin F. Davis

ARMY OF NORTHERN VIRGINIA

Gen. Robert E. Lee, Commanding

LONGSTREET'S CORPS: MAJ. GEN. JAMES LONGSTREET

McLaws's Division: Maj. Gen. Lafayette McLaws
Kershaw's Brigade: Brig. Gen. Joseph B. Kershaw
Cobb's Brigade: Lt. Col. C. C. Sanders
Semmes's Brigade: Brig. Gen. Paul J. Semmes
Barksdale's Brigade: Brig. Gen. William Barksdale

Anderson's Division: Maj. Gen. Richard H. Anderson
Wilcox's Brigade: Col. Alfred Cumming
Featherston's Brigade: Col. Carnot Posey
Armistead's Brigade: Brig. Gen. Lewis Armistead
Pryor's Brigade: Brig. Gen. Roger Pryor
Mahone's Brigade: Col. William Parham
Wright's Brigade: Brig. Gen. Ambrose R. Wright

Jones's Division: Brig. Gen. David R. Jones
Toombs's Brigade: Brig. Gen. Robert Toombs
Drayton's Brigade: Brig Gen. Thomas F. Drayton
Pickett's Brigade: Brig. Gen. Richard Garnett
Kemper's Brigade: Brig. Gen. James L. Kemper
Jenkins's Brigade: Col. Joseph Walker
Anderson's Brigade: Brig. Gen. George T. Anderson

Walker's Division: Brig. Gen. John D. Walker
Walker's Brigade: Col. Van Manning
Ransom's Brigade: Brig. Gen. Robert Ransom

Hood's Division: Brig. Gen. John B. Hood
Hood's Brigade: Col. William T. Wofford

Law's Brigade: Col. Evander M. Law
Evans's Independent Brigade: Brig. Gen. Nathan Evans

JACKSON'S CORPS: MAJOR GENERAL THOMAS J. JACKSON

Ewell's Division: Brig. Gen. Alexander Lawton
Lawton's Brigade: Col. Marcellus Douglass
Early's Brigade: Brig. Gen. Jubal A. Early
Trimble's Brigade: Col. James A. Walker
Hays's Brigade: Brig. Gen. Harry T. Hays

Hill's Light Division: Brig. Gen. Ambrose P. Hill
Branchy's Brigade: Brig. Gen. L. O'Brien Branch
Gregg's Brigade: Brig. Gen. Maxcy Gregg
Field's Brigade: Col. John M. Brockenbrough
Archer's Brigade: Brig. Gen. James J. Archer
Pender's Brigade: Brig. Gen. William D. Pender

Jackson's Division: Brig. Gen. John R. Jones
Winder's Brigade ("Stonewall Brigade"): Col. Andrew J. Grigsby
Taliaferro's Brigade: Col. James W. Jackson
Jones's Brigade: Capt. John E. Penn
Starke's Brigade: Brig. Gen. William E. Starke

Hill's Division: Major General Daniel H. Hill
Ripley's Brigade: Brig. Gen. Roswell Ripley
Rodes's Brigade: Brig. Gen. Robert E. Rodes
Garland's Brigade: Col. D. K. McRae
Anderson's Brigade: Brig. Gen. George B. Anderson
Colquitt's Brigade: Brig. Gen. Alfred Colquitt

CAVALRY DIVISION: MAJOR GENERAL J. E. B. STUART

Hampton's Brigade: Brig. Gen. Wade Hampton
Lee's Brigade: Brig. Gen. Fitzhugh Lee
Robertson's Brigade: Col. Thomas Munford

NOTES

ABBREVIATIONS

OR: United States War Dept., John Sheldon
Moody et al. *The War of the Rebellion:*
Official Records of the Union and
Confederate Armies

NYH: *New York Herald*

NYT: *New York Times*

NYTrib: *New York Tribune*

NYW: *New York World*

INTRODUCTION

1 Davis, *Essential Writings*, 198–203, 224–29; Davis, "Message to Congress," Apr. 29, 1861, in *OR*, Series 4, Vol. 1, 268.

2 Lincoln, "Annual Message to Congress, Dec. 3, 1861," in *Speeches and Writings*, 2:292.

3 McPherson, *Tried*, 30–45.

CHAPTER 1 Lincoln's Strategy

1 Donald, 357–58; McPherson, *Tried*, 98.

2 McClellan, *Civil War Papers*, 316–23.

3 Ibid., 289–90.

4 *Hartford (CT) Courant*, "Good News . . . ," June 30, 1862; *NYT*, "Affairs . . ." and "Our Army," July 1, 1962.

5 Goodwin, 445, McPherson, *Tried*, 99.

6 McClellan, *Civil War Papers*, 322–23, 326; Sears, *McClellan*, 226; Hay, *Inside Lincoln's White House*, 191; Lincoln, *Collected Works*, 5:292.

7 Sears, *McClellan*, 226.

8 Henry Adams, *The Education of Henry Adams*, edited by Jean Gooder (New York: Penguin, 1995), 103.

9 The following analysis of the development of Federal strategy is based on McPherson, *Tried*, chs. 1–5, and Stoker, chs. 1, 3–6, 9. Lincoln's admonition to McClellan is in Lincoln, *Collected Works*, 5:289–90.

10 Ibid.

11 On the development of Lincoln's policy toward slavery and emancipation, see Guelzo, chs. 1–2; Foner, *Fiery Trial*, chs. 6–7.

12 McPherson, *Tried*, 99–100; Lincoln, *Collected Works*, 5:292.

13 Browning, 537–38; on Halleck's appointment, see McPherson, *Tried*, 111–12.

14 On McClellan's background, character, and preparation for command, see Sears, *McClellan*, chs. 1–4, and Rafuse, chs. 1–4. Rafuse pays particular attention to the development of McClellan's political views and associations. Waugh, chs. 1–9, provides an overview of the ongoing tensions between the two.

15 Sears, *McClellan*, chs. 5–6; Rafuse, chs. 6–9; McClellan, *Civil War Papers*, 71.

16 Ibid., 70, 82.

17 Perret, xiii–xv.

18 McPherson, *Tried*, 54–60; Weber, 27–37.

19 Donald, 478–80; Goodwin, 463–68, 491–95, 563–70.

20 The Post and Tribune Company, Publishers, 1880, "Facing Treason," 192: William C. Harris, Ph.D., *Public Life of Zachariah Chandler, 1851–1875* (Lansing, MI: Michigan Historical Commission, 1917), 54, 66.

21 Browning, 554.

22 McClellan, *Civil War Papers*, 71–73.

23 Lincoln, *Speeches*, 1:512.

24 Ibid., 598–99.

25 William A. Blair, "The Seven Days and the Radical Persuasion," in Gallagher, *Richmond Campaign*, 156–57; Silbey, chs. 1–2. On McClellan's ties to Barlow, Aspinwall, and Belmont, see McClellan, *Civil War Papers*, 3, 127, 154, 213, 306, 365, 369, 376, 482, 490, 500, 525, 550, 556; Rafuse, 52, 68, 81, 93, 125, 148–53, 157, 172, 196–97, 212, 220, 244–46, 250; Katz, ch. 6, esp. 106, 112.

26 McPherson, *Tried*, 51; Sears, *McClellan*, ch. 5.

27 Sears, *McClellan*, 128; Rafuse, ch. 4; Stephen A. Douglas, in Lincoln, *Speeches*, 1:598.

28 Foner, *Fiery Trial*, chs. 3–4.

29 McClellan, *Civil War Papers*, 81–82.

30 Lincoln, *Speeches*, 2:294–95.

31 Ibid., 81–82, 87, 89, 91, 114.

32 Ibid., 85–86.

33 Sears, *McClellan*, 106–7; McClellan, *Civil War Papers*, 71–73, 75.

34 Sears, *McClellan*, 116–18; McJimsey, 38–39.

35 Sears, *McClellan*, 137–67.

36 Ibid., 132–36.

37 Sears, *McClellan*, ch. 1, esp. 5–6, 25, 132–36; McClellan, *Civil War Papers*, 477–48, 482.

38 Sears, *McClellan*, 132–34.

39 Segal, 155–56; McClellan, *Civil War Papers*, 164–67.

40 Sears, *McClellan*, 142–43.

41 Thomas and Hyman, ch. 6; Sears, *McClellan*, 136–56, 177–78.

CHAPTER 2 **McClellan's Strategy**

1 On McClellan's strategy for achieving a decisive battle at Richmond, see Sears, *Gates of Richmond*, esp. 9–10. McClellan had been a staff officer under Winfield Scott in 1847 and had seen Scott combine the moral effect of battlefield victories with conciliatory diplomatic gestures to persuade the Mexican leadership to come to terms. See Bauer, esp. ch. 17. Further confirmation came from his more recent experience of the Crimean War (1854–57), which McClellan studied as part of the U.S. military mission. The capture of a single major city, on the periphery of the Russian Empire, had compelled the czar to sue for peace (Sears, *McClellan*, 23–27, 44–49).

2 Ibid., 164–65.

3 See Sears, *McClellan*, 101–6, for a good overview of the defects in McClellan's intelligence gathering and analysis; for his failure to develop an effective cavalry, 114. The lack of capacity for an independent analysis by the War Department is reflected in the similarly inflated estimates of Rebel strength given out by cabinet officers—see, for example, Seward, in Segal, 151. Lieutenant General Scott had the kind of expertise that might have served to correct McClellan, as when (August 1861) he scoffed at McClellan's assertion that Beauregard had 100,000 men and was preparing to invade Maryland. McClellan not only rejected Scott's views, he assailed Scott as a "dotard" and demanded the old general's resignation. See McClellan, *Civil War Papers*, 79–80.

4 Sears, *McClellan*, ch. 5; Taafe, ch. 1.

5 McClellan, *Civil War Papers*, 183–84.

6 For example, see McClellan, *Civil War Papers*, 110–11, 219–20.

7 Hay, *Inside*, 36.

8 The best study of the Peninsula campaign is Sears, *Gates of Richmond*. For McClellan's judgment of Lee, see McClellan, *Civil War Papers*, 244–45.

9 Ibid., 231, 235, 239.

10 McJimsey, 34–35; Sears, *McClellan*, 229–30; Crouthamel, 122–31; Long and Long, 169.

11 *NYT*, "The Submission Party," July 1, 1862.

12 McClellan, *Civil War Papers*, 304.

13 Sears, *Gates*, 337, 347.

14 Sears, *Gates*, chs. 10–11, is the most complete treatment of the subject—see esp. 280–81, 308–9. See also Sears, *McClellan*, 203; McClellan, *Civil War Papers*, 234–35, 305–6. Rafuse, 237–43, takes a more favorable view of the campaign, but even he says that McClellan's absenting himself from the battlefield of Glendale "defies belief."

15 Sears, *Gates*, 233–34, 250.

16 McClellan, *Civil War Papers*, 322–23, 326.

17 Sears, *McClellan*, 213–15.

18 John T. Hubbell, "The Seven Days of George Brinton McClellan," in Gallagher, *Richmond Campaign*, 28–43.

19 Ibid., 37–38; Sears, *Gates*, 281, 331; Sears, *McClellan*, 218–19.

20 McClellan, *Civil War Papers*, 305.

21 Catton, *Mr. Lincoln's Army*, 88.

22 Lincoln, *Collected Works*, 5:289; McClellan, *Civil War Papers*, 367.

23 Sears, *McClellan*, 229–30; *NYT*, "Ill-Timed and Mischievous," July 10, 1862. *Harper's Weekly* refused to admit that McClellan had actually been defeated: his retreat was a move long planned, and it left his army "nearer the accomplishment" of his objective "than it has ever been." "On to Richmond!" (July 19, 1862, 450).

24 McClellan, *Civil War Papers*, 349.

25 Ibid., 346.

26 The full text is in McClellan, *Civil War Papers*, 344–45. See also Sears, *McClellan*, ch. 10; McPherson, *Tried*, 105–6.

27 He would say the same thing in a letter he wrote to Secretary of War Stanton that evening: "The nation will support no other policy . . . for none other will our Armies continue to fight" (McClellan, *Civil War Papers*, 247).

28 Ibid., 348, 351.

29 Lincoln, *Collected Works*, 5:312–13, 317–18, 322, 328–31, 336–38.

CHAPTER 3 **President Davis's Strategic Defensive**

1 Davis, *Papers*, 8:293.

2 The discussion of Confederate policy, politics, and society that follows owes a great deal to the analyses of Confederate nationalism, and the nationalist principles of President Davis, in Gallagher, *Confederate War*, and Faust, chs. 1, 2, and 5. See also Rable, chs. 3–7; Thomas, *Confederacy as a Revolutionary Experience*, chs. 2–4; and McPherson, *Battle Cry*, ch. 8, which accurately describes secession as a preemptive counterrevolution.

3 Davis, *Papers*, 8: 293–94; *DeBow's Review*, May 1, 1862, 44.

4 "The Conduct of the War," reprint from *Savannah Republican* in *Charleston Mercury*, May 10, 1862; *Richmond Daily Dispatch*, "Invasion of the Enemy's Territory," May 6, 1862; *Charleston Mercury*, "The Crisis," May 8, 1862.

5 Rable, 154–57, 161–63, 166–67, 249.

6 Davis, *Papers*, 8:285–86, 289; 299, 308.

7 *Richmond Whig*, "The Defensive Policy," quoted in *Charleston Mercury*, Aug. 29, 1862.

8 The most thorough analysis of the evolution of Confederate strategy during this period is Harsh, *Confederate Tide*, ch. 1. See also Stoker, chs. 10–12; Woodworth, chs. 3–4; Davis quoted in Long and Long, 229; Davis, *Papers*, 8:279, 287.

9 Davis, *Papers*, 8:293; Harsh, *Confederate Tide*, ch. 2; *OR*, Series 1, Vol. 11, Pt. 3, 690.

10 Hattaway and Beringer, ch. 1; Strode, chs. 11, 17; Woodworth, ch. 3, esp. 80–81; McPherson, *Battle Cry*, 365–67, 394–97, 857.

11 Rable, ch. 7, esp. 138, 145–47.

12 Harsh, *Confederate Tide*, ch. 2. On Lee's background, character, and ideas, see Thomas, *Robert E. Lee*, chs. 1–14. On Lee's generalship and strategic thinking, see the excellent group of essays in Gallagher, *Lee*, especially Charles P. Roland, "The Generalship of Robert E. Lee," 159–88; Gallagher, "Another Look at the Generalship of R. E. Lee," 275–90; and also Woodworth, 151–53, 249–51, 157–59, 220–45. For criticism of Lee's generalship, especially his predilection for the strategic and tactical offensive, see Nolan, esp. ch. 4; Thomas L. Connelly, "Robert E. and the Western Confederacy: A Criticism of Lee's Strategic Ability," in Gallagher, *Lee*, 189–208; and McWhiney and Jamieson, esp. chs. 7–8 and Pt. 3.

13 Woodworth, 57; William C. Davis, "Lee and Jefferson Davis," in Gallagher, *Lee*, 291–308.

14 Woodworth, 164–65; Sears, *Gates*, 204–6; Harsh, *Confederate Tide*, chs. 2–3.

15 Hubbard, 107, 115.

16 Harsh, *Confederate Tide*, 98, 108–15.

17 *Richmond Daily Dispatch*, "Follow Up the Victory," July 5, 1862.

18 Harsh, *Confederate Tide*, 60–73; ch. 4.

19 Connelly, *Army*, chs. 10–11; Davis, *Papers*, 8:288, 292, 301.

20 Ibid., 8:296, 298, 299, 305.

21 Woodworth, 174–75; Strode, 289–91; Davis, *Papers*, 8:302–3, 305–6; *NYW*, "Important War Papers," Aug. 14, 1862.

22 Davis, *Essential Writings*, 259.

23 Harsh, *Confederate Tide*, 115–18.

24 Ibid., 119–22.

CHAPTER 4 **Self-Inflicted Wounds**

1 Guelzo, 111–44; Lincoln, *Collected Works*, 5:337–38.

2 Guelzo, 120–21.

3 Ibid., 121–23; Thomas and Hyman, 229–39; Sears, *McClellan*, 140–44; McClellan, *Civil War Papers*, 300.

4 Sears, *McClellan*, 235.

5 Lincoln, *Collected Works*, 5:343, 350–51; Lincoln, *Speeches*, 2:344–46.

6 Blair, "The Seven Days," in Gallagher, *Richmond Campaign*, 157–68, 174–77.

7 See, for example, *NYH*, "Fighting in Earnest—Down with All Traitors," July 15, 1862; *NYW*, "The End of Peaceable Warfare," July 11, 1862; *NYW*, "A Sterner War Policy," July 12, 1862; *NYW*, "Jeff. Davis's Last Lying Appeal

to Europe," Aug. 11, 1862; *NYW*, "Important War Papers," Aug. 14, 1862. The *World* nominally favored emancipating the slaves of Rebel leaders, but not general emancipation, and was a strident advocate of racial theories of white supremacy. See "The Emancipation Bill," June 20, 1862; "A Movement of Malcontents," June 25, 1862; "An Argument for Gradual Emancipation," June 27, 1862; "The Anglo-Saxon and the Colored Races," July 8, 1862; "A Sterner War Policy," July 12, 1862.

8   *NYH*, "The Past and the Future," July 11, 1862; "Moral, Social and Political Revolutionary Movements of Greeley and His Fraternity" and "The New Conservative Policy of the Government," July 21, 1862. For treatment of Pope's proclamations and the Confiscation Bill, see *NYH*, "Pope's Proclamation" and "Fighting in Earnest—Down with All Traitors," July 15, 1862; *NYH*, "The Confiscation Bill," July 13, 1862. Also see *NYH*,. "The Retaliatory Orders . . . ," Aug. 10, 1862. These editorials favor Pope's measures and Lincoln's moderate revision of the Confiscation Act, while opposing the Radical version of the latter.

9   Sears, *McClellan*, 230–32; and *NYW*: "The Great Battle Before Richmond," June 30, 1862; "Gen. McClellan's Army" and "Military Strategy on the Peninsula," July 1, 1862; "Gen. McClellan's Army," July 3, 1862; "The Crisis," July 4, 1862; "Wanted—A War Cabinet," July 7, 1862; "The Crisis" and "The Right Man in the Right Place," July 8, 1862; "The Removal of Secretary Stanton," July 9, 1862; "General Halleck," July 14, 1862; "The Military Situation," Aug. 1, 1862. The *Herald* agreed: see the coverage of the Richmond fighting, July 4 and 6, 1862; and "The Army of General McClellan," July 6, 1862; "Mismanagement and Mismanagers of the War Department," July 7, 1862. *Frank Leslie's Illustrated*, a popular weekly, supported the *Tribune*'s view, that McClellan's "Napoleonic genius" was fraudulent and his operations marked by "military incompetence." See editorial of July 19, 1862.

10   *NYT*: "The Crisis of the War," July 7, 1862; "Secretary of War," July 10, 1862; "Audacity as a War Energy," July 11, 1862. Compare *NYH*, "A Vigorous War," Aug. 2, 1862.

11   McClellan, *Civil War Papers*, 365; Guelzo, 106–9, 286 n. 91. Articles from *Spirit of the Times* are collected in Wilkes, 8–9.

12   Guelzo, 130–31; Foner, *Fiery Trial*, 221–30.

13   McPherson, *Tried*, 111–13.

14   On Pope's political background and wartime experience, see Cozzens, ch. 3; on his orders to his army, Cozzens, 83–88.

15   McClellan, *Civil War Papers*, 368, 378, 382.

16   Ibid., 369; Sears, *McClellan*, 240.

17   Ibid., 239–41.

18   Ibid., 235; McClellan, *Civil War Papers*, 360–62; Marvel, 99–100.

19   Kearny quoted in Catton, *Mr. Lincoln's Army*, 88–89; de Peyster, 350; Guelzo, 98. For reaction of McClellan's officers, see Sears, *Gates*, 337–39.

20 Hay, *Inside*, 231–32; Fehrenbacher and Fehrenbacher, *Recollected Words of Abraham Lincoln*, 230.
21 McClellan's estimate of Lee's force was ludicrously excessive, triple his actual troop strength. However, he seems actually to have believed he was outnumbered. He was certainly aware that the administration hoped to use his refusal to advance as an excuse to relieve him. See his letter to Aspinwall in McClellan, *Civil War Papers*, 365.
22 Ibid., 372, 380–81.
23 Ibid., 383, 385, 388–89.
24 Ibid., 349; *NYW*, "A Sterner War Policy," July 12, 1862.
25 McClellan, *Civil War Papers*, 389–90, 376–77; quoted in McPherson, *Crossroads of Freedom*, 80–81.
26 McClellan, *Civil War Papers*, 387–88.
27 Ibid., 390.
28 Ibid., 378, 382, 388; and compare Wilkes, 3–4, 6, 8–10, on McClellan as "false prophet."
29 *NYW*: "The Military Situation," Aug. 1, 1862; "Army of Virginia," Aug. 6, 1862; "News from Washington" [Lincoln defends Stanton], Aug. 7, 1862; "General McClellan's Campaign," August 7, 1862. For the *World*'s take on the McClellan/Pope conflict, see "Jeff. Davis's Last Lying Appeal to Europe" (Aug. 11, 1862), which defends Pope, and "Important Move by Gen. McClellan" and "General McClellan's New Orders" (Aug. 15, 1862), in which their different styles are contrasted, with an outcome favoring McClellan. See also McClellan, *Civil War Papers*, 358–59.
30 Ibid., 397; and see correspondence among McClellan, Fitz-John Porter, and Burnside, in *OR*, Series 1, Vol. 12, ch. 24, Pt. 3, 615–16, 651–52, 661–62.
31 Lincoln, *Collected Works*, 5: 370–75; Foner, *Fiery Trial*, 221–30; Guelzo, 130–44.
32 Lincoln, *Collected Works*, 5:389.
33 Ibid., 388.

CHAPTER 5 **Both Ends Against the Middle**

1 Woodworth, 174–75.
2 This account of the campaign follows Harsh, *Confederate Tide*, ch. 5.
3 See ch. 3 n. 12 above; and Harsh, *Confederate Tide*, ch. 5.
4 I think Harsh, *Confederate Tide*, 136–37, overstresses Lee's reluctance to risk heavy casualties.
5 Ibid., 132–33.
6 Ibid., 67–68, 142–43, 230, 278.
7 McClellan, *Civil War Papers*, 389–90, 404.
8 Ibid., 405.
9 Ibid., 407–12.
10 *OR*, Series 1, Vol. 12, ch. 24, Pt. 3, 691.

11   McClellan, *Civil War Papers*, 413.
12   *OR*, Series 1, Vol. 12, ch. 24, Pt. 3, 709.
13   McClellan, *Civil War Papers*, 414.
14   Ibid., 415–16; Sears, *McClellan*, 253.
15   Hay, *Inside*, 37; McClellan, *Civil War Papers*, 416; Sears, *McClellan*, 255.
16   *OR*, Series 1, Vol. 12, ch. 24, Pt. 3, 706, 709, 723, 739–40; McClellan, *Civil War Papers*, 413, 415–16.

CHAPTER 6   **McClellan's Victory**

1   McClellan, *Civil War Papers*, 421–23.
2   Welles, 100–104.
3   Hay, *Inside*, 37; Sears, *McClellan*, 255; Welles, 93–95, 102, 104–9.
4   Sears, *McClellan*, 257–58; an alternative interpretation of McClellan's actions during this crisis is Rafuse, 255–67.
5   McClellan, *Civil War Papers*, 423.
6   Adams Jr. et al., *Letters*, 176–80.
7   *OR*, Series 1, Vol. 19, ch. 31, Pt. 2, 808.
8   *NYTrib*, "The War in Virginia," Sept. 1, 1862. "If Jackson is not captured the responsibility will rest with Gen. McClellan, who was ordered to move three days since, but failed to obey. The order was repeated to march this morning, but still the movement was delayed . . . inexplicable inactivity at a most critical moment." It is worth noting that the *Tribune* estimates the Rebel force at 200,000—an indication of just how bad Northern intelligence was, even outside McClellan's circle.
9   Wilkes, 3–4, 6, 9, 20–23.
10   *NYW*, "The Battles Before Washington . . . Charges Against Gen. McClellan"; *NYW*, "Are We Losing What We are Defending?," Sept. 2, 1862, defends against the *Tribune* editorial "accusing Gen. McClellan of cowardice, indolence, or treachery."
11   Adams Jr. et al., *Letters*, 178–80.
12   Hay, *Inside*, 38–39.
13   Ibid.
14   McClellan, *Civil War Papers*, 427; Sears, *McClellan*, 258; *OR*, Series 1, Vol. 19, ch. 31, Pt. 2, 788, 798, 838, 1018.
15   Welles, 102; Segal, 192–94.
16   Sears, *McClellan*, 263–65; McPherson, *Tried*, 121.
17   Welles, 103, 107.
18   Historians have generally exonerated McClellan of deliberately treacherous intent. Stephen Sears sees his resentment of Pope as an unconscious drag on his operations but finds it hard to believe McClellan would deliberately abandon to destruction the soldiers he loved—including the corps led by his closest comrade and disciple, Fitz-John Porter. Yet as Sears himself notes, in the Seven Days McClellan abandoned Porter and his beloved army to sepa-

rate himself from a potential debacle. See Sears, *McClellan*, 254. Rafuse, 271–72, offers a more positive defense.

19 Sears, *McClellan*, 255–56.
20 Hay, *Inside*, 38–39.
21 Lincoln, *Collected Works*, 5:403–4.
22 McClellan, *Civil War Papers*, 435, 438.

CHAPTER 7 **Lee Decides on Invasion**

1 Harsh, *Taken*, 51.
2 Ibid., ch. 1, esp. 23–25, 31–32.
3 Davis, *Papers*, 8:373. I disagree with Woodworth, 185–87, who sees Lee and Davis thinking along different lines and interprets Davis's silence on the invasion of Maryland as a sign he was too surprised to respond.
4 *Jackson Mississippian*, "Forward," quoted in *Charleston Mercury*, Sept. 2, 1862, and *Richmond Whig*, quoted in *Charleston Mercury*, Sept. 6, 1862.
5 Davis, *Papers*, 8:377; Davis, *Essential*, 255–56; Strode, ch. 20, esp. 237–38, 289; Rable, ch. 7; Glatthaar, 164.
6 Davis, *Papers*, 8:376, 382.
7 Rable, ch. 7; Strode, chs. 23–24; Hubbard, 107, 115–23.
8 Davis, *Papers*, 8:373, 377.
9 Harsh, *Taken*, 107; *OR*, Series 1, Vol. 19, ch. 31, Pt. 2, 600–601.
10 Harsh, *Taken*, 81–83; Strode, 301.
11 Davis, *Essential*, 261.
12 Hubbard, 115–23.
13 Harsh, *Taken*, chs. 1–2. On Lee's troop strength (real and imagined) see Harsh, *Sounding*, 138–39.
14 Harsh, *Taken*, 70–71, 83–84.
15 Ibid., 72–76; Glatthaar, 166–67.
16 Harsh, *Taken*, 76; Davis, *Papers*, 8:373.
17 Harsh, *Taken*, 72–73.
18 Ibid., 39, 43–45, 117, 382; Harsh, *Sounding*, 102–3.
19 Sears, *Landscape*, 69, estimates 50,000. The higher estimate is from Harsh, *Taken*, 38–39, 170–71; and Harsh, *Shallows*, 139.
20 Lee himself had been disturbed by a much lower rate of straggling during the campaign against Pope: 9,000 stragglers from a force of 55,000 straggled, roughly 16 percent. The Army of Northern Virginia did indeed suffer extraordinary losses to straggling during the Maryland campaign, but a rate of 43 percent suggests a degree of demoralization that no officer observed at the time. The 65,000–70,000 estimate is also consistent with Harsh's data on the losses and gains to Lee's original force from battle casualties at Second Bull Run, postbattle reinforcements, and the return of stragglers (Harsh, *Shallows*, 138–39, 143–46).
21 Sears, *Landscape*, 69, estimates 50,000; the higher estimate is from Harsh,

Taken, 38–39, 170–71. Lee's inflated estimate owes something to the fact that his army now contained an extraordinary number of regiments—205 in total, a third of all units in Confederate service.

22 Harsh, *Shallows*, 152–53; Glatthaar, 164–65.

23 Harsh, *Taken*, 70–71, 83–84.

24 Judkins, "History of Co. G, 22nd Georgia," 36.

25 Ibid., Sears, *Landscape*, 83–86; Harsh, *Taken*, 169.

26 Harsh, *Taken*, 107–11, 124–27; Strode, 301–2.

27 Harsh, *Taken*, 117–19; Glatthaar, 166.

28 Harsh, *Taken*, 133ff.

29 Sears, *Landscape*, 89.

30 Harsh, *Taken*, 145–67.

31 Ibid., ch. 3 and 149–51, 186–87.

32 The discussion of Lee's plan is based on Harsh, *Taken*, ch. 3. See also Woodworth, 90–91; Sears, *Landscape*, 90–91.

33 Sears, *Landscape*, 87; Harsh, *Taken*, 175; Glatthaar, 166–67.

34 The account of Confederate movements that follows is based on Harsh, *Taken*, ch. 4.

CHAPTER 8 **McClellan Takes the Offensive**

1 Catton, *Mr. Lincoln's Army*, 34.

2 Sears, *McClellan*, 266–8; Sears, *Landscape*, 79–81.

3 At Glendale, for example, he fought a successful rear-guard action to protect the Union retreat, but nearly negated its effect by refusing to follow the army's withdrawal. Sears, *Gates*, 308.

4 Rafuse, 281–82.

5 Sears, *Landscape*, 101–7.

6 McClellan, *Civil War Papers*, 439.

7 The following discussion of McClellan's plans and actions is based on Rafuse, 278–88; Sears, *Landscape*, 105–11.

8 Marvel, 111.

9 Cox, 354–59.

10 McClellan, *Civil War Papers*, 438.

11 *NYH*, "National Capital Safe . . . We Now Take a Fresh Start. No More Mistakes to Be Made," Sept. 4, 1862; *NYH*, "The Enthusiasm for Gen. M'Clellan" and "The Virginia Campaign—The New Order of Things," Sept. 5, 1862; *NYH*, "The Radical Plan," Sept. 6, 1862.

12 *NYW*, "General McClellan," Sept. 3, 1862; *NYW*, "Gen. McClellan Restored to Command" and "The Military Situation," Sept. 4, 1862; *NYW*, "Strategy and Anti-Strategy," Sept. 6, 1862; *NYW*, "A Rebel Army in Maryland" and "Gen. Pope in a New Command," Sept. 8, 1862. The latter notes Pope has been sent to fight Indians, whose savage methods mirror his own treatment of civilians.

13 *NYTrib*, "The Crisis," Sept. 4, 1862.

14 Strong, 255–56; Welles, 108, 112–13, 116–18.

15 Sears, *McClellan*, 272; Sears, *Landscape*, 111; Sears, *Controversies*, 134–35.

16 *NYTrib*, "Northern Independence," Sept. 12, 1862; "Usurpation Threatened," Sept. 13; see also Strode, 301.

17 Sears, *McClellan*, 268; *NYH*, "The Important Position of General McClellan," Sept. 11, 1862; *NYTrib*, "Northern Independence," Sept. 12, 1862. See also *NYH*, "General McClellan and the Chief Organ of the Radicals," Sept. 20, 1862, and "McClellan and the Fire in His Rear," Sept. 15, 1862, which responds to the *Tribune*'s charge of usurpation.

18 Sears, *McClellan*, 268, 272.

19 Rafuse, 280–81.

20 Sears, *Landscape*, 106.

21 McClellan, *Civil War Papers*, 440–44.

22 On the lost order and McClellan's plans to exploit it, see Sears, *McClellan*, 280–87; Sears, *Landscape*, 112–21; Rafuse, 288–94. For Lee's side of the story, see Harsh, *Taken*, 152–67, and ch. 5.

23 Sears, *McClellan*, 287.

24 Ibid., 284–87.

25 McClellan, *Civil War Papers*, 456–57.

26 Harsh, *Taken*, 240.

27 Sears, *Landscape*, 116–21; Sears, *McClellan*, 283–88; Rafuse, 292–94.

28 McClellan, *Civil War Papers*, 454–55.

29 Harsh, *Taken*, ch. 5, esp. 245, 249.

30 Sears, *Landscape*, 123–24.

CHAPTER 9 **The Battles of South Mountain**

1 This account of the fighting on Sept. 14 is based on Harsh, *Taken*, ch. 6, and Sears, *Landscape*, ch. 4.

2 Catton, *Mr. Lincoln's Army*, 139.

3 Ibid., 149.

4 Ibid., 150.

5 Harsh, *Taken*, 288, 300.

6 Sears, *Landscape*, 151; Wittenberg, 32–33.

7 Sears, *Landscape*, 151–52.

CHAPTER 10 **The Forces Gather**

1 For Lee's decision to reconcentrate his army at Sharpsburg see Harsh, *Taken*, ch. 7.

2 Ibid., 300–306.

3 Sears, *Landscape*, 154.

4 Harsh, *Taken*, 306, 315–22, 326–29.

5 McClellan, *Civil War Papers*, 461.

6 Ibid., 462–63.

7   Ibid., 463. It is worth noting that McClellan never positively affirmed the 15,000 casualties as his own estimate but attributed it to the reports of others, which gave him deniability. A later survey of the battlefield by officers reporting to McClellan's staff estimated that 500 Confederates had been left dead on the field. Given the usual ratio of killed to wounded, and Hooker's initial claim of "nearly" 1,000 POWs, an estimate of 3,500 would have been reasonable. However, it is not known when McClellan received the report of that survey. In his "Preliminary Report" (Oct. 15, 1862), McClellan reduced his estimate to a more reasonable 3,000 killed, wounded, and captured. *OR*, Series 1, Vol. 19, ch. 31, Pt. 1, Reports, 38. Sears, *Landscape*, 143, estimates 2,300 Confederate casualties, including 400 captured.

8   Harsh, *Taken*, 310–12; McClellan, *Civil War Papers*, 464.

9   Harsh, *Taken*, 346–47.

10 Col. Jacob Hays, Report of September 22, 1862, *OR*, Series 1, Vol. 9, ch. 31, Pt. 1, Reports, 491–93.

11 McClellan, Report of Oct. 15, 1862 ("Preliminary"), *OR*, Series 1, Vol. 19, ch. 31, Pt. 2, Reports, 29–31. Sears, *Landscape*, 164. Rafuse, 308 ff., says McClellan was uncertain about the arrival of Confederate reinforcements and sent Hooker to develop Lee's left but reserved his main force until Lee's strength and position were ascertained.

CHAPTER 11   **Preparation for Battle**

1   McClellan, *Civil War Papers*, 465.

2   Ibid., 464.

3   Ibid., 397.

4   Ibid., 473, 464; Lincoln, *Collected Works*, 5:426.

5   Estimates for Lee's troop strength at Antietam range from 38,000 to 40,000, including A. P. Hill's Division (2,500–3,000); so that the estimated strength for Lee's force at Sharpsburg on the morning of Sept. 17 falls between 35,000 and 37,500. Harsh's analysis of Lee's troop strength seems to me the most credible, because of Harsh's close attention to the accounting procedures followed by Lee's HQ. I have therefore generally accepted the estimates he gives in *Taken*, 218–20, 559 n. 1; Harsh, *Sounding*, 201.

6   Judkins, 38.

7   Priest, 3.

8   The discussion of Lee's defensive preparations that follows is based on Harsh, *Taken*, 354–61.

9   McClellan, "Report of August 4, 1863," ("Final"), *OR*, Series 1, Vol. 19, ch. 31, Pt. 1, 67. McClellan counted as "present" all troops accredited to units in the field, whether they were actually at hand or absent (on leave, in hospital, on detached service); and he counted noncombatant elements (cooks, musicians, teamsters, etc.) as well as riflemen and cannoneers. In tallying Confederate strength he made the additional error of assuming that each

regiment was at or near its authorized strength, although deep into a campaign there were scarcely any units in either army that mustered anything near their authorized strength. He and his officers also accepted uncritically the estimates offered by naïve civilians. These estimates ought to have been corrected by intelligence gained through cavalry probes and the interrogation of prisoners. On Confederate accounting see Harsh, *Shallows*, 139, and *Taken*, 169.

10 The evidence of earlier campaigns suggests that McClellan sincerely believed his erroneous figures. Some of the unwonted confidence with which McClellan approached the battle may have come from an awareness of the reduced numbers, the weakened physical strength and morale in Lee's command.

11 Sears, *Landscape*, 173.

12 Sears, *McClellan*, 298–99.

13 In his "Final Report" (*OR*, Series 1, Vol. 19, ch. 31, Pt. 1, 55), McClellan says he intended Hooker's force to deliver the main attack, to be *supported* by II and VI Corps, but there are good reasons to doubt this was actually his plan. If Hooker's was supposed to be the main assault, then McClellan intended a flank or oblique attack. The textbook method for staging such an attack requires strong demonstrations or diversionary attacks, to pin enemy units in place and draw reserves away from the point of impact. Hooker's column should also have been reinforced to give it a preponderance of strength, and if possible its approach should have been masked to conceal its strength. None of these conditions pertained to Hooker's attack. His onset was to precede, not follow, attacks from McClellan's center and southern flank. There was no attempt to conceal the assembly of Hooker's force. Given McClellan's estimate of enemy strength, the resources he gave Hooker were inadequate for any purpose other than that of a strong diversion. If Lee's supposed 65,000 were evenly distributed, Hooker's 20,000 were probably facing an equal number of Confederates, posted on good terrain for defense, with ample reserves nearby, on a line so long that Hooker did not have enough men to cover it, even with the addition of XII Corps. Moreover, the units McClellan gave Hooker were among those he considered second-rate.

14 McClellan, "Report of October 15, 1862," *OR*, Series 1, Vol. 19, ch. 31, Pt. 1, 30. Sears, *McClellan*, 299, says Burnside's attack was intended to strike the decisive blow, presumably after earlier attacks had drawn Lee's forces northward. As it happened, the morning attacks did draw troops away from Burnside's front, creating the opportunity for a decisive attack. But there is no evidence that McClellan anticipated such a development or made plans to exploit it. Burnside's was the weakest maneuver element, and McClellan never indicated an intention to reinforce it from the army reserve; his orders to Burnside were vague but suggested a diversionary attack rather than a main assault.

15 Harsh, *Taken*, 347.

16 Sears, *McClellan*, 299.
17 Ibid., 297–99; Sears, *Landscape*, 169–73.
18 Sears, *McClellan*, 299; Marvel, 125–32.

CHAPTER 12 **The Battle of Antietam: Hooker's Fight**

1 My discussion of this phase of the battle is based on Harsh, *Taken*, 368–85 (decisions by Lee's HQ and Confederate movements); Sears, *Landscape*, ch. 6 (Federal movements and decisions by Hooker and by McClellan's HQ); and Priest, chs. 3–7 (esp. for timing of particular troop movements). See also the maps at "Antietam on the Web," http://antietam.aotw.org/ maps.php?map_number=main, Detail Maps 1–3; and George W. Davis, E. A. Carman, and H. Heth, *Atlas of the Battle of Antietam* (1908), maps 1–8.
2 Priest, 332–33; Harsh, *Sounding*, 201.
3 Hess, 113–14.
4 Sears, *Landscape*, 191.
5 Ibid., 194–202; Priest, ch. 5.
6 The Second Virginia was detached during this battle.
7 http://14thbrooklyn.info/ShortRegtHistory.htm.
8 Sears, *Landscape*, 193–94.
9 Ibid., 188.
10 Ibid., 188–89.
11 Harsh, *Taken*, 373.
12 Quoted in Glatthaar, 171.
13 Sears, *Landscape*, 191, 201–2.
14 Ibid., 214; Harsh, *Taken*, 378–81.
15 Ibid., 380–81.
16 Ibid., 383.
17 Sears, *Landscape*, 195.
18 Sears, *Landscape*, 235; See Burnside's "Report" in *OR*, Series 1, Vol. 19, ch. 31, Pt. 1, 416–17.
19 Sears, *Landscape*, 215.
20 Ibid., 261.

CHAPTER 13 **The Battle of Antietam: Sumner's Fight**

1 My discussion of this phase of the battle is based on Harsh, *Taken*, 385–404 (decisions by Lee's HQ and Confederate movements); Sears, *Landscape*, ch. 7 (Federal movements and decisions by Hooker and by McClellan's HQ); and Priest, chs. 8–12 (esp. for timing of particular troop movements). See also the maps at "Antietam on the Web," http://antietam.aotw.org/maps .php?map_number=main, Detail Maps 4–7; and Davis et al., *Atlas*, maps 9–11.
2 Sears, *Landscape*, 221.
3 Ibid., 224.

4 Harsh, *Taken*, 381.

5 Sears, *Landscape*, 224, says 1,400, but troops were continually arriving from McLaws's and Walker's commands.

6 Harsh, *Taken*, 385, says 6,600 CSA troops were on this line, but it is not clear whether he includes D. R. Jones's Division.

7 Sears, *Landscape*, 238–39.

8 Ibid., 236, 241.

9 Priest, 3; Judkins, *39*, 84.

10 Priest, 180; "Report of Francis C. Barlow," *OR*, Series 1, Vol. 19, ch. 31, Pt. 1, 289–90: Patrick R. Kelly, ibid., 298.

11 Sears, *Landscape*, 244.

12 Ibid., 245, 247.

13 A single battery from that sector (Captian John A. Tompkins's) had fired in support of French's right flank for two hours before retiring to resupply with ammunition. McClellan had sent only one battery from his artillery reserve (Battery K, First U.S.) to Richardson's support, but its guns were short-range smoothbores. It managed to drive off a Confederate battery that was within range but was itself damaged by fire from Confederate-rifled cannons, which had longer range.

14 Harsh, *Taken*, 404.

15 Sears, *Landscape*, 247ff.

CHAPTER 14 **The Battle of Antietam: The Edge of Disaster**

1 Harsh, *Taken*, 407.

2 My discussion of this phase of the battle is based on Harsh, *Taken*, 397, 401–29 (decisions by Lee's HQ and Confederate movements); Sears, *Landscape*, ch. 8 (Federal movements and decisions by Hooker and by McClellan's HQ); and Priest, chs. 8–12 (esp. for timing of particular troop movements). See also the maps at "Antietam on the Web," http://antietam.aotw.org/maps .php?map_number=main, Detail Maps 8a–12; and Davis et al., *Atlas*, maps 11–14.

3 Sears, *Landscape*, 241.

4 Wilson, 1:112–15; Sears, *Landscape*, 272–73.

5 Sears, *Landscape*, 271–74.

6 McClellan, *Civil War Papers*, 467–68.

7 Sears, *Landscape*, 270–74; Harsh, *Taken*, 407–12.

8 Lincoln, *Collected Works*, 5:460.

9 Harsh, *Taken*, 413; Sears, *Landscape*, 272–73.

10 In its tactical effect, the movement (made by Griffin's and Stockton's Brigades of Morell's V Corps division) was entirely inconsequential: the two brigades had gone less than half a mile when they were ordered to halt and hold their position. However, the timing of the order (if it could be established) might yield some insight into McClellan's decision-making process. In their official reports both McClellan and Porter affirm that the brigades

were sent to support Sumner and Franklin—to aid in defense rather than
lend muscle to an assault. One of the battlefield tablets (No. 26) says that
the order was given at 2:00 PM; Sears, *Landscape*, 272, says the brigades
were ordered to Sumner's aid shortly after the capture of the Sunken Road
(perhaps 2:00 PM); see also Harsh, *Taken*, 414; and Johnson and Buel, 2:656,
Editors' Note. However, General Griffin's after-battle report states that he
did not get the order until about 4:00 PM (*OR*, Series 1, Vol. 19, ch. 31, Pt.
1, 349–50); and Davis, *Atlas*, maps 12 and 13, confirm the brigades did not
move before 4:00 PM. It is likely that McClellan sent the order from Sumner's
HQ, at the end of their meeting (ca. 3:00 PM), and that it took half an hour or
more for the courier to bring the order to Porter and for Porter to forward it
to Morrell.

11 Harsh, *Taken*, 421.

12 Tim Reese, "On the Brink: The Confederate Center, Boonsboro Turnpike,"
"Antietam on the Web," http://antietam.aotw.org/exhibit.php?exhibit_
id=371; and Sears, *Landscape*, 284–85.

13 Leslie J. Gordon, "All Who Went into the Battle Were Heroes: Remembering the 16th Regiment Connecticut Volunteers at Antietam," in Gallagher,
Antietam, 174–80.

14 Sears, *Landscape*, 290–91.

15 Reese, "On the Brink."

16 *OR*, Series 1, Vol. 19, ch. 31, Pt. 2, Reports, Correspondence, etc., 316.

17 *Battles and Leaders* 2:656; Sears, *Landscape*, 291; McPherson, *Battle Cry*,
544.

18 Sears, *Landscape*, 292.

19 Rafuse, 326–27.

CHAPTER 15 **The Day When Nothing Happened**

1 Sears, *Landscape*, 295–96.

2 See Harsh, *Taken*, 414ff.

3 Ibid., 425.

4 Ibid., 425–26.

5 Ibid., 436–37.

6 Ibid., 426; Sears, *Landscape*, 304; Taylor, 136.

7 Harsh, *Taken*, 441–43.

8 Ibid., 441–44.

9 Taylor, 136; Harsh, *Taken*, 437.

10 Ibid., 443.

11 Sears, *Landscape*, 298–303; Sears, *McClellan*, 318–20; Rafuse, 326–27.

12 Sears, *Landscape*, 298.

13 *OR*, Series 1, Vol. 19, ch. 31, Pt. 1, 66.

14 Sears, *Landscape*, 298–99.

15 Harsh, *Taken*, 438–39; McClellan, *Civil War Papers*, 468–69.

16 *OR*, Series 1, Vol. 19, ch. 31, Pt. 1, 65.

17 Fitz-John Porter, "Report," *OR*, Series 1, Vol. 19, ch. 31, Pt. 1, 339; Burnside, "Report," *OR*, Series 1, Vol. 19, Pt. 1, 416–17; Marvel, 145–47.

18 Sears, *Landscape*, 304–6; Catton, *Mr. Lincoln's Army*, 85.

19 Rafuse, 328–29; Harsh, *Taken*, 445.

20 Ibid., 447.

21 McClellan, *Civil War Papers*, 470.

22 Ibid., 470, 473.

CHAPTER 16 **Lincoln's Revolution**

1 Sears, *Landscape*, 298–301, 308–11; Sears, *McClellan*, 320–28; McClellan, *Civil War Papers*, 473, 476; Rafuse, 332–26.

2 Sears, *McClellan*, 324; Segal, 203–4; Rafuse, 335; Smith, 144–45.

3 Cox, 354–59.

4 *Harper's Weekly*, "McClellan," Sept. 27, 1862, 610.

5 Hay, *Inside*, 230–32.

6 Cox, 358–59. References in McClellan, *Civil War Papers*, 476, suggest that this meeting was on Sept. 21.

7 Rafuse, 329; Sears, *McClellan*, 320–28; Sears, *Landscape*, 312–15.

8 *NYTrib* [editorial], Sept. 19, 1862; *NYTrib*, "The War for the Union . . . ," Sept. 20, 1862; *NYTrib*, "Leaving Maryland . . ." and editorial, Sept. 29, 1862. See also Segal, 298–99.

9 Sears, *McClellan*, 324; Rafuse, 335; Segal, 204–7.

10 Ibid., 207–8; Fehrenbacher and Fehrenbacher, 38; Hay, *Inside*, 40; Welles, 142–45. For a full discussion of the ideas behind the Proclamation, see Guelzo, ch. 4; Foner, *Fiery Trial*, ch. 7.

11 http://eh.net/encyclopedia/article/ransom.civil.war.us.

12 Foner, *Fiery Trial*, 249; Long, 706.

13 *NYH*, "A Proclamation by the President of the United States" and "Important from Washington—The President's Proclamation," Sept. 23, 1862; *NYH*, "Signs of Peace at Richmond," Oct. 1, 1862.

14 *NYTrib*, "Northern Independence," Sept. 12, 1862; *NYTrib*, "Usurpation Threatened," Sept. 13.

15 Hay, *Inside*, 38–39; he later (231–32) took the view that McClellan's hesitation was due to timidity, not conspiracy.

16 Welles, 146–48; Hay, *Inside*, 41.

17 Lincoln, *Collected Works*, 5:442–43, 508.

18 Sears, *McClellan*, 328; *NYH*, "The Convention . . . ," Sept. 25, 1862, sees the conference as favorable to both McClellan and the president's Proclamation, which the *Herald* was (for the moment) supporting. See also *NYH*, "Important from the South," Oct. 4.

19 In November, after he had decided to fire McClellan, Lincoln would famously describe him as "an auger too dull to take hold." But apparently that disparaging characterization was already current in the Republican press. A *Tribune* editorial titled "Augers That Won't Bore" was printed

Sept. 4, just after McClellan's reappointment, and the paper would recall the phrase in its later criticisms of the general's passivity. See Fehrenbacher and Fehrenbacher, 32; Segal, 203–4; Rafuse, 343–44; McClellan, *Civil War Papers*, 477.

20 Hay, *Lincoln's Journalist*, 315–16.

21 Sears, *McClellan*, 324.

22 Sears, *Landscape*, 319–20.

23 McClellan, *Civil War Papers*, 482.

24 Sears, *McClellan*, 326; Rafuse, 339–41; Catton, *Never Call Retreat*, 357–59.

25 Cox, 359–64.

26 *NYW*, "The Emancipation Proclamation," Sept. 24, 1862; *NYH*, "Important . . . ," Oct. 4, 1862.

27 Sears, *Landscape*, 320–21.

28 Rafuse, 341–2.

29 Sears, *Landscape*, 319.

30 Rafuse, 87–89.

CHAPTER 17 **The General and the President**

1 Sears, *Landscape*, 325; Hay, *Inside*, 232; Rafuse, 344–45.

2 Ibid., 344.

3 McPherson, *Tried*, 151–55.

4 Rafuse, 343–46; Sears, *Landscape*, 324–25; McClellan, *Civil War Papers*, 488.

5 Ibid., 490; Rafuse, 346; Sears, *Landscape*, 325–26.

6 Welles, 163; Weber, 65.

7 *NYH*, "McClellan's Great Victory," Sept. 16, 1862; *NYH*, "The Campaign in Virginia," Sept. 20, 1862; *NYH*, "The President's Visit," Oct. 7, 1862; *NYW*, "The Proclamation and Great Military Vigor," Oct. 1, 1862; *NYH*, "The War . . . ," Sept. 30, 1862; McClellan, *Civil War Papers*, 490, 492–93.

8 Ibid., 493–94.

9 Sears, *Landscape*, 331; Hay, *Inside*, 232; Strong, 1:256, 267. There is a revealingly ambivalent set of editorials in *NYH*, "The President's Visit," Oct. 7, 1862, and "General McClellan's Recent Order," Oct. 8, 1862. The first asserts that McClellan and Lincoln are partners, planning a swift and decisive campaign that will force the Rebels to make peace before the Proclamation can go into effect; the second contrasts McClellan's patriotic and realistic order with the president's "ineffective" proclamation.

10 Harsh, *Taken*, 468–75.

11 Ibid., 468.

12 Ibid., 468, 471.

13 Davis, *Papers*, 8:437; Connelly, *Army*, ch. 14.

14 Welles, 176–77; Sears, *McClellan*, 328; *NYW*, "The Proclamation and Great Military Vigor," Oct. 1, 1862; *NYW*, The Discussion of War Measures" and "Gen. McClellan and Cabinet Officers," Oct. 6, 1862.

15 Lincoln, *Collected Works*, 8:460–61.

16 Ibid., 474, 479.

17 Sears, *Landscape*, 329, 331, 337; McPherson, *Tried*, 41–45; Rafuse, 356. While he was supposedly granting McClellan a last chance to prove himself, he was already discussing possible replacements.

18 Sears, *McClellan*, 340–43; McClellan, *Civil War Papers*, 520–51; Rafuse, 375–79; *NYH*, "The Democracy Exultant," Nov. 11, 1862.

CHAPTER 18 **Dubious Battle**

1 Hay, *Inside*, 40–41.

2 Gallagher, "The Net Result Was in Our Favor: Confederate Reaction to the Maryland Campaign," in Gallagher, *Antietam*, ch. 1.

3 Ibid., 5.

4 Hubbard, ch. 9.

5 Connelly, *Army*, 278, says Davis should have insisted that Bragg and Smith combine forces and attack Buell instead of allowing them to go separate ways. However, given Davis's distance from the scene of operations, it was reasonable and even wise for him to rely on the judgment of his field commanders; and practically speaking, it is likely that Smith and Bragg (like Lee) would have acted on their own judgment rather than adhering to the letter of orders issued by someone out of touch with their immediate situation.

6 Gallagher, "Net Result," 17, 19; "Our Army in Maryland," *Richmond Daily Dispatch*, Sept. 10, 1862, defends the invasion despite evidence its military result will be limited.

7 Lincoln, *Speeches*, 2:434.

8 Adams Jr. et al., *Letters*, 194.

9 Rafuse, 332.

10 Sears, *Landscape*, 339.

11 http://civilwar.ilgenweb.net/articles.html.

12 Lincoln, *Collected Writings*, 5:444; McPherson, *Battle Cry*, 561–62.

13 See Wood, chs. 2–4.

14 Jones, *Union in Peril*, 138–90.

15 Foner, *Fiery*, chs. 8–9; McCurry, ch. 7.

16 Slotkin, ch. 7.

17 Long, 706. This estimate relates the mean of total enlistments for the period, roughly 850,000, to the mean of total black enlistments (90,000).

18 Frederick Douglass, "Should the Negro Enlist," *Frederick Douglass' Monthly*, August 1863, 851.

19 Lincoln, *Collected Writings*, 5:371–72; Lincoln, *Letters, Speeches*, 2:498–99.

SELECTED BIBLIOGRAPHY

WEBSITES AND DATABASES

Brian Downey et al., *Antietam on the Web*, http://antietam.aotw.org/.
Harpweek, LLC, *Illustrated Civil War Newspapers and Magazines*, linc.alexander
  street.com.
Proquest, *Proquest Civil War Era*, proquest.umi.com.

NEWSPAPERS AND MAGAZINES

Charleston Mercury, May 1–December 1, 1862
DeBow's Review, 1862
Frank Leslie's Illustrated, July 1–November 30, 1862
Frederick Douglass' Monthly, May 1862–August 1863
Harper's Weekly, 1862
New York Herald, June 25–December 31, 1862
New York Times, June 25–December 31, 1862
New York Tribune, June 25–December 31, 1862
New York World, June 25–December 31, 1862
Richmond *Daily Dispatch*, May 1–December 1, 1862

BOOKS

Adams, Charles Francis, Jr. et al. *A Cycle of Adams Letters, 1861–1865*. Vol. 1.
  Edited by Worthington Chauncey Ford. Boston: Houghton Mifflin Co., 1920.
Alexander, Edward Porter. *Fighting for the Confederacy: The Personal Recollec-
  tions of General Edward Porter Alexander*. Edited by Gary W. Gallagher.
  Chapel Hill: University of North Carolina Press, 1989.
Bauer, K. Jack. *The Mexican War, 1846–1848*. Lincoln: University of Nebraska
  Press, 1974.
Blair, William. *Virginia's Private War: Feeding Body and Soul in the Confederacy,
  1861–1865*. New York: Oxford University Press, 1998.
Browning, Orville Hickman. *The Diary of Orville Hickman Browning*. Vol. 1,

1850–1864. Edited by Theodore C. Pease and James G. Randall. Springfield: Illinois State Historical Library, 1925.

Carman, Ezra. *The Maryland Campaign of September 1862: Ezra A. Carman's Definitive Study of the Union and Confederate Armies at Antietam.* Edited by Joseph Pierro. London: Routledge, 2008.

Carmichael, Peter S. *Lee's Young Artillerist: William R. J. Pegram.* Charlottesville: University Press of Virginia, 1995.

Catton, Bruce. *Bruce Catton's Civil War: Mr. Lincoln's Army.* New York: Fairfax Press, 1984.

———. *Never Call Retreat: The Centennial History of the Civil War.* Vol. 3. New York: Doubleday and Co., 1965.

Connelly, Thomas L. *The Army of the Heartland: The Army of Tennessee, 1861–1862.* Baton Rouge: Louisiana State University Press, 1967.

Cox, Jacob D. *Military Reminiscences of the Civil War.* Vol. 1. New York: Charles Scribner's Sons, 1900.

Cozzens, Peter. *John Pope: A Life for the Nation.* Champaign: University of Illinois Press, 2005.

Crouthamel, James L. *Bennett's New York Herald and the Rise of the Popular Press.* Syracuse, NY: Syracuse University Press, 1989.

Davis, George, W. E. A. Carman, and H. Heth. *Atlas of the Battle of Antietam.* [Washington, DC], 1908.

Davis, Jefferson. *Jefferson Davis: The Essential Writings.* Edited by William J. Cooper Jr. New York: Modern Library, 2003.

———. "Message on Constitutional Ratification," in United States War Dept., John Sheldon Moody et al. *The War of the Rebellion: Official Records of the Union and Confederate Armies,* Series 4, Vol. 1. Washington, DC: Government Printing Office, 1900.

———. *The Papers of Jefferson Davis,* Vols. 7–8. Edited by Lynda Lasswell Crist et al. Baton Rouge: Louisiana State University Press, 1995.

Dell, Christopher. *Lincoln and the War Democrats: The Grand Erosion of Conservative Tradition.* Rutherford, NJ: Fairleigh Dickinson University Press, 1975.

de Peyster, J. Watts. *Personal and Military History of Philip Kearny, Major-General United States Volunteers.* New York: Ricer & Gage, 1869.

Dew, Charles B. *Apostles of Disunion: Southern Secession Commissioners and the Causes of the Civil War.* Charlottesville: University Press of Virginia, 2001.

Dirck, Brian R. *Lincoln & Davis: Imagining America, 1809–1865.* Lawrence: University Press of Kansas, 2001.

Donald, David Herbert. *Lincoln.* New York: Simon & Schuster, 1995.

Durden, Robert F. *The Gray and the Black: The Confederate Debate on Emancipation.* Baton Rouge: Louisiana State University Press, 1972.

Dyer, Frederick H. *Compendium of the War of the Rebellion.* 2 vols. Seattle, WA: Morningside Press, 1994.

Faust, Drew Gilpin. *The Creation of Confederate Nationalism: Ideology and Identity in the Civil War South.* Baton Rouge: Louisiana State University Press, 1990.

Fehrenbacher, Don E. and Virginia Fehrenbacher, eds. *Recollected Words of Abraham Lincoln.* Palo Alto, CA: Stanford University Press, 1996.

Flower, Frank Abial. *Edwin McMasters Stanton: The Autocrat of Rebellion, Emancipation, and Reconstruction.* Akron, OH: Sallfield Publishing Co., 1905.

Foner, Eric. *The Fiery Trial: Abraham Lincoln and American Slavery.* New York: W. W. Norton & Co., 2010.

———. *Free Soil, Free Labor, Free Men: The Ideology of the Republican Party Before the Civil War.* New York: Oxford University Press, 1970.

Frank, Joseph Allan. *With Ballot and Bayonet: The Political Socialization of American Civil War Soldiers.* Athens: University of Georgia Press, 1998.

Freeman, Douglas Southall, ed. *Lee's Dispatches: Unpublished Letters of Robert E. Lee, C.S.A., to Jefferson Davis and the War Department of the Confederate States of America.* New York: G. P. Putnam's Sons, 1957.

———. *Lee's Lieutenants: A Study in Command.* New York: Charles Scribner's Sons, 1944.

———. *R. E. Lee: A Biography.* Vols. 1 and 2. New York: Charles Scribner's Sons, 1934–1935.

Gallagher, Gary W. *The Confederate War.* Cambridge, MA: Harvard University Press, 1997.

Gallagher, Gary W., ed. *The Antietam Campaign.* Chapel Hill: University of North Carolina Press, 1999.

———. *Lee the Soldier.* Lincoln: University of Nebraska Press, 1996.

———. *The Richmond Campaign of 1862: The Peninsula and the Seven Days.* Chapel Hill: University of North Carolina Press, 2000.

Glatthaar, Joseph T. *General Lee's Army: From Victory to Collapse.* New York: Free Press, 2008.

Goodwin, Doris Kearns. *Team of Rivals: The Political Genius of Abraham Lincoln.* New York: Simon & Schuster, 2004.

Goff, Richard D. *Confederate Supply.* Durham, NC: Duke University Press, 1969.

Griffith, Paddy. *Battle Tactics of the Civil War.* New Haven, CT: Yale University Press, 1987.

Guelzo, Allen C. *Lincoln's Emancipation Proclamation: The End of Slavery in America.* New York: Simon & Schuster, 2004.

Hagerman, Edward. *The American Civil War and the Origins of Modern Warfare: Ideas, Organization and Field Command.* Bloomington: Indiana University Press, 1988.

Harsh, Joseph L. *Confederate Tide Rising: Robert E. Lee and the Making of Southern Strategy, 1861–1862.* Kent, OH: Kent State University Press, 1998.

———. *Sounding the Shallows: A Confederate Companion for the Maryland Campaign of 1862.* Kent, OH: Kent State University Press, 2000.

———. *Taken at the Flood: Robert E. Lee and Confederate Strategy in the Maryland Campaign of 1862.* Kent, OH: Kent State University Press, 1999.

Hattaway, Herman and Richard E. Beringer. *Jefferson Davis, Confederate President.* University Press of Kansas, 2002.

Hay, John. *Inside Lincoln's White House: The Complete Civil War Diary of John Hay.* Edited by Michael Burlingame and John R. T. Ettlinger. Carbondale: Southern Illinois University Press, 1997.

———. *Lincoln's Journalist: John Hay's Anonymous Writings for the Press, 1860–1864.* Edited by Michael Burlingame. Carbondale: Southern Illinois University Press, 1998.

Hess, Earl J. *The Union Soldier in Battle: Enduring the Ordeal of Combat.* Lawrence: University Press of Kansas, 1997.

Hubbard, Charles M. *The Burden of Confederate Diplomacy.* Knoxville: University of Tennessee Press, 1998.

Johnson, Robert U., and C. C. Clough Buel. *Battles and Leaders of the Civil War.* Vol. 2. New York: The Century Co., 1887.

Jones, Archer. *Civil War Command and Strategy: The Process of Victory and Defeat.* New York: Free Press, 1992.

Jones, Howard. *Union in Peril: The Crisis over British Intervention in the Civil War.* Lincoln: University of Nebraska Press, 1997.

Jordan, Ervin L. *Black Confederates and Afro-Yankees in Civil War Virginia.* Charlottesville: University Press of Virginia, 1995.

Judkins, W. P. "History of Co. G, 22nd Georgia," http://www.mindspring.com/~jcherepy/memoir/judkins.txt.

Katcher, Philip. *The Complete Civil War.* London: Cassell, 2005.

Katz, Irving. *August Belmont: A Political Biography.* New York: Columbia University Press, 1968.

Levine, Bruce. *Confederate Emancipation: Southern Plans to Free and Arm Slaves During the Civil War.* New York: Oxford University Press, 2006.

Lincoln, Abraham. *The Collected Works of Abraham Lincoln.* Edited by Roy P. Basler. Vol. 5. New Brunswick, NJ: Rutgers University Press, 1953.

———. *Speeches and Writings.* 2 vols. New York: Library of America, 1989.

Livermore, Thomas L. *Numbers and Losses in the Civil War in America: 1861–1865.* Bloomington: Indiana University Press, 1957.

Long, E. B., and Barbara Long. *The Civil War Day by Day: An Almanac 1861–1865.* New York: Da Capo, 1971.

Marvel, William. *Burnside.* Chapel Hill: University of North Carolina Press, 1991.

McClellan, George B. *The Civil War Papers of George B. McClellan: Selected Correspondence, 1860–1865.* Edited by Stephen W. Sears. New York: Ticknor & Fields, 1989.

McCurry, Stephanie. *Confederate Reckoning: Power and Politics in the Civil War South.* Cambridge, MA: Harvard University Press, 2010.

McJimsey, George T. *Genteel Partisan: Manton Marble, 1834–1917.* Ames: Iowa State University Press, 1971.

McPherson, James M. *Battle Cry of Freedom: The Civil War Era.* New York: Oxford University Press, 1988.

———. *Crossroads of Freedom: Antietam.* New York: Oxford University Press, 2002.

————. *For Cause and Comrades: Why Men Fought the Civil War.* New York: Oxford University Press, 1997.

————. *Tried by War: Abraham Lincoln as Commander in Chief.* New York: Penguin Press, 2008.

————. *What They Fought For, 1861–1865.* Baton Rouge: Louisiana State University Press, 1994.

McWhiney, Grady, and Perry D. Jamieson. *Attack and Die: Civil War Military Tactics and the Southern Heritage.* Tuscaloosa: University of Alabama Press, 1984.

Miller, William Lee. *President Lincoln: The Duty of a Statesman.* New York: Alfred A. Knopf, 2008.

Mitchell, Reid. *Civil War Soldiers.* New York: Viking Press, 1988.

Nolan, Alan. T. *Lee Considered: General Robert E. Lee and Civil War History.* Chapel Hill: University of North Carolina Press, 1991.

Nosworthy, Brent. *The Bloody Crucible of Courage: Fighting Methods and Combat Experience of the Civil War.* New York: Carroll & Graf, 2003.

Perret, Geoffrey. *Lincoln's War: The Untold Story of America's Greatest President as Commander in Chief.* New York: Random House, 2004.

Potter, David M. *The Impending Crisis, 1848–1861.* Completed and edited by Don E. Fehrenbacher. New York: Harper & Row, 1976.

Power, J. Tracy. *Lee's Miserables: Life in the Army of Northern Virginia from the Wilderness to Appomattox.* Chapel Hill: University of North Carolina Press, 1998.

Priest, John Michael. *Antietam: The Soldiers' Battle.* New York: Oxford University Press, 1989.

Pryor, Elizabeth Brown. *Reading the Man: A Portrait of Robert E. Lee Through His Private Letters.* New York: Viking, 2007.

Rable, George C. *The Confederate Republic: A Revolution Against Politics.* Chapel Hill: University of North Carolina Press, 1994.

Rafuse, Ethan S. *McClellan's War: The Failure of Moderation in the Struggle for the Union.* Bloomington: Indiana University Press, 2005.

Sears, Stephen W. *Controversies and Commanders: Dispatches from the Army of the Potomac.* New York: Houghton Mifflin, 1999.

————. *George B. McClellan: The Young Napoleon.* New York: Ticknor & Fields, 1988.

————. *Landscape Turned Red: The Battle of Antietam.* New York: Ticknor & Fields, 1983.

————. *To the Gates of Richmond: The Peninsula Campaign.* New York: Ticknor & Fields, 1992.

Segal, Charles M., ed. *Conversations with Lincoln.* Piscataway: Transaction Publishers, 2002.

Silbey, Joel H. *A Respectable Minority: The Democratic Party in the Civil War Era, 1860–1868.* New York: W. W. Norton & Co., 1977.

Slotkin, Richard. *No Quarter: The Battle of the Crater, 1864.* New York: Random House, 2009.

Smith, William Ernest. *The Francis Preston Blair Family in Politics*, vol. 2. New York: Da Capo Press, 1969.

Stoker, Donald. *The Grand Design: Strategy and the U.S. Civil War*. New York: Oxford University Press, 2010.

Stone, DeWitt Boyd, Jr. *Wandering to Glory: Confederate Veterans Remember Evans' Brigade*. Columbia: University of South Carolina Press, 2002.

Strode, Hudson. *Jefferson Davis: Confederate President*, vol. 2. New York: Harcourt, Brace and Co., 1959.

Strong, George Templeton. *The Diary of George Templeton Strong: The Civil War, 1860–1865*. Edited by Allan Nevins and Milton H. Thomas. New York: The Macmillan Co., 1952.

Taafe, Stephen. *Commanding the Army of the Potomac*. Lawrence: University Press of Kansas, 2006.

Tap, Bruce. *Over Lincoln's Shoulder: The Committee on the Conduct of the War*. Lawrence: University Press of Kansas, 1998.

Taylor, Walter H. *Four Years with General Lee*. Edited by James I. Robertson, Jr. Bloomington: Indiana University Press, 1996.

Thomas, Benjamin P., and Harold M. Hyman. *Stanton: The Life and Times of Lincoln's Secretary of War*. New York: Alfred A. Knopf, 1962.

Thomas, Emory M. *The Confederacy as a Revolutionary Experience*. University of South Carolina Press, 1971.

———. *Robert E. Lee: A Biography*. New York: W. W. Norton & Co., 1995.

Time-Life Books. *Echoes of Glory: The Illustrated Atlas of the Civil War*. Alexandria, VA: Time-Life Books, 1991.

United States War Department. *Atlas to Accompany the Official Records of the Union and Confederate Armies*. Washington, DC: Government Printing Office, 1891–95.

———. *The War of the Rebellion: Official Records of the Union and Confederate Armies*, Series 1, Vol. 40, Pts. 1–3. Washington, DC: Government Printing Office, 1892.

United States War Dept., John Sheldon Moody et al. *The War of the Rebellion: Official Records of the Union and Confederate Armies*, Series 1, Vol. 12, Ch. 24, Pts. 1–3. Washington, DC: Government Printing Office, 1885.

———. *The War of the Rebellion: Official Records of the Union and Confederate Armies*, Series 1, Vol. 19, Ch. 31, Pts. 1–2, Reports and Correspondence. Washington, DC: Government Printing Office, 1887.

Warner, Ezra J. *Generals in Blue: Lives of the Union Commanders*. Baton Rouge: Louisiana State University Press, 1992.

———. *Generals in Gray: Lives of the Confederate Commanders* Baton Rouge: Louisiana State University Press, 1987.

Waugh, John C. *Lincoln and McClellan: The Troubled Partnership Between a President and His General*. New York: Palgrave Macmillan, 2010.

Weber, Jennifer L. *Copperheads: The Rise and Fall of Lincoln's Opponents in the North*. New York: Oxford University Press, 2006.

Weitz, Mark A. *More Damning Than Slaughter: Desertion in the Confederate Army*. Lincoln: University of Nebraska Press, 2005.

Welles, Gideon. *Diary of Gideon Welles, Secretary of the Navy Under Lincoln and Johnson*. Vol. 1, 1861–March 30, 1864. Boston: Houghton, Mifflin Co., 1911.

Whitman, George W. *Civil War Letters of George Washington Whitman*. Edited by Jerome M. Loving. Durham, NC: Duke University Press, 1975.

Wilkes, George. *McClellan: From Ball's Bluff to Antietam*. New York: Sinclair Tousey, 1863.

Williams, David. *Rich Man's War: Class, Caste, and Confederate Defeat in the Lower Chattahoochee Valley*. Athens: University of Georgia Press, 1998.

Wilson, James Harrison. *Under the Old Flag: Recollections of Military Operations in the War for the Union, the Spanish War, the Boxer Rebellion, Etc.* Vol. 1. New York: D. Appleton & Co., 1912.

Wittenberg, Eric J. *The Battle of Brandy Station: North America's Largest Cavalry Battle*. Charleston, SC: The History Press, 2010.

Wood, Forrest G. *Black Scare: The Racist Response to Emancipation and Reconstruction*. Berkeley: University of California Press, 1968.

Woodworth, Stephen E. *Davis and Lee at War*. Lawrence: University Press of Kansas, 1995.

Wyatt-Brown, Bertram. *Honor and Violence in the Old South*. New York: Oxford University Press, 1986.

INDEX

Page numbers in *italics* refer to illustrations.

Adams, Charles Francis, Jr., 130–32, 367, 404

Adams, John, 131

Adams, John Quincy, 131

African Americans:
colonization policy and, 86–87, 88, 105–6, 365, 412, 421
in military service, 86–87, 105–6, 365–66, 396–97, 410–12
and right of self-defense, 365–66
see also Emancipation Proclamation; slavery

Alabama, 66, 411

Alexander, Porter, 344

Altoona governors' conference, 359, 370, 372

American War of Independence, 67

Anderson, G. B., 239, 272, 295–96, 302, 304

Anderson, G. T. "Tige," 239, 273, 284, 286, 291, 296

Anderson, Richard H., 154, 163, 167, 216, 234, 238, 272, 273, 289–90, 296–97, 303, 306, 321

Andrew, John A., 372

Antietam, Battle of, xiii, 156, 210–13
A. P. Hill's flank attack in, 327–30, 332–33, 335, 425–26
assessment of, 394–96
Burnside's attack in, 316–17, 319, 323–27, 334–35, 447*n*
campaign leading to, *see* Maryland, invasion of
casualties in, 267, 330, 346, 349, 357, 426
Cemetery Hill in, 324, 326

Confederate artillery in, 221, 240–41, 255–56, 258–59, 261–62, 284, 324, 330
Confederate counterattack at Dunker Church in, 306–9
Confederate defensive positions in, 210–13, 219–21, 233–40
Confederate food shortage in, 234–35
Confederate forces in, 217–22, 223, 227–28, 234, 238, 240–42, 250–51, 312–13, 340, 342
Confederate order of battle in, 432–33
Confederate preparations in, 236–41
Confederate reserves in, 238, 272, 296
Confederate retreat in, 352–54, 426
Confederate supply line in, 236–37
cornfields in, 212–13, 238, 253, 255–56, 259–60, 264–65, 270, 275, 278–79, 293, 304
Dunker Church in, 212–13, 245, 254, 256, 259–64, 270, 272–74, 277–78, 280–81, *280*, 284–85, 286, 287, 290, 291, 293, 295, 302, 305–9, 311–16, 318, 324, 343, 349
East Woods in, 212–13, 237–38, 253, 255, 256, 261–63, 264, 265, 270–71, 278–79, 291, 307, 314, 318, 320, 322, 349
1862 election and, 235, 397
first public account of, 362
foreign intervention issue and, 235
French's attack in, 291–97, 301–5
Hood's counterattack in, 264–66, 270, 273, 275
Hooker's advance in, 225–26
Hooker's attack in, 253–64, 447*n*
Irish Brigade in, 299–303

Antietam, Battle of (*continued*)
Iron Brigade in, 256, 259–66, 275, 277
Jackson's flank attack in, 320–21, 323, 331–32, 336–37
Jackson's reinforcements in, 223–26
Lee and midday crisis in, 319–20
Lee's decision to continue battle in, 340–44
Lee's decision to fight at, 210–11, 221, 236, 399
Lee's tactical command in, 271–74, 394–95
Lincoln-McClellan meeting and, 379–82, 427
Lincoln-McClellan telegram in, 233
lost order and, xvi–xvii, 226
Louisiana Tigers in, 262–63
Lower Bridge in, 213, 226, 239–40, 243, 247, 272, 275–76, 281, 289–90, 294–95, 312–13, 316, 318, 323, 335–36, 337, 349
McClellan and midday crisis in, 313–19
McClellan-Halleck telegrams in, 216–17, 231, 313
McClellan's "all is lost" outcry in, 336
McClellan's attack decision in, 233
McClellan's communications failure in, 247–48, 250
McClellan's decision making in, 449*n*–50*n*
McClellan's decision to discontinue battle in, 347–52
McClellan's Final Report on, 241, 348, 351, 447*n*
McClellan's indecision in, 247–48
McClellan's missed opportunities in, 221–22, 226–27, 231, 289–90
McClellan's overestimates in, 223, 241–42, 250, 319, 446*n*–47*n*
McClellan's political ambitions and, 334–35
McClellan's postbattle inaction and, 361–63, 369–70, 384–85
McClellan's Preliminary Report on, 243–44, 388, 446*n*
McClellan's refusal to advance after, 405
McClellan's risk-aversion in, 222, 236, 322–23, 338
McClellan's sense of mission accomplished and, 357–59

McClellan's survey of Confederate positions in, 224–25
McClellan's tactical command in, 274–77, 280–81, 288–91, 313–15, 318–19, 331–34, 336
McClellan's tactical plans for, 241–47
McClellan's victory criteria for, 226–27, 246
midday crisis in, 313–16
Middle Bridge in, 212, 220, 239, 243, 244–47, 275, 281, 289–90, 312–14, 318–19, 320, 324, 333, 335, 349
Nicodemus Heights in, 213, 225, 237, 267, 284, 331, 337–38, 345
ordeal of wounded in, 351–52
Richardson's attack in, 297–303, 305
Roulette Farm in, 212, 225, 238–39
significance of, xiii–xv, 396
Stonewall Brigade in, 260–62, 284–85
Sumner's attack in, 283–88
Sunken Road in, 239, 272–73, 285, 288, 290–305, 311–14, 318, 320–22, 324, 343, 346, 349, 450*n*
surrender of Harpers Ferry and, 213–15
tactical patterns of, 266–67
tactical stalemate in, 339–43
terrain of, 237–38, 241, 246
Texas Brigade in, 264–65
XII Corps attack in, 269–71, 277–79
Union advance to Sharpsburg in, 217–20, 222–23
Union artillery in, 226–27, 245, 262, 265–66, 305–6, 307, 309, 330, 331
Union forces in, 221, 227, 240–41, 242, 250–51, 312–13, 340, 349
Union order of battle in, 429–32
Union reserves in, 227, 245, 324–25, 333–34
Union's center concentration in, 244–46
as Union victory, 357
Upper Bridge in, 221, 246, 267, 281
West Woods in, 212, 225, 238, 264–66, 277, 283–88, 291, 293, 307, 331, 337, 345, 349
Archer, James J., 203, 330
army, as military term, xxx
Army of Northern Virginia, C.S.A., xxx, 72, 73, 131, 257, 340–41, 400
artillery of, 154–55, 240–41

flexible command structure of, 237

marching style of, 158–59

at onset of Maryland invasion, 151–57, 174–75

post-Antietam status of, 385–86, 395, 428

straggling problem of, 234, 386, 399, 443n

Army of Tennessee, C.S.A., xxvi, 5, 65, 76, 100, 400

Army of the Cumberland, U.S., 411

Army of the James, U.S., 411

Army of the Potomac, U.S., xxii, xxv, xxx, 4, 13, 31, 32, 39, 42, 61, 104, 119, 132, 175, 255, 257, 361, 387, 396, 403, 411, 428

Burnside declines command of, 98–99

as "last army of the Republic," 334–35

McClellan cult of personality in, 45–47

McClellan's last review of, 391–92

McClellan's personal bond with, 45–46, 54–55, 170–71, 391

reorganization of, 134, 172–74

Stuart's raids and, 384–85, 387–88, 418, 427

Army of Virginia, U.S., 96–97, 109, 117, 120, 172, 420

Aspinwall, William, 26, 99, 130, 372–73, 378, 382–84, 391

Austria, 146

Ball's Bluff, Battle of, 33

Baltimore and Ohio Railroad, 157, 161, 361

Banks, Nathaniel, 93, 118, 124, 172, 173, 248, 269, 318, 417

Barksdale, William, 286, 289

Barlow, Francis C., 300, 302–3, 304–5, 307, 309

Barlow, Samuel L. M., 26, 28, 30, 34, 42, 48, 91–92, 99, 103, 178, 378, 382

Bates, Edward, 129, 393

Bates, John C., 106

battery, as military term, xxx–xxxi

Beauregard, Pierre, 70, 437n

Belmont, August, 26, 90–91, 378, 382

Bennett, James Gordon, 37–38, 92–93, 177, 372, 376, 383

Big Bethel, Battle of, 196

Bismarck, Otto von, 146

Blacks, *see* African Americans

Blair, Francis P., Sr., 88, 374, 376, 383

Blair, Montgomery, 27, 31, 37, 129, 133, 367, 376, 383

Emancipation Proclamation opposed by, 88–89

McClellan's correspondence with, 358–59, 374

Blood Tubs, 44

Bolshevik Revolution, 365

Border States, xvii, xx, xxi–xxii, 19, 87

Emancipation Proclamation and, 88, 90, 408

invasion of Maryland and, 143–44, 149

slavery issue in, 11–12

Boteler's Ford, 240, 324, 353

Bradford, Augustus, 370

Bragg, Braxton, xxvi, 5, 10, 62, 70, 76–77, 79, 81, 100, 119, 143, 149, 150, 174–75, 235, 386–87, 390, 396, 398, 399–400, 418, 420–21, 422, 424–26, 427, 428, 453n

Branch, L. O'Brien, 330

Breckinridge, John C., 25

Brockenbrough, John M., 331

Brooke, John R., 300–301, 302, 303–5

Brown, Joe, 64, 65–66

Brown, John, 115

Buchanan, James, 16, 34

Buchanan, Robert, 316, 318, 324, 326, 331–32

Buell, Don Carlos, xxii–xxiii, xxiv, xxvi, 5, 13, 32–33, 76, 79, 95, 386–87, 390, 399, 401, 415–16, 417, 419, 422, 426, 427, 428, 453n

Bull Run, First Battle of, xxi, xxii, 15, 17, 21, 33, 36, 161, 171, 205, 260, 261, 300, 303

Second Battle of, *see* Second Bull Run Campaign

Burnside, Ambrose, xiii, 13, 79–80, 96, 100, 105, 118, 133–34, 136, 151, 173–74, 175, 182, 186, 187, 197, 202, 209, 217–18, 220, 226, 241, 254, 342, 347, 348, 351, 353, 374–76, 380, 382, 383, 403, 405, 421, 428

at Antietam, 243–44, 246–50, 275, 276–77, 281, 290, 294, 312–13, 316–17, 319, 323–27, 330–35, 338

army command refused by, 98–99

Burnside, Ambrose (*continued*)
and criticism of McClellan, 176–77
McClellan replaced by, 391, 404
Turner's Gap fight and, 198–99, 205

Caesar, Julius, xvii
Caldwell, John, 300–302, 303, 304
Cameron, Simon, 37–38
campaign, definition of, xxxi
Canada, 179
canister, xxxi
case shot, xxxi
Castiglione, Battle of, 183–84
Cedar Mountain, Battle of, 80, 260, 269, 421
Cemetery Hill, 324, 326
Census Bureau, U.S., 64
Century, 334
Chancellorsville, Battle of, 235
Chandler, Zachariah, 20, 21, 27, 42
Chantilly, Battle of, 126, 423
Charles I, King of England, 374
Charleston Mercury, 65, 143
Chartist movement, 43
Chase, Salmon P., 19–20, 21, 27, 31, 36–37,
128–29, 133, 136, 173, 178, 367–68, 374,
393, 402
Emancipation Proclamation opposed by,
89
Christ, Benjamin, 326
Christian, William, 258, 263–64
civil rights, 413
Civil War, U.S., xiii, xiv–xvi, xx, xxi, 3,
18, 21
attack and defense in, 256–57
battlefield tactics in, 256–57
Border States in, *see* Border States
casualties in, 413
conciliation policy and, 11–12, 21–22, 28,
59, 61, 63, 85, 401
early military operations in, xiii–xvi
foreign recognition issue in, 33, 72–73,
145–46, 396, 410
naval blockade in, xx, xxi, xxii, 146,
150–51
revolving character of, xv, xix, 150
slavery issue in, *see* slavery
as "total" war, 150
Union coastal operations in, xxiii–xxiv

war aims in, xix–xx
western offensive in, 75, 76–77, 79, 100,
143, 149–50, 174, 175, 235, 386–87, 390,
396, 398, 399–400, 418, 420–21, 422,
425–26, 427, 428, 453n
Cobb, Howell, 201
Cobb's Legion, C.S.A., 201–2, 287, 295
Cochrane, John, 374–76, 383
colonization policy, 86–87, 88, 105–6, 365
412, 421
Colquitt, Alfred, 196, 198, 205, 212, 273,
278–79, 285, 286–87, 295
Confederate States of America, xiii, xvi,
xix–xx
American Revolution as model for, 67
foreign recognition issue and, 33, 72–73,
145–46, 396, 410
foreign relations and, 63, 72–73
growing rancor in, 91–92
military power of, 396–97
"peace" movement in, 407
plantation system of, 66, 68
radicalized federal policy and, 77–78
social system of, 66–68
states' rights fundamentalism in, 64–65
Twenty Negro Law of, 410–11
war strategy of, 63–69
western offensive of, 75, 76–77, 79, 100,
143, 149–50, 174, 175, 235, 386–87, 390,
396, 398, 399–400, 418, 420–21, 422,
425–26, 427, 428, 453n
see also Border States
Confiscation Act (U.S.), 86, 93, 97, 106
Congress, Confederate, 145, 407, 427
Congress, U.S., xx, 12–13, 21, 27, 77, 92, 179,
373, 387, 402, 420
conscription, 65, 70, 85, 155, 397, 416
Conscription Act (C.S.A.), 65, 70
Constitution, C.S.A., xix, 64–65
Constitution, U.S., xix, xx, 18, 413
Fifteenth Amendment of, 413
Fourteenth Amendment of, 413
slavery question and, 23–24, 29
Thirteenth Amendment of, 413
war powers in, 21
Continental Army, 68
Cooke, J. R., 307
Copperhead movements, 400
Corinth, Battle of, 386, 396, 414, 427–28

cornfield, 212–13, 238, 253, 255–56, 259–60, 264–65, 270, 275, 278–79, 293, 304
corps, as military term, xxx
Couch, Darius, 186, 202–3, 226, 345, 347–48, 351
Coulter, Richard, 263
Cowpens, Battle of, 67
Cox, Jacob, 131, 174, 185, 195, 196–97, 201, 248, 249–50, 277, 281, 294, 312–13, 319, 324, 325, 330–31, 361, 374–76, 380–84, 405
Crampton's Gap, 193–94, 201–3, 206, 217, 425
Crimean War, 15, 41, 437n
Crittenden, John, 145, 378
Cromwell, Oliver, xvii, 179–80
Crook, George, 197, 295, 316
Cross, Edward, 300, 307–8
Cross Keys, Battle of, 417
Curtin, Andrew, 175, 255, 359, 370
Curtis, Samuel R., 95
Custer, George Armstrong, 217, 219

Davis, Benjamin "Grimes," 207–8
Davis, Jefferson, xiv, xv, xvii, xviii, xix–xx, xxvi–xxvii, 11, 15, 21, 62, 93, 96, 97, 159, 164, 235, 240, 278, 402, 404, 411, 416, 421, 424, 453n
background and personality of, 69–70
Lee's Antietam report to, 342, 385–86
Lee's strategic partnership with, 71–72
Maryland invasion decision and planning of, 142–44, 147–50
war strategy and, 63–69, 73–77, 79–80, 81, 394, 396, 398, 400, 418
DeBow, James D. B., 64–65
DeBow's Review, 64
Declaration of Independence, 23, 24, 25
Delaware, xx, 12
Democratic Party, U.S., xiii, 12, 14, 20, 30, 31, 42, 59, 90, 99, 360, 361, 372, 379, 380, 397, 400, 409, 427
Copperheads of, 408
Douglas wing of, 15–16, 22
1862 election and, 428
1864 election and, 408–9
expansion of slavery and, 23–24
factions of, 23–26
McClellan and, 15–16, 26, 48–49

Denmark, 147
Dennison, William, 16, 359
District of Columbia, 77
division, as military term, xxx
Doubleday, Abner, 255–56, 259, 266–67, 378
Douglas, Stephen A., xviii, 15, 27, 145, 379, 397
Lincoln's debates with, 22, 23, 25
slavery question and, 24–26, 59
Douglass, Frederick, 412
Douglass, Marcellus, 258
Drayton, Thomas F., 200, 324–25, 327, 330
Dryer, Hiram, 326, 331–32, 336, 338
Dunker Church, 212–13, 245, 254, 256, 259–64, 270, 272–74, 277–78, 280–81, 280, 284–85, 286, 287, 290, 291, 293, 295, 302, 305–9, 311–16, 318, 324, 343, 349
Duryee, Abram, 255–56, 258–59, 271

Early, Jubal, 237, 277, 284, 285, 286–87
East Woods, 212–13, 237–38, 253, 255, 256, 261–63, 264, 265, 270–71, 278–79, 291, 307, 314, 318, 320, 322, 349
Eckert, Thomas, 7
Eighth New York Cavalry Regiment, U.S., 207–8
Eighteenth Georgia Regiment, C.S.A., 265
Eighty-first Pennsylvania Regiment, U.S., 300, 303
Eighty-fourth New York Regiment, U.S., 260–61
Eighty-eighth New York Regiment, U.S., 299, 302
elections, U.S.:
of 1857, 20
of 1858, 24
of 1860, 26, 88, 96–97
of 1862, xxvii, 27, 72, 88, 143, 147, 148, 370, 382, 384–85, 390, 392, 397, 403, 405, 428
of 1864, 26, 42, 53, 360, 378, 392, 398, 400, 408–9, 410
XI Corps, U.S., 173, 175
Eleventh Mississippi Regiment, C.S.A., 265
Emancipation Proclamation, xiii, xiv, xv–xvi, xviii, 105, 106, 357, 371, 380, 393, 395, 414
Altoona governors' conference and, 372

Emancipation Proclamation (*continued*)
 Black enlistments and, 410–12
 cabinet meeting on, 86–89
 character of war and, 395
 colonization policy and, 88, 365
 1862 election and, 408
 effect of, xxvii, 409, 410–12
 final draft of, 61, 85–87, 90–91, 363–64,
  365
 foreign intervention issue and, 409
 issued, xiii, xv, xvi, xxvii, 61, 85–91, 92,
  94–95, 364–65, 406–8
 Lincoln's decision to issue, 85–86, 364–
  65, 406–8
 Lincoln's spiritual crisis and, 364
 McClellan's response to, 372–78, 383–84
 military victory and, 89–90, 95, 357, 410,
  413–14, 426
 press and, 91–94
 public opinion and, 91, 94–95
 racial politics and, 400, 408–9, 412–13
 revolutionary aspect of, 364–65, 367,
  412–13
 slavery and, xiii, xv–xvi, 365–66, 375,
  378, 395, 413
 Southern cause and, 410–11
 Union war effort and, 367
 as war measure, 407–8
 war strategy and, 401–2
English Revolution of 1640–52, xvii
Evans, Nathan "Shanks," 239, 326
Ewell, Richard, 238
Ewing, Hugh, 327, 330–31

Fairchild, Harrison, 327, 330, 332
Farragut, David, xxiv
Featherston, Winfield S., 304
Ferrero, Edward, 317
V Corps, U.S., xxv–xxvi, 5, 50, 102, 110,
 124–25, 172, 175, 182, 200, 217, 226, 243,
 244, 255, 274, 275, 281, 288–91, 312–13,
 318, 324, 325, 333–34, 338, 347, 353,
 417, 418
 see also Porter, Fitz-John
Fifth New Hampshire Regiment, U.S., 300,
 303, 305, 307–8
Fifth Virginia Regiment, C.S.A., 189, 260
Fifteenth Amendment, 413
Fifty-first New York Regiment, U.S., 317

Fifty-first Pennsylvania Regiment, U.S., 317
I Corps, U.S., 173, 182, 185–86, 197, 199,
 202, 204, 220, 222, 224, 243, 249, 254,
 255, 267, 270, 274, 277, 281, 285, 288,
 289, 294, 316, 318, 320, 331, 332, 337,
 343, 346, 349
 see also Hooker, Joseph; Iron Brigade
First Massachusetts Cavalry Regiment,
 U.S., 130
First Texas Regiment, C.S.A., 265
flank, flanking maneuver, xxxi–xxxii
Florida, 411
Foner, Eric, xvi, 412
Ford, Thomas H., 190–91
Forsyth, John, 68–69, 143
Fort Donelson, xxiv, 4, 39, 415
Fort Henry, xxiv, 4, 415
Fort Sumter, xxi, 16, 25, 63, 378
IV Corps, U.S., 186
Fourth Rhode Island Regiment, U.S., 326,
 330
Fourth Virginia Regiment, C.S.A., 260
Fourteenth Amendment, 413
Fourteenth Connecticut Regiment, U.S.,
 292
Fox's Gap, 193, 196–99, 201, 207, 216–17
France, xvii, 21, 29, 33, 68, 72–73, 75
 intervention question and, 146–47, 151,
  235, 409–10
 Mexico project of, 146–47, 409
 recognition question and, 145–46, 396,
  410
Franklin, William, 36–37, 53, 172, 175, 183,
 197, 346
 at Antietam, 243, 275, 281, 288, 307,
  313–18, 323, 325, 331, 332, 336–37, 338,
  345, 347, 351, 362
 at Crampton's Gap, 201–3, 206
 in Harpers Ferry relief operation, 209–10,
  217–19, 220, 223–24, 422, 425
 Maryland invasion and, 186–87, 190,
  225–26
 as McClellan loyalist, 176, 244, 361–62
 in Second Bull Run Campaign, 120–23,
  128, 134, 422
Frederick II "the Great," King of Prussia,
 235
Fredericksburg, Battle of, 396, 404
Free-Soilers, 88

Fremont, John C., 19
French, William H., 275, 283, 288, 306,
    307, 325, 346, 349
    in Sunken Road fight, 291–94, 296–97,
    301, 304–5, 311, 313, 316, 318, 338
French Revolution, xvi, xvii, 178
Fugitive Slave Law, 77
Fuller, Margaret, 91

Gaines' Mill, Battle of, 50, 54, 200, 321–22,
    418
Garland, Samuel, 196–97, 199, 217, 273, 278,
    285, 295
Garrett, John, 361
Georgia, 66, 113, 410
Gettysburg, Battle of, 72, 153, 255, 398, 410
Gibbon, John, 183, 205, 256, 261–63, 264,
    266, 283, 287
Gladstone, William, 146
Glendale, Battle of, 50, 51, 53–54, 113, 135,
    419, 444n
Goodwin, Doris Kearns, 88
Graham, Captain, 309
Grant, Ulysses S., xxiii, xxiv, xxv, xxvi, 4,
    13, 32, 39, 68, 76, 79, 95, 315, 380, 401,
    415–16
Great Britain, xiii, 33, 43, 72–73, 75, 131
    American Revolution and, 67–68
    Emancipation Proclamation and, 89
    intervention question and, 146–47, 151,
    235, 397–98, 409–10, 424
    recognition question and, 145–46, 396
    Revolution of 1640–52 in, xvii
    Second Bull Run and, 150–51
Greeley, Horace, xviii, 91–92, 177, 362
    coup threat and, 179
    open letter to Lincoln of, 106–7, 421–22
Greene, George S., 269–70, 278, 279, 291,
    293, 302, 306–7, 311, 314, 316, 325
Greene, Nathanael, 67
Gregg, Maxcy, 329–30, 331
Griffin, Charles, 131, 353, 449n–50n
Grigsby, Andrew Jackson, 260, 262, 284
Groveton, Battle of, 423

habeas corpus, 64, 366, 369–70, 371, 414,
    426
Halleck, Henry W., xxiii, xxiv, xxv, xxvi,
    3, 4, 5, 10, 13, 32–33, 39, 63, 65, 78, 90,
102, 104, 105, 107, 111, 116, 118, 175, 181,
    184, 185, 242, 345, 359, 367, 383, 398,
    401–2, 406, 416, 417
    background of, 95–96
    McClellan's Antietam telegrams to,
    216–17, 231, 313, 347–49, 353, 358
    McClellan's command debate with,
    160–61
    McClellan's Harrison's Landing meeting
    with, 86, 95–96, 98, 100–101, 416,
    420–21
    McClellan's reappoinment and, 128, 130,
    132–34
    military inadequacy of, 108–9, 119
    promoted to overall command, 61,
    85–86, 92, 95, 420
    Virginia theater reorganized by, 95–96
Hamlin, Hannibal, 408
Hampton, Wade, 201, 265
Hampton Legion, C.S.A., 265
Harland, Edward, 327, 329–30
Harpers Ferry, 142, 182, 187, 194, 203–4,
    206, 223, 395, 399, 424–25
    Confederate three-pronged movement
    on, 162–68
    Crampton's Gap fight and, 201–2
    Jackson's operations against, 184–85, 186,
    210–11
    in Lee's operational planning, 152–53,
    157, 160–61
    surrender of, 213–15, 425
    terrain of, 161–62
    Union cavalry's breakout from, 190–91,
    207–8
    Union relief operation and, 185–86,
    188–90, 209–10, 217–19, 425
    Union reoccupation of, 354, 358, 385, 387
Harper's Weekly, 360
Harsh, Joseph, 112, 342, 443n, 446n
Hartford Courant, 8
Hartranft, John, 317
Hartsuff, George, 258, 261, 263–64
Hatch, Ozias, 379
Hay, John, xvii, 20, 57–58, 132, 136, 364,
    379, 393, 403
    McClellan conspiracy and, 367–68, 370–71
Hayes, Rutherford B., 196
Hays, Harry, 262–63
Heintzelman, Samuel P., 53, 102, 110, 118, 172

Henry VIII, King of England, 365
Hill, A. P., 194, 203, 215, 234, 240, 312, 321, 322, 324, 326, 348, 354, 446n
   Antietam flank attack of, 327–29, 331–33, 335, 426
Hill, D. H., 154, 157, 164, 166, 188, 210, 239, 264, 272–73, 275, 276–79, 289
   background of, 195–96
   at South Mountain, 189, 195–96, 198–200, 203, 206, 234
   in Sunken Road fight, 285, 288, 292, 306–7, 312, 321
Hood, John Bell, 70, 200, 205, 207, 238, 258, 263, 264–66, 267, 275, 278, 279, 341
Hooker, Joseph, 133, 185–86, 195, 199, 206, 217, 219–20, 224–25, 226, 234, 237, 241, 248, 249, 270, 275, 276, 288–91, 313, 315, 318, 325, 336, 338, 342, 346, 349, 446n, 447n
   in attack at Antietam, 243–44, 246, 253–54, 257–58, 266
   leadership of, 279–80
   Lincoln's challenge of, 403
   military background of, 173
   wounding of, 279–80, 283
House of Representatives, U.S., 408
Humphreys, Andrew A., 347, 348
Hunter, David, 100, 105

Illinois, 19, 24
Illinois Central Railroad, 15–16, 26, 43, 99
Indiana, 19
Irish Brigade, 299–303, 340
Iron Brigade, 183
   at Antietam, 256, 259–66, 275, 277
   at South Mountain, 205–6
Island No. 10, 97
Italy, 146
Iuka, Battle of, 426
Ives, Malcolm, 37

Jackson, Andrew, 88, 374
Jackson, Thomas J. "Stonewall," xxv, xxx, 5, 6, 10, 15, 76–77, 79, 81, 96, 97, 98, 113, 124, 126, 134, 203, 207, 213, 219, 222, 267, 273, 277, 285, 289, 294, 306, 311, 319, 327, 329, 353–54, 370–71, 386, 390–91, 418, 420, 428, 442n
   Antietam defense sector of, 237–39

Antietam flanking movement of, 320–21, 331, 336–37
   background and personality of, 114
   Harpers Ferry operation of, 157, 161–68, 184–85, 186, 189, 191, 194, 201, 210–11, 214, 424–25
   in march to Sharpsburg, 215–16
   Maryland invasion and, 153–54
   and reinforcement of Lee, 223–27, 233
   in Second Bull Run Campaign, 109–11, 116–18, 120–21, 124–26, 421–23
   Valley Campaign of, 3–4, 48–49, 74, 114–15, 416–17
   West Woods fight and, 286–87
Jackson Mississippian, 143
Jenkins, Micah, 326
Johnston, Albert Sidney, xxiv, 415–16
Johnston, Joseph E., 16, 40–42, 47, 70, 415–16, 417
Joint Committee on the Conduct of the War, 20–21, 27, 32, 232, 347
   McClellan's testimony to, 33
Jomini, Antoine-Henri, 95
Jones, David R., 239, 272–73, 289–90, 317, 320, 323, 325
Jones, J. R., 215, 227, 238, 253, 258, 262, 263, 267, 285, 312, 329
Juárez, Benito, 300
Judkins, W. B., 234, 296–97

Kanawha Division, U.S., 174, 185, 195–96, 249, 294, 324, 327, 359
Kansas-Nebraska Bill, 22–23
Kearny, Philip, 100, 126
Kelly, Patrick, 302
Kemper, James L., 324, 325, 327, 330
Kentucky, xx, xxi–xxii, xxvi, xxvii, 3, 72, 400, 420, 421, 425
   Confederate invasion of, 76, 77, 79, 149, 175, 235, 386–87
Kershaw, Joseph B., 286–87, 291
Key, John, 368–69, 388, 404, 427
Key, Thomas, 179, 359–60, 361, 368
Knights of the Golden Circle, 44
Korean War, xviii

Law, Evander, 264–65
Lawton, Alexander, 215, 227, 238, 256, 261, 262–63, 264, 267, 277

Lee, Fitzhugh, 207, 212

Lee, Harry "Light Horse," 70–71

Lee, Robert E., xiii, xiv, xvii, xviii, xxv–
xxvi, xxx, 10, 15, 44, 58, 62–63, 69,
96–98, 100, 105, 108, 116, 119, 121,
134–35, 136, 150, 155, 170, 171, 176, 181,
193, 196, 200, 212, 214–15, 217, 222–23,
227, 233–34, 238, 246, 251, 295, 296,
306, 311, 324, 327, 329, 354, 357, 377,
390, 402, 405, 417–18, 419, 421, 423, 428
    at Antietam, see Antietam, Battle of
    Army of Northern Virginia reorganized
        by, 153–56
    command system of, 111, 113–15
    decision making by, 398–99
    described, 70
    family background of, 70–71
    lost order and, 188–89, 394, 425–26
    Maryland invasion and, 141–45, 147–48,
        151–53, 423–26
    McClellan's misjudgment of, 47, 58, 71
    in Peninsula Campaign, 47, 49–50, 52,
        54, 58, 73
    Second Bull Run and, 110–11, 116–17, 124
    Sharpsburg decision of, 210–11, 221, 232,
        236
    as strategic thinker, 111–12
    war strategy and, 66–68, 73–79, 81

Lee, Stephen D., 212, 238, 256, 258, 274,
    279, 286, 341, 343, 344

Leuthen, Battle of, 235

Lincoln, Abraham, xiii, xiv, xv, xx, xxii–
xxiii, 3, 5, 22, 30, 41, 43, 54, 77, 81, 85,
98–99, 104, 111, 119, 127, 150, 153, 175,
182, 299, 321, 334, 357, 415, 416, 418,
420
    attempts to usurp authority of, 19–20
    cabinet of, 19, 27, 394
    colonization policy and, 86–87, 88,
        105–6, 412, 421
    conciliatory strategy and, 11–12, 21–22,
        28, 401
    decision making of, 398
    depression of, 3, 5
    on divine will, 136–37
    Douglas's debates with, 22, 23, 25
    Emancipation Proclamation and, xiii,
        xv–xvi, xxvii, 61, 85–91, 92, 94–95,
        364–65, 406–8, 426
    Fremont relieved by, 19
    Greeley's open letter to, 106–7, 421–22
    habeas corpus suspended by, 366, 426
    Halleck-McClellan exchanges and,
        122–23
    Halleck promoted to overall command
        by, 61, 85–86, 92, 95, 420
    Key affair and, 368–69, 371, 427
    McClellan reinstated by, 129–33, 136–37,
        423
    McClellan relieved of command by,
        388–92
    McClellan's Antietam meeting with,
        379–82
    McClellan's character doubted by, 136,
        175–76
    McClellan's "grand design" letter to,
        57–61
    McClellan's misjudgment of, 102
    McClellan's political conflict with, xvi–
        xviii, 14–15, 34–35, 359–61, 371–74
    McClellan's "treason" telegram to,
        52–53, 55–57, 418–19
    military self-education of, 9–10
    Peninsula Campaign and, 5–9, 42, 48
    Pinkerton's meeting with, 363–64, 371
    Radicals and, 20–21
    Scott's strategy meeting with, 6
    slavery question and, xix, xx, xxvii,
        11–12, 23
    Union strategy and, 394, 401–3, 407
    war policy of, 19–20

Lincoln administration, 77, 78, 109, 148, 152

Lincoln-Douglas debates, 22

Longstreet, James, xxx, 80–81, 97, 115, 118,
    157, 162–63, 187, 195–96, 200, 202, 203,
    206, 208, 209, 210, 216, 219, 221–22,
    223, 234, 271, 306, 307, 311, 320–22,
    335, 341, 353, 390–91, 422–23, 424,
    425, 428
    Maryland invasion and, 153–54
    as military commander, 113–14
    in move to Sharpsburg positions, 211–12
    in Second Bull Run Campaign, 110–11,
        117–19, 124–26
    lost order, xvi–xvii, 164, 168–69, 226, 394,
        424–25
    finding of, 182–83
    Harpers Ferry relief operation and, 185

lost order (*continued*)
McClellan's reaction to, 183–84, 186–87, 193, 209
Louisiana, 66, 90
Louisiana Purchase, 23
Louisiana Tigers, 262–63
Lowe, E. Louis, 147
Lower Brigade, 213, 226, 239–40, 243, 247, 272, 275–76, 281, 289–90, 294–95, 312–13, 316, 318, 323, 335–36, 337, 349

MacArthur, Douglas, xviii, 403–4
Malvern Hill, Battle of, 50, 51–52, 54, 100, 419
Mansfield, Joseph, 248, 254, 267, 269–71, 275, 277, 281, 325, 336
Marble, Manton, 48, 91–92, 93, 177, 376, 381, 383
Marcy, Randolph, 8–9, 16, 37–38, 176, 204
Marx, Karl, 91
Maryland, xiv, xx, xxi, xxvii, 72, 175, 373, 400
Maryland, invasion of, 141–91, 216, 227, 395, 396
army reorganization and, 141, 153–56
assessment of, 398–99
Battle of Antietam in, *see* Antietam, Battle of
Border States and, 143–44, 149
Confederate artillery in, 154–55
Confederate western movement in, 181–82
Davis's proclamation in, 149–50
decision for, 142–44
foreign recognition issue and, 145–47
Harpers Ferry operation in, 152–53, 157, 159–68, 188–91, 217–19
Lee divides army in, 161–62, 170, 182–84, 399
Lee's operational plan for, 147–48, 151–53
Lee's proclamation in, 148–49, 159
lost order in, 164, 168–69, 182–83, 186–89, 210, 425–26
McClellan's excessive caution in, 209–10
political objectives of, 145–49, 460
public opinion and, 143
South Mountain battles in, *see* South Mountain, Battle of
states' rights and, 148–50

stragglers problem in, 154, 156–57, 159, 165–66, 216, 221, 234, 443n
strength of opposing armies in, 174–75
Union Army reorganization in, 172–74
Mason, James, 73, 146–47
McClellan, George B., xiii, xvi, xxvii, 4, 62, 65, 74, 80, 90, 96, 99–100, 107, 108, 109, 114, 125, 134, 151, 164, 175, 202, 203, 308, 311, 343, 400, 412, 423, 437n
anger at perceived enemies of, 102–4, 119, 178
at Antietam, *see* Antietam, Battle of
army reorganization and, 134, 172–74
Aspinwall's correspondence with, 372–73
assessment of, 403–6
background of, 15–16
Blair's correspondence with, 358–59, 374
coup threat and, 18, 21, 103, 119–20, 176, 178–80, 358–60, 402–3, 405–6
cult of personality and, 13, 45–47
Democrats and, 15–16, 26, 48–49
divine will and, 137–38
1864 election and, 42, 53, 360, 375, 392, 408–9, 410
Emancipation Proclamation reaction of, 372–78, 383–84
excessive caution of, 209–10, 213, 222, 236, 403
grand strategy of, 28–29
Halleck's command debate with, 160–61
Halleck's Harrison's Landing meeting with, 86, 95–96, 98, 100–101
headquarters staff of, 45–46, 99–100, 102, 176–77
Joint Committee testimony of, 33
Key affair and, 368–69, 374, 407
last review of, 391–92
Lee misjudged by, 47, 58, 71, 102
Lincoln contrasted with, 57
Lincoln's Antietam meeting with, 379–82
at Lincoln's council of war, 36–37
Lincoln's doubts on character of, 136, 175–76
Lincoln's firing of, 388–92, 428
Lincoln's mistrust of, 175–76, 423
Lincoln's political conflict with, xv–xviii, 14–15, 34–35, 136–37, 359–61, 371
lost order and, 168–69, 183–84, 186–87, 193, 209

military dictatorship threat and, 18, 21, 29–30, 373–74, 382
overestimates of enemy strength by, 42–45, 100, 209, 217–21, 223, 231, 344, 441n
in Peninsula Campaign, *see* Peninsula Campaign
political ideology of, 27–28
political supporters of, 94, 176–78, 359, 427
Pope's defeat and, 106–8, 130–32, 367, 370, 395, 401–2, 423
Pope's rivalry with, 97–98
popularity of, 13, 29–30, 46–47, 170
Porter as confidant and surrogate of, 99, 103–4, 132–33, 176, 244–45, 274–75, 335, 361, 374, 376, 378, 381
press and, 37–38, 48, 60, 91–92, 94, 131, 232, 360, 361
as railroad executive, 15–16
restored to command, 130–34, 136–37, 423
risk-aversion of, 31–33, 38–39, 40, 44, 47–48, 49, 54, 402–3
Scott defamed by, 28–32, 406
Scott telegram of, 218, 232–33
Second Bull Run and, 120–23
self-conceit of, 17–18, 29, 30–31, 32, 38, 46–47, 227
on Seven Days defeat, 102–3
Stanton's early relationship with, 34, 36–38, 56
Stanton's feud with, 89, 98, 104–5, 128–31, 136, 176, 232, 358, 363, 376, 421–22, 424
strategic approach of, 135–36
ultimatum to Lincoln considered by, 136–37
victory criteria of, 226–27
and violation of Articles of War, 405–6
as War Democrat, 14
in West Virginia Campaign, xxii, xxiv–xxv, 16–17
McClellan, Mary Ellen Marcy, 16, 18, 182, 327, 354, 363, 382–83
McClernand, John A., 379–80, 403
McDowell, Irvin, xxi, 17, 36–37, 48, 118, 137, 170, 172, 416
McKinley, William, 196

McLaws, Lafayette, 154, 186, 219, 228, 238, 272, 274, 276, 284, 286, 287
in Harpers Ferry operation, 162–63, 167–68, 189–91, 201–3, 206, 208, 209, 215–16, 424–25
McRae, D. K., 278–79
McWhiney, Grady, 111–12
Meade, George G., 253, 255, 264, 265, 267, 274, 345, 346, 349, 381
Meagher, Thomas, 299, 301–2, 303
Meigs, Montgomery C., 8, 36–37
Mexican American War, 6, 15, 17–18, 23, 46, 69, 95, 96, 113, 114, 173, 195, 205, 232, 235, 240, 259, 297, 329, 361, 437n
Mexico, 146–47, 409
Michigan, 20
Middle Bridge, 212, 220, 239, 243, 244–47, 275, 281, 289–90, 312–14, 318–19, 320, 324, 333, 335, 349
Miles, D. S., 160–61, 162, 167–68, 190–91, 197, 207–8, 210, 213–14, 425
Miles, Nelson, 300
Military Department of Maryland and Southern Pennsylvania, U.S., 160
Miller (land owner), 238
Mississippi, 66, 411
Missouri, xxi–xxii, 19, 66, 88, 97
Missouri Compromise, 378
Missouri Republican, 370
Mitchell, Barton, 182
Morrell, George W., 324, 331–32, 347, 349, 351, 449n
Morton, Oliver P., 423
Munford, Thomas, 190

Napoleon I, Emperor of France, xvii, 179, 183–84, 236
Napoleon III, Emperor of France, xvii, 29, 146
Napoleonic Wars, xvi, 329
National Road, 164–65, 166, 184–85, 193, 196, 198–99, 205
Navy, U.S., 73
Netherlands, 68
New Orleans, xxiv, 3, 63, 77
New York Herald, 37–38, 42, 56, 92, 93–94, 104, 179, 366, 372, 376–77, 383, 384
New York State, 9
New York Stock Exchange, 100

New York Times, 8, 49, 56, 91, 94, 177, 384
New York *Tribune,* 56, 91–92, 93, 131, 177,
    315, 334, 345, 362, 368, 370, 384, 442*n*,
    451*n*–52*n*
    coup threat in, 178–79
New York World, 42, 48, 91–92, 93, 94, 103,
    104, 177, 376, 378, 383, 384
Nicaragua, 16
Nicodemus Heights, 213, 225, 237, 267, 284,
    331, 337–38, 345
Nicolay, John, 20
IX Corps, U.S., 96, 110, 118, 126, 151, 173,
    175, 176, 182, 185, 195, 197–99, 202, 217,
    220, 222, 226, 243, 247, 248–50, 277,
    288, 295, 316, 318, 329–30, 332–33, 335,
    336, 349, 426, 447*n*
    see also Burnside, Ambrose
Nineteenth Indiana Regiment, U.S., 205,
    259–60
Nolan, Alan, 112
North-Western Police Agency, 43
Northwest Territories, 24

118th Pennsylvania Regiment, U.S., 354
124th Pennsylvania Regiment, U.S., 270
125th Pennsylvania Regiment, U.S., 270,
    284, 285, 286–87, 291
126th New York Regiment, U.S., 190
128th Pennsylvania Regiment, U.S., 270–71,
    277–78

Paige, Nathaniel, 178–79, 367–68
Palmerston, Lord, xiii, 151, 397, 409–10
Parliament, British, 146, 374
Patrick, Marsena, 259, 260, 262, 263, 283,
    285, 287
Pender, William D., 330–31
Pendleton, William, 236–37, 353–54
Peninsula Campaign, 40–58, 115, 226, 232,
    241–42, 244, 255, 291, 299, 301, 361,
    404, 405, 417
    calls for reinforcements in, 44–45, 48
    defense of Washington in, 41–42
    forces engaged in, 49–50
    Halleck-McClellan meeting in, 95–96,
    98, 100–101, 416, 420–21
    Harrison's Landing fortifications in,
    54–55
    intelligence failure in, 43–45
    Jackson's Valley Campaign and, 48–49

Lincoln-McClellan meeting in, 57–60, 419
    McClellan's abandonment of army in,
    51–54, 135, 419, 442*n*–43*n*
    McClellan's Harrison's Landing letter in,
    57–61, 419
    McClellan's "treason" telegram in,
    52–53, 55–57, 418–19
    Napoleonic model for, 41
    overestimates of Confederate strength in,
    42–45, 48–50
    Seven Days Battles in, *see* Seven Days
    Battles
    training for, 47
    Union retreat in, 50–52, 54, 418
    Urbanna plan and, 40–41
    Yorktown siege in, 47, 415–16
Pennsylvania, 148, 157, 175, 180
Pennsylvania Railroad, 153
Perryville, Battle of, 386, 390, 396, 414, 427
Phelps, Walter, 259, 260, 261–62
Pinkerton, Allan, 43–44, 103
    Lincoln's meeting with, 363–64, 371
Pinkerton National Detective Agency, 43
Piper (farmer), 297
plantation system, 66, 68
Pleasonton, Alfred, 174, 182, 184, 195,
    242–43, 275, 291, 313, 316, 319, 324,
    326–27, 353
Polk, James K., 18
Pope, John, xxiii, 6, 13, 73–76, 78, 80, 85,
    87, 90, 93, 95–98, 102, 128, 133, 137,
    143, 150, 151, 157, 170, 172, 176, 182, 200,
    218, 220, 223, 244, 248, 269, 304, 322,
    406, 419–23
    McClellan and defeat of, 106–8, 130–32,
    367, 370, 395, 401–2, 423
    in Second Bull Run Campaign, 109–11,
    115, 117–19, 121, 124–27, 395
Porter, David, xxiv
Porter, Fitz-John, 5, 46, 48, 91, 102, 105, 110,
    172, 182, 255, 422*n*
    at Antietam, 274–75, 319, 325, 327, 332,
    335, 351, 353–54, 358, 449*n*–50*n*
    as McClellan's confidant and surrogate,
    99, 103–4, 132–33, 176, 244–45, 274–75,
    335, 361, 374, 376, 378, 381
    in Peninsula Campaign, 50–51, 200, 442
    at Second Bull Run, 118–19, 124, 131, 133,
    244–45
    and violation of Articles of War, 405–6

Port Republic, Battle of, 417
Posey, Carnot, 304
Potter, Robert, 317
Price, Sterling, 62, 77, 386, 426
Prussia, 146–47
Pryor, Roger, 297, 304

Quaker guns, 42

Rafuse, Ethan, 404
Raymond, Henry, 91
Reconstruction, 413
Reformation, 365
regiment, as military term, xxix–xxx
Reign of Terror, 178
Reno, Jesse, 173–74, 197–99, 248–50
Republican Party, U.S., xix, xxvii, 9–10, 22,
    72, 88, 97, 375, 397, 403
    expansion of slavery and, 23–24, 26
    Radical, 20–21, 28, 42, 45, 49, 54, 89,
        91–92, 93, 102–3, 106, 108, 109, 136, 177,
        179, 227, 232, 233, 334, 375, 383, 384, 402
Revolutionary War, 67
revolution of 1848, 116
Reynolds, John, 381
Richardson, Israel, 234, 275, 281, 325, 338,
    346, 349, 449n
    in Sunken Road fight, 293–94, 297–309,
    311, 313, 316, 318
Richmond Daily Dispatch, 65, 74–75
Richmond Whig, 66, 143
Ricketts, James, 255, 263–65, 266, 267, 283
Ripley, Roswell, 198, 239, 262, 272, 277, 279
Rodes, Robert, 198, 200, 292, 295, 303–4
Rodman, Isaac Peace, 197, 294, 317, 323–26,
    330, 346
Rosecrans, William S., 428
Rossbach, Battle of, 235
Roulette Farm, 212, 225, 238–39
Ruffin, Thomas, 365
Russell, Charles, 191, 197
Russell, Lord John, 151, 397, 409–10
Russian Revolution, xvi

Sackett, Delos B., 317
Saratoga, Battle of, 67
Savage's Station, Battle of, 50, 419
Savannah Republican, 65
Saxton, Rufus, 105
Scammon, Eliakim, 196–97, 294–95, 346

Scott, Winfield, xxi, xxii, 6, 15, 16, 17, 38,
    71, 235, 437n
    McClellan's defamation of, 28–32, 406
    McClellan's telegram to, 218, 232–33
    in Mexican War, 41
Sears, Stephen, 53, 180, 442n
Second Bull Run Campaign, 108–25
    assessment of, 125, 127
    Chantilly fight in, 126
    Confederate reinforcements in, 112–13
    Confederate turning movement in, 110–
    11, 115–17, 125–26
    foreign recognition issue and, 127
    Lee's flank attack in, 124–25
    Lee's strategy for, 109–12
    Manassas raid in, 116–17, 120–21, 123, 134,
    421
    McClellan-Radicals conflict and, 108–9
    McClellan's command status debate in,
    120–23
    Second Bull Run Battle in, 124–25, 134,
    136, 141, 423
    Union inexperience in, 117–18
    Union withdrawal from, 126
Second Confiscation Act of 1862 (U.S.),
    77–78, 92, 97, 104, 420, 427
II Corps, U.S., 102, 120, 121, 125–26, 151,
    172, 175, 217, 220, 225, 226, 243, 244–46,
    275, 281, 288–90, 291, 297, 313, 346,
    349, 422, 447n
    see also Sumner, Edwin Vose
Second Mississippi Regiment, C.S.A., 265
Second Sharpshooters, U.S., 259–61, 262
Second Wisconsin Regiment, U.S., 205,
    259
Sedgwick, John, 275, 283–88, 291, 306–7,
    318, 338, 346
Seminole War, 88, 255, 259, 329
Semmes, Paul J., 287
Senate, C.S.A., 416
Senate, Roman, xvii
Senate, U.S., 20, 21, 408, 415
    Military Affairs Committee of, 178
Sepoy Mutiny of 1857, 89, 409
Seven Days Battles, xxv–xxvi, 10, 49–54,
    68–69, 72, 73, 94, 104, 113, 115, 145, 172,
    173, 200, 235, 236, 241, 245, 260, 299,
    301, 321–22, 337, 343, 357, 387, 388,
    394, 418, 442n–43n
    casualties in, 75, 419

Seven Days Battles (*continued*)
  McClellan on defeat in, 102–3
  see also Peninsula Campaign; *specific battles*
Seven Pines, Battle of, 5, 47, 49, 173, 232, 241, 299, 301, 303, 417
Seventh New York Regiment, U.S., 300, 303
Seventh Wisconsin Regiment, U.S., 205, 259–60
Seven Years' War, 235
Seward, William, 13, 19, 27, 31, 36–37, 61, 86, 129, 364, 420
  draft mission of, 8, 9–10
  Emancipation Proclamation favored by, 89
Sharpsburg, *see* Antietam, Battle of
Shepherdstown Ford, 236–37
Sherman, William T., 411
Shiloh, Battle of, xxiv–xxv, 4, 68, 75, 95, 415–16
Sigel, Franz, 116, 118, 172, 173
VI Corps, U.S., 100, 102, 120–21, 124–26, 134, 151, 172, 175, 176, 186, 188–89, 193, 201, 215, 220, 223–27, 243, 244, 250–51, 275, 281, 288–90, 307, 313, 331–32, 333, 334, 337, 338, 345, 422, 423, 425, 447n
  see also Franklin, William
Sixth Wisconsin Regiment, U.S., 205, 259, 264
Sixteenth Connecticut Regiment, U.S., 326, 329–30
Sixty-first/Sixty-fourth New York Regiment, U.S., 300, 302–3, 304
Sixty-third New York Regiment, U.S., 299, 301, 303
Sixty-ninth New York Regiment, U.S., 299, 301, 303
slavery, 14, 20, 22, 396–97, 401, 418
  abolished in DC, 77
  Border States and, 11–12
  colonization policy and, 412, 420–21
  Emancipation Proclamation and, xiii, xv–xvi, 365–66, 375, 378, 395
  Jackson's attitude toward, 114
  in McClellan's "grand design" letter, 59–60, 61
  territorial expansion issue and, 22–25

White supremacy and, xiii, 24–25, 27–28, 59, 93, 106
Slidell, John, 73, 146–47
Slocum, Henry W., 201–2
Smalley, George, 315, 317, 333, 335, 345–46, 362, 388
Smith, Caleb, 368
Smith, Edmund Kirby, xxvi, 62, 76, 78, 149, 420–22, 423–24, 425, 428, 453n
Smith, William "Baldy," 100, 176–77, 201–2, 316, 320, 360–61, 383
Snavely's Ford, 250, 317, 323, 336
South Carolina, 66, 411
South Mountain, Battle of, 163, 189, 218, 226, 232, 234, 241, 248, 249, 278, 321, 325
  casualties at, 206
  Crampton's Gap fight in, 193–94, 201–3, 206
  Fox's Gap fight in, 193, 196–99, 201, 207
  Iron Brigade in, 205–6
  terrain of, 196, 198–99
  Turner's Gap fight in, 193, 195–200, 206–7
Spain, 68
Special Order No. 191, *see* lost order
Spirit of the Times, 94, 131
Sprague, William, 372
squatter sovereignty, 25
Stanton, Edwin M., 4, 7, 8, 54, 95, 101, 103, 108, 109, 133, 135, 175, 177, 178, 208, 334, 362, 374, 382, 402, 406, 417
  blamed for Peninsula Campaign defeat, 42, 93–94, 104–5
  Emancipation Proclamation favored by, 89
  McClellan's early relationship with, 34, 36–38, 56
  McClellan's feud with, 89, 98, 104–5, 128–31, 136, 176, 232, 358, 363, 376, 421–22, 424
  McClellan's "treason" telegram to, 52–53, 55–57, 418–19
  press criticism of, 93
Starke, William, 258, 261–62, 263, 265, 267
states' rights, 64–65, 148–49, 400, 411
Stephens, Alexander, 64–65
Stevens, Isaac, 126
Stockton, T. B. W., 449n

Stone, Charles, 20, 33–34
Stones River, Battle of, 396
Stonewall Bridge, C.S.A., 260–61, 262, 280, 285
strategy, as military term, xxxi
Strong, George Templeton, 178
Strother, David H., 345, 346–47
Stuart, J. E. B. ("Jeb"), 111, 115, 126, 423
    at Antietam, 237, 255–56, 258, 267, 277, 284, 320, 322, 331, 332, 337–38, 343
    at Crampton's Gap, 201, 209, 216
    in Maryland invasion, 154, 157, 159, 163, 166, 168, 174, 187
    in raids around Union Army, 384–85, 387–88, 418, 427
    at South Mountain, 188–89, 194
Sturgis, Samuel, 197, 295, 316–17, 323–24, 331, 346
Sumner, Charles, 20–21, 121
Sumner, Edwin Vose, 128, 131, 133, 175, 226, 274, 306, 317, 320, 322–23, 324, 325, 349, 450n
    background of, 172–73
    confusion and hysteria of, 314–15, 318–19, 331, 338, 346
    as corps commander, 245
    in northern front fights, 275–76, 280–81, 283–91, 293–94, 332, 334
Sunken Road, 239, 272–73, 285, 288, 290–305, 311–14, 318, 320–22, 324, 343, 346, 349, 450n
Supreme Court, North Carolina, 365
Supreme Court, U.S., 373
Sykes, George, 220, 275, 316, 319, 326–27, 331–34, 345

tactics, definition of, xxxi
Taft, Elijah D., 245
Taylor, Zachary, 297
Tennessee, 3, 11, 66, 77, 143, 415–16, 420
Tenth Maine Regiment, U.S., 271
Texas Brigade, C.S.A., 200, 205, 264
III Corps, U.S., 102, 110, 172, 173, 175
Thirteenth Amendment, 413
Thirty-second Ohio Regiment, U.S., 190
Thirty-third Virginia Regiment, C.S.A., 260
Thouvenel, Edouard, 146
Tod, David, 359, 370

Tompkins, John A., 449n
Toombs, Robert, 239–40, 272, 294–95, 312–13, 317, 324, 327, 330
Traveller (Lee's horse), 271
Trenton, Battle of, 67
Trimble, Isaac B., 253, 258
Turner, Levi, 368
Turner's Gap, 193, 195–200, 206–7, 216–17, 425
XII Corps, U.S., 151, 172, 173, 175, 182, 217, 220, 226, 243, 248–49, 254, 267, 272, 274, 281, 283, 285, 288, 289, 290, 291, 305–6, 316, 318, 320, 337, 346, 349, 354, 358
    northern front attacks of, 269–71, 277–79
    see also Mansfield, Joseph
Twelfth Illinois Cavalry Regiment, U.S., 208
Twelfth Massachusetts Regiment, U.S., 261–62, 263
Twelfth North Carolina Regiment, C.S.A., 196–97
Twenty Negro Law, 410–11
Twenty-second Georgia Regiment, C.S.A., 158, 234, 296
Twenty-second New York Regiment, U.S., 259
Twenty-third Ohio Regiment, U.S., 196
Twenty-seventh Indiana Regiment, U.S., 182
Twenty-seventh Virginia Regiment, C.S.A., 260
Twenty-ninth Massachusetts Regiment, U.S., 299

Upper Bridge, 221, 246, 267, 281

Van Dorn, Earl, 62, 77, 119, 386, 396, 420, 427
Vicksburg Campaign, 410
Virginia, xxi–xxii, 114
Virginia Central Railroad, 80, 109–10, 152
Virginia Military Institute, 114
von Kleiser, Albert, 245

Walker, John G., 162–63, 167–68, 181–82, 191, 194, 203, 213, 215–16, 228, 240, 272, 273–74, 289, 293, 295, 314, 320, 424–25
Walker, William, 16

War Democrats, 14, 25, 402–3
War Department, U.S., xxv, 3, 6, 7, 43, 52, 93, 94, 132, 175, 362, 437n
War of 1812, 6, 160
Washington, George, 67
Washington, Martha, 71
Webster, Daniel, 261
Weed, Stephen H., 245
Weigley, Russell, 112
Welles, Gideon, 61, 86, 89, 129, 133, 135, 178, 368, 388, 420
West Virginia, 17
West Woods, 212, 225, 238, 264–66, 277, 283–88, 291, 293, 307, 331, 337, 345, 349
Whig Party, U.S., 9, 20, 91
White, Julius, 161, 167–68, 191, 207, 214
White supremacy, 93, 365, 400, 408, 410–11, 412

slavery and, xiii, 24–25, 27–28, 59, 93, 106
Wilkerson, Samuel, 56
Willcox, Orlando, 197–98, 295, 324, 325–27, 330–31, 332, 346
Williams, Alpheus, 173, 269, 270, 271, 277–78, 279, 283–84, 288, 291, 293, 294–95, 306, 380
Wilson, Henry, 178
Wilson, James H., 314–15, 317–19, 320, 338, 345, 346
Winchester, Battle of, 417
Wood, Fernando, 99, 360, 378
Wool, John, 160–61
Wright, Ambrose "Rans," 296, 297, 302, 303, 304

Yorktown, Battle of, 67

ABOUT THE AUTHOR

RICHARD SLOTKIN is the Olin Professor of American Studies (emeritus) at Wesleyan University, where he began teaching in 1966.

His nearly lifelong interest in the Civil War began in 1951 when, at age nine, he took a summer automobile trip with his family to Florida, visiting several battlefield parks, and coming face-to-face with the exclusions and humiliations of the Jim Crow South. As a historian his chief concern has been to understand and interpret the role of racism, and of racial violence, in our national history.

Slotkin has twice been a finalist for the National Book Award. He is best known for an award-winning trilogy of scholarly books on the myth of the frontier in American cultural history: *Regeneration through Violence* (1973), *The Fatal Environment* (1985), and *Gunfighter Nation* (1992). In *Lost Battalions* (2005) he combined military and social history to show how war transformed the nation's understanding of race and ethnic difference. His latest book is *No Quarter: The Battle of the Petersburg Crater, 1864* (2009), a study of the political and military forces that shaped the war's largest racial massacre.

He has also written three historical novels: *The Crater: A Novel of the Civil War* (1980), *The Return of Henry Starr* (1988), and *Abe: A Novel of the Young Lincoln* (2000). The latter received the Michael Shaara Award for Excellence in Civil War Fiction (2001).

Praise for **Eva's Berlin**

Life in Hitler's wartime Berlin is illuminated by this eloquent, beautiful memoir. EVA'S BERLIN *is essential reading, recalling a half-Jewish girlhood and bittersweet post-war California years.*

COLIN EISLER, Ph.D.
Robert Lehman Professor, Institute of Fine Arts, New York University
Author of *Masterworks in Berlin, A City's Paintings Resurrected*

EVA'S BERLIN *is a rich and subtle telling of a very moving story that captures the complexity of a history that still shapes our lives today. Eva Leveton gives us one more crucial piece of the history of the holocaust essential to our understanding of what was suffered. A beautiful and compelling book.*

SUSAN GRIFFIN
Author of *Women and Nature* and *A Chorus of Stone; A Private Life of War*

Eva Leveton has created a deeply moving memoir. Like Anne Frank, she documents the ethos and poignancy of wartime life with the curiosity of a lively child who is fully present to the world of adults around her. This is an important book that makes palpable the experiences of those who lived through World War II, not on the battlefield, but in the devastation of an embattled enemy city, and affirms the knowing innocence of the child.

ELINOR W. GADON, Ph.D.
Cultural Historian
Author of *The Once & Future Goddess*

I think it is important, especially for my generation, to understand the memoirs, stories, and myths of our grandparents, but even more the "myth" of the culture. Being part of the "German" culture, I feel a deep sense of responsibility to understand this complex time. This book provides a guide.

MANUELA MISCHKE REEDS, M.S.
German student

Also by Eva Wald Leveton

A CLINICIAN'S GUIDE TO PSYCHODRAMA

ADOLESCENT CRISIS: FAMILY COUNSELING APPROACHES

Eva's
Berlin

Eva Wald Levitan

Eva's Berlin

Memories
of a Wartime
Childhood

Eva Wald Leveton

Thumbprint Press

Second Printing, November 2000

ISBN 0-9654951-6-7

10   9   8   7   6   5   4   3   2

Thumbprint Press
Post Office Box 518
Fairfax, California 94978

For my husband Alan,
and my sons, Sasha and Julian,
whose love has transformed my
orphaned self and allowed
me to belong.

Acknowledgements

This book has had many supporters without whose encouragement the memories would have been too painful to explore. I thank Kathleen Burgy for her unique, sensitive, and loving understanding of my soul, George Hitchcock for his steadfast encouragement and helpful critique of all my writing efforts, and the two writing groups in which this project became a reality: the Dawn Seminar at the California Institute for Integral Studies with Don Johnson, Elinor Gadon, Jurgen Kremer, Mike Acree, and Tanya Wilkinson and its at-home follower with Marilyn Kriegel, Alan Leveton, Don Johnson, Corey Fisher, and Jonathan Greenberg. Their feedback was invaluable. Once written, Rosemary Davies, Susan Griffin and Gloria Hale helped simplify both the ideas and the all too frequent Germanic turns of phrase, and my dear friends Carol Wallace, Nancy Spring, and the late Erin Dienstag urged the suddenly shy author of these memoirs into publication with their belief in her story. Finally, this book would not exist were it not for the fine editorial eye of Guy Biederman and Laura Jane Coats' unique sense of design which made an aesthetic whole out of an unwieldy amalgam of words, quotes and photographs.

Contents

	Prologue	3
CHAPTER 1	You Can Go Home Again	7
2	Relocation	47
3	Who Is My Father	73
4	The Zoo	91
5	Bombs Over Berlin	109
6	Battling the Dragon	135
7	Nazis	157
8	School	171
9	Jewish	181
10	Potatoes and Onions	195
11	My Sex Educaton	207
12	Grandfather's Lap	219

13 Baden-Baden, A Lull in the Storm   235

14 Ciro's   257

15 Spring 1945   263

16 The Conquerors   277

17 The Aftermath   291

18 The War Is Over   307

19 Changes   321

20 The Struggle to Survive   343

21 Despair   359

22 Living and Dying   373

    Epilogue   391

Eva's
Berlin

Prologue

World War II is the center from which I grew. I was eleven years old when the war ended and my Aryan mother and I left Germany to be reunited with my Jewish father in San Francisco. Living in America, I tried to forget that the war had ever happened. But, as the years passed, memory defeated the will to forget, and I remembered more and more.

Eva's Berlin

I hadn't really intended to put the war behind me. But San Francisco taught me to focus on the present. Neither the children I met nor my father's German Jewish friends wanted to hear about the war. It gradually dawned on me that, when they asked where I came from, they wanted to hear something pleasant about my arrival here.

"So how do you like being liberated?"

"Aren't you glad you left Germany?"

"Aren't you the lucky one to come here to California?"

"Well, the war's over now. You have to put the past behind you and start all over again."

Remembering something nobody wants to hear about was a difficult proposition. I decided to forget. But the past was unaccommodating. My best efforts to put it behind me failed, and as I grew older and my companions became more diverse, I began to tell some of the stories. Talking about the war never became easy. Like many a trauma survivor, I was willing, even eager, to describe the past, but when emotions threatened to emerge, I found a style that kept the hounds of memory at bay. I was a plucky survivor, a child playing in the ruins. It was not until I had children of my own that I realized the intensity and size of the pain locked up inside these 'entertaining' vignettes. The simple exercise of imagining either of my sons in Berlin made my head reel. I could not picture their innocent faces in an air-raid shelter, or coping with hunger, or hearing the sounds of battle as the city was taken. My pain, of course, unrealized and unexpressed for many years.

Although I'm half-Jewish, this is not a story about hiding. Nor is it about belonging. It is the story of a child caught in the in-between. Between Nazis and Jews. Between her mother and her grandmother. Between the ruins of her mother's Berlin and the promise of her father's America. Is it all true? I'm not sure. Others have written their stories of the war. From time to time, I've included their voices, in search, I suppose, of the community I never had. Like any memoir, this one is patched together from actual memories — mine and others' — dreams, fantasies, and historical accounts, leavened, one hopes, by a layer of understanding. It is the nature of memory that what we remember becomes embellished by what we imagine, and impoverished by what we forget. The child who came to the United States after the war had cooperated when I silenced her. Now she needed a voice. These are my memories of Berlin.

Eva's Berlin

CHAPTER ONE

You Can Go Home Again

AMBIVALENCE Thoroughly American in 1952, all of seventeen in loafers and cashmere sweaters — *Lisle of Scotland* was the *in* brand at Lowell High in San Francisco — I was afraid to go back to Berlin. I'd made my adjustment to my new home, and it hadn't been easy. What if Berlin had changed as much as I had in those six years? Modernized, Americanized? Would my memories get all mixed up with some new version of the city I loved? Berlin was the repository of my German origins. Going back was a risk.

My first return visit was surprisingly reassuring. Contrary to all my expectations, Berlin seemed to say, "you can go home again." The dialect alone warmed me. Slow and

Eva's Berlin

comfortable and full of fat syllables, it nurtures an attitude. *Icke dette kieke mal* — untranslatable words for: I'm here, look at this — is a Berliner's code meaning "we're Berliners, pal, people who know what's going on." The community took me in with expressions like *Mensch*, used as an opener, a Berliner code which means 'human being.' Here, it's an expression like "hey, man," a kind of connective tissue.

"*Mensch*, it's so hot even the flies are sweating."

"*Mensch*, the way that doctor treats you, you might as well stay home."

In Germany it is said of the Berliner dialect that it is spoken directly from the liver, *frisch von der Leber weg*, and there is something oddly surreal and homey in the metaphor, a combination that is pure Berlin.

Staying with friends in a villa just outside the city, I felt at home immediately. Caressed by the soft Berlin air, exhilarated by the thundershowers that turn the skies violet at a moment's notice, my walks in the small forest of the *Grunewald* area restored a sense of oneness with nature more comforting than the language of San Francisco's eucalyptus trees. I sat on the veranda, drank my *Kaffee* with rich, postwar *Schlagsahne* — whipped cream — and welcomed my German self back into my body.

None the less, post-war Berlin was different from the Berlin I had known and loved. Instead of a metropolis,

> The language, of course, is Berlinerisch, the pass key to a club, a secret dialect, like Swiss German, that other Germans cannot relate to and do not care to hear.
>
> F. GRUNFELD

awake with crowds, busy and noisy, I found a stage-set representing the "West." No longer the capital, a city cut in half for no discernible purpose, West-Berlin had been reduced to two or three posh streets rebuilt with American capital. The *Kurfürstendamm* glittered with sidewalk cafes and their

elegant patrons. The *Gedächt-niskirche*, The Kaiser Wilhelm Memorial Church, still stood, its ruined towers left intact, a memorial to the destruction. Inside, carefully selected photographs provided the tourist with an aesthetic version of the war. In the side streets groups of shadowy people moved through the same ruins I had left six years before. Interrupting the bleak landscape here

and there were apartment houses rebuilt by *Bauhaus* style emulators, whose enthusiasm for glass and steel ignored the homeyness of the four-story buildings they replaced.

Yet what bothered me about Berlin was not in these details. In a different context, I would have embraced them all. What upset me on that early visit was that Berlin had lost its meaning. Going back was like meeting an old friend who'd attempted to cover the mutilating wounds of an automobile accident with carefully applied make-up: heartbreakingly

Eva's Berlin

familiar, heartbreakingly altered. Returning to San Francisco after that early visit, I was overcome by a mélange of old and new impressions too upsetting to sort out. I didn't. Instead, I found myself forgetting the place I had just come from. My real home was the Berlin I remembered.

MY BERLIN   Berlin. *Grossstadt*, the big city. My first memory is of sitting on the upper level of a double decker bus. I am four years old; the *Kurfürstendamm* is spread out before me, its bright lights dimmed by falling snow. On the other side is the *Gedächtniskirche*, good watchful lady that she is, snow swirling around her towers. Gray-blue buildings, most of them four stories high, wide boulevards lined with black silhouettes of trees. The snow falls in thick, soft flakes. As I watch, ribbons of white cotton enclose the bus and me in a dreamlike cocoon.

Berlin is the love of my mother's life. *Mit Spreewasser getauft*, baptized with the waters from the river Spree, she never tires of telling me how important Berlin is, how central to all of European culture. She is a native, *waschecht*, the city so ingrained in her, nothing can wash it away. Her eyes grow big as she recites Berlin's virtues. So many restaurants and cafes where intellectuals, musicians and theater folk gather. The famous people at *Kempinski's* or the *Romanische Café*, "at the next table, as close as you are to me right now!" Dietrich, walking down the aisle of the theater ahead of my mother, a vision in sequins, with an entourage of four young men. Brecht, arguing with such furious intensity that anyone would know he was a genius. Furtwängler, tall, quiet, refined, walking a little dog down the *Kurfürsten- damm*. Magical names, so familiar. She uses the French *soigné* to describe the women in the latest clothes, silky, and perfectly cut. Not a hair out of place. Elegant. Glamorous. The chic little outfits she herself wears, shot velvet, satin, and Italian embroideries, purchased with money saved from her salary as a legal secretary.

Berlin is the background for a melo- drama in which my mother has the starring role. She sings Berlin's praises as others might the national anthem. The theater, the opera, the premieres, the jazz, the new tall buildings, all within reach. She can't count the times she stands in line at the kiosk to see the opening of a Kaiser play, or Brecht and Weill's *Threepenny Opera*, or the latest cabaret. The queues don't bother her. She is aware of her good fortune. When the time comes to take me to my first plays and operas, we dress to the nines; she in black chif-

Try as he might, Hitler was never able to capture the Berliners. Long before the city was demolished by bombs, a frustrated and angry Hitler was already planning to re- build Berlin and shape it to the Nazi image. He even intended to change its name to Germania, for he had never forgotten that in every free election in the thirties Berliners had rejected him.

JULIUS RYAN

11

Eva's Berlin

fon and black patent platform heels, I in blue velvet and shiny patent leather shoes. I am being initiated as a Berliner.

Berliners don't give themselves airs. They're easy to talk to in a cafe, at the stores, waiting for the subway. They advertise their sense of humor and their calm in the middle of the hubbub. *Immer mit der Ruhe und dann mit 'em Ruck!* — always take it easy

and then, when it's time, act fast! The Berlin idiom is comical. Rhymes like:

> *Ick sitze da und wundah mir*
> I sit there wondering
> *uff eenmal geht sie uff, die Tür.*
> Suddenly the door opens
> *Ick sitze da und kieke*
> I sit and look
> *und wer steht draussen? Icke!*
> and who's there? Me!

It makes no sense. It sounds funny. I say it over and over again. We Berliners form a tribe of our own.

IN DENIAL My mother's loyalty to her home town was only strengthened by a ten year absence. When she married my father, she had to move to Münster, Westphalia, where I was born. I imagine she was persuaded to leave her beloved Berlin by the promise of life as Frau Doktor Eichenwald, a role that was to have fulfilled the dreams of luxury she had concocted during the depression that preceded World War II. But Münster was never to become home for my mother.

From the time they were married in 1929, the laughing couple photographed on their honeymoon hanging onto their Mercedes, a sepia-toned flapper and her handsome, dark doctor, my mother tried quite rightly to convince my father that he was in danger. The brown uniforms shouldering their way into her territory frightened her. She showed him newspaper accounts of arrests, boycotts and book burnings. She pointed to his brother Karl

who had already begun to plan his escape from Germany with the help of his wife's relatives in Holland.

But my father ignored her warnings. He was an optimist who believed that his wife and his brother were overreacting. While his brother was moving heaven and earth to get out, my father was revelling in his thriving practice in Münster. He couldn't understand why Jews were leaving Germany. There had been some incidents, he knew that. Supposedly some businesses had been closed, some books burned. But he felt Hitler and his little cadre of admirers

Eva's Berlin

represented a mere fraction of a people that were basically warm and caring. The reports were probably exaggerated. "One can't believe everything one hears," he said.

In 1927, when he was a medical student in Munich, he had actually been in a small beer hall when Hitler gave a speech.

"Look," he said to my mother, when she mentioned emigration, "I understand crazy people. When I interned at the mental hospital, I was locked in a room with a profes-sional wrestler. A huge guy. I had to think fast. What was I going to do to keep him from hurt-ing me?"

Here my father paused for effect. "But then I used my head," he continued, "and deve-loped a strategy. All I had to do was remember the fellow was a poor madman. He needed my support. I paid the man one compliment after the other: What an interesting life you've led! How did you ever manage to overcome so many opponents?" Another pause before he scored his final point. "And the guy chatted with me quite amiably until the nurse came in! That's exactly what those hangers-on are doing with Hitler. They're just flattering him until he cools off."

His voice deep with emphasis, he finished his speech. "That short, crazy Austrian will soon be recognized as a fanatic, an impractical dreamer. Germans are known for their

Such nonsense, most people thought at first. The man was nothing more than a political crackpot with a small band of followers.

LILA PERL

efficiency, for their practicality, and for their realism," he said. Soon, he was convinced, they would recognize Hitler's histrionics for what they were. "Nonsense," he liked to repeat, "is simply nonsense."

My father's argument was full of holes, even he knew it, but he wanted to stay in Germany. He felt German, not Jewish; he'd been raised that way. His family did not attend synagogue. He had married a woman whom Hitler would have called a "pure Aryan" and no one in his family had objected. She was the bright, charming and beautiful secretary whom he dated after they met at a medical convention where she was working. He hadn't asked whether she was Jewish and neither one of them cared about the fact that she had been raised Lutheran. Religion wasn't an issue. They had married in 1929 in the city hall. He was fond of saying, "We are as German as anyone we know," unaware that the very statement questioned the premise.

My father was living his dream. He had moved to Münster from Borghorst, a tiny village not far away. He had achieved exactly what he wanted: a thriving medical practice, a beautiful wife, a library full of the classics he liked to cite, an apartment decorated with antique furniture and filled with friends and admirers. In Münster in1930, my father was the *Theaterdoktor* for the municipal repertory company.

> **A**nd in 1931, Paul von Hindenburg, president of Germany, is reported to have said of Hitler that he was a queer fellow who would never become chancellor: the best he could hope for was to head the police department.
>
> VICTOR NAVSKY

Eva's Berlin

Actors, producers, and directors pronounced their *Herr Doktors* in reverent tones. After their visits, his famous patients left little presents: pots of marmalade, bottles of wine, a rare cactus for the garden. Surely, such privileged people would make it their business to protect him. Even when massive arrests and the horror of *Kristallnacht* made it more and more difficult, he stuck to his position

My parents' good life continues for a few years — a round of vacations in Italy, dinner parties at our house, visits

to my grandmother in Borghorst. I am born in December, 1934. A series of nannies is added to the household. My mother wears elegant clothes, *complets*, a French term adapted by the Germans to mean that everything matches: the chic little dress made from the same material as the lining of her coat. She has her picture taken wheeling me through the park in my carriage. My father is delighted to have a child, soon to be nicknamed *Ideltidel*, the first grandchild in his family. Two maids, Cissy and Marie, cook and clean for us. As a toddler, I spend much of my day with them. When they hang up the white laundry in our back yard, I hide in the wet, soap-smelling sheets until they find me because I can't help but laugh out loud.

LESSON ONE   Just after my fourth birthday in 1938, on a cold winter morning, the Nazi newspaper, *Der Stürmer*, is delivered to our front door. Now, everything will change. The headline, in fat black letters, says: CITIZENS WARNED AGAINST KIKE DOCTOR ERNST EICHENWALD. Not that I can read it. I'm only four. But my chest tightens as I watch one adult after the other picking up the paper incredulously, and then dropping it. The space around the table where the paper lies is a danger zone, emitting frightening vibrations. I don't want to go near it. The adults are talking just out of my earshot. I hear them repeat the word, *kike*, a terrible word I've never heard before. The folded newspaper on our delicately carved hallway table is a curse. Our cheerful, sunny house becomes suddenly hushed and quiet.

The adults talk with the intensity of conspirators. I try not to listen. My mother keeps urging my father to leave Germany. Leave Germany! They could be talking about jumping into the sea or flying to the moon as far as I'm concerned. Leave Germany! Darkness surrounds the phrase, witch-heavy, like a call into a nightmare. My father sounds less and less certain. It hasn't blown over. The Germans show no signs of coming to their senses. He looks beaten, his head bowed slightly, a bluish tinge to his skin. He knows my mother is right: we have to leave Germany. He wants to stay. But he, too, smells the witch's curse. His inability to make up his mind irritates my mother.

"You're not even as smart as your younger brother," *Mami* teases, knowing that my father's always been the one with book learning while his brother failed school.

"You're stuck in a rut and you're so afraid of getting muddy trying to get out that you'll stay stuck there forever," she says.

He answers, "I never believed this could happen."

My father's patients seem to know what *kike* means because they are staying away. From one day to the next, a crowded waiting room has become empty and silent. My father's face changes overnight. His confident smile is replaced by a stunned expression. Instead of running lightly up and down the stairs between the apartment and his office, he sits quietly in one spot, lost in thought, ignoring the paper on his lap. He no longer jokes about the *Nazis*.

A month after the *Stürmer* arrived, I find my father in the bedroom, carefully packing his silk suits into a large trunk. Stunned, I watch for a long time. Then he turns to me with a small, self-conscious smile. "I guess she was right," he says. "Your mother has always been very intuitive."

LESSON TWO   That headline in the *Stürmer* marked the beginning of the end of our family's life in Westphalia.

My fourth year, 1938, was to be a year of hard lessons. The evidence kept coming, evidence that even my father's optimism couldn't conquer.

Our next lesson takes place at the house of my favorite grandmother, my father's mother, in Borghorst, a rural village not far from Münster where my father was born. Few cars drive on the narrow lanes lined with comfortable farmhouses, white with gabled roofs. The air smells of hay and flowers with a hint of manure; the children behave as though the place is as much theirs' as the adults'. In Münster, I live primarily among grown-ups. My mother has to make arrangements by a telephone call or we have to go to the playground to meet other children, but in Borghorst children are everywhere. They work on the farms; they play in the streets; they ride horses, herd cows and goats, and feed the chickens. I

spend hours of my third, fourth, and fifth summers following them around: learning about farm chores like milking, haying, and stuffing sausage meat into casings.

My enthusiasm disappears when it comes to killing chickens. When I react to seeing one flap around the yard with piercing shrieks and her head cut off, I'm told chickens can't feel anything. But I remain skeptical. There is a photograph of me crushing a white chicken to my

19

chest, its feathers all splayed out. Her name, Hennchen, means "little hen" and she is my favorite — white, with a little black on her wings. She clucks her welcome every morning when I visit her to feed her grain. How could I ever agree to cut off the head of one of her relatives?

One hot Sunday afternoon, just a little after *Mittagessen*, the big noon meal, I go out to play on the main street. I'm rolling an old hoop, looking for company. The old bicycle tire rattles across the cobble-stones and makes my hand shake. I'm a little surprised at how empty the street is,

only a few chickens wandering around pecking at the weeds that poke up here and there, and a small spotted dog that often joins our games. Then I am aware of a peculiar silence and I am frightened, though I don't know why. A stone lands near me. It looks like a piece of plaster from one of the houses. Puzzled, I look at the sky. Is it raining stones? The silence is becoming unbearable. What's going on? Suddenly, a volley of rocks lands near me and I begin to panic. I drop my hoop. It traps me as I try to run away from the pursuing rocks. I still can't see where the stones are coming from but I don't care. I'm running as fast as I can. I can feel the blood running down my leg where one of the stones hit and a bump forming on the back of my head from another. I see the bushes move and a bit of printed cotton by which I recognize my friend Gerda. Then I hear her voice and the voices of Hans and Johann and others I don't recognize, yelling, and I run faster toward my grandmother's house.

"*Judenschwein*." They are calling me a Jew pig. Again and again, "*Judenschwein*."

I'm bleeding from the blow on the back of my head; my legs and arms are scratched. The shock blocks out physical pain. My world is spinning. "No. They can't. They couldn't possibly. No! No! No!" I say to myself as I stumble toward shelter.

The house is only yards away and I get there within minutes, breathing hard in the dark doorway. Badly shaken, I arrive in my grandmother's front room so disoriented I might as well be on an ice floe in a swiftly moving river. I sit down, looking to my grandmother for help. She looks distracted, says something about a talk with the farmhands about a lame horse, and examines my leg and head wounds.

"Nothing to worry about," she tells my parents who have come into the room. "These are just scratches and bumps. She'll be just fine in a little while."

I can't stop shaking while she cleans my wounds. She doesn't seem to grasp that what has happened has rocked me to the bottom of my soul, and I can't find words to express my sense of betrayal. My parents also stick to details that don't matter to me.

Eva's Berlin

"Nothing serious," my father keeps saying. "Thank God."

"It's got nothing to do with God," I want to say, "and it is serious," but all I can do is sob.

My mother glares at my father as though the whole thing were his fault. She starts to say something about those kids being *Schweinehunde* themselves, but my father and grandmother shush her.

"Not now, *Bielein*, there's no point," my father says, calling my mother by her pet name, "it'll all blow over, you'll see. Let's concentrate on getting the child calmed down."

I don't even know what a Jew is. I ask them when they take me to the kitchen and fix me hot chocolate, the same as they do with any other bruise. "It's just something about a person, like being blonde, or being a doctor," my mother says.

"But why do they yell like that? Why is it bad?"

"It isn't bad at all. It's what your father's family is. But you know how children are, they just got wind of something political that they don't understand. It's too hard to explain." My grandmother strokes my hair and tells me I'll forget this soon, but I know she's wrong.

A CHICKEN LEG   I have another memory of that year in which Nazism becomes associated with my grandmother's German Shepherd, Lord.

Piling out of the Mercedes just before dark on that particular day, we find my grandmother in the kitchen holding out a piece of cold roast chicken she has wrapped in a brightly colored napkin for me as a special treat. The juices start flowing in my mouth. Clutching my chicken leg, my *Böllchen*, I go out for a walk with Lord, the huge tan and black dog who is my friend and protector. Walking with him makes me feel taller and stronger. Embraced by the country dusk, with its smells of fresh plantings and cut grass while I inhale the familiar aroma of roast chicken, I am experiencing one of those rare times when everything is right with

the world. And then, just a few minutes after leaving the house, in one of those moments that is both longer and shorter than any other, Lord grabs the *Böllchen* out of my hand and eats it. His thick, coarse fur brushing my side as he leans into me, his eyes fierce and close, crunching the bone with his teeth; it's so unexpected that, for a moment, I think I'm imagining it. But when I look, my hand is empty. Lord growls at me when I try to get my *Böllchen* back from him, and lopes off to eat it by himself.

Eva's Berlin

I walk slowly back to the house, feeling wounded, as though I'd had a bad fall. Back in the living room, the adults are sitting around talking and reading the paper. Still stunned, I want to tell them what happened, but I feel strangely slowed down. It takes a while to get their attention.

"*Oma.*" I stand by her side, speaking softly. "*Oma*, Lord ate my *Böllchen.*"

They start to laugh before I finish telling what happened. Embarrassed, I feel tears streaking my hot face. I lose track of what I'm saying, stuttering, "Lord, Lord, Lord," between sobs. I watch the tears falling onto the tops of my brown shoes, coloring the cracks in the leather a darker brown than the rest. For the second time, my favorite grandmother sitting near the window with her lists of farm chores, shows no sign of understanding.

"It will pass, it will pass," she says, laughing with the others. "Tomorrow is another day and who knows, maybe another *Böllchen.*"

My grandmother's laughter hurts. No one understands about me and Lord. There's no point in trying to tell them. I try to rid myself of Lord's image before going to sleep. But I can't do it. Ferocious dragons blend with Lord in my dreams. When I wake up, my pillowcase is wet with tears.

Lord fit the German ideal. He was pure-bred, fit, and strong. Even his fur was the right color, brown and black. As I grew older, the brown uniforms became symbolic of Lord's betrayal.

LESSON THREE   The "official" Nazi persecution of my family began in the fall of my fifth year, also in Borghorst. It was September, 1939, just before Hitler invaded the *Sudetenland* and war began in earnest.

Asleep in my bed on the third floor of my grandmother's house, I am awakenend by loud knocking on the front door. The country silence is shattered by harsh voices.

"Open up. Open up. Police." I can hear heavy footsteps on the wooden floors and then the front door opening.

"Ernst Eichenwald and Karl Eichenwald. *Dalli. Dalli.* On the double."

A scuffling noise. A door slams. Silence.

Burrowing down into my soft feather bed I concentrate on the blackness behind my eyes. Nothing is happening. The nubs in the fabric of my pillowcase press into my face. Slowly, images come. First concentric circles, deep blue and yellow, then houses, and a silver moon. When I see a chicken running, I follow it, laughing.

> "**I**t was the Gestapo, the secret state police," Mama said, "They asked for papa by name. "Get dressed," they said," and come with us." Just like that. "Get dressed and come with us."
>
> LILA PERL

The next morning my father and uncle are not in the dining room that faces the country lane. The aroma of freshly baked rolls fills the house, as it does every morning. It's not the first time we've eaten breakfast without my father and uncle. Everyone in Borghorst knows Ernst Eichenwald

Eva's Berlin

is a doctor; sometimes he gets called in an emergency and my uncle, who knows everyone in the village by name, goes along to chat with the family. I tell myself nothing out of the ordinary is happening as I dip bits of the crunchy roll into the yoke of my soft boiled egg. But I can't make the fantasy work. I know they are not making a sick call. I wish my grandmother would tell me exactly what is going on, but she is busy talking to one of the farmhands about some slaughtering. The harsh noises in the middle of the night ring in my head until I can't ignore them any longer and ask my grandmother what happened.

"Your father and your uncle were taken to the Borghorst jail last night," she says, as though it is nothing out of the ordinary.

I have heard of horse thieves being put there. It's a small, gray building on the outskirts of town.

"Why? They didn't steal any horses."

She looks at me, straining for an answer, while I search her face for the laugh crinkles I depend on to cheer us both up.

"I know. They didn't steal anything. I really can't explain it to you, it's one of those things that maybe you'll understand when you're older."

"Why can't I understand now?"

"It's just because they are Jewish," she says.

There is that word again. I still don't know what it means. I look at her questioningly but her laugh turns bitter and her voice harsh.

"The men who arrested them said they were housing them in jail for their own protection," she says.

She's right. I don't understand. Isn't she Jewish, too? And my aunt?

"Why didn't they arrest everybody Jewish?" I ask. But they don't answer because my mother and aunt are laughing about that word, "protection." I don't get it. What's funny about it? Why would they need protection? They aren't in danger. No one attacked them. I conclude that the Nazis took them to jail for no reason at all.

We pack a basket with food and cigarettes and go to the jail, where, to my surprise, we find my father and uncle Karl in relatively good spirits. The jail is a small grayish building with bars on the windows. Otherwise, it looks like any of the little farmhouses or shops in the village. Inside, it smells of urine and old clothes. My father and uncle are sitting in a cell on some wooden chairs. Although they're locked up, they're unharmed. The jailers, old friends from the Borghorst grammar school, are hanging onto the bars of their cells talking when we come in. I hear one of them say, "Remember when Karl brought a whole herd of sheep into the school yard?"

I see them laughing together but, even when they come out to talk with us for a little while, I can't get rid of the tightness that settled in the pit of my stomach when I heard the knock on the door in the middle of the night.

After a few days, they are released and life really does go back to normal. At breakfast, my uncle is back in the dining room telling my father stories about the people passing by outside. The farm house is quiet and calm. Soon afterwards, my uncle leaves for America. From then on, our contact with the Nazis will be more impersonal.

THE FINAL LESSON   The final blow is dealt later that fall of 1939. One early evening, after visiting my grand-

mother in Borghorst, we come home to our Münster apartment. As Cissy and Marie have the weekend off and aren't expected till the next morning, we hardly notice that no lights are on in the apartment. As soon as we open the door, we find ourselves in the middle of a disaster. The apartment looks like a battleground: rugs turned up and ripped, chairs upside down, wallpaper slashed. In the living room, the blue damask upholstery of the Louis XIV chairs is bleeding gray felt stuffing. My favorite little chair sprawls on the floor with one of its legs splintered off and its fluted back slashed.

Old Flemish paintings, which my father collects, have been ripped from the walls; one looks like it's been peed on. Cigarette butts, circled by charcoal from being stamped out mark the parquet floor. Dirty bootmarks spot the light bedroom carpet. We walk through the rooms like zombies. In the kitchen, pots, pans, knives, forks and spoons cover the floor. The refrigerator doors are open as though in protest. In my father's office, desk drawers have been turned inside out and the contents torn and scattered. His precious books are on the floor.

My mother is crying and my father is shaking his head over and over again. I watch my mother pick up this object or that as though it were a wounded bird. Absurdly, my father stands reading a book as he puts it back on the shelf.

My mother's pain seeps slowly into my skin like lead. Her face looks as though someone just slapped it, disoriented and wild. I go to put my arms around her. From the floor, she picks up a *Meissen* figurine, her favorite shepherdess whose porcelain basket of roses is now in a million pieces. She doesn't notice me. My father says, "It's just things, *Bielein*, none of us are hurt. Things can be replaced."

But my mother doesn't hear him. Her skin blotchy, tears in her eyes but making no sound, she continues to pick up this thing and that, then letting it drop back down to the floor. I can't find a way through the magic circle that protects her from my

Once Hitler had been confirmed in power, Nazi thugs rampaging through the streets had official blessing. Truckloads of storm troopers broke into homes, businesses and bars all over the city...

ANTHONY READ AND DAVID FISHER

touch. My father goes to make my bed and then he puts me in it. He shrugs his shoulders again and again.

As soon as my parents get over the first shock, they send me to stay with my grandmother in the country. Relieved, I spend a week sitting in the warm comfort of the chicken coop, collecting and sorting eggs, and playing with Hennchen. At the house, the talk is about egg and sausage production and the baby that one of the maids will soon have. My grandmother's laughter mixes with hot chocolate to make me feel that Münster and the apartment are far, far away. Except that I don't play on the street anymore. We all know why, but we don't mention the day the rocks came. It's tacitly agreed that I'll remain on our grounds. The granddaughters of some of my *Oma's* friends come over and play with me in the afternoons. We eat tomatoes that grow on vines in the garden and carry Hennchen, swaddled in blankets, to my baby carriage. Everything is just as it was, but different.

When I return to Münster, the apartment appears much as it was before. The people who are repairing what can be fixed have lent us furniture and paintings. I don't care. Furniture is furniture as far as I'm concerned. Everything looks normal again — that's what matters — and we all concentrate on behaving that way.

MY MOTHER'S STORY   If it weren't for what my Berlin grandmother says — or doesn't quite say — when we go to live with her the following year, I might never have discovered the depth of my mother's sorrow about the ransacking of our apartment. Soon after we arrive in Berlin, I overhear my grandmother talking to my great uncle Robert in a way that makes my skin crawl.

"How could she do that with the child right there?" Her eyebrows twitch like cat playing with a half-dead bird. "It's just unthinkable. A woman her age. A mother."

With an air of icy superiority, she hints at something my mother did after the Nazis broke in. Something that has to do with me.

"Imagine being so irresponsible. And then to go to a sanatorium just when she is needed at home."

I don't understand. I thought irresponsibility had to do with not looking both ways before crossing the street. Then I overhear my grandmother arguing with my mother.

"Are those sleeping pills on your bedside stand?"

My mother looks away from her, flushing a deep red.

"How many do you take now?"

No answer. The questions keep coming,

"Isn't it dangerous? So soon? Have you seen the doctor about this? Did Ernst give these to you?" until my mother leaves the room.

After months of feeling squirmy when I hear her talking this way, it suddenly comes to me when I'm lying in bed. I don't want to put words to it. A tight feeling closes my throat. I pull the pillow down over my head and look for images to come and comfort me but I can't keep the words away. That night in Münster, my mother tried to kill herself. Kill herself. I can't really understand or imagine what it means and that is very hard for me because I make it my business to understand everything. I try to imagine my mother wanting to take her life. To look the horrible truth right in the face, like I tried to look at the chicken flying around the yard with her head cut off. My mother wanted to leave me. How could she, when I love her so much? How could she say that she loves me and then do this? I try to feel what she felt the night of the ransacking. But I don't know what happened afterwards. That night, before I was sent away, she looked like I felt when the rocks were thrown at me. Then I was sent away.

Our Münster apartment was my mother's pride, hard evidence that she had succeeded. She was the mistress of the house with two maids — two — not the failure of her mother's tireless prediction. When she crossed the border in my father's Mercedes, she brought back treasures from large Italian outdoor markets. She never tires of telling the tale of her bargaining: "They recognized a lady when they saw one. I told them what I would pay for those embroideries and then I left. And wouldn't you know it, by the time I got to where the Mercedes was parked, there they'd be! They'd followed me and they were begging me to buy! At my price, of course!"

Apricot silk embroidered in blue, or pink silk with

salmon colored thread, she decorated our apartment with these materials, and added Belgian lace curtains, Persian carpets, and ornately carved oak furniture in the dining room. Her Bohemian wine glasses shimmered crystaline green; goblets of three different sizes picked up the carved planes of her silverware.

The night of the ransacking, her familiar features looked different, out of focus somehow. I didn't want my beautiful mother to look like that. Why didn't she try to put the ransacking behind her? She was safe. We were all safe. Why wasn't she relieved?

"Because we're Jewish." She wasn't. She was German. And the Germans were persecuting her and her child. After she discovered the chaotic mess, she took an overdose of sleeping pills. I believe that's how it happened, but it's hard to accept.

I want to sit her down and say, "It was just furniture. We don't need it. We still have each other. How could you think of leaving me and *Papi?*"

I want to punish her, shake her, and then crawl into her lap. But she is opaque. She doesn't let me play the scene that would make everything all right. When my grandmother retells parts of the story in the hushed, dramatic tones reserved for the family shame, I want to scream that it's a lie. My mother would never do anything like that. I want to, but I can't, and so I come to hate my grandmother because I know that what she's saying is true.

Eva's Berlin

LEAVING In the late summer of 1939, I return to Münster from my grandmother's house in Borghorst, hoping against hope that somehow everything will return to normal.

In the library, my father is looking at his books, shrugging his shoulders and shaking his head. "What will happen to them? Perhaps I'll leave them with a friend."

He explains to me that some of his books are very old, too delicate to travel across the world with our furnishings. I know that he loves his books because he touches them with soft hands. I feel very close to my father in that moment. We feel lost. Our entire lives have been lived right here. This is where we belong. But my father is packing.

With the help of the Seesemann's, the same relatives who helped my aunt and uncle emigrate, my mother succeeds in getting all of us to Amsterdam. For her, this is the beginning of an adventure. We rarely talk to our neighbors any more, because they cross to the other side of the street when we appear, but when we do, my mother talks big.

"We're stopping off in Amsterdam, and we'll see some of my husband's theater friends, but really we're on our way to America," she says. "I think my husband will be very successful there. It's still a young country. They need well-trained doctors."

She has been eager to leave the country, and now, finally, her chance has come. Silky and languid before, ever the elegant hostess, my mother is burning with a new energy. But, although she knows what to do and does it with gusto, there is an undertone of bitterness. Over soft-boiled eggs, she tells my father that the household goods have to be organized and packed as soon as possible. He butters his roll and looks at her encouragingly but he doesn't respond. She gulps down her scalding hot coffee as though it were cold water and leaves the table abruptly.

"Your father," she says to me *sotto voce*, "is a fool."

In another minute, we hear her voice as she orders the maids to pack our furnishings into large wooden crates to be sent to America. These crates, standing empty in our apartment for a week or so, had been my playhouses, quickly filled with my dolls and stuffed animals, tattered blankets and old lace curtains. I had welcomed the crates, only dimly realizing their purpose. Now it was all becoming real. We would be taken from this house just as my dolls were going to be taken from the crates in another minute. As I rush to protect my cherished possessions from the maids, my mother announces that our house will be sold. I feel the ground shifting under my feet.

Finally, everything is packed. We leave Münster for a short stay with my grandmother in Borghorst before starting on the first leg of our journey, to Holland, where we'll obtain visas for the United States. Up to now, I had placed grandmothers in the same category as my parents: eternal presences. Despite all the obvious signs, it had never occurred to me that we might really be separated. Now we are preparing to be separated, perhaps forever. Farewell to my favorite grandmother, to the chickens, and to Lord, the German Shepherd. I strain to imagine life in a new country, but my mind is filled only with a vague sense of dread.

My parents and grandmother behave cheerfully, but nothing feels quite real. When the family gathers for the midday meal, my father tells the same old jokes but, for the first time, my uncle isn't there and the easy flow is gone.

"So one German Jew meets another one on the boat and says: How do I get to San Francisco from New York, once we're in the USA? And the guy answers: That's an easy one. First you get to California, and then you turn left."

The reception is lukewarm and he tries another one.

"So, the German Jew asks the other guy to give him some tips about how to get along in America. First, says the guy," and my grandmother starts to laugh in anticipation of the punch line, "first *müssen Sie können die language.*"

Another laugh — the mixture of English and German strikes a chord — and then another silence. And so the meal continues. The adults' faces seem distracted, like they often do when I ask a question, but they seldom look like that when they talk with each other. I am having trouble locating myself in this new atmosphere. I feel as though I'm encased in brittle glass that any impact could shatter instantly. But it doesn't happen. The dinner just ends. When we leave, my grandmother's eyes well up with tears, and my father's reassurances sound hollow.

AMSTERDAM, A WAY STATION We leave Borghorst that evening and we are finally on our way. In the train station in Münster, I feel lost among the crowds of people and suitcases. I'm afraid of losing my parents, who seem to have eyes only for our belongings and the railway tickets which they check over and over again. The largest suitcase becomes my lifeline. I hold onto its luggage tag until we are safely settled in our sleeping compartment. Lying on my stomach on the soft mattress of my upper berth, I can spy snatches of other lives through the half-opened blind. I see a man in shirtsleeves drying his hands on a soiled towel, then a child sitting on her bed crying. She is older than I, maybe ten, and wears a blue ribbon in her reddish hair. I think about how she must have felt when she put the ribbon on this morning, happy and expectant.

The iron wheels grind underneath me and I snuggle into my bunk-bed, feeling the anticipatory excitement of former vacations. Then I remember, with a start, that I don't know where we're going and it's not a vacation.

We arrive in a cold, unwelcoming city: Amsterdam. Tall, narrow houses crowd against each other like so many disapproving relatives. Waterways appear in unexpected places, like black, forbidding fingers, warning us to stay away. I feel lost and small, clinging to my parents more than any of us are used to, afraid I'll disappear into the dark waters.

At the Seesemann's home, the cramped, over-furnished rooms also feel unwelcoming, although our hosts

Eva's Berlin

assure us daily that we can stay with them until our visas for America arrive. But it feels like we are too many for their small quarters. I share the bed with both my parents who keep repeating that we are lucky to be there. It's not easy, feeling lucky, when what I feel is grief over everything I've lost, and there's no comfort in the outside world. I practice concentrating on what I like and sit by the yellow and orange tulips near a window facing the canal, trying to enter the flowers' elegant, delicate structure in my imagination.

The Seesemanns often ask how the emigration is proceeding. But, because of a strange and surprising set of circumstances, our emigration is not proceeding at all. Back in Münster, fearful that the Nazis would discover that I was half-Jewish, my mother secured a baptismal certificate for me. In Amsterdam, it proves to be our undoing. A few weeks after our arrival in Holland, the Dutch government informs us by letter that asylum can be granted to my father because he is Jewish, but that my Aryan mother and I have to return to Germany. This is totally unexpected. My parents are convinced there's been a mistake. At government offices, my mother explains and explains to the authorities that she is married to a Jew, that her half-Jewish daughter was never raised in the Christian faith, but the authorities turn a deaf ear. My father swears affidavits that he is my father, my Jewish father, and that I had never been baptized. But it's no use. They will not change their decision. It's difficult to believe. Holland demands our immediate departure because we're not Jewish enough.

How did they decide, I often wondered. Were the Dutch racists, too? Had they taken seriously the Judaic law that the mother's race determines the race of the child? Had my mother been Jewish and my father Aryan, would they have let us stay? How could they separate a family? Take my father away from me? Did they put greater faith in the phony certificate than in what we said? Weren't they supposed to be good and the Nazis bad? I couldn't let it go. We were sent back because I was half-Aryan. I thought the trouble was that I was half-Jewish. It was a lot to think about.

SNAPSHOTS   I am looking at photographs of my parents. In front of Heidelberg's castle on their honeymoon, the elegant young couple stands out from the crowd of tourists. She, with fingerwaves and a cloche hat, manages to look both

sexy and, at the same time, demure. He is typecast as the successful and beloved doctor, she as his glamorous wife.

"Your father was very handsome, don't you think?" she would say later, showing me

his picture. "You can't really see how elegant my clothes were, but I wish you could. Just look at that bit of black and white print on the dress under that black silk coat. Anyone would recognize it as Paris *couture*. No one else had anything like it. You can't imagine how many people asked me where I shopped."

It was, in fact, hard for me to imagine clothes as beautiful as she made her's sound, rubbing her fingers together over the imaginary silk, her eyes shining. When she showed me pictures of the famous actresses whom she was said to resemble, their dresses inhabited my fantasies, as much a symbol of all that is beautiful and feminine as the piles of jewels that I imagined in fairy tale castles.

After Amsterdam, the *joie de vivre* in the earlier photos disappears. My parents still look elegantly dressed, but the "yes" to life, so evident earlier on, is gone. Downward lines of disappointment appear on my mother's face. She looks sorrowful.

BACK TO BERLIN Within a week or so of getting our notice from the Amsterdam authorities, we are on our way to Berlin. Getting tickets and re-arranging our suitcases, my parents tell me our separation will be short. We'll leave most of our things with my father in Holland and get them as soon as we rejoin him. We are Aryans, after all, and it should not be difficult to get passports to leave Germany, now that my Jewish father is no longer with us. Their words have an air of bravado. Something happened to my parents when the authorities intervened. It is as though the hand of God has reached down and stopped us. I try to believe it will all work out. But just under our attempts to be cheerful and confident looms the feeling that we are caught in the wheels of the terrible machine, like so many others.

We never really said good-bye. I remember my father's face at the airport in Amsterdam, smiling, putting on a great show of confidence in the future. But my mother's face was wet with tears.

What a day it must have been for my mother. Her life shattered. No more Frau Doktor Eichenwald, except in a more and more uncertain future. The name she thought would legitimize her forever as a member of the professional class now made her an outcast. Eichenwald — another part of the Jewish botany, as Jewish as Rosenbaum or Schildkraut or Lilienthal, as Jewish as the yellow stars people were beginning to wear in Münster. She wasn't even Jewish.

My first airplane ride. I trace the pattern of the seal-brown upholstery with my fingers and look out of the tiny windows, trying not to see the tears in my mother's eyes. Soaring, I look for angels in the puffy clouds that welcome me as Holland never did. I want to live here, dart in and out of soft white castles and preen my huge white wings while the tiny world below me continues its toy life.

But thoughts about my mother take me away from my cloud life. She'd been so glad to be married. Walking to work through the Linden lined Berlin streets with her best friend Ursel, she'd had great plans. They wanted large airy rooms instead of the small, crowded apartments their fathers' civil service salaries afforded. They dreamt of limousines and handsome chauffeurs. Together they vowed to escape the lower middle class and become something important, major figures in the glamour of the city. Ursel had planned to be a fashion designer. My mother would become a famous trial lawyer. She'd actually attended law school until, as a result of the depression, her parents were no longer able to pay and she began to work as a legal secretary. When Ursel married a banker, my mother felt she'd lost the competition. Filled with envy, she pictured her friend in a mansion while she was still working for a living like a shopgirl! My father's appearance must have been the answer to her prayers. It was 1925. I wonder how much thought she gave to his being Jewish.

Now it was all over. No more husband — handsome, tall, well-positioned, much-loved. No more servants, space, money, clothes, food. Back to the parents she'd left more than a decade before. Back to the small apartment from which she'd planned to rescue them.

I worried about my mother. We were so close. I could detect what was wrong by the look on her face and the tone of her voice, when others were fooled into thinking she was having a good time. But knowing her moods didn't mean I understood them. Sometimes what caused her moods seemed to be just the opposite of what had caused them the time before. Coming back to her parents' apartment caused her despair this time. On the other hand, just a few weeks ago, she seemed so happy to be back in her beloved Berlin that I wondered whether she had arranged the whole scene just to return. Could she have used the phony certificate as a ruse to get us back here? She often told a story about my birth that made me wonder.

When I was born my mother became ill with a breast infection while still in the hospital. "The worst pain I ever experienced," she told me many times, "was because you tried to drink from my breast."

She had been taken to a sanatorium, a place in the *Schwarzwald* with verandas and views and people catering to her which she described in glowing terms. She had hated giving birth. The sanatorium was a well-earned reward. While I was left behind with a nurse who fed me bouillon and vitamin drinks, she luxuriated in massages, special baths, and a diet that consisted of delicate custards and nourishing soups.

"You were born allergic to my breast milk anyway," she said, as though the whole thing could have been avoided if I had only acted more in accord with both my own and her nature. She never mentioned being happy that I was born. Or any sadness about leaving me, a tiny baby, in the care of a stranger. Listening to her tales of the care received after the exhausting birth, her success as the favorite patient at the sanatorium, I wondered sometimes whether she had exaggerated her illness so she could get away from me.

Now, our flight to Berlin brings another separation.

Eva's Berlin

This time we are leaving my father. I can't imagine being without him any more than I could imagine leaving Germany. He is part of me. How can I picture life without him? A sense of impending disaster makes itself known by a heaviness in my throat and stomach. I can't eat. I don't know how to be cheerful, though I know my mother expects it.

"Don't go around with a long face," my mother tells me. "It won't be long and then we'll meet *Papi* in Amsterdam. And then we'll all go to America!"

I feel a burden of guilt. If it weren't for whatever it was that was wrong with me, my mother wouldn't have gotten a breast infection. If it weren't for me and my false baptismal certificate, our family would be together. My mother's looks seem to confirm my fears. She doesn't come out and tell me that we had to leave Holland because of me, but whenever Amsterdam or my father are mentioned, her eyes land on me and then bounce skyward and I experience a confusion as vague as snowdrifts.

Berlin begins with forgetting. We hardly mention our life in Münster. Nor do we talk about Holland. Gradually all that remains of my memories of Holland is an ache just below the surface of my consciousness and a lesson I'll never forget: that the good guys can turn into the bad guys just like that.

After we have squeezed ourselves into my grandparents' small apartment, my mother makes one final trip to the Dutch border to hand my father her jewelry to use as a nest-egg for his emigration. She is conflicted. Her heavy gold chains and bracelets are part of a hoard she began when she got her first paying job. My father fleshed it out with ribbons of diamonds and rings set with pearls and rubies, and an emerald set in a tiny diamond border, trinkets polished to a bright gleam by her maids. She keeps only a pin that looks like a golden wish-bone with ruby and emerald tips, a couple of thin gold chains, and two thick, red-gold bracelets. The rest she wraps for him in one of her flowered chiffon scarves.

Heavy border patrols on both sides make the situation almost impossible. My parents are both so afraid of endangering my father's escape that they barely exchange a word. Afterwards, back in Berlin, my mother, who usually crows about her adventures, can hardly keep from crying. But her trip serves its purpose. My father is on his way to America a few days later. It is 1939.

Eva's Berlin

CHAPTER TWO

Relocation

WAITING Our packed suitcases in the hallway look like rumpled dwarfs. When I pass them I'm filled with a mixture of hope and fear. How wonderful it will be to see my father! I can imagine him waiting for us in a big shiny car. When we arrive, he will step towards us and scoop me up in his arms and everything will be all right. That's what I imagine some of the time. But, at other times, I get frightened. How can I leave Germany and everything I know and love? What is America? A big question mark, as far as I'm concerned. I've heard America is very large, that everyone there has lots of money, and I've seen a few pictures of cowboys and Indians. They don't look like anyone I've ever met, bearded and wild,

Eva's Berlin

with funny headgear. They scare me. I'd rather stay in Germany than take my chances with them.

O n March 12, 1938 …it seemed all too likely that the U.S. immigration authorities would issue even fewer quota numbers than the 27,000 that had already been allotted for the year.

LILA PERL

We want to alight like butterflies on my grandparents' apartment for a few moments and then dash off to Holland and America, but we are quickly disappointed. As the days pass in fruitless efforts to get visas, our wings become heavier and heavier. We can't get there. Lead after lead, path after path leads to a dead end. Days become weeks and the weeks turn into months.

My mother and I visit consulates and bureaus. We have introductions to important people. I stand near my mother as she fills out forms in triplicate and listen to her repeat her hopes for success, only to have them dashed the next day.

"The quota for the day was smaller than we expected."

"The boat is in drydock."

"Your papers were lost or misplaced."

My mother makes more visits to the authorities and fills out more papers. Sometimes she comes home exuberant.

"Our exit visas have been granted. Any day now, can you believe it, any day, we'll be on our way to meet *Papi*."

But it is not to be. Each time, for new and mystifying reasons, the visas are cancelled at the last minute.

"The quota was filled yesterday."

"The quota was reduced by the authorities."

"Only complete families could go."

The authorities are playing cat and mouse with us. Our bags remain in the hallway.

My mother looks very pretty in the photos taken in a studio that promised to get them to my father: her hair is impeccably coiffed in a roll, her diamond and ruby wishbone pin displayed against her black silk dress. It must have been the equivalent of "dressing for success," but neither her looks, her clothes, nor her charm helped her get visas.

I learned in that period just after war had been declared that waiting meant inevitable disappointment. The lesson stuck. My impatience has vexed many of those I love. I feel sure I was born with it, a part of a temperament too quick for convention, pushed to an extreme by those waiting years. Instead of learning to wait, I learned to avoid waiting, to fear it and to seek comfort in speed. When the United States entered the war, in 1941, our waiting came to an end. Berlin, it turned out, was to be our destination — our destiny — until the war finally ended.

Eva's Berlin

BERLIN, RANKESTRASSE 33 My mother's parents live at the rear of a large, four-sided apartment house near the *Gedächtnisskirche* on one of West Berlin's oldest streets. The streets are lined by four-story high apartment houses, graying old ladies, their balconies spilling geraniums and petunias, like lace cascading down a woman's blouse. The

Gedächtniskirche, a slate-blue cathedral lit up by the deep reds of a long stained-glass window, stands on its own island in the middle of traffic like a sentinel, calm and quiet. Streetcars, steel cages with beautifully polished wooden benches inside, stop near it and double-decker buses arrive from the *Kurfürstendamm* and the *Tauentzienstrasse*. From there it is only a few blocks to my house.

Our street is quiet, but not entirely residential. On the first block of *Rankestrasse* is *Miericke's Konditorei*, a pastry shop that would make a perfect setting for the light operas my mother loves so much, all mirrors and chandeliers lighting up beveled display cases for all the pastries in the world. From my mother's descriptions and my few visits before the rationing began, I can see every-thing behind the glass cases in my imagination. There are cream puffs and apple cakes and strawberry fruit tarts and Napoleons with their pink and chocolate frosting, and enough whipped cream to decorate the cakes and top steam-ing cups of coffee and chocolate. In the warm summer after-noons, the place is filled with ladies in long gloves and hats with little veils which they raise to consume their delicacies. After 1942, when the pastries disappear and serious ration-ing begins, the memory of *Miericke's* will become an image of a past I barely remember.

A little further down the street is another restaurant, quite different in tone. Its sidewalk tables and dark bar provide a gathering place for the men in the neighborhood. There, they read the paper in the morning with their coffee and crisp, warm rolls, discuss the news over a beer in the afternoon, and stop in for a drink after work. In the con-spiratorial tones reserved for gossip about the famous, a neighbor tells my grandmother that the Dutch Queen Juliana's future consort, Bernhard, used to be one of the regulars there. My grandmother — in one of those odd associations of proximity and success — takes his presence so near her as confirmation of her own aristocratic rank as the wife of my grandfather who, paradoxically, has re-nounced his Polish title, *Graf Bielinski* for the simple *Herr*.

The first floor of our house front is occupied by Ciro's, an elegant restaurant, where people come for lunch and dinner. Dressed to the nines mostly in browns and blacks, they look cleaner to me than anyone else on the street. I watch them disappear quickly behind the black door decorated with a large, silver C, uttering wisps of conversation too sophisticated for me to understand. The C remains in my awareness and, as I walk past, I often list all the 'C' words I know, not an easy task in German, because there are so few.

WHERE WE LIVE   Our house is large and gray. It faces the sidewalk without embellishment and, like the other large houses on our street, lacks a front garden. Entering through the heavy gate, dark wood carved with scrolled designs and ornamented with brass, I pass the *Portier-Frau's* little room in the dimly-lit hallway. The *concierge* is a buxom blonde who sits near her half-opened window night and day, missing nothing and no one. Her name is Frau Grass. For me, she is a figure in a diorama; I cannot imagine her room as anything but a backdrop for all of us who pass by daily, sometimes several times. Perhaps there are other rooms behind it — there must be, she has to cook and go to the bathroom — but I imagine them empty. Her life is completely devoted to watching us, her tenants. She knows all our comings and goings. My mother, who thrives on the gossip the *Portier-Frau* dishes out, adores her.

"She told me Frau Meyer's husband snores so loud that they had to move his bed to the front room."

"Herr Paasch is seeing a lawyer. He is very high up in the business world. Someone from Siemens or Krupp is trying to ruin him and he's fighting back."

"The Janovski sisters have bought a new baby grand."

It is to Frau Grass that my mother looks for confirmation of her hunches about who is flirting with whom, whose relatives are visiting from the country, who has made or lost money.

At the end of the hallway, a large door opens onto an inner courtyard leading to the other three wings of the house. This common area, where we meet going in and out of our apartments, consists of brick walkways laid out in a cross with dandelions pushing up between the cracks. There are two staircases, each with a straggly rhododendron near the bannister, the sole attempt at decoration made in the dim and distant past. Although it is drab, for me, the courtyard has a kind of magic. From our kitchen window, I can keep up with all the animals in the apartment house. When Fräulein Walter walks past our back windows with her Pekinese, I rush out to pet the round blonde waves over his black velvet eyes. Sometimes, I sit watching the Schmidt's cat, Miese, stalk birds.

"Abra-cadabra. Bird-angels protect the sparrows. Abra-cadabra. Let the cat get tired."

Due to my efforts, many of the birds are saved.

Once, a beggar comes with an organ and a monkey dressed in red velvet and gold braid. The old man sings

Eva's Berlin

Italian folk songs in a thin, reedy voice while the monkey turns the organ's handle. After he finishes, coins come pelting down into the courtyard from windows all around the house and the monkey, small and deft, collects them, doffing his porter's cap. He is the company I have been looking for, straight out of one of my fairy tales, yet real. In my mind, he remains a permanent resident.

Directly across the courtyard, through another dim hallway, is our apartment. Written on the brass plate by our door is O. Bielinski, my grandfather's name, as elegant and exotic among the German names as the man himself. It is a melodious name, I wish it were mine. I spell it out loud over and over again, because its letters — especially the last three — have a particularly winning rhythm in German: *ess...kah...eee.*

MY PLACE The bedroom that I share with my mother when we first arrive from Holland is on the immediate right as we enter the apartment. My grandparents have given up their dining room and furnished it for us. In typical child's fashion, I am not aware of the sacrifice this must have been for my very proprietary grandmother. But soon after we arrive, I realize that we are unwelcome guests. She rigidly patrols the house to see whether a bed has been left unmade, or clothes left lying on one of the chairs. When my mother objects, the tension between them builds.

I like my room. The small white bed has slats hinged

at the sides to keep me from falling out. My mother often forgets to put them up, leaving me with mixed emotions: on the one hand I feel grown up and independent, on the other, endangered and abandoned. I want to appear strong and happy. *Kraft durch Freude* — strength through joy. The Nazi slogan is on everyone's tongue. Before I go to sleep in the little white bed, I imagine myself on an adventure where fairies and kind animal spirits help and guide me.

THE FIRST FIRE Sometimes my bravado gets me into trouble. Although it is not allowed, I stay up long past my bedtime, turning the pages of the hoard of books I collect from other parts of the house. Fairy tales  mixed with books of photographs and paintings of foreign lands which I like to look at when the others think me asleep. Easy to do in summer but not in the winter darkness. One night, unable to locate a candle, I confidently make a small bonfire by stacking a few kitchen matches in the place where the candle usually sits. The resulting flare enables me to read quite well, if only for a short time. But, to my surprise, the bed catches on fire. The flame at my side is small and yellow, not much larger than the candle at first and I lie there, fascinated, unable to comprehend the adults' alarm as they rush in. My grandfather, having smelled the smoke, quickly puts it out with my blanket, speaking to me in a tone of voice I hardly recognize.

"This was not a good idea, child. You put yourself in danger! Please understand this. You can't use matches except when one of us is around."

My mother and grandmother tell me that I could have burned the house down. Alhough I register the seriousness on their faces, I don't really believe them. I'm still excited by what happened. The fire looked beautiful. Only the bed was slightly blackened.

The charred hole leaves a permanent mark on my bed which I regard with a certain amount of pride. But my mother and grandmother refer to the fire whenever they want to point out my foolishness:

"It's just like her," they say, shaking their heads, my mother hiding a smile, "she won't listen to anyone."

My mother seems to like my rebelliousness, despite her words to the contrary. My grandmother is dead serious. She's right, of course, but I tune out their warnings and go about having my own adventures. Why should I listen? My grandmother seldom really watches me. Neither does my mother. Most of the time, they seem perfectly content to let me do things my own way.

MY LITERARY LIFE CONTINUES Books and stories are the magic carpets that take me where I want to go. My mother and grandfather read me fairy tales from every country and continent, the poetry of Schiller and Göthe; sometimes even little stories from the newspaper or moral tales whose child heroines accomplish miracles of one kind or another. My favorites come from far, far away — Eskimo tales that let me travel to vast snow-laden landscapes, or African stories studded with lions and tigers. By the time I'm four, however, my mother starts to become less enthusiastic about following my insistent, *"Les' weiter,"* keep reading. When I approach her with my latest favorite, she sometimes waves me away impatiently.

"I wish you could read," she says.

It is a wish I fulfill without much trouble. I learn to read like I learned to eat, hardly aware of the effort. My love for books gives me wings: I devour the letters and their combinations. It's as if I already know them and only need my grandfather and mother to legitimize my guesses. From then on, I read whatever I can find.

When I reach the age of five, my mother gets me a library card. I devour the books in the children's library. *Nesthäkchen*, a nickname meaning "the last to leave the nest," is one of my favorites, the center of a series of books which trace her life from early childhood to grandmotherhood. A bit of a spoiled brat, surrounded by a huge and doting family who make her the center of their lives, *Nesthäkchen* is who I want to be. In a corner of the living room, where I've rigged blankets and pillows off the arm of the sofa as a special place for my secret fantasies, I pretend to

Eva's Berlin

be *Nesthäkchen*. In one of the last episodes, she is a grown-up doctor in Sao Paulo. Geography means absolutely nothing to me and I have no idea where such a wonderful sounding place might be located, but it sounds exactly like what I want for myself.

The *Ahmelang* library is an old brick building with large low-ceilinged rooms full of books. Going there is deeply satisfying; it is one place — perhaps the only place I know — where all I have to do is ask, and I get what I want. Hours and hours are spent roaming the imaginary streets of London, away from the consulates, away from the packed bags, safe in the middle of an adventure. Reading Dickens makes me glad I live in Berlin. England is so crowded. The rooms are tiny and the streets narrow. And none of the characters have the Berliner sense of humor. By the time I'm six, I've read all of Dickens, skipping what I don't understand.

At the checkout desk, I barely notice the strange looks the adults at the *Ahmelang* library send my mother over my head.

"Isn't she a little small for all those big books?"

My mother replies, "She's really an adult in disguise. She isn't five; she's more like fifty."

At home with my books I work out the pronunciation of the English words using German phonetics. Shakespeare, for example, becomes *Shah kes pee ah ray*. Romeo and Juliet are my favorite characters although I don't understand the fuss everyone makes about their dying so young. Fifteen seems like a ripe old age to me. When I run out of children's books at the library, I turn to the adult romances serialized in the newspaper like *Courths-Mahler's* stories about poor serving wenches rescued by adoring gentlemen who risk their noble names in a marriage far below their station: more interesting even than Dickens' London, which was apparently populated mostly by boys.

Once I open a book, I live in the author's world. Wrapped in words that nourish my senses, I feel safe. Quickly, I become addicted. Even when others think me totally engrossed in an activity like eating or talking, I am actually calculating how much time it will take for me to get back to my book. Wherever else I am, I'm usually willing myself to return home to the overstuffed chair with the hunt pattern on the upholstery and the scratched arm-rests, to continue reading my current novel. Like the heroines of fairy tales who suddenly go through a mirror or down into a rabbit hole and find themselves in another world, I disappear into my book and remain there, far away. Again and again, when someone attempts to talk to me while I read, they find me almost unrousable until I come to with a loud shriek and frighten us both.

Facing the courtyard is a small bedroom that becomes mine when I'm seven. At night, shadows fall on the curtains like willowy ladies approaching my small white bed. A tall, dark, oak wardrobe dwarfs me. I'm afraid ghosts might come in through the mirror, people who lived and died here before we moved in.

In the middle of the night, a recurring nightmare often wakes me: I am riding through the countryside in a black carriage drawn by six white horses. Gradually but inexorably the carriage goes faster and faster until, certain that the next moment means death, I jerk awake breathing rapidly, petrified, sure that the carriage has plunged over a rocky promontory. It takes me a while to realize that I'm in my bed, but, I can't rid myself of the fear. I cry myself back to sleep. No adult comes in to comfort me because I don't call out when I'm afraid. I often exhaust myself yelling for them to come and bring me glasses of water before I go to sleep, but I keep my nightmares to myself.

When I am seven, my grandfather blesses my new bedroom with a gift that allows me to read far into the night: a lamp above the bed controlled by a switch I can reach with my hand. Some nights my shoulder aches from the effort of holding my arm up hour after hour to make sure I can switch the light off at the slightest noise. If they catch me, the lamp will be removed. I can't take that chance. The lamp allows me to enter the big world without restrictions. Reading, I'm an adventurer in foreign lands or a princess in a castle. Gradually, I become less afraid.

SEDUCED   My mother's bed with its royal blue satin comforter is in the far corner of my first bedroom. Despite the pain she frequently causes me, I love my mother with a fierce and sensuous love. I see in her all that is feminine; she is beautiful, charming, alluring. In the late morning, I crawl in beside her, feeling her smooth silky skin, secure in the fantasy of how much she loves me. Every curve of her body belongs to me. Since my mother can do no wrong where I am concerned, I believe the same holds true for me. When she objects vehemently to my pulling myself up by putting my elbow on her breast, her anger surprises me. I can't believe that I could possibly harm someone I love so much.

PETERCHEN   Our living room looks like a storeroom in a run-down club, faded and out of date, crowded with furniture every shade of brown. There are two easy chairs by the windows, over-stuffed and threadbare, the brown spangled with faded gold. A table on one side of the room holds the budgy's cage. He is a spiffy bird, pastel green glinting with black and downy yellow accents. I watch him preening much of the day, flinging tiny feathers into the air until he is perfectly smooth and shiny. Sitting on a pine wood perch my grandfather built, he warbles, *"Wo ist denn mein Spiegelchen?"* It means, "Now where is my little mirror?"

My grandmother taught it to him, as she will teach it to every bird we will own — why, I don't know. Perhaps the bird is the only being in her world that is to be allowed its vanity. She often stops by his cage, on her rounds of cleaning and tidying, for a duet where they repeat the phrase one after the other, faster and faster, until it's almost a song.

Eva's Berlin

On the opposite side of the room is an empty fish-bowl, irridescent with the colors of the rainbow. Once in a while, Peterchen takes a flight around the room and alights on the glass bubble, a magical bird. The dark oak dining room table where Peterchen searches for leftover crumbs is surrounded by six dark oak chairs, visiting elders. During the day, his feathers are illuminated by light that enters through lace curtains but soon loses its stamina, leaving the room in semi-darkness. In the evenings, Peterchen, quiet in his darkly shrouded cage, the room is given a soft, rosy light by a burgundy-colored, fringed lamp.

THE DARK ROOM On the far side of the living-dining room is my grandparents' dark bedroom. I don't know much about what goes on in this, the most remote room of the house. When I glimpse it in semi-darkness, I see that it holds their large bed, an armoire, and a few family treasures. My mother's mauve lace confirmation dress and the myrrh from my grandmother's wedding bouquet are stored in one of the many drawers of a black lacquered Chinese chest. Once in a while, my grandmother has an attack of benevolence and delves back into the darkness to show me one of her treasures. The myrrh has an ancient, tea smell. My mother's dress is a very light, almost grayish, pink, made of lace so fine I'm afraid to touch it, for fear it will tear. I'm not sorry that I am kept out of my grandparents' room. It speaks of age and coming death with a certainty that inspires a kind of awe.

On certain days in late fall and winter, when the light is low, and the air outside chilling, a terrible smell emanates from the back bedroom. Sour and insistent, it permeates the whole apartment. My mother holds her nose and tells me it's Baldrian, an herb used since medieval times. I imagine forests of it boiled down to make salves. My grandmother suffers from *Hexenschuss*. The word literally translated means witch-shot, a magical word, bringing the world of fairy tales into our apartment. I picture a witch — my grandmother — being shot, of course, not the reverse. Severe pain across the middle of her spine causes my grandmother to stop dead in her tracks and remain slightly bent over, frozen in a posture of the old hags that gave the pain its name. With a determined expression on her face, she forces herself to move and hobbles to the bedroom, calling my grandfather for help. Soon afterward, Baldrian's unpleasant aroma wafts through the apartment and my grandmother reappears, still somewhat bent but straighter, on the road to triumph in the war of the witches.

My mother and I are gone by then, the horrible smell our ticket to freedom. No one can be expected to remain in an apartment where the pungent, green air makes our throats dry and our eyes tear. We flee to Fräulein Walter's apartment upstairs, where we sip tea and eat dry crackers while Fräulein Walter shows us her pre-war negligées.

Eva's Berlin

GRANDMOTHER'S BEDTIME In the late evening, at nine o'clock or so, when the apartment building is quiet, my grandmother gets ready for bed. She takes off her carefully pressed black or navy dress — always with a pattern, tiny little dots or flowers, pinkish or *écru,* never white because that would mean too much contrast. Then she disappears into her closet to finish undressing. I guess that under her dress is starched white cotton underwear, like the nightdress she wears under her dark brown robe. Last, she comes back out and walks down the hall, carrying a tall lit yellow candle to be placed by a mirror equipped with a narrow shelf. Her hair, pinned up in a tight bun during the day, hangs down her back in a long braid. White around her face, her hair gets darker as it gets longer until, down by her hips, her braid is dark brown. Sometimes I try to imagine how the color has run out; other times I try to see the color rising up again until it is brown all around her face. But I never succeed, because my grandmother has been old since I can remember. Her face takes on a waxen sheen from the candle as she undoes her braid and her hair falls down her shoulders like waves, incongruously soft, like a song whose words are long forgotten. My grandmother always frightens me a little, she is so much of what she is, so majestic and overbearing and I so small, but when she stands in the dim light of the corridor she loses some of her ferocity and hints at the ghost she'll soon become.

FATHER TIME Behind the bedroom is a long porch lit by dim greenish light filtered through the maple tree outside. There stands my favorite object: a grandfather clock, pale bluish green, with a face that depicts Father Time as an old man carrying a scythe to mark the hours. The four corners are decorated with the sun, the moon, and the planets. I visit him often. Hoping against hope that the old man in the long blue gown and the wizard's hat will suddenly move, I imagine him meeting the characters in my fairy tales. I picture myself at Father Time's side in a brocade dress, tight around my chest, with a velvet train and a pointed hat like his, trailing lace as delicate as dew. He is a visitor from a world of darkness, part fairy tale and part real, almost alive but not quite. Looking at him makes me sad in a way that I like.

We sit on our porch in the dusk of a late summer afternoon, waiting for darkness to fall like a warm cloak around our shoulders. A long dusk, a chance to watch the pink and purple shadows turn to brown on the apartment house walls, a chance to call the darkness to us, to embrace it. When I think of it now, I marvel at the feeling of utter safety in those first years of World War II. In the early 'forties the skies are still the known and predictable roof of our world.

Eva's Berlin

FRIENDS Just outside the porch is the backyard where, for the first time, I smell lilacs, their color so delicate I'm not quite sure whether it's white or violet, their aroma as sweet as the honey I learn to suck from their flowers. The yard faces the house across from ours, a mirror image of our own, separated by a few feet of garden on either side of a black wrought iron fence. Thea, a girl of my age with brown hair and freckles and a soft, sweet voice, lives there and often plays alone in her yard. Shyly approaching the fence, we become friends. We play house on a table under the lilac bushes, where we make sandwiches from oak leaves and lilac blossoms and feed them to her doll and my teddy bear.

Thea is half-Jewish like me, but her Jewish father lives in the house, a fact that confuses me. I know that Jewish fathers can't stay in Berlin, but here is one who does. Since my mother discourages any questions about my Jewishness because, as she tells me, the less I know the safer I will be, I never find out how Thea's father can perform such a miracle. My own explanations change over time. At four and five, I imagine he is protected by a witch, or perhaps he has a guardian angel my father didn't know about. Later, I imagine he promised the German government a patent to an invention crucial to winning the war, or that he bribed one of the Nazis with an inheritance we didn't know he had. He will remain at home until the last year of the war, when, suddenly he is taken to a concentration camp.

Thea's family seems to be following the same rules as

mine. They tell her nothing. Thea and I, playing in the backyard, sometimes try to puzzle out what is going on. The word
"concentration camp" is scarey. We know that people who
are taken there often do not return. But we know no details.
Thea's father isn't there long. On his return, he tells us nothing about where he was or about what happened. We are
nine years old and feel that our maturity deserves a full
accounting, but he turns his face away or changes the subject when Thea asks. Soon, we realize that he is different.
He isn't the same man who left. His eyes have seen something terrible. I can't say anything to anyone about it. It's
just a feeling I can't explain that makes me want to turn
away. Thea and I don't even talk to each other about what
might have happened.

Thea's mother is a pear-shaped, heavy woman with
jet-black hair and white skin. It is ironic: she's the one with
Semitic features but it is her sandy-haired, blue-eyed husband
who is Jewish. She keeps an eye on us when we play and
often shares a little food with me, a piece of bread she baked,
or a green apple from the tree in their yard. Once, she
manages to squirrel away the ingredients for that German
delicacy *Pflaumenkuchen*, a cookie-like tart covered with
sugared plums and served with whipped cream.

Thea, who is pear-shaped like her mother and a little
taller than I, plays with me for hours at a time. She uses her
superior knowledge about how much things cost and what
can be bought in stores to set up play shops where we sell

carefully displayed stones, scraps of material from my grandmother's sewing basket, broken jewelry. She helps me cook fancy dishes by wrapping tiny pine cones in leaves and sticking them with thorns. In front of each dish, she places a large leaf and the amount of little seeds it will cost to purchase it. My job is to bring in customers — imaginary rabbits, deer, birds, dolls, and stuffed animals — and negotiate the price.

After playing store, we choose new characters, put on costumes, and find the right place for our next drama. Our play takes place in the throne room of an imaginary medieval castle, decorated with velvet and furs. I reign as an empress who walks like my grandmother. Thea, my lady-in-waiting, wears her mother's bathrobe. She walks a step behind me and carries the train, made from a tattered velvet bedspread. The empress has made a sacred pledge to bring justice to her country, now that her husband, the cruel emperor to whom she was betrothed when she was only fourteen, is dead. Much of her time is devoted to pardoning those who have been wrongfully imprisoned. Potted plants stand in for the defendants while Thea pleads for them. My huge court with its many ladies-in-waiting and servants of all kinds is represented by twigs and branches placed carefully around the throne in intricate patterns. I am known for kindness, generosity and wisdom.

Thea, as the devoted servant, carries out my slightest wish. When the empress raises her scepter, Thea lies flat on the ground on her stomach, begging to be of service. She runs to the edges of both our yards to get lilac blossoms to feed the empress's canary. She digs large holes and lines them with rose petals to please the empress's nose. As empress, I graciously accept these favors.

One of Thea's duties is to oversee the care of my exotic animals. My park is filled with lions and peacocks, ferrets and birds of paradise, but the snow leopard is my favorite. He pads about the castle on his large velvet paws, fire glinting from his eyes; his silky fur provides the perfect footrest for a tired empress. Thea and I are perfectly cast. In full cooperation, we dive again and again into our fairy tale, to surface only when one of our mothers repeatedly calls that a meal is ready.

On the side of our yard, another fence separates us from the neighboring house to our right. Horstl, our mortal enemy, a year or two older than Thea and I, moves there when we are seven. He stands by his fence and watches us, always ready with a derogatory epithet, like *"Du alte Pflaume,"* which means "you old plum." The phrase feels even more insulting because it resembles no swear words we know. He is a skinny, knock-kneed boy with freckles and stringy brown hair who is alone a lot. I believe that he spends hours by the fence waiting for one of us to turn up, so he can call us names and scoff at our "stupid girls games." We are enemies until we become friends.

Standing at the back fence, Horstl changes his tone

one day and tries to interest me in a game of doctor and patient.

"Do you know how to play doctor?" he asks, his voice a little hoarse.

"I should know. My father is one!" I answer, though I really don't know exactly what he means.

He beckons me closer. "Well," he says, conspiratorially, "both of us have to undress."

I am surprised. Something isn't quite right. My father has an office where people undress before he examines them, but I believe that he is always fully dressed underneath the white coat. I give Horstl the benefit of the doubt because I have been curious about what boys really look like.

"Sure," I say, and, after a few short minutes, we stand in the yard bare as wintry trees. Just after he lets his pants down, my horrified grandmother catches us.

"How could you? Didn't you know that a young girl should never ... Wait until your grandfather finds out ... I always knew it would turn out this way!"

My punishment is to stay at home for the rest of the day, helping my grandmother dust shelves and wash glass jars for canning. Nothing happens to Horstl because my grandmother doesn't speak to the neighbors.

"There's no point at all trying to teach anything to the class of people that would let their child do something like this," she says.

After the incident, Horstl stops calling me names,

and even asks me over to the fence once in a while to show me his gleaming metal pocket knife and a rock that looks like a witch's face.

I make two more half-Jewish friends through Thea: Erika, three years older than my seven years, and her older brother Günther who is fourteen. They are both dark, with almond-shaped eyes and olive complexions. Erika is petite but strong. Günther is tall and clever. Like me, they are adventurous and free to roam the city as they please. Erika and I often ride through the *Tiergarten* on Günther's bicycle, one of us on the crossbar, the other behind Günther, who pedals as fast as he can. To complete the picture, we pose like circus riders. Standing on the back rack, I extend one arm and one leg, elated, precarious, imagining my bulky knits replaced by a glittering leotard and tights.

Günther, seven years older than I, strong and deft, is my first crush but we are the most practical, unromantic sort of companions. He treats me as an appendage to his sister. If he wants her along, he puts up with taking me. Although I hang on his every word and make tremendous efforts to impress him, he seldom talks to me. When he has to give me a hand climbing a tree or rock, I carry his touch with me the whole next day.

Chapter Three

Who Is My Father?

SILENCE As my life in Berlin begins to take on its own color and shape, our battle for visas lost, and we know that we will be staying until the war is over, my father begins to be forgotten. Except for the times my mother breaks out in tirades against him for leaving too late and without us, he is rarely mentioned. My grandfather cautions her against the tirades. The less said about a Jew, the safer we are.

My mother's parents live inconspicuously. We are secure with them because they are old enough to be almost invisible in the bureaucratic paper maze. They no longer work. They have few friends. No one comes to ask them questions. Eventually, of course, the others in the apartment

Eva's Berlin

building find out that my mother and I are not just the blonde and blue-eyed Germans we seem to be. Our name is Eichenwald. We receive letters from America delivered through the Red Cross. And there is my mother's loose tongue telling anti-Nazi jokes and giving pro-Jewish sermons. But my father, as a living breathing person, disappears from view. His name. Where he lives now. What he does. What kind of a person he is.

When I try to recall the man, I remember him in Holland. He is just under six feet tall and smells of cigars as he bends over me. My hands remember the texture of his skin with its satisfying soft resilience. I recall hugging him from behind when he sits on the bed to undress, my surprise at the long silky hairs on his chest. His voice has a deep, humorous lilt. He takes pleasure in words. Sounding them out. Expounding their derivations with an air of making important announcements.

"Educate, from the Latin *ducare*: to lead. And 'e' from *ex*, meaning out. To lead something out from another. Isn't that wonderful? To draw it out of them, that's exactly what education should be. Something already inside, but not complete, has to be lead out."

He speaks seven languages. My father is large and real, and at the same time, more and more shadowy. Some-

> **E**ven greater is my wish to make people aware of the fact that not all Germans were Nazis; there were some who, though not falling in the category of 'heroes,' were brave enough to risk their lives in their own special way of resisting.
>
> ILSE MARGRET VOGEL

74

times I try to remember Holland, longing for a memory to hug close like the other children do their fathers. As time goes on I'm not sure whether I really remember him from Münster or Amsterdam, or whether I'm just recalling what my mother told me, or, worse yet, which of the stories about him I made up.

Who is my father? Every now and then, in my bed at night, a fairy tale brings back my longing.

THE SNOW QUEEN   A little girl loses the boy, her playmate and her soul mate, to the Snow Queen, one of the most horrifying and fascinating characters in my books of fairy tales. Her appearance alone is stunning: glowing dark eyes, white strands of hair adorned with ice crystals that sparkle from her billowing white gown. Wrapped in blankets of snow, she rides in a sleigh drawn by six white wolves. Time and again she lures me into a landscape studded with infinitely patterned ice flowers, like those that grow on the windows of my room in winter. Her palace is vast, spacious and cold. Evil incarnate, she takes the child to her icy palace, where he becomes a non-human zombie. Boys I know disappear into the *Hitlerjugend*. They don't turn into zombies, but they, too, are transformed into something mysteriously impersonal. Aided by magical helpers disguised as forest denizens, the little girl travels to the palace and, after many ordeals, rescues her friend so that they can return home together.

I, too, would go to the ends of the earth to rescue my love, if only someone could show the way. But in my bed at night, my heart goes out to the little boy who is held captive by the Snow Queen. Her terrifying sweep fascinates and repels me. Had I been told that it was the Snow Queen who had taken my father, I would have understood and happily braved an alien world to bring him back.

TWENTY-FIVE WORDS OR LESS Letters forwarded by the Red Cross about nine or ten months after they are written provide the only contact we have with my father. Letters that say he loves us, he is waiting, has bought a house in a place called San Francisco, California, we would love the garden, hugs, kisses, Ernst. Twenty-five words or less, what can he say? I can't find my father there. My mother has a different experience.

When she sees American stamps on the flimsy light blue envelope with its red and blue border, she tears it open and quickly scans the page. I don't know what she is hoping for, but it never arrives. I imagine she wants a romantic love letter that tells her he can't work, eat or sleep because he misses us so much. Or perhaps that he's come down with some fatal illness because he can't stand imagining us in war-torn Berlin. He, on the other hand, seems to spend his twenty-five words trying to sound as normal and cheerful as possible, but the more he succeeds, the more my mother's eyes fill with tears.

I want her to be happy to find that my father was still alive when he wrote the letter. I want her to thank God that we still are a family. Instead, the letters arrive like so many dark clouds on my mother's horizon. She hates my father for having used the escape made possible by the sacrifice of her jewelry.

"Why did he leave us?"

"What entitles him to live in a house when we're guests in the back room with my parents?"

"Why didn't he take us with him?"

Over and over again, she says, "I wanted to leave in time. How many times did I say it? He didn't listen."

"He and his love of languages. I wish he loved common sense just a little."

"Men are stupid," she tells me, "stupid and helpless and leave you holding the bag."

I don't want her to talk this way because I know that the bag, in this case, is me.

A TORTURER Once started, my mother gives vent to ever more frightening stories. My father's office in Münster with its waiting room and several examining rooms with white curtains blowing in the usually open windows, is located on the floor below our living quarters. I am seldom allowed to go down but I am curious about the glass cabinets full of surgical apparatus.

"Those cabinets," my mother announces, "are filled with horrible steel instruments," then she lowers her voice and pulls me closer to her, "and you'll have to wait until you're older before I can really explain to you what *Papi* uses them for. But wouldn't you know it, they're only used on women."

She drops hints about "things that go on between men and women" and "private parts," from which I infer that she would like to talk about something secret. I am four years old — I only know that men and women do something together, something they get excited about that has to be kept from children. My mother doesn't fill me in on the particulars, but she takes a certain amount of pride in her familiarity with these instruments of torture. She actually says, "Don't ever let a doctor use those things on you," but she means, "Don't let a torturer like your father ever talk you into letting him examine you."

I develop an insatiable curiosity about medical instruments, read about them in the books my father left behind and look for them in museums. But I only find the ones my mother talked about when my mother and I visit a castle in Heidelberg with medieval exhibits of crude tongs and pincers that look like they could easily tear a woman to pieces. My mother doesn't come right out and say it, but I know what she is thinking.

These talks with my mother are very hard. I don't want to be frightened of my father. Or angry with him. Yet these letters and conversations are the only ties I have to a father I don't want to forget. In my bed at night when the house is quiet, I tell myself my own stories about him. They begin with Münster.

THEATER DOCTOR   Handsome and charming, he strides around the theater with a basket of remedies — handing this one a pill, finding just the right words for the actress about to go on stage despite a high  fever, taping a sprained ankle for a ballerina. Only a very talented person like my father could be chosen for such a glamorous job.

In my fantasy it is my father who is on stage, brightly lit by a spotlight of his own. The prematurely gray hair and large dreamy eyes in the photo in my mother's album, his love for big cigars and hand-tailored suits give him the appearance of a matinee idol. He is different from the German men I know. He bears no resemblance to the goose-stepping soldiers nor to the older bespectacled shopkeepers in our neighborhood. He is taller, smoother, darker, and more dignified: a healer of artists.

I remember him in an Amsterdam cafe surrounded by show people. There was Kurt Gerron, the tall, rotund actor

Eva's Berlin

with the oily voice, who thought he had a way with children and stooped to pick me up the minute he saw me, despite my loud objections. Fräulein Nina Auerbach always arrived with two or three others engaged at the cabaret where she sang *chansons*. Short red hair surrounded her heart-shaped face like feathers. She wore little silk dresses like my mother, but with an exotic touch. I was especially taken with a fringed silk wrap shimmering with the colors of dawn. I listened, mesmerized, as my parents gossiped and cigarette smoke colored the cafe walls with the faintest blue. It was the kind of atmosphere both of my parents enjoyed — lively and full of glitter, with my father at its center. Exuding a warm, expansive glow, he'd fix his dark soft eyes on one of the talkers and I could see that person expand with pleasure.

In the summer of 1944, the Nazis assigned Kurt Gerron, a well-known Berlin character actor and an inmate in the ghetto, to direct the movie. He had played opposite Marlene Dietrich in the Blue Angel and had been in the original production of Brecht's Threepenny Opera.

I liked to watch my father. But I didn't like his friends. There was Merkel, the opera singer who would hide under a table in the hallway until I came by and then suddenly jump out, rising to his full six foot two height, yelling, *"Du alte verschimmelte Kröte!"* — you moldy old toad — a phrase which didn't seem funny to me. No matter how I tried to prepare myself as I walked upstairs, I found myself trembling with fear of the large ungainly man.

One of the last social get-togethers I remember in Amsterdam was with Kurt Gerron, just after Disney's *Snow White* was released. He was immensely pleased with the voice-overs he had done, but his deep actorly voice scared me. When he bent down to talk to me, I wanted to find a knob to turn down the volume as I tried to avoid the inevitable hug. But my memory of him is marred by an act of even greater betrayal than his uncle-ish, chuck-you-under-the-chin-I-know-kids-love-me routine. He managed to come between me and the fairy tale. Sitting in the cinema, hearing his voice narrating Disney's strangely menacing version of *Snow White,* I was terrified. I had always pictured her in the romantic, slightly fading colors of the shiny illustrations in my books: pale and languid, a suffering little girl. Betrayed by her stepmother, she was already working herself to the bone for dwarfs too stupid and preoccupied with their "work" to keep her from a living death. Now Gerron and Disney changed her into an ugly stranger. Instead of a forest of green trees, ghastly brown sticks with green flames attacked the audience and Snow White herself looked like a kewpie doll. I couldn't understand. What did this have to do with *Snow White*?

They'd turned my favorite fairy tale into something

Gerron's attempts to feel like a productive artist again, though his cast was made up of sick and starving inmates...though he kept losing women to transports to the East, are the painful illusions that underline the tragic, cabaret-like piece that is Sweet Theresienstadt.

ELINOR FUCHS

crude and foreign. And there was Gerron, my father's rotund friend, narrating the story as though it were a waltz through the Vienna Woods. My whole world was changing — Münster trashed, my favorite grandmother left behind, this cold new country and now Snow White. For me, her place was in the shadowy region of myths. I had endowed her with an uncanny, ethereal beauty. Now the shadows were colored in with crayons and illustrated with song books. I never wanted to see the movie again.

A GENIUS My father is a martyr. My mother credits him with the discovery of a cure for a life-threatening disease. Perhaps it is tuberculosis or heart disease. Her story changes with each telling. In one version, two Aryan doctors on the same project arrange to have my father fired and then take all the credit. He is about to take them to court and make a million *Deutschmarks* when he has to leave Germany. Now others are reaping his rewards. He bears the injustice without complaint.

As the tale is repeated, I ask more and more questions. If they fired him from such an important project, wouldn't he have got wise and left the country earlier? My mother just rolls her eyes. Then I begin to wonder whether my mother invented this story.

A daydream about my father, the scholar, helps quell my doubts. I see him sitting up late at night in a room filled with books of fairy tales, looking for stories to tell sick children. From his medicine bag spill tales from China, Finland or Italy, stories that heal little girls dying from diphtheria, bringing wizards with magic potions and trees equipped with ladders that lead down past their roots to golden cities.

One of the languages he speaks, my mother tells me, is Latin. I picture him walking up and down a university hallway repeating the phrases I remember him saying, *Quod licet Jovem, non licet bovem*. It means that what is allowed to Jupiter isn't allowed to an ox, and it's my father's way of expressing contempt for the masses. He considers himself a cut above; I have to agree with my mother's complaints about his snobbishness. He is brilliant, talented, and educated and he expects to be looked up to by the hoi-polloi. Then I imagine him old and gray, surrounded by other graybeards looking like the old saints in Flemish paintings, saying, *E pluribus unum*, the only other Latin phrase I remember. I don't know what it means, but it has a nice ring.

AN EGOIST At the other extreme is my father, the greedy, selfish pleasure seeker. He is tall but not slim. He has a round face and the kind of body that says flesh rather than bone. When the few pictures that arrive from America show his full belly, my mother takes it as an insult.

"We're starving and he's cramming the food into his mouth," she says, as though a man with any sensitivity at all would surely go on a starvation diet, just to show his sympathy for us.

Eva's Berlin

My mother talks about a man who never walked when he could drive, an almost unimaginable quality in a German.

"Imagine, the lord of the manor," my mother would say. "In the olden days, he probably would have had servants carry him from one room to another."

The man she is describing is not my father, not the man I picture curing diphtheria, generously laboring into the dark night for the sake of children. My favorite holy picture shows Jesus surrounded by children. "Suffer the little children to come unto me," he says, and I picture myself, the little girl closest to his knee. I'm sure my father is like Jesus. If, somewhere in America, he is eating enough to gain weight, I forgive him. But I don't take his part when my mother complains. She is so alone, and I am her only friend.

The litany of my father's self-indulgence is delivered whenever my mother is particularly frustrated: "Your father has to wear silk suits. You can't tell me that men aren't at least as vain as women. Silk suits, and always from that tailor who tells him he learned on Savile Row in London. I don't believe a word of it, but he does, of course, because it makes him feel more important. And those cigars of his. *Cigarillos.*" She imitates my father's deep voice caressing the Spanish word.

"Of course, your father is too good for German cigars. He has to buy a whole case of *cigarillos.* Talk about particular. He didn't learn that in Borghorst! Did you notice the tone of his voice when he sent back the food at *Homburg's* before we left? Just because it wasn't perfect he made the waiter feel like he was a peasant."

In the middle of her harangue, my mother begins to smile. She can't help but be amused by my father's snobbishness.

"He wanted two servants in Münster, of course. I would have made do with one, but no, that wasn't good enough for your father. Well, it was all right in the end. It was a very large apartment."

She loves to talk about his playing sick. "And then there are his aches and pains. My God, how often that man is seriously ill. But you know, it's funny. He's so calm with his patients, yet when it comes to himself, he exaggerates. Where anyone else would say they have indigestion, he says he's *vergiftet*."

My father, poisoned. I imagine him surrounded by competitors for the cure he has invented, all in white coats with stethoscopes around their necks, this one slipping him a lethal medicine, that one putting a bit of poisoned mushroom in his coffee.

"Poisoned. What an idea! Everyone else gets a little sick but your father is poisoned! If men had cramps like we do they wouldn't talk that way. "

I don't know what cramps my mother is referring to. Is it my grandmother's *hexenschuss*? I don't have anything like that. Perhaps my mother does. But there's no point in interrupting her in the middle of a cascade of insults. She goes on and on, laughing sometimes, sometimes with a mean tone in her voice, like Frau Meyer upstairs has when she's fighting with her husband.

I can't believe my father's as bad as all that. Maybe he does exaggerate, but so does my mother. It's one of the things I like about all of us. We like to tell a good story, with dramatic emphasis. Shyly, in my bed at night before I go to sleep, I tell my father that she doesn't really mean it. It's just that waiting so long is hard for her.

ART COLLECTOR Paintings join us in Berlin along with other furnishings that failed to reach California, just like my mother and me. They make me wonder about my father. Our walls in Münster were decorated with sepia-toned Flemish landscapes of country roads leading past farm-houses, with perhaps a cow or a horse or two grazing off to the side.

Try as I might during my late-night musings, I can't understand my father's taste in art. Nothing is happening in these pale pictures of dusk or early morning. The houses look as though no one lives in them. The animals are scratched into the top of the paint with a few strokes that make them look like ghosts. I prefer the bright colors of the illustrations in my books of fairy tales, pictures of castles and roses twined over bowers where princesses sit dreaming.

I imagine my father must have needed these pictures to rest under when he was exhausted from his work with sick people. I picture him coming home on a dark, rainy night, fog blowing in as he opens the door to our house. The maid greets him, takes his coat and offers him a warm drink in our sitting room. There he relaxes, surrounded by the golden Dutch landscape, his cares leaving him with the wisps of steam evaporating from his cup.

My favorite painting is a madonna and child from my parents' bedroom in Münster. It is done in dark browns, gold tones and bright red for the madonna's dress. The Jesus is a fat, awkward baby with bluish skin and a square healthy head of red hair. The baby is balancing on one toe and looks like he's about to jump off his mother's lap onto my parents' bed. The madonna and her baby must be another sign of my father's love for children. I come to the picture to look at the madonna. She is beautiful and kind, her face full of tenderness for her child. When she arrives in Berlin, I visit her often in the living room, imagining her soft glance directed toward me.

These are the stories I repeat to keep my father alive in my imagination. But, as time goes by and I get older, the letters delivered through the Red Cross get fewer and farther between and my mother talks about him less and less.

I make new friends in Berlin whose fathers are hardly more present than mine, coming back from the front for a day or two of difficult communication. These men look exhausted. Their eyes have a haunted look. When they visit, they don't spend much time at home with their wives or children, but go out to look for the company of other soldiers.

Eva's Berlin

I watch them sitting at large tables in the outdoor cafes talking loudly about what is going on at the front. They sound like the boys playing soldiers, using language that puzzles me: "Outflank the enemy... strategic positions... fall back... *Stukkas*... eradicate the targets."

More visitors than fathers in their worn uniforms, they don't help me learn what fathers do. At six years old, I no longer fantasize about leaving Berlin to meet *Papi* in the United States of America. He has become a shadow. I can't imagine recognizing him. I come to believe that seeing him again would mean meeting a total stranger who'd expect me to love him, and I wouldn't have the slightest idea how to do it. Sometimes I indulge a fantasy that quickly turns to shame. I wish he had died in the war like so many of the other fathers. It would be so much simpler.

CHAPTER FOUR

The Zoo

DEER

In winter, the zoo has few visitors.

    Animals huddle in their stalls.

    Trees loom gray in the mist.

Wearing thick brown stockings, coats lined in red wool,

the children approach,

footsteps crunch the frost-hardened ground.

    Holding bags of potato peel for the deer

    gathered at the distant hayrick,

they stretch out their hands

    prepared to stand a hundred hours

    still as trees.

Finally, a flicker of movement

    a doe inches forward, her fawn at her side.

    Then, nostrils wide, necks taut with apprehension,

    the whole herd approaches the children;

Eva's Berlin

Cave paintings,
a mauve sea carrying waves of deer.
Suddenly, a white buck appears
rutting, his antlers gone. Instead
    a double-crown on his silvery forehead
    corona of frozen blood.
"An emperor" whispers the child,
    "enchanted by a witch."
Black mouths grasp food from the children's hands.

On the way home through ruined
streets, they trudge silently,
hands deep in flannel pockets
    breathing white clouds
    into the wintry air.

IN TOW In Berlin, we learn to adjust. My mother works during the day. I spend a lot of time with my grandmother, who takes me to the zoo every day. Her hand feels like fine glove leather, soft and dry. Glancing up at her as she pulls me along, I see a small dark blue straw hat with just enough of a brim to shade her sun-sensitive eyes and frame her set, determined face. She attacks these outings with a combination of energy, duty, and pleasure. Walking at a pace so fast and inattentive that traffic screeches to a halt, my grandmother drags me past the glittering windows of the shops on the *Tauentzienstrasse* where I want to linger. The mannequins are dressed in the latest fashion: long velvet ball gowns, black wool suits with gray silk blouses. My mother would give anything to buy them; my grandmother Gertrud doesn't give them a glance.

She believes in the salutary effect of fresh air the way other grandmothers worship God and while she doesn't "ooh" or "ah" when she encounters a particularly pretty sight like other grandmothers do, her eyes take on a particular glow when the first crocuses appear and, later in the spring, when rows of pansies border the paths of the zoo. Softness enters her glacial blue eyes, hinting at a long-gone girlish self, a self I know mostly from brown tinted photographs in the family album. She smiles a thin-lipped smile but she doesn't slow her pace. She walks rapidly with her head held high, glancing neither to the right nor to the left. My job is to keep up with her. To my relief, when we get to the zoo, we go our separate ways.

Just before we reach the playground, my grandmother goes to sit on one of the green, wrought-iron chairs that congregate around the large flower beds. There she receives bits of gossip from other grandmothers. On the heavy side, wearing flowery print dresses and dark woolen sweaters they have knit themselves, none of them are as well turned out

Eva's Berlin

as my *Oma*. They are blousier, plainer, and more comfortable in their aging bodies. Afterwards, in her most confidential tone, my grandmother tells me they are not her kind.

"It isn't just the way they dress," she says. "They neglect themselves."

Now and then, my grandmother opens her dark blue leather handbag, takes out an immaculately white linen handkerchief, and polishes her gold rimmed glasses, looking about discreetly to see whether the others noticed that she is a cut above.

Everything about them, body and soul, is judged harshly. Isn't she different from those others? She "keeps up." Never an unironed dress or a hair that strays from her tortoise shell combs. She tells me about how the ladies were discussing their washing methods for delicate clothing. "Talking about Frau Meyer's underwear, indeed! I am the daughter of a civil servant and the wife of a civil servant and I know my place."

I ponder the question of what it means to have a place. Does everyone have one? How did my grandmother arrive at such certainty about hers? I'm guessing that my own place is in the background. My grandmother's version of the old adage is that children should be neither seen nor heard. But I, her granddaughter, am not content with the place she assigns me. Defiantly, I imagine myself becoming an empress many times more impressive than she, a real empress with jewels and pearls and a dwarf to bring me hot chocolate. Perhaps, just before she dies a slow and painful death, I will allow my grandmother a visit. Her gray-blue eyes narrow as she straightens my hair and closes the buttons of my cardigan for the walk home. The empress's place, the one I want, is already occupied.

STRUWELPETER My grandmother's favorite story is a teaching tale about a boy called *Struwelpeter*, Messy Peter. Her eyes sparkle with disapproval and her back straightens a bit more when she takes the book from the shelf. The cover shows a grotesquely messy child with long dirty fingernails, his hair a tangle.

"Lice," she says with a shudder, "would find a perfect home in that nasty child's head and his wrinkled, dirty clothing. No pride in himself. It's easy to see why nothing will ever come of him."

I feel sorry for *Struwelpeter*. He's the kind of boy nobody likes. He looks a little like a harlequin in his old-fashioned clothes; but everybody teases him and, worst of all, the grown-ups think it serves him right. Too lazy to cut or clean his nails? Then he deserves his terrible death, the story tells us. His head in the clouds, he slips and falls into the canal and drowns.

Eva's Berlin

The story makes me feel the world is a hopeless place. I don't understand why *Struwelpeter* should be punished for looking at the sky. I wish the men on our block would look at the clouds. They spend all their time looking at the way their shiny boots strike the ground. But then *Struwelpeter* would never make the German army. I fail to convince my grandmother of his good possibilities. The worst part of the story comes after they bury *Struwelpeter*. Like me, he liked to pick his nose. Now his forefinger grows through the coffin, and through the earth that covers it, a hideous memorial to a little boy's transgressions. They never say it in so many words, but I suspect *Struwelpeter* is Jewish. Only Jews are picked on the way he is.

THE PLAYGROUND When we get to the zoo, I run to the playground as soon as my grandmother is seated, hoping to find my friend Alia. She is my idol, lithe and long, a champion at the acrobatic tricks we practice on the single and double bars and rings. Five sets of double bars of various sizes await us, their wood polished by constant use. A little further back are four sets of metal rings covered with leather, suspended by ropes like a swing. Most of the girls who come to practice here are in their teens; at six, I am the youngest and have to work to keep up.

Hard callouses are forming on my palms from gripping the bar. My goal is twenty *Sitzwellen*, rotations. Leaning back with my full weight, head thrown back, letting myself fall and then making a complete turn around the bar, the sensation of the cold, polished wood hard on the backs of my knees, I make the earth revolve around me. Sitting. Letting go. Sky. Treetops. Trees. The benches behind me. The gray soft sand below. Coming up into the sky, into the light grey clouds backlit by the sun. My eyes blinded for a moment. Tree tops. Sitting again. And again and again.

Alia's silky brown hair falls down to her shoulders, surrounding her oval, tanned face. She moves with a soft, effortless grace. She can perform forty *Sitzwellen* without apparent strain. She approaches a single metal bar set in green wood, leaps up to it and lets herself revolve as though it was as easy as breathing.

One day, however, she looks different. Paler than usual, and suddenly breathing heavily, she begins to falter. When she gets off the bar, she clutches her head. We all gather around her and make her lie down on one of the green slatted benches that flank the playground. She is very white. Terrified that she could die, I breathe a sigh of relief when I hear her say, very softly, that it's only a headache. She presses her long fingers to her temples and lets me bring her a cup of water. Overcome with empathy and longing, I would do anything to help her.

"I have a headache, too," I say, offering up my healthy body in the name of love. Later, walking home from the playground and hugging the image of Alia close, I ignore my grandmother as she sails along.

Eva's Berlin

FEATHERS   I often meet my friend Erika at the zoo. With Erika's guidance — she is the older one; I am seven, she is ten — I learn to explore the zoo. The animals become as much a part of our world as the other children. When Erika and I bring home some feathers we have gathered just outside the birds' cages, my grandfather equips us with special poles with pins at the ends to poke through the cage. With these poles, we fish for feathers. Watching our strenuous efforts for a while with some amusement, the bird keeper allows us to enter the bird cages at the end of the day to gather the feathers directly.

Soon we become authorities, collecting feathers of every size and color: flamingo pinks, imposing eagle and vulture feathers with their waxy brown and white sheen, the shimmering blue-greens of ducks and the pearled black and white of guinea hens. Even tiny, soft hummingbird feathers find their way into our bags.

At home, I unpack the feathers carefully and slowly, piling them up according to size and color. Then I give them a bath in soft soapy water and lay them out on a white tea-towel to dry, before fluffing them out again and putting them away in the shoe-boxes I've lined with tissue-paper. My collection is kept in the drawer of a little table I use for drawing and writing. A fairly awkward and messy child (I drop china cups, and even the treasured breakfast eggs have been known to slide out of my grasp), I lose my clumsiness with feathers. They remain whole, remarkably clean, and orderly.

Sorting and re-sorting the feathers brings the birds closer. Owl feathers are my favorites. I take them out again and again to look at their watery patterns. Touching their softer than soft threads, I imagine them attached to my skin at the shoulder blades, glittering rows of them, until I am flying out over our courtyard with angel wings, feathers rustling as I soar out over the zoo, dipping in and out of my favorite cages.

AUTUMN LIGHT In the fall, the zoo has its special pleasures. The summer visitors have gone and the Aryan children are back in school. Erika and I feel that being half-Jewish gives us an advantage. Since our mothers don't want to alert the authorities by registering us for the *Kinder-schul-verschickung*, a program that sends Berlin's children to the country, we enjoy the unique privilege of being among the few children free to come to the zoo. It is quiet enough to hear the first falling leaves rustle under our feet. Some-times, in the midst of a warm breeze, Erika and I sense the sudden coolness of autumn's arrival.

On sunny days, we bring string bags lined with paper, full of whatever leftovers retain even the slightest promise of nourishment for the animals. There is nothing that can't be fed to some creature or other. Fish skin and scales go to otters and seals; sugar cubes and pieces of burnt cake are thrown to bears who sit on their huge haunches and beg, clapping their gigantic paws. Bags of vegetable peels, apple cores, and a few dry heels of bread get an enthusiastic reception from pigs and chickens.

When the leaves have fallen, I spend hours and hours hunched over, gathering smooth bullet-shaped acorns with their prickly hats. I lose myself in the crunch of the leaves, the smooth silky feel of the acorns, their soft castanet sound as they slip into the paper bag, and the golden fall light. Later when snow covers the ground, they will be a proper surprise for the deer.

TOOTHLESS AND PURRING My fantasy companion, the leopard, becomes a reality in the zoo. Not the snow leopard; he is too young and agile to be trusted with visitors. But there is a very old, toothless leopard who rubs his graying yellow back on the bars of his cage and purrs like a chorus of twenty alley cats when my friend Erika and I visit. We press ourselves up against the green wire of the cage to stroke him with the part of our fingers we can push through the wire. His fur feels incredibly soft above a body that is sinewy and bony at the same time. Like visitors to a cherished prisoner, we return again and again. The more we know him, the more we ache to lay our hands on his fur and run them down his back without the separating metal of the fence.

Our strategy is to make friends with the keepers who feed our friend his portion of bloody bones at three o'clock every afternoon. The one who takes care of our leopard is Dieter. After seeing us stand in front of the cage at feeding time for weeks, he tells us about the leopard's home, Africa, and his age, twelve years. Watching the leopard eat is like watching an animal's ecstasy. With half-closed eyes, he pushes his soft head into the pile of bones; the pleasure of it sends shivers through his spotted fur. On a warm March morning, Dieter calls Erika and me over to the walkway behind the cages and prepares us for the thrill we hardly dared hope for. He has gained permission for us to enter the leopard's cage.

"Now girls, you can't talk or giggle when you're in with a wild animal, no matter how sweet and old you think he is. Always remember, he's a wild animal, and anything you do could make him do something you don't expect."

I get shivers down my spine anticipating the adventure.

"Be very careful when we first go in," Dieter says. "Always approach the leopard from the front, so he doesn't pounce in surprise, and then make all your movements very slow. Nothing sudden, do you understand?"

Of course we understand. We would swear to anything for the privilege of entering the sacred domain. Feeling tall and important, we enter the cage through the rectangular wooden door the keepers use. Tentatively, we approach the green wire fence where our old friend is lying on a bare tree branch, his body stretched out the length of the long white limb, his front paw dangling down. When he sees us, he stretches and then — we are thrilled! thrilled! — he comes down to our level. The keeper, who has followed us in, nods his head encouragingly. Shyly, we extend our hands to touch his long, articulated back. When I place my hand on his silky fur, it ripples slightly. Worried, I look at the keeper, who nods again. I continue to stroke the leopard, Erika's hand behind mine. We are very still, so still that we can hear his breath evening out and then — it is a great surprise even though we've heard it before — he begins to purr. After a few minutes, the keeper beckons us to come out and we do, changed forever by a spiritual communion with the animal world.

At first, our visits last a few minutes. Then, after a couple of weeks, we are allowed to stay a little longer. Gradually, we learn to feed him a few special pellets handed to us by Dieter, with instructions to keep our hands very flat, almost bent backwards. The leopard's tongue is long and narrow and very pink, rough to the touch, like one of the special cleaning sponges my grandmother uses in the kitchen.

During the winter months, we become regular visitors to the leopard's indoor cage. The once offensive acrid smell of the *Raubtierhaus*, the house where the lions and tigers live, no longer bothers us. We are always watched by one of the keepers when we enter the cage and we never spend more than ten minutes. But those ten minutes mark us as the ultimate insiders of the zoo, separating us from other children.

On rainy days, Erika and I enter the photo studio where children regularly have their pictures taken with lion cubs and watch enviously as child after child sits on the sofa holding a lion on his lap. Oh, the softness of the cubs' roly-poly bodies, their long downy fur, their square heads as large as those of the children holding them! The awkward golden paws splayed out on a child's lap!

My grandmother does not share our enthusiasm. She wears the contemptuous smirk she reserves for anything I truly want.

"I wouldn't dream of paying for a photograph," she tells me with an air of superiority that forbids challenge. But I ignore it.

"Oh please, *Oma*, please, please, please! I wouldn't ask for anything else for my birthday or for Christmas, please!"

She remains impervious.

"Your mother has a camera. She already takes far too many pictures of you. It's giving you grand ideas. No, we'll leave the lions to the tourists."

Once her mind is made up, there is no changing it. I stop asking. Day after rainy day, we go to the studio and sit for hours, bathed in longing.

Eva's Berlin

ADULT ANIMALS Adults count for little in our private zoo world. As spectators or policemen, they skim the surfaces of our domain. Perhaps some of them observe us playing, but what do they really know of our existence? The adults live in the city and visit the zoo, while for us children it's the other way around. For us, the zoo is central; the home of our special family. The keepers, whom we exempt from "grown-up" status, help and guide us. Older animals, like the large, bony leopard, hold us in their gaze like any loving mother; parrots and monkeys entertain us as warmly as any eccentric aunt or grandparent. It isn't always safe, of course, but the animals aren't the only source of the danger.

I am seven when a stranger sits down next to me on the bench where I am resting from practicing shoulder stands. He is tall and thin, a grown-up not quite old enough to be a "father." He's wearing a dark tweed jacket and horn-rimmed glasses. I don't take much notice of him until he moves closer and then closer still, asking me whether I'd like to see his pocket-watch, which he wears on a gold chain on his vest, like my grandfather. I'm not really interested — a sour cigarette smell combined with a violet soap on his hands offends me — but, not wanting to be impolite, I look at the flowery scroll that surrounds his initials, and listen to the ticking of the clock. Putting it away, in a gesture as sudden as the strike of a cat stalking a bird, he lifts me onto his lap. I'm so stunned that I don't move. Strong tobacco odors, combined with the sourness of his breath, overwhelm me. I feel the texture of his tweed jacket through the cotton sleeve of my dress and a long, thin armbone underneath. Under my buttocks, the soft, squishy texture of his thighs. This feels wrong in a way I can't name. I want to say something, but no words come to me. I want to get away, but I can't move. I feel isolated, as though a soft, transparent wall had come between me and the rest of the children who are playing near us.

He is talking to me but his voice is far away. I am stuck in a transparent cocoon. He pulls me closer, talking and talking, and, slowly, the words become comprehensible. I mustn't be frightened, he says, because he already knows me, he's been watching me for weeks, and he can tell that the two of us will do wonderful things together. He tells me I am special, different from the other girls in so many ways. Suddenly, I come back to life. How can this stranger with the sour smell possibly assume I want to do anything with him? None of what he's saying is true. I try to wiggle off his lap. He holds onto me firmly, talking on and on. I feel the slender metal pin that holds his tie pushing into my shoulder. Frightened and at a loss, I notice I am smiling, that is, my face is smiling without my wanting it to. He is whispering into my ear, stroking my body with his free hand. I am struggling with my face. My voice has disappeared. More than anything else, I wish that someone I know would look my way but no one does.

Then, suddenly, I am not smiling any more and my

body is full of an unknown strength. Yelling I don't know what at the top of my voice, I leap off his lap and run across the playground to the rounded flower bed where my grandfather sits waiting for me because my grandmother is home with a back ache.

The story spills out of me like a spray of water, half-crying, half-trying-to-get-out-of-there-as-fast-as-possible, I tell him what happened. He shakes his head.

"No, no no!" and he pulls me back to the playground to identify the culprit — but the man is gone.

"That was a bad man," my grandfather says to me, shaking his head. "How strong you are. How right you were to run."

I walk along the path with a sour feeling in my stomach. Something important has been spoiled. I notice the dust on my shoes. The sourness rises to my mouth. Grabbing my grandfather's hand, I pull him toward the bushes where I am sick.

"You are as white as a piece of cardboard," my grandfather says, when we're back on the path that leads away from the zoo. I hold his hand tightly. At home, I go straight to my room and bury myself in a book.

LUMINOUS EDGES Most of the time, the zoo fulfills its promise. In the summer, there is a yearly *Fackelzug*, a torchlight parade, in the Berlin zoo. The clown who leads it has a special relationship with us children. He knows how to twist balloons into fabulous shapes: animals, pretzels, hats, and puzzles. He can imitate the gorilla's walk and cock his head and screech like a parrot, and when he does, we children roar with laughter. His name, Onkel Pelle, has a wonderful Berlin sound.

Following behind Onkel Pelle with the other children in the warm dark night, I feel the exhilaration of attending an ancient ritual. Lit by my torch, I see faintly reddened tree trunks and rounded bushes along the path, a gleam of metal from a cage here and there turned silver by the passing light. I imagine the zoo immense and unending beyond the little glimpses I can catch, surrounding me like a vast, dark ocean. As we walk, I can sense the presence of the animals, especially the big ones — elephants, water buffalo, giraffes — in the blue night air around us. Our footsteps fall on the same ground on which the animals lie sleeping. We are all one in the dark.

CHAPTER FIVE

Bombs Over Berlin

FIRE

The city is illumined by volcanoes.
Human lava spills from their cores
on streets overflowing with rubble.

Birthday candles decorate fences.
Broken windows multiply
reflections dancing on rubble.

Winds introduce the living to the dead.
Old wood, wet wood.
And children, lost in the rubble.

Eva's Berlin

A NEW SENSE OF TIME The torchlight parades in
the zoo marked the time before the bombing started; my
childhood memories are sorted into that before and after.

In the first years of the war, when I was six and
seven, I hugged the last remnants of material security close
to myself. Though our circumstances had teetered wildly
this way and that and our waiting had been disappointed,
though my father had gone and I now lived with my
grandparents, I still moved in a familiar, stable world. I
recognized the large gray apartment houses in my neighborhood by their individual markers; this one had large
brown carved doors, that one had a restaurant on its
ground floor. Most of the time, the ground under my feet
was firm and predictable. It never occurred to me that
any of this — my world — was subject to change. Berlin
was Berlin, my street was my street. It was a close atmosphere, sometimes dangerous, it is true, but the dangers
were normal dangers that face children the world over,
having to do with accident, human and nonhuman. After
1941, when I was seven, the bombs shattered not only my
material world but my sense of the stability of time, of
sky, of neighborhood. What could once be counted on
had become fragmented.

THE REHEARSAL Up until about the middle of
1941, Berlin practices for the bombing. Electric lights in
our homes must be turned off for several hours each

evening and street lights are cut off as well. On these nights, equipped with low-powered flashlights we are permitted to use, my grandfather and I make a dark round, a *dunkle runde*, through the empty streets of our West Berlin neighborhood. Hand in hand, we walk through the shadowy streets, past restaurants and darkened shops, past the houses that appear black except for the liquid reflections of the window panes. Every once in a while a bus or a car comes by with a gentle whoosh. The streets are quiet and soft. Secure in my grandfather's presence, I imagine vast blue seas lapping on either side of us just beyond the houses, seas from which giant turtles may emerge into the luminous shadows, ready for us to mount for a night's journey. The silvery gray of the sidewalk, the dark of the street below, the watery windows, and the black stalks of the street lights take on the quality of a dream garden on the glittering edges of a dark world.

> **B**erlin, September 3, 1939, the first air-raids: "the ugly shrill of the sirens, rushing to the cellar...the utter darkness of the night — how will human nerves stand that for long?"
>
> WILLIAM L. SHIRER

One early evening, I hear the low tone of the siren for a practice air-raid and my mother and I go out to watch as gunners rehearse anti-aircraft maneuvers in the area of the *Gedächtniskirche*, where several light beams illuminate the towers in the dark night sky. It is spring; the night is balmy and the small crowd of spectators exchanges jolly comments as they might before a theatrical performance or at a fair. Soon after we get there, a tiny, brightly silvered plane can be seen in the square formed by two crossing beams. For me, the silver bird is a vision from a fairy tale. It is tiny and gleams like a perfect jewel in the night sky. Entranced, I am rudely awakened when I hear a voice saying, "That one's a goner," and I learn that the silver cage formed by the criss-crossing searchlights is a deathtrap. That there will be men up there flying planes and other men waiting to catch them in the searchlight in order to kill them. The darkness I believed would forever cloak me in its soft velvet caress will never be the same again.

THE SHELTER I didn't know there were storage rooms under our apartment until I heard hammering and sawing one morning and asked the workmen what they were doing.

"We're building a bomb shelter."

Bombs were filled with ice cream as far as I knew; the Germans call an ice cream dessert surrounded by a meringue an *Eisbombe*. What was he talking about?

"We're at war, little lady," he told me, "and pretty soon the Tommies are going to come here in airplanes."

"Tommies? The English! The English!"

I was thinking of an English family with a lot of boys named Tommy arriving at the Tempelhof airport, where we'd landed coming back from Holland. I still didn't understand.

"They're coming in airplanes and then they drop

bombs. There's a war going on, young lady! Vroom vroom! Bombs! They can blow up a building just like that. They're explosives."

"What do they look like?"

"They're sort of like the little packages that your mother brings home from the grocery store. Only where they land, there's a big bang, and then there's a big mess. Do you understand?"

I was beginning to. Somebody in England was like the Nazis and they, too, were trying to get us, only these men weren't going to put us in jail, they were going to blow our house up from under us.

"So you're making a place where we can hide?"

"We're making a nice, cozy little place for all the people who live here. Those Tommies don't know the first thing about Berliners or else they wouldn't even think of trying to blow us up. Don't you worry about a thing."

I don't worry all that much after I get used to the basic idea. Bombing becomes a fact of life like thunderstorms or diphtheria or the Nazis. It takes a few months to fortify the rooms, including one the size of a classroom, for all of us to fit into. I get to know the workers by going down at lunch time hoping they'll offer me parts of their liverwurst sandwiches made with the thick, black bread we seldom eat at home. Once I get my grandmother to let me take down part of a raisin cake she'd baked to share with the men. It doesn't take long before I can't imagine a house without a bomb shelter.

Eva's Berlin

The first time we use the shelter is like nothing I've ever experienced before. It happens about one o'clock at night and begins with a marrow-splitting noise. The sound of the sirens slices the night into pieces. It is called *der Alarm*, the piercing call that signals fear. I see panic rising in the adults' haste to leave the apartment. I can feel fear constricting my own chest and throat. But my sheets are warm and, for a moment, I wonder whether I'm in a dream. Then my mother's urgent call moves me to action.

"Come on, Eva, into your clothes and let's go! Now! Right now!"

Called away from the green forests of my dream world, I realize I must move quickly. I have trouble focusing my eyes in the room lit only by a flashlight. My wool dress and my overcoat have been at my bedside for several weeks, ready to put on over my pajamas. Next to them is a suitcase packed with a frayed grayish teddy bear and the sailor doll made of dark blue velvet.

We meet other odd-looking shapes in overcoats, carrying suitcases as they cross the yard to go to the shelter. We are nervous, alert, disturbed. Once arrived in the large room with the low ceiling and dim light, we sit on wooden benches and await disaster.

Nothing happens for quite a while. It is quiet in the shelter. Some of us are sleepy, others silenced by fear, others

Nearly every night, the fierce, ear-piercing howl of the air-raid sirens cut into me. It frightened me just as much as it frightened everybody else. But the face I showed the people around me — even to my friends — was a smiling face.

ILSE MARGRET VOGEL

are listening intently. Can an airplane be heard? Are any bombs exploding in the distance? We try to divert ourselves with small talk, but our attention keeps returning to the terrible possibilities. Off-hand remarks become heavy, deflated by our distracted listening.

"Can't you just see Göring in his special air-raid uniform? Midnight blue with silver buttons in the shape of the moon? On that fat body!"

"Has anyone gone up on the roof to watch? Don't we have a list?"

"Kunze, it's your turn."

"All right, I'm going." Frau Kunze starts to cry and is comforted by the *Portier-Frau*.

"How long's it been since it started?"

"Can you hear anything?"

"No. Maybe they turned around and went home."

I amuse myself by injecting my blue sailor doll with water from a syringe left in my father's medical kit. To my surprise, the water always comes out in a different place from where I placed the needle, as though the velvet body had a life of its own. Slowly, we wake up more and the adults begin the patter that usually passes among the residents of the house.

"Hitler and his gang are probably in some luxurious underground mansion with dancing girls and caviar."

"Imagine what the *Partei Bonzen* are eating. They probably have a private bakery down there just for them."

Eva's Berlin

"I heard some officers right here in Berlin requisitioned a restaurant, *Kempinski's* I think, just for private parties."

Some people sleep. Others stare quietly ahead saying nothing. We hear the sounds of airplanes passing overhead and a few, muffled explosions far away. We begin to talk about going back upstairs.

"Not until they sound the all-clear siren."

"What's the difference? They're gone."

Then we hear the come-and-go shriek of the siren again. It sounds like a female ghost screaming; I imagine a woman whirling, her gauzy clothes flapping like sheets. We get up from our chairs. The first raid is over. Back in our apartments, we go back to sleep in rumpled beds. The next morning, we talk about how easy it was. Soon the trip to the basement will become a normal part of our routine.

As the bombings become a nightly event, my mother and I become part of a small group that sits near the entrance of the shelter under the stairway. In contrast to those who huddle in the big room, more often than not sad, frightened, sometimes shivering and crying, our little club is dedicated to laughter. In some of the shelters there are signs: *Weinen verboten*, crying forbidden. My mother agrees. Using a snobbish brand of

---

We Berliners are living through harrowing days and nights... Almost daily we are "visited." In the daytime the Americans drop their bombs on us. And at night the British do their murderous job.

ILSE MARGRET VOGEL

116

humor, we express our contempt for those who trudge past us.

"Did you see Frau Schmidt? She looked like she's wearing her clothes inside out, didn't she?"

"That one, look at Hans Bohr!" Here my mother breaks into giggles, but still in a whisper, "Doesn't he look like he's been caught with his pants down? Do you think he was sitting on the toilet when the alarm rang?"

"Did you hear Frau Scholle crying? Really! That woman will surely whine all night."

We are not like those other people. We are superior. *Weinen verboten*. Later, when all the adults are well caught up in their conversation, I sneak over to the other room and try to cheer up some of the ones my mother despises.

Ours is a makeshift shelter, strengthened with what pieces of iron and heavy crossbeams the men in the house could find, but not nearly as safe as it should be. Sometimes, during a near explosion, plaster rains down on our heads and once a whole lamp drops down from the ceiling. No one is hurt but we listen when our district air-warden advises us to go to the heavily fortified neighborhood shelter in the *Tiergarten* for greater security. Walking past the zoo in the middle of the night is almost enjoyable, like an adventure, a secret mission. Hand in hand, my mother and I follow the crowds of people headed in the same direction.

> The zoo tower was the biggest of the three...the two lower levels formed an air-raid shelter for 15,000 members of the public.
>
> ANTHONY READ

Eva's Berlin

Once there, we enter a large, low, rounded building with a thick roof holding loaded anti-aircraft guns. It is a spooky sight. Going through the tall, heavy doors, we push through two large, well-lit rooms with rows of metal chairs and wooden benches filled with people who got there ahead of us. We find a seat in the third room. I lean on my mother's lap, my elbows on her thighs, and watch the throngs arriving from outside. They are walking slowly now, in the orderly manner expected at all times of Germans. After about ten minutes, the doors are heard to close and we sit in muffled silence. Unlike our house shelter, this one is sealed off from the noise of the outside world. People compare notes on whether it was worth coming.

"It's a long walk and we could have been killed on the way."

"Once you're here, though, you feel so much safer."

"I'm worried about my aunt. She's sick. We had to leave her behind."

My mother is worried about her mother, as well, because she refused to come with us.

"If I die, I'd rather be in my own house, thank you very much," my grandmother had said with a characteristic upward thrust of her chin.

After an hour or so, the all-clear sounds, and we walk the few blocks back to our house. Nothing appears any different from when we left. My grandmother feels superior because she saved herself the trip. We go back to our beds.

In the beginning, the bombs interrupt our sleep once or twice a week and our trips to the basement or the bunker make us irritable and nervous but we don't experience the worst until later. Since we hear only distant shelling, we begin to believe that the danger has been exaggerated. Some people even consider staying in their beds during the raids.

But after a few weeks, the flight paths begin to include the inner city. We hear the roar of the planes just above our heads, waves of them coming closer and closer until the sound overwhelms everything else and I am convinced that they will fly directly into our street. The bass drone that seems about to shatter my eardrum will shatter our house and I am certain we will explode with it.

When bombs begin to drop in our neighborhood, we learn to distinguish between the less dangerous incendiary bombs and the frightening explosives. The first resemble large firecrackers, weighted down with a heavy metal cylinder to help them reach their targets. They hit with a popping noise, no louder than a single gunshot, and anything hit by them breaks into flames. Berliners take turns watching the roof tops, equipped with pails of water for

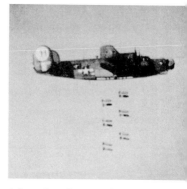

putting out the fires. In the daytime, we children collect the lead weights and splinters of shrapnel — *Splitter* — and give them to our parents to use as paperweights.

Eva's Berlin

The explosive bombs are confusing. We observe the destruction they cause: a whole house blown up so that

nothing remains except an unrecognizable ruin. But we don't know what the actual bomb looks like because it, too, disintegrates in the explosion. When these bombs arrive, the noise is unmistakable. A few blocks away, there is a high whine that comes closer and closer, then a noise like firecrackers, or gunshots. But within a block or two, it feels like time stops just before the worst happens. The airplane noise stops, people stop talking, the whole house seems to gather itself into a momentary silence. Our bodies taut, our eyes wide, we are suspended until we hear the explosion.

The bombs that drop nearby make our walls tremble and our bodies shake so much that we can feel the liquid inside. Plaster snows down from the ceiling. The noise is deafening. People start moving around anxiously. Some people scream with terror. Some can't stop moving. Others weep, hanging onto the person nearest to them. Our family is among the stoic ones that sit and wait it out.

When it is over, we meet each other's eyes with immense relief. Some offer a prayer of gratitude. We have survived once more. In our corner of the shelter, the joking begins again as we wait for the "All-Clear."

Between 1941 and 1945, we survive attack after attack. Other houses on our street are hit. My friend Horstl disappears when the house next door is bombed. I don't think he was killed. Most people manage to escape from the burning buildings through basements connected to each other by entry ways of loosely placed bricks. Horstl joins those we refer to as "bombed out." The vernacular makes it sound like a he lost a tile in a game. In fact, it means that the house was totaled. One day the house was there; the next it was gone. Gone also all the inhabitants, including Horstl, who will be forever caught in my memory facing my grandmother, both of us with bare bottoms.

The *Gedächtniskirche* is bombed several times. For a while the church remains standing; only the towers are hit again and again, becoming shorter as we watch. The day after its final, most destructive bombing, I sit in its ruined entrance sifting through ashes to collect pieces of gold mosaic that no longer glitter in the candlelight.

As planes come and go more and more frequently, there comes a time when the overhead drone becomes a predictable part of the night's stay in the shelter. The ever increasing noise causes my body to fold in on itself protectively. I can't adapt to the terrifying sound.

> At the top of the battered Kurfürstendamm, Berlin's Fifth Avenue, bulked the deformed skeleton of the once fashionable Kaiser Wilhelm Memorial Church. The hands of the charred clock were stopped exactly at 7:30; they had been that way since 1943.
>
> JULIUS RYAN

Eva's Berlin

FALLING I have the same dream over and over again. I am a tiny figure in a huge amphitheater, white alabaster columns towering over me; below, a pool of green water the color of emeralds. Slowly, my ant-self inches along the marble floor. I can barely glimpse the water, a shimmering spot in the far distance, but I must get to it. I feel as small as I do when I stand in the courtyard watching the planes fly overhead, as small as I feel when the sirens scream and the fires start. But I am determined. With tremendous exertion, I pull myself toward the edge of the

pool and find steps leading down to it, greenish white, glowing in the dim light. Pulling myself down the giant staircase, I know that nothing can stop me from entering the magic pool. Finally, in an ecstasy of anticipation, I push off the last step. And then I fall and keep on falling. I fall into the great moment, into freedom, into lightness. Just before I hit the water, I startle awake.

What is frightening at night brings adventure during the day. The changed landscape of shelters and ruins affords us hours of exploration. Childhood's sameness is replaced with constant change that my friend Thea and I pursue on bicycle rides through the neighborhood, climbing trees to see what houses have been bombed and searching the ruins for treasures.

Berlin is becoming pock marked. The streets are studded with skeletons: a staircase in the midst of an empty block, bricks laid bare, charred beams sticking out of buildings. These holes are both disturbing and fascinating to us, like seeing adults we had always seen fully clothed suddenly undressed. The apartments, their inner walls exposed, wallpaper torn, tiles broken, electrical wires exploding like eels, lure us into their maze. My grandmother's warnings of slides, smouldering fires, and avalanches serve only to whet our appetites.

> A dark puffy veil that hung like a pall covered the capital city.
>
> JEFFREY ETHELL

My grandmother has reason to worry. On one memorable occasion she watches, her anxious face framed by petunias in the window box, as I break through a floor and disappear. One minute she is sternly admonishing me to avoid a thin piece of decking that covers an entrance to our shelter, and the next — *RUTSCH* — I am sitting on a ledge in the basement. My back is scratched, but I'm alive and well, listening to the panic-stricken grown-ups search for me. The moment of losing all control is a little like my dream of the deep pool — that delicious sensation of falling — and then the arrival in the basement, a startling anti-climax.

Eva's Berlin

Touched by bits of light coming through the gap where I fell, the benches, chairs and tables of our shelter come into view. The place has a useless, forgotten look, like a dusty attic. The adults who arrive out of breath expecting to see me frightened and hurt find me smiling. I have survived another adventure. My mother and grandmother are torn between relief and the urge to punish me for my carelessness.

"Now, don't move. You could have hurt yourself. Let me help you down. Let's take a look at you. You could save us this kind of worry," my mother says.

They insist on checking me for injuries, though I'm sure I have none.

"You got away with it this time. But you won't always be so lucky. One day, something will happen and the seriousness of life will make itself felt. Then you'll wish you'd been more cautious."

Der Ernst des Lebens, the serious side of life, was one of my grandmother's favorite lecture topics.

"All right. No disasters. Thank your guardian angel. I'll bet your grandmother can find a little bit of cocoa in the cupboard," my grandfather says and then he takes me back upstairs to the kitchen.

"Don't scare me like that, okay? What a relief! Every thing is just fine."

My mother puts her arms around me. I savor the secret pleasure of adults worrying about me.

TREASURE HUNTS After that, I walk more carefully. Fooled so easily in our own house, I resolve to slow down in the ruins. I learn to walk and climb hesitantly, like a blind person, exploring each new area with my foot or hand before trusting it with my full body weight. Erika and Günther are quicker. Both of them move with the speed and agility of born athletes. But much as I wish to imitate them, I move slowly. So often what looks secure enough at first glance becomes unstable in an instant: the floor gives way to large splintered boards or the walls begin to shake and shower us with plaster.

Bombed houses outnumber standing ones; we claim blocks of ruins for our own. No longer in the adult world, no longer rigid and staid, no longer proper, with the right time for breakfast and supper. Now, sun and wind sweep the rooms clear and make patterns on the remnants of walls to be gathered up as scenery for fairy tales. The cellar where I discover the corpse of a spotted dog becomes the dungeon where we throw our enemies. A large empty space, backed by a single wall, can be the ballroom.

Inside the ruined houses, rubble makes hills for us to climb. Creating small avalanches beneath our feet, we scramble up to reach what is left of the house. We jump through glass-less windows like pirates boarding a ship to discover treasures we had never imagined: Delft blue tiles with scenes of sail boats and windmills; a feather boa, once, and a taffeta dress. We find sacks filled with potatoes and onions, a basket

Eva's Berlin

full of towels and sheets, half-rotten from the combination of fire hoses, rain and snow. All this once belonged to real people living real lives. Were they old? Did children live here? We feel our way around: here was a closet, here, a large bedroom, here, a kitchen.

I find a room that must have been a boy's. A box of tin soldiers, tiny but exact, has survived the fire. A boy must have lived here, playing on this floor, covered with a Persian rug instead of splintered boards. I picture him the same size as Günther, maimed by a bomb, a hole in his head, bleeding.

Slowly, we make our way back again. Then the wind blows, and we suddenly stop dead in our tracks because the dust in our eyes keeps us from seeing anything.

The skeletons of the bombed out houses threatened to collapse. There was no longer any part of the city that did not have rows and rows of ruins.

ILSE MARGRET VOGEL

RUINED CELLARS The basements frighten us. Left intact by the bombing, they smell of decay from fire-hoses used above. They have a different feeling than the upper floors. For one thing, they are never empty. Whatever the former inhabitants left behind — blankets, books, dishes, a bit of carpeting, exposed springs, ragged clothing — can be found in the dark little storage rooms off the main shelters. These signs of previous life, treasures in the open air, frighten us here below.

Above ground, where the wind blows and the sun shines, we are confident. In the basements something else

126

takes over. When we hear a rustling noise or a breath of wind, we stop dead in our tracks. Every noise seems to be human. Perhaps we'll find a dead body, or even worse, someone not quite dead, groaning or gasping his last breath. Perhaps it'll be a ghost with yellowed skin and white scraggly hair and rattling teeth, exuding the sweet stench of the dead, reaching a skeletal hand toward ours. And though we never do encounter either a person or a ghost, the fear never lessens.

THE BOMBING CONTINUES The first years of the war taught us a lot about air-raids. We got used to interrupted sleep. We were bombed two, three, four times a week, almost always at night. On the other nights, we recovered. We took a breath and went about our ordinary lives for a short interval. During the last years of the war, 1944 and 1945, we lost our chance to recuperate. It seemed as though the bombing never stopped. Air-raids occurred every night and every day, sometimes more than once. Despite the constant threat, we shopped, went to the parks and the zoo, and even to an occasional concert or theater. But every move we made occurred against a backdrop of sirens, threatening to bring the moment that could change our lives forever.

I am at my friends Günther and Erika's apartment when I hear the first sounds of wind and whine coming closer and closer. The windows rattle. What to do? What happened to the siren? They're already here! Should we hide under the table? We stay frozen where we are playing. Even

Eva's Berlin

Günther can't think, the noise is too great, the building is shaking. A bomb has fallen close by. Where is my mother? The walls collapse inwards on the house next door. We can see it from where we stand. We hear screams and windows breaking. Then we lie face down under a table trying to avoid the ceiling of the room we're in. It's coming down and the plaster dust and the splintered furniture are falling on us. Then, finally, the sound diminishes. We check. The house is still standing. Our damage was the result of the bomb hitting next door. All three of us are safe and sound. What about my mother? Was it as bad in our district? The phone is busy. I don't get through for a while. Everyone is checking on everyone else. Then I talk to her. We're both fine. We laugh. We reassure each other. *Unkraut vergeht nicht*, weeds don't perish.

Back to next door. What happened? Where are the dead? There must be dead. Then the first count — five — and the ambulances and the quiet returning to the street where small clutches of survivors stand talking quietly. Gone is the radio and the rocking chair and everything that they imply, gone the routine comfort of breakfast in the morning. The ominous sound is lurking in the background now, the sound that tears up time and leaves its shreds clinging to mind and heart. The warning for all Berliners. It could happen any time to any one of us. We learn to live in the moment during the last two years of the war.

SCHOOL'S OUT 1943, Berlin's children have been sent to the country with the *Kinderschulverschickung*. I have never known whether I could have gone away with the others or not. Those who are left in the city by 1943 are not officially there at all; we are "hidden children" though we are not actually in hiding.

After the other children are evacuated, our time together takes on a special quality. Long and generous like a summer vacation, it is at the same time very short, like a terminal illness. Although sirens send us home or to an air-raid shelter every few hours, we feel free as birds without school or schedule. Left to our own devices, we spend most of our days exploring the *Tiergarten* and the zoo, and playing in the ruins. My mother allows me to play with Thea and the older children as much as I want. My grandmother limits herself to sour commentary: "I don't know why you let that child be watched by other children. Heaven knows you weren't brought up that way."

THE ISLAND After the bombs destroy its formal gardens, Erika and I spend a lot of time in the *Tiergarten*. There are bushes to play hide-and-seek in, a partially destroyed bandshell which becomes our stage, and, best of all, an island where a bomb caused a tree to fall into the water spanning the shore. We spend several days wrestling with its protruding branches, smoothing it out to form a wobbly bridge. Crossing the murky pond, we set foot on the island. It is neither large

Eva's Berlin

nor small, about the size of a quarter city block, a small plot of land that belongs just to us. Working until we have blisters on our hands, Erika and I clear away blackberry brambles and nettles, and, with what small trowels and rakes we can snatch from the garden, carve paths that wind through the brush.

Having found a great cause, we become ever more lawless. To find plants, we become accomplished thieves. At the zoo, where there are wide stretches of flower beds between the animal cages, one of us stands guard while the other puts as many young plants as possible into net bags we brought filled with food for the deer. In late spring, we dig up crocus and tulip bulbs, and a few carrots in case we go hungry. In summer, we favor the yellow pansies whose faces are supposed to make us feel guilty for stealing but fail to. From the zoo we continue to the *Schrebergärten*, small plots of earth Berliners planted during the war. Here, in the loamy compost, baby roses, violets, and mosses are fenced in by barbed wire that catches on my jersey pants on my way home. Clothes such as these sweatpants are about as hard to come by in Berlin as food. I wear the same pair of thick woolen *trainingshosen* every day during the winter and early spring. If my grandmother finds out that they are torn, I'll never hear the end of it. Patching the small, navy blue triangles takes up hours I'd rather spend reading by my night lamp, but it works, and my life of crime remains hidden from my severest judge.

The island calls Erika and me at all hours of the day.

There, we celebrate birthdays and tell each other secrets we swear to keep. Our hands dig into the black loam we free from roots and brambles to plant the flowers we have hoarded. Oval paths are decorated with white stones and shells brought home from summer trips. In a special place, we plant a large bush of daisies that serves as an umbrella for miniature dwarves who live under large red mushrooms with white spots, called *Glückspilze*, lucky mushrooms. They will be our island's guardians. To keep strangers away, we leave a hedge of brambles at the edge of our secret garden. From the shore, the island looks no different than before we claimed it.

We seldom visit our island in winter because of the slippery condition of our bridge in the snow, but as soon as the melt starts we are there, cleaning up and waiting to greet the first crocus. We have a cemetery for birds; even the insects we find dead are buried there with special rituals. At each burial, one of us creates an appropriate dirge and the other decorates the grave with twigs and gravel and any costume jewelry saved up from our basement explorations. The green finch gets a twig cross with a green paste jewel stuck in its center; the mouse is buried with a pearl necklace. In early spring, the island is full of birdsong. It cradles us in April breezes and teaches us something about the sacred.

We permit no visitors except my mother, once; a visit which she wears like a medal of honor. Wearing high heels, she carefully makes her way across the tree bridge and surveys our gardens with the complicit air she uses to hide things from my grandmother. We lead her down a spiral path to a special stone chair where we decorate her with a chain of pansies. She gives us a generous seal of approval and reminds me often of her status as our only adult guest. I vacillate between being sad because she only visited once and being glad that I've come up with something she admires.

By now dusk had come. With horror we saw the moonless sky over the inner city was not turning dark, but instead was tinged with streaks of red and dusty yellow...the smoke-filled air burned our eyes and made us cough. Fire engines, their sirens shrieking, rushed past us.

ILSE MARGRET VOGEL

AWE   For some of us, the horror of the raids is mixed with the uncanny beauty of the fire. Coming out of the air-raid shelter, we follow the pink color in the night sky to the bombed out buildings, giant castles of flame. Orange, yellow, red and gold, the flames light up the street as we stand back, whispering the names of any we know who lived there.

The flames are the cause of our fear; yet we can't take our eyes off them. They draw us in as spectacle, as symbol; we are servants of the fire god. Though the flames spell terror and destruction with an undeniable clarity, we can't leave them. After the drone of the engines of planes flying overhead, the flames reconnect us with nature. Again and again we stand in front of a burning building, riveted by the dancing flames. What started with book burnings and burnt out Jewish stores is continuing. The German nation is burning up.

Oddly, Berlin in flames is the only event that matches the Nazi promise of glory in its apocalyptic dimensions. So many battles won, so many marching soldiers, so many buildings splendidly erected, the voices of Hitler, Göring and Göbbels inspiring Germans to acts of glory. The *Thousand Year Reich*, Hitler calls it. It doesn't work. Battles are lost, soldiers come home wounded and discouraged, buildings are bombed, and voices become hysterical. But Berlin burning, Berlin in its worst defeat, is an apotheosis. In its terrifying beauty, we get in touch with our spirits again, our true spirits, not the ones Hitler is addressing. The flames determine whether, where and how we live. We stand in awe, gazing at the spectacle. We appreciate its vast scale, its world-ending beauty. Walking home, we turn back again and again to see the yellow flames leaping toward the black sky before opening the door to our apartment to see what the night's damage has been.

The city stretched out below me as I had never seen it before. The heavy smoke clouds were aglow with the reflections of the raging fires on the ground

ILSE MARGRET VOGEL

CHAPTER SIX

Battling the Dragon

SITTING DUCKS

The ducks in the Berlin zoo live on an island.
They waddle over ornate bridges
and lay their eggs under azalea-topped pavilions.

Now and then, on the far side of the moat,
a keeper appears. His long, looped pole
scoops up an unsuspecting bird and
deposits it in his green van.

At home, my grandmother is conducting
business of state. Head erect, gray hair held
in place by loops of tortoise shell,
she keeps the contents of the kitchen
from getting out of line.

Eva's Berlin

Safe in my corner, where I sit bandaging
a wounded teddy bear, I observe her:
a gray eminence
in an atmosphere of boiling onions.
When will her keeper come?

RIVALS   World War II wasn't the only war going on in my life. The war between my mother, Elisabeth Eichenwald and my grandmother, Gertrud Meister, shook my life with equal intensity. My grandmother's energy was as unstoppable as the bombers that crossed our sky every night. My mother wasn't equal to her fury. Arguments arose almost every day and, much as I hated and feared them, I couldn't leave my mother to face the battle alone. So I sat quietly, listening and watching.

Slender and fair with light blue eyes and the regular features of gothic madonnas, my mother and grandmother resemble each other. But her daughter's beauty hasn't been earned. Beauty is as beauty does. A daughter's good looks should be the crowning touch of a life of virtue.

Elisabeth is not interested in being the moral example her mother raised her to be. Not neatly or tastefully dressed in the Meister respectability. Not quiet and dignified in her language. Not to be located in one of the predictable German bourgeois lives: the hardworking *Hausfrau* with the kerchief over her head to protect it from the flying dust; the dark-suited, white-bloused lady with her hair neatly twisted into a chignon, who makes weekly visits to the graves of her relatives.

My grandmother judges everything my mother does. The way she walks, talks, dresses, eats, and drinks: every gesture demonstrates her lack of respect for the way my grandmother raised her. Gertrud Meister has encountered rebels among her own otherwise strait-laced relatives. One brother, Onkel Erich, sings soprano arias at parties and his daughter, Tante Margo, smokes cigars. She speaks to them only when the situation demands it. My grandmother honors simple self-sufficiency, like baking one's own bread, and sewing one's clothes, and a respectable appearance. My mother eats oysters at *Kempinski's* on the *Kurfürstendamm*, values a good story above plain truth, and wears sheer black stockings and short, flippy dresses.

Elisabeth Eichenwald gossips on the telephone with Fräulein Wagner about the passes Herr Paasch, a married man, makes at her, a married woman. My grandmother bristles: "Not in front of the child," while I, unseen in the corner, savor a feeling of superiority because I already know what they're talking about. It's a short-lived pleasure. Momentarily, the poisonous fumes begin to rise.

Eva's Berlin

Now the Berlin dialect is the topic. My mother prefers its working class vulgarities to *hochdeutsch*, high German. When my grandmother overhears it, she begins to lecture anyone who happens to be in the room: "She didn't learn it from me . . . but I can guess who taught her." Then she flounces off, her head held high.

The martyred tone and the raised eyebrow let any insider know that the father, my grandfather, is the culprit. Without his influence, my mother might have grown up properly. My grandmother's anger is fed by her husband's attitude in the face of these accusations. He hasn't the slightest regret about the way he raised his daughter; in fact, he's proud of her.

It could have been different. There is one story both my grandmother and my mother love to tell. In it, they gleefully recount the time they joined forces to humiliate my grandfather. The story goes that my grandmother got wind of the fact that my grandfather had invited a young woman who worked at his office to a show at the *Eispalast*, a huge Berlin skating rink. Pulling strings at the box office through a neighbor who worked there, she managed to buy two seats right next to them for my mother and herself. They made sure to arrive early so that they could be discovered sitting there practicing nonchalance when my grandfather appeared with his date.

"The expression on your *Opa's* face when he saw us," my mother breaks into gales of laughter before she finishes the phrase. I can imagine my grandmother's *hauteur* and the pretty young woman crumpling under her gaze.

GRANDMOTHER'S DUBIOUS GIRLHOOD Gertrud Meister's photograph bothers me. It shows her at twenty with white gleaming shoulders and a mass of curls, laughing with a girlfriend. Her cheeks are round, her eyes merry.

No matter how hard I try, I can't match that image to the grandmother I know. I try to work my way backwards in time. But my grandmother's features lack mobility. Her "Aryan" profile is carved in stone, the narrow eyes have nothing in common with the girl in the photo. My grandmother's face is lined with furrows as old as the bark of the huge oak in

our garden. What happened to the girl in the photo? Did the clock strike the way it does in fairy tales, leaving her forever sour? Or is the young woman still alive somewhere inside? Perhaps she's the one who insists on my grandmother bringing romantic novels to the air-raid shelter

and she who shushes us when her favorite song plays on the radio, *Dunkelrote Rosen, bring ich, schöne Frau.* She looks as severe as ever sitting there, straight as a ramrod, listening. But I know that, inside, she is the beautiful woman receiving a suitor with his arms full of roses.

I decide that as a girl my grandmother believed the romantic tales she found in novels. She'd grown up in respectable, modest circumstances the daughter of a civil servant, one of four children, the only girl. She had chased the rainbow of marriage, and just when she thought she'd found the pot of gold, she became disenchanted. Raised on Göthe and Tolstoy and visits to innumerable German castles, what a triumph her engagement to a Polish count must have been! Marrying into the nobility was the goal of every German girl of her generation. Growing up in a country practically devoid of foreigners and a social class far below her aspirations, I imagine my grandmother found Otto Bielinski as exotic as a Chinese emperor. Safely ennobled with a name like Bielinski, Gertrud Meister probably saw her future self living in a castle surrounded by devoted servants.

The fact that my grandfather's sense of humor rendered him incapable of taking his background seriously probably escaped my grandmother altogether, oblivious as she was to irony or paradox. How could my grandmother guess that her fiancé really didn't care about being a count, when popular novels assured her a true aristocrat only pretends to simplicity, even poverty, to save others from painful comparisons? I can imagine my grandfather's rich descriptions of his family background when he courted her. I know how easy it is for him to tell stories about castles. But, in real life, he was one of three heirs to a Polish estate they had relinquished, along with their titles. He was a democrat who wanted to become an ordinary citizen in this country that was so clean, so orderly, so simple by comparison to his own.

But he never could resist embellishing a story and his tales of grandeur must have eclipsed whatever real information he could give her.

It was sad. He married her to live a simpler life; she married him to become a countess. Trapped and betrayed, she turned into a dragon, fiery, and proud; her disappointment smouldered in a blaze of rage.

THE BATTLE ZONE I get up before anyone else in the Berlin apartment. After removing the bird-cage cover, I sit at the dining room table and listen to Peterchen once again search for his lost mirror, "*Wo ist denn mein Spiegelchen?*"

Few noises penetrate from the courtyard except for the occasional steps of an apartment dweller leaving for work. Inside, the apartment is blessedly quiet, allowing me to stare into the distance, dreaming of sitting on the shoulders of a bird like Peterchen, but much larger, and flying into the warm summer day.

My reverie is interrupted by the clatter of my grandmother's heels on the hallway floor. She comes from the back bedroom fully dressed, her hair neatly captured into a chignon at her neck. In her energetic, righteous manner, she begins to bustle about, straightening up the kitchen with an air of correcting a terrible wrong. I try not to reliquish my fantasy, holding on to Peterchen's silky green feathers we float in air yellowed by Linden blossoms as my grandmother sails past me. Soon, she brings me a cup of milky tea and a roll.

Eva's Berlin

"It's time to have breakfast, *Prinzessin*," she says, rolling her eyes upward.

Stirring my cup of tea while she busies herself in the kitchen, I can't escape her stormy energy. A bevy of sharp notes flies in and circles in the air with the restless flutter of a flock of birds caught inside. She sets a pot down, and I can hear the stove top quivering. A cup and saucer clang together and I begin to shake inside. Has she broken something? Will it be my mother's fault because she's put it in the wrong place?

Nothing unusual happens. Nothing is broken. The clatter is part of her speed, like sparks that fly from the wheels of a train. She comes to the dining table. *Schlank wie eine Tanne*. She likes to characterize her posture as "straight as a fir tree." She sits next to me, stiff and erect, with a cup of watered milk and a small glass of foul-smelling herbal juice. Her teaspoon, as though it has a life of its own, starts beating a tattoo against the delicate white porcelain of her cup. I watch her carefully. She seems friendly enough when she butters my roll, but I sense that something is wrong. I haven't a clue as to what it might be and concentrate on chewing my roll and drinking my hot tea to avoid provoking her. My grandmother opens the bird's cage but Peterchen chooses to remain on his perch and we eat our meal in a tense silence.

When we are almost finished, my mother comes in, her sleepy eyes slightly out of focus, her hair stiff and bristly, a few wisps escaping the fashionable roll that frames her face. Now I can feel waves of disapproval begin to collect. Rearranging jam pots and creamers on the table, my grandmother darts quick, angry glances at my sleepy mother. I am worried. Looking at the two of them, I want to give my mother strength to fight whatever it is that is coming with the inevitability of blue-black Berlin clouds gathering for a thunderstorm. I want my mother fiery, tall, quick. But she is short and soft in appearance with the dreamy far-away look of a 'thirties movie star in her feathery white mules and her blue satin bathrobe. She sits down and stares into her cup of coffee as though a treasure lies buried at the bottom.

Then my grandmother begins.

"*Die Jugend von heute,*" a frequent preamble to an argument, meaning "the youth of today" is reiterated several times with increased venom. "*Die Jugend von heute.*"

My mother does not respond but my grandmother doesn't seem to notice. "I suppose it's customary among your sophisticated friends to leave the towels on the floor after you take a bath?"

Her voice is beginning to take on a metallic sound. My mother shakes her head slightly, a smile playing around the corners of her mouth. My grandmother responds quickly, "You're smiling. Of course, you're smiling. I should have known it would come to this. I'm not surprised. Why should you listen to me with respect just because I'm your mother? You have no idea about how deeply your conduct offends me."

Eva's Berlin

She draws her breath in through her nose and throws her head back. I sit quietly and say nothing.

"One might imagine that you'd know better, but no, of course not. A grown woman with a child living in her parents' small apartment, who doesn't know enough to pick up after herself!"

My grandmother's face has contorted into an angry mask, her eyebrows high and drawn together, her eyes piercing, a deep red color rising from her throat. My mother makes a small, "No, no" sound now and then but she doesn't answer. I would give anything for a place where my mother would be safe from my grandmother's voice. If we could only leave the room. But my mother just sits there and shakes her head wanly while my grandmother continues.

"A woman who gives herself airs to cover her lack of house and husband. Fräulein Walter upstairs, who we all know is a prostitute, knows more about how to behave than you do."

I force myself to concentrate on finding a solution. My grandmother wants my mother to feel ashamed, I think, to beg her forgiveness for having a Jew for a husband, for being sloppy and failing to appreciate the work our arrival has placed on her mother. But I have to admit that, even if my grandmother weren't so angry, my mother wouldn't do that. I've never heard her say she was wrong about anything. But then my grandmother doesn't apologize, either. I sit back in my chair, exhausted.

My grandmother raises herself up, stretching her long neck like a goose. "I'm not surprised," she says. "I've seen it coming all along. At the very least, you should divorce that Jew for the sake of the family. Not that I expect that from you. I know my own daughter, I'm sorry to say. I've learned not to expect anything."

Dragon's fire leaps from her eyes as she continues to beat an angry tattoo with her spoon. I sit trying to quell a queasy feeling rising from my stomach.

My mother has perfected the art of appearing unfocused, as though she really is somewhere else, so that my grandmother's diatribe is lost in an empty room. But I know nothing about disappearing. I am frightened into hyper-alertness by my grandmother's rage. Will she hit my mother? She could throw both us out of her apartment. Or keep me and send my mother away. Then what would we do? Meanwhile, the quarrel continues.

"You always were your father's daughter, not mine. No one can say you learned to behave this way from me. Answer me! Only a whore would marry a Jew."

I don't know what a "whore" is, but it must be terrible because my mother reacts by waving her hand across her face, as though she's trying to avoid an insect headed for her eyes, and says, "Enough, mother."

I feel as though I'm alone in a vast, empty space. I lose the sense of my own body. A feeling of doom.

With no warning, my mother stands up, shrugs her

shoulders, and walks out, winking at me conspiratorially. I follow, trembling with fear. My legs feel rubbery as I walk and I grab my mother's hand. I'm immensely relieved to get away. My mother drops my hand as soon as we're outside the dining room and disappears into the bathroom. Alone in my mother's bedroom, I listen to my grandmother thrashing in the kitchen. Through the open doorway, I see my grandfather coming toward me, his gray felt slippers so soft I barely hear him. I feel suddenly shy and self-conscious. I know he heard what went on; our apartment is too small to ignore my grandmother's rising voice. Why hadn't he come to help my mother? He notices the look on my face and winks at me,

"Your grandmother has missed her calling. She should have been an actress in Schiller's tragedies."

I can't help but smile and wink back, the thought of his desertion completely forgotten. Theater appeals to me. My grandmother, the great tragedienne, raging, but not in earnest. With another smile, *Opa* disappears into the back room. I want to feel the way he does and try to look back on what happened as a big act but I can't. I'm too afraid of my grandmother to applaud or boo. The war between her and my mother is real. My mother also winked at me before we left the dining room but I don't believe she is taking this lightly. She seemed so small and delicate, sitting there, pretending not to care while her mother raged. I want to laugh with *Opa*, but I can't. Instead, I try to come up with excuses for him. He probably couldn't say or do anything to change things. My grandmother has the force of a tidal wave and he's more like a little brook. My grandfather and my mother are good and my grandmother is bad. Why isn't the good winning?

Suddenly, I have a terrible premonition. What took place today will be repeated time and again. I will watch, frightened and in awe, as my dragon grandmother devours my mother bit by bit. I can see her at the cutting board, deftly removing a succulent bit of my mother's body which she drops into the soup. Sometimes it is just a fingernail. But just as often she gets vital organs. The certainty that she means to eliminate my mother terrifies me.

THE DRAGON'S SOFT UNDERBELLY There are times when my grandmother delights me. Christmas holi-

days at the beginning of the war were suffused with the aroma of her baking, of vanilla blending with lemon and chocolate. Among the brown earthenware cake molds, the sieves, the double-bladed knife that looks like a cradle, and the wooden spoons, she looked like a grandmother should. Surrounded by flour, butter, chocolate and sugar and armed with her magical tools, her long slender arms and hands moved gracefully as she pummelled the glistening

Eva's Berlin

dough. I watched as she added, reduced, sifted, chopped, mixed and kneaded the dough, and, finally, oiled the pans. When she let me help, I ladled the dough into the heavy pans and decorated star-shaped cookies with sugar crystals.

These few Christmases when I was five and six years old are islands of memory in which even my grandmother is surrounded by a golden haze. On Christmas eve, over the roast goose, Gertrud Meister thawed out; her eyes became soft and there was a hint, just a hint, of the lovely young girl in the photograph. She told me stories of her childhood — the day her mother gave her the cameo brooch I am to have after she dies, the time her brother got a Pekinese dog from a distant relative, only to have to give it back because her father wouldn't have it in the house.

"We didn't have much when we were children. We'd use string for a leash and tie a carton to it and pretend that the Peke was still with us."

I felt myself warming to my grandmother, wanting to be her friend, but, even then, the feeling failed to blossom. I couldn't forget her regular, non-Christmas self, after all, and I kept my distance.

On Christmas Eve, my grandmother and I wait together in the bedroom for Santa Claus's arrival. I hold my breath with fear and anticipation while my grandmother's eyes widen with pleasure. Then the door bell rings and, after the door is opened noisily to let Santa into the hallway, we listen as my mother is interviewed by Santa Claus.

"Is this where little Eva lives?"

"Yes, it is, Santa Claus. Have you brought her some presents?"

"Well, slow down here. First, I must find out whether she's been a good girl or not."

"Oh, she's a good girl, Santa Claus."

"All year long?"

"Well, sometimes she's a bit quick with her tongue, but she's been good."

"Anything else?"

"Just a little thing. She gets impatient at times. But she's been good, really."

"I'm happy to hear that she's been a good girl and, of course, here are her presents."

There are clumping noises as cartons are placed on the floor, the front door is shut, and I know the visit has ended. The excitement is rising to my throat like a swarm of bees. I can hardly wait to go in.

While we are waiting, *Opa* and *Mami* have been trimming the tree with silver ornaments and tinsel, screwing long metal candle-holders into its trunk and lighting long yellow tapers. When I'm finally let in, the light from the tree softens the room and bounces from silver to silver. I feel I'm among angels. My grandfather tells me a tale of long ago, when the people who lived in the forests came out of their snow-laden caves to decorate a tree with suet, nuts and grain for the winter-starved animals as a prayer to bring back the light. I always imagine our tree in the forest, surrounded by snow and animals eating their fill.

My dear *Opa*. It is only after he dies, on my eighth Christmas, that I put two and two together and realize that he was the voice of Santa Claus.

THE BATTLE CONTINUES On ordinary days, my grandmother's presence makes me feel uneasy. I'm afraid of her moods and, even more, of the quarrels with my mother. The worst scene of all starts the same as all the others, except that, during a moment's pause in my grandmother's harangue (just after she's delivered the one about my mother being no better than a prostitute), my mother surprises me by looking directly at Gertrud Meister and saying quietly,

"Don't you wish somebody'd call *you* a whore? Your life is so boring and sexless. I know you've always envied me."

My grandmother's eyes narrow, acquiring the light blue color that signals her anger, a quality she attributes to nobility, as she shares it with Frederick the Great. After a short, ominous silence, she slaps my mother across the face.

It is a terrible moment and long. We are suspended, as in the silence that comes just before the explosion of a bomb very close by. I don't feel anything nor can I look at either of the combatants. Then my mother shrugs her shoulders the way she always does when we leave the room at the end of a fight, and we begin to walk out. But there is a difference. She is crying. It is the first time I see my mother's face crumple, and her tears are as surprising to me as her anger was when it appeared. Despite everything, I always counted on her stoicism as a kind of strength. Now that picture is shattered. She looks so fragile that I'm afraid to hug her when she sits down at her dressing table and picks up a tissue. I shuffle my feet on the fluffy white rug.

What would I do, who would I be without my mother? I can't imagine myself without her. I only know I'm terrified of losing her, or of her losing me. "My mother needs me. I am her protector" — words engraved on my heart. In my fantasies, I eliminate her enemy.

There is a fairy tale in which dwarfs help the mayor's wife by cleaning her kitchen every night while she sleeps. Being a vain creature, the mayor's wife takes the dwarfs' hard labor as her due and never leaves them the delicacies or gold coins they expect as a reward. They work and wait and work and wait until, finally, they become exasperated. One night, they lard the stairs that lead from her bedroom to the kitchen with dried peas. The mayor's wife breaks her neck on her way to breakfast the next morning.

COLLECTIONS I dream of locking my grandmother up in a tower like the witch did Rapunzel, so I can force her to listen to me until she understands. If I could only find the power. But I know I can't. I try to comfort myself with the thought that she will die soon, and my beautiful young mother and I will live happily ever after. But I'm afraid of

Eva's Berlin

death. Even my grandmother's.

To ease the moment for my mother and me, I resort to a tried and true strategy. My mother loves coffee and misses it terribly when she runs out of rations. Regularly, I steal some from my mother's own cache and hide it from her, wrapped in pink tissue paper and tied with ribbon ready to be taken out in a time of need, as I save the acorns for the deer in the zoo. This is such a moment. Silently, I place the ribboned package on the center of her blue satin bedspread. Later that morning, when the coffee's pungent aroma fills the air, I feel a secret pride.

My mother's love of coffee starts my compulsive saving. Having accumulated a pile of little pink tissue bags full of coffee, I become a hoarder of treasures. Scraps of paper to make little notebooks. Old clothes for dress-ups. I can't stop. Theater tickets, matchbooks, postcards, letters, dance programs, round pebbles sculpted by mountain streams, plants pressed between pages of my diary, feathers, Christmas cards that were especially pretty. I am collecting evidence of my existence. When I arrive at St. Peter's gate and he asks, "And what did you do with your life on earth?" I'll be prepared. "Here," I'll say, and show him my collections and go directly to heaven.

I'm terrified of vanishing without a trace, like the fairy tale girl without a shadow. Soon, my collections become larger than my storage space and I have to cast out one set or another. But then, of course, a new collection begins.

A HOUSE OF DRAGONS German lore is full of dragons. Siegfried, the hero, slays one. In my father's books of reproductions, they are fierce creatures, spiny and red-tongued, the size of a dinosaur. Breathing fire, they devour unsuspecting victims. I can feel their pulsing force in the paintings. Dragons are incapable of stillness.

My grandmother, too, is incapable of stillness. She, too, is continually casting about for prey. I can imagine our lineage. Though the dragons' bodies are lost, their energy survives in women like Gertrud Meister. In our family, women can breathe fire. Through them, we pass on the power of destruction.

My mother's dragon nature is pitted against a tree. Her friend Frau Paasch complains that the maple outside our bedroom bothers her.

"Its foliage," she says, "makes my bedroom window on the second floor so dark, I can hardly wake up in the morning."

Soon afterwards, my mother tells us at breakfast that the trunk darkens her bedroom, too. The tree is a young maple, the smallest tree in our backyard, surrounded by scruffy looking weeds and black earth. In spring, it sends out delicate candles of chartreuse velvet. In summer, it gives shade to the starlings and green finches that visit our window box. The maple is part of the household. I often sit near it and listen to the birds. How could my mother turn against it? It's just a pencil in my mother's window.

Eva's Berlin

Paying no attention to my attempts to save it, my mother and grandmother set out to destroy the tree. United once more by a common enemy, their arguments diminish. Their talks about how to do away with the tree are short and to the point. They decide on poison as the least detectable method. Then they take turns using my grandfather's drill to bore holes in the maple's trunk. With one of the syringes from my father's medical kit, they inject it with a smelly greenish brew that foams in the bottle.

Early in the morning and late at night, so as not to be seen by other tenants, one of them is out in the garden using the large syringe. The tree wilts slowly. Its lush green leaves curl and turn brown at the edges, as if singed in a fire. More and more holes are drilled; more and more injections given. Branches turn into wood so dry it creaks and breaks off. The tree begins to look so worn and disheveled that the birds avoid it.

The two women take a grim pleasure in its demise.

CHAPTER SEVEN

Nazis

A CONTRAST I remember a year before the war, when my grandfather was still alive.

He takes me to Charlottenburg castle for a review of the palace guard. In the middle of the gray city, large trees flank its park-like courtyard. The air is humming with festivity; white-plumed horses draw gleaming black carriages and the marching band is playing a fast tempo for a small troop of soldiers whose glittering medals and peaked helmets reflect the sun. Sitting on my small grandfather's bony shoulders, I watch the parade, surrounded by a crowd not much taller than myself. The excitement of the occasion makes my skin tickle. I don't know the important graybeard in the gilded

Eva's Berlin

carriage among horse-guards and uniformed soldiers, but the people around us wave to him the way they might to a venerated member of the family. Something festive and very important is going on. People whisper to each other as the carriage approaches,

"There he is...lucky we got here in time...he looks well...his health is holding up...I believe he looked at me just then" — trivialities that make me think they know him personally.

> Hypnotized by flags, banners, speeches and marching feet, the German people did not awaken from their organized delirium.
>
> MAX VON DER GRUN

He acknowledges the guards who parade before him with a friendly wave, and occasionally recognizes someone in the crowd with a smile and some words we can't hear — the old man doesn't seem so different from the grandfather whose shoulders are supporting me.

VOLKSFESTE After we arrive in 1939, Berlin becomes the scene of *Volksfeste* — rallies of a very different sort. On a sunny afternoon in my fifth year, I catch the excitement of marching music and crowds and pull at my mother's hand to get her to stop in the square where thousands are already gathered. My mother shrugs her shoulders. She doesn't want to stay, but the crowd is making it hard to get away and she, too, loves a parade on a sunny afternoon.

Soon they begin to come. Men are marching in perfect unison wearing extravagantly clean, brown uniforms.

Their faces are set, heads lifted in anticipation of victory, their expressions so alike they might be carved out of stone. The crowd screams, *Sieg Heil*. Some women near us are crying. My mother and I are on an island by ourselves. We are observers of a scene so large it feels threatening. Something, I don't know what exactly, but I feel something terrifying could burst through the gleaming show at any moment. I clutch my mother's hand.

When the marching stops and the speeches begin, my stomach starts to hurt. I can't follow the words, partly because the *Heil* still rings in my ears. They're talking about the German nation and taking over the world. And I keep hearing something about "will." I don't understand. I recognize the word because my mother accuses me of having too much will. It means that I've been bad, disobedient. This man seems to be  saying will is a good thing, but he sounds scary, screaming at us in a hoarse voice. What does it mean when he says that we have one will? We don't; we all want different things. I lose track of the speeches. My mother's face has frozen into a mask. I want to leave.

Eva's Berlin

"Please, *Mami*, let's go."

But she doesn't move, and she doesn't look at me. We stand there, trapped by words.

After the speeches, more soldiers. They look ready to fight. I'm frightened. What if they suddenly shouldered

their guns and started shooting at us? I probably know someone in the regiment from our neighborhood or from the apartment house, but I couldn't recognize them if I tried. Their faces are vacant. They've been changed, the way the boy is in the *Snow Queen*; they've been turned into zombies. I imagine them marching right over us without even noticing.

"Please, *Mami*, let's go home." I give her hand a good yank and she responds. She looks dazed. "All right, but you have to find all the holes in the crowd for me. You're small. You go first."

While the crowd yells, *"Heil! Heil Hitler! Heil!"* I pull my mother by the hand as we push through the mass of bodies. We talk very little on the way home.

Even when there isn't a parade, military convoys roll

through the streets. I go the other way when I hear the tanks, clumsy and heavy like pre-historic animals, guns mounted on top looking oddly like horns. Men in civilian clothes all but disappear from our streets: brown shirts and green and grey military uniforms, worn with a swagger take their place. They are seldom accompanied by women. Berlin streets, once spring filled with light green Linden trees and elegant ladies drinking coffee at sidewalk cafes, now hold men in grinding boots, accompanied by loud music and louder speeches. Public radio addresses screech victory at us at all hours of the day and night, victory after victory for the *Thousand Year Reich*.

GÖRING, FAMILIENVATER When I am five, Göring comes to speak near the *Gedächtniskirche*, his wife and two of his daughters, only a little older than me, sitting next to him. There he is, his large, fat body encased in a splendid white uniform sparkling with medals and ribbons, a family man. My grandmother nudges me,

"Now you can see how quiet and well behaved some little girls can be."

Eva's Berlin

She tells me that ten seamstresses were kept busy for weeks and months sewing uniforms for Göring out of materials specially woven for him. I observe the family  closely, trying to ferret out a clue about their particular life, to imagine what it is like to have that man as a father. They are blonde and blue-eyed, like me and they look a little strained up there on the platform, sitting ramrod straight next to their mother looking out at us. I can't find anything that distinguishes them from children I know, but I keep thinking, "Nazis and children," two words that just won't fit together. What are they doing on the platform with that bellowing man? Surely they don't ride on his back or listen to him telling stories. I am afraid of him. Are they? Or are they only his children on this great occasion; their private life different, smaller, like that of all the other children whose fathers are away at war?

Back at home, my grandmother can't wait to tell my grandfather and mother the news.

"We saw Göring today," she says, with the air of importance that comes from partaking of greatness. "We saw Göring today and he wasn't any further away than you are."

She sounds like when she talks about how her eyes are the same shade of blue as Frederick the Great's. We are royalty, she is saying, but my *Opa* winks at me to signal that she's off on one of her tangents again.

PLAYGROUND HITLER The zoo playground has become our club house by the time I'm seven. With Günther as president, we meet regularly by the green slatted benches to discuss weighty matters, such as who may belong to our club. One spring afternoon, we decide to play a trick on Heinz, a boy with a big bulbous forehead, disliked for his use of large words and his academic recitations. In order to label him, once and for all, as the egghead he is, we measure our foreheads.

The result is staggering. After the measuring is done and the numbers recorded, Günther announces with a derisive laugh,

"You've won the contest, Eva. Your forehead is even bigger than Heinz's."

I feel the earth moving under my feet; I'm hot and then cold. Instead of conversation, I hear a loud buzzing in my ears but I manage to hide these feelings. Now everyone will know I'm different. Or maybe they've known all along, I just didn't know it showed. It's as bad as finding myself a *Mischling*, half-Jewish in a world of Aryans. At night, I dream that I am watching other children ride the merry-go-round, but I can't join them because I'm stuck behind a window, while an acquaintance of my mother's says matter-of-factly, "Of course, you can't go in there. You're half-Jewish."

Try as I may, I can't evade Hitler's voice when it comes on loudspeakers in the *Tiergarten* or zoo or in stores where I'm doing errands. I can't follow his message because the yelling confuses all meaning, but some words come through and I grow to hate them, words like, "*Reich ... Grösse ... Völkertum ... Kraft ... Sieg ... Macht ... Entschlossenheit.*"

The words themselves are new in my vocabulary as neither family nor friends are given to talking about "empire, greatness, patriotism, strength, victory, might, determination." I will never be able to hear them without the hysterical high whine and the white noise of the P. A. system.

At the playground, we're in the middle of a game of knives-in-sand — a game that requires us to throw pocket-knives into a small mound of sand from our wrists, elbow, shoulder, and head — when the voice comes over the public address system and, in a flash, we're divided. Klaus, a Hitler Youth who is new to the playground, is accusing Günther, my older half-Jewish friend, of being racially impure. For a moment I'm panicked that he knows something.

"You're one of them. You shouldn't even be here. The *Führer* hates you and so do I! This is for us Germans. You can't even play here."

"What are you talking about? I was playing here when you were a little kid."

"You're a Jew!"

"So are you."

Günther is using "Jew" as a hate word. I don't have time to think about it because they're already rolling on the ground, while Erika and I scramble to get the knives out of the way. Wrestling and kicking up dust, they pummel each other until Günther wins. Erika and I go to hug him and clean his cuts with our already grimy handkerchiefs. We barely notice that Hitler's speech is over. Klaus leaves soon afterwards and we don't see him again. But we vow that from now on, when we hear Hitler's voice coming over the loud-speaker, we will leave the playground. That was a close call.

S.S. AND S.A. The Nazis bark their talk and clang their boots and censure anyone who doesn't quickly *Sieg Heil*. Stores, movie houses and apartments are decorated with pictures of our *Führer* looking like he is just about to arrive in a glorious future with the rest of the country trailing behind him. The S.S. and S.A. men are there to make sure we salute every picture.

Berliners quickly develop an awareness of what signals possible trouble. We speak and move carefully. We're not only required to obey the rules: to register with the police every time we move, to inform the authorities of any travel plans, to report new or suspicious people in the neighborhood: we're expected to obey enthusiastically. There are fewer and fewer private spaces. When we sit in sidewalk restaurants, play in the playground, or go for walks at dusk, S. S. men are apt to appear demanding special accomodations or meting out punishment. I'm terrified that my mother could be arrested. Our former *Gemütlichkeit* is replaced by a shared paranoia.

My mother comes home to tell us that her best friend Fräulein Wagner was sitting at the *Romanische Café* with one of her boyfriends, Herr Schmidt, when two S. S. men walked up to their table and just stood there until the two of them got up and left. Fräulein Wagner seemed to think the whole thing was pretty funny, but her friend had been shaken.

My friend Ingrid's mother had to delay a day's bread baking in her bakery to make a special order for an S. A. Bonze. A hundred pounds of flour were delivered to bake special cakes for the big wig's birthday party.

When I am seven, my mother's friend Ursel is forced to move to the country with her two children because her villa in the *Grunewald* has been turned into a Nazi headquarters.

DIE GEMÜSEFRAU, THE VEGETABLE LADY

It's not only the uniformed Nazis we have to watch out for. They're just the known enemies. The unknown enemies are people who are Nazi sympathizers but pose as friends. Neighbors report neighbors and one never knows whether strangers are listening for something to report.

My mother's loose tongue worries me. Frau Meyer, for example, could report her jokes about the Nazis' brown (turd) shirts. When I see uniformed men approach her truck to buy the morning produce, I tremble, imagining the knock at our door and my mother being taken away. With relief, I notice that *Mami* buys Frau Meyer's most expensive vegetables — black asparagus spears we peel carefully to reveal their immaculate whiteness, and toy cabbages the Germans call *Rosenkohl*, and wild mushrooms. When the selection is reduced to potatoes and onions, she takes a scarf, and sometimes a slightly worn silk nightgown, and gives it to Frau Meyer for her daughter.

So far so good. But I'm not allowed to talk about my fear of the Nazis. *Weinen verboten*, crying is forbidden. My mother laughs whenever I bring it up.

"I know how to handle people, don't give it another thought."

But I do, because my mother's first encounter with the Nazis back in Münster almost ended in a permanent separation.

A NAZI SPORT Being half-Jewish and living in Nazi Germany means living on a fringe where it's hard to figure out who's on what side. Not even all Nazis fit the stereotype.

Eva's Berlin

Although the official cloak is Nazi garb, Berlin is hiding many Jews and political rebels. We learn to tread carefully and keep an open mind. A potential enemy could turn out to be a friend, just as easily as the reverse. Herr Kunze, our Nazi boarder, is one of the surprises.

In 1944, toward the end of the war, when Berlin's apartments are becoming more and more crowded with people who have been bombed out, we, too, take a roomer. Most of the houses on our street are gone, replaced by piles of rubble and a few burnt-out husks and free standing brick walls that survived the bombs. Our Boarder, Herr Kunze, had lived in a large apartment in a house on the next block. After it was destroyed by an explosive bomb, he came to our house through the connecting basements with nothing but his long black overcoat covered with dust.

Large and broad, with white hair and a deep voice, he gravitates to our corner of the shelter and immediately begins to tell jokes. My mother is taken with his wild sense of humor and my grandmother is impressed by his size.

Ein wirklicher Mann, a "real man," my grandmother calls him and, for once, my mother and I have to agree. We take to him immediately, a warm, fatherly man — just what we need.

They offer him my front bedroom with the large wardrobe and I move back in with my mother. After a few weeks, my mother and grandmother find a uniform in the tall wooden wardrobe. I overhear them saying that he must have been something of a big shot in the *Partei* but . . . it's strange to say, but it really doesn't matter. By now we know that he's as careless as my mother. He makes enough remarks against the regime to get himself arrested many times over and, like my mother, he doesn't get caught. His participation in party activities appears to consist of wearing his grand brown uniform with its shiny black boots and glittering medals and attending a Nazi function about once a month. The rest of the time he spends reading, writing, and playing with me.

A Nazi who likes to play! He endears himself to me, not only because he tells me stories and makes up endless puzzles for me to solve, but because he is messy. He often leaves an island of dirty dishes and food spots in my grandmother's immaculate kitchen, accompanied by little notes.

Ich bin eine Sau. Richard, Prince von Feydinau, meaning "I am a sow. Richard, Prince von Feydinau." Not much of a joke, but the German rhymes, and we children are loyal to those who cross over.

CHAPTER EIGHT

School

THE FIRST DAY   On the first day of school in the *Third Reich*, I dress carefully in the pleated frock that marks me as a member of the upper classes, my navy felt hat covering Lord Fauntleroy curls. I'm carrying the *Schultüte*, a cardboard cone covered with silver paper, printed with multi-hued balloons and filled with sweets and little toys. Finally. It's not just the bag of toys I've been waiting for; I have great hopes for school. For what seems like an eternity, adults have been squelching my curiosity with, "Wait 'til you're in school."

Now, I expect my questions to be answered. Since I already know how to read, I anticipate becoming the star of the class.

Eva's Berlin

Stardom comes easily. My mother and grandfather applaud me at age five when I sing, *Ich bin die Chansonette vom Stern, ein jeder hat mich gern* — I am the singer from the star, everyone loves me — making an extravagant swimming bow.

My mother claps and tells me she already knew when I was four that I would become an entertainer. She imagined me another Shirley Temple with my blonde curls. Then, with a sudden change of direction, she sees me as a diplomat's wife, a millionairess or a tennis star, even though I've never seen a tennis court and don't know what a diplomat does.

My grandmother, too, feeds my sense of self-importance. "You know how to get your way," she says and sends me, "the child," to push to the head of the queue. It's a barbed message, this assurance that I'll succeed. Neither my mother nor my grandmother have what they want, and they don't know how to get it. I'm supposed to be different, for their sake more than for my own. There's something in the way they urge me on that makes me feel bad at the same time I'm feeling good.

Later, I learn that something about their disappointment in men is connected to their wish for my success. When my father wanted to visit the hospital room shortly after I was born, my mother defiantly announces that she sent him away. Why let him gloat over his child? What right had he? He didn't know about labor pains or swollen breasts. I can imagine my mother eying me on the day I was born, breathing the mission into my brain and body, "This birth was a terrible thing God and your father did to me. You'll have to make up for it."

I never questioned my role. School was just a rung on an immense ladder that I would climb to the top. For my mother. For women. For all of us.

A MINOR SET-BACK It isn't working the way I expected. My writing skills are far below average. I expected to learn everything the way I learned to read, as though the skill was already in me, ready to blossom, and my mother and grandfather only had to say a few magic words to activate it. I thought it would be like those white glistening pages we used to rub with a damp sponge to reveal colorful illustrations. But writing is different. The familiar letters are devilishly hard to make. I pass from incredulity to disappointment and rage. We use a little slate board and delicate paper-covered chalk pencils decorated with swirling spirals. How can anything so appealing be so hard to control? For homework, I have to cover the slate with drawings of combs. Why combs? My teacher Fräulein Stodt, assures me that I will master the intricate curves of the first writing exercises after sufficient practice. But I can't seem to do it. I prove the futility of the exercises by failing to learn German script.

I put failure behind me with a shrug of my shoulders.

Eva's Berlin

I can't stand my mother and grandmother's *Leiden*, that particularly German suffering with its ability to hold onto pain, no matter how minute, over weeks and months and years. *Beleidigt. Leidend. Schwer leidend.* Insulted, suffering, suffering heavily. No. I am the best in the class in reading. Forget about the rest.

IN THE CORNER I can't understand why the teacher doesn't let us talk. Most of the subjects are familiar to me. The adults sitting around our table have been discussing problems of good and evil, religion and politics, every night that I can remember.

"Can the Nazis possibly hold their own if the Americans really back the British?"

"Let me tell you what Churchill said on the short-wave."

"Does Frau Paasch have any idea what her husband is doing?"

"Say some of these people are real criminals. Is it right to just take them away?"

"The child keeps asking me to go to church. I just can't stand exposing her to all that crap."

School is my first opportunity to join the discussion. But the teacher insists on lecturing about subjects far removed from my questions, like neatness and order, and the importance of making several copies of anything we hand in. I've learned to call attention to myself by flinging my fingers together so that the bones crack noisily when I raise my hand. She disapproves. Frustrated, I turn to a neighbor to express my opinion. My punishment consists of standing with my face turned to the corner, a place I gradually grow to like. The jagged white line worn into the light-green wall of my niche lets me follow my own thoughts, as the class is led through its ponderously slow routine.

MAMI DOESN'T SEEM TO MIND "I've always liked your spunk. It reminds me of myself when I was a girl," she says, laughing at my accounts of Fräulein Stodt approaching me, ruler in hand, to condemn me to the corner.

My suffering is short-lived. Soon after I reach second grade, Hitler closes Berlin's schools and orders the *Kinderschulverschickung*. Berlin's children are to be placed with families or in camps in the country, where they can enjoy more food and fewer bombs. For me, the risks are too high. My father is a Jew in the United States. My mother and grandparents are in Berlin. Should anything happen to them, what would I do? So far the Berliners have closed an eye to my half-Jewishness. Evacuation could put my name on a roster. Unlike the Berliners, provincial Germans pride themselves on following the letter of the law. We spend a lot of time trying to figure out what to do. In the end, a doctor friend of my mother's provides a certificate telling the authorities that I have asthma and am too ill to be moved. I remain at home in Berlin.

I'm trying to ignore the fact that I've been left

behind. Over and over again the tide carries me away from what was supposed to be — first our life in Münster, then my father, and now school. Roaming Berlin with my few half-Jewish friends, I learn to depend on my sense of adventure to carry me from day to day.

SHELTER LESSONS The end of school is not the end of my education. In the shelter, I become the house mascot. The adults pass the time telling me stories and playing games with me, until a bomb falls and diverts their attention. Herr Kobler teaches me history and geography by bringing down the stamp collection his son has left behind. Frau Kern teaches me to crochet.

The Janovsky sisters, who taught mathematics in high school before the war and occupy one of the posher apartments facing the street, now pay me the kind of attention I'd expected in school.

"Could Eva come and sit with us?" they ask my mother timidly.

Small and delicate in their movements, like brown ducks, the two sisters come up with an endless supply of puzzles and games that teach me enough mathematics to pass entrance exams to the Lyceum — middle and high school — after the war. We often play "hangman" and I watch the pencil become steadier in my hand as we erect gallows on a piece of paper. More directly related to schoolwork, the sisters arrange numbers helter-skelter on a piece of paper, and

I use my pencil to connect them while they quiz me about their properties.

JURCZEK The best part of my education takes place after the second grade, when the *Kinderschulverschickung* closes our schools. My mother finds someone to continue my education in Dr. Jurczek, an old professor who, having spent a short time in *Theresienstadt* for speaking out against the Nazis, agrees to give me private lessons even though he is now under *Lehrverbot*, no longer allowed to teach. Since I am not permitted to learn, we are a perfect match. But there is much more to it than that. Dr. Jurczek is personification of the wise old man from my fairy tales: small, delicate, with a halo of white hair surrounding his balding head. I take to him right away.

I go to him twice a week in the small apartment on the third floor of the *Friederichstrasse*, where his wife keeps the white lace curtains freshly starched and serves me weak milky tea with a bit of honey. He greets me wearing dark slacks worn shiny and thin, and a soft gray sweater. He's the first person I have met who reminds me of my grandfather. From the moment we start, I am ready to learn anything he wants to teach me, and I find out that this is going to be very different from school. He believes I need to learn what he knows best: medieval lays, the songs of the troubadors. He knows unending verses of these ballads by heart, many of which are fifteen to twenty pages long. Each lesson

consists in his reciting two sagas in a quavery voice, as sure
of every syllable as if he'd been born reciting the words. I
listen like someone leaning on an ancient tree, comforted
and awed. Afterwards at home I write a composition about
one of the tales.

I'm in heaven. Tales of valor and nobility, of Sieg-
linde, Adelbert, Wolfram and Gudrun, dragons, witches,
dwarves, tricksters, treasures, curses and magic are as good
as my grandfather's tales, as good as Grimm and Andersen.
We talk about my compositions. Dr. Jurczek understands me
and I understand his ballads. No standing in the corner here.
He praises my writing. He writes a poem in my *Poesie Album*
— poetry album — a journal kept by German girls, in which
every teacher, relative, and friend writes words of guidance.
It speaks of the light that sometimes appears in the darkness
and the difficulty of finding a friend, not in times of sorrow,
but in times of joy. We are such friends.

It is all illegal, of course, but piano lessons are permitted in Berlin and he is posing as my piano teacher. While
we're working, we both keep an ear on the stairs leading to
his apartment. At the slightest noise, one of us sits down at
the piano to play one of the only tunes we know. Dr. Jurczek
plays *The Last Rose of Summer*, or I play *Hänschen Klein*, a
simple nursery song about a boy called little *Hans*. I have
learned to sing it by the numbers of the fingers I use: *Fünf,
drei, drei; vier, zwei, zwei* — five, three, three; four, two, two;
Eins, zwei, drei, vier, fünf, fünf, fünf — one, two, three, four,

five, five, five.

When the steps outside are no longer audible we return to our knights and ladies.

CHAPTER NINE

Jewish

WHAT IS IT? *Jüdisch sein*. To be Jewish. The word crops up in so many conversations:

"Of course, his being Jewish didn't help with the authorities."

"They have money; they're Jewish, you know."

"With that nose, could she be anything else but Jewish?"

"Well, the name used to be Rosenbaum, but that sounded too Jewish, so they changed it to Ross."

"You can say what you want about Hitler, but I say the Jews deserve what they're getting."

"They're going to miss them in the arts, those Jews."

Jewishness. What on earth does it mean? I only know

Eva's Berlin

how the adults feel about it by what it isn't. It certainly isn't good to be Jewish, I know that at the age of three. A jumble of impressions: stones thrown at me in Borghorst, my father being taken to jail, our having to leave Münster, Holland letting my father stay but kicking us out, whispers about so-and-so having been "taken away" or someone else having "got out." My grandmother says that my father is one of my mother's worst mistakes. She has nothing against Jews, she likes to repeat, but she feels their place, as foreigners, is not in a pure German family. Throughout my childhood, I will be am aware that I am Jewish. Half-Jewish. But besides the fact that this is not a good thing, I don't know what it's all about.

> There were about five thousand Jews in the city of Berlin who had decided to go underground, becoming U-Boats in the German slang, to sit out the war.
>
> ANTHONY READ AND DAVID FISHER

I DON'T LOOK JEWISH My mother likes to tell the story of the photographer who asked me to be the poster girl representing the ideal Aryan child. With a bitter laugh, she relates that she got me out of there as fast as possible. But the story is also a feather in her cap, proof that her blonde and blue-eyed child does not look Jewish.

Even though I experience few acts of overt persecution, my Jewishness remains a constant threat, an abyss just under the neat parquetry flooring. The problem is so disturbing, I later realize, that focusing on it would destroy our illusion of safety, and we depend on that illusion to keep going from one day to the next. Like earthquakes in San Francisco, my insecurity is a condition of life, accepted and pushed away at the same time.

It is strange, this feeling of being a part of something so huge, and, at the same time, so veiled. At home, we don't talk about being Jewish. Even I, known for my insistent questions, learn not to ask. The few conversations about our Jewishness stay with me, like my mother's giggles about watching my Grand Uncle Sigmund, wearing a tasseled prayer shawl over his shoulders and balding head, bowing over and over again. I want to see him pray — the way he does it sounds so different from what I've seen in church with my friends — but I never get a chance to. I can make sense of my mother's giggles because the picture of my wizened uncle in a shawl reminds me of the man I saw dressed up in ladies clothing in the play *Charley's Aunt*, but I suspect something else. My mother thinks praying is ridiculous. I pray often, but I don't talk to her about it because prayer, too, is a taboo subject at home.

I hear that synagogues are being burned, but I don't know what a synagogue looks like or what one does in them. I know from my mother's Jewish jokes that rabbis have

It was 1938 in Berlin and 19 year-old Hannah was shocked to hear that her father had been arrested by the Nazis. She had been raised in the Lutheran faith of her mother, and her father's being a Jew had never been an issue, much less a deportable crime. So she went to the Gestapo to complain. Officers said they couldn't help her... "We don't help your kind," she remembered being told.

WARREN HOGE

183

beards, and I like beards, but I've never seen a rabbi. I know that Jews are good people because my father is a Jew. I also know that most everyone else says bad things about them and my mother always defends them. I work so hard at not believing the bad things that I end up believing all Jews are good.

What about God? Another taboo subject in our house. I spend hours ruminating about what kind of a God could let these things happen. He wouldn't let the synagogues get burned if he was in them, I decide, so he probably wasn't. But I'm sure he is in some of the Catholic churches I have seen; I can feel him in the dark wood carvings and the benches worn down from kneeling. I can feel his presence more in nature, where I make my root gardens in our back yard. He's where the spring rains turn the meadows outside Berlin into a carpet of flowers. But then I have to ask myself again: if he's around, why didn't he stop Hitler? Slowly, I come to the conclusion that he, like my father, is basically a good man, but too much of an optimist. Like the Sorcerer's Apprentice, having got things started, he probably couldn't stop them once they had a life of their own. I keep up my own conversations with him at night because I feel he'll do what he can, even though, by now, it isn't much.

I MAY LOOK JEWISH SOON My mother likes to make remarks about the Jews' crooked noses and flat feet. She uses the Berlinese expression *Wüstenlatcher*, which literally means "desert-waddlers." She is worried about me.

"Let me look at your foot," she says, and takes it in her hand. "I'm afraid that you have your father's flat feet. We've got to do something about that."

The orthopedic inlays make me feel like socks are wadded up in my shoes. I hide them under my mattress among my books.

My nose is also inspected regularly for signs of growing larger. My curly hair — another dead give-away, according to my mother — is braided to make it look straight. I am a *Mischling*, a *Halbjüdin*, the German for half-breed, whose impurities could bring disaster on my family. At any moment, my nose, my hair, or my feet could cause me to be recognized. My Jewishness — at least, the traits that I gradually come to associate with it — lies just below the surface, an invisible stigma that threatens to mark me as one of the doomed.

I become alert to the slightest sign of disapproval. I learn to please. I learn to charm. Since my family expects me to be strong and unafraid, I behave as though nothing bothers me. "Passing" as a full German becomes a vital necessity, much as "passing" as fully American would later on.

Sometimes my attempts to represent myself as purer than pure German misfire:

On a playground outside a hotel in Baden-Baden, where we are on vacation, a new friend and I are playing dolls. While our dolls are eating a family meal, my new friend talks about her father.

Eva's Berlin

"My father is at the front, fighting for Germany," she says, glowing with pride.

Wanting to impress, I say, "Mine is a general in the German army!"

Neither one of us knows exactly what a general does, but my new friend is properly impressed. We play the rest of the afternoon, having one of the doll family's sons go to war, come home wounded, and find love with teddy bear nurses in a hospital. Later that evening, her mother, in a flutter of excitement, approaches mine.

"Well, my little girl told me something I certainly didn't know. It must be marvelous to be married to such an important person."

My mother was worried. What had I said?

"Oh, actually, we've never thought of it that way."

My friend's mother continues, "But how else could one think of it? A general in the *Reichsarmee!* What could be more special than that?" She is fawning now.

I watch the tension increase in my mother's neck and jaw muscles. In Germany, any such reference can be checked and found to be fraudulent within hours.

"Oh, this is quite embarrassing," she says, quickly inventing a story. "I hope you'll forgive my little daughter. My husband wanted to join up, you see, but he's really quite ill. And Eva has always made the world up the way she wants it to be. I'm so sorry."

My ears fill with the loud hum of fear. What if they

check on us and find out my father is a Jew? I watch for signs of hidden officiousness in my friend's mother, but see only a softening of her face as she smiles, "No need to apologize. She's just a child, and a patriotic one at that. I understand completely."

It looks as though we'll be all right, but it was a narrow escape. My mother tells me not ever to mention my father again to a stranger.

LEARNING TO ACT I shrug my shoulders when I think about it. Oh, well! So my father isn't a general. What difference does it make? But shrugging my shoulders isn't enough. I have to find a place for myself in a world that defines me by what I am not. Not Jewish enough to leave Holland with my father; and the new regulations say I'm not Aryan enough to join the Hitler Youth, not that I want to. But when there are no practical solutions, my imagination can always be counted on. I begin to make up a more suitable self. My books supply characters ranging from the fairy tale princess to Huckleberry Finn to a passionate Latin Catholic nun, whom I envy for having carved a cross in the palm of her hand to prove her faith. I take on a part of this one and try on a part of that one. It's different from "putting on an act" for entertainment. I am acting in earnest. I believe I am the per-

> Jews are notably absent in films of the Third Reich...by the 1940's they had almost disappeared from Nazi film, a cinematic "final solution."
>
> TOM REISS

son I'm trying to become. One day I give orders and mete out favors among my friends with an air of *noblesse oblige*. The next day I am a limping orphan. The fact that my behavior changes, with what someone else might consider alarming frequency, doesn't bother me or my family. Most of the time they don't even notice. On the few occasions when they do, they tell me I'll become an actress some day.

A GAME   On particularly lonely days I walk up to the busy corner of *Rankestrasse* and *Tauentzien* and watch the passers-by. I am looking for a special someone with whom I will play my scene. He should be tall and attractive, in a suit, and, if possible, a raincoat. When the right person nears the intersection, I enter the crosswalk with a pathetic limp, moving ever so slowly until my target, full of sympathy, offers to help me across the street.

"I can do it by myself," I say, becoming even more pathetically handicapped, dragging a foot behind me. The man puts his arm around my waist and supports me as I limp to safety.

"Thank you so much. I hope it wasn't too much trouble."

"Not in the least, no trouble at all. None at all."

What a strange mixture of feelings — true and false all mixed up, until I don't know what's what. There's my true need for a grown-up's attention, and the false limp, and the true pleasure of play-acting, and the false joy of putting something over on an innocent bystander. The excitement of doing something illicit makes me repeat it again and again.

All the characters I play are cute. I have perfected a look that, mirrored in the photographs that trap it, will embarrass me when I am older. The little girl in the taffeta dress or the raincape, the one playing on the beach or skiing down the hill — all of them pose coyly, smiling with just the touch of flirtatiousness popularized by the current magazines. It is a role that earns instant applause. My mother threatens to photograph me whenever I cry. I learn to keep smiling. The girl seen by others is neither sad nor Jewish: she's cute.

YELLOW STARS   I can't get the different roles I play to fit together. Under a surface of charm and ease lies a passionate intensity which I recognize as my real self. This is the self that loves God and makes up rituals and prayers centering on her favorite trees and animals. This Eva is serious and committed and, physically at least, fairly competent, but — and this will puzzle her for years to come — she isn't recognized by the grown-ups, who talk to her as though she's a slightly retarded

pet. On the other hand, the adults often ask her to do things they should do themselves. She feels powerful and powerless all at the same time.

Eva's Berlin

Becoming a cool judge of reality, I expect less and less from adults. They don't help me with my terrifying dreams. I often wake up, sobbing, from nightmares in which German eagles rip me to shreds in their cages or witches butcher me and wrap parts of my body in wax paper to sell at the village market. Nobody comes unless I scream for help.

In our neighborhood, I see yellow stars proliferate on the overcoats of some of the grown-ups, but I don't have to wear one. They're large, two inches across, and stand out garishly on dark city clothes. A scuffle occurs near *Miericke's Konditorei*. About five S. S. men surround two small Jews, thin old men in long, thick woolen overcoats and dark hats. The Nazis are pushing them back into a storefront and then pulling them out again, searching their overcoats, barking questions at them and then shoving, almost throwing them back.

What's happening makes me feel crazy inside. I want to go and hug the two strangers. I want to yell at the Nazis. But

just as in a dream, when I couldn't move away from tanks bearing down on me because my feet were stuck in mud thick as molasses, I feel paralyzed. The Nazis load the men into vans just like the keepers do the ducks in the zoo. After that, I hide in doorways when I see Nazi uniforms coming. My star is invisible, yet I'm afraid they'll see it anyway. When the Nazis pass, I learn to get so interested in the window display that they don't know I'm there.

OMA KLARA'S LAUGHTER   My Jewish grandmother Klara has eyes that laugh even when she is serious. Her gray curly hair bounces around a face that is perpetually amused. Like my Berlin grandmother, she wears the dark clothes of old women, but on her they have a draped, generous quality. Nothing throws her. There is a story that, during a formal dinner for twenty, when one of the cousins dropped the casserole to the floor just as she entered the dining room, my grandmother said, "Well, now we know where dinner's being served," and began to scoop hers from the floor, inviting the  others to follow. My Uncle Karl has the same laughing eyes. When he tells jokes, he hardly ever gets to the punch line, because by then he is laughing so hard that tears are rolling down his cheeks.

Eva's Berlin

In Berlin nobody ever mentions them; they might as well be dead. When I ask my mother whether we can visit my grandmother's house, she changes the subject. Except for a few short letters that tell us they are still alive and well, my father's family drops from our conversation. Once, my mother says that my grandmother and Uncle Sigmund are so old that they probably won't have to go to a camp. I cling to that bit of information. Though I don't really know what a concentration camp is, the expressions on people's faces tell me it's a dark, frightening place. My mother refuses to give me any detailed information. She says it would be bad for me to know.

At night, before I go to sleep, I ask God to protect my grandmother and Uncle Sigmund. In the daytime, I put special stones on the altars I've made in the roots of trees — a black one for my Uncle Sigmund, and a rose-colored one for my grandmother. Breathing on each three times and folding my hands, I pray:

> *Lieber Gott, mach mich fromm*
> Dear God, make me faithful
> *dass ich in den Himmel komm*
> that I may go to heaven
> *Und beschütze meine Oma*
> and protect my Oma
> *Und meinen Onkel Sigismund,*
> and my Uncle Sigmund
> *dass sie zu Hause bleiben dürfen.*
> that they may stay at home.

Toward the end of the war, my mother reads me a letter telling us that my grandmother Klara died in her sleep. It is written by a neighbor who found her on the floor by her bed, in a peaceful, curled up position.

"We should be grateful," my mother says, "because she never did have to go to a concentration camp. How wonderful that she died at home."

How can I be grateful for my favorite grandmother's death? I spend a long time practicing curling up in my bed and then rolling out and dying, to see what it might have felt like. I believe it hurts to fall out of bed and I think my grandmother curled up in a cramp of pain before she died. I grieve her quietly and for a long time. About a year later, my mother tells me that my Uncle Sigmund, my grandmother's brother — the one who prayed — has been taken to *Theresienstadt*, a concentration camp.

> **B**ut Marion had a fixed idea, one that was important for her to hold onto. If she could find four pebbles of almost exactly the same size and shape, it meant that her family would remain whole.
>
> LILA PERL

"We should be grateful," she says. "I've heard that *Theresienstadt* is one of the best camps."

I have stopped asking about concentration camps. But I wonder what can be "best" about something so horrible you can't even talk about it? My Uncle Sigmund is said to have carried his best overcoat over his arm, hiding a hunk of his favorite sausage. He had a gift for essentials.

Eva's Berlin

CHAPTER TEN

Potatoes and Onions

COFFEE AND CAKE

The soft summer rain of my childhood
fell on ruins that smelled of wet stone and dust.
In the warm, empty afternoons,
it whispered secrets of meadows
heavy with camomile and mint.

Rain fell in soft cadences,
blanketing the city in muffled sound.
Inside, watered coffee and sugared bread
were served to aunts and uncles,
while children traced the paths
of raindrops along window panes
moistened by their breath.

Eva's Berlin

We hang onto the remnants of normalcy with an iron grip. The Sunday afternoon *Kaffeeklatsch* is more than just a get-together for gossip and coffee; it is our way of continuing what Germans in my part of the country have been doing for about one hundred years. Every Sunday morning, in the early years of the war, finds me looking forward to the afternoon, the smell of coffee, the table set with our best china — white with gold rims — and cakes baked by my mother and grandmother. My mother bakes a black and white cake with swirls of chocolate, and paints frosting into the fluted grooves of the cake. Afterwards, I lick the lukewarm chocolate from the spatula.

Sometimes we buy cakes from my friend Ingrid's bakery around the corner. Danish coffee cakes with jam and and *Bienenstich*, sticky and yellow like honey. Ingrid takes me into the warm back rooms where the baking is done in huge ovens and lets me help myself to the ragged edges cut off coffee cakes. The smells alone are enough to send me into ecstasy, but free cake! An egg-yellow mannah topped with buttery *Streusel*. Back at home I listen to gossip from Frau Paasch or Fräulein Wagner and concentrate on eating as much cake as possible.

The idyll doesn't last long, of course. Soon there are no more cakes. Rationing means we can eat only essentials. Sweets are a luxury. When the rolls aren't available any more, my grandmother bakes a wet, gluey concoction from dark rye flour, graced for the *Kaffeeklatsch* with a bit of sugar she's saved for special occasions. I can't get used to crunchy sugar on top of wet bread. It makes my mouth curl around my tongue.

HUNGER PANGS Berlin is one of the worst places to be during the war years because we rely on ration cards. While the privileged few *Parteibonzen* high up in the party seem to have an unlimited supply, most Berliners learn to make do with less and less. People with relatives on farms supplement their share with a little extra butter or milk, or the occasional carrot or cabbage. Our own diet is sparse and dull: lots of potatoes, a bit of butter and meat, and lots of onions. Fresh fruits and vegetables are a thrill; an egg a miracle.

Occasionally, on summer vacations on the Baltic coast, we pick blueberries. Sunlight catches the beach sand on the forest paths; the sky overhead is stained dark blue, almost violet. Barely aware of the sting of my sunburned skin, I strip the fruit from scratchy branches, eat a handful and put a handful in my pail. The sweet-tart flavor of berries stays with me the entire day.

Such days are few. At home, we leave the table hungry most of the time. Before a meal, the smell of food makes juices run in my mouth. Potatoes with their odor of warm steam, the sourness of onions, the slightly burning aroma of flour being browned for a gravy: I sit down at the table ravenous with expectancy. But I have learned not to dig in. Calculating my fair share, I arrange it carefully on my

Eva's Berlin

plate so I can stretch it. My favorites, like potatoes mashed in gravy, have to be divided so that some is eaten right away and the rest is saved for the end of the meal. In the middle, I arrange and re-arrange the food in different patterns so that I don't have to sit and watch the others eat, or, worse yet, have them offer me some of their portion. A piece of potato can be a head, with carrot sticks arranged as a crown. This way I finish when they do, with the scratch of hunger still in my mouth.

Once upon a time — and it seems long ago — when the words 'I am hungry' meant I'm ready to eat again, I did not know what hunger was. I did not know that hunger was a mind-killer, a growling beast inside you demanding to be fed and occupying all your thoughts.

ILSE MARGRET VOGEL

It is a strange experience, this constant hunger, because, although it never leaves, it doesn't announce itself by name, either. It's there in the background, a gray, dismal feeling, like sand scratching the back of one's neck after a day at the beach. There's no point in thinking about it since nothing can be done, but I can't rid myself of it, either. It's a feeling of void, of absence where there should be presence, and it seeps into every corner of my life.

LIES Sheets of blue and yellow paper marked off in squares, our ration cards look like the lotto cards I play with. Bringing them to the various stores in exchange for goods feels like a game to me. Ten yellow squares for a quarter pound of butter. Twenty blue squares for two slices of ham. My grandfather is pleased that, at the age of seven, I'm old enough to shop.

But one windy day on my way to the bakery, a strong gust blows through the ruins, sweeps one of the cards out of my hands, and my luck turns. The ration card, our allotment of bread for a whole month, is gone.

My frantic search in the piles of rubble that flank the street comes to nothing. I can't find it. Panic closes my throat. Automatically, I walk to the bakery as I was supposed to, stand there for a moment looking vacantly at the counters, and then turn around to walk home, trying to tell myself that everything will be all right if I can just think of an excuse.

I decide to tell them the card was stolen. Why lie? The card is gone either way! But I have to convince them a thief is to blame for this disaster. Back at home, I stand in the kitchen, empty-handed, and rattle off my tale of woe.

"I put it down on the counter and I turned my head just for a minute, and then, when I turned back around, it was gone and I saw this big man leaving the store really fast."

I'm convinced; my tears are flowing. But my grandfather doesn't believe me.

"No, this doesn't sound quite right to me," he says. "Something's murky here. I'll go back to the bakery with you and we'll get to the bottom of this."

Each person received seven different ration cards a month, each a different color: blue for meat; yellow for fats, cheese and other dairy products, white for sugar... green for eggs... orange for bread... pink for flour, rice, cereals, tea and coffee substitutes...purple for confectionary, nuts and fruit.

ANTHONY READ AND
DAVID FISHER

199

Eva's Berlin

I can't stand it. It'll all come out! Worried, I say, "The thief probably fled a long time ago, *Opa*, there's no point in trying to find him!"

But my grandfather won't be dissuaded. I drag my feet as we walk the few blocks to my friend Ingrid's bakery in the dusk. My grandfather's silence is unbearable. When we reach the lights of the bakery, I have a moment of completely irrational hope that everything will be all right. For a moment, I'm convinced that there really was a thief, that someone caught him and our ration card will be restored. Then my grandfather asks the storekeeper to tell him what happened and I realize that I can't stand the charade any longer. Quickly, I pull my grandfather out of the store and tell him the real story,

"I lost the card and I lied about it."

He gives an almost imperceptible nod and remains silent as we walk home. If he were only angry I would feel some relief. But my *Opa* is not angry, he's disappointed, which is much worse. I walk by his side, feeling more ashamed with every step.

Back at the apartment, standing by the rainbowed fishbowl, I am shamed by all of them: grandfather, grandmother, even my mother. Through *Opa's* silence I understand, perhaps for the first time, that there are some things one doesn't lie about. What if someone else had been blamed for the theft? I am heavy with the weight of what I might have done. My punishment, a week's house arrest, is soon forgotten, but the look in my grandfather's eyes is with me still.

ORGANIZING FOOD   *Organisieren* is a term used by the Germans to mean getting something any way one can. Günther, Erika and I learn that we can "organize" food in the zoo, where park-like flower beds are planted with carrots. In the late afternoon, when the keepers are busy feeding the animals, and the ticket takers are counting money in the tills, we make our move. Using our knives to break the topsoil, we pull the carrots out of the dark rich earth and stuff them into our bags. When my mother asks, "Now where did these come from?" I answer, "There's a lady that had too many in her garden" or "Frau Meyer had them left over on her truck."

As well-known feather collectors, we are able to enter the bird cages without attracting much notice. Günther calls our attention to the fact that feathers are not the only treasures to be found there. Birds lay eggs! Would anyone notice if we took an egg now and then and slipped it in among the feathers? Our plan works. Delicate and small, light blue or powdery green, speckled or plain — they find their way into our bags.

At home, my mother quickly breaks them into a bowl, a feast of fresh yolks, deep yellow, melting in our mouths. My explanation is easily accepted. The eggs are gifts from our friends, the keepers.

Eva's Berlin

Our luck doesn't hold, of course. After a few months, a zoo official in a dark uniform runs into us in the narrow corridor between the bird cages.

"What do you think you're doing here?"

Oh no! He is a small, older man, whose eyes look at us piercingly from behind wire-rimmed glasses. He must have watched while we stuffed the eggs into our bags. He stands very close to us and lectures us long and hard. I smell garlic on his breath.

"Don't you know that the zoo is a museum and the museum is part of the *Reich*? We have laws here, just like the rest of the country, and we expect the German youth to obey!"

Fear rises in my throat. What if he finds out we're part Jewish? My hands are cold and clammy. I barely hear him as he warms to his main topic: the eggs.

"These birds are pure breeds, you know. We have to collect each egg carefully in order to propagate exotic species. Whole bird groups could die out here because of people like you!"

My body, tense at first, now begins to dissolve in rubbery waves while insect wings beat a tattoo in my mouth. Soon, I am floating down into the pit, barely present as he drones on. From his far-away voice I understand that we are to appear at the administration building the next day.

We dress somberly for the occasion, Erika and I in the dresses we wear on Sundays, Günther in knickerbockers.

After waiting meekly in front of the tall, wooden partition that admits us to the office, we are taken to see the director, a tall, thin woman with braids on top of her head, in a brown wool dress with a high collar.

"Having a zoo card is a privilege. You children seem to think it entitles you to do whatever you want in the zoo! As German children, you should know better, especially you, young man," casting a devastating glance at Günther, the oldest.

"The zoo belongs to Berlin, to the *Reich*, don't you know that? It is our duty to be on our best behavior here at all times. What kind of home did you grow up in that would permit stealing from the zoo?"

Though Günther and Erika's faces look serious and collected, I believe they are as frightened as I am. Will she call our families? Worse yet, will she look us up in one of the many registers that would tell her we are not pure Germans?

"Lack of discipline is the last thing we want in a German home. I'm going to send a note to your parents. I hope it makes an impression."

We shift in our shoes, look down at their scuffed tops and the ribbed brown wool stockings we are wearing.

"Don't you know that our country is at war and we must think of Germany, not ourselves? Don't we know that Germans are honest? That stealing is a crime? What if everyone behaved as you do? Then we wouldn't have the victories we're all so proud of, would we?"

The longer she talks the less frightened I feel. She is delivering a well-rehearsed speech. She believes she is addressing pure Germans. She hasn't recognized us, after all. Slowly, I feel the warmth of blood returning to my face and hands. What a relief! We just have to bear up until the sermon's over, then we can leave.

"Of course, we will withdraw your privileges here at the zoo. Please hand me your zoo cards."

Losing the *Zookarte*, the card with my picture that entitles me to enter the zoo without charge, is a serious punishment. I will not be able to visit the playground or my animal friends. For a moment, the three of us are properly humbled. We hand over the cards and learn that we will get them back after three months. Then we go home.

Once outside the zoo, the relief of not being found out to be half-Jewish sweeps over us and we start to laugh uncontrollably. Günther starts us off with an imitation of the director's moralizing tone and Erika and I take turns playing outlaws who couldn't care less about the consequences.

"*Scheisse mit Reis! Scheisse mit Reis!*" I yell, skipping down the pavement toward my house and imagining her brown dress covered with turds and rice.

"We don't care. We don't care," Erika and I start chanting, and pretty soon we are bounty hunters whose cleverness allows us to thumb our noses at the *Reich* and everything that goes with it.

POTATOES AND ONIONS In the last year of the war, 1944, our meals consist of potato soup, onion soup, potatoes with onion sauce, and potato salad. The food looks gray and soggy, and, try as my grandmother does to vary the taste, it tastes gray as well, starchy and thick. Again and again, the mouth gets ready to taste something and what it gets is the flat, mealy taste of potatoes and flour. After a while, even the onion tastes like stucco.

We watch as each other's faces become pale and our bodies thinner and thinner. The grown-ups seem to be slowing down. None of them moves as fast as they used to. We are all tired a lot. Walking becomes strenuous after one block or so. No one lifts me up any more, though I'm not very tall. When we cuddle in bed in the mornings, I can feel my mother's bones stick out. When the war ends, my mother who is of average height, will weigh eighty pounds and I, aged eleven, sixty.

CHAPTER ELEVEN

My Sex Education

GRANDMOTHER'S ADVICE   I'm hoping to remain flat-chested. At the playground where we climb bars and rope swings in shorts and undershirts, being flat-chested is a mark of beauty in a girl. Breasts don't look right. The older girls are embarrassed by the way they jiggle and bounce on the bars and rings. Boys are lucky. They don't have any, and compare ours to pudding.

My grandmother tries to interest me in romantic possibilities.

"Soon you'll begin to swell under your blouse," she says, with a look that drives me wild with its pretensions to know better. "And you'll love it. The boys will pay attention to you. You'll blossom like all young girls do."

It is one of the rare occasions when my grand-mother says anything with a positive tilt, and I hate her for it. I won't grow breasts. I will stay strong and flat. The only boy I like is Günther and he couldn't possibly like those jiggly things.

"Breasts," I tell my grandmother, "are ugly and I hope I never get any."

HOT GOSSIP   Every night, my mother and grandfather glue themselves to the crackling short-wave radio, listening for news from abroad to find out what is really going on in the world outside of German propaganda. The news is never good news as the "short" war goes on longer and longer. But that isn't what makes me tremble. I am expecting the arrival of men in brown shirts to take my mother and grandfather away because listening to foreign news is a crime.

When the radio is shut off, the rest of the long evening is spent with the grown-ups sitting around the table under the fringed rose silk lampshade gossiping, while my grand-mother clatters her disapproval in the kitchen.

February 4, 1940. In Germany it is a serious penal offence to listen to a foreign radio station.

WILLIAM SHIRER

Fräulein Wagner, who lives directly above us, brings a bottle of wine. She looks like a yellow pansy with her bouffant hairdo and her soft *écru* silk blouses. The war is forgotten as I watch the women sip their wine and warm to their topic. They are discussing Herr Paasch's latest advances.

"Can you imagine, a man bald as a newborn baby? I wouldn't even dance with him with that protruding belly!"

"He was wiggling those bushy eyebrows at me and suggesting we meet for lunch! It's really too much!"

"Where does he get those shiny, checked suit coats?"

"And then he sent me roses. You too? And boxes of candy?"

With the conspiratorial look that women get when they discuss a flirtation, they exclaim, in turn,

"NO! Never could I imagine . . . " and their eyes widen and their giggles continue.

I try to imagine either one of them in Herr Paasch's arms and start to giggle myself. I recognize that they're playing, just like Thea and I play empress and court. In real life, they're happy to leave him to Frau Paasch, who gives everyone within earshot household advice.

"Have a pot of hand cream on every sink in the apartment to keep your hands soft and pretty," she has told us more than once.

"Lubrication is so important," she often whispers to my mother, trying to evade my ears for a reason that escapes me. I don't understand this last piece of advice or why it makes my mother and Fräulein Wagner laugh.

My mother and her friends repeat the phrase when she leaves, accompanied by more giggles. They pity her for being married to Herr Paasch, who is clearly dying to be unfaithful. I, on the other hand, feel justice is being served because Frau Paasch doesn't like children. She is a snob who ignores me like she ignores Frau Meyer of the vegetable cart. She carries her blonde, beautifully coiffed head high and ignores my bids for attention with a pained, bothered expression.

"Do I have to endure this?" it says to my mother. "Can't you do something about her?"

Then I remember the stories about her husband and smile a malicious smile.

THE MEANING OF RED Fräulein Walter lives in the wing to our left. On the wall of her living room is a photo-

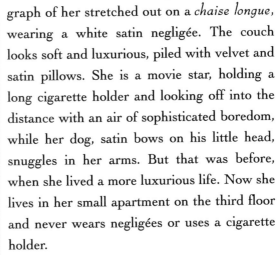

graph of her stretched out on a *chaise longue*, wearing a white satin negligée. The couch looks soft and luxurious, piled with velvet and satin pillows. She is a movie star, holding a long cigarette holder and looking off into the distance with an air of sophisticated boredom, while her dog, satin bows on his little head, snuggles in her arms. But that was before, when she lived a more luxurious life. Now she lives in her small apartment on the third floor and never wears negligées or uses a cigarette holder.

Red is her color. Her immaculately clean apartment is full of it: bright, fire-engine red. She has a red toilet seat, a red kitchen table and chairs, red shelves, a red velvet bedspread, and she is always buying new red pots and pans for the kitchen. In my mother's mind, the languid woman in the photograph, together with all that red, leads to a single conclusion: Fräulein Walter was a call girl in the upper echelons of the *Reich*. Unwittingly, she became a party to secrets that would have cost her her life if she hadn't changed her identity and moved to our house.

I have a hard time decoding this story. There seems to be a connection between these secrets and that other mysterious subject, sex, but, at age eight, I don't understand enough to figure out what might have happened. Was she having an affair with a married Nazi, like Herr Paasch wanted to have sex with my mother and Fräulein Wagner? Did the Nazis tell her something about somebody Jewish? There's no use asking my mother because, while she clearly likes to include me in these conversations, she never explains. She refers to Fräulein Walter as a *"grande horizontale."* The fact that her apartment contains neither *chaise longue* nor Pekinese is proof to my mother that Fräulein Walter had to hide all traces of her former life.

"But *Mami*," I say, "then why does she have the photograph on her wall for everybody to see?"

My mother does not bother with such petty objections coming from a child. Swearing me to confidence, she insists she'll never tell the Nazis when they come to question her about it. As far as I know, they never do.

Eva's Berlin

Fräulein Walter is my friend. Though her skin is beginning to look puffy and her hair is an inky blue-black that must be from a dye-pot, I admire her looks. She is langourous and slinky, with long legs usually clothed in slacks, different from the housewives on the other floors with their printed flower dresses and kerchiefs to keep their hair from getting dusty. She wears more make-up than anyone else in the house: mascara to emphasize her already dark brown eyes, and bronze-colored rouge on white powdered skin. She looks like someone special, an actress, or a medium, someone who knows things others don't. But instead of giving herself airs like Frau Paasch, she acts like she could be my older sister. We spend hours looking through her clothes, many of them red. Sometimes she models them for me while I sit on the couch, drinking mint tea out of a delicate porcelain cup.

On special days, she shows me her lingerie. She has a lot. Bras of white satin with violet lace and violet ribbons, black bras and panties edged with red lace, slips made of shiny materials with scalloped edges, some heavily embroidered with white and pink flowers and birds. Her nightgowns are the *pièce de résistance* in reds, pinks, grays and blacks — shiny, voluminous yet transparent, clothes fairies or princesses to float in. Could my mother be right about Fräulein Walter's past? I imagine her young and raventressed, with handsome noblemen and officers feeding her candy as she lies back on her satin pillows.

ROUMANIAN LOVE AND POKER One of my best friends in the apartment house is Petri, a Roumanian ill with tuberculosis in the upstairs apartment he shares with his girlfriend Else in the wing to our right. I visit them regularly to play poker with Petri. We play for pennies, pretending we are wagering large amounts of foreign money. Rubles, dinars, and francs are our favorites. Hours pass. Playing is serious business. I learn to order the cards with aces high, through kings, queens and jacks down to the lowly deuces, taking care that he doesn't see my hand so that I can bluff to my heart's content. Sometimes I catch him smiling behind my back. I often win. Later, he will tell my mother that my financial future is assured.

He is a handsome man, so thin there isn't much to his body, but his head is dark and intense with large coal-black eyes that sparkle when he talks. His long hands, the streaks of

gray in his black hair, and his olive skin make me think of the djinns and sorcerers in my illustrated fairy tales. He longs for the Black Sea as I imagine my mother wishes my father would long for us. My mother tells me that he'd been high up in the Roumanian embassy when war broke out and, because of his TB, couldn't return to Roumania.

"Else is a prostitute, too," my mother says. "She saved Petri's life by taking him in and nursing him."

I search the apartment for the red items that are the dead giveaway, or remnants of luxury like satin negligées or *chaise longues*, but finding none, ask my mother why it's so different there from Fräulein Walter's.

"Else worked in a lower-class brothel," my mother explains. "She was a *Matrosenmatratze*, a sailor's mattress, not a *grande horizontale*, like Fräulein Walter."

I still don't know what a prostitute does but I know there's something wrong with this story. After all, Petri is hardly a sailor.

Now that I am eight years old I am more and more doubtful about some of my mother's stories, and yet I don't want her to stop telling them. Small-boned, short and slim, with her light brown hair and her animated face, she is a wonderful storyteller. When she imitates the characters in her story, her eyes get large and her voice and intonations change. With a novelist's soul and no inclination to write, her stories go back and forth between the world we live in and the one she imagines. For her, imagination wins over reality every time. She talks about what she sees in front of her, but she can't resist embroidering it. I know some of it is true. Petri really is from Roumania, and Fräulein Walter did lead a very different life once, and I know people have secrets, because we do.

I learn to listen without either believing or disbelieving her. I put what she says in a special compartment in my mind with things I can't be sure about. Time will tell me what is true or false.

BIRTH CONTROL My mother scares me with tales about the many children she aborted. When we come to the corner of *Tauentzien* and *Rankestrasse*, she reminds me that she lost babies on a corner just like this one, dropping pieces of them on the ground.

"I was just coming home from shopping for a new dress, and then, right here on this corner, I lost a baby. I remember a nice man carrying me across the street and calling an ambulance."

I suspect the point of the stories is a fantasy I so often play out myself, the beautiful, helpless victim, but I can't get the mutilated babies out of my mind. I've learned that babies are carried inside the mother's body until they are born and I don't want to believe they can just drop out. I take to watching the pregnant women I see on the street striding along, apparently confident. When I come upon an actual newborn baby, I'm proud and relieved that it survived. I take these stories as evidence of my own strength and resilience. Where others were lost, I remained. But when I see a pregnant woman, I worry.

Eva's Berlin

THE LOVE AFFAIR   I decide that married sex must be unspeakably boring from the way my mother rolls up her eyes when anyone mentions it and how she keeps saying that she can't understand that my father could want so much of it. Clearly there is only one thing to look forward to: the love affair. Her stories are filled with examples: her friend Renate, for instance, who came to the office every Friday with an overnight bag, ready to meet a gentleman friend for the weekend. Her married friend Barbara, who met an actor for forbidden trysts in the posh Eden hotel, and had breakfast served to her in a canopied bed with lace flounces.

My mother lets me know that she, too, had many offers. There is a glint in her eye when she tells me that men often compared her face to that of a medieval madonna. I think she wants me to believe that she is a medieval madonna and when a man recognizes it, he has no choice but to fall fatally in love. I believe her, of course; I'm in love with her myself. Her white oval face would grace any painting, I agree.

"I don't understand it," she tells me, "but they all compare me to the same painting — a van der Weyden in Amsterdam."

I never actually see the magic working. Though I observe my mother in the company of various men when we go to plays or the opera together, or sit in a restaurant, I never hear them talk about her classic nose or mention

Flemish painters. I give her the benefit of the doubt and assume they're behaving differently because extravagant compliments can't be paid in front of a child. Only Herr Paasch lets me see the dogged admiration my mother feels is her due, and he behaves the same way with Fräulein Wagner. It is difficult to figure out what's really going on. As far as my mother's swains are concerned, I'm not quite sure if she ever takes one of them up on their offers, or even whether there are any offers — but for myself, I am looking forward to having love affairs. My mother's eyes tell me they are going to be a delicious surprise.

CHAPTER TWELVE

Grandfather's Lap

BANANAS

As a sapling, a dapper Polish
count without job or country,
my Berlin grandfather
explored Philadelphia.
They grew bananas there,
he said, as large as
new-born babies.

The pharmacy, where
he clerked, throbbed
with emergencies.
At midnight, he'd
mount the cow pony hitched
to a post in front of the store
to give first-aid
to wounded cowboys.

Eva's Berlin

When he returned,
hottentots danced
in the streets, "Like this,"
he said, and my grandmother
marched out of the room.

Bananas big as babies.
My mother believed every word.

EXCURSIONS   I keep in step with *Opa*, my body
brushing against his thick, black overcoat. Its texture feels
rough, important, the opposite of the softer, more pliable
textures women wear. Despite his short, delicate appearance,
he is my ideal man.

  We collect old bread and crackers all week for our
excursions to parks, castles, and the zoo. At the *Alexander-
platz*, we feed pigeons that land on any available part of
our bodies. Sometimes there are forty or fifty of them in
the square. The whir of their wings, the soft-hard touch of
their delicate claws on my wrist, the fluff of the gray down
when a breath of wind catches it: I feel as if I'm in another
world.

  In the early years of the war, 1940 and 1941, when
there is still food to be bought, we go for foot-long hot dogs,
Wienerwurst, washed down with apple cider at the *Kadewe*,
West Berlin's biggest department store. Leaving the big
store with its displays of fashionable clothing, we can't pass

the hat section without trying on a few until we are caught by a salesgirl's disapproving eye.

"Really, I could understand better if the child were unsupervised, but sir, I'm sure you know better than to set such a bad example."

My *Opa* takes off the wide-brimmed straw with the yellow veil. I remove the taupe flapper cloche. We maintain our serious, dignified, but chastened expression until we are out of the salesgirl's sight. Then giggles overtake us. On the way home, I can still taste the crunchy spiced sausage combined with the tartness of the amber-hued cider.

We are visiting *Sans Soucis*, the palace of Frederick the Great copied from the *Petit Trianon* at Versailles. Gathered for the tour in a light, airy room, we are given felt slippers, like the ones *Opa* wears at home, to protect the highly polished parquetry. Mine are too big for my six-year-old feet; I feel as though I'm pushing two boats across the floor. While our guide points out Frederick's love of everything French — the high windows, the ceilings decorated with angels — *Opa* winks at me, our signal to slow down. Making sure the tour has moved on, we dance. My grandfather always waltzes — that is his tempo — whether there is music playing or not. He is just the right size for me, his touch familiar and light. Where my head reaches only the waist of most of the adults I know, I come up to his shoulders. I am flying around the room; his mustache is bobbing. After a few turns, we stop because I am dizzy, overcome with whirling

pleasure. When we rejoin the tour, we wear our most stu-
dious expressions.

STORY TELLER   Sitting on the edge of his chair at
home, I rearrange *Opa's* sparse gray hair, making sure that
all the hairs are evenly aligned and the part over his right ear
perfect. He is wrinkled and skinny and his clothes more comfortable than fashionable. At home he wears corduroy slacks
and well-worn flannel pajama tops and gray felt slippers. I
can't think of anyone whose looks please me more.

My grandfather is the answer to my prayers for
escape from my duty-bound grandmother; he believes in
fun the way she does in work. I can usually find him reading in his favorite chair near the bird cage, while the sun
plays on his book and Peterchen walks up and down the
edges taking small bites out of the pages. He never objects
when I curl up on his lap where I can feel his skinny legs
under my buttocks. He can always be depended on for a
story that adds an additional character to Grimm's and
Andersen's tales: a curly-haired, blonde little girl growing
up in Berlin.

"Once there was a very sad queen who lived in a
dark, dark forest and yearned for a little girl."

My grandfather describes the castle, its dark towers,
its beautiful tapestries, and its delicate tea sets, and assures
me that none of this brought the poor queen any pleasure.
Finally, he gets to the point I've been waiting for.

"And then, one fine morning, the queen's steward opens the castle's wide gates, and guess what he finds? A little blonde girl about six years old and very appealing, dressed in poor, ragged clothes."

I knew I'd have a part in this story.

"The queen summons the steward to bring dark, hot chocolate and delicate white biscuits for both of them. The little girl's name is Evelyn."

So close to my name! Delighted, I follow adven-tures that give the queen someone to love and allow Evelyn to develop into a beautiful princess.

Opa's ever-available lap holds me sobbing after I've fallen down outside.

"Oh, my knee hurts so much, it's killing me, *Opa*."

Then he rocks me, and says with a little dry laugh,

"There, there. I know it hurts, but it's not the worst thing in the world. Just imagine, if all the children with hurt knees in the whole wide world got together, you'd be one of them."

I can't help but laugh when I think of all of us children hobbling toward our grandfathers.

Eva's Berlin

THREE ARISTOCRATS An early photograph, delicately tinted in tea browns and engraved with a florid advertisement, shows my grandfather and his two brothers. In pure white shirts and swallow-tail coats, they are the epitome of young aristocrats. My grandfather is sitting elegantly poised on a banquette, his two brothers casually standing in front of a potted fern. They look like they've taken a moment out of an afternoon at a great lady's salon, chic, rakish and without purpose.

My grandfather's sister Anna neither worked nor married. She was the Bielinski who fainted when a meal, party, or ritual needed dramatic punctuation. The family then broke into gales of laughter, preparing my grandfather for my grandmother's tragic declamations. All three brothers played the piano. Strauss and Mozart, mostly. Every now and then, with an eye toward my grandmother, who sat with her knitting like madame Defarge, they broke out into some "hot jazz" they'd picked up on a trip to the United States.

THE MAN WE LOVE My grandfather's romantic appeal thrills my mother and me.

"Your grandfather had quite a way with women," she tells me.

"He still gets letters from one of his old girlfriends. I have seen them. They're scented, can you imagine?"

I really can't, but I like to imagine him as sought

after by women — young and light, waltzing any number of ladies around fern-filled ballrooms.

My mother is the apple of his eye. She makes a point of asking him how she looks before she goes out in the evening. He pays her extravagant compliments and winks at her when she is dressed up in her little black suits and platform patent leather heels.

I find my romance in the movies. Black and white and sepia-toned, just a few delicately tinted with color, the ones I prefer invariably deal with the love affairs of married people. Marriage is dull, they say, and husbands and wives are entitled to excitement and intrigue. The women in these films are beautiful and seductive; they can sing and dance and send out sexual rays so powerful that any man in their presence is disarmed by the mere hint of a smile. Their language is soft,  their clothes silky; they slink and whisper hoarsely and smile Mona Lisa smiles.

In one particular film, perhaps it was called *Wiener-blut*, after the Strauss waltz, a young actress fascinates her director in a love scene improvised using only the alphabet (they are using my language — I am just learning to spell in

Eva's Berlin

the second grade!) and I'm so completely enchanted that I lose track of time and come home late for dinner.

My ears ringing with waltz music and the romance of the plot, I dawdle through the darkening streets. The director will make a star out of the young actress in a film set in a chalet in the Tyrolean Alps; the waltz — still ringing in my ears — will be a signal of her later triumphs. I am waltzing home. How can I be expected to remember the time?

On my return, I am confronted by three stern faces. Where have I been? Don't I know it is dark outside? Of course I know, I used a flashlight! Don't I care that they worry? At the very back of my mind, I probably care a little. But I'm not going to admit it. I'm going to tough it out. My grandfather is having trouble keeping his stern expression. I feel sure he would have made the same choice. Staring at the rainbow reflected in the glass fishbowl I tell myself, "I don't care what they say or how they punish me, they'll never be able to take this away from me, never!"

I can see myself living in the Alps, rehearsing my next scene for the director. I even come up with a variation of his technique. Perhaps we could try numbers for our special dialogue: I would open the door, saying,

"*Eins.*" He would deliver an arm full of roses.

"*Zwei.*" I would hand them to a tiny, perfectly dressed, maid, waving her off stage.

"*Drei.*" He would kiss my hand.

"*Vier.*"

My grandmother has left the room in a huff. She can sense my lack of contrition. I promise to come home before it gets dark. Then I am sent to bed without dinner.

OPA'S ANGER I expect my grandfather to be on my side when I'm in trouble but I learn, on at least one occasion, that he can get angry as well. I have a cat named Miezerich, black with white markings and long silky fur, who sits on my lap for endless hours of reading. One day I decide to test my friend Horstl's belief that cats are indestructible by swinging him around by the tail.

When *Opa* comes into the room, he stops me just as I grab the cat's tail for another try and takes the cat in his arms. Stroking him gently, he talks to me in a stern, unfamiliar voice, "So that's what was going on in here. I heard the thumping but I couldn't believe you would do anything like this! Never, never do anything to an animal that you wouldn't have done to yourself. Have you lost your senses entirely? You're torturing your friend!"

He doesn't stay to explain or make things better. He just leaves the room. I am too crushed to respond. What just happened? My grandfather looked like he might hit me. I hear a soft voice inside tell me that I do know what he's talking about, but I am too proud to admit it. I repeat to myself that I intended no harm. I want to tell *Opa*, "It's my cat. I know it would have let me know if it was hurt. Cats have nine lives. They don't care."

Eva's Berlin

But I don't say any more about it. I just sit on my bed staring into space. Later that day he takes me aside to tell me that, although he was angry, he loves me no less, that he will always love me, no matter what I do. He is my dear familiar *Opa* again. Immensely relieved, I believe him and he keeps his word.

ILLNESS My grandfather has asthma. Before we go anywhere, my grandmother and mother remind him to take his pills. Every once in a while, he becomes short of breath and looks pale as a ghost as he leans on a wall gasping for breath. I keep very quiet to help him recover.

It's strange, but even though he is the only one of us with an illness, my grandfather is the only person I trust to know what to do for himself. I try to help everyone else. My mother, my friends, even strangers seem to me to be in constant need of assistance. I save coffee for my mother and try to invent ways to help her win the battle against her mother. During the brief period I'm enrolled in school, I help my friend Ingrid with her reading. When I see a stranger looking lost on the street, I go up and offer assistance.

Only grandfather has managed to convince me that he is taking care of himself. With him I can be sure that, if there is to be any taking care of, he'll take care of me. The idea that he could be taken from me is unthinkable, despite the unmistakable signs of his illness. On the days when his breathing is labored and his skin takes on a bluish tinge, he uses an inhalator, an amber glass tube equipped with a rubber ball that he squeezes to force medicine down his chest. On those days, I am not allowed on his lap. He sits reading quietly, with only the budgy for company. But I fail to read the signs. He is my own indestructible *Opa*.

DEATH AND WITCHES   The night my grandfather dies starts out like so many others. The siren sounds. We go down to the basement, where my grandparents stay in the big room with the others while we sit and joke under the stairway. A few bombs fall but nothing very near us. It lasts a little more than an hour.

After the last siren calls us back upstairs, I hear adult voices saying my grandfather is unable to walk and has to be carried back up in his chair. Three neighbors carry him. I think to myself he's probably had one of his attacks, but, of course, I'm not worried. I am afraid, however, of going to the back room to see him. Though I am eight years old, take streetcars by myself, walk to the zoo through the city streets unaccompanied, this is different. To get to my grandfather, I have to pass by a windowless storage room at the end of the corridor. I am convinced that witches live there, and I make sure I always cross that corridor quickly, with my eyes straight ahead, so they won't be able to grab me. Why does he have to be in the back room? I don't go in there unless I have to.

Eva's Berlin

The next morning, the house is silent except for my mother's weeping. Dressed in dark clothes, she and my grandmother are sitting in the kitchen when I come down. They don't have to say anything. I know. I sit with them, staring at a fly that is making its way along the patterns of the wax cloth on the kitchen table.

When the undertakers come to carry *Opa* out on a stretcher, I see that my mother has put a lily in his folded hands and a candle by his head. He looks waxy, his skin yellowed, almost transparent. I have never before seen a body without any sign of movement. He looks like my grandfather and, at the same time different, as though someone had used him to make a copy. His silence is unbearable. Before, I counted on his talk, quietly burbling, like a little spring running over rocks. Now his silence is cold and empty.

He was so alive just yesterday. Walking back into the apartment, I am sure that my real grandfather is still in the room I was afraid to enter.

During the day, I soldier on. At night, I bargain with God, Mary, the saints and the angels to bring back my grandfather. I promise to make any sacrifice they might want — my bed-lamp, my friends, my visits to the zoo — if only I could have my *Opa* back. For months, my hopes are kept alive by glimpses of my grandfather. There, that small man on top of the escalator at the *Kadewe* department store... surely that is... or the small man in the raincoat huddled in the doorway waiting for the rain to stop? Sometimes I start to run to meet him before I remember. In my dreams he looks the same as always: my *Opa*, telling me stories, taking me on walks, his pockets filled with chocolate. On waking, the pain of his absence is scalding.

Little by little, he begins to disappear. Gradually, I get used to the world without my grandfather. It feels different, like the sensations just before I get sick. Nothing feels quite right. The length of each single day is oppressive, like a weight on my chest that grows heavier with the hours. I become a maker of schedules:

> Get dressed.
> Eat breakfast.
> Brush teeth.
> Brush hair one hundred strokes.
> Help in the kitchen. Ask to cut vegetables.
> Take care of feathers.
> Call Erika.
> Read *Nesthäkchen*.
> Ask if I have to do errands.
> Go to the zoo, don't forget pocket knife.
> Visit Erika.
> Help in the kitchen.
> Eat dinner.
> Listen to the radio-operetta tonight.
> Arrange clothes for next day –
> *Trainingshosen*, sweatpants.
> Read Shakespeare.
> Go to sleep.

Eva's Berlin

If I don't know what I'm doing next, I'm afraid I'll sit and stare and cry forever.

Now that there is no more grandfather to make little jokes about his wife's drama, I am my mother's sole protector. I cuddle with her in the mornings and march through the rest of the day trying to be cheerful and strong. I don't like feeling sad. At the playground, I practice on the bars and rings until the callouses form little mounds on the palms of my hands. At home, when my grandmother begins her criticisms, I draw attention to myself. I start swearing. I tell jokes in which sex and the toilet play a big part.

When food is served I yell, *"Scheisse mit Reis!"* because it shocks my grandmother and makes my mother laugh. My grandmother is so upset with me that she stops making roast chicken just to prevent me from asking for its *Aschloch*, its asshole. When all else fails, I claim I have a headache that needs immediate attention.

After a while I stop seeing and hearing my grandfather in my dreams. I can't feel him anymore. He's gone, like last year's Christmas tree.

CHAPTER THIRTEEN

Baden-Baden, A Lull in the Storm

MOTHER

Outside the casino in Baden-Baden
on white gravel paths
I draw runes, invoking your name.

On a darkened basement stage
dressed in the tatters of
the old Regime: tea-colored lace,
velvet, brocade
Russian marionettes speak Pushkin's lines.
I learn them by heart
waiting for you.

Eva's Berlin

In the soft green vapors of the spa,
my feet part the water of
your pearl bath into fans of
peacock feathers. On a slab,
a lady kneads and pummels
the white dough of your body.

At the *Kurhaus*, I train
sparrows to eat from my hand.
The grand white shell in the park
is filled with players who
know my name.

In the long nights,
I learn to weave
cloth for your night gowns
using mirrors, scented amulets
peacock feathers.

Eyes full of hate and longing
you accept my gifts
sealed in your dream.
I am still waiting for you.

THREE STARS   My mother's vacation rituals require
first-class hotels. Every spring, from 1940 to 1944, we leave
Berlin and take the train to Baden-Baden, where we stay for
the entire month of May at the *Kaiserin Elisabeth*, a small

hotel with a dignified atmosphere and French decor, some-where between a fine house and a sanatorium. The large bedrooms are bright with window boxes full of pansies and petunias. Small reading and writing rooms substitute for the more imposing lobbies of bigger hotels. The dining room welcomes its guests with starched white tablecloths and lace curtains. Our own table is close to the large French window where I practice, without success, refolding the napkins into the intricate fans that greet us at each meal.

The smallness of the *Kaiserin Elisabeth* lets me get close to the cooks and chambermaids who appreciate the interruption in their routine and help me with my explorations. I collect paper forms from the concierge, get rides on the cleaning carts, and help the gardeners dig in the dirt to plant pansies and weed the flower beds. Below our rooms is an expansive lawn filled with white deck-chairs, usually empty, looking like spectators at an invisible event. There, I practice handstands and cartwheels to the applause of the gardeners, and get large green grass stains on my white cotton dresses.

Long corridors, painted a subtle mauve color, run through the hotel's three floors. When it rains, they become lanes for a race-course with small Persian rugs for a final slide at each end. Sometimes, like *Till Eulenspiegel*, the German trickster, I get up early to switch the shoes, carefully set out in front of each room for polishing. Balconies facing the forest become circus trapezes from which I hang suspended in precarious positions designed to frighten unsuspecting guests. The basement houses the laundry where moist air smells of starch and soap and the washer-women let me play with newborn kittens, tiny, blind, and soft.

Close to the Alsace, Baden-Baden's style is more French than German with its mansard roofs and lacy balconies. Flowers appear everywhere. Even the lanterns are surrounded with flower beds. Every house is decorated with planters filled with a profusion of roses, geraniums, lobelia and petunias. The huge *Kurpark* with its old trees and paths lets visitors walk for miles until they reach the country. Winding its way through the park is the River Oos with its banks of pinkish-white magnolia blossoms. Baden-Baden's spring breathes lightness: light yellowish loamy soil, light green leaves in the budding trees, and light, soft breezes.

In the *Kurpark's* center, near the casino and the band-shell, the rich shop for expensive goods in small boutiques. There are shops filled with small clocks enameled with birds and flowers, shops for elegant leather goods, for diamond and gold jewelry, and lace-edged linens. The tourist can listen to music from the bandshell while having an *Eiskafe* in the casino's restaurant or drink the waters for which Baden-Baden is famous. In the *Trinkhalle*, the sulphuric smell is almost absorbed by potted ferns and high glass ceilings. I don't know about the healing properties of these springs, but I recognize the smell of rotten eggs and gratefully down a glass of grape juice instead.

To my great surprise and relief, Baden-Baden is not a target for bombers. In the balmy, sweet air, the quiet hotel lets us forget the war. But it's more than just the air that gives us our reprieve. Even food is more plentiful here. The hotel cook manages to use our ration cards to make delicious meals because the hotel is surrounded by fields of potatoes and asparagus. A small chicken coop at the far end of the garden even produces the occasional soft-boiled egg for breakfast. The forest is dense, with wild mushrooms that carry the musk of the forest floor and add an exotic taste to our meals.

FEVER Painted with chalky greens and oyster shell pinks instead of the unrelenting Berlin gray, Baden-Baden's houses are nestled against forests and mountains. The contrast to Berlin's gray streets is shocking, like plunging from hot water into cold. Perhaps that is why I always get sick.

Almost as soon as we arrive in Baden-Baden, I get pneumonia. Each time, I arrive believing that it won't happen this time because I am a year older — seven, eight, nine — and more resistant, and each year it happens again. I dread the signs that begin with a tickling sensation in my chin and gradually take over my body. My lungs ache in each of their many branches, limbs shake, shoulders heave from coughing, and chills and fevers take their turns. Pinned to my damp bed by pain and weakness, I look forward to the fevers. The waves of heat coursing through my body carry me to the outer reaches of fantasy. I fly through the air with the swarms of birds that pass by my window, small, light, emitting chirps from fever-dry beaks. I shape-shift into a giantess who steps lightly from mountain to mountain surveying her domain. The wide spaces I inhabit are filled with operetta music, Strauss, Lehar, Friml. Accompanied by swirling waltzes, I move swiftly, crossing valleys and streams, touching my toe to the highest fir trees and laughing at the mite-sized people down below. When the hotel maid urges cold drinks, I refuse as long as possible because I don't want to come back to the moist, painful present. Dryness and heat are my passport to freedom.

When I finally return, it is hard to remain quietly in bed. Every wrinkle in the sheets cuts into my skin. My head explodes with pain and feels as though a train were running through it. I get up prematurely only to faint, briefly revisiting the magic kingdom where the light is golden and space vast and swirling before I pass out into blackness. Fainting is one of the few sensations that lives up to its description in the novels I read: the light-headedness, the feeling of being lifted — lifted! — followed by a slow glide into velvet darkness. I practice holding my breath to make it happen, but I lack patience.

Although the room is pretty enough, with its view of the Black Forest behind the pink magnolia trees, I don't like being confined. In this small world, four walls, a nightstand with books with blurry pages, and occasional visitors whose cheery remarks make me feel even more isolated, how can I help but get more and more depressed? I make resolutions. This time will be different: I will get well before I get worse. This time my mind will remain clear, instead of soaking up the illness like a sponge and giving me nothing but dim threads of thought. I will write in my diary. I will write a story. I will draw.

It never works. I come to hate the doctor who assures me that I will be well "in no time." His "no time" is an eternity for me. When I try to get up again after a few days, my head throbs with a low hum and my ears feel as though they are stuffed with cotton. Wobbling and depressed, I return to bed for the usual ten to twelve days. There, gradually, I develop a role with which I entertain myself. Lying back in the hotel's frequently changed, crisp linen sheets, their coolness a blessing on my fevered body, I spread my hair on the pillow and pretend I'm Violetta, the wronged, languishing heroine from *La Traviata*, one of my first operas. I imagine a handsome suitor about to visit and my cough takes on a tragic note. My small, high voice, delightfully altered and hoarse, reminds me of a movie star's. With time, the romance of illness appeals to me almost as much as the restrictive fact of it depresses me. A little stronger, I drape myself in my sheets and blankets, comb my hair so it falls in curls over my nightgown, and bid a hoarse *adieu* to my phantom lover, Armand, who appears reflected in the window pane. Since I can't help but notice that nothing I do makes my eight-year-old body resemble that of the famous courtesan, I develop a great fondness for the curve of my back which, from my kneeling position on the bed and draped with a sheet, looks just right in the mirror.

After the usual ten days or so of illness, I walk around Baden-Baden in a daze of gratitude. The spring air is sweet with blossoms and as clear as the purest water. On the *Merkur*, the highest mountain in the area, the Black Forest's every tree is etched so clearly I can distinguish the needles of the pines. The blue-black of the mountain contrasts with the delicate pink of the fruit trees on the path to our hotel. I run and jump to try to catch a bit of the blossoms in my hand.

FOUR STARS For the last years of the war, we stay at *Brenner's Park Hotel*. Large and spacious, it stands on the banks of the Oos and its front windows look out on Baden-Baden's main promenade and the *Kurpark*. It has terraces and gardens, places to eat inside and out, and a bevy of servants who remain in the shadows, always at the ready. Unlike the *Elizabeth's* staff, they look on me with suspicion. The adults play cards or listen to intimate concerts in the common rooms on the ground floor where the wallpaper is light green and champagne colored and the furniture Louis XV. In our own

> **B**renner's Park Hotel looks like a mini-Buckingham Palace. It is set in a carefully landscaped park through which a charming little river, the Oos, cascades down man-made steps while families of mallards paddle about. The place oozes with bucolic charm.
>
> MALABAR HORNBLOWER

large bedroom, with its down comforters and inlaid mahogany desk, my mother points triumphantly to the flowers and little packets of soap placed there to welcome us, incontrovertible proof of our special position.

In World War II's Germany, children are expected to fit into an adult world. Because I feel there's nothing for me to do at the hotel, I soon learn to find the hidden places that were meant to be played in, but mistakenly used for something else. Like Eloise, the girl whose exploits at the New York Plaza have spurred on so many American girls, I slide down the banisters on the grand stairway with abandon, find greenhouses and trees to climb in, and make a nuisance of myself in the laundry and the kitchen. My mother receives discreet notes from the management beginning, "The hotel staff would appreciate it if children refrained from..." but they simply goad me on to greater adventures. In the early morning, before my mother wakes up, I work my shoe trick again, making sure to replace men's shoes with ladies' and vice versa. Before breakfast, I practice climbing the magnolia trees that reach out to me with their thin, brittle limbs.

FREUDE DURCH KRAFT   Joy through strength. The pile of gravel behind the kitchen is high enough to be used for sledding or skidding. The quality of the stones, white mixed with gray, glistening in the early morning sun, calls for a ritual. Mumbling magical words from all the fairy tales I know, I lay out mystical spirals and geometric designs:

Eva's Berlin

"Elysium ... Abracadabra ... Hexen ... Rübezahl ... Rumpel-stilschen ... Maria's Ruh." After I have acquainted myself with the individual pebble, and laid out an oriental maze of circles and ovals, each with its own magic purpose, I walk around it ceremoniously, adding flowers, mosses and prayers in the appropriate places.

Then the gravel pile makes a new demand. Every morning before breakfast I visit the stones, and after saying the magic words by the maze, I take off my shoes and socks and walk barefoot on the pile of gravel as long as my feet can stand it. Up, down and around the pebbles, slipping and sliding, each painful stab in the arch of my foot a triumph over weakness. *Kraft durch Freude*, strength through joy, is reversed into joy through strength in my mind. Threads of illness still clinging to my body, I am impatient with weakness. This will help me to get stronger. The callouses on my feet are badges testifying to my strength, like those on the palms of my hands from using the bars in the playground. My sense of accomplishment isn't merely physical. Surviving the pain is the most important part. Alone in the early morning hours, I'm mortifying my body like the would-be nun in the story who carved a cross into her palm.

My friend Lilo lives in Baden-Baden. My mother met her mother at the casino and never tires of telling me what a strong, aggressive, able woman she is. Frau Riedel has a strong, athletic body and plays tennis every afternoon. She has the kind of energy the Germans call *draufgängerish*, ready for anything, adventurous. Lilo, who is my age, eight, when we meet, is everything her mother is not: tenderhearted, kind, and shy. Having grown up in the Black Forest, she is my guide on the wooded paths and shows me which trees are easy to climb. Later, when I take her into my confidence,

she finds ancient trees for the root garden I teach her to plant and joins my prayers.

As I get stronger, my mother and I, together with my friend Lilo and her mother, go to a swimming pool at the end of the *Kurpark*. We walk across the large, empty lawn that surrounds the pool in the last morning coolness. Putting on my bathing suit in the large women's dressing room, I am surprised by how beautiful the naked women are, young or old, slim or fat. The reproductions of Renoir and Rubens nudes in my father's art books had always seemed like the illustrations in books of fairy tales, beautiful, but probably imagined. Now I can see that women do look like that.

This new aquaintance with the soft curves of the women's flesh, their breasts and hips, introduces me to the community of women. Sagging breasts are laughingly compared with the taut bodies of young women. One old woman insists on showing us her appendectomy scars every time we see her. The others tease her about being too old to have been at the front. My mother and Frau Riedel don't come into the dressing room with us. They arrive with long flowery robes over their bathing suits; there is no need to change. I like it here. Often, I make up excuses just so I can go back into the changing room and listen to the women.

After we change, my friend Lilo and I spend the morning soaking up sun and water, while our mothers gossip in the shade. The hot sun isolates me in a hot circle and lets me see spiraled swirls of red and yellow and violet that lead to ever more fantastic landscapes, where there is no war and everyone has enough to eat. After a while, back in the pool, water fights with Lilo and the other children return me to reality.

RÜBEZAHL Sometimes Lilo and I and our mothers hike on the old paths that lead to the *Merkur* or to inns at small villages nearby. The blue-black color of the fir trees lends the forest a mysterious quality; its floor is moist and fragrant with velvet mosses. Powdery blue-green wisps of lichen hang from the trees. I remember each of the trails from the year before and pride myself on predicting when a certain root will cross our path.

"If you stumble, it is because a dog lies buried there," my mother says. *Da liegt ein Hund begraben.*

After much thought, I decide it can't be true. Not only have I never seen anyone burying a dog in the forest — and there are many, many roots — but, even if I had, I wouldn't believe that dogs carry grudges beyond the grave and take revenge on perfect strangers.

Lilo shows me where wild forget-me-nots grow and where the trees have roots large enough to make reclining chairs for us. When we reach the spring meadows, our mothers stop to talk and rest on one of the benches, and we make daisy chains from *Gänseblümchen*, tiny blossoms with their egg-yolk yellow centers and frilly white skirts and stems so flexible that we can weave hundreds of them into heavy wreaths for our heads.

The forest leads Lilo and me along its paths, whispering stories. Usually, one of our mothers shouting brings us back, and we return to go to one of the umbrella shaded decks of an inn for black bread and a glass of milk.

Rübezahl is the mythic ogre who lures children deep into the woods and devours them. He is gigantic, his body and limbs made of branches and roots of trees, his hair of moss and fern. Lilo and I never tire of interpreting signs of his presence: that piece of lichen must be part of his beard, this twiggy sound means he is walking very near. We imagine him huge, his legs like ancient trees, his head a tangle of gray, carrying a sack to stuff us into. It is a deliciously frightening game because, in fact, I feel safer in the Black Forest than anywhere else.

Eva's Berlin

THE CASINO   My mother comes to Baden-Baden to gamble. The casino was built to serve the richest people in Europe and it suits her perfectly. Servants dressed like the footmen in Strauss's *Rosenkavalier*, in powdered white wigs and sky blue toreador pants, take her coat. The restaurant is elegant with its crystal chandelier and Bohemian glass mirrors, and its soft, deep, red plush carpet. But my mother goes to the casino for more than the decor. Every day, sometimes twice, she approaches the roulette table with the same obsession she will later devote to alcohol. She never tires of her tales of success when she comes back.

"When you come right down to it, it's the smart ones who win. And your mother is just a little smarter than the others."

"Count von Brandenburg was there betting thousands of *Deutschmark* and winning. Of course, I followed his bets, and then, when I could smell that he was going to start losing, I got out. The others, especially that poor fat blonde Frau Strauss, lost their shirts."

"Marika Süss, the film star was there. She just doesn't have it. I could see it immediately. And so beautiful, with that red hair. She lost everything, and then that rich admirer of hers paid. But you can tell, he's going to drop her."

"One of the Trupps was there. They're big in paint. What a winning streak. But not as good as mine, and then he just couldn't see that it wouldn't last and lost his shirt. I think they're not going to let him play there for a while."

My mother likes to say that she wins at the races by betting on the jockeys, not the horses. At the casino, she doesn't use the mathematics of chance, she reads the players. Every now and then an uneasy flutter in my stomach tells me something went wrong, but my mother never reports a loss.

Despite her tall tales about her winnings, my mother isn't gambling for money. There's an intensity about her when she's about to enter the casino, an expression that reminds me of a movie heroine in a love scene. Perhaps she goes to the casino the way others go to church, regularly and with a beseeching attitude. I believe she's trying to find out whether God loves her.

Winning means she is lucky. When she feels lucky, her eyes shine with delight, like the eyes of nuns I see on excursions to churches, who make me wish to be one. When she's lucky, she knows why she's on this earth. When she loses, she's a lost soul. The light in her eyes goes out. My mother never speaks of God, but I believe that she is looking for him in the casino.

THE PUPPET THEATRE No children are allowed inside the casino's hushed red velvet halls. When the footmen open the doors for my mother, I try to get a glimpse inside, but all I can see are a few shadowy adults standing around large tables covered with green felt. After the doors are shut, I am on my own. I am used to it. Lilo is my only friend, and since she lives in Baden-Baden, most of her time is taken up with school and after-school activities. Here at the *Kurhaus*, I know my options. There is a large restaurant, popular for afternoon tea, a place with potted ferns and roving violinists; there is the glassed-in *Trinkhalle*, always a little steamy, where sulphur water and grape juice are served, and there are other public rooms for grown-up entertainments like lectures and billiards, and there is the puppet theatre.

The *Marionettentheater* is one of the *Kurhaus's* few concessions to the presence of children. There, dolls costumed by Russian refugees who once held jobs with the Moscow Opera perform Shakespeare and Göthe. I see Faust there for the first time, and Lear, extravagantly dressed in velvet and brocade, speaking with heavy Russian accents. Though I watch these plays often enough to know most of the lines, it takes a while to get into the story. I can see the puppets' strings glisten in the spotlight, and their wooden, angular movements look inhuman. In Berlin, I remember seeing *Cinderella* in a large and colorful production. I wanted to move into the castle and marry the prince with his red velvet cloak and his beautiful legs in tights. I wait for these marionettes to convince me that they're human, like me, and after a while, they do. As the plays develop, I forget that they are just puppets and enter the plot.

The theater is meagerly lit because of wartime restrictions and filled with dust, and the marionettes perform their precise, glittering movements in semi-darkness. Scratchy music from a Victrola accompanies the action. Faust and Lear — such sad heroes. I know I could help both of them. If I were Gretchen, I would tell Faust that I would go to another city and raise the child — my mother is raising me without my father — and no one would be the wiser. And as for Lear, I would be just like Cordelia, but smart enough to outwit her wicked sisters so that she could keep her father from going mad. I would keep the tragic plot from unfolding if only I could, but I can't. Then, just before dusk settles in, I am outside in the fresh air again, crying silently because I feel the sadness of the characters as though I knew them in real life.

PASTIMES   Sometimes I play with the white gravel of the *Kurpark's* pathways, rearranging the white stones to make patterns. I make spirals as I do at the Brenner but I forego magic and prayer because this is a public place. Instead, I work on mosaics of stars, horses, rabbits, and cats. Sometimes I draw a plan for an elaborate house. Occasionally, an adult who takes pity on me talks to me for a while, and, in the early years of the war, buys me a sweet. Every now and then, the most glamorous of my mother's younger friends, Marilla, a dashingly fashionable twenty-year-old, takes me for an ice cream at one of the cafes and shows me how to pour a fancy liqueur over the dessert, winking conspiratorially at the waiters. This is what it must be like to be a princess, I think to myself, with waiters for servants. Marilla, who has a complexion like fresh peaches, and chestnut hair down to her

Eva's Berlin

waist, just has to snap her fingers and three young men dressed in fancy red vests jump to attention.

Most of the time, however, I wait near the bandshell, where I can see my mother coming out of the casino, and dawdle around talking to members of the orchestra and to the Russian gardeners. These gardeners are aristocrats brought down by the Communist regime. My mother has told me that they used to come to Baden-Baden to live in the huge villas on the Oos with an entourage of servants, but now they are poor and have to work for a living. I am full of questions.

"Did you live in a huge house near a forest just like this one? Did you have your own personal servant?"

"Yes, he was called Feodor and he was short and fat like the conductor here."

"And was there a park as big as this one to play in?"

"Yes, bigger, and there were none of these silly shops."

"And are you still rich?"

"No," and a smile comes over the large, sad face. "All we could rescue were a few jewels. My wife keeps them under the mattress."

"And the rest is gone?"

"Yes."

It sounds just like what happened to us, only worse. My nine-year-old heart aches for these men, with their almond-shaped eyes, their long black and gray beards and their gentle manners. If I could only have been a powerful empress like Catherine the Great, I would have sent my armies to protect them. I try to imagine them defending themselves against Cossack soldiers brandishing swords and knives. How could they do anything but run? Not one of them looks like he's ever been in a physical fight. They're just like those little Jewish men I saw being tortured by the Nazis in front of *Miericke's Konditorei*. I can see them on a long trek, dropping their many possessions little by little until they end up here.

The white lace of the bandstand's ironwork entrances me. Surrounded by the ever present magnolias and chestnuts with their wobbly white spikes, it is perfect for the waltzes and polkas that are the specialty of the orchestra. I like to imagine myself in a private home, probably a Russian dacha, where a young woman is about to get married, and the orchestra hired to play for the celebration.

When my mother finally appears, my waiting is overshadowed by her success. But I have been waiting and waiting and I know that she hasn't given me a thought the whole time. I am furious at her.

I'd like to say, *"Mami*, what about me? Where is my reward for my patience? For my ability to take care of myself?" But I know she wouldn't listen.

I'd like to say, "I wish the casino would be bombed into a thousand pieces! I hate you for going away all the time!" But there's no use. Instead, I listen.

"No one at my table believed that the number I picked would win again, but it did! It was thirty-nine, my age, can you imagine? Then I put all my winnings on the red, taking an enormous chance, and sure enough, red came up!"

Her eyes are shining, her intensity enormous. That's when she has a good day. On other days it can be different. Then she walks quickly toward the park's exit, almost dragging me behind her, without speaking. I know not to ask her anything because she looks brittle, like she might shatter into a million pieces.

Later, in the United States, when my father and his friends talk about her gambling, they will insist she lost more than she won, much more. They will speak with the certainty of male authorities analyzing a woman's failure. They are doctors, after all, and lawyers. But whether in Baden-Baden or the United States, I don't care whether she won or lost. I resent my mother's gambling with the jealousy of a lover. What is it about gambling? It takes her away and makes her eyes shine like diamonds. If she wants to play games, why doesn't she play with me?

CHAPTER FOURTEEN

Ciro's

A RESTAURANT FOR ADULTS Occupying the entire front section of the first floor of our apartment house is a restaurant called Ciro's. The letters are written in neon across the windowless wall facing the street. I smell its sour smell of alcohol and yesterday's tobacco and increase my pace on the way to the zoo.

On an early spring day in 1944, when I am nine years old, my mother takes me to Ciro's for a special treat. She hints at a business success with a property she owns in Westphalia. We both dress up: I wear my royal blue silk with the white felt *Edelweiss;* she a dark brown suit with a creamy blouse and gold earrings. In the dark restaurant, red plush banquettes, shining white linen tablecloths, tall crystal glasses, and waiters in red coats await us. We sit at a table for two.

Ciro's is different from the hotels in Italy we visited before my father left and those I knew in Baden-Baden. It is so dark, it could be winter or summer, day or night. There are no other children in the room. The familiar feeling of listening unobserved to adult conversation magnifies: I am a spy. My new territory is ominously quiet. I decide to explore.

FOOD MAGIC My first mission is in the kitchen, which happens to be on the way to the bathroom, a place where I have legitimate business. It, too, has a refined, quiet air. The toilet, instead of gurgling like the one at home, flushes subtly, like a glass of water being poured down the sink. On the way to the kitchen, I take one of the flowered napkins put out for the guests and stuff it into my pocket. The cooks are preparing *Krebschwänze*. For me, in that fourth or fifth year of the war, seeing plates piled with saffron-colored rice decorated with jumbo prawns (for that's what they are even though the literal translation is crab's tails) is as exotic as visiting the kitchen of one of the palaces in my father's book of Chinese fairy tales. Soothed by the buttery smell and the soft lights, I return to our table.

I am overwhelmed by the aroma of saffron and fish and the warmth of the large room. Although I've never seen rice the color of a sunset, the smell is so inviting that it feels familiar. When the waiter finally comes and serves us, I am not disappointed. This is the rice of my imagination; this is how rice should taste. The pink color of the shells on the yellow rice reminds me of roses on sentimental birthday cards. I wish I didn't have to peel the color off the prawns. Crunchy and white, they have a surprisingly delicious taste. I wouldn't be surprised if the little black dwarf from the *Rosenkavalier* brought hot chocolate for dessert.

COCKTAILS FOR ONE What surprises me are the "cocktails." It's a new word with an odd sound. Before I can assimilate its newness or inquire exactly what it means, an array of them arrives at the table. There is the pre-meal cocktail, the cocktail that accompanies the meal, and the one that follows, all served to my mother, of course, not to me; I am given a glass of watered apple juice decorated with a tiny paper umbrella. In between courses, several more cocktails are served to my mother by winking, smiling waiters. She is delighted. Smiling back, she drinks the contents of every one of the glasses put before her. Slowly, I begin to have a sense that something is wrong. I'm noticing a change in my mother but I can't put my finger on anything specific. My mother doesn't sense my misgivings. She is in her element. Beaming "thank you's" and leaving a large tip, she lets me know that the waiters have fallen for her outfit. The brown was calculated to set off her pale complexion and her dark blonde hair. These cocktails are part of the flattery she can't possibly refuse.

Eva's Berlin

Back in our apartment, my mother goes to bed immediately, complaining in a weak, unfamiliar voice that the prawns poisoned her. She wants to call the doctor. She is pale. She vomits. I am afraid she's going to die. My grandmother, who can hardly bring herself to enter the room, calls in our Nazi boarder to advise us. He questions me about the meal, and, to my surprise, advises against the doctor.

"Don't be ridiculous," he says to my mother, "you're drunk."

My grandmother, who has been watching from the doorway, leaves the room, slamming the door. My stomach contracts. Herr Kunze tells me not to worry,

"She'll sleep it off," he says, and I notice that she does look sleepy as we leave.

He takes me to his room to show me some new postcards in his collection but I can't focus my attention on them. I'm not really there. Though I can see my feet on the ground, I can't feel them. I am floating around, perceiving blurry sounds and bits and pieces of what he's showing me, but I can't make sense of it because I'm so confused and worried about my mother. I don't know exactly what it means to be drunk, but the way he said it made it seem hideous. One word stays with me. Drunk. My mother?

I've only heard the word once before. When my grandmother and I returned from a mid-morning errand, two women were lolling on the steps leading up to another apartment house, dishevelled, a confused expression on their faces. Surrounding them, a circle of strangers was making insulting remarks.

"They're drunk," my grandmother explained, adding, "and at this time of the day!"

Her tone of disapproval was so intense that I asked no further questions when she pulled me rapidly away from the scene. Instead, I filed the experience in my own private cabinet of horrors, next to the witches in the dark room at the end of the hall. Drunken women. Women who couldn't get up. Their faces had a fluid quality that horrified me. I could imagine them dissolving like the faces I've seen in carnival mirrors. They couldn't talk right. Why not? The crowd that had gathered to watch them, as though they were freaks at the circus, made me want to run away. I wished I had never seen those women. Women who were taunted. And now my mother. I had a difficult time completing the thought.

CHAPTER FIFTEEN

Spring 1945

DREAMING

Snow still covers the flower beds.
Here and there a crocus pushes violet
through a dark circle of earth.
Embraced by the roots of a giant oak,
a child dreams
>> defying lightning bolts
>> under a metal sky.

Eva's Berlin

STANDING IN QUEUES The nightmare begins in April. Rumors are flying.

"They're fighting on the outskirts of Berlin."

"Germany has lost the war."

"Germany won't capitulate."

"Berlin — what is left of it — will be destroyed."

In the last few weeks of the war everything speeds up. There is a feeling of crisis, of something coming to a head. Sirens go off at all hours of the day and night. We are waiting for news about what is to happen, wondering whether we should just go to the shelter and stay there or continue to dodge bombers and flak while gathering last-minute supplies. Feeling frazzled, tired, rushed and frightened is the order of the day.

I am ready to run errands for anyone who asks. Overhead, bombers cross and re-cross our neighborhood. When no requests come my way, I bandage my teddy bears and line them up under the flannel blanket in their special box. They, too, are waiting, and listening to the whistle of exploding fire bombs close by.

We spend the last weeks of the war standing in queues waiting to buy the remaining supplies from stores that finally decide to let them go without ration cards. It is so typical of the Germans that, in those last days of the war, with bomber planes overhead and

> Though it was dangerous to expose yourself to the hail of shrapnel, some housewives stood for hours in front of grocery stores. Many were hurt. Some were killed.
>
> ILSE MARGRET VOGEL

shelling audible from East Berlin, there's not a hint of disorder. No looting; no running amok. Chaos is constantly threatening to break through, making inroads with new craters on every street and blowing dust this way and that, but we Berliners stand in queues, quietly chatting, for a pound of butter or a loaf of bread to take down into the shelter.

I stand in line, armored by my clothes — thick dark pants, wool dress, thick sweater, winter coat. My whole being is concentrated on one goal: to take advantage of the sales and bring home food. I feel absolutely safe. The dust kicked up by flak and bombs bothers me more than the explosions. When a bomb hits close by I watch as others run away frightened while I remain, stoically pleased with the advantage of the shortened line.

Back at home, my mother and I stand at the kitchen table unpacking our string bags and comparing our booty. I take out bread and butter; she has meat. Outside we hear the pop-pop-pop of shooting a few blocks away, and the nasty drone of airplanes flying low overhead to drop their bombs. Now that I'm home and with my family, I can feel the war again. The explosions are so near that the walls shake and plaster falls on our hair and on the table. The sound alone is devastating, a whine that gains in intensity until I feel I'm in the center of

One and a half million buildings were ruined, and 150,000 Berliners were dead. When the air-raids ended in April, 1945, Russian artillery — 22,000 pieces of ordnance — fired shells into Berlin at the rate of one every five seconds.

ANTON GILL

Eva's Berlin

the coming blast; at any moment, I'll be blown to smithereens. Waves of panic run through my chest and stomach. When the explosion finally comes and we find out that, although the bomb has hit close to us we are safe, and it is relatively quiet for a bit, the tension is relieved by the excitement of survival. We are alive! We're still here!

I can hardly wait to eat. Real bread with real butter! But the mixture of fear and rush and crisis eclipses our hunger. Not one of us can think of eating the food until we reach the safety of the shelter.

On our way down, my mother tells me that, coming back, she saw that one of the stores where she had been had been bombed in just the few minutes she was gone. She had been walking home, proud of her acquisitions, in a sort of daze, when she saw that the last bomb had actually hit the house where she'd just stood. Some of the people that had been in line with her minutes before were lying dead on the street. She looks small and pale as she tells us what she saw, the horror of it plain in her voice. She had bent down to see whether a woman she had talked to was still alive and had found her body warm but without breath. The woman had clutched her purse fiercely even in death. My mother shudders and shakes her head. I don't know what to say. I don't want to hear about dead bodies. We survived, didn't we? My mother and I congratulate each other. We are the lucky ones.

THE FINAL DAYS Bunkers are being readied for a longer stay as the fighting approaches our house. The food we have is carried down into the shelter. We have the meat we got at the last minute, the butter, some bread Frau Meyer traded to us for a few slices of sausage. My grandmother brings raisins and the sugar she's been saving in a small net bag. Cots are made ready for overnight stays. We are preparing to meet the soldiers who are shooting the guns we hear approaching closer and closer.

My mother says, "Conquering armies do what they want. We won't have any say-so at all." She says it without fear, with an air of finality, as though she were announcing the news.

In my mind, I can hear the trumpets blaring the accompaniment to an army arriving on *Rankestrasse*, four

Eva's Berlin

abreast, marching in the goose step. Will we try to block their way? Will the men in our house fight to the last? I am praying that they won't, that somehow we'll manage to welcome the conquering army. After all, they are my father's allies, but no one will talk to me about that. When I ask our Nazi boarder, he just shrugs his shoulders and sighs.

Artillery shells, the first to reach the city, burst all over the square. Bits of bodies splashed against the boarded up store front. Men and women lay in the street screaming and writhing in agony. It was exactly 11:30 a.m. Saturday, April 21. Berlin had become the front line.

JULIUS RYAN

"Of course, we don't want to fight, but you know Herr Meyer."

I do know Herr Meyer. He is the husband of our *Gemüsefrau*, the vegetable seller my mother has been coddling, and the only really enthusiastic Nazi in our house. There's no telling what he'll do, or what he'll be trying to force on the rest of us.

In these last weeks before the war ends, we live with a constant awareness of impending disaster combined with hope. Although we've lived in a state of crisis for several years, this is different. For the first time, we can sense that the end is near. Our forecasts alternate between delirious hope that it will all be over and we'll lead a happy life with my father in America, and a conviction that Berlin won't survive these final struggles and we'll go down with it. When I see anyone I haven't seen for a while, I don't know whether I should stay and try for a hug or a deep searching look that says good-bye forever, or hurry on by pretending all will be well.

SPRING BULBS The city is bleeding from every pore. In some places, water mains are broken and people are sloshing through the streets ankle-deep in water. New bomb craters are everywhere. People are scurrying, trying to survive in what is surely the end of the world. Conversations are short and hurried.

"Did you know they had meat left at *Schmidt's?*"

"Did you take bedding down to your storage room?"

"Do you hear them shooting? They sound just a few blocks away."

"Are you still in your apartment? When are you going down?"

Götterdammerung — the twilight of the gods. Twilight it is. Will there be gods as well?

I planted bulbs in winter. They are just beginning to bloom. Looking out of my mother's bedroom window just before we leave our apartment for the shelter, I am caught by their fragile beauty — purple hyacinths, lillies of the valley, and Persephone's temptation, the delicate white and yellow narcissus. I can't abandon them to the bombs whistling all around me. Without another thought, I go out into the garden and kneel on the dark earth, carefully clipping the blossoms for a bouquet. My mother and grandmother, seeing what they consider the height of childish irresponsibility, start screaming,

"Come inside! Right now! Come into the house immediately!"

Eva's Berlin

Their voices sound far away. I move slowly as in a dream. I don't hear my mother, the bombs, or the flak. I feel perfectly safe, as if I am doing exactly what I am supposed to do. I have to pick every flower, without tearing a single petal. The pleated white hearts that make the star of the narcissus, the purple ovals of the crocus, the pink and white and purple hyacinths studded with blossoms must all be carefully arranged.

Afterwards, my grandmother says, shaking her head and making a sour face, "Picking flowers, with shrapnel from the anti-aircraft guns flying everywhere!" My mother cries and hugs me, and helps me find vases.

STREET FIGHTING We can hear the Russian armies on the outskirts of Berlin. A new crackling sound has been

added to the sirens, the exploding bombs and anti-aircraft fire. It's a strange feeling. A beautiful April day, the light green leaves of the Linden trees transparent in the sun, and that crackling in the distance, drawing nearer and nearer.

Hitler is still recruiting. Every male over the age of twelve is lining up near the *Gedächtniskirche* to get a uniform to fight for a Germany that die-hard Nazis still believe will lead the world. They look so ungainly, those little boys in their oversize and torn uniforms, frightened and confused.

I recognize one of Günther's friends, fourteen years old, his face white and drawn, trudging toward a group of them. They are tense and serious. What are they thinking? Is it like playing war, only better? Are they doing it with the blind obedience taught in the *Hitler Jugend?* Or are they just plain scared?

Before we go down to the basement shelter, my mother and the other women in our house care for the wounded soldiers returning from the front, now only a few miles away. There are no physicians, no medicines, just a few untrained women doing their best in rooms rigged with cots. I want to go and help, but they won't let me into that part of the house. The young soldiers often die.

"Not much older than you are," my mother keeps repeating when she tells me the story. I am ten.

Approaching my house I saw an elderly man in an S. A. uniform swing a broad brush and write in big letters BERLIN WILL REMAIN GERMAN on a wall... my house proclaimed WHO BELIEVES IN HITLER BELIEVES IN VICTORY.

ILSE MARGRET VOGEL

THE LAST PATRIOT   Alone in our garden, I make offerings of stones and feathers to the stone gods who live in the large protruding roots of an oak tree.

Eva's Berlin

Just before we are ready to move down into the shelter, we hear Herr Meyer's voice coming over the megaphone, interrupted by sounds of gunshots.

"We are going to win this war," he intones. "Don't even think of raising the white flag. Fly the flag of the *Vaterland*. We can win. We will win and show the world the glory of the German *Reich*."

His voice echoes in the empty street. He is addressing the army of teen-aged boys dressed in the drooping uniforms they inherited from men killed in the war. Berlin is in shambles. The Russians are literally just around the corner. Herr Meyer is alone in his pick-up truck with his megaphone, the voice of the Nazi, screaming, breaking, and continuing with unshaken conviction: completely, utterly insane.

TAKING SHELTER   Soon afterward, we go to our shelter, which has an almost cozy, lived-in look by now. The common area doesn't have enough space for all of us to sleep, so we're using our own storage compartment, a large closet that smells of wet cement. Crumbling walls reveal bricks behind the plaster. We've managed to rig a cot in the long, narrow cell of a room lit by a single bulb. There, my mother, my grandmother and I take turns sleeping. Although we've loaded it up with lots of blankets, the cold seeps through the covers as well as through the many layers of our clothes.

When I learn I won't be able to go up into the air

again for weeks, perhaps even longer, I feel as though I'll be shut in a bricked up-tower for the rest of my life. My throat and chest feel tight, but I talk incessantly. My mother — impatiently — tells me to be patient. But I can't stand waiting, and this is the worst waiting I've ever done. I make a pest of myself.

"But, *Mami*, what is going to happen?"

"When are they going to come?"

"Why can't I go up to the apartment, just for a little while?"

"When are we going to eat?"

"Did you bring my books?"

"What can I do to pass the time?"

My mother makes a meal of the supplies we picked up earlier in the day. Watching her spread butter on the pumpernickel cheers me up a little. I place a white towel on the cot and the three of us sit down to eat our meal with focus and concentration.

Eating calms me for a while, but then I get restless again. The cubicle is so small and so dark that I can't read, and in the common room where people gather, the atmosphere is even grimmer than it was during the air-raids. People are sitting quietly for the most part, some obviously frightened, others busy discussing the possibilities.

> Under ideal conditions, Bemann believed, 200,000 fully trained and combat seasoned soldiers would have been needed to defend the city. Instead, what he had to hold Berlin's 321 square miles, an area almost equal to that of New York City, was a miscellaneous collection of troops ranging from 15 year old Hitler Youths to men in their seventies.
>
> JULIUS RYAN

Eva's Berlin

"Let's hope this goes with a minimum of violence."

"It's hard to give up hope for Germany, even now."

"The honorable thing to do would be . . . "

"Those Ruskies have one hell of a reputation."

"Will they put us in a camp?"

They look like people sitting around a corpse. I can feel the tension in my own body. For once, even my mother and her friends can't find their sense of humor. Conversation dries up quickly. Everyone is so worried about having to share that they eat furtively, taking a bite out of a slice of bread hidden in the pocket of a thick winter coat, or hiding it away in their storage compartments like we did. The latrines, rigged in pails, fill up and give off a foul stench because no one dares to go up above to empty them. I try not to go to the bathroom even though I have to. Some people sleep, others sit and stare. It is as if we've used up all the camaraderie during the last years of the war. Now all that's left is dread. It's the worst time of all, this waiting for it to be over.

CHAPTER SIXTEEN

The Conquerors

AT THE PLAYGROUND

On a spring morning
after the thaw
a child exploring dirt
on the playground
picks up a handful of skin.

A well-used rag
it has its own consistency
neither
leather nor flesh.

She imagines it
attached to the hand
of a very young soldier
who died, fighting a lost battle
on the playground
of the Berlin zoo.

Eva's Berlin

RUSSIAN SOLDIERS The shots come closer and closer. Finally, we hear tanks entering our street and the shelling gets even heavier. We remain in the shelter, waiting. Every once in a while someone goes up for a moment, only to return to tell us that the fighting is still heavy. My mother worries about what will happen to the wounded boys who now have no one to take care of them. Then we hear high Slavic voices approaching our cell. Moments later, Russian soldiers wearing heavy boots and massive winter coats enter the shelter.

Listening as they walk past our little closet, I am about to congratulate my mother on our invisibility when I see two soldiers standing in the doorway of our storage room. One pulls out a gun and holds it to my mother's head, gibbering Russian and pointing to the prone body of my grandmother on the cot behind us. He is tall, with high tartar cheekbones and small deepset eyes and wears a big military winter coat that almost covers his boots. The other soldier is slighter in stature and milder looking, wearing the brown uniform of the Russian army. My mother quickly analyzes the situation and tells me that they believe my grandmother is a soldier. Moving slowly and gently, she gestures that they are mistaken, that my grandmother is an old woman, her mother, demonstrating the relationship by showing that she is my mother.

I am frightened. I feel the poignancy of every moment: the soldier might actually pull the trigger and my mother crumple dead on the floor. I can see her lying there and his gun pointing at me, next. Behind the panic lies a detached curiosity about how the plot will turn out. Perhaps this really is the end and we'll all be dead and never see my father again. But maybe not. Maybe we have a chance. I hold my breath.

The soldiers are gruff, their faces unmoving, like masks. Minutes become hours as we stand there, our bodies exploding with the desire to live. After what seems like an eternity, though it could only have been a few minutes, the one holding the gun motions the other one to go to check my grandmother who has been asleep through the whole drama. He approaches slowly, carefully, like one approaching a mine. Then my grandmother lets out a snore and he sees her old woman's face. He smiles. He motions to the other that it's all a joke. They've been looking at a grandmother. We are saved.

> Instantly, the light was cut off by a large figure, filling the door frame: a Russian soldier with a gun slung over his shoulder and a pistol in his left hand.
>
> ILSE MARGRET VOGEL

Seeing and hearing more and more Russian soldiers enter our cellars is like nothing I've ever experienced before. They are all men, for one thing, and we almost all women. Men acting as if they have a perfect right to enter our house. What will they do with us? Soon the Russians are giving orders and threatening us in a language we can't understand. Some pull guns, some swagger. We sit huddled together surrounded by our few possessions, desperately worried.

Eva's Berlin

URI, URI The soldiers' demands are difficult to decipher. "Uri, Uri," they keep saying, and after we consider all kinds of exclamations they might be making in Russian, we understand that they want our watches, the German word is *Uhr*.

We could never have guessed. Jewelry, yes, and money, perhaps, but watches? Later, we learn that these can be traded for land and animals back in the Russian villages.

Smiling broadly, the soldiers add watch after watch to their wrists with the pride of children winning tokens in a game. They seem to like children. When they see my mother and me, two of them come over and show us worn, yellow photographs of their own children, wearing dark blouses with lace collars for the portrait. Soon I have an important role to play. Whispering instructions to each other and to me, Frau Meyer surreptitiously places her watch in the deep pockets of my dark blue winter coat for safekeeping and encourages the other women to do the same. Proud to be useful, I walk around with my secret stash, knowing that no one will ask what I have in my pockets. The ruse works. No Russian soldier suspects and, after the first week, I return the watches to their rightful owners.

FRAU KOMM' Then they rape the women. After a few women sitting near us have been taken, we come to believe my mother has been spared because of "the child," and I am serially adopted. Careful to avoid being seen by the same soldier twice, I am passed around so that those whose child

I'm pretending to be can escape the ominous, *Frau komm*. Literally translated, it means, "woman, come," and it is uttered in a terrifyingly commanding voice.

At first it seems like a game to me, the men coming down into our basement and calling out this woman or that. But then, when the women return, slowly and alone, I realize that something hideous is going on. Their mouths are contorted in a way I've only seen just before someone vomits. Their eyes stare and their pale faces lack expression; they look blank, in shock.

"What's happening?" I ask my mother.

"It's part of the war. Men do it at the end of every war," my mother tells me. "They do what they want with the losers. The women just have to take it."

Frau komm, words like manacles. There is a lot of talk afterwards. One woman shakes all over and keeps repeating, *Schreckliches Schwein*. She's calling to the soldier a horrible pig. Another woman affects bitter humor and says, "It could have been worse." I don't know what they're talking about and for once I don't want to find out. What I see in their faces frightens me.

WHAT WE EAT The next few days are a blur. We're surviving on the food we brought down with us. Strange, those moments of pure joy over the taste of smooth, sweet butter or the pleasure of biting into meat in the midst of this chaos. Soldiers are coming in and out of our shelter; at the same time, we hear that some others are moving their wagons into our courtyard and making their quarters in our apartments. We don't know what's really going on except that we have to stay where we are, in a basement teeming with people and the stench of close, unsanitary living. After a week or so, as one or another of the adults stealthily takes a peek into the upper world, we learn that our incarceration won't last much longer. The adults begin to make forays into the streets.

Herr Paasch returns from above with meat that Frau Krause cooks on a camp stove without asking where it came from. Biting into it eagerly because I'm used to the taste of meat again, it tastes odd but I eat it anyway. I've learned not to complain. Later, Frau Krause tells me that it had been cut from the carcass of a horse lying dead on the corner of our street. She is proud of Herr Paasch's resourcefulness. I feel like I've been tricked into eating the corpse of a friend, and I vomit. After that, I stop eating altogether for a while.

> **W**onderful meal at noon — potatoes with salt. In the evening potato pancakes fried in cod-liver oil. Taste isn't so hot.
>
> JULIUS RYAN

As more adults venture upstairs to their apartments, they return to tell us that the Russians are camping in our courtyard. They're setting up huge supply wagons with bedding inside and large campstoves. This is not at all what we expected. A conquering army that's willing to camp outside? We were sure they'd take over our apartments and, if we were lucky, offer us a room. Now we're beginning to hope that we can return to our own homes.

My mother and I decide to go have a look. As we enter our apartment, we see a large military uniform hanging on the coat tree in the hallway. A few of our things have been moved to make room for boots and a dark coat lined with sheepskin. Someone is living here but he must have gone out.

Blessing the occasion that allows me to escape the disgusting pail, I go to the bathroom. While I'm there, I hear voices, my mother's and a deeper male voice, but I can't make out any words. As I'm coming out of the bathroom, I see my mother running out the door of our apartment and across the courtyard, screaming my name. At the same time, a tall, uniformed soldier is speaking to me in Russian. I'm looking at him, trying to understand what he wants, when my mother's screams become more and more hysterical and I start to walk backwards toward our front door and then quickly turn, running to join my mother. Why is she so hysterical? I feel no danger. Later she tells me,

> **S**he told how she took care of the wounded soldiers in the cellar, how she butchered a horse found shot on the street and carried a pail of the meat home to eat.
>
> URSULA VON KARSDORFF

"I ran because I was sure he'd rape me, I was just sure of it. And then I ran but as I was running, I thought, my God, he could rape you. That's why I started screaming."

THE RUSSIAN MESS A week or so later, the soldiers let us go back to our apartments. They are fully encamped in

Eva's Berlin

our courtyard. We've heard that they came to Berlin through farmlands, taking what they wanted as they went. Still, when we see several horses and a cow in our courtyard, it's hard to believe our eyes. Cattle in the middle of downtown Berlin! I find a horse tied to our window frame. He pushes his big brown head with a white flame down the center through the cardboard replacing the long-gone glass, and starts to gnaw our radio. I couldn't have wished for anything more magical. A horse eating a radio! The exchange is definitely to our advantage, since the old set gave off nothing but horrible squeals, anyway.

> In their crude way ... the Russians tried to help us as best they could. They were extremely good to me.
>
> LILA PERL

Our animal visitor warms the room scarred by falling plaster during the final battles. When I sit in my grandfather's chair he pokes his head inside and lets me feel his velvet nostrils and scratch the silk of his ears.

Fräulein Meyer, who used to live in the country and knows about milking, makes use of the cow. Early in the morning, before the Russians are up, she sneaks past their wagons to the backyard where the animal is tied to a tree, and fills a tin with warm milk. Another miracle: this milk, compared to the blue watered liquid we've been buying with our ration cards.

Gradually, the Russian camp in our courtyard becomes the center of our neighborhood. Seeing how hungry we are, the soldiers offer to feed us from their canteen. It is hard to trust that an army can be kind as well as cruel. But we're too hungry to give it much thought. We accept the food enthusiastically. Every day at noon we line up with cups and plates for our measures of soup and bread. The soup is red with tomatoes and slivers of beef floating in it. The bread is dark and chewy.

Little by little, we're getting to know the Russians and we find ourselves liking them. They're a gruff lot and we don't understand their language nor they ours, but, gradually, we come to understand that they are trying to find a way to live with us, rather than to exploit us. They are different from the Nazis. After the first week, they neither steal nor rape, nor do they make a show of their authority with us or with each other. They remain strangers, but strangers who try to be helpful and, in doing so, reveal an endearing human awkwardness. I learn some Russian:

Maslo — butter.

Nye ponyemayo — I don't understand.

Dos vedanya — good-bye.

Spassibo — thank you.

The soldiers enjoy teaching me, much like the adults in the shelters did during the bombing. They are big, jolly men who smell of garlic and onions, which they eat raw. When I try to imitate them, they laugh themselves silly.

ROMANCE One day, a short, squat man with a reddish mustache and watery blue eyes comes to our door with his

Eva's Berlin

cap in his hand. He hems and haws in the doorway until my mother persuades my grandmother to invite him in. My grandmother is petrified. She hasn't forgotten her first encounter with these soldiers — but my mother has the unstoppable expression that comes over her at the outset of an adventure.

Seated at our dining room table, the mustached soldier produces a bottle of vodka and a raw onion and looks at my mother with intense, admiring eyes. In pantomime, because he speaks no German, he directs my mother to first drink a slug of vodka and then follow it with a bite of raw onion. My mother, insisting that my grandmother and I witness the scene from the door, upright sofa just behind her, does as she is told. After a few cow-eyed glances and several drinks, the Russian produces a rhinestone bracelet and hands it to my mother, who accepts it reluctantly. She is flattered, of course, but I can tell that she is worrying about what will happen next. Nothing happens. The point of the visit was to give her the gift. The soldier's smile lights up the leathery old face like sun breaking through morning mists and, with an exaggerated bow, he makes his departure.

Here is another story for my mother's collection. She

On May 4th, Ilse Antz slowly stepped from her Wilmerdorf cellar for the first time in daylight since April 24th. The streets were strangely quiet. "At first, unaccustomed to the brightness, I saw dark circles before my eyes. But then I looked around. The sun was shining and spring had come. The trees were blooming..."

gathers an audience and highlights the soldier's clumsy bows, invents extravagant compliments addressed to her beauty, and, then, with a triumphant air, shows off the bracelet. To her great surprise, Fräulein Walter, who has been following the story with great interest, declares it as her own! A soldier apparently took it from the third floor and delivered it to the first. After a few more cow-eyed, well chaperoned visits, the soldier is transferred along with his regiment, and my mother, greatly relieved, returns the bracelet to the giggling Fräulein Walter.

NORMAL LIFE BEGINS AGAIN We grew fond of the soldiers' rough country faces and the sing-song of their voices. Most of them were peasant farmers who sat whittling little pieces of wood and singing sad songs in the evenings, people like ourselves, missing their families. It's true, they were cruel when they arrived. But then they changed. We were to look back on those few weeks of Russian occupation as an interlude between the cold steel of the Nazi regime and the bureaucratic militarism that followed when the Four Powers took over. Times were still chaotic, but we had food and shelter and, for a brief moment, we were not caught in a machine.

"...The air was soft. Even in this tortured and dying town nature was bringing back life. Up to now nothing had touched me, all emotions were dead. But as I looked over the park, where spring had come, I could not control myself any longer. For the first time since it all started, I cried."

WILLIAM L. SHIRER

Eva's Berlin

It was odd to be in the light again. Though we weren't in the shelter all that long, in that week or two our world had shrunk as it does in illness. For a while, the shelter seemed to be all there was; our past, present and future, lived in dim, greenish light and narrow, low-ceilinged rooms.

After the shooting stopped we began to realize that, for the first time in years, skies were just skies. No planes, no bombs, no anti-aircraft shelling. It was hard to believe that nights could pass without the sound of sirens. At first, we woke up frequently listening to the unaccustomed silence, anxious without knowing why. But gradually, sleep returned and with it, infinitesimally small amounts of trust began to appear, like spores carried by spring winds.

CHAPTER SEVENTEEN

The Aftermath

THE BUGS Relief proves to be like a gulp of air to one who is gagging, exhilarating but brief. Weariness quickly takes over, then sickness. My mother and grandmother both come down with the *Ruhr*, dysentery, a combination of diarrhea, vomiting and fever, dangerous for these already emaciated women. Packets of camomile and mint tea are passed around from household to household. I take my place at my mother's bedside as she tosses and turns and uses me as a cane to walk to the bathroom.

Her pallor frightens me: she is white with a tinge of green. I hold her hand. She says little. Her breathing is soft and shallow, her eyes closed. I sit, feeling more alone than when she isn't there. I want to take her by the shoulders and shake her awake, but I resist. Sometimes she trembles. I pray that she won't die. After three or four days, color returns to her cheeks, and she asks for an apple. We don't have one; I get a glass of water instead. Then I run out to the yard where I can jump up and down with happiness and gratitude that she'll live.

Soon, I get the next plague: head lice. My mother never mentions it without lowering her voice. Germans are humiliated by this filthy illness. It must have been brought by the Russians. My grandmother douses my head with vinegar every night to "burn the creatures up." My sleep is disturbed by images of lice in flames coming out of my head. The acrid smell of vinegar lingers. I blame my grandmother, of course. The lice have to live somewhere, too.

THE BLACK MARKET   In the grip of fatigue and illness, the city loses its hold on reality for a while. The stores are still shut during this time. Then my mother finds out about the black market on the *Siegesallee*, a part of the *Tiergarten*. Going there is like going to a large fair. There are people trading everywhere: an old couple with their things spread out on a rug, housewives like my mother, with a few items in their open bags. Americans and Englishmen deal from jeeps. We Germans are trading in our valuables for food. My mother trades my father's Leica to a young American who offers a carton of cigarettes. Deftly, she talks him into an additional two pounds of butter and two cans of Spam, as triumphant about out-bargaining him as she was with the market women in Italy. Butter and meat! What treasures! Then she trades half the cigarettes to some other Germans for a jar of marmalade and some soap.

We come home proud and, for once, my grandmother is happy with what we've done. Happy, but worried about the Allied Command's raids.

"Don't go again," she warns my mother, "and don't take the child because they can throw you in jail, just like that."

My mother ignores her warning. A few days later, she comes home with two loaves of bread and a dozen Hershey bars, bragging that they only cost her only six Italian silk nightgowns. She is triumphant.

"There was a raid, all right," she tells us, her eyes glowing, "and I was rounded up with the rest of them, but you'll never guess what I did."

In fact, we have not the slightest idea.

"They're so stupid, those soldiers. When we were being herded into the office, I just slipped the bread and the chocolate under some bricks in the ruin next door. Nobody noticed a thing, and when I came out, I just picked them up again!"

> This is what's become of Berlin. Fascinating and depressing at the same time. Hunger everywhere. All the people here have a half-mad look, the fight to survive occupies them totally. Still they are warm, generous and witty. But as a whole, it's horrible.
>
> WILLIAM SHIRER

Eva's Berlin

Although her stakes remained small my mother would be an inveterate smuggler all her life.

THE FIRST LETTER

June 1, 1945

Dearest EE,

I have already tried several times to let you know that we're still here and alive. Perhaps this letter or another letter will reach you. We have more or less survived here and are waiting anxiously for a sign of life from you, and most of all, that I can bring back to you our really dear — and despite everything — spunky Eva. I imagine that you are trying every possibility there and since it is the conquering nation, perhaps you'll be able to make a connection sooner than I can.

We're the same as everyone else here. Almost all the houses in our block on the Ranke-strasse are gone except for the little Miericke Konditorei, and even that has the upper floors shot away, but we are still standing and I often think one could call that a miracle. God willing, we will survive the time it takes to get back together again. The last period of time, the endfighting around the Zoo shelter, wasn't easy but one gets used to anything and then wonders later how one could have stood it. Eva is a child and still manages to be pretty tough and without worries. Corpses or parts of them don't bother her. She passes by them without a care on the way to the first Russian movie. I guess she has the same temperament as your mother, who, thank God, was spared every-

thing. Whether Onkel Sigismund will return, I don't know; I packed for him and for Tante Rosa before they left for Theresienstadt. I think he would come to me first, since he has no one else.

Perhaps I am writing too little about what you want to know, but that would take a novel and I still hope to be able to talk with you again. I am unbelievably skinny but generally healthy, except for my heart and resting now and the hope of seeing you again should help me get better. In any case, Eva has to get out of these ruins as soon as possible. You will probably have seen newsreels of how we have to live. She herself doesn't know what she's missing, but that's all the more reason for my wanting a normal life for her. Next week, I'll try to get her enrolled in a school. She had private lessons while we could still leave the house before the last battles, because higher education was forbidden for her.

I'm going to stop here because I still hope that you will already have some news of us and because I place my hope in you. How are you? How is the practice? When will we hear from you? Oh, there is so much I want to know. That I have remained the same, you will already know and now I hope to get news of you, also. My mother sends hearty greetings. She survived everything with her seventy three years and is still quite fit.

I kiss you and send you my warmest greetings,
                    your old Bielein

P. S. Yesterday we received a Red Cross letter from you written last year.

Eva's Berlin

A DEATH AND FRIED POTATOES   A few weeks after the war ends, the *Ruhr* kills my grandmother. One moment she is helping me with the lice, the next she is lying in bed in a coma. Standing at the door of her bedroom, I try to quell my enormous fear of anything dead or dying to go to see her, but I freeze in the doorway listening to her rasping breath, labored and regular, like dry leaves being raked in fall. She looks very still and as regal as ever, propped up on two immense embroidered pillows, her hair loose around her shoulders, a statue with a heaving chest. For a few minutes, I stand there in the presence of death. Then I leave quickly, shuddering.

Playing in the yard later that day, I glance through the window from outside. I can hardly believe what I see. My grandmother is in the kitchen, puttering around as though it were a day like any other. For a moment, I believe I'm seeing a ghost but her quick gestures and the clattering pans are undeniable signs of life. She pays no attention to me. I am trembling, afraid she'll turn to me and something unnameable will pass between us. But she doesn't notice me.

She's wearing my grandfather's tartan bathrobe, her hair straggling over her shoulders; it's the first time I've seen her less than perfectly dressed. But she still has an air of queenly authority as she moves about the kitchen, headed for a pan of *Bratkartoffeln* left on the kitchen stove in a dark metal frying pan. Fried potatoes are one of her favorite foods; I guess she doesn't want to miss her last chance to eat them. I watch her, fascinated, as she scrapes out every last bit of food left in the pan with a soup spoon. She stuffs the crusty brown potatoes into her mouth and then scoops up more. She belches. Finished, she heaves a loud sigh and starts to turn back. I'm suddenly aware that her breathing has been normal the whole time. After stopping at the stove to take one last look into the pan, she goes back to her room. A shudder passes through my body like a rush of birds' wings.

A few hours after eating the potatoes, my grandmother dies. My mother comes out of the back bedroom that early evening, coldly announcing her mother's death.

"Well, it's all over. She had an easy time of it."

I imagine she is relieved. There are no tears in her eyes. I don't want to see my dead grandmother. I'm still afraid of her capacity to surprise. But when they carry her to the hearse, her hair spread out in waves on the white pillow, she doesn't frighten me, her expression is so familiar. In death, my grandmother looks satisfied, almost proud.

Her death is so different from my grandfather's. There isn't any funeral. She dies. Then they take her away. I picture her in the cemetery we used to visit together to place fresh carnations, red and sweet-smelling on the graves of her relatives. In fact, I have no idea where she is buried. Her death was just one incident in the chaotic months after the war ended, months that spelled humiliating endings for many of Germany's dragons.

Eva's Berlin

Now that she's gone, her absence adds to my sense of unreality. Later, I realize that she was the ballast that kept our family balloon from floating into the sky. She anchored us in the kitchen. We learned by pitting ourselves against her stern commands. Unlike my grandfather, my mother, and me, she was not confused by her imagination. She knew the difference between her real life and her romantic fantasies, and she kept her well-shod feet firmly on the ground. Without her, our sense of who we are will become more and more precarious.

My mother and I believe my grandmother could have lived through the *Ruhr* had she wanted to, but that she chose to die. There was a reason. In her youth, a fortune teller told her to avoid crossing a large body of water. Heeding this warning, my grandmother had avoided boat trips on even the smallest lakes, including Berlin's sweetly tree-lined *Wannsee*. The end of the war challenged her resolve. My mother expected her to come with us to join my father. Going to America meant crossing the Atlantic and to her, certain death. I don't think she ever seriously considered it. Instead, she chose to die at home with the help of the *Ruhr*.

SOLDIERS After the Russian soldiers settle in, the allied troops arrive and with them, gradually, the city begins to regain a sense of continuity. It isn't easy. The soldiers — French, English, American — are healthy and strong, a different breed from the people we've lived with all through the war. Their Jeeps dot our streets, sounding like a swarm of angry bees. Their uniforms are spanking clean with immaculate white spats covering their boots, and helmets with the initials MP. They walk around in groups, speaking French or English, smoking cigarettes, and, if we're lucky, distributing their rations, with the air of royalty dispensing alms. These soldiers put me off though I'm not quite sure why. No one is robbed, raped or wounded, as far as I know. But they swagger around with an air that says,

"Here we are at last and aren't you lucky!"

And I can't find the bridge to this new kind of human being. The older girls don't seem to be bothered. Romances start up on every street corner. Every allied soldier walks around accompanied by at least three German girls. The girls flirt with them, teach them German, show them what's left of the town and come back home with an exotic new delicacy: chewing gum. I pronounce it "shaving goom," reading the wrappers, and find it disappointingly bland, tasting neither like chocolate nor like the sugary cakes from my friend Ingrid's bakery. After so much hunger, biting into something that doesn't yield any nurturing substance baffles me. Why chew if you can't eat?

I don't like what's happening to the girls who are hanging onto the strangers, laughing and flattering them. It makes me wish I weren't a girl. I watch from the sidelines, taken with a sudden shyness. I'm the wrong age: ten, skinny and leggy; I don't even have fantasies of romance with these men. There must be a better way to get at their rations.

A future in a place full of people like these soldiers frightens me. I wish my father lived in Russia. Soon I'm going to have to leave Germany. I am filled with dread but I'm surrounded by optimists.

"Aren't you glad that now, finally, your family will be reunited?"

"You must be so thrilled that you'll finally get to see your father."

"Just imagine, going to America, where you can get anything you want!"

Their assumption that I want to leave Germany and can hardly wait to get back together with my father upsets me. What do they know about me? The truth is that I want to stay in Berlin. I don't remember my father and can't imagine that I'll like him. I don't want to go to a country where everybody speaks a strange language and is sure to want something from me. But there is no room for such feelings in the scripts that are being handed out. My mother has been waiting to leave for seven years. I keep my worries to myself.

THE ANIMALS: 1945 We children check on the zoo as soon as the war's end allows us back on the streets. The destruction there is not too bad: just a few bombed-out buildings. The hayloft we played in on so many rainy days has burned down. The lion house — an oriental structure — was blown up. But quite a few animals in unbombed cages return our enthusiastic greetings. The bear and gorilla enclosures are unharmed but empty of animals. The keepers tell us what happened.

"These Russkies just came in with their rifles and started shooting," Dieter, the leopard keeper, says. "They got the gorilla, a wildebeest, and a couple of bears before we could stop them. They were drunk I think."

I look for our leopard. Then Dieter tells me, "He died before the end of the war, thank heavens. All the noise was too much for the old guy, I guess."

We ask to see the graves of our leopard, the black Russian bears and the gorilla and place offerings of flowers on the mounds.

The reptile house was a nightmare that had already happened before the war ended. An explosive bomb had hit it one morning, just a few hours before we got there. I stood with a crowd of people looking at a roped-off pile of stone almost covering the crocodiles, which, every now and then, twitched, shot a leg forward or swished a tail. They were all dead, we were told; the movements were reflexive. The crocodiles were dead, but not quite. It just proved what I had always feared: anything dead might begin to move, to move toward me. I remember pushing through the crowds to make my way back to the live animals.

> At the Tiergarten, a stable was hit and the horses that were not killed or maimed broke loose and galloped screaming down the Kurfürstendamm, their manes and tails on fire.
>
> ANTON GILL

Eva's Berlin

We learn from the keepers that Babu, the zebra, a wildebeest, and a couple of brown bears used escape routes left by the bombs to make their way out of the zoo during the last days of street-fighting. The empty cages have a ragged, pathetic appearance. We walk from one to the other, guessing what happened to those that are missing. Then one of us comes up with an inspired notion: we will search the neighborhood for the escapees. We enlist the willing keepers and, armed with a little zoo food and a lot of rope, set out on a search. We fan out on streets almost empty of traffic and, since most of the animals have only got to the adjacent *Tiergarten*, we succeed quickly. We find Babu first, surrounded by children. He is so tame that they are petting him. We corral him easily and set out to bring him back to the zoo, singing and beating metal rods together in a festive parade.

The bears are found in the park nearby, snarling when we attempt to get near. They are just inside a rocky cave, one of them prowling back and forth, the other lying in front of the entrance, very much the new home-owner. Slowly, the keepers encircle them, offering scraps of food and making familiar guttural sounds to which the bears eventually respond with a weary but docile look. Shuffling along like circus bears behind the

> So we got back Berlin. My abiding impression of that bombed city is that of the Trümmerfrauen — the women of the ruins — working their orderly German way through the piles of rubble, setting aside usable material in neat rows, ready to rebuild what had been lost.
>
> ANTON GILL

keepers, they are brought back to the zoo. The wildebeest is never found. I imagine it, with its bright African pelt, lying at the bottom of a mound of rubble.

On our rescue mission, Erika and I see that our island's part of the *Tiergarten* has been roped off and labeled "out of bounds" by one of the armies. Our island lost to us. We learn that, even when we regain permission to walk near it, children will not be allowed to visit the island. Our bridge will be cleared away. There are already trucks with pulleys taking away other dead trees. We share our loss without ceremony. The island  is no longer part of our lives. We don't go there anymore and we don't talk about it.

CLEAN-UP CREWS Despite tiredness, illness, and apathy, we begin the hard work of cleaning the city of rubble soon after we leave the shelters. Every street is filled with rubble from the many bombed houses. Pail brigades of *Trümmerfrauen* form to take care of the problem: women who heap the debris into orderly mounds, clear the streets, and hose everything down. For weeks, we stand in lines in

Eva's Berlin

ruined houses, handing pails and more pails filled with rubble to our neighbors. Like the lines at the stores when the
war was almost over, we are creating order out of chaos. It
seems like there's enough rubble for the rest of our lives, but,
for some reason, we are not discouraged. With every pail
that's passed, we're making progress.

Later, when I walk down our street to survey our
finished work, I realize how fond I'd grown of the ruins.
They have a special quality. They breathe with the spirits of
their former inhabitants. Now, no one gives them a thought.
The clean-up feels heartless. But *Ordnung muss sein*. Order
must be. It makes it easier to think of leaving.

PURIM The event that most deeply connects me to my
Jewishness occurs soon after the war. The city is just beginning to get back some semblance of normalcy when a Jewish
family moves into the apartment across from ours. Curious to
learn anything I can about being Jewish, I make it my business to get to know them. I learn they have just been released
from the camps. There are three of them, all in their twenties,
cousins, thin as rails, who act a lot younger than their age and
welcome me as their playmate. In the evenings before it gets
dark we play a kind of volley-ball in the back yard or we play
with marbles, which they had secretly done in the camps
using tiny pine cones. We become friends, but they don't
want to talk about the camps to me or anyone. Their bruised
looks when the subject arises silence all my questions.

Shortly after we become friends, one of them surprises me with an invitation to a Purim celebration. I learn that it is the Jewish spring festival, and expect something like an Easter egg hunt. Instead, I find what I have been seeking.

The celebration is attended by hundreds of concentration camp survivors — most of them Polish — caught up in a ritual of passionate affirmation. Standing three deep in a large circle, they play instruments and dance horas. They sing songs and pray in Yiddish, Hebrew and Polish. I find myself standing in their midst, clapping, holding hands and watching as one and then another comes into the center to thank God for a particular story of survival while the rest of us weep.

"Thank you God for sparing Gittel."

"I thank you for my life and my mother's."

"Thank you for my family . . ."

I don't understand a word of what they are saying, except in the few instances where the Yiddish resembles German, but there is no need for a translation. Stories of torture, despair, loss and transcendance are conveyed with tenderness and with rage. Words are unnecessary. I feel I have come home. These people — their passion, their rhythms, their music — are deeply familiar. When they weep, I weep. I dance the hora, first with the family that brought me, then with the others. For the first time, I understand that we have come through an ordeal. There will be a new beginning.

CHAPTER EIGHTEEN

The War Is Over

THE MESSENGER   The first American soldier we see comes with a letter from my father. He is a small, dark man accompanied by a German girl with white blonde hair whom he introduces as his fiancée (I hate her from the moment she comes into our house). She is not yet twenty, but she is carefully made up: pink cheeks, a beauty spot, white powder, blue eye-shadow to highlight her cornflower-blue eyes. I don't want the Germans to dress up for the Americans who bombed us.

He begins by making us a present of his box of rations. Among strange little cartons I don't recognize is a slice of the most unbreadlike white bread I've ever seen. Then I discover something I've only seen in illustrations: an orange. I am overwhelmed. Its smell, its texture, so like the skin of an animal with its pores, the startling color. No German fruit or vegetable looks like that. When the juicy pulp explodes in my mouth I barely register the messenger. I'm suspicious of this short, stocky man with his dark complexion. He smiles incessantly. His young, confident, unworried face is so different from ours. We sit with frozen smiles while he tells us about the wonderful future that lies ahead for us in San Francisco and his happiness about his engagement to the platinum blonde. We thank him for coming and he goes, his girlfriend in tow, a self-satisfied expression on both their faces.

LETTERS FROM A FATHER As soon as they're gone, we read my father's letter:

> *Dear Bielein and Eva,*
>
> *How can I tell you how much I miss you? And how much I hope that you will like your new house with its large garden? I deeply and truly hope, that you, dear Bielein, and our Ideltidel are beginning to fare a little better now. I'm sending some vitamins (one in the morning and one at night — at least — on a full stomach). They'll help as a basis for recovery.*
>
> *Thursday night (today is Saturday) I operated on Ernst Hill (Cohen) for a serious appendicitis. Am even a bit proud of my work. But some-*

*thing always sees to it that trees don't grow up
into the sky. Soon enough something will come
along and dampen my high spirits.*

*I am fine. Except for one thing: I miss you
both more every moment. The day after tomorrow,
I'll find out whether it'll all work out, and then I
hope to have you here shortly. I am constantly trying to imagine how you will like it here.*

*I let a street photographer take my picture.
Just became a citizen.*

Yours with a hearty kiss,

EE and Daddy

So that is my father. I feel a certain animosity about
his calling me *Ideltidel* as though I were still four years old.
Perhaps my mother was right. We were suffering and he was
eating regularly and pretending we, too, were just the same
as ever. I don't think I'm going to like him. Nothing he writes
speaks to me. I can't picture my father nor does the house
beckon the way he wants it to. He's a stranger from a strange
country. I comfort myself with the memory of the orange, its
symmetrical wedges sheathed in lace and its exciting, sweet
and sour taste.

Rereading it as an adult, I see that he is careful not to
leave his self-congratulation without balance: life will see to
it that his tree doesn't grow into the heavens: that he doesn't
over-reach. His letter is warm and caring. I had been reading
it through my mother's lens — and I wasn't ready for a father,
anyway.

Eva's Berlin

"YOUR LIPS, THEY KISS SO HOT" Berlin is changing. The city is divided up into sectors: French, English, American, Russian. What does it mean? Isn't it one city any more? Different languages all around us, French, English, Russian. Different flags in different parts of the city. Ours is English. New laws are being written. The war is over, but we're still being ordered around by soldiers. Women wearing turbans to avoid head lice line up in queues for the first fragrant warm loaves of white bread. We are still hungry and thin. It is not the scene of joyous rescue often shown in the movies.

The wind blowing through the dusty ruins seems to be blowing me around as well. I don't know where I am. I find myself missing the sense of community of the nightly air-raids. Music and theater come to my rescue.

Berlin's theater and night life had continued throughout the war, stopping only on the days of commemoration of the dead after battles like Stalingrad (I remember the odd silence of the streets and the ominous repetition of the word Stalingrad — it came to sound like it meant death — and the hushed voices). The Berlin Philharmonic played regularly up to the end. The immense concert hall, where the audience sat in immaculately clean seats and drew their Sunday clothes more and more tightly around their thinning bodies, represented another world. Beethoven and Mozart brought me landscape, poetry, and new language. All of it was familiar in its rhythms and tonalities, as clear as the forest brooks on

Baden-Baden's trails, as mysterious as the fog on the Baltic Sea. The music took me into its confidence and guided me like my grandfather had on our visits to the old castles.

Of course, everything stopped when the Russians came. But now, as we take our first steps back out into the city, the theater comes alive again and, by complete chance, I get to witness its premiere performance. When my mother sends me to an agency to get our new ration cards — food is as scarce as ever — I wait in the same line with a couple who turn out to be actors applying for a permit to give the first post-war cabaret performance. Ever since my visit to the children's theater, actors have replaced the nobility in my fantasies of glamor and fame. They are special people. Their voices are more vibrant. These two have angular faces with deeply set eyes. With a sense of backstage privilege, I listen to them explaining their requirements for the musical revue. I am so in awe that I don't even try to talk to them. On the way home, I decide that I must convince my mother to let me see the show. She is, after all, responsible for my love of theater — she's taken me to operas and plays since I was four years old — and she agrees to let me attend the performance at the *Marmorpalast*, just a few blocks from my house, by myself.

> The Berliners not only survive but even perform in the theater. To get enthusiastic about a four-hour performance of Macbeth at several degrees below zero. Oh, loveable Berlin, who on earth could emulate you?
>
> RUTH ANDREAS FRIEDERICH

Eva's Berlin

A few days later, on an early spring evening on the *Kurfürstendamm*, I am sitting in the orchestra section on a red plush seat that feels much too large for me. Electricity hasn't been restored yet in Berlin; the artists perform holding candles. I sit in the darkened theater, eagerly awaiting the man and woman I met earlier. An array of performers appears: jugglers, comedians and singers; then there's a tap-dance act and a tango. My eyes are glued to the stage. The event delivers exactly what it promises.

My two occupy a place of honor at the end of the program. He wears top hat and tails, she black velvet *décolleté*. He dances and sings and plays the piano. She sings in that throaty German cabaret voice made famous by Dietrich and Leander,

> *Deine Lippen, sie küssen so heiss,*
> Your lips, they kiss so hot,
> *Deine Arme so liebsam und weiss.*
> Your white, adorable arms.

Who knows whether these are the actual lyrics; they're the ones I will remember forever. Transported and utterly seduced, I forget where I am and begin to dream. Surely this is how life will unfold. A handsome man, witty and talented, will sing to me, dance with me, and together we will conquer the world. I feel much older than my actual ten years as I make my way back to our apartment, hoping that no one will be home to ask questions. I want to treasure this experience and keep it for myself and only share it when I meet the one who will understand.

MAY I SPEAK TO THE CONSUL? In 1945 and early 1946, my mother and I go from office to office trying, once more, to get visas to join my father. American Army Headquarters sends us to the American Consulate. They aren't open yet. Back to American Army Headquarters. They don't handle those papers. Wait two weeks. Back to the consulate. Every office is the same, whether it's located in an old villa just outside the city in the *Grunewald* or in a hastily constructed quonset hut in East Berlin. Some involve interminable changes of streetcars and subways; others are easily accessible. The waiting rooms smell of human anxiety.

Every now and then we meet someone crucial. It is always a man. We stand in front of the desk of this vice-consul, or general secretary, or immigration officer, so tense we can't look at each other and even my mother finds it hard to talk, though she does her best to use her charm. I stand by feeling as if a pool of ice water is slowly numbing me from head to foot. One phone call, one signature, that's all we need.

> **P**lease, please, may I speak to the consul? The consul is busy.
>
> GIAN CARLO MENOTTI

But we can't get it. The official is brusque. He informs us that he is eager to help but his powers are limited. He glances at our carefully assembled papers and has us fill out new forms.

Eva's Berlin

"Your case is unusual."

"I will have to look into it."

"Perhaps I can communicate directly with your American relative in San Francisco, but that will take time."

"I will get back to you very soon."

We know from the coldness in his eyes that nothing will happen. Our bodies become knotted and our minds confused. I want to beg him to do us a favor. I'd promise anything just to get this interminable suspense over with. Sometimes my mother does just that. But we are shown the door after ten minutes or so and then it begins again.

In May, 1946, after almost a year has gone by, we meet the right man. He is young. He is moved by the number of visits we have made to his consulate, or perhaps he has heard from my father. Thirty minutes after entering his office, we are given the form that guarantees our passage to New York. Our boat will be the *Marine Perch*, the second ship to leave Bremerhafen with a cargo of German emigrants.

LEAVING AGAIN   Life in Berlin is just beginning again. I've been in a regular school for the past six months and I'm enjoying it. For the first time since the second grade, I am one among many children. I don't have to hide anything. I'm not in any special categories except for those I earn. My classmates elect me the *Vertrauens-Schülerin*, the trusted student who represents her class at school council meetings. Academic work is as easy as it was in the second grade without the dreaded handwriting practice. The other students often look to me for help. Me, who hasn't had any schooling while they've been continuing their education. I credit my dear Dr. Jurczek and the shelter classrooms. My homeroom teacher, Frau Gravenstein, is teaching me to draw. I have many new friends: Christa with brown hair, finely arched eyebrows and rosy cheeks; Renate, who likes to talk as much as I do and phones me every day. And now, just when my life has begun to take on a semblance of normality, we are going to leave.

I try to embrace our move for my mother's sake. Going to America was what had kept her going throughout the war. How could I even think that it wasn't for the best?

Now that it's finally happening, there's so much to do that I can't think at all. In the flurry of packing and saying good-bye, I lose track of what is happening. I do what I have to do without really believing I am leaving Germany, my home. Walking through the neighborhood, the day seems so much like any other that sentimental farewells seem overly dramatic, just like our friends' stories about how fortunate we are.

My friend Thea says, "Everything is golden in California. It's going to be like paradise."

Much as I try, I don't believe her.

Christa's mother says, "What a lucky young girl to be going to America, where everyone is rich and life is easy!"

I don't want to think about it. My feet are used to these grey stones, my mouth and my heart belong to the soft Berlin air.

Eva's Berlin

BREMERHAFEN   On arriving in Bremerhafen, we are taken to a refugee camp in the middle of a city bombed so flat that it makes Berlin's wounding appear mild. Not even ruins remain standing here, just the outlines of former buildings on the flat ground and a few remains of walls here and there. It is as though whole streets have been erased.

The camp consists of a few quonset huts. We sleep in bunk beds in a dormitory with many others, most of whom are concentration camp survivors. A tight community, they consider us privileged outsiders and seldom include us in their talks. For once, my mother doesn't try to use her famous charm. Perhaps she's grieving Berlin as much as I am, or more. Perhaps she doesn't want to find out about the world of the camps. I am so trapped in my own sadness that I don't even think of trying to help her or of making friends on my own. Once more, we are outsiders.

The others, thin and intense, sit on their bunks swapping stories of survival. We don't know the vocabulary. But, sitting on our own beds, reading or joining the others for the few meals we have together before the *Marine Perch* leaves, we begin, despite our resistance, to get a picture of the horror.

I hear about death camps. It takes a while to get the idea. I had imagined hard work and little food. But in camps like Auschwitz it was just a matter of time before everyone died. Lines were being formed where every person was assigned a number; even numbers went to the gas chamber, odd numbers did hard labor. The next day the process would be repeated. I hear descriptions of huge gas ovens where hundreds of Jews were killed every day, of piles of skeletons so high that they formed small mountains. I had wanted to know about the camps. But these stories are so nightmarish that I can hardly bear to listen. I don't ask questions. I don't join in. There's nothing I can say except to thank God fervently — and silently — for letting these people stay alive. I can't think about the dead or those who killed them. The evil is so huge that all I can do is run from it.

THE VOYAGE   Life on the boat revives us. My mother and I have our own small room with a port-hole on the side of my upper berth. I can lie on my bed and look far off into the gray-green distance and imagine travelling on and on without ever reaching shore. I look for gulls and dolphins to break up the monotony and feed them bits of bread that I've saved from breakfast. Sometimes the dolphins swim close to the ship's prow, playing in its wake. I can't take my eyes off them, leaping and diving, silvery beings that have nothing to do but play.

In my hotel mode, I set about exploring everything from the top deck with its railings good for practicing the bar work I perfected on the playground, to the hold, the lowest part of the boat, where many people are camped on the floor. There are no other children on the boat. Like the help in the *Kaiserin Elisabeth* in Baden-Baden, the sailors become companions. With them I practice the English I learned during my one school term after the war from Mrs. Kyper.

"Good morning, class!" We all stood beside our desks, ready to answer, "Good morning, Mrs. Kyper."

The sailors encourage my halting English and teach me to say, "Swell," when asked how I'm feeling. They show me exotic foods like peanut butter which gets stuck in my throat like glue, and cereal which reminds me of the food in the bird-house in the Berlin zoo. They are amused by my grimaces and keep trying to interest me in new American flavors. When they show me the catsup bottle, they succeed. The color of it alone is so unlike that of any food I've ever seen that it demands to be tried. It's been so long since I've eaten candy that its tomato sweetness wakes up my taste-buds. The tall red bottle on our table is a gift I use daily. I put catsup on everything from bread to peas.

ROUGH SEAS When the seas get rough, I am one of the few passengers in the dining room. Even my mother stays in her bed. My hardiness is rewarded with extra sweets for dessert. I savor each bite of my first piece of apple pie and my first dish of ice cream. The sweetness makes my palate tickle.

High seas don't frighten me at all. I turn the unsteadiness of the ground into a challenging game: I have to walk down the long, narrow corridors without ever touching the walls. At night I lie in my rocking bunk, looking out on the green, storm-tossed waves. I don't think about drowning. I think about riding the boat like the horsemen on stormy nights on the heath in fairy tales.

> *Wer reitet so spät durch Nacht und Wind?*
> Who rides so late through the stormy night?
> *Est is der Vater mit seinem Kind.*
> It is the father with his child.

The myth of the *Erlking*, a dark figure who wraps his child in his cloak as they ride in the raging winds, both fascinates and repels me. I would like to be held, to be feverish and ill, and then swept up into the darkness. There are times when even drowning takes on a fascination for me. To become one with the ocean. I imagine myself in the tall waves, swimming at first, gradually weakening and filling with salt water and finally pulled down into the depths. I wouldn't try to fight it. I would let the sea take me into its wide embrace, knowing I was returning home.

The ten days of our ocean crossing pass quickly. I become accustomed to the salt air on the upper deck, to the birds and the dolphins that accompany us, and to my English lessons. The boat trip is a vacation. The war is over. The new country feels far away. There is nothing that needs to be done.

CHAPTER NINETEEN

Changes

A FATHER   Our arrival in the United States is talked about for days before it happens.

"Only four more days, and the day after tomorrow, we should see land."

"This is exciting."

"What will await us there?"

"Can you imagine what we'll find?"

We see land the day before we arrive. It still looks far away, a faint brown line that could just as well be a shadow. I wish it were. I don't want to arrive.

I don't want to meet my father. Not because I anticipate meeting a villain. Quite the contrary. I never believed

Eva's Berlin

my mother's stories about how selfish he was to leave us. I defended him in my imagination. I built up a picture of a glamorous father who worked in the theater and could speak many languages. Yet I don't really want to meet him. What has he to do with me? How would speaking seven languages make it easier for me to speak with him? The photographs make him look large. I'm small. Who needs a father, anyway? I haven't needed one all these years. Why should I want one now? I want to hide on the boat and go back to Berlin.

On the day after we first see land, the skyline of New York appears in view and, before we know it, we are all crowding on deck to look up into the huge greenish folds of Liberty's garments. After that, the milling about on the deck reaches wild proportions. Every passenger seems to want to be the first to leave the boat. Luggage is everywhere. Some passengers are already desperate because they can't find theirs. My mother and I get separated for a while. Reporters come on board and start interviewing people and taking pictures. Immigration officers give instructions about how to proceed. And then, suddenly, right here on the boat: my father.

He is tall, with graying dark hair and a tanned face. He's wearing a trenchcoat and a hat with a press pass clipped to the hat band. When he hugs my mother and me, I feel his largeness. It's odd, being hugged by such a large man when I'm only used to women. Do I remember him? Not really. He looks like a more wrinkled version of the man in the photographs. As I watch him busying himself with our luggage, I don't feel anything special. My mother looks both excited and worried. She is proud of his coming on board with a press pass. She nods and smiles over and over again when he succeeds in getting us to be among the first to disembark. We are getting special treatment.

As we set foot on American ground after leaving the gangplank, my mother gives me her two golden necklaces and tells me to touch them to the ground we must kiss for good luck in our new country. I do what she says. But I don't understand what she is talking about. I already miss Berlin.

Next we go to an office in the harbor where, near the sign 'Displaced Persons,' we are to wait for clearance from immigration. There is a circular bench where we sit, surrounded by our luggage. When I want to go off to explore, my father comes after me and offers his hand. I take it, not knowing how to avoid it without being rude. And then, suddenly, I remember him. The touch of his large, fleshy hand, the rhythm of his walk, and the voice — the husky, soft baritone that tells me about our home in San Francisco brings him back to me. I am overcome by a sense of deep familiarity, one that I didn't expect. I sink into the rhythm of his walk as though I'd walked with him all my life. And although it's difficult for me to understand everything he says because I can't see his face, I am comforted by his conversation. Trying to understand this strange new-old intimacy, I remember the quality of his voice, the odd combination of snobbishness and warmth, the linguist's careful pronunciation of certain words. The smell of his cigar, combined with cologne, once again isolates us, and I am intrigued. When he brings me back to my waiting mother, he is beaming from ear to ear.

"We have discussed everything," he tells her, and she, too, smiles.

A NEW NAME   Not quite. We haven't discussed everything, because I only find out when we get to the hotel that he has changed our name. His name is not Dr. Eichenwald anymore. His name is Dr. Wald. My mother and I will become Elizabeth and Eva Wald.

"You'll see that it's impossible for people to pronounce, let alone spell, Eichenwald," he says. "Karl and I got everything from Ickenwall to Eyeshenwool. So we compromised."

I'm so taken aback that I don't even think to object. He says that the change means nothing, that it's for the better, and that's that. But somewhere inside I raise an objection. I like my old name. An Eichenwald is an oak forest. The word carries weight. I like the rhythm of three syllables. A *Wald* is just any old forest. My new name lacks character; it doesn't sing. We never return to the subject. The German oaks are left behind unmourned, but not forgotten.

A NEW COUNTRY   Everywhere, people are speaking English. Despite Mrs. Kyper's efforts, I can hardly catch a word here and there. A chattering toddler walks by holding his mother's hand. I marvel at how such a small child can already be speaking so fluently.

The absence of hunger takes some getting used to. Instead of the joy my father expected, my mother and I are paralyzed by our first meal in New York. Hailing a taxi to drive down the crowded streets with their gigantic skyscrapers, he takes us to Reuben's for plate-size steaks and baked potatoes piled high with sour cream and chives. The German version of steak would have been startling enough. *Rumpsteak*, we called it and it always reminded me of Rumpelstiltsken because it, too, was usually wrinkled and small. But the American version looks like an entire roast for just one person. At the sight of so much food, my stomach rebels and my mouth constricts. Eating so much when others have so little seems like a betrayal.

Berlin has shrunk our stomachs and got us used to feeling unsatisfied. Now there is a whole new challenge. I pretend that this is just a normal, everyday meal but the feeling of fullness overwhelms me long before I finish. My mother, too, sits jabbing at her meal. Feeling guilty, we send our plates back covered with the food we know somebody in Berlin is craving.

BEGINNING   Outside on the wide streets again, I see myself in the plate glass windows. I am dressed in new clothes bought at *Bergdorf Goodman's*. I see an Eva who looks transformed, elegant enough to become a part of the bustling New York scene that reminds me of Berlin. My wool coat, light green like young ferns, feels warm on my shoulders. These first few days as a tourist let me hear New York's familiar big city hum. I'm beginning to soften. Perhaps coming to America wasn't such a bad idea after all.

I gawk at the window displays, holding onto my father's hand while he tries his best to interpret this new culture to my mother and me. But his best efforts and my new clothes aren't enough, after all. There's just too much of everything. New York is more crowded, larger, healthier and less human than what I am used to. I am more confused than ever about where "my place" might be.

My mood goes up and then down again often in those first few weeks. One minute, I'm ready to conquer this big exciting new country. The next I feel like a worm crawling along the bottom of the skyscrapers.

My father takes us to meet his cousin Lulu who serves us strawberries and vanilla ice cream in her apartment on the East Side. The adults talk over old times and I go outside to explore the new neighborhood. For the first time in my life, I see streets peopled by Jews. Old men in long black overcoats and gray beards, young men with tall hats and dark curls as long as mine, Jewish women with Jewish children. I can hardly believe my eyes. It's as though I've entered forbidden territory, yet none of these people seem the least bit self-conscious. Looking at the children, I try to imagine growing up feeling that it's all right to be Jewish. I can't talk to any of them because I'm too shy to try out my new language, but I watch carefully. They're tossing a small ball around, running, yelling. Sometimes a mother leans out the window to call to her child and the child answers carelessly. There's not a sign of self-consciousness or worry. They don't seem to know about Jews being hunted.

Later, my father takes us to one of the many Jewish delicatessens. He explains that many of these people are German Jews who got out earlier than he did and other American Jews who sponsored German Jewish families and helped them come over before the war. I am amazed. What would my life have been like had I come here at age five? Looking around at how different many of these people look from my mother and me, I am drawn to their dark, dark hair, their deep eyes, their long, skinny bodies. That's what I want to look like when I grow up, I tell my father, and my mother laughs at the absurdity.

If only life could continue like that: three people, pleased and shy, on the threshold of possibilities. We are a family again. I'm beginning to dream about what it might be like to have a father, someone older and bigger who cares about me, asks me questions, guides me, and whose skin and walk are as familiar as the land I just left. My father is dreaming of our arrival in the house he bought for us. A house with

a large garden in the middle of the city, a marvel of a house where my mother can grow roses and I can have as many cats as I want. And my mother? She expects the fulfillment of her romantic dreams, a man who will carry her across the threshold, ask her to soothe the wounds caused by her absence, nurture her, and make her feel beautiful.

It wasn't to be. Perhaps dreams never are, and these, incubated during the war, had very little relationship with the realities that faced us. We were challenged by demands far beyond what we had imagined. A new language had to be learned in a new culture. From the beginning, the expectation of happiness dogged us. Over and over again, we heard people respond in a way that we couldn't.

"How are you?"

"Just fine, thank you."

"How's it going?"

"Great!"

For my mother and me, the new routine has to be learned in the context of transition, not only from one country to another, but from war time to peace time. When we arrived in New York, my father told me the sign for 'Displaced Persons' in the immigration office was for people who were not being met by their American sponsors. Now the phrase fits me. Here, anyone who was not feeling "fine" is out of place.

My father is not the man we knew in Münster. His face no longer carries the air of success that characterized *Doktor* Eichenwald. Dr.Wald began life in the U. S. as an intern who had to re-earn his medical degree as he learned the language. Even when he achieved it, instead of being able to play the role of respected researcher-physician, he had to start over again. He is helped by my uncle, who'd started a textile business even before my father arrived. When my father set up his office in one of the poorer parts of the city, many of the drunks and dope addicts who came to him did so because my uncle left my father's card in the cheap hotels he supplied with sheets and towels. Though my father's face still sparkles in conversation, in repose, he looks heavy and sad. He seems to be caught in-between his new world where he is successful and busy and his desire to join my mother and me in our slow and difficult adjustment. It won't be long before each of us will feel abandoned by the others, more alone than before, when the hope of getting back together had kept each of my parents from despair.

Eva's Berlin

SAN FRANCISCO   After New York, San Francisco seems small. New York's echoes of Berlin had comforted me. Now I feel confined. I'm so alienated by the lack of metropolitan hum that I can't appreciate the beauty of the place. The ocean looks dark and frightening without the elegant esplanade I'm used to from our trips to the Baltic, nor the teeming sidewalk restaurants full of people enjoying themselves. The forest behind our house is constantly covered with a cold, dense fog. I long for the camaraderie of streets teeming with people, of strangers talking to one another.

The houses that make up our neighborhood look Lilliputian to me. I am so used to apartment houses that having a separate house for each family seems like solitary confinement. The hills make the city look small. You have to get on top of one to see the horizon. From there you see an ocean so vast that the city looks smaller still. There's only one theater, and an opera season that lasts only a few months. There is no cabaret. At night, when we return from dinner at a restaurant, the streets are empty and quiet. I hear that San Francisco has no snow and I'm not surprised. All the essentials are missing here.

We're not safe in San Francisco. Walking down Stanyan Street on a sunny day I look from the glinting sidewalk up toward the houses that line our street. Small, Victorian one-family houses with turrets and fancy windows alternate with more modern and box-like two or three story apartment buildings and flats. Furthermore, I am shocked to discover that the houses on our street are made of wood! How can such a rich city be so incautious? There are no bomb shelters. One bomb attack and our whole street would be gone! I watch for burning matches or cigarettes on the ground, terrified that fire could sweep through the whole neighborhood. Why hasn't anyone thought to protect these houses?

Our house stands in the back of a large garden filled with tropical plants I've never seen before. My father collects them with the same devotion he has for words. Plants have exotic names that roll off his tongue, like Aechium, with its large fuzzy leaves the color of blue-gray pigeons, and Pitosporum. He's proud of the monkey puzzle tree that wraps its arms around itself like so many spiders. For me, the garden speaks a more familiar language. Fuchsias and impatiens grow in a friendly array of pinks and, near the kitchen table where we eat breakfast, a window faces a full hedge of blood-red roses. I bring armfuls of them inside to keep me company.

My parents have selected a hideous pink for the walls of my new room and bought a bedspread to match. They've given me a make-up table with a large mirror and pink satin skirt, all because they love me and all without asking. I hate pink and I don't have any use for the make-up table. I would have liked a large desk and bookshelves and a bed for my cat. But they are so proud of their perfect little girl's room that I table my objections.

My room overlooks a fuchsia nursery: rows and rows of red, pink and violet bushes, the blooms ruffled like a can-can dancer's petticoats. Behind the nursery lies Sutro Forest. The eucalyptus trees, with an aroma that reminds me of my grandmother's Baldrian cure, frighten me at first; the elephantine trunks with their peeling bark have so little in common with the fir and pine I am used to. But they are trees, after all, with large root systems where I will be able to make moss gardens. When I sit by my open window at night, their rustling comforts me.

A STRAWBERRY Soon after we arrive in San Francisco I come down with a serious middle ear infection. With a high fever, I feel much like I did in Baden-Baden so often, located in a strangely dry and fantastic world, barely aware of the others who come and go in my room. A pink light enters my new bedroom through gauzy curtains. A friend of my father's, a doctor with snow-white hair and thick glasses, comes to examine me. He leaves a basket of deep red, juicy strawberries on my nightstand and urges me to eat them. Although my dry tongue is begging to wolf them down without pause, I am unable to because I have to share with my mother. It will take a long time for me to believe that a basket of straw-berries can be bought any time they're in season.

ENGLISH LESSONS My father's office is in a large gray building on Market Street, a street crowded with people, a few large department stores and theaters. Located on the edge of the better downtown area, it has a tacky, cheap flavor. Small stores that sell inexpensive clothes alternate with low-budget movie houses. The street has no trees, no flower beds, just storefronts and gutters full of trash.

Sometimes, my mother and I go clothes shopping in the stores near my father's office. I am not interested in clothes. My mother's ideas about what I should be wearing are similar to her ideas about decorating my room. At eleven years, I'm all angles and legs. The flouncy dresses my mother selects for me make me feel even more gangly and awkward.

Downtown isn't all bad. The salesmen and ladies on the first floor of department stores like *Woolworth's* or *The Emporium* put on acts every day selling make-up, health aids, and novelties. Their eyes shine and they make contact with their audience. Sometimes they hand out free samples and I come home clutching a tiny vial of perfume or a smaller tube of cleaning fluid. Never in the least tempted to buy one of their products, I'm a devoted listener nonetheless. They communicate clearly, using gestures and props that leave no doubt as to what they are saying. Much of my beginner's English vocabulary comes from their performances.

Eva's Berlin

At *Woolworth's* large tiered counters, greeting cards become another English textbook for me. Germans send very few printed cards. I only recall the black frames around death announcements. Here, like everywhere else in America, everyone is wishing someone else something wonderful — happy birthday, happy anniversary, get well soon, congratulations on your graduation. Waiting for my mother to get her hair done at the beauty shop upstairs, or while she shops for clothes, I read these anonymous messages, using the generous illustrations of roses, hearts, candles, crosses, and hospital beds to figure out what they mean.

In Germany, I was the best student in my English class, but now that I'm here in California, I realize that Mrs. Kyper's German-accented British English bears little resemblance to the American voices around me. I have a hard time understanding the simplest sentences. Much of the time, when anyone addresses me, I can only come up with a confused, "What do you say?"

To help me learn the language, my father sends me to a summer school where I practice interminable exercises to help my pronunciation.

"A dillar, a dollar, a ten o'clock scholar."

My teacher asks me to open my mouth wide when I say it so he can see whether I am placing my tongue correctly to the roof of my mouth in order to say the 'r.'

"Think of this. Think of that."

The 'th' is the most difficult sound. I felt a little silly

making it, as though I'd developed a lisp.

English isn't hard to learn. It has far fewer grammatical rules, cases and genders than German. But it is hard to pronounce and hard to love, without rhythm or melody. In those first years, before I could appreciate its jazzy informality and its Shakespearean depths, English seemed to me matter-of-fact, clear, and unlovely.

A LETTER FROM A FRIEND

October 30, 1946

My Dear Eva!

Many, many thanks for your dear letter. I was really very happy to get it. My hearty congratulation for 'not having got seasick.' You see, your wish was answered in the form of a cat. Sadly enough, I'm going to have to wait a long time for mine. Did you 'go to the dogs,' too? Then you have to write me all about them, okay? I still go to the zoo as much as possible. The former Circus Busch was there and I palled around with those folks enough so they let me go to the performances free, and help lead the horses back to the stable (at the Zebra house) and even ride them. Of course, that was fabulous and led me to hang round the stables all the time. Too bad they're gone for the winter and the zoo is boring again. On the meadow where the wolves' area used to be, they still have some wild horses and ponies running around free, and that's where you can find me and Helga. One little wild horse let me ride him and we rode

Eva's Berlin

at a gallop through the herd and felt like cowboys. But since we didn't have reins or a bridle 'Ingrid' ran wherever she pleased. Now she, of all of them, has been locked up in a stable so that's all over. But I go there every day and meet Ingrid, Bärbel, Lothar and Matzel and they all send greetings.

It's great that you are in a school, but isn't it hard to keep up? In the beginning you must have had a hard time understanding anything the teacher said. It's a good thing that you're not a shy little girl, otherwise you would have died of shame. I can imagine that the little Americans gather to look at this new being in their midst. We only have school on half days. Gaby and my whole class want me to send you greetings. You probably already know more English than I learned in five years! You enviable creature, you! I would love to visit you and see your garden. It must be wonderful. Please write me about whether you've been to your zoo because I'd love to know what an American zoo looks like. Did you at least get airsick on the plane? How was that, anyway? Oh, I'd love to know so much. Please write me often. Please, please!

It's the first time that we can't be together on your birthday. So I can only send my best birthday wishes through this letter. I wish every possible good thing for you, a terrific amount of happiness and even better health! The only gift I can give you is my promise that I will try to write often! I congratulate you this early because your letter took eight weeks to get here and we can't send any air-mail letters from here yet.

I hope you can tolerate all the good food except for fruit so that your stomach can celebrate your birthday! But it probably has got used to all those good things by now!

Please pet your little (black?) cat Peter one extra time for me and greet him from me and greet yourself especially   *from your,*   *Erika*

SORROW I have been trying to read one of my German books every night before I go to sleep, but on most evenings, the book remains shut. Sitting by my window, I listen to the wind in the eucalyptus trees and I cry. There are many reasons. Because my working father is more absent now than when I hadn't known him well enough to miss him. Because my mother is unhappy and I'm the only friend she has and I can't seem to help. I'm crying because I miss Berlin. I miss Berlin. I miss Berlin.

Once, at school, they show a film with a Strauss waltz as background music. Though I sit quietly in my chair, I am racked with sobs threatening to surface like howls. *Tum de tum, tum, tum-tum, tum-tum.* Long flowing chiffon, *Biedermeyer* furniture, angels laughing down on us from the ceiling. *Tum de tum-tum.* A whole world lost to me.

Eva's Berlin

Warmth, lightness, charm, humor and promise of romance are caught in music that falls on the deaf ears of Grattan

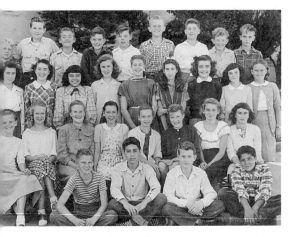

grammar schoolers, who are chewing gum and hoping the film will soon be over.

I'm not like them. I'll never be like them but I don't know how to remain European, either. Americans know so little about war. Their efforts to join in with tales of saving string and gasoline rationing don't bring me any closer. My father's German Jewish friends let my mother and me know that the suffering of Germans during the war was infinitesimal in comparison to that of the Jews. Everybody is right. Everybody is sincere. But I feel more and more isolated.

I make a stab at explaining where I come from, what kinds of games we played in Germany, what kind of music I like. But the other children look at me and then at each other as though they're trying to make sense of a creature from another planet, one that doesn't interest them in the slightest. Unfortunately, the less they understand, the more vigorously I praise everything German.

"In Germany, we don't play baseball. We play soccer.

They play it all over Europe."

"It's a stupid game. You hit the ball with your head. It makes you stupid."

"No, it does not. It's much harder to play than your stupid baseball."

"In Germany, we have concerts that everybody can go to and everyone likes classical music."

"Classical music stinks."

"You just say that because you don't understand it."

"It stinks."

Finally, Cordelia, a fat girl sitting across the aisle, who wears black patent Mary Janes and plaid skirts that are too tight for her, says, "Why don't you go back where you came from?"

I wish I could. Nobody speaks up for me, not even Celia Melendez, whom I consider the nicest and most beautiful girl in our class because of her delicately arched eyebrows and her wisps of dark, curly hair.

The teacher was staring at me. Then it hit me. I'd used the wrong language. I clammed up immediately and wished with all my heart that it was possible to sink beneath the floor... Within a few days we found we'd been singled out for bullying by the older boys... Name-calling and fists were the two main weapons.

WILLIAM KURELIC

In Germany, I had learned only gradually that I didn't belong, and even when I did, I felt thoroughly German. The language, the music, the landscape, were all mine. It just turned out I didn't have the right credentials. Here, the knowledge of being an outsider is clear from the

Eva's Berlin

outset. I am a fish out of water. I don't know how to behave in this strange new country, and that's bad enough. But what's worse is that very little calls to me. I am so homesick that I can't find a place to land.

My father's hand can't guide me through the maze of my new school. He knows no more about American children than I do. Perhaps he doesn't know much about German children either. He had, after all, spent his childhood reading Greek and Latin under his mother's dining room table. These children upset me. It isn't just that some of them view me as the enemy and tell me to go back home where I came from. It's that I feel alone even when they're being nice.

On an overnight at a classmate's house, a woman wearing flowered pants and a lot of bright orange lipstick turns out to be the grandmother, who chain-smokes Camel cigarettes and talks in a hoarse voice I have difficulty understanding. Her mother's boyfriend is an amputee who spends the evening drinking bourbon and water and whistling complicated tunes along with the radio. His whistling is lyrical, like a young girl's soprano. But soon, the bourbon takes him away. My new friend shows me her flouncy skirts and her collection of net crinoline petticoats that stand in her closet like a row of dancing midgets. I don't know whether it's my poor English, or because the smell of fried food permeates everything — but I can't find my way into this crowded apartment.

Going to the movies with another girl and two boys,

I'm shocked by something entirely unexpected. As soon as it gets dark, the girl is kissing and hugging one of the boys we came with, and I can smell the acrid cologne the boy I'm with is wearing. His hand is on my shoulder pulling me towards him. I'm not ready for this. Why would I want to kiss him? I don't even know him. I push him away and try to ignore his anger, determined to watch the movie to keep the situation from being a total loss.

Back in Berlin, boys and girls were almost interchangeable. Except for that notable occasion when Horstl and I were caught playing doctor, I haven't given much thought to boys as an opposite sex. Romantic fantasies are about men in the movies and these boys look nothing like them. Boys are just like girls, as far as I'm concerned, perhaps a little stronger. But here, it's like what those German girls were doing with the American soldiers who gave them chewing gum. I stop going to the movies.

CHAPTER TWENTY

The Struggle to Survive

MOTHER ISN'T WELL I am a little more than eleven years old and we live in San Francisco. My parents and I have just returned from a German movie about the war years. It takes my mother and me back to the times when we were saving bits of food for special occasions and listening for the sirens to announce air-raids at night. We leave the theater a bit disoriented. Are we really living here where it's so different from the Germany we've just revisited?

A little while after we come home, I hear a clatter in the kitchen and find my father looking at a large bottle spilling brown liquid on the kitchen floor. Above it, my mother is standing on a chair, her hands reaching far back into a high cabinet.

"You're a drunk," my father says to her. "I should have known it."

My father has been puzzled about my mother's breath for some time. It smells of "acetone," he says, a word I don't understand. He had wondered about the diagnosis. Now he understands.

"Of course," he says, "that accounts for her moodiness as well."

He is talking in a voice I later come to recognize as his doctor voice, detached and final, like the one he probably uses to convey bad news to the families of his patients.

My mother denies everything. "It's just this once because the movie made me remember so many terrible things. And I miss Berlin. I don't drink, you know that. You do know that. Now let me just lie down. The wind in the trees outside makes me so nervous. I hate these eucalyptus trees."

A pattern is set.

PRIVATE STRUGGLES At fourteen, I sit in my bedroom banging my head against the wall. My mother is in the next room, lying on the double bed, one arm dangling to the floor, her head thrown back, snoring. She is disheveled, her white sandals soiled, her blouse hanging partly over her skirt, strands of hair in her face. I would give anything not to have to see my beautiful mother falling apart this way.

The next day, when she gets up, pale and shaky, I

am full of pity. She's miserable. I know she didn't mean to hurt me. I want to forget yesterday as much as she does. I resolve to make her life better. I bring her presents, put bouquets of baby roses on her bedside stand, translate the jokes in the comic section. I invite her to take hikes with me like we used to in Baden-Baden, to get massages, to get beauty treatments.

For a day or two, I feel my efforts are rewarded. She doesn't drink. After that, she is drunk again. I am more and more desperate. Something has to be done. Talking to my father doesn't help. He shrugs his shoulders. He looks away. He comes home from the office later and later.

When I try to talk to my mother directly, I run into immediate counter-attacks.

"You're trying to spoil one of the few times when I'm enjoying myself." She looks so unhappy. It's true. She checkmates me in one move.

I keep hoping she'll change, because on the days when she doesn't drink she becomes her old familiar self again, not a mother exactly, but a very good friend. We sit gossiping at the *The Emporium*, having our feet tickled by coin-fed machines in the ladies' lounge and laughing our heads off at the other women and their aching feet. My

Eva's Berlin

mother tells me that the one in the flowered dress can hardly move her lacquered head because she's married to a hairdresser, and the one in the row in front of us must be on a diet. She is stuffing down candy as though it were her last chance on earth. We are accomplices again, allies in a world we understand but don't value.

The next day, coming home from school, I follow the familiar clues: the hose left on the garden path, the smell of something burning in the kitchen, a piece of clothing in the hallway, a spill on the bathroom floor. The end of the line is easy to predict: my mother, the stranger passed out in the hallway or on her bed or, even worse, staggering towards me. Her face, coarsened by age, has a dim, angry expression, as though she's been hit by something but can't quite tell what happened. When she is able to talk, I am her target. In a thick voice that exudes hatred, she begins her accusations. I don't love her. I am selfish and egotistical, just like my Papa. When my father arrives, she reels off the list of injuries, starting with his enjoying himself while we suffered. My father leaves. I understand. There is nothing one can say to her when she is like this.

But I can't leave her. I'm the only one she has. After she falls asleep, I listen to radio serials like *The Whistler.*

> **B**efore he even walked in the door, she would wonder if he would be high. Would he . . . talk about stuff he wouldn't remember tomorrow? Julie was always scared to bring friends over because she didn't want them to see her father drunk or passed out on the kitchen table.
>
> FRANCES
> SHUKER-HAINES

Leaning against the pillows piled high on my pink satin bed-spread, I hold onto the radio's antenna to bring the voices in more clearly.

"Who knows about the terrors that lurk in the human heart?" The voice teases the listener.

I know. But what I know isn't all that entertaining. Sometimes I call my friend Erin to tell her what happened. Her mother, too, has a close relationship with the bottle. We don't need to go into detail; each knows what the other is up against. At breakfast the next morning, my mother plays with the cat.

CHARADE OR TRANSFORMATION It's hard to give up being valued for myself. Every now and then, I still try to talk about the war with my American friends. They look like children trying to be patient but failing while they listen to parents talk interminably about the hard lives they led.

Discouragement creeps in. I realize that there is no way to communicate what it was like. I lived on the wrong side of the world and I'm beginning to understand that their feeling of safety depends on remaining unable to imagine what happened to me and others in similar circumstances.

My pillow is wet every night before I go to sleep. I cry in the school bathroom, when I'm picked last and unwillingly for a team. When Keith, who sits behind me, hits me on the head with a hammer, calls me a Nazi and tells me to go home, I cry at my desk, hiding my face in a book. What an

Eva's Berlin

irony! I'd give heaven and earth to go back to Berlin. I cry for a year. Then I give up. This can't go on. I have to find another way, or I'll end up *leidend*, long-suffering like my mother and grandmother.

At night, looking out over the moonlit fuchsia garden, just before entering high school, I make a vow. I will stop trying to hang onto being European in the presence of others.

I will blend in. I will become an American girl, at least on the outside. First, my grandmother's posture has to go. I have noticed in Mrs. Bengston's classroom that everyone slouches. Slowly, I learn to slide downwards in my chair until my bottom contacts the very edge of the wood and my legs sprawl forward. Second, I have to drop my accent. I work hard to perfect my American English. Next are my clothes. I will wear the tight straight skirts and cashmere sweaters the others wear.

The most important change, however, is in the way I act. I force myself to stop answering truthfully, no matter how I feel, when others talk to me. I learn to say, "Hi" and "Fine" whenever anyone says hello to me. I stop praising Germany. I stop voicing opinions. I go out with Jerry, who has oily hair and smells of chewing gum, and Karl, whose eyes look more frightened of me than I am of him. I become a good listener who knows how to show approval the American way. I am playing a role. Inside I remain as European and as argumentative as ever, but I only let that part out at home with my parents and at night, in my bed. It's a hard bargain that will take decades of my adult life to undo, and it allows me to survive.

High school goes well. My act works. My accent is gone. I wear the right clothes. It's easy for me to get A's. I make it my business to find out what my teachers are looking for and I give it to them with the same attention to detail I give my dress and my language. One of our history teachers likes thick papers bound in cardboard folders, the contents fully outlined and rendered with appropriate chapter headings and page numbers. I hand in what I think of as a laughably superficial paper using as many words as possible. My outline alone is three pages long, written in green ink and underlined in red. The folder is bright orange and it is returned with the A I've come to expect. It doesn't take long before other students depend on me to get them through the harder courses.

My role as a successful high school junior keeps me occupied; it is something to do. By the time I'm a senior, new acquaintances can hardly believe I've been here for such a short time.

"It can't be," they say, "you, a German! Why, you're as American as apple pie."

Eva's Berlin

The part of me that feels genuine has gone underground. I make one friend with whom I risk the real me. Erin is my secret treasure. Convinced that no one appreciates her

Botticelli beauty the way I do, I'm disappointed when I find out that they vote her the Most Beautiful Eyes in our class. I want her only for myself. Still, she comes to my house after school and when we talk I allow myself a more German voice than I use with anyone else. I teach her to say

Du bist gut. Du bist schön — you are good, you are beautiful. We practice cooking chipped beef in cream sauce and other horrible concoctions we've learned to make in our cooking class. We look at my father's art books and, when nobody's home, dance in the living room. My European background doesn't shock her, nor does my mother's drinking.

At night, when I sit by my window and look out across the pink fuchsias to the dark trees of Sutro Forest, I don't cry as often as I used to. I don't know who I am becoming. I'm not quite myself but I'm a lot less miserable than I was before. My plan is working.

EMERGENCY One early summer day when I am fifteen and returning from school, the situation worsens by another notch. I hear an unfamiliar sawing noise before I see my mother lying on the floor in the hallway. Then I recognize it as the slow rasping breath I heard when my grandmother was in her last coma. I begin to shake. Is my mother dying? I push away the panic and call my father. The conversation is short.

"Hello, Dr. Wald's office."

"Could I speak to my father please, this is Eva."

"Sorry, he's with a patient."

"Could you have him call me as soon as possible?"

"I will tell him you called."

Then, when the phone rings after what seems like an eternity, my father's voice, hurried and impersonal,

"What is it?"

"It's Mama, she's passed out again, but her breathing's so weird and I can't rouse her."

"Oh, that's terrible. Really terrible." A long pause.

"Listen, I just can't get away. Let me give you the emergency hospital's number. They'll come and take care of it. I really can't get away, the waiting room is full. Do the best you can."

I call the number. The medics come quickly. They're students from the medical center just up the street. Nothing disturbs their good mood; they hum tunes and joke as I lead them to my mother. Passing by the television set in the living room, one of them turns it to a station playing a football game.

"Just got to get the score," he tells me, smiling broadly.

They go back out to get the gurney, and load my

mother into the ambulance. On our way to the emergency hospital, one of them looks at me and shakes his head.

"Your mother needs to be in a hospital," he tells me, "no kid — not even a young lady as smart as you — should be left to care for someone like this. And in the hospital, they'd know how to help her."

I don't know what to say. I know he's right. At the same time, the way he says it has a false ring. I hate flattery. I hate false promises. I can't help but suspect that they don't really care about me or my mother.

At the emergency hospital near the entrance to Golden Gate Park, they pump her stomach while I sit in the waiting room imagining a large black hose attached to my mother, throbbing like the engine of a train. Faintly, I hear the football game coming from the direction of the operating room. When it is all over, the medic comes to talk to me. He seems completely different from when he spoke with me before.

"Don't worry about her," he says, "she'll be all right. What a smile."

My mother's much advertised charm has worked its wonders once again. It made me feel terrible. For a moment, a stranger had seemed to glimpse the seriousness of her problem. He hadn't really helped, but at least he seemed to know what I was up against.

She won't be all right. There will be days and days when her walk is heavy and her speech slurred and the food burned or uncooked. Then, in a month or two or three, the whole process will repeat itself. I will sit on my bed and listen to the repetitive bass of her breathing, and my head will feel like a time bomb waiting to explode. I'll bang my head against my pink wall, over and over again. Then I will call the emergency hospital.

At the end of such a day, my mother still in the hospital, my father takes me out to dinner at a fancy restaurant and praises me.

"You're a pro. I couldn't have done any better."

I'm glad that I'm doing a good job. Even a hint of recognition elates me. But I am confused by these dinners with my father. Exuding charm, he praises the food, speaks French to the waiter and Italian to the busboy. Taking me into his confidence, he describes a case of gall bladder surgery and promises to show me the operation in his book of medical illustrations when we get home. He compliments my appearance and my intelligence. I love feeling grown-up and going to fancy restaurants with my father, but I feel that something's wrong. Far away, at the back of my mind is the feeling that I want to talk to him about my mother, but I can't quite bring it to the surface

HORSES I learn to ride from Charley Rowley, a tall man with a black mustache who wears his tailored jodhpur suits with elegance. The stables are close, at the bottom of our street, just across from Golden Gate Park. I'm petrified at

Eva's Berlin

first. Riding was my mother's idea, another of her attempts to groom me for an upper-class life. There were no horses in the Berlin zoo and my first acquaintance with them doesn't inspire confidence. With Charley next to me on his horse, I sit on mine, trembling. When we begin a slow trot, I'm convinced I'll fall, and become so stiff that I almost do. But Charley puts his hand over mine as I hold the reins and teaches me to connect to the horse's soft mouth. Slowly the rhythms of the various gaits blend with the sound of hooves on the soft earth of the bridle paths and I begin to look forward to my treks through the park.

After a while, I make my first friend in San Francisco, Judy Petersen. It was she who responded to my question, "What does it mean, popsicle?" and went on to interpret much of what I saw on the playground. She soon joins me on my rides. There is a summer when our parents rent horses so that we can ride any time we want to for an entire month. We learn cowboy songs and pack picnics. We ride from morning to night.

In high school, Carol Wallace and I cement our friendship by riding in pairs. We take medals in all the horse shows, dressed as perfect Englishwomen or wild Arabs in Bedouin costume. I make an effort to come in second in the horsemanship competitions because I know winning is important to her. The fact that she has a right to her blue ribbons without my help never occurs to me.

On horseback, I'm in a different world. In nature, on paths lined with old trees, giant ferns and rhododendrons, I forget my mother. I even forget that I'm a foreigner. For a short while, I am able to continue the life that started in the Berlin zoo.

SHAME I am terrified that anyone except me and my father might see my mother like this: her hair a mess, her stockings uneven, walking unsteadily. I become as watchful as I was in Berlin taking forbidden private lessons from Dr. Jurczek. When I hear anyone on the stairs leading to our house, I run outside inventing excuses intended to keep them from coming in.

"I am just leaving for the doctor's to pick my mother up from an appointment."

"My mother has left town."

"My mother and my father are out to lunch together."

When I manage to avert disaster, the waves of panic cease for a little while. But her drinking becomes more and more difficult to hide. We have fewer and fewer "normal" dinners. On one occasion, when my father has invited some of his German doctor friends and their wives for a roast beef dinner, the subject of "what the Germans knew" comes up. My mother, who, while preparing a wonderful meal, has had several glasses of wine, ends the discussion by putting her hand through one of our porch windows. She drinks almost every day now and fights any attempt at talking about it. Two or three times a year, I have to take her to the emergency hospital.

After another year or so, when the time between hospitalizations begins to decrease, we realize that my mother is not just drinking to forget, she is drinking herself to death. Every hospitalization follows an attempted suicide. Frightened and helpless, my father suggests she try a sanatorium or, when he's angry, a state hospital. She listens just long enough to hear what he's getting at and then runs to the bedroom and bangs the door shut. I know he's right and she's wrong, but I can't take his side. Weeping, I plead with him to let her stay home.

"She's unhappy enough here with me who understands her. How would she feel in a hospital with utter strangers?"

"She and I belong together. She didn't send me away with the other children during *Kinderschulverschickung*. How can I send her away now?"

To let my father prevail would be such an enormous betrayal.

"Your talking about the hospital was enough," I tell him, even though I know that this is not exactly true.

"You've helped her understand the seriousness of her problem. I'm sure she'll stop drinking now."

My mother remains at home and for a few days after one of these scenes she will remain sober.

My father can't hang onto his conviction. He, too, wants desperately to believe that everything will be all right. He disappears into his work again and leaves my mother to me. I give up the slim hope that he will know what to do. In fact, I give him the bare facts about what is happening and assure him that I'm handling it. When my mother is hospitalized, he telephones the nurses to leave instructions. The possibility of sending her away for more than a few days is forgotten.

CHAPTER TWENTY ONE

Despair

DISAPPOINTMENT   For my parents, despair conquers the will to survive. Like swimmers who've given their all to reach the goal, they collapse after they reach it; but, unlike professional athletes, they never recover. Disappointment undermines their buoyancy.

A little after I turn fourteen, the snowball effect of my mother's repeated suicide attempts finally succeeds in involving my father. Suddenly, he becomes authoritative. He tries to talk to her like he does to the drunks who come to his office. She doesn't listen. He tries rages and threats and, when these don't work, he brings in psychiatrists, puts her in clinics and takes trips with her to Mexico and Europe. He can't believe that he can't help her.

I try to explain her to him and then him to her. But he can't understand her despair. The war is over now and we're all together and she should be happy. She can't profit from his optimism. She receives it as a slap in the face, a denial of all the pain she went through.

"How can she be so dissatisfied?" he asks. "She has everything a woman could want: her family, this beautiful house, enough money, her health."

"How can he be so superficial?" she asks. "Doesn't he see that I'm at the end of my rope? No one here understands the slightest thing about what I've sacrificed. I'm a stranger here. His Jewish friends look at me as though I were a Nazi. My daughter's growing up American. I can see when I'm not needed."

In a desperate attempt to give her meaningful work, my father fires his receptionist-secretary and employs my mother to sit in his office, and when that doesn't work because she misses so many days, he asks her to do his billing with him every two weeks. Sitting at the typewriter together gives them a chance to talk over his patients and, for a while, my mother drinks less.

In the long run, nothing works. Slowly, the lines on

my father's face grow deeper until one summer day during my fifteenth year he comes down with pleurisy. He has to stop working for a month. My mother stops drinking entirely and devotes herself to taking care of him. She looks happier than I've seen her look for a long time. Then he gets well and goes back to the office and her downward spiral continues.

AN ECCENTRIC SISTER Through a friend of my father's, my parents meet the German Olympic fencing champion of 1936, Helene Mayer. She looks like my idea of a hun, over six feet tall and stately with blonde braids worn on top of her head. The aura of fame that still clings to Helene excites my mother, who remembers the newsreels of her successes. I am captivated with her stories.

Arriving here soon after winning the gold medal, she was at Mills College when she had her first blind date. When her date made a pass at her in the back seat of a convertible, she picked him up and, at the next stop sign, deposited him on the street. As a contrast to my depressing experience at the movies, this is nothing short of inspirational.

She rides horses in Golden Gate Park, just like I do, she owns a cocker spaniel and lives in a small apartment near us. When she takes a bath, she tells us, she likes to find as many uses as possible for the bathwater. So she bathes fully dressed and takes the spaniel into the tub with her!

She calls me *Wörmchen*, her version of *Würmchen*

Eva's Berlin

meaning little worm. I take it as a mark of affection. With my mother, she giggles about love letters she has been receiving

from a German count. We invite her to dinner once or twice a week. I begin to think of her as an older sister. When she comes to visit, my mother doesn't drink.

Helene is the cause of the only temper tantrum of my childhood. I am fifteen years old. During a family dinner, when the plate piled with chicken is passed around, my father encourages her to take whatever she wants. He knows that I still feel as committed to the chick-

en leg as I did the day my grandmother's dog grabbed one from me in Borghorst. The chicken leg is reserved for me. He has broken an unspoken rule. Just as I thought, Helene takes advantage of the situation and puts the leg on her plate and eats it.

After dinner, I go downstairs to talk with my father who is working in his office. When I tell him that he shouldn't have offered the chicken leg to Helene, he laughs. That's when it begins. I hardly hear his answer because I'm crying and screaming at the same time.

"You don't understand. She's not even a member of the family! You know how much I like that piece! How could you?"

My father keeps smiling, and my crying and scream-ing takes on gigantic proportions. I cry and scream as he pushes me upstairs again and as my mother puts me to bed. I cry and scream for at least two more hours. No matter what either one of them says when they come and try to talk rea-son to me, I cry and scream so much I can't hear them. I've changed my mind. I don't want an eccentric sister after all, not one who takes my place at the table.

SOLACE These are the years I devote to the small Lutheran church I discover on one of my first exploratory walks. I can get there easily walking or taking the streetcar without help from my parents, who are not happy about my insistance on going to Sunday School but don't prevent my doing so, either. Reading Bible stories is more satisfying than what we're learning at school. The children here don't reject me. A new friend named Barbara with long black hair has an angelic soprano voice. I like dressing up and walking there every Sunday morning.

The pastor is a handsome man with sandy curls, who preaches sermons resounding with humor and common sense. We are urged to be kind to one another. We are reminded that hope often lies hidden in dark corners. We are invited to do good works, not for the sake of the after-life, but for this one. But the experience isn't all I'd hoped for in my desire for spiritual learning: the sense of mystery I feel lying in the moss of my root gardens is missing. I come closest to it the day I faint.

The story begins with shoes. My mother persuaded me to buy my first pair of high-heeled shoes a size too small over my objections and those of the salesman. She prided herself on the aristocratic smallness of our feet.

Having taken a little longer than usual to complete my outfit, with the small hat, the navy-blue suit, the blue suede shoes and white gloves, I go to church without breakfast that morning. Sliding into the pew beside my friend Barbara, I feel a bit light-headed but think nothing of it. When the sermon is finished, we rise as the choir files out, singing. They are carrying candles and, as I rise, the candles form an arc that circles from their arms across the ceiling bathing the church in a warm light and I hear Barbara whispering, "Sit down," but I can't. I feel myself sliding softly and smoothly past the pew and onto the floor; my soul braided into the choir's hymn I become part of the revolving light.

When I return to ordinary consciousness, Barbara is holding a handkerchief with cologne to my nose and a few other women have gathered around me. They help me get up slowly and walk toward the daylight pouring in through the church's wide-open doors. I hardly notice them because inside I'm still suffused with light. I've been part of a miracle. The light I saw was surely the light of heaven that makes us all one. Atonement. "At-one-ment," our pastor says. Saying prayers of gratitude, I make my way home. There, my parents notice my pallor, and, in an unusual show of solicitude, feed me a special breakfast and urge me to rest.

MY FATHER LEAVES US A SECOND TIME In my sixteenth year my father and I are having a very pleasant summer while my mother visits her friend Ursel in Berlin. I spend my days on horseback. In the evenings, *Papi* often takes me to the houses of his friends for dinner. Sometimes we visit my aunt and uncle and my two twin cousins who are six years younger than I am. My father had been close to his brother's family during the war; in fact, he'd delivered my cousins himself. But my mother was jealous. Even in New

York, she had raged at him when he wanted to buy presents for the twins. She expressed so much resentment about any generosity he showed his brother's family that he began to see them less and less. With my mother away, he is able to resume the connection and

I roll around on the floor laughing at my uncle's jokes because he's laughing so hard himself.

I spend a lot of my time with a boyfriend named Tony, whose brown suede jacket leaves marks on the nap of my red wool coat where he put his arm around me. Part of my decision to pass as an American means tolerating the attentions of boys. I feel very little when he touches me, just the sensation of his weight and a little curiosity about what he might be experiencing. But having a boyfriend is a sign of success.

Just before my mother is due back and my senior year in high school starts, my father falls ill with what looks like a recurrence of his pleurisy. When she learns of his illness on the telephone, my mother, in a rare moment of intuition and an unfamiliar spirituality, goes into a Catholic church in Berlin.

She lights a candle and prays to the Madonna to save him. But the Madonna is called in too late.

THE NUNS COME TO VISIT Shortly after my father returns from the hospital, where he was diagnosed with inoperable cancer, the three of us are sitting on our porch drinking tea from our old silver tea service. They haven't told him. We don't know what he knows and, true to our family tradition, the most important subject remains undiscussed. In the three weeks of his illness, he has lost at least twenty-five pounds and looks thin and wan. A parade of nuns, dressed in full black habits, comes up the stairs through our garden. It's a surprise visit from the Portuguese convent my father has taken care of for years. These are the nuns who make him cards on the thinnest parchment painted with delicate water-colors and lettered by hand in jet-black ink. On holidays they give him gifts of exquisitely delicate linen handkerchiefs and napkins bordered with handmade lace. But they have never visited my father before.

"Oh no," he says, shaking his head and smiling. "I'm not ready to go just yet."

He is attempting a joke and now we know that he knows. It is the first and the last time he alludes to his death.

His illness is like a veil descending on our already sad house. When I come home from school, I devote myself to him entirely. He grows thinner and thinner. His skin has taken on a bluish tinge. He lies back on his pillows, weak but usually ready for a joke I prepare for him. I bring him little bouquets of the pink Cecile Brunner roses from our yard. I tell him which of his patients called with messages to get well. He is happy to learn that so many of them miss him. My mother and I have very little contact. When I come home, she feels she is off duty. She drinks, but not as much or at least not as conspicuously as before. I pay very little attention. We hire nurses to help take care of my father.

SILENCE Three months go by with my father becoming more and more gravely ill. They are months during which I live the life of the sixteen-year-old high school student that I am, but only peripherally. My real life is with my father. One night, I come home from a coffee date and go directly to his room. He asks me about the boy. We have one of those short conversations necessitated by his shortness of breath. He smiles at me, but I'm not convinced.

Eva's Berlin

Later on, sleep is difficult because I can't help listening to my father's deep cough. In the middle of the night, I get up to check on him. He is very hot. He seems happy that I came in and lets me turn his pillow for him. It is hot and wet. Then I fall asleep. I wake up at four a.m. to silence. The house feels so empty that the emptiness seems to be creating its own sound, hollow and vast. When the first light enters my room through the pink curtains, the nurse comes in to tell me what I already know. My father is dead.

THE FUNERAL It's only been four months since we first learned my father was ill. They called it "galloping cancer." I hold on to the memory of turning the pillow for him, the last intimate gesture, the last smell of my father's oily, cologned face. I hug it close during the nightmare that follows. Waves of grief shake me. The house is empty and silent. My mother drinks continuously.

Just before the funeral, I walk into her bedroom to hand my mother some black stockings and discover her cramming handfuls of Seconal into her mouth. Enraged that she could be so unfeeling, I scream at her and place my fingers on her jaws to force her to open her mouth and spit out the pills. I'm only partially successful. She weaves her way through the service. Full of hatred and disgust, I try to steady her gait.

The funeral takes place at the local synagogue. It's the first time any of us have ever been there. An elegant rabbi comes to shake our hands and exchange platitudes, while our

German lawyer and my uncle are engaged in conversation about how little money is left for my mother and me. I listen to them criticize my parents' extravagant spending habits, their trips to Mexico and Europe, and my father's taste for handmade silk suits.

The funeral itself is an empty ritual. No one there speaks of my father's death with any feeling or knowledge of who he was. It ends in our viewing a numbered spot on a wall of a cemetery building where his urn will be housed. Afterwards, my aunt hands us a bill for the pair of black stockings and the black veil she'd bought my mother for the funeral.

ALONE   He never quite became my father. I could not rely on him for advice or look to him for protection. But there was a real intimacy between us. When he and my mother fought, a look at his awkward, pained face told me exactly why he was about to leave the house. When he listened to music, it was music I also wanted to hear. I learned to dance the samba with him to Xavier Cugat's music. We understood each other's puns.

There were times when he upset and confused me. When I was fifteen years old, he wouldn't eat breakfast with me because I'd cut my bangs. The first time I wore lipstick, he left the table again. Both times he shouted at me that what I was doing was inappropriate for a young girl but not for a prostitute. Then he stomped out. These sudden, angry outbursts not only frightened me but they made no sense until I was much older. Then I understood that he was worried, and possessive of the daughter he wanted for himself. Then I could see that he was behaving not so much like a father but more like a jealous lover.

I am sixteen when he dies. Alone in my room, inconsolable, I cry until I think I've exhausted all the liquid in my body and then I cry some more, surprised by the relentlessness of grief. A friend had died. But I'm not grieving a friend. I'm grieving the father I never had. He left me when I was four years old in Amsterdam. Now, not quite five years after I'd finally found him, he's left me again. I learn that, although he was very close to dying from his cancer or perhaps because of that, he gave himself the final injection. I understand. He was afraid of dying a death like some of his patients. My agony is about finding and not finding a man who remains a mystery to me. In the end, what remains is the smell of cigars mixed with cologne.

RAGE It's not until I'm in my thirties that I get in touch with my rage. My father killed himself. I knew about the final injection and I still don't blame him for it. I am enraged because he didn't say good-bye. He must have thought about his own death. I can't believe that he didn't give a thought to the women he was leaving behind. He must have thought about his wife's alcoholism and his daughter's despair. It's hard for me to believe that he convinced himself that his strong, capable daughter would be able to cope, but I suppose that if he had talked with me about his leaving us, I would have accepted his opinion. My father, however, said not a word. Perhaps his own guilt made talking as difficult for him as my mother's had always made it for her. He may have wanted to say a thousand things. He may have wanted to, but he didn't. His last testament to me was my mother.

CHAPTER TWENTY TWO

Living and Dying

LIVING I have been out of school for a month since my father died. On the advice of my father's doctor, my mother has agreed to go to a sanatorium in Menlo Park "just for a rest" and my girlfriend Erin has moved in to keep me company. She helps me remember that we are just sixteen, old enough to believe that we can handle anything that comes our way.

We fix our old favorite chipped beef on toast for dinner and dance around the living room to *Kiss Me Kate*. Perusing our yearbook, we gossip about the girls who look like advertisements for Prell shampoo. Erin is far more beautiful than any of them. In my graduation picture, I look like one of the nuns sitting by Christ's body in one of my father's books of Renaissance paintings: thin, drawn and martyred. I am looking up out of the picture. Perhaps it's an indication of where I'm going. I often have the uncanny feeling that my feet have left the earth. Inside, I'm still my old familiar self, but when I talk with my mother or friends or teachers at Lowell High, I experience a floating sensation. I sense air, not ground. Once more, and in a new way, I am a 'Displaced Person.'

SENIOR TEA   I do all the things expected of me. I have dates with boys who walk me home from school, invite me on picnics, and take me to Sock Hops and to Proms. My name

appears on the Honor Roll. My photograph can be found on several pages of the yearbook. In contrast to my graduation picture, in these snapshots of dances and parties and committee work, I manage to look as vacantly happy as the other girls.

But, much as I try, I can't quite bring it off. A trail of clues — some subtle, some glaring — would lead an astute observer to discover that I am not quite the person I appear to be.

Since my father's death, time hangs heavy for me. Sadness has arrived with a crushing weight. My father gone, my mother is almost constantly drunk. To keep from being overwhelmed with helplessness and grief, I keep busy. School is full of opportunities for distraction. I volunteer for everything I can, academic and social. My efforts succeed in keeping me going, but, my performance lacks smoothness. My real self begins to show through.

In my role as 'Big Sister' I am supposed to help incoming freshmen get acquainted with the complexities of the school. My 'little sister' puts up with me, though she knows her way around better than I do. She appears to appreciate my company and doesn't complain. As part of my duties, I attend meetings and do special chores for Mrs. Close, the biology teacher in charge of the Big Sisters. I am on the committee that buys Mrs. Close an expensive Maltese cat for her birthday. When the four of us, carefully done up in our cleanest cotton dresses, deliver the cat to her house, I forget to sit carefully balanced on the edge of her damask couch sipping my glass of egg-nog because I become entranced with the kitten. In the midst of our play, the kitten suddenly attacks Mrs. Close's lace curtains as though they were so many trees and I spill my entire glass of egg-nog on the light-blue silk cushions of her sofa. Despite my embarrassment, I am flooded with an odd sense of relief. I've been working too hard to do the right thing. For once, the cat is, literally, out of the bag. I could use a few more spills, but I quickly drown my relief in embarrassed apologies.

Lowell High School's class of '52 is known for celebrating its graduating girls with fancy tea parties. We are expected to wear white gloves, high-heeled shoes, and hats. I usually leave the house properly dressed, but, after walking down the garden steps and along the long drive-way that leads to the street, I succumb to temptation. I remove my large brown felt hat and leave it in the mailbox.

It is one of these teas, given by one of the more affluent families at my school, that fully exposes my inadequate understanding of the American way of life. Even as I enter, I am impressed by the butler who takes my coat at the door and the maid who goes in and out of the kitchen to replenish the rich array of teacakes and hors d'ouevres. Dressed in one of my best suits, brown wool with satin piping, I head for the table where tea is being served to pile my plate with as much food as possible. Alhough I haven't been hungry for years, I still attack every opportunity to eat free food with the energy of a starving person. After I have eaten, I'm at a loss. I try to stay a while but, I can gush, hem, giggle and haw only for so long. Before I go home, I leave a generous one dollar tip in the hands of the butler. Some years later, at a class reunion, I learn that the person I took to be the butler was the host, my classmate's father.

STANFORD   Leaving home after high school is something I have looked forward to for a long time. Though I've grown to love the beaches and the ocean despite the freezing temperatures, the Bay Area's perennial wisps of fog have come to be associated with our sorrows. I want to leave my mother yet I know I have to remain within calling distance in case I am needed. Stanford, with its cloudless sky, its Moorish arches, and its quiet, monastic air, seems like an oasis.

The letter arrives late. When I pick it out of our mailbox by the large bay tree, it exudes the faint odor that I will always associate with 'the farm,' as it was then called: very dry grass, hot sun, and a faint herbal aroma. The letter tells me that I am accepted for the summer quarter. It's a mixed blessing: despite my best efforts I have failed to

be as acceptable as one of the girls who will start in fall. But it is a blessing none the less; a qualified acceptance is better than none at all.

When I arrive, I find that life in the dormitory is another challenge. We are wearing the 'New Look,' full skirts worn with Gibson girl blouses. I observe the other girls as they compare clothes and figures, exchange gossip about their families, and dash about getting ready for dates with an energy that baffles me. I'm afraid that I don't belong here, either.

But Stanford is small enough and large enough to permit outsiders to meet. I become a member of a group of four with my friends Annie Hoag, the story-teller, Barbara Armstrong, the actress, and Barbara von Briesen, artist and foreign student coordinator. Together, we sit up late at night debating philosophical issues, find ways of defying the stringent dormitory rules, shock the prim and proper Stanford girls with our lack of attention to decorum, and give support

when one or the other (I was one and Anne the other) gets suspended from campus.

At the back of my dormitory lies Lake Lagunitas, large enough for short boat trips and long swims in the hot Palo Alto sun. In this time before boom boxes, beepers, and cell phones, it is a place where quiet reigns. Students come out to talk and study and the occasional blue jay is heard with its raucous call. I am to be found there almost anytime I'm not in class, reading my assignments or one of the German novels I've found in the library stacks.

Stanford's small classes provide the academic challenge I have been looking for. A course in medieval history brings back my years with Dr. Jurczek and lets me submerge myself once more in tales of knights and battles, of wimpled ladies and romantic love. I spend hours in the Bender Rare Book Room on the top floor of Cubberley Library, turning the dry yellowed pages of ancient texts and, for the first time, following the curlicued golds and reds that illustrate illuminated manuscripts. Our mandatory English course demands that we criticize modern essays dealing with everything from Momism to *The Man in the Gray Flannel Suit* — from sociology to politics, philosophy and religion in a class small enough to permit us to voice our views. Here is the opportunity awaited since my efforts were thwarted in the first grade. Slowly, I find friends whose minds show traces of the originality, rebelliousness, and wit that I have been searching for.

FOREIGN STUDENT   Stanford has students who come from all corners of the world: India, China, Japan, France, Italy, Sweden and Germany. They need a coordinator and my friend Barbara von Briesen is perfect for the job. She carts them around in a borrowed car to classes, coffees and orientations. Shyly, I join in. Once more, I question where I belong. Unlike the others, I attended an American high school. Like them, English is my second language. Foreign students, like actors, attract me with their colorful eccentricities. The sheer exoticism of the Indian Sikh, who is said to have yards of black hair hidden underneath his turban, appeals to me. Students from the highly politicized

Eva's Berlin

Eastern Bloc draw me into entirely new debates and discussions. At Stanford in the 'fifties, where both the spoken and the unspoken rules are on the strait-laced, conservative side, foreign students usually ally themselves with the more rebellious groups. Among the girls, the Lone Woman Rule which allows a girl to visit one of the men's (unregulated) dormitory rooms only in the company of another woman is broken regularly.

When one of us has to appear before one of the many committees that enforce our strict girl's dormitory rules, we meet afterwards to laugh together. When we are punished with moral lectures by the Dean of Women who asks us to take seriously the responsibilities of being a 'Stanford girl' we counter with an argument that praises Stanford's academic values while holding the social environment in contempt. Of course, my friend Anne and I are suspended in our sophomore year, and my friend Barbara barely avoids it.

My conversations with the foreigners echo my own experiences. They are going through mild forms of the same difficulties I have had, and that is a comfort. My Czech friend Antonin finds me an enthusiastic listener when he delivers a vituperative lecture on the barrenness of American culture, but I can't quite join him in his total rejection of American values. I find that just as I can't fully become American, I can't quite identify myself as a foreigner, either. Being identified as a German isn't the same, after all, as being Czech or Italian or Indian. Germany has become synonymous with the plagues of racism and dictatorship. Where ever I go, even such 'good' German qualities as orderliness, cleanliness, and mechanical genius are derided. Whenever German is quoted as part of an article or essay, several words are misspelled. I don't know anyone who wants to learn German yet I continue to love my language, with its echoes of landscape and music, of Göthe and Mozart. Whereas my struggle in Germany centered on the question, "What does it mean to be Jewish?" I am now struggling with, "What does it mean to be German?"

It is in these conversations that I discover that although I began my Americanization for the sole purpose of 'passing,' so much time has been spent perfecting my American role-play that some of it is sticking. I'm becoming more American every day, even as I gradually take back the parts of my soul rooted in European soil. So I listen to Antonin's diatribe with pleasure. But I point out the virtues of jazz and democracy. My 'place,' unlike my grandmother's, will always be in more than one location. I will remain a *Mischling.*

When I go back to visit Germany during my college years, I find many changes. Of my best friends Günther and Erika, only Erika survives. Both got ill in the stressful and hungry aftermath of the war, and both were sent to a Swiss sanatorium. We corresponded and I watched sadly as their letters became more and more restricted to the minute details of their tuberculosis regimen. I grieved when Günther died a few years after the war, but because he was so far away and

Eva's Berlin

I hadn't seen him since we were children, his death blended with Mann's accounts of the illness in *The Magic Mountain*. I had lost him when I lost Berlin.

Erika has married a pediatrician with whom she leads a stolidly German life. I can't find the person with whom I shared the island in the *Tiergarten*. With three young children, she extols the pleasures of motherhood and insists

that she had never even thought of a career. When she describes the appliances that came with her new apartment with an enthusiasm matched only by American advertising, I realize that she has become a woman of post-war Germany, and that means she's ahead of me in adopting American values. I wonder what happened to the close and intricate fantasy life we led during the war. Perhaps it was only needed to counter the crisis of being half-Jewish in Nazi Germany. Perhaps the sanatorium took it out of her. Perhaps a little of both.

Most of the Germans I talk with show a similar fascination with material things while foregoing the kind of philosophical-political discussions I had hoped for. No matter, Berlin's humor and its comfortable dialect can still be found on any streetcorner, and the landscape echoes the experiences of my youth: the soft *Berliner Luft*, the quality of air that so unmistakably identifies Berlin, the Linden trees with their powdery yellow bloom, the old gray houses.

In Baden-Baden, I find my friend Lilo again. She has become a beautiful young woman but in her I find the same person I had left behind. We talk over tea at the *Kurhaus*, comparing Stanford and the University of Heidelberg, exchanging views about the opposite sex. She is as lively as ever, but our lives have become too divergent and, though we correspond for a while, we gradually lose contact.

MOTHER On the few quick visits home during the summer of my nineteenth year, my mother doesn't drink. On one of the rare occasions when she allows discussion, she confesses that she believes she drinks more when I am with her. She doesn't know why and I don't press her: I'm so relieved that she seems to be making progress that I don't even care that she seems to be saying that that it's my presence that harms her.

In the fall quarter, I come home to stay and discover one more time that nothing has changed. My mother has dropped her thoughtful attitude and continues to drink. She no longer remembers that my going away to Stanford had been a relief. Instead, it becomes a topic of unending accusation.

"You're just like your father," she says. "He had no

problem leaving us, either."

When I show her my first college A's, she responds, bitterly, "That's what I mean, you're just like him. He was successful, too."

From now on, despite my efforts to cheer her and cajole her or to find therapy for her, our good times together will become fewer and fewer and her bouts of drinking more and more closely interspersed with suicide attempts. Then, when I am a sophomore in college, she begins to have epileptic seizures that terrify her. Now, suddenly, she doesn't want to die. She consents to go to a sanatorium in Menlo Park, a place with cottages and rose gardens and a doctor who reminds her of my father as a young man.

When she returns home, she is filled with tales about her fellow patients. The one who found her three-year-old dead in the swimming pool and had to have shock treatments. The one who murdered her husband and his girlfriend. She is fascinated by the problems of others but her own remain untouched. I visit her often but never enough to avoid reproach. I take psychology courses to find out how to help. It doesn't work, of course. She looks on any attempt to help as an attack. I don't give up and neither does she.

CELESTIAL NAVIGATION Just after my nineteenth birthday, the housemother in my dormitory calls me into her office. She begins by saying, "You look particularly nice today," and goes on to compliment me on my black and white skirt and my starched white blouse, "just perfect for this sunny day."

I make the correct social responses, but I'm puzzled when she asks me to take a ride in her Chevrolet sedan. We are not friendly. What does she want?

A large, horsey woman, she used to be a celestial navigator in the WAVES. The term has been a source of many a biting remark, since we associate the word celestial with choirs of angels and her appearance is anything but angelic. We drive away from campus through softly curved spring-green hillsides to a more wooded, shady area. We make more small talk. I still don't know why we're here. She compliments me on my grades. I grow more and more uncomfortable.

Finally, she parks the car on top of a rise overlooking the rolling hills that already have a hint of the yellow hue they'll wear all summer.

"I have some very bad news," she says. "We've had a call from the police. I don't know how to say this any other way but plainly. Your mother was found dead this morning."

The feeling of unreality makes oceans roar in my head. I can hardly breathe and I am stuck here alone with this horrible horse-faced woman.

"She can't be dead," I say. "I just called her this morning and she didn't answer."

From very far off, I can hear that what I'm saying is absurd. I am having a hard time breathing. The horse face is attempting a tender expression and failing.

"I don't expect you to know what to do. It will take some time to absorb this."

I am smiling. Perhaps the horse face turned out to be a celestial navigator after all. Will she take me to my mother? She starts the car again. We drive back toward Stanford. I am wrapped in a cocoon, enclosed in dense cotton. She stops by our dormitory. Somehow, I get out of the car. We are walking toward my room in the dormitory when I hear her say,

"Look, just rest for a while, and then, if you want to talk, feel free to come around to my office any time, okay?"

I want to pound something with my hand. I hear my voice crying,

"Now I don't have anybody." I'm faintly aware that she is standing at my doorway. Perhaps she is saying something. I can't hear her. I am furious. My breath is shallow. My eyes are focused on my doorknob.

"I want to be alone now," I say, and she turns to walk away.

WHO WAS SHE I never see my mother again. Her physician identifies her body at the morgue where the police had taken her. I am left with bloody sheets and a house that looks as bruised as I imagine she was. Caught between my shame about exposing the evidence of my mother's degradation and my helpless grief, I don't know where to turn. When Anne and the two Barbaras show up on my doorstep, having heard the news from our housemother, we turn our sadness and confusion into an energetic housecleaning.

My parents' old friend Dr. Hill arranges a very small funeral at one of those anonymous cemeteries that house hundreds of the dead on our peninsula, conducted by a minister I've never met. Only Dr. Hill and my aunt are in attendance. The minister says a few words. Someone puts an arm around my shoulders. The day is cold and the hillside shrouded in thick fog. We scatter the earth over her grave. I feel immeasurably sad.

Back at home, I sit at her dressing table holding the handkerchief she used to blend her make-up and smelling its familiar aroma for the last time. *Eau de Cologne,* powder, Roger and Gallet's carnation soap: the downy, soft handkerchief recalls my mother's most feminine self. I remember her giggling with Else, the Roumanian's girlfriend, about *nightshade*, the sexy hue of a pair of stockings garnered on the black market. Or dressed in black chiffon and platform patent leather heels. I don't know if any men admired her the way she felt she deserved, but I did. I saw her charm. I sat at her feet and listened to her extravagant embroideries. Through her I learned to appreciate gossip, fiction and intrigue. Her spirited imitations of our friends and relatives were my first lessons in psychology. My love for her, though it was liberally sprinkled with hate, survived what seemed, at times, to be inhuman messages of rejection. And, although she left a legacy of immense pain, she also left me her conviction that life was an adventure to be entered fully — absurd and difficult, perhaps, but full of dramatic situations to be embroidered and, with a little bit of luck, rewritten.

In the end, she felt she had run out of luck. Perhaps that was the saddest thing of all, her conviction that she had been deserted by the angel who looked over her shoulder at the gaming tables and brought her through the war, only to show her that the promised Eden had no more reality than a dream.

Epilogue

The story of the girl who grew up in Berlin ends with her mother's death. The old cast of characters is gone. The scenery has changed. From now on, her story will blend into the great story, the one that each of us can tell about the trails that led us here. Yet wisps from that time cling to the present like the fingers of fog that shroud the San Francisco hills, to be included in the life of the woman she was to become. These pages cannot describe that woman's life. They are intended to give the reader a bare outline of her progress.

Eva's Berlin

THEATER My love of theater started at age six, when my mother took me to a performance of *Sleeping Beauty* and I fell in love with the prince in his glittering coat and white tights. Entranced by everything theatrical — the larger-than-life figures, the make-up, scenery, costumes and lighting — I sat in the darkened theater rapt with attention. At Grattan Grammar School in San Francisco, my own theatrical career began as Miss America (with a heavy German accent) and continued with parts as angels and snowflakes in the Christmas plays of church and school. Although I acted very little in high school, I read aloud interminably to any friends who would listen.

In my senior year in college I met George Hitchcock, an actor. We were dating steadily when he was cast in Shaw's *Arms and the Man* and I recognized an opportunity to do

something I had always wanted to do that now had the additional advantage of keeping me occupied while he was rehearsing. I tried out for a play. My first part was that of Dolly, one of the voluble, witty twins in Shaw's *You Never Can Tell*. I took to the theater like a duck to water. Rehearsals took place on warm, spring evenings. They were a time out of life, hours in which I had no responsibilities and could let my imagination play. My twin and I hit it off from the beginning. An experienced actor, he helped me by running lines and supporting my wobbly body during a dancing entrance. My dress was made of pink organdy with a thousand flounces and, to my great surprise, I ran away with the reviews.

My happy relationship with the theater continued for a long time. I acted my way through college and graduate school playing classic ingénues, and once, to my great delight, a whore in Giraudoux's *The Madwoman of Chaillot*. Black satin slit to the waist and net stockings provided a thrilling contrast to my 'good girl' image, even if only for a moment.

The theater became home to me. I loved its atmosphere and its energy. Reading for a part came naturally. I had had practice, both in jumping into another existence in and reading aloud. The sense of belonging bestowed by having 'got the part' made me feel at home. The circle of actors assembled for a first reading gave me my first intimation of what it was to know one's place, a place, in fact, that allowed an unknown freedom. An hour before the performance, in that empty space of time before the mirror, without obligations except to make up my face, I could let my imagination roam the world of dreams and fantasies. Then, as the character I was playing began to appear in the mirror, a different self began to emerge until, in my role, I could join the others and enter the world of the play.

The struggle to belong was to continue to plague me. Something was missing in my stage persona — not for those watching, perhaps, but for me. Even when I appeared in several plays a year, I could never really make myself believe that I acted on a stage. While I had no trouble entering the imaginary world of theater, I found it impossible to bring the actress into my real world. As an audience member watching others act, I found myself marvelling at the actors' courage, as though it was something I could never do. When I came to the theater and saw myself advertised, I often thought it must be someone else's picture behind the glass in Shakespearean dress, some other person who was reviewed in the paper. Not me, not the self I could visualize doing my schoolwork or talking with my friends. I could never picture the actress in my mind's eye. She escaped the rest of me, took on another personality, headed for the spotlight and did as she pleased.

FATHERS I continue to look for the father I lost before I ever really knew him by seeing men who are years, even decades, older than I. As a teen-ager, I date Arne Sorenson, a thirty-year-old Dane who entertains at Lutheran church socials with a pantomime of a woman struggling into her girdle. Not only a member of that glamorous community — actors — he is European and exudes a sort of leathery, sweatered masculinity that makes me feel secure in his presence. My Greek friend Dimitropolous, another multi-linguist in his thirties, is so tyrannical that he refuses to speak to me for days after I've served him the wrong brand of bread for lunch, but he also takes me on long evening walks to help me sleep. At Stanford I find a French professor in his fifties who wears a Homburg and speaks nine languages, a man rumored to have been a spy during the world war. Monsieur Le Notre, dressed for our date in a long black overcoat and the famous hat, warns me that dating older men will ruin my reputation, but I pay no attention.

Years later, I fall in love with a music professor thirty-five years older than I, another dictator, this one a German whose tyranny is mitigated by care and an apparent appreciation of my real self. He coaches opera singers. Together, we stage scenes from classic works for his students' recitals. In him I find the first real father. I know now that while I first went to him for vocal coaching for a role in an outdoor Shakespeare festival, it was through him that that I discovered a more important voice, the one that would become the foundation for a self I could trust.

My first husband is George Hitchcock. Handsome, charming, and twenty years older than I, he is the actor and writer who not only distracts me and enchants me, but shape-shifts into the mountain man who takes me on hikes and camping trips that help to ground my floating self. Convinced that he was placed on this earth to reassure me, I

marry the father I always wanted: a playwright, warm, tender, and calm, who writes roles for me in his plays and sits with me while I try to deal with the fears and nightmares of a budding actress. Joining his large circle of friends, I become a part of the San Francisco community. And through him, I begin to develop a fragile trust in the future. He fathers me successfully enough to let me divorce him after fifteen years and marry the man who would be the father of my children.

A SENSE OF PERMANENCE The understanding that nothing lasts came early on in my life. From the time we left Münster for Holland, my sense of what is lasting was challenged again and again. When neither country, neighbor, family, sky, or earth can be counted on, roots become worn from the effort to take hold in shifting ground. Although I had already learned to enjoy the present moment, I found it difficult to unlearn the lesson that the next moment could bring disastrous change.

In the dormitory at Stanford, I found it difficult to join conversations about the future. When girls planned to buy furnishings and jewelry they hoped to keep all their lives, it sounded to me like so many pipe dreams. Only the very naive could believe that anything owned today would still be there in several more years. I tried to live simply, with few expectations.

And so I became a beginner on the road to Buddhist non-attachment without knowing it. I let myself possess a few things as long as I knew myself fully prepared for their sudden disappearance.

I spent very little money. If it didn't cost a fortune, it was easier to let it go. At least there would be enough money left for a sudden departure if all was lost. As more and more years in America passed without a sign of war, however, I had to acknowledge that, for years now, houses, furnishings, and food supply had remained intact. Having permitted a bit of hope to enter the script of predictable loss and abandonment, I allowed myself to buy furniture for the apartment I shared with my first husband. The rule was that any single item had to be bought for less than fifteen dollars. I learned to refinish wood. A round oak table with eight leaves and some Windsor chairs, long-slatted and elegant, are still in my possession. I lived with my bags packed. Clothes had to be made on my sewing machine, or bought on sale, or second-hand. My only pets were cats who could be counted on to take care of themselves.

After another decade passed in relative peace and I entered my thirties, I began to realize that what I experienced was simply a more intense version of what the whole human race was facing: impermanence, the immanence of death. That insight made a glimpse of the future possible. Now I could permit my desire for children to surface. I could even buy a house and furnish it with items costing more than fifteen dollars, as long as I was prepared to let them go.

It took ten more years and a second marriage to dare to have children. My second husband is not a father to me. With him, I was able to join the larger community, to allow myself the hopes and dreams that had eluded me in my college years. With Alan as a partner in life and in work, I could dare to hope for children. They did not, however, come easily, and when they did, I realized that it had taken forty years of my life for me to believe in the possibility of a future. Even then, the belief was tested. Our first adopted child, a beautiful dark-haired boy named Aaron, was with us only for an instant. He died at the age of seven weeks of that mysterious illness: crib death. But once I had held a baby in my arms, they would not remain empty. We adopted Sasha four months after Aaron died and our biological son, Julian, was born a year and a day after Sasha came into our lives.

Even now, my hold on material reality is tenuous. When my women friends tell me, "I know where everything is in my house," I'm awe-struck. The conviction that giant forces are constantly rearranging the objects of the material world behind my back is still with me. When I misplace something, it's hard for me to believe that it still exists. Were someone to tell me it had just been swallowed up, on the other hand, I'd understand completely. When things are stolen from me, I can't avoid a nagging doubt as to whether I had owned them in the first place. Objects are loosely attached to the earth, in my view, and when I read pre-war German authors like Hermann Hesse or Thomas Mann, who lovingly describe certain old gates and cobblestone streets, I am overcome with nostalgia for something I have longed for but never had. The knowledge of permanence came too late to be convincing.

HUNGER REMAINS In this land of plenty, where landfills could be stocked with thrown away food, hunger is still with me. I'm seldom aware of it when I am alone. But in company I am compelled to eat as quickly and as much as possible, convinced for the moment that this plenty cannot last. The only difference is that I no longer feel compelled to share. It's as though what I have learned about America's rich resources applies to others, but not to me. Sharing dessert with a friend, I recently found myself nearly having a spoon fight over the ice cream in the middle of our apple crumble. I've invented a term for it, 'competitive eating' — humiliating and unavoidable as my devotion to Hestia, the goddess of the household, whose demands range from the simple baking of bread to the saving of everything edible.

I have met other refugees with such compulsions. Food scraps considered garbage everywhere else must be transformed, frozen, melted, canned, baked or dried. Only vegetable scraps may be thrown on the compost. Everything else must be eaten by someone or it will be weighed against me in Hestia's final judgement. Bread must be saved to be fed to the ducks and seagulls. Second leftovers go to the dog and cat. On any vacation, the food plan is visited and re-visited in my mind. I must buy just enough and no more.

"*Auf das nichts umkomme*," said my grandfather; that nothing shall be wasted.

DEATH   Perhaps my fear of dying began with bringing my mother to the emergency hospital. Or perhaps it began in the last year of the war when the reptile house was bombed and I stood watching the reflexive movements of the animals I was told were dead. For a long time, the fear of the not quite dead made it difficult for me even to enter a room where the cat proudly deposited a dead bird or snake. The uncanny feeling that the dead aren't quite dead drew in my breath and made me lose control of my body. Once I jumped sky-high trying to sweep a dead sparrow out of the way with a long broom because I kept expecting it to rustle its wings.

Now I am old enough to have survived the death of close friends. My friend, the music teacher, died in his eighties. I was there as his brain deserted him through a series of strokes. After he died, his wife and I went to see his body in the hospital's morgue. For the first time in my life, I had no fear as I placed some flowers into his hands and said a silent prayer. I was thanking the body for holding him for so long, aware that he, himself, or whatever made him so, was long gone. Together with her husband and son, I sat with my friend Erin, as she died of cancer. We had a chance to review our lives together, to laugh and to cry. Right now, her urn rests on an altar in my bedroom — ashes waiting to be scattered on her favorite hiking path. Although my grief has taken me through many dark woods, these friends have helped me accept the finality of death. I can hold a dead bird with tenderness, no longer afraid that its wings will begin to flutter in my hand.

WORK The reader will not be surprised to learn that my experience in life and the theater yielded more information about the human psyche than most professions required. It seems only natural that when the choice came between becoming a professional actress and a psychologist, the latter won out. I loved the theater, it's true, but there were many reasons I could not make it my profession. The competetive commercial demands of a theatrical career frightened and distanced me. I did not want to spend time hoping to act in a commercial in order to put food on the table. I was afraid of a future without a steady job. I did not have the kind of talent that demanded I serve it. On the other hand, I needed a place to continue to try to solve the puzzles of my personal history. I needed to keep helping, so that I could, by proxy, heal my family and myself.

Happily, I could combine drama with the practice of

psychotherapy. Helping to develop and use both psycho-drama and drama therapy proved to satisfy my desire to practice my profession in a way that allowed me to express myself creatively and help others to do the same. I have worked together with adults and children, seen families and groups, professionals and graduate students, to help untie some of the knots of our human dilemmas. It has been satisfying, this ancient combination of theater and healing, and I believe it has untied a knot in my own life. When, about five years ago, I stopped taking new clients, I explained it by saying, "I believe I've cured my mother."

THE COMPELLING PRESENT My two sons Sasha and Julian have entered their mid-twenties. Their presence in my life has been the most enduring reassurance. Without knowing it, they helped me confront the ghosts of the past.

Hearing the story of their grandparents' early death, my five-year-old son Sasha held my hand. "Don't worry, Mom," he said, "you and Dad'll stay up till we're very old." When they were older and watching violent movies on television with their pre-teen peers,

I asked them how they could watch so much blood and murder. Again, it was Sasha who patiently explained it to me.

"It isn't real, Mom," he said, shaking his head. "It's just special effects. If it was real, Julian and I would be the first to get out of there."

Both of them are known for stopping fights rather than starting them. They were part of a Conscientious Objectors Group in their teens. I had to admit they knew more about the difference between truth and fiction than I did.

BERLIN AGAIN   Now, as Berlin readies herself to become the capital again, the city is returning to her old self. There are troubles now as there were then. Economic and class differences cause rifts and dissatisfaction. But it isn't a trouble-free Berlin I come to visit with my husband and my younger son. It's a real Berlin, a Berlin that pulses with the same vigor it had during its most dreadful years. I find it in the 'nineties.

Throngs of people crowd the streets; the sidewalk cafes bursting, a huge contingent of students and international hippies are buying and selling their way around the *Gedächtniskirche* where as a child I amused myself by making a *Schlitterbahn*, a path smoothed for sliding on the ice. The crowd feels young. *Frech*. The word describes a special Berliner impudence, talking loudly in the dialect that seems to survive everything — the Kaiser, Hitler, bombs, street fighting, division, the Wall, Honecker, the Western Powers. To all those many people in the streets, there is no question that Berlin is the place to be. After all that has happened, Berliners are still Berliners.

The new-old city confronts me with typical direct-ness. Re-animated by the crowds in the streets, every stone feels familiar as I walk past the Berlin zoo where I spent so much of my early childhood. On earlier visits when I couldn't find the crowds of people or the familiar metropo-litan spirit, my emotions had remained locked up. This time, the trees beckoning from behind the gray brick walls of the zoo could have been my grandmother's hands urging me to walk faster. The same giant stone elephants at the orange gate. The soft, caressing air lets my young self re-enter my body. Berlin is mine again. My steps quickening, I pull my large son along faster and faster until we reach the *Kurfürstendamm*, where I recognize the *Romanische Café*, the sidewalk restaurant where my mother and I ate ice cream so long ago. As my husband Alan and my son Julian sit down to order pastries, I am overcome with intense emotion. For the first time since the war ended, I feel I've come home. For a moment, I feel as though I've just left the *Marmorpalast*, which is right next door. I can still hear the lilt of the love songs in that first cabaret performance just after the war.

Ordering, I see myself through the eyes of the wait-er, not the eleven-year-old girl who left after the war, but an American woman of late middle age, accompanied by her husband and son, and I'm suddenly overwhelmed by a com-bination of sadness and rage. Crying, I feel like a lover returning to her beloved, only to find someone else has taken her place. What are all these people doing here? At the table next to ours, two couples are in animated conversation. They're in their early thirties, dressed with the kind of chic natural to the inhabitants of any metropolitan area with a little cash. Probably office workers, married a short time, having a drink before going home at the end of a working day. I can't take my eyes away from their table. Objectively speaking, we have little in common. Yet, listening to their conversation, their inflections, the slightly sexual innuendo that turns ordinary talk into a game, I'm overcome with raw envy. They're leading my life! They're living in my city, speaking my language. They never had to leave. They never had to translate, to learn another language, another way to behave. I want to grab their bodies, their souls, their clothes, their walks, the drinks they ordered and make them mine. I should be that woman speaking the dialect my mother taught me. I can feel Berlin in my body. I can feel myself having grown up German, marrying, living in a cramped apartment. My real existence. What are these strangers doing living it? This is my soft summer air, my gray pavement. Tears come. I can't stop weeping. Then I become self-conscious. Slowly, I return to my adult self where I meet the rage of my eleven-year-old counterpart. Rage at having been torn away from my home. Rage at the lack of understanding about how much I'd lost. As I regain my composure, I see my husband looking concerned and understanding and my son, who looks puzzled. I ask him, "Could you understand any of that? I know you don't like it when I cry."

"Sure, Mom," he answers. "You feel like you've been here all along, but you haven't."

The surprise is that some time during the second day of my visit the feeling leaves me entirely and I find myself occupying my own life again, the one I do have as opposed to the one I never had. Suddenly, as though the spell has lasted its time and not a moment longer, I'm back in the present.

Freed, I can embark on reparations. As I give Alan and Julian a tour of the zoo, I remember the lion cub photographs. My grandmother is long gone. Could it be possible that the studio remains? We walk past the elephant house on our way to the old playground and there it is! The photo studio for children who want to pose with the lion cubs. It is located outdoors where a ticket kiosk has been built in front of the cubs' cage, surrounded by lawn where they can play.

The coveted photograph remains elusive. When we first arrive, the cubs are asleep in the shadow of a tree. We are told to wait until they wake up. To pass the time, we walk to the playground where I spent so many hours. Here everything is changed. Modern playground equipment, see-saws and slides and swings abound, but the old bars and rings have disappeared. I bend down to crumble the earth between my fingers. It feels as familiar as an old shoe, and I can feel my young self standing at the double bars, ready for a shoulder stand, hoping that Alia is watching.

When we return to the studio, the cubs are far more interested in playing together than in having their picture taken with us. They romp and chase each other around the trees, their downy fur like feathers against the old gray bark of the trees, oblivious to the fact that they have a job to do. Tempted with snacks, beguiling words from their keeper, and all the sweet enchantments we can think of, a small cub finally settles down on my lap to permit the photograph for which I've waited half a century.

Eva Wald Leveton
San Francisco, December 1999

Bibliography

DANES, MAGDA (1997) *Castles Burning*. W.W. Norton: London.

ETHELL, JEFFREY AND PRICE, ALRED (1981) *Target Berlin; Mission 250: 6 March, 1944*. Jane's Publishing, Inc.: New York.

FRIEDERICH, RUTH ANDREAS (1984) *Battleground Berlin: Diaries 1945-1948*. Paragon House Publishers: New York.

FRIEDMAN, INA R. (1982) *Escape or Die; True Stories of Young People Who Survived the Holocaust*. Addison-Wesley Publishing Co., Inc.: Reading, Massachusetts.

GILL, ANTON (1993) *A Dance Between Flames: Berlin Between Wars*. Carrol and Graf: London.

V. KARSDORFF, URSULA (1962) *Berliner Aufzeichnungen aus den Jahren 1942-1945*. Biederstein Verlag: München.

KRAMER, JANE (1996) *The Politics of Memory: Looking for Germans in the New Germany*. Random House: New York.

KURELIC, WILLIAM (1985) *They Sought a New World*. Tundra
   Books: Canada, United States.

LADD, BRIAN (1997) *The Ghosts of Berlin; Confronting German
   History in the Urban Landscape*. University of
   Chicago Press: Chicago.

PERL, LILA AND LAZAN, MARION BLUMENTHAL (1996) *Four Perfect
   Pebbles: A Holocaust Story*. Greenwillow books: New York.

READ, ANTHONY AND FISHER, DAVID (1993) *The Fall of Berlin*.
   W.W. Norton & Co., Inc.: New York.

RYAN, JULIUS (1966) *The Last Battle*. Simon and Schuster:
   New York.

SHIRER, WILLIAM L. (1941) *Berlin Diary, The Journal of a Foreign
   Correspondent*. Alfred A. Knopf: New York.

SHUKER-HAINES, FRANCES (1994) *Everything You Need to Know
   About a Drug-Abusing Parent*. Rosen Publishing Group:
   New York.

VOGEL, ILSE MARGRET (1992) *Bad Times, Good Friends*.
   Harcourt, Brace, Jovanovitch: New York.

Glossary

Deutschmark: German currency.

Der Stürmer: German Nazi newspaper.

Führer: leader, term used to address Hitler.

Gemütlichkeit: cozyness, comfort.

Gestapo: Secret Police.

Hausfrau: housewife.

Hexenschuss: German dialect for sciatic pain.

Heil Hitler: the Nazi salute, hail Hitler, given with raised right arm.

Hitler, Adolf (1880-1945): leader of the Nazi party, which ruled Germany from 1933 to 1945; his book *Mein Kampf* (My Struggle) describes his plan to conquer Europe and form a master race by eliminating the Jews.

Hitlerjugend: Hitler Youth, German Youth Organization.

Ideltidel: Eva's baby name for herself.

Judenschwein: Jew pig.

Kaffeeklatsch: afternoon coffee get-together.

Kaiser: emperor.

Kinderschulverschickung: children's transports out of Berlin to the country for schooling.

Kristallnacht: the night of shattered glass when the Nazis trashed the Jewish businesses, 1938.

Kurpark: a park at a spa.

Marmorpalast: Marble Palace, Berlin movie house.

Mensch: human being.

Mischling: a person of mixed race.

Nazi: short for *Nationalsozialistische Deutsche Arbeiterpartei,* National Socialist German Party.

Oma, Opa: grandmother, grandfather.

Parteibonze: a big wheel in the Nazi party.

Portierfrau: Concierge, house manager.

Raubtierhaus: house where wild cats are caged.

Reichsarmee: Hitler's army.

Rutsch: zoom.

S.A.: short for *Sturm-Abteilung*, storm troopers of the Nazi party.

S.S.: short for *Schutzstaffel*, originally Hitler's body guards, later Hitler's intelligence and secret police.

Scheisse mit Reis: Shit with rice.

Schwarzwald: Black Forest.

Schweinehund: German swear word, literal meaning: pig dog.

Sieg Heil: hail victory, another Nazi salute.

Sitzwelle: revolution around the horizontal bar.

Streusel: butter crumbs on cake.

Struwelpeter: Messy Peter, a children's book.

Stukkas: German fighter planes.

Theresienstadt: Concentration camp in Czech. Republic.

Photograph Key

PAGE   CAPTION

XXX   Eva, age four, Berlin

XIII   *Gedächtniskirche*, Kaiser Wilhelm Memorial Church, Berlin viewed from Tauentzienstrasse, around 1905

6   Eva, age eighteen, Baden-Baden

9   *Gedächtniskirche*, Kaiser Wilhelm Memorial Church, post-war Berlin

10   Elisabeth Bielinski, age twenty-six

12   Tiller Girls, Berlin, 1920's

13   Elisabeth and Ernst Eichenwald as newlyweds, 1929

16   Eva, age twelve months

17   *Der Stürmer*, Nazi newspaper

19   Eva, age three, with Hennchen

20   Eva, Hans, and Gerda, Borghorst

22   Eva, age four

23   Lord, the German Shepherd

28   Eva, age four, with Mami

39   Elisabeth (first on right) and Ernst Eichenwald (third from right) as newlyweds, Heidelberg, 1929

45	Ernst Eichenwald on the beach in Holland, 1939
46	Eva, age five, with Papi
49	Eva, age five, with Mami
50	*Rankestrasse* 33, Berlin
55	Otto Bielinski, Opa
64	Gertrud Bielinski, Oma
72	Eva, age two and one half, with Papi
75	Eva, age ten months, with Papi
79	Ernst Eichenwald, 1938
90	Elephant Gate, Berlin Zoo, 1905
93	Eva, age three, with Oma
95	*Struwelpeter*, Messy Peter
103	Eva, age five
108	Allied Bombers over Berlin
119	Allied Bombers over Berlin
120	*Gedächtniskirche*, Kaiser Wilhelm Memorial Church, Berlin
122	Aerial view of Berlin air-raid
134	Gertrud Meister Bielinski, age thirty
137	Gertrud Meister Bielinski, age sixty-five
139	Gertrud Meister Bielinski, age twenty, with girl friend
147	Oma with Eva, age two
156	German soldiers
159	Germans salute a Nazi parade, *Heil Hitler*
160	Hitler addresses the crowds
161	Nazi demonstration
162	Hermann Göring receives flowers from his daughter
163	Adolf Hitler and Hermann Göring
170	Eva, age six, first day of school
180	Jewish storefront, glass smashed by Nazis, 1939 Kristallnacht
189	Jewish star
190	Jewish storefront, glass smashed by Nazis, 1939 Kristallnacht
191	Klara Eichenwald, Oma
194	Bombed street, Berlin, 1945
206	Berlin night club scene

210	Berlin night club scene
213	Petri Sindele (above) Petri Sindele and Else, after the war in Roumania (below)
218	The three Bielinski brothers, with Otto in the middle
223	Eva, age three months, with Opa
225	Marlene Dietrich in the "Blue Angel"
234	Brenner's Park Hotel, Baden-Baden
245	Eva, age five, with Mami
256	Hotel Kempinski, Berlin
262	Berlin, the final battle, April, 1945
267	Berlin, the final battle, April, 1945
270	Last-minute recruits, teen-agers in battle, April, 1945
276	Russians declare victory over Berlin, May, 1945
290	Post-war Berlin, the British sector
303	Bombed street, Berlin
306	1191 Stanyan Street, San Francisco, the garden
320	The family re-united: Elisabeth, Ernst, and Eva Wald, Market Street, San Francisco, 1946
326	Dinner at the Fairmont Hotel, San Francisco, 1946
328	Eva, age eleven, with Papi, Carmel, 1946
331	Eva, age sixteen, in the garden at 1191 Stanyan Street, San Francisco
337	Erika Liebeschütz, 1947
338	Fifth grade, Grattan Grammar School, 1946
342	Eva, age eleven, with Mami, 1946
345	Elisabeth Wald, 1946
348	Eva, age twelve, a girl-scout fashion show, 1947
350	Erin Walsh Dienstag
354	Judy Petersen
355	Eva, age fifteen, with Carol Wallace (middle), St. Francis Riding Academy
358	Ernst and Elisabeth Wald, Palm Springs, 1950
360	Ernst Wald, 1951
362	Helene Mayer, 1932
365	Elisabeth Wald, Ruth Wald, Eva, and Karl Wald (Eva's cousins Barbara and Caroline Wald in foreground)

372   Eva, high school graduate

374   A tea for Mrs. Close with Eva, age sixteen, second from right

375   Eva, high school graduate

377   Summer quarter registration card, Stanford

378   Eva, age seventeen, on the Andrea Doria, 1958

382   Erika Liebeschütz

383   Lilo Riedel

390   Eva Hitchcock, 1965

393   Eva, age eighteen, in Stanford production of Shaw's
You Never Can Tell

394   Eva, age twenty, in German production of Shiller's
Maria Stuart

396   George and Eva Hitchcock, 1965
402   Julian, Alan, Eva, and Sasha Leveton, 1998

407   Eva with lion cub, Berlin Zoo, 1996